# THE
# SUCCESSOR

MIKHAIL FISHMAN is one of Russia's leading political journalists. Active since the late 1990s, he has chronicled Russia's dramatic political life. He served as editor-in-chief of *Russian Newsweek* and *The Moscow Times*, as well as hosting the Friday night news round-up at TV Rain, Russia's leading independent news network. In 2017, Fishman and Vera Krichevskaya released *The Man Who Was Too Free*, a documentary feature on Boris Nemtsov. It was the highest-grossing documentary in Russia in at least a decade and laid the groundwork for this book, which was an instant bestseller on Russian publication in 2022. Fishman faced increasing intimidation and suppression from the state; when Putin launched the invasion of Ukraine in 2022, he left for Amsterdam, where he now lives and works in exile with his family.

MICHELE A. BERDY is a writer, translator and journalist who lived in Russia for over forty years, and wrote a long-running column for *The Moscow Times*.

# THE SUCCESSOR

## BORIS NEMTSOV, VLADIMIR PUTIN AND THE DECLINE OF MODERN RUSSIA

**MIKHAIL FISHMAN**

TRANSLATED FROM THE RUSSIAN BY MICHELE A. BERDY

PUSHKIN PRESS

Pushkin Press
Somerset House, Strand
London WC2R 1LA

Copyright © Mikhail Fishman, 2022
English translation © 2026, Michele A. Berdy

*The Successor* was first published as *Преемник* by Corpus Publishing House in Moscow, 2022

First published by Pushkin Press in 2026

The right of Mikhail Fishman to be identified as the author of this Work has been asserted by them in accordance with the Copyright, Designs & Patents Act 1988

ISBN 13: 978-1-78227-725-5

All rights reserved. No part of this publication may be reproduced, stored in a retrieval system or transmitted in any form or by any means, electronic, mechanical, photocopying, recording or otherwise, without prior permission in writing from Pushkin Press

A CIP catalogue record for this title is available from the British Library

The authorised representative in the EEA is eucomply OÜ, Pärnu mnt. 139b-14, 11317, Tallinn, Estonia, hello@eucompliancepartner.com, +33757690241

Designed and typeset by Tetragon, London
Printed and bound in the United Kingdom by Clays Ltd, Elcograf S.p.A.

Pushkin Press is committed to a sustainable future for our business, our readers and our planet. This book is made from paper from forests that support responsible forestry.

www.pushkinpress.com

9 8 7 6 5 4 3 2 1

# CONTENTS

Prologue — vii

## PART 1

1. 1987–89: How It All Began — 5
2. 1989–90: Great Expectations — 24
3. 1991: The Last Battle — 47
4. 1991: A New Country — 63

## PART 2

5. 1992–93: The Capital of Reform — 83
6. Winter 1992–Spring 1993: Two Centres of Power — 101
7. Summer–Autumn 1993: Breaking the Deadlock — 117
8. 1993–95: The Successor — 141
9. 1991–94: Chechnya and the Unnecessary War — 158
10. 1995–96: Peacemaker — 178
11. 1996: Communism or Democracy — 204

## PART 3

12. 1997: First Deputy Prime Minister Nemtsov — 237
13. 1997: A Boat Going Over a Waterfall — 261
14. 1998: The Emperor's Last Journey — 287
15. 1998: The Point of No Return — 297
16. 1996–98: Putin — 317
17. 1998–99: President 2000 — 326
18. 1999–2000: Successor 2.0 — 349

## PART 4

| | | |
|---|---|---|
| **19** | 2000–01: First Blood | 375 |
| **20** | 2002: Nord-Ost | 395 |
| **21** | 2003: The Other Russia | 419 |

## PART 5

| | | |
|---|---|---|
| **22** | 2004: Life on the Sidelines | 451 |
| **23** | 2004: The Orange Revolution | 457 |
| **24** | 2005–09: The End of the Revolution | 477 |
| **25** | 2005–08: Sovereign Democracy | 490 |
| **26** | 2004–08: Putin's Warrior | 515 |

## PART 6

| | | |
|---|---|---|
| **27** | 2008–10: The Thaw | 531 |
| **28** | 2010: Arrest | 555 |
| **29** | 2010–11: The Rook and King Change Places | 571 |
| **30** | 2007–11: The Dude from Marino Who Reinvented Politics | 580 |
| **31** | 2011: Bolotnaya Square | 589 |
| **32** | 2012: The Rout of the Bolotnaya Square Movement | 612 |

## PART 7

| | | |
|---|---|---|
| **33** | 2013: Two Campaigns | 629 |
| **34** | 2013–14: Euromaidan | 649 |
| **35** | 2014: Russia after Crimea | 665 |
| **36** | 27 February 2015 | 685 |

| | |
|---|---|
| Epilogue · Five Years Later: 2020 | 705 |
| Endnotes | 729 |
| Index of Names | 771 |

# PROLOGUE

## Navalny's arrest

I was working at TV Rain and finishing this book when Alexei Navalny announced that he was returning to Russia from several months in Germany after being successfully treated for Novichok poisoning. My first thought was: "What, already?" It was clear that he would return at some point—this was Navalny, after all—but why the rush? He hadn't fully recovered from being poisoned. What would a few months change?

I'd been writing this book for several years and had recorded an interview with Navalny a few years earlier. There was something I wanted to clarify—and then I caught myself. No, I won't bother him. He only has a few more days of freedom. I had no doubt that Navalny would be arrested as soon as he returned.

The TV Rain channel first peaked in popularity when it broadcast live reports during the Bolotnaya Square protests in 2011–12. Three weeks before the annexation of Crimea, TV Rain was prohibited from airing on Russian cable networks for its broadcasts from Kyiv during Euromaidan. But by the time that Navalny was returning, it was already at its second peak of success. The independent TV channel, still resisting state ideological pressure, was rapidly growing in popularity, no longer on cable but accessible on YouTube.

On 17 January, TV Rain broadcast live coverage of Navalny's return, showing him and his wife Yulia getting on a plane in Berlin and turning on *Rick and Morty*; tens of thousands of people coming to meet him at Vnukovo Airport in Moscow and then their arrest when the plane was diverted to another airport; Navalny saying he was happy to be back home and not afraid of anything at an impromptu press conference before going through border control; and a few minutes later showing him giving Yulia a quick hug before the police took him away for ever. It was the most popular broadcast in the history of TV Rain. The live coverage was watched by a record half-million concurrent viewers.

Of course, Navalny was counting on people coming out to protest his arrest. If millions had come out, Russia might have had a chance to get off its destructive path, but only about 150,000 people took to the streets across the country—far fewer than during the protests in winter 2011–12. Fear had enveloped the country. Protesters were beaten and detained, thousands of demonstrators received several days of detention, and there were soon more than one hundred criminal charges. Protesters were tracked through security cameras and then expelled from universities and fired from their jobs for "committing an immoral act."

I had been detained before—no rallies had been authorized in Russia since the Covid era—but I'd recently had a chance to see how the system worked. In early February, my eldest daughter, Anya, was detained. She and her boyfriend had protested outside the court when Navalny's sentence was announced. The police released her on the same day since she was a minor—she was seventeen years old—but she was registered at the police department and had to go to the district office so that the commission on juvenile affairs could consider our case. The commission wasn't made up of police or FSB officers. It was made up of ordinary Moscow civil servants, mostly teachers and directors of neighbourhood schools. They had to punish us; otherwise, they would have broken the rules of the game and would have come under suspicion themselves. But I saw how easily they slipped into the role of inquisitors. This must have been how party trials were conducted in the Brezhnev era.

The Soviet power structure was built on a clear-cut party hierarchy. Since Stalin's death, power in the Soviet Union had never depended on the will of just one man; it was the power of the corporation. Putin's system of one-man rule seemed more vulnerable. Polls showed that his approval rating was continuing to decline gradually, while Navalny's popularity was growing even though he was under arrest. When he returned to Russia, he posted on YouTube about Putin's palace, a huge estate built for him on the Black Sea. It was viewed by more than 100 million people—still a record for non-entertainment videos on Russian YouTube. Navalny's team found procurement documents for the palace interiors: one toilet brush had cost €700.

"Let's look inside, and you'll see that Vladimir Putin is mentally ill: he is obsessed with wealth and luxury," Navalny said in the film's narration. The extravagant but tasteless palace instantly became a symbol of caste and corruption. At rallies for Navalny, people came out waving toilet brushes.

It wasn't just Navalny. The public atmosphere was reminiscent of the period nine years before when the Bolotnaya Square protests were broken up. Repression was growing, but it didn't produce love for the regime. On the contrary, discontent was growing. I could see it myself. The TV Rain channel was growing increasingly popular, and the other anchors and I were recognized on the streets more frequently and thanked for our work.

And so I sat in the district office, watching the members of the juvenile affairs commission zealously denounce my daughter and me as alienated, unworthy members of society—they apparently didn't recognize me—and thinking that Putin's power might be stronger than I'd thought. Yes, the corporate rule of the Communist Party of the Soviet Union had been replaced by the tyranny of one-man rule, but it still relied on a vast army of clerks and bureaucrats who enthusiastically carried out the will of the government.

After Navalny's return and arrest, it quickly became clear that things would never be the same again. In the past the authorities hadn't felt the need to justify their persecution of dissidents, but now they took another step. In the spring they simply outlawed all Navalny's supporters. The court declared that his headquarters throughout the country were extremist, and the parliament passed a special law banning anyone who had publicly supported or sympathized with Navalny over the past few years. A social media post was enough to break the law. The government now deemed it "association with the activities of an extremist organization."

At the snap of a finger, the government crushed a peaceful political organization and deprived tens, if not hundreds of thousands, of

Russian citizens of their civil rights—simply for a like on Facebook. The zeal to destroy the entire sphere of lawful political expression—any dissent against the regime—was breathtaking. It was swift, brazen—a blatant misuse of power. And journalists were next in line.

Previously, the label "foreign agent"—someone who is paid by or under the influence of a foreign government, i.e. an enemy of Russia—had been applied to non-profit organizations. Now it was being applied to the press. Putin began his reign in Russia with the arrest of media magnate Vladimir Gusinsky, and censorship had increased over the twenty-odd years he had been in power. Now it had reached a new height. *Meduza*, the most popular independent online news media outlet in Russia, had been operating out of Latvia since 2014 when the first harsh wave of censorship hit the Russian press during Euromaidan and the annexation of Crimea. In late April, it was declared a foreign agent. TV Rain was named a foreign agent in August.

But that wasn't all. The Kremlin got personal: it began to label individual journalists as foreign agents—journalists like me, who was put on the list in December 2022. I knew almost all of them personally, and I had worked with many of them for years in the same newsrooms. Now they were officially recognized as second-class citizens. They had to put humiliating disclaimers under their posts on social networks: "This material has been created, disseminated and/or sent by foreign agent Ivan Ivanovich Ivanov, who is registered as a foreign agent, or concerns the activities of foreign agent Ivan Ivanovich Ivanov, who is registered as a foreign agent." They also were required to submit reports to the state on all their spending. It was outrageous. I suppressed a sharp pang of anger and, like everyone else, realized that this did not bode well for us journalists.

It still wasn't clear that a war was imminent, but since the beginning of the fall, I was quite aware that the finale was near: soon my usual life would be over, and I would no longer be able to continue working as I had done for more than twenty years under Putin. Nor would my colleagues.

## Purging the rear guard

The word "war" made headlines in late March 2021. Putin's statements suddenly became threatening. In a speech on the anniversary of the annexation of Crimea, he said he would never accept the "generous gifts from Russia" being used against it: "I hope this will be heard."[1] The word "gifts" had long been familiar. It was first heard in 2005, when he told Condoleezza Rice, then in Russia as secretary of state, that the post-Soviet states received their institutions and resources from the Soviet Union. And, therefore, Russia had the right to take them back.

After his speech, Putin went on vacation in the taiga with Sergei Shoigu. Shoigu was one of the men who had brought him to power—he had headed Putin's supporters' list in the 1999 elections, remained a close confidante and become defence minister in 2012. The Kremlin published photos taken when they holidayed together. In one they are getting ready for the sauna; in another they are drinking tea together. Putin went to Siberia with Shoigu several times. We journalists laughed at their bromance, not suspecting that during this joint holiday Putin had given his defence minister his first orders. A week later, Russian armoured vehicles began to line up near the Ukrainian border. The US military's European Command even raised its security alert to the highest level: imminent attack likely. But the word "war" was only used in the context that, of course, there would not be a war. Why would Putin need a war and its consequences—tough new sanctions from the West? Besides, there weren't enough troops for a major military operation.

At that time, no one realized that Putin had begun preparations for an invasion and was moving part of his army to the Ukrainian border under the guise of exercises. Then, on 12 July he published an article entitled, 'On the Historical Unity of Russians and Ukrainians'. This was his second commentary on a historical topic in recent months. The first, an hour-and-a-half lecture delivered to the leaders of the CIS countries who came to St Petersburg on the eve of the year 2019, was devoted to the Munich Conspiracy, which had opened the way for Hitler's war. The practical meaning of this lecture was to justify the Molotov–Ribbentrop Pact: Munich had somehow induced Stalin to conclude a non-aggression pact with Germany. But Putin delivered another important message in his lecture: the injustice of the Treaty of Versailles, which had humiliated Germany, and the arbitrary borders in Europe created grounds for a future crisis. In his speech, Putin noted that after the First World War, Germany was victimized by a hypocritical West that arrogated to itself the right to determine the borders of states and shape world order.[2]

The article about Ukraine published in July was written along the same lines. Starting from the Middle Ages, it asserted that the Ukrainian nation did not exist. Ukraine was just a part of the larger Russian nation, and the modern country of Ukraine was an entirely artificial construct of the early Soviet era, based on borders that were arbitrarily drawn by the Bolsheviks. In this text, international law and world order were irrelevant against the background of issues of blood and Russian borders formed in the distant past. The article also contained a direct threat: Ukraine was being turned into an anti-Russia, Putin wrote, and he would not allow "our historical territories and the people related to us who live there to be used against Russia." In essence, it was a manifesto justifying military intervention.

It later became known from publications in the Western press that US intelligence had learnt of the invasion preparations in October. At that time, Putin was holding the Valdai Discussion Club, his annual meeting with international experts. One of the questions prepared in advance concerned Ukraine: how can we prevent its transformation into an anti-Russia? What should be done? Putin answered that he did not know yet, but that "military development of the territory is already underway, and this poses a real threat."[3]

But the journalists there were much more interested in his conversation with *Novaya gazeta*'s editor-in-chief, Dmitry Muratov. Muratov and the Filipino journalist Maria Ressa had just won the Nobel Peace Prize for their "efforts to defend freedom of speech." This was the Nobel committee's way of standing up for independent Russian journalism. Muratov knew that Putin was furious about the prize—he clearly took the committee's choice as an attack on him personally. When the committee's decision was announced, he did not congratulate Muratov, but instead threatened him, saying he shouldn't get the idea that he could "hide behind the Nobel Prize." Muratov was given the floor, and he said that journalists and human-rights activists were designated as foreign agents—enemies of the motherland—without trial and without warning. They were branded and that's it. Perhaps, Muratov suggested, we might consider a procedure to be taken off the "foreign agent" list? Putin looked daggers at him.[4]

The designation of journalists and human-rights activists as foreign agents had become a weekly routine. Every Friday we waited to find out who was next. Meanwhile, the authorities began arresting all of Navalny's associates still in Russia. By the end of October, the number of political prisoners in the country—more than four hundred people—equalled the number of political prisoners in the late USSR for the first time. And reports from parliamentary sessions looked more and more like Stalin-era editorials. It was as if a time machine had malfunctioned and was jumping from one date in the past to another.

In November Memorial, Russia's premier human-rights project, was put on trial. It had been founded in the late 1980s under glasnost and perestroika when the country had begun to talk about Stalin's repressions. It was created as a mission to return the memory of millions of victims to the new generations. At the time, Memorial was a mass movement, a social force. By the late 2010s, it had become a cultural and educational institute, as well as a human-rights organization. The charges were ridiculous: Memorial was sued because several pages of its website did not include the foreign agent text.

We watched the destruction of Memorial incredulously. The memory of Stalin's terror still seemed sacred—four years before, Putin himself had unveiled a monument to the victims of political repression in Moscow. And we couldn't believe it because we could not answer the question: why? What was the point? Unlike Navalny, Memorial did not cause trouble for the Kremlin. These bans and repressions were even more frightening because they seemed irrational and excessive. Why were they twisting everyone's arms? What was the reason for it? At Putin's end-of-year press conference, a BBC correspondent asked him that very question with genuine bewilderment: "What has happened in Russia recently to make the number of people the authorities consider extremists, undesirable organizations and foreign agents grow so rapidly?"[5]

Nothing had happened. Putin was simply acting according to plan: if you're going to attack your neighbour, first make sure you're in complete control of your country. Putin was preparing for an invasion and cleaning up the home front.

## War

Publications about a new massing of Russian troops near the Ukrainian border appeared at the end of October, and from mid-November signs of preparations for a major war were already clearly visible. The Americans, already aware of the preparations for an invasion, sent to Moscow the head of the CIA, Bill Burns, an experienced diplomat who had worked extensively in Moscow. He returned home even more alarmed: Putin was talking tough. Washington soon warned Moscow publicly that more aggression against Ukraine after 2014 "would be a serious mistake." Putin talked about NATO's creeping expansion in Ukraine. He was shifting the red lines that he himself had previously drawn. Now his words made clear that he didn't consider just Ukraine's accession to NATO unacceptable, but Western military assistance to Ukraine in general. The main thing was clear: he was no longer satisfied with the status quo of the last few years—neither war nor peace. One way or another, Ukraine must return to Moscow's sphere of influence.

"Ominous signs indicate that Russia may conduct a military offensive in Ukraine as early as the coming winter," wrote American military expert Michael Kofman in late November.[6] He and other analysts reasoned as follows: first, the Russian army's manoeuvres near the border went far beyond exercises. Second, Putin saw no other way out: Ukraine was moving towards the West, and he could not stop this movement except by military force. Recognizing the independence of the already captured territories of Donbas or even incorporating them into Russia would not resolve the problem. A local military operation in Eastern Ukraine would not help either. Everything suggested that Putin was preparing for a big war.

This reasoning made perfect sense to me. I was just finishing this book, for which I reconstructed day by day how Putin's obsession with Ukraine had grown. A clear picture had emerged: Putin bet on Yanukovych in 2003; he congratulated him on his victory in the presidential election in 2004—and lost to the Maidan and Orange Revolution. He had convinced himself that Ukraine did not exist as a state; he bent Yanukovych to his will in 2013, and for his efforts got Euromaidan, already a fully fledged uprising—and lost again. He took Crimea and part of Donbas, and then for many years tried to hobble Ukraine with the Minsk Agreements—and lost again.

For more than twenty years Putin had been destroying public and state institutions and crushing the opposition. He had seized absolute power and completely subjugated the country—but he had never been able to vanquish Ukraine. All these years, he stored up his anger and thirst for revenge. Putin had become an autocrat, his megalomania had long since become limitless, and there was no one to bring him out of this state. He had spent the last two years since the outbreak of the epidemic in isolation, surrounded by aides and courtiers. He dreamt of war: you could see how eager he was to try out his toys—all those missiles he so passionately advertised in his addresses to the nation. No one knew what Putin was up to—until the invasion began, few people were privy to his plans—but my sources in the Kremlin and the Duma also confirmed my conclusions: yes, he seems to be preparing to go to war for real. "War may not happen yet—common sense may yet prevail," I said on air in early December. "But looking at the situation today, that outcome would be a great stroke of luck."[7]

In winter 2022, war was getting closer by the day. Putin gave NATO a deliberately impossible ultimatum—he demanded legal guarantees that the organization would not expand eastward. By the end of January, Washington was well aware that Moscow was not interested in negotiation and that its demands were a ruse, a pretext for invasion. A week before the invasion, the head of the State Department, Antony Blinken, spoke at the UN: in the next few days, Russia would attack Ukraine, rain bombs and missiles down on it, and tanks and infantry would march on Kyiv. Later, the Western press would describe vividly how, despite clear warning signals from Washington, neither Kyiv nor most European capitals believed in the prospect of a full-scale war until it began.

War can be predicted, but it is impossible to imagine. You can't conceive of it. Bombs exploding in Kyiv? Kharkiv's subway turned into a bomb shelter? Odesa's boulevards sandbagged and lined with anti-tank hedgehogs? How could this be possible? All this had already happened—eighty years ago. Neither in Ukraine nor in Russia was there a family that had not suffered in the Second World War, what people in the USSR called the Great Patriotic War. To imagine the black-and-white newsreel familiar to every Russian, Ukrainian and Belarusian from childhood coming to life again, in colour, in reality? Unthinkable.

The war was approaching every day; rational analysis showed its inevitability, but it was almost impossible to comprehend this inevitability. In the middle of February, my large family gathered for lunch at a café: my wife and I, my sister and her husband, all our children, my parents. The conversation, of course, turned to the war. It's a matter of a week or two, a month at the most, I said.

"So you mean bombs hitting Kyiv?" Igor, my stepfather, asked me. He always served as a model of common sense for me.

"Yes, they will," I answered.

"How could that be?"

The same thing was said in the Ukrainian city of Vinnitsa, 250 kilometres south-west of Kyiv, by my wife's parents. (Vinnitsa is not in the path of the Russian troops' offensive, but we warned them anyway and tried to persuade them to leave. In July 2022, the city's central square, one bus stop from their home, came under missile attack. But they never left.) Friends, acquaintances, co-workers said the same thing. No one believed that the war would really happen.

Intellectually, I understood that war was inevitable and that it would be the end of the world order and the end of Russia—not symbolically, but in actual fact. Our whole life would change irrevocably. But what would it be like? I could not say. Nor could I imagine bombs falling on Kyiv. Two weeks before the war, I said on air: "It's hard to believe in a full-scale war with Ukraine—a war of the kind you see in movies, a war from the distant past but impossible to imagine today, in February 2022. Alas, that's no guarantee that this war will not happen."[8] It was as if we were in the movie *Don't Look Up*, about a comet hitting the earth, which had been released a month and a half earlier.

# PROLOGUE

On 21 February, an emergency meeting of the expanded Security Council recognized the independence of Donbas. Putin made each of his courtiers, the highest officials of the state, appear on camera. It was important for him to hold them responsible for the invasion. It soon became clear that this was the first move in the war: by recognizing the independence of the territories in Eastern Ukraine and concluding "mutual assistance agreements" with them, Moscow, as Putin would later explain, gained the legal right to provide them with military support. But even after recognizing the independence of Donbas, the world still did not believe in the prospect of a major war. It took two more days to see it for themselves.

On 22 June 1941, the German invasion of the USSR began with the bombing of Kyiv. A famous war song captures this moment:

> On June twenty-two
> At four in the morning
> Kyiv was stormed
> And we were informed
> That we were at war with no warning.

Russia's invasion of Ukraine also began early in the morning. This time the enemy came not from the west, but from the east. On 24 February 2022, at 6.00 a.m. in Moscow and 5.00 a.m. in Kyiv, Putin gave a televised address: he was launching a special military operation "to demilitarize and denazify Ukraine", calling on the Ukrainian military to lay down their arms, while the West, if it intervened, would face consequences "it had never faced before in its history." Putin made it clear that he was ready to use nuclear weapons. Half an hour later, through the howling of air raid sirens, the first bombs were already falling on Kyiv, as well as on Kharkiv, Odesa, Dnipro, Kherson and Mykolaiv. Russian troops crossed the Ukrainian border simultaneously from the south, north and east. The subways in Kyiv and Kharkiv were immediately turned into bomb shelters. As Ukrainian women and children tried to squeeze onto westbound trains, men joined territorial-defence units. The comet fell to earth. The world collapsed.

## The end

From the very first minute of the war, we knew that TV Rain would not last long. But what is "long" anyway? The war started on Thursday. We kept working. The Kremlin and its propagandists immediately switched to the language they had specially invented for the war: not Ukrainians, but neo-Nazis and Bandera-supporters; not the Ukrainian army, but nationalist formations; not war, but a special military operation. For us, the most important thing in those days was to describe what was happening and call things by their proper names: Ukrainians as Ukrainians, Volodymyr Zelensky as the legitimate president of Ukraine, and the invasion as a war of conquest, armed aggression, violating both the UN charter and the Russian criminal code, which also has an article on the waging and planning of a war of aggression.

At the very outset of the war, no one thought that it would last for years, because no one believed that Ukraine could withstand the onslaught. It seemed obvious to everyone that Kyiv would be captured within a few days. The international media (along with us) discussed what would happen next: whether the puppet government that the Kremlin would install in occupied Ukraine would hold, how powerful the partisan movement would be, etc. But by Sunday it was already clear that the plan conceived in Moscow was being thwarted: the Russian paratroopers near Kyiv had been defeated, Zelensky was leading the defence from the capital, demonstrating to the whole world the steadfastness and courage of Ukrainians by his personal example, and the whole country was united in its desire to fight back against the enemy.

Meanwhile, in Russia, some people came out to protest the war. On just one day—24 February—about two thousand people were detained. Others were leaving—in protest, in disagreement or disgust, but also out of fear: There were rumours that the borders were about to be closed. It was almost impossible to buy a ticket for any flight abroad even a week in advance.

The more obvious it became that the blitzkrieg was failing, the riskier it was for independent journalists. How much longer would the Kremlin be willing to tolerate us? Despite my parents' entreaties, my wife Yulia and I both worked at TV Rain, and we decided that we would stay in Russia as long as TV Rain was functioning and we could go on air. We couldn't abandon our colleagues and our work at a time like this.

On Monday, 1 March, I had a free evening. What do you do when your house is on fire? You finish up important chores and pack. For some reason I decided to fix my glasses—I put in new lenses. On my way to the shop, I was listening to Ekho Moskvy radio, an uncensored Moscow radio station founded in the days of the 1991 August coup attempt. Dmitry Gordon, a well-known Ukrainian journalist, was saying live from Kyiv that Putin was a fascist. And at that moment I realized that we had only days. Neither Ekho nor TV Rain would be there in a week.

I was overly optimistic. The next day, Tuesday, was the sixth day of the war. I was broadcasting live with TV Rain's editor-in-chief, Tikhon Dzyadko, when the Prosecutor General's Office demanded that both TV Rain and Ekho Moskvy be shut down. Ekho Moskvy had already been disconnected from the airwaves, and TV Rain's website had been blocked. Roskomnadzor could not disable YouTube, where TV Rain was broadcasting, so technically we could continue broadcasting. But it was clear that this was the end: we would no longer be able to work.

Amendments to the criminal code were urgently prepared to criminalize critical statements about the war: up to fifteen years in prison for spreading "false information" about the actions of the Russian armed forces. In two days, these amendments would be adopted. A month later the first arrests would be made, and three to four months later the first sentences would be handed down. That Tuesday evening, everyone at TV Rain was nervous. No one knew what the Kremlin's next move would be. Someone called to say that the police were on their way to the newsroom; someone else called to advise me not to spend the night at home.

While I was on air, my sister Sasha, who had flown out of Russia with my parents the day before, bought us tickets to Baku, Azerbaijan for the next morning. We didn't have visas to Europe, and it was the only city my wife Yulia, our four-year-old daughter Katya and I could fly to. That evening we quickly packed some things. Early in the morning of 2 March we were at the airport. We fled.

• • •

When was the moment that Russia lost its freedom? Was there a chance when we shattered—for ever, it seemed—the shackles of communist dictatorship to build a democratic state where the rights of the individual would be respected? Could Boris Nemtsov have become president? Could Alexei Navalny have become the leader of the nation?

Today, in 2025, the answers to these questions are far more pessimistic than they seemed several years earlier when I sat down to write this book. Was the abhorrent war that Putin began unavoidable? Was the disaster that he led Russia into predetermined?

Today, after more than thirty years have gone by, the miracle of August 1991 still stays with me. I remember the happiness, the almost palpable feeling of a fresh wind blowing away the evil of Soviet rule. Another image from the 1990s remains in my memory. It's 1997, I am twenty-four, and it's an average day, nothing important happening. I'm walking down a Moscow street—not the glamorous Moscow of the Putin era, when everything shimmered with gold and money, but the crude and chaotic Moscow of the 1990s—and I am filled with joy, because I believe in my own future and the future of Russia. Russia is part of a greater free world, and therefore I am, too, and it's for ever. Nothing will change that.

In a few years, I would learn that I was wrong. But today, almost thirty years later, in exile and after nearly four years of this devastating war, I can't stop wondering: what was that? Could we have succeeded, or was it nothing but an illusion, a hallucination?

Back then, in the 1990s, the sceptics remained pessimistic: consumed by the trauma of collapse, haunted by its imperial syndrome, Russia would never succeed in abandoning its historic path as the Empire of Evil, merciless to its own people and bringing misery and destruction to the outside world. The present seems to have proved them right. Russia failed to break the vicious circle of despotism and lawlessness and is now spreading death and violence. Russia failed and is doomed to fail. Boris Nemtsov didn't have a chance. Neither did Alexei Navalny. None of us had a chance.

And yet, I refuse to accept this judgement. I refuse to accept that my emotions in the 1990s were a delusion. Nemtsov probably would not have become president of Russia, regardless of the specific political situation in the late 1990s. He was carried aloft by the revolution at the end of the 1980s and early 1990s. A few years later, he was already too free and too idealistic for the times. A revolution is always followed by revanche. The elites had succumbed to lust for money and power; the people had faced harsh reality and were beginning to long for a strong arm and the country's past greatness. Boris Yeltsin's second presidential term was a failure and cleared the pathway to autocracy.

But not all autocracies are the same. Some transform into civilized states. Others mutate into ghastly tyrannies. Putin's highly personalized one-man rule has emerged as a worst-case scenario. Built on violence and deception, it brought out the most immoral and destructive traits of governance. It combines a mafia code of honour, the Stalinist relationship between the state and its subjects, and a fascist, militarized leadership.

I refuse to accept that this kind of government was inevitable and the inherent characteristic of Russia. Now that I have experienced the entire journey—together with Nemtsov, and later with Navalny—I still believe that Russia could have had another future.

Is this other future still possible today? The Russian edition of this book was published two weeks before the start of the war. I wrote then that Nemtsov's life story, his values and ideals would still be needed, that there would be a happy ending. Russia would finally throw off the yoke of tyranny, violence and inequality. I still believe that today, although I am not sure that I will still be here when it happens.

AUGUST 2025
AMSTERDAM

# THE SUCCESSOR

# PART 1

# CHAPTER 1

## 1987–89

## How It All Began

### Put the executioners on trial

Nikolai Ashin, a twenty-four-year-old employee at the Gorky Radio Research Institute, was unhappy with perestroika. The policy to reform the political system in the USSR wasn't dealing with the right issues, and it was too slow. He thought the reforms initiated by Soviet leader Mikhail Gorbachev were only halfway measures and that even the premise was wrong. How could a communist system reform itself? In Gorky, a large city on the Volga River now called Nizhny Novgorod, Ashin was interested in politics, so he decided to start a newspaper—not a standard newspaper, but a wall newspaper. There would be one copy printed, and it would be put up on the wall right next to the entrance to the institute cafeteria, where everyone would see it.

The first issue of the paper came out in November 1987 with an introductory article signed by Ashin. It began: "There are appeals made from the pages of newspapers and TV screens to nominate, elect, actively participate, actively discuss—all within the bounds of socialist legality, of course. There are calls for democratization—within the framework of socialist pluralism. Transparency, openness, freedom to criticize—yes, but objectively and constructively. Excuse me, but it was the same under Stalin—everything within certain limits. And these limits are now set by the same organizations they were set by back then."

Both the wall newspaper at the Radio Institute and Ashin's article were signs of the times. On the one hand, glasnost—the policy of openness, speaking truthfully about the situation in the country—reached its peak in 1987, communist ideology was already bursting apart at the seams, and even the official Communist Party press was discussing topics that had been under a veil of silence for decades. Magazines published millions of copies of fiction written by once-banned writers. Films that had been collecting dust on the shelves for years were released in movie theatres. Young TV talk-show hosts instantly became stars like no one Soviet viewers had ever seen before. None of this was imaginable even a year and a half or two years earlier.

On the other hand, the power of the Communist Party was still strong, and the conservative opposition to perestroika and Mikhail Gorbachev, which was led by Yegor Ligachev, the second man in the Communist hierarchy, was already gaining strength within the party. Just as Ashin was working on the first issue of his wall newspaper, Boris Yeltsin, then the progressive and popular head of Moscow, was clashing with the old guard at a meeting of Communist Party leaders.

The contours of the political struggle that would determine the events of the coming decade were beginning to emerge: Gorbachev was being pressured by the Communist orthodoxies of the Politburo (the top policy-making body in the Party and government) and country on the right, while Yeltsin's star was rising on the left. Freedom—first and foremost, freedom of the press—was suddenly sweeping the country. But the enormous Communist Party machine was not about to give up without a fight, and to some, like the young anti-Communist Ashin, perestroika seemed incomplete and hypocritical.

The beginning of the era of glasnost might be dated to January 1987, when the film *Repentance* was released. Directed by the Georgian filmmaker Tengiz Abuladze and shelved for two years, it was a parable of a tyrant who resembled both the head of the Soviet secret police Lavrenty Beria and leader Joseph Stalin. Glasnost became synonymous with de-Stalinization. A flood of evidence of mass repressions poured from the mass media, a river of truth that turned readers' blood cold. At the time Soviet people had only vague notions about the repressions; the archives had not yet been opened, Alexander Solzhenitsyn's

*Gulag Archipelago* had not yet been published in *Novy mir* magazine, and few grasped the scale of the number of victims. "Anyone opening a major Russian newspaper or magazine in 1987 or 1988 was instantly surrounded by names, faces, voices—the ghosts of thwarted lives of one's compatriots: slandered, arrested, tormented, shot, starved, or worked to death," wrote Leon Aron, a scholar of the perestroika era.[1] Of course, the Party's general line could not keep up with the spirit of the times. Official Party documents were already condemning the repressions while still celebrating Stalin's exceptional contributions to what was still called "socialist construction."

Nikolai Ashin was uncompromising. He demanded that the executioners be put on trial. "The arbitrary actions and impunity of even the rank-and-file officers and agents [of the KGB] have for decades bred an instinctive fear in people, a fear that has become a hereditary Russian national trait, 'genetically' transmitted from generation to generation," he wrote in his introductory article. "To overcome this legacy, it would help if we could hold our own Nuremberg trials of those who perpetrated repressions in those years."

The newspaper caused an uproar, but the spirit of the Radio Institute was liberal, even for those years. The institute's Komsomol (Young Communist League) Committee studied Ashin's personal file and made its decision. "We consider the newspaper's aim of creating an atmosphere of glasnost in the institute to be correct."[2]

Ashin's article was avidly discussed throughout the institute, including in his department of theoretical physics. Boris Nemtsov, a twenty-eight-year-old physicist, colleague, supervisor and close friend of Ashin's, decided to write a response, which was published in the next issue of the newspaper. This was Nemtsov's first political statement. "The article is written with civic spirit, honestly, courageously and emotionally, which naturally attracts the reader. Nevertheless, I cannot support a number of the author's proposals," Nemtsov wrote.

> First of all, the proposal to hold a Nuremberg trial of those who carried out repressions under Stalin. Most of them are either dead or helpless old men. Of course, the desire for revenge is great, but a desire for revenge and bloodthirst can hardly be called a sign of high

moral principles, and it is precisely moral cleansing that should be the goal of such endeavours. Besides, even if trials were held, juries would immediately face insurmountable difficulties: lack of access to archives and documents, not to mention lack of official support. In short, the proposal is tempting, but hardly feasible. It seems to me more realistic to organize a fund-raising event to build a monument (even a modest obelisk or plaque) to memorialize the victims of Stalinist terror.

## Nemtsov the physicist

Nemtsov was born in Sochi, a resort town on the Black Sea, where his parents married and worked. His mother, Dina, was from Gorky, where she graduated from the Gorky Medical Institute and worked as a paediatrician. His father, an engineer, held a senior position in the Sochi construction headquarters. His parents' marriage was not happy, and Nemtsov's childhood memories of his father were fraught. The tension between them lasted right up to his father's death in 1988.

Nemtsov's parents divorced when he was seven years old and in first grade. His father left to take up a promotion in Moscow, and he and his mother and older sister Yulia returned to Gorky. That is where they continued to live, in a small two-room apartment in a Khrushchev-era apartment building, first the three of them, then the five of them when his sister married and had a baby. They were very poor. His mother worked in a hospital, they couldn't make ends meet, and by the sixth grade Nemtsov was unloading goods at a nearby store to make some extra money. "If you don't do well in school, you will live in poverty," Nemtsov later recalled one of his mother's main admonitions. "She said this all the time, and by the ninth grade, I knew it by heart."[3]

Nemtsov was a good student and graduated with a gold medal, but his mother described him as always lacking in discipline, and his school record was full of comments that in class he was constantly chattering, laughing and generally being disruptive. Somehow Nemtsov managed to avoid joining the Komsomol. In the 1970s this was a rarity, and a high-school student without a Komsomol badge was something of an outcast. His high-school transcript noted that Nemtsov was "politically unstable", and both factors nearly shut the door to higher education. When his mother saw the evaluation, she panicked and ran to the school. "But Boris really *is* politically unstable," the school principal said, exasperated. He let himself be talked into making the criticism milder, however: "He can make politically ill-considered statements."[4]

The young Boris Nemtsov wasn't deemed politically unstable because he was militantly anti-Soviet. In fact, Nemtsov had no interest in politics when he was young. He became a dissident largely due to one of his chief character traits—a lack of self-censorship: Nemtsov always said what he thought. A few years later he clarified his position in an interview: "I am not a Communist by conviction. But to call me an anti-Communist— that's too strong, and it implies that I'm actively against it."[5]

Boris Nemtsov was a very gifted young man. He studied physics and mathematics seriously in his last years of high school and was accepted in the prestigious Radio Department of Gorky State University. In the mid-1950s, the Radio Institute was founded by the top physicists of the time, and two decades later the Institute of Applied Physics (IAP) was also founded nearby. Gorky was located near the most important secret military production facilities in the country, where submarines, fighter planes and other military equipment were built. Because physics and mathematics were essential to the development of the nuclear bomb and the arms race, the two subjects always held a special and privileged place in Soviet science, and the Soviet authorities allowed mathematicians and physicists a little more freedom than others. Thanks to all this, the best of the Soviet scientific intelligentsia settled in Gorky, and the local institutes became hotbeds of freethinking.

After graduating with honours, Nemtsov went to work in the theoretical department of the Radio Institute, where his scientific adviser was his uncle Vilen Eidman, a famous scientist and disciple of Academy of Sciences member Vitaly Ginzburg, who would win the Nobel Prize in 2003. "My father was a stern, tough man and would not have spent time on his nephew if he wasn't a good physicist," Eidman's son, Igor, said of his cousin. "He thought Boris was incredibly gifted and had a brilliant scientific career ahead of him."[6]

Physicist Lev Tsimring, one of Nemtsov's classmates and friends, explained what Nemtsov worked on. "The faculty instilled in us the idea that everything is based on the theory of nonlinear wave oscillations," he said, "and from that basis you can then apply it to different areas. We were taught to apply it to radio waves and plasma physics. That's what Boris was doing at the Institute."[7] His mother recalled that "scraps of paper with formulas on them were all over—on the tables and floor. Even when he visited my parents, he kept writing those formulas."[8]

Later, the journalist Yegor Vereshchagin wrote that, in Nemtsov's Ph.D. thesis, "it seem[ed] like he was trying to cover a lot of topics, as if he were being pulled in different directions instead of focusing on one particular area."[9] But this is a question of approach: a person can become an expert in a particular field, or he can take a broader view, see analogies in other fields and find universal patterns that are invisible to specialists working more narrowly. "We were studying fluid dynamics," Tsimring recalled. "Waves in the ocean, the instabilities that wind waves produce—that sort of thing. And he had the idea of seeing what would happen if you did roughly the same thing in acoustics. So just like that he went into acoustics. He had no trouble jumping from one field to another."[10] That was the idea that led to the acoustic laser, which Nemtsov was involved in developing.

Nemtsov the physicist was the precursor to the future Nemtsov the political orator: without an in-depth, detailed understanding of issues—a trait he would often be criticized for—he could explain the essence of a matter in a way that people understood. This would be one of the sources of his popularity.

The Radio Institute gave their researchers free rein to do what they wanted, so there was no pressure on him. He was also well-known at the neighbouring IAP because he regularly attended their seminars. And he worked with students. His future assistant and secretary, Alexander Kotyusov, met the twenty-seven-year-old Nemtsov in 1986 in his fourth year. He clearly remembered their first meetings at the Radio Institute. Since classified military work was done at the institute, there was a special system of passes, and no one without a pass was permitted above the first floor. Nemtsov worked with students on a window ledge on the landing between the first and second floors.[11]

## The freest man

Everyone in Gorky's scientific community knew Nemtsov—in fact, he was well-known outside it, too. Even then the character traits that would play a decisive role in his career and in his life were on display: tremendous self-confidence, a complete lack of self-consciousness that verged on impertinence and a total absence of subservience that was almost insolent. Described as "arrogant and a super-extrovert" by Pavel Chichagov, a physicist at IAP, he stood out in any company, especially among the other scientists: a tall, sexy, curly-haired, handsome playboy. He didn't look like a scientist at all.[12] His success with women was legendary, even in his student days.

In the centre of Gorky were two clay tennis courts in a park that the institute rented for several hours a week. Since the 1970s, young physicists went there to play tennis. A fashionable foreign sport, tennis was then something like a postcard from forbidden Western life—especially in Gorky, in those years a depressing and gloomy city made up of scientific institutes surrounded by dreary working-class neighbourhoods. The Gorky Automobile Plant, which made the famous Volga car, was like an entire city within the city. In the early 1980s, at the peak of Brezhnev's stagnation, it was chic to get a tennis racket—even if it was, at best, made in Estonia—and pick up a tennis ball—even if was completely bald. Nemtsov loved sports and working out, known for being able to do thirty pull-ups in a row nonstop. When a ski resort appeared in the hills near the city, he took up alpine skiing; when he started going to Sochi, he immediately learnt how to surf. Nemtsov was not going to pass up tennis.

Natalia Lapina, a student at the Gorky Theatre School, saw Nemtsov on the tennis court in 1981. "What a handsome guy! Probably a foreigner," she thought—that's how much Nemtsov, tennis racket in hand, stood out in Gorky. She sat down next to him and waited while studying a role she was playing. She wasn't disappointed. "Young lady, you have such a discerning gaze," Nemtsov told her. "Wow," thought Lapina, "what a word—discerning."[13] They soon started an affair. Lapina lived in the village of Sormovo, an industrial suburb of Gorky where submarines were made and where the streets were lined with beer stands and the drunks who frequented them.

In six or seven years, Lapina would become a famous actress and one of the sex symbols of late-Soviet cinema. But on those evenings the twenty-two-year-old Nemtsov, dressed in a red tracksuit, would escort the eighteen-year-old beauty on the bus back to working-class Sormovo. They couldn't afford a cab.

Nemtsov loved women, but he loved science even more. He wouldn't come to the institute until the afternoon but could then sit at work and write formulas until late at night. Nemtsov was an efficient worker who could easily switch from one topic to another. His work habits were good in part because he didn't drink much. "People drink to relax, and he just didn't need that," Tsimring said. "He was never tongue-tied. Why drink?"[14] He was so liberated from rules and conventions that, when he was a student, in good weather he would walk around the city barefoot—until one day he got electrocuted when he put one bare foot on the running board of a trolleybus before lifting his other foot off the ground.

In her memoirs, physicist Margarita Ryutova gives another example of Nemtsov's lack of self-consciousness. Impressed by Nemtsov's work on emissions from moving sources, she wrote, Vitaly Ginzburg invited him to scientific conferences that the renowned physicist Vadim Tsytovich had been organizing in Sochi since 1984. The idea of the conferences was to bring together scientists, both famous and up-and-coming, and to discuss the problems of modern science at the intersection of various fields. The Sochi conferences were very prestigious, and for a young scientist an invitation meant being one of the chosen few. Nemtsov took the invitation as a matter of course.

Ryutova described a typical scene at the Sochi conference in 1986, the first time Nemtsov was invited. Isaak Khalatnikov was at the chalkboard. Khalatnikov was the founder of the Landau Institute for Theoretical Physics outside Moscow and one of the country's most renowned and respected scientists. "Khalatnikov was speaking in his soft voice, neatly drawing graphs and covering the board with equations, not referring to any papers at all. As he spoke, people asked questions, which he answered clearly and politely, until Nemtsov spoke up.

"'Isaak Markovich, do you have any idea what you are writing there?'

"Khalatnikov, very politely, replied, 'Yes, Boris, these are components of the five-dimensional metric tensor.'

"'When you're working in five-dimensional space, you need to keep your mind on it.'"[15]

Nemtsov spoke that way with everyone at the conference except Ginzburg, but even with him he spoke freely, much in the same way he'd talk with Boris Yeltsin in a few years. "He never ingratiated himself with anyone," Tsimring said, "and he always behaved exactly the same way in his lectures: very free. He was a free man. I was not as free as he was."[16]

Everything seemed to come to Nemtsov easily, effortlessly: success in science and the joys of personal life. Nemtsov met his future wife Raisa in a queue in the cafeteria at the Gorky Kremlin. Called the Communist Party canteen, it had decent food and an arcane system of Soviet privileges. Only officials and high-ranking Communists were allowed in until two o'clock in the afternoon, and after that the common folk were allowed in. Naturally, there was a line. Nemtsov, then twenty-three years old, came along and, with his usual impudence, jumped in line closer to the cash register. It was the beginning of 1983. Nemtsov was having an affair at the time, but that didn't stop him from flirting. Raisa, an employee of the local library, was three years older than him and married to a military man, although by then the marriage was all but over. "Boris entered the dining room, and all the girls gasped at this extremely handsome young man with a very striking appearance: tall, with almond-shaped eyes, a thick mop of hair and a beard. He was very noisy and was immediately in the centre of attention," recalled Raisa. "I knew that this man was not for me. First I was older. Second, I was not quite available. And Boris was also not available. When we saw his girlfriend, we realized that we weren't in his league. The girl was also really good-looking."[17]

However, the parents of the girl Nemtsov was courting at the time, who were wealthy and successful people, thought that marriage to a researcher at the Radio Institute was a mésalliance. They pressured their daughter to break up with him, a young man so poor he couldn't buy a decent pair of trousers. Nemtsov and Raisa began seeing each other, and in March Nemtsov invited Raisa to go with him to Moscow. They were to stay at his father's house. Raisa wondered whether this meant their relationship was serious? It seemed so. Although they slept in different rooms, Nemtsov's father treated her like his son's bride-to-be. But Nemtsov didn't take relationships seriously and had no intention of getting married, even when Raisa told him she was pregnant. But Raisa insisted: "He wanted it to be business as usual. And I thought: 'How am I going to have a baby with a man I'm not married to?' I said: 'No way!' And so we got married."[18]

The wedding was very modest: just a few close friends gathered at the home of one of Nemtsov's friends. Instead of buying rings, the newlyweds spent the money on essential household goods. They also had nowhere to live, so Nemtsov and Raisa lived in his two-room apartment together with his mother, his sister Yulia, her husband and their child. By March 1984 they were able to rent a one-room apartment, where Zhanna was born. Friends told Nemtsov that he wouldn't be able to keep up with science due to sleepless nights, but Zhanna was a very calm baby. She slept well, and Nemtsov sat next to her and wrote his thesis.

Perestroika was in full swing, but the young physicist did not pay attention. "There was talk about politics, of course," Raisa recalled, "but not as much as about science. When we visited friends, we talked only about science."[19] Nemtsov was entirely taken up with physics, sports and his new family. So when Nemtsov responded to his friend Ashin's article in the institute's newspaper in December 1987, he could not have imagined that politics would become his life's work.

## Gorbachev versus the Communists

Gorbachev and his few like-thinkers in the Politburo, most notably Alexander Yakovlev and Eduard Shevardnadze, had progressive ideas and were embarking on the most important reform—political reform. During the seventy years of Soviet rule, the Communist Party and the government had merged, and now Gorbachev was attempting a surgical operation of unprecedented scale to separate state management from Party control. He wanted to do nothing less than take away the

Communist Party monopoly on power and hand it to the Soviets—the legislative branch—to finally implement the well-known but long-forgotten Leninist slogan "All Power to the Soviets!"

After seven decades of dictatorship, this was the birth of parliamentary democracy. Alexander Yakovlev was already imagining a two- or three-party system. It had not come to this—Gorbachev said that "the time wasn't right yet"*—but the 29th Party Conference, scheduled for the summer of 1988, was fateful. Gorbachev thought that it would mark the true start of perestroika.

The conference was to approve the rules for the country's first alternative elections since February 1917: the election of delegates to the Congress of People's Deputies. The election of deputies was to take place a year later, in the spring of 1989. The conservatives in the Communist Party were already bitterly fighting the reformist pro-Gorbachev wing of the Party. In March 1988 they published a Stalinist article, 'I cannot compromise my principles', signed by "Party activist" Nina Andreyeva (in fact, Yegor Ligachev personally handled the publication). "This impertinent attack by the orthodox [Communist] opposition was something like a cross between the denunciation of Dr Lydia Timashuk, which set in motion the anti-Semitic trial of 'the doctor's plot' [supposedly to kill Stalin] in 1952, and 'A Word to the People', which appeared in July 1991 in the newspaper *Sovetskaya Rossiya* and formulated the position of the State Committee for Emergency Rule [the conspirators who carried out the coup attempt]," Gorbachev's press secretary Andrei Grachev later wrote in his memoirs.[20]

Gorbachev responded with his well-known tendency for indecision, and from the very start political reform was ambiguous. Gorbachev believed in freedom and was ready to take on the Party hacks. But he took a soft stance because it was in his character, and because he sincerely believed that the country and the political regime would change by themselves if nudged in the right direction. Gorbachev was what might

---

\* Gorbachev's aide Andrei Grachev wrote in his memoirs: "Yakovlev recalls that in late 1985, he wrote a note to Gorbachev, proposing to split the Communist Party into two parties: liberal and conservative, keeping them within the framework of one Union of Communists. Gorbachev read the note and just wrote, 'Not yet.'"

be called a true Leninist; he believed that the Communist Party had a future if it returned to the principles of Leninism. And he expected to make concessions to the Party functionaries to get reforms through.

He proposed a compromise: power would go to the Soviets, but in the first stage the Soviets would be headed by Party functionaries, including Gorbachev himself, and the Communist Party would maintain control over the nomination of candidates for the congress. There was certainly no question of abolishing Article 6 of the USSR's constitution, which guaranteed that the Communist Party would be the "leading and guiding force of Soviet society." According to this plan, perestroika would continue to be "managed", and democracy had to coexist, at least temporarily, with the dictatorship of the Communist Party. This special "half-congress" harnessed together a raging steed and a trembling doe.

Physicist Pavel Chichagov, soon to be a member of Nemtsov's team, recalled how he became a political activist. Before the conference, the Party officially invited work collectives to send their proposals on how best to organize the election of deputies. After all, it was perestroika, and the motto was letting the people have their say. Chichagov and several other scientists wrote a letter outlining their thoughts on this matter. It was very liberal, of course. "For me it was a choice," Chichagov recalled. "Either I sit in silence, or I am politically active."[21]

Chichagov personally took their letter to Moscow, to the newspaper *Izvestiya* and to the Communist Party headquarters. He became very nervous when he saw his name and an excerpt from the letter in *Izvestiya*. Who could guarantee that perestroika was irreversible and that no one would come after him? The spectre of the KGB still loomed over the country—and, with it, remnants of fear. As a popular rhyme based on a poem by Alexander Pushkin's had it:

> Now we're in the age of glasnost,
> But this will pass, all the same.
> Then our local KGB post,
> Will remember all our names.

But there was no going back. That's how Chichagov entered politics.

## The ghost of Chornobyl

Life in Gorky became politicized overnight. Informal political groups ranging from democratic to monarchist appeared in the city at the same time as local independent social movements, such as environmental and city protection groups, gradually became stronger. At the state-organized May Day parade for International Workers' Day, local students unfurled a banner bearing the words: "Power to the People!" They had certainly crossed a line, but nothing happened to them.

At about that same time, in May 1988, a small group of activists put up a tent city on Gorky Square in the city centre to protest the construction of a metro, which would entail destroying the historical square. Residents had been fighting the metro for a long time, but all their appeals to the authorities and even protest rallies had made no difference. Stanislav Dmitriyevsky, one of the activists, recollected, "It was a gesture of despair: we didn't think anything would come out of it. But we woke up in the morning and saw we were surrounded by thousands of people."[22]

At the same time, another high-profile engineering project was resumed in Gorky: construction of a nuclear-powered heating plant (Russian abbreviation: AST). The idea for the project dated back to the late 1970s. At that time the slogan "Atoms for Peace" was very popular. But the AST project was started and stopped several times over the next decade. Then in April 1986, the Chornobyl disaster struck. A year and a half later work was set to resume on the plant in Gorky when frightened residents began to protest.

The accident at Chornobyl terrified physicians. The children's hospital where Nemtsov's mother worked took in children from Ukraine with irradiated thyroids. She became an activist. First she asked her son, a physicist, to speak to the doctors, and when the tent city grew on Gorky Square, she went there, too. Her son couldn't stay away. "Mom began collecting signatures," he later recalled. "I was afraid that she would be arrested and put in jail, so I went with her to make sure nothing happened to her, God forbid."[23] Nemtsov's mother stood on the square and held up an anti-nuclear banner. Dmitriyevsky recalled: "One of them [i.e. Nemtsov or his mother] came up and said, 'Can we sit here on the sidelines with our protest?'"[24] The two protest movements joined together.

The tents stood there for about a month, and while they were on the square the *Gorkovsky rabochy* newspaper asked Nemtsov to comment. Although the local physicists considered the fears after Chornobyl to be exaggerated and in general trusted the integrity of the Soviet nuclear equipment, they didn't always trust the human beings running it—some worker somewhere might forget to flip a switch. And besides, the era of Soviet mega-projects was in the past. Nemtsov took that position in his article 'Why I'm against atomic power plants':[25] the construction might be flawed (there were examples), data on radiation levels were not made public and a ground-based plant like this would be an obvious target for sabotage or in a time of war. He proposed a gas-powered heating plant instead.

The article had great resonance. "The anti-nuclear movement read the article and exclaimed, 'Oh! Now we have a physicist!' Nemtsov began to be invited to all the discussions and rallies," recalled Askhat Kayumov, leader of the Volga Region Environmental Movement, then a member of the Gorky University Environmental Movement. "That's how we met,"[26] he said, and it was how Nemtsov became a well-known and popular figure in the city in the summer of 1988. The institute even had a special box for letters to Nemtsov. He spoke at rallies, laying out his objections to the positions of specialists supporting the power station. And he handled criticism well.

Soon after, Ginzburg put Nemtsov in touch with Andrei Sakharov, inventor of the Soviet hydrogen bomb, Nobel laureate and the most famous Soviet dissident. For almost seven years—from January 1980, when he publicly condemned the invasion of Afghanistan, to December 1986—Sakharov lived in internal exile, in Gorky, completely cut off from the outside world. A policeman was always on duty outside the entrance to his apartment, which was on the ground floor of a nondescript building in the city outskirts. The KGB watched and wire-tapped the apartment from two buildings next door, and a jamming device was installed in the basement of Sakharov's building so he couldn't listen to Western Russian-language broadcasts on the radio. Neighbours were urged to avoid Sakharov. "I grew up in a neighbouring building, and we used to run to get a look at his wife, Yelena Bonner, when she came from the capital to visit her husband," recalled Yekaterina Odintsova, who would become a well-known journalist in the city and have two children with Nemtsov. "To us third-graders, she seemed like an emissary from another planet. Our parents yelled at us and told us to have nothing to do with the exiled professor and his wife. So we just admired them from a safe distance. We also knew the men on duty who were guarding the family. Incidentally, because of these guards our yard was the quietest and safest in the neighbourhood. Everyone tried to avoid it."[27]

Exile was agony for Sakharov. He spent many years alone, and from May 1984, when Bonner, who was his only link with the world, was also sentenced to exile with him, Sakharov said he turned into "a living corpse." He went on several hunger strikes and was force-fed until 15 December 1986, when suddenly a telephone was installed in Sakharov's apartment. The next day Gorbachev called him. A week later Sakharov walked back into his classroom at the Physics Institute of the Academy of Sciences to the applause of his colleagues. The release of Sakharov from exile was the true start of perestroika.

In September 1988, Nemtsov was sitting in the kitchen of the Moscow apartment of Sakharov and Bonner. This, Nemtsov later said, was the only time he worked as a journalist, interviewing Sakharov for the popular Gorky newspaper *Leninskaya smena*. Sakharov fully supported Nemtsov: yes, nuclear energy was necessary, and yes, the plant planned for Gorky was much safer than the one at Chornobyl, but at the same time nothing was absolutely safe, and, in the end, a plant operator might get distracted for a moment. So yes, he agreed, ground-based nuclear reactors should be banned. The interview ended with two quotes:

> NEMTSOV: "In spite of the fact that many people in Gorky are against the AST, construction continues."
> SAKHAROV: "I hope that you will be able to turn the tide. I'm completely on your side."[28]

These words were spoken not just by a moral authority, not just by a celebrity, and not just by a Nobel laureate. Nemtsov was being supported by Andrei Sakharov—a political giant, a hero of the era. Opinion polls—perhaps the first in Soviet history—showed that by autumn 1988 Sakharov was ahead of Gorbachev in the political ratings.

## When fear departs

"Great and dramatic" is how the year 1988 is described in the diaries of Gorbachev's aide Anatoly Chernyayev.[29] The Cold War was over. The Soviet Union began to withdraw its troops from Afghanistan. Ronald Reagan came to Moscow in May and stopped using the label of "evil empire" to describe the Soviet Union. And then the Union itself was shaken for the first time. In February, dozens of Armenians were killed in the Azerbaijan city of Sumgait. The Sumgait pogrom was the first outbreak of mass violence in modern Soviet history.

Gorbachev decisively condemned Stalinism, which had become the rallying call for orthodox Communist reactionaries. Every single Soviet ideological concept—the dictatorship of the proletariat, the guiding role of the Party, friendship among nations, the struggle against global imperialism, the ban on private property, the socialist legal system—all this collapsed. The 19th Party Conference held that year played an enormous role in their destruction.

The conference went down in history for many reasons, including the role it played in the career of Boris Yeltsin. Yeltsin had headed the Sverdlovsk regional government in the Urals until 1985, when Mikhail Gorbachev brought him to Moscow, first to work in construction organizations and then as head of the Moscow city government. After Yeltsin's démarche at the October 1987 Plenum,* Gorbachev told

---

\* On 21 October 1987, Boris Yeltsin unexpectedly took the floor at the Central Committee Plenum, a routine Party event to discuss the report on the 70th anniversary of the 1917 Revolution. He gave a rather confused criticism of Central Committee Secretary Yegor Ligachev and the Politburo in general, and of Gorbachev for his emerging cult of personality, and asked to be withdrawn as a candidate member of the Politburo. In response, one after another the Central Committee members branded Yeltsin a renegade who opposed the Communist Party.

him, "I will not let you back into politics," and demoted him from the Moscow leadership back into construction.[30] Politically isolated, Yeltsin had a hard time even getting admitted to the 19th Party Conference. He was seated in the gallery, and at first Gorbachev had no intention of giving him the floor. But Yeltsin almost physically forced his way to the podium and gave a sharply critical speech. Asking the Party for "political rehabilitation", he criticized the permanent status of Politburo members, supported abolishing privileges for the *nomenklatura*\* and advocated open discussion within the Party. "Boris, you are wrong," Ligachev famously told him from the rostrum. With this, the Party split into two wings: the orthodox communists and the democratic movement. Yeltsin had returned to politics.

Soviet people watching the Conference on television suddenly saw for the first time that disputes and discussions were possible within the Party, that voting might not be unanimous, and, most importantly, that this was all normal. You can speak out against the official Party line, and they won't do anything to you—they won't repress you, lock you up, fire you from your job or even, at the very least, remove you from the hall.

This was a turning point in the history of perestroika, the moment when people began to lose their fear of the state. The power of the Communist Party was still strong on the surface, but in reality it was already wobbling. Boris Yeltsin described the atmosphere that emerged after the conference: "A new time is beginning, completely unexplored and unfamiliar. This is the time to find ourselves."[31] Elections to the Soviet legislature were scheduled for March of the following year. Later Nemtsov wrote, "I had already defended my Master's degree and started writing my doctoral dissertation. I wasn't even thinking about a career in politics. But I began to be included in all sorts of environmental projects, and I was invited to meetings and protests."[32]

Nemtsov was no longer just a successful young physicist. Towards the end of autumn 1988 he was an authoritative opponent of the Soviet atomic lobby and the leader of the anti-nuclear movement in Gorky who had received a blessing from Sakharov himself. But Nemtsov already had

---

\* The *nomenklatura* was the list of key state positions filled by Communist Party appointees, the highest and most privileged positions.

a little experience with election campaigns. In October 1988, Nikolai Ashin, who had published that first article in the Radio Institute wall newspaper, was nominated to the district council, and Nemtsov became his proxy. They campaigned together. Nemtsov spoke at voters' meetings, and Ashin personally went around to talk to all his constituents. He won handily. When the winter campaign for the elections of deputies to the First Congress of the USSR began, Ashin dragged Nemtsov into the elections.

Ashin and his colleagues considered Nemtsov to be an ideal candidate: young, famous, talented, right-minded, smart, successful and easy-going. What's more, he was charming and a favourite among women voters. But Nemtsov had to be persuaded to run. He had no desire or intention to go into politics. He was still deeply involved in science. But his ambition made itself felt, and, in any case, neither Nemtsov nor his friends thought that he had a chance of being elected. "It was obvious that he wouldn't make it past the district level," Ashin recalled. "We thought: well, if he doesn't get elected, that's OK. At least we'll make some noise."[33] With that, the Radio Institute nominated Nemtsov.

Ashin feared, and rightly so, the district-level conventions, which were the Party's instruments for maintaining control over the first true elections in Soviet history. These were meetings to discuss candidates and determine who would be nominated to run. In big cities, where political life was already in high gear, some pro-democracy activists managed to get into district conventions by collecting signatures in support, which was easy enough to do. In those districts the conventions hotly debated issues, often all through the night. But the Communist Party structures still had the advantage, even though they no longer reflected the balance of power in society.

The convention for Voter District 158 in Gorky was held on 17 February 1989 in the city administration building. Besides Nemtsov, there were two other candidates, both representatives of the urban elite of the time: Valentin Naidenko, rector of the Gorky Construction Institute, and Alexander Khokhlov, rector of Gorky University. Next to them, the twenty-nine-year-old bearded and curly-haired Nemtsov stood out, even in appearance and certainly with his presentation. Despite being ill with a high fever, he spoke clearly and expressively. "He presented an absolutely liberal electoral program," recalled Viktor Lysov, at the time a democratic activist and also Nemtsov's future assistant. "He talked about private property, about a multi-party system, about the need to abolish Article 6 of the Constitution. It was so strange to hear such tough words."[34]

Nemtsov was booed. The majority of people at the convention represented the Communist Party, and the small group supporting Nemtsov from the Radio Institute and the IAP could not tip the balance of power to their favour. The district convention ended at around one o'clock in the morning with no surprises. Nemtsov was not approved as a candidate. But his little election campaign did not go unnoticed. From the end of winter 1989, Nemtsov was already considered one of the leaders of the local democratic opposition in Gorky.

When a new election campaign began less than a year later, this time to elect deputies to the Congress of the Russian Republic—that is, Russia as part of the USSR—Nemtsov's colleagues would come back to him.

# CHAPTER 2

## 1989–90
## Great Expectations

### Yeltsin's triumph

By the time of the First Congress of the USSR, which was the starting point for Boris Yeltsin's meteoric rise, the entire Politburo, both reformers and conservatives, had already come out against him. The conservatives, led by Ligachev, had long seen him as a traitor to Party principles. Yeltsin's decisive victory in the March 1989 election to the congress had made a strong impression on Gorbachev. Yeltsin won 91.5 per cent of the vote—5.2 million people voted for him. It was a triumph. This is when Gorbachev realized the magnitude of Yeltsin's popularity. He was no longer a renegade, no longer a reckless loner thrown off the Party's ship. He was a real political leader, supported by millions of people.

And this is when their competition began, a struggle destined to play an enormous role in the history of not only the Soviet Union, but the entire world. Yeltsin described their meeting in mid-May 1989, a week before the congress began. Gorbachev asked him to think about working in the cabinet, but he refused. Yeltsin was no longer interested in deals with Gorbachev. He had tremendous momentum, which Gorbachev realized. Gorbachev's aide Georgy Shakhnazarov recalled a conversation with his boss a few months later: "Why not satisfy Yeltsin's ambitions? Say, make him vice-president?" Gorbachev, who would become President of the USSR in May 1990, replied: "He's not fit for this role, and he won't go for it. You don't know him. He is extraordinarily ambitious. He needs to have all the power."[1]

However, for the democratic intelligentsia that were the leaders in Moscow and Leningrad in those years, Yeltsin was not yet one of their own. He was a Communist, until recently a candidate member of the Politburo, who was, moreover, inconsistent—one minute sharply criticizing Communist ideology, the next arguing about "Leninist principles"; one day trashing the Party nomenclature, the next day repenting before it and asking for "political rehabilitation." He wasn't anything like the "aggressively conformist majority"—a famous phrase by Yury Afanasyev, rector of the Institute of History and Archives, one of the leaders of the democratic movement and one of the finest orators of the time. Yeltsin had an unusual personality: impulsive, abrupt, capable of defying the official line (as everyone had witnessed many times) and sensitive to public opinion. He had declared war on the privileges of the Party elite, calling for more stringent reforms. But what did Yeltsin stand for? His views were very unclear at the time. On the eve of the congress, Sakharov also noted: "I have respect for him. But from my point of view, he is a figure on a completely different scale than Gorbachev. Yeltsin's popularity is, in a sense, Gorbachev's 'anti-popularity', the result of the fact that he was seen as opposition to the existing regime and its 'victim'. This explains Yeltsin's phenomenal success [in the elections in Moscow]."[2]

A young economist and future head of Yeltsin's government named Yegor Gaidar had a similar impression. "You could clearly see the strength and political potential, the ability to grasp the problems that really concerned people. But it was totally unclear where this potential would be directed. Everything connected to the economy was especially vague. Gradually it became clear that Yeltsin was ready to use his weapon that had grown blunt over time against the decrepit socialist regime; it was vigorous social populism."[3]

A year earlier the 19th Party Conference had heralded irreversible changes in the country. Now they were coming to fruition. In the Soviet Union, legal political opposition—an opposition to that "aggressively conformist majority"—had appeared for the first time in the hall of the First Congress. Called the Inter-Regional Deputies Group (IDG), its core was a group of Moscow deputies led by economist Gavriil Popov. The group was one of the most influential democratic platforms at the time. It would soon become the Democratic Russia voting bloc, a powerful movement—indeed, a proto-party—and, by the autumn of 1991, it would be the country's main political force. The question of what to do with Yeltsin was left unanswered. Yeltsin himself claimed leadership, but in the IDG there were doubts about whether they should even invite him to join. Yes, Yeltsin was popular, but wasn't he part of the system that he was now fighting against?[4] In the end, to his displeasure, Yeltsin became only one of the five co-chairs of the IDG. Another co-chair was Andrei Sakharov.*

A few months before the congress, in late December 1988, a letter arrived at the television programme *Spotlight on Perestroika*. "We can't go on living like this, the way we are living now [...]. In the canteen and cafeteria, they feed us whatever they can scrounge up. Sometimes you can't even take the sandwich because the luncheon meat is inedible [...], there are no towels, no soap, no steam room." The letter was written by miners from one of the Kuzbas coal mines in Siberia, among the richest in the world.[5] The miners also complained about falling wages, but the main problems were food and soap—neither of which was available. The Soviet economy was in a deep crisis. The relative if stagnant prosperity of the Soviet system in the second half of the 1970s and first half of the 1980s had come to an end.

In 1986, the price of oil plummeted and the Soviet Union instantly became a debtor state. In 1987–88, the country was saved by good harvests, but in 1989 there was a poor harvest, and the economy collapsed. Western banks refused loans, the government didn't even have enough money to import grain, not to mention everything else it needed. Without price liberalization the steps towards the market taken by the government—giving economic autonomy to so-called "self-supporting" (i.e. not financed by the state) businesses—only worsened the situation. Enterprises began to raise salaries across the board, and printing money with a huge budget deficit set off a new wave of inflation as goods flew

---

\* The IDG was headed by Yury Afanasyev, Gavriil Popov, Andrei Sakharov, Boris Yeltsin and Viktor Palm.

off the shelves. In Gorky in 1989, not only was there no meat or oil available on the open market, but even grains and macaroni products could be bought only with food coupons. In July 1989, Kuzbas and all of the country's mining districts went on strike. This was the first mass strike in Soviet history. It scared the Politburo and the Council of Ministers to death. In exchange for Western loans, Gorbachev withdrew Soviet troops from Europe.

"Increasing economic hardship and growing consumer market deficits [...] are undermining the legitimacy of the authorities and spurring massive support for anti-communist protests. This particularly affects the situation in capitals and major cities," Yegor Gaidar wrote.[6] This was the historical context for the Yeltsin phenomenon: everyone who was dissatisfied with the state of affairs in the country, from miners and workers to teachers and scientists, pinned their hopes on him. And when the election campaign to the Congress of the Russian Republic began at the end of 1989, it was already clear to everyone that Yeltsin was the leader of the democratic movement. He was the battering ram that could break down the discredited communist system.

This fact became even clearer on 14 December 1989 when Sakharov died. Six months earlier, Sakharov had spoken from the rostrum of the First Congress: "I have a mandate higher than the mandate of this congress," and no one needed to explain what he meant. His microphone was cut off, the deputies drowned him out by clapping, but he kept going. It was a majestic moment: sixty-eight-year-old Sakharov, looking much older than his years, standing alone against a jeering crowd of Communists. Now he was gone. The anti-Communist movement had lost its moral leader.

A month later, Nemtsov led a solemn ceremony in Gorky to place a plaque on the house where Sakharov had lived in exile. "I believe that today is the first step towards repentance," Nemtsov said. "The first step we must take to earn forgiveness. But it is not the last. We need to raise our heads and live not by lies. And then maybe the horror that took place here in this house won't happen again. Some people have immeasurable guilt on their souls. They mocked Andrei Sakharov, followed him, searched his apartment, force-fed him in the hospital. We should not be like the angry mob and shout, 'Crucify!' But we must calmly and firmly say, 'Resign. Do not anger God. They have to go, and they will go.'"[7]

Nemtsov had just celebrated his thirtieth birthday. He was running for the First Congress of the Russian Republic.

## Deputy Nemtsov

Nemtsov was initially hesitant about running. The Russian-level congress elections were a bit of a comedown—slightly second rate—compared to elections to the Union-level congress. Things were hopping at the union level. The whole country sat on the edge of their seats watching the Union congress, new stars and new leaders appeared, coalitions were formed, all the most important problems were discussed, and it was real politics. But beyond that, Nemtsov was faced with a dilemma. What should he do about his scientific career? Physics or politics? He had a serious choice to make.

By the end of 1989, Soviet science was in a very poor state. People working in the sciences could barely make ends meet, but the fall of the Iron Curtain opened up new opportunities. People began to leave for the West, some temporarily under contract with scientific institutes, and some permanently as Jewish émigrés. Nemtsov couldn't decide. He had no intention of emigrating, but several of his close university friends had already gone to work abroad, and their example looked very attractive. It was a change of scenery, life in another country, a decent salary, all while continuing to do what they loved.

When his friends asked him to run in the elections, Nemtsov refused at first but was eventually persuaded. Shortly before his nomination, he went to consult with his friend Lev Tsimring. Should he stay or go? Science or politics? "I said to him, 'Boris, what can I advise you? The only thing is, don't have any illusions—you won't go back to science,'" Tsimring recalled. "But it seemed to me that even then he had already decided. He needed to get support from the people he was working with. He wanted to get our blessing before he left."[8]

This time Nemtsov was nominated by the IAP. At the institute meeting, Communist Party members grumbled about the nomination, but life had already changed in the country. The Party couldn't block nominations, and candidates no longer went through the "filter" of district-assembly elections. Nemtsov was nominated almost unanimously.

He began his campaign with a relatively small election team—the first real election campaign in his life. The whole city of Gorky was his electoral district. Nemtsov joined the Candidates for Democracy association, which put him at the vanguard of a whole team of people running for office at different levels of government, from district and regional councils to the Congress of People's Deputies of the Russian Republic.

Judging by the huge rally organized by the Candidates for Democracy in the city centre in early February, this was probably the most powerful electoral coalition in Gorky. Nemtsov made a speech along with his future ally, Sergei Kiriyenko, who was from the Komsomol and running for the regional council. The city's top leaders also came. Politics was made in the street, and even the Party bosses who didn't know anything about street campaigning understood that that they needed to go out to the people. The liberal campaign statement of the Candidates for Democracy was published in local newspapers.[9] In politics, they advocated for Russia's sovereignty within the USSR; transfer of power to the Soviets; separation of legislative, executive and judicial powers; equality of political parties; and freedom of the mass media. In the economy they supported equality of all forms of ownership and abolition of the command system of economic management.

The campaign was a series of interviews and meetings at community centres, institutes and factories—up to four meetings a day. Not everything went smoothly, and Nemtsov wasn't allowed to speak everywhere. They wouldn't let him into factories. "At the last minute it would turn out that 'there was a power outage', 'the work shift wasn't over' or some requisite permission was missing," Nina Zvereva, a well-known TV journalist in Gorky who also joined Nemtsov's small campaign headquarters, later recalled.[10] Back then, Nemtsov and Chichagov, who was in charge of scheduling and holding meetings at the headquarters, would take a bag of leaflets, wait for the end of a work shift, stand at factory exits and hand them out to the workers. They travelled by the institute bus, allowed by the Communist Party committee at the IAP. When they couldn't get the bus, they had to use whatever they could find, including a cheap, two-door Moskvich car with a metal box instead of a back seat. Nemtsov and Chichagov would climb inside the box and head for another meeting with voters.

In February 1990 another rally was held in Gorky, the first in the outskirts of the city, where there were factories and most of the workers lived nearby. Most of the workers came. "I remember this black mass of people," said Valery Kulikov, then a member of the Communist Party Committee at Gorky Aviation Plant.[11] The point of the rally was simple: the conditions of the workers in Gorky were not much better than that of the Kuzbas miners. They demanded change. Kulikov spoke, urging the workers to quit drinking and take to the streets.

Nemtsov also spoke, but the audience didn't receive him well. "I had a pretty radical programme for those years," Nemtsov wrote later. "Freedom of speech, private property, open borders, returning the historical name to the city of Gorky and, of course, closing the nuclear power plant."[12] Private property was not accepted by the workers, who grumbled when Nemtsov spoke of it. Nemtsov was not allowed on the territory of the plant by the order of the KGB. In 1990, the KGB was still trying to derail independent candidates before the elections and keep the country's politics under their control, but they were acting more out of habit than conviction and had little success. Photocopies of each issue of the wall newspaper that Chichagov and his comrades made at IAP, and which hung in a prominent place near the entrance to the institute's cafeteria, were sent to the KGB and the Regional Communist Party. After an interview with Nemtsov was printed in the newspaper at the start of the campaign, Chichagov was summoned to the Communist Party headquarters and told to take it down. They told him Nemtsov's criticism of the Communists could be considered a criminal offence and that it was the newspaper's editorial board that would be charged, not Nemtsov. Although there were no direct insults in the text, Nemtsov, shooting straight from the hip as usual, wrote that the Communists were "small-minded people" who would "immediately raise a fuss" at the least criticism.

After Chichagov discussed it with his colleagues, they decided to leave everything as it was. Chichagov was summoned by a KGB officer assigned to the institute. "I told him I wasn't going to pull the interview,"

Chichagov recalled.[13] He had a bad feeling in the pit of his stomach, but he'd made his choice, and the KGB couldn't change anything. The Soviet regime's machine of violence had broken down, and, without it, the Communist regime had lost control over society.

However, the KGB was still quite capable of petty acts of retribution. During the election campaign, Lev Tsimring suddenly saw a note he had written to Nemtsov a year earlier pasted on a utility pole. He'd written about a meeting when Nemtsov was being attacked and booed. Tsimring wanted to support him, so he wrote, "Don't get upset over crap." And he signed it. And now—a year later—this note had been copied and pasted up around the city. Tsimring had no doubt that this had been done by someone in the KGB.[14] The point was also quite clear to local residents: the Jews Nemtsov and Tsimring thought that Russians were crap.

Perestroika freed public thought and discourse, and by the end of the 1980s anti-Semitism had also found its niche in the public space. Liberals and Westerners attacked the Soviet government on the left, nationalists and monarchists on the right. Pamyat (Memory), an organization built on the belief in a Zionist conspiracy, became a significant political force. Nemtsov's Jewish blood on his mother's side did not go unnoticed. "Boris immediately said, 'I want my name to go on the ballot as "Boris Nemtsov, Jew"—why try to hide it when it's scrawled on every fence and written in every leaflet? Better that I say it myself,'" Nina Zvereva recalled later. The problem was that, in his passport, under "nationality", Nemtsov was listed as "Russian" after his father. "So I came up with the idea," Zvereva said, "to write 'Boris Nemtsov, mother—Jewish, father—Russian.'"[15] "I am an internationalist," Nemtsov said in an interview with the Gorky newspaper *Leninskaya smena* in February 1990. "My father is Russian, my mother is Jewish. My wife is half-Russian, half-Tatar. So, three nationalities are combined in my daughter. I have never divided people by nationality. That's barbaric. In civilized countries nationality is not indicated in documents. Only in Nazi Germany and in our country."[16]

Once a group of nationalists came to one of Nemtsov's meetings with voters. When he started talking about what to do to make things better for the people, they shouted "What people? You're a Jew! What people are you going to fight for?" Nemtsov responded the way he had in the interview, saying that he was an internationalist, that nationality was not determined by a word in a passport but by culture and traditions. It wasn't so much his words but how he took the attack that impressed the audience. "I realized how strong Nemtsov was in a confrontation," Chichagov said. "When he's attacked, he's hard as nails. He responded, the guys shut up, and that was the moment I knew he'd win the election."[17]

Twelve people ran against Nemtsov, all of them from the Communist Party. Nina Zvereva described a live TV debate. Nemtsov spoke last— young, curly-haired, wearing a stylish jumper (borrowed from a friend for the occasion). Zvereva had prepared a speech, but by the time it was Nemtsov's turn to speak, everyone was tired. The previous ninety minutes of speeches had merged into one thick wall of noise. Zvereva was watching the debate from home: "I was thinking, come on, don't read your speech, think of something else to say. And he did. He said, 'You know, so many people are promising everything in the world. I won't promise anything, except one thing.' He paused. 'I won't lie.' He said it and stared right into the camera. 'I won't lie.' It was brilliant. After that he tried to repeat that as often as he could: 'I won't lie.'"[18]

Nemtsov stood out against the backdrop of a dozen high-status politicos as the embodiment of innovation. He was a new kind of politician: modern, young, free and yet completely "one of us." He won by a good lead in two rounds of voting and became a deputy of the First Congress of the Russian Republic. In the spring of 1990, Nemtsov began his political career. A time of great hope was coming Russia's way.

## Russia vs the USSR

The question of Russia's sovereignty was the first item on the political programme of the democratic coalition in Gorky. By the spring of 1990, this idea had become the main driving force of Russian politics. Gorbachev believed that, for Yeltsin, Russia's sovereignty was a kind of crowbar to break into power in the country. As Gorbachev's aide Shakhnazarov wrote in his memoirs:

The positional struggle between the rival leaders soon reached the stage of open warfare on every conceivable front. At times they would clash in hand-to-hand combat, so to speak, with sharp political statements and demeaning characterizations of each other. But Yeltsin always took the initiative. At first, he stayed in the background, engaging in battle only after the artillery rounds shot from the Democratic Russia headquarters and activists—mass attacks on the government in the press, mass demonstrations in Moscow and Leningrad, miners' strikes. But after Sakharov's death he took the lead. The idea of Russian sovereignty was the battering ram against the Union leadership and the president.[19]

The personal feud between the two leaders, Gorbachev and Yeltsin, largely determined the agenda. When Yeltsin took a step down from the Union level to the republic level, he began to undermine the central government. He attacked and Gorbachev defended. And then Gorbachev dealt the *coup de grâce* to the Soviet regime: he broke the monopoly of the Communist Party. In March 1990 he oversaw the abolition of Article 6 of the Constitution on the guiding role of the Communist Party, introduced the post of President of the USSR and took office.

But the list of complaints from the hardline Communists continued to grow while the democratic public now suspected that Gorbachev wanted to usurp power in the country. This, in historical perspective, was unfair. Gorbachev didn't increase his personal power: he decreased it. But the intelligentsia had turned its back on him. Gorbachev looked weaker and weaker, unable to score a victory on any front. The weaker Gorbachev was, the stronger Yeltsin seemed.

The idea of Russia separating from the Soviet Union sounded almost ridiculous. The USSR (at least in its Stalin–Brezhnev sense) was "Big Russia", a new version of the Russian Empire. How could it secede from itself? The paradox was well illustrated by the scene that Yeltsin's widow Naina described in Boris Minayev's book. She recalled a day in early spring 1990 when Yeltsin came home and said, "We have to save Russia!"

> To be honest, I did not understand a thing, and I was even frightened. What Russia? At the time there was only the Soviet Union, and no one was thinking of anything else. So I asked:
> "Boris, what are you talking about, what Russia?"
> "Our Russia!"
> I made him lie down, gave him some medicine, some herbal remedies. I even felt his forehead. Maybe he was running a fever?[20]

The outskirts of the empire were already in open rebellion. Estonia was the first country to put its declaration of independence on Gorbachev's desk in November 1988. Then Lithuania and Latvia followed, and in August 1989 on the fifty-year anniversary of the Molotov–Ribbentrop Pact a human chain surrounded all three republics—every fifth citizen of the Baltic countries stood hand-in-hand across all three countries. At that point even Moscow understood that they couldn't hold the Baltic republics in the Union without violence.

Pro-independence movements were also growing in the south of the Soviet Union in the southern Caucasus, the three republics of Georgia, Azerbaijan and Armenia. Blood had already been shed. In April 1989, the Soviet army brutally suppressed an independence rally in Tbilisi, the capital of Georgia, and a few months later they put down unrest in Baku. The nationalist movement in Ukraine was growing stronger. A wave of revolutions swept through Eastern Europe as soon as the Soviet Union began withdrawing its troops. In November 1989, the Berlin Wall fell, giving new impetus to the disintegration of the Soviet Union. The Soviet system ceased to exist, first of all in people's minds. But Gorbachev still believed in it. "Faced with the hard choice of continuing perestroika or preserving the Union, Gorbachev chose the Union at that moment, hoping that he would be able to manoeuvre without sacrificing perestroika," his aide Andrei Grachev wrote in his memoirs. "That's how he started on the path that led to the loss of both."[21]

If the empire no longer existed, then what would become of the mother country, Russia? By the spring of 1990, the answer to this question had appeared. Russia and its people were also victims of a stagnant, deceitful and authoritarian union—that is, Communist—government.

This answer suited everyone. The right-wing camp was able to promote the nationalist idea. Since June 1989, the Russophile writer Valentin Rasputin had stood at the speaker's podium of the First Congress, pontificating on whether Russia should leave the Union: "Without the fear of becoming nationalists, we can say the word 'Russian' and speak of national self-identity."[22] For Western-looking democrats, Russian sovereignty symbolized a break with the Soviet totalitarian past, a foundation on which to build a new free state. Sovereignty became synonymous with national identity and freedom. At the First Congress of the Russian Republic, Yeltsin put it this way: "The most important, primary sovereignty of Russia is the human being and his rights."[23] Finally, against the backdrop of the emerging economic disaster and the Union government's lack of will, all hope for an improvement in life was already being pinned on Yeltsin and the Russian government. People were hoping that by shedding the ballast of the Soviet republics, Russia would quickly become a rich and successful country. Sovereignty promised decisive reforms, and at the same time embodied the economic interests of the nascent Russian elite already eager to push aside the elderly Soviet bureaucrats.

"The Russian 'revival' became an acutely relevant idea for absolutely all classes, strata, and political movements," wrote Boris Minayev. "Yeltsin endowed this idea with some features of dry pragmatism."[24]

## The people want freedom

Nemtsov first saw Yeltsin at Sakharov's funeral on 17 December 1989. "Yeltsin stood there like a bear," he later recalled, "and when he turned his head, his whole body turned, too." They met four months later on 14 April 1990. Deputies from the democratic coalition gathered to discuss the upcoming congress. Privileges were still in effect, and deputies were beginning to enjoy the perks. They could buy train tickets to Moscow at a special ticket office, were put up in the Rossiya Hotel with a view of the Kremlin and could order gourmet smoked fish and red caviar in their cafés. Nemtsov, who opposed these privileges, even gave the waitress a dressing down when she tried to sell him a box of candy that was hard to find. By then the bloc of deputies called Democratic Russia had more than two hundred people. Nemtsov was a member of the congress's organizational committee. He dictated key ideological guidelines from the Democratic Russia platform to journalists. "The First Congress of People's Deputies of Russia must do what has not yet been achieved at the Union level—take complete power of the government of the Russian Republic."

Just a few months previously, democrats had been looking askance at Yeltsin. But by the spring of 1990, he was a different man and a different politician. Gone was the populist Communist who had broken with the Party. Here was a rebel and a true leader of the people. "Populist—I don't consider this an insult," Yeltsin calmly explained in an interview at the time. "Many leaders aren't in touch with the masses. They don't even know how to go about it."[25] Yeltsin had a huge personality that overshadowed even then all his conceivable shortcomings, no matter how much official Soviet propaganda exaggerated them. Leaflets and newspaper articles depicting him as a drunkard had the opposite effect and only increased his popularity. If they said he was a drinker, it was probably slander. But if it was true, it meant he was one of us.

Russia had never seen anything like the rallies that were held in the squares of Moscow and other Russian cities in early 1990s. These were not just rallies in support of Yeltsin. They were pro-freedom rallies. "There are moments in history when people yearn for freedom," Nemtsov said many years later. "And there was a moment like that in modern Russian history. It was the late 1980s and early 1990s. The people thirsted for freedom! When a million people gathered on Manezhnaya Square [right next to the Kremlin] and demanded to crush communism and give people freedom, it was a real breakthrough!"[26]

Yeltsin's famous charisma, multiplied by the love of the people, was unbeatable. He was a very big man, very Russian, with handsome chiselled features, perhaps a bit rough around the edges but full of life, determined, courageous and honest. Yeltsin embodied the hopes of all strata of society for a happy future—a future that would come very soon if the path of reform was followed, a future where freedom meant full store shelves. Nemtsov looked at Yeltsin the same way. For him, Yeltsin was a superman, a giant capable of turning the wheel of history.

"I realized that I was meeting with someone legendary. I thought that he would give a lecture on freedom, democracy and human rights," Nemtsov recalled.

> But when we said hello, Yeltsin immediately asked, "So what ideas do you have, what should we start with in the Supreme Soviet,* what do you suggest?" And for almost the entire two and a half hours that the meeting lasted, Yeltsin was silent. He took in what we said, which impressed me enormously. He may have said a few general words at the end—that he really liked the meeting, that there were important proposals, and they concerned not only the state structure of the country, but also the problems of the development of entrepreneurship, taxes and so on. Yeltsin's remarkable modesty simply astounded me. I had expected something very different...[27]

The two main goals of the democratic bloc at the congress were to elect Yeltsin chairman of the Supreme Soviet and to fulfil the first point of their political programme: proclaim Russian sovereignty. These tasks complemented each other: sovereignty gave the future chairman real power, and, with a leader like Yeltsin, it was clear why sovereignty was needed. Work on the declaration was already in full swing on the eve of the congress. "I remember it very well," Chichagov said. "Nemtsov came running over and said, 'Let's write a declaration of independence.' I started looking at other countries' declarations, then we discussed what should be included. I sat down to type our text. And then Nemtsov grabbed it and ran."[28]

Nemtsov took his version to a session of the commission specially created to work on the declaration. Nemtsov needed a rough outline, a draft, to have something to discuss. All the democrats felt the romantic appeal of the declaration. The Russian Republic was a half-empty formal division within the large country called the USSR. But now there would

---

\* The Supreme Soviet was the permanent and highest body of the two-chamber congress. Although on paper it was the most powerful body of government, during the Soviet period it was largely a rubber-stamp body that passed unanimously decrees and laws sent to it from the Communist Party.

be a real democratic state in its place, with a separation of powers, an independent court, guarantees of political rights and freedoms. And it would not be subject to the dictates of the Communist Party.

Of course, the ambiguity of Russia's status inside the Soviet Union remained: the congress of the Russian Republic noted in the text of the declaration that it "declares its determination to create a democratic state based on the rule of law within a renewed USSR", and this renewed USSR was to be based on some kind of new agreement between the republics. But then another important point appeared, stating that Russian laws would take precedence over Soviet ones. This meant that Russia wanted to have control over its own budget and not support the other republics of the Union.

Boris Yeltsin, who was at the time just one of more than a thousand deputies at the congress, used that text in his speech. Soon he was elected chairman of the Supreme Soviet of Russia. The position, which made him effectively the head of Russia at the time, was of great historical significance. This was the decisive round in the battle between Gorbachev and Yeltsin. Alexander Lyubimov, a deputy who was also one of the hosts of *Vzglyad* (Viewpoint), the most candid and popular talk show on television in those years, recalled how he, Nemtsov, and other young democratic deputies lobbied the Communist deputies to vote for Yeltsin instead of the Politburo candidate. Deputies like Lyubimov who were already making money all chipped in, exchanged their roubles for foreign currency and bought a case of imported beer—an unthinkable luxury at the time. They gave the Communist deputies cans of beer in return for their promise to vote for Yeltsin. "They'd ask, 'What if I take the beer but vote against Yeltsin?'" Lyubimov said. "We told them that if Yeltsin won, everyone would be able to buy this beer, including them."[29] The Communists and Gorbachev fought against Yeltsin's election as best they could. Gorbachev himself even came to the congress to campaign against Yeltsin. In the end, Yeltsin won in the third round by four—just *four*—votes. This victory cleared Yeltsin's path to the top post. It was the moment that determined Gorbachev's defeat.

But no one knew this then, including—and especially—Gorbachev who, as his aide Shakhnazarov wrote, at that moment "wouldn't have bet on Yeltsin for anything and was convinced that his opponent had used up his potential and tried to convince society of this."³⁰ After winning the election, Yeltsin was lifted to the top of the Russian hierarchy. In his memoirs, Yeltsin recalls entering his airy new office in what came to be called the White House, the very building he would order tanks to fire on in three years' time, and hearing an aide say, "Look at the office we seized!" and thinking to himself, "What next? After all, we didn't just seize an office. We seized all of Russia."³¹

The Declaration of State Sovereignty, the prototype of the future constitution, answered the question of what it meant to "seize Russia" and what Russia actually was. On 12 June 1990, it was adopted, to thunderous applause, by an overwhelming majority in the congress. Of more than a thousand deputies, more than nine hundred had voted in favour. "The most important achievement of the congress is that we elected Boris Yeltsin chairman of the Supreme Soviet of the Russian Republic," Nemtsov later told journalists. "This is a man of truly great potential, a man of clear intelligence, who is progressive and very hardworking. I think that our desire to change the system—both political and economic—is also important. By now everyone probably understands that it is impossible to make an economic revolution without a radical change in the political system."³²

A month later, Yeltsin would defiantly resign from the Communist Party right at the Party congress in front of Gorbachev and the entire Politburo. The Russian leader would close the book on his past, and from this point on a new historical era would begin: the building of a democratic, free Russia.

## Last chance to save the Union

In the Yeltsin-led Supreme Soviet of Russia that began to work after the congress ended, Nemtsov wanted to join the Legislation Committee.* Sergei Shakhrai, who would soon become a key member of Yeltsin's

---

\* The Supreme Soviet was formed from deputies according to a complicated procedure. The regulations allowed Nemtsov, who was a deputy but not a member of the Supreme Soviet, to sit on the Legislation Committee.

team, had just been tagged to head up this committee. He recalled vividly how Nemtsov came to him.

> It was a hot summer day. I remember perfectly. He was in light-coloured pants, sandals, a short-sleeved shirt, smiling, hair sticking out every which way. He said, "I want to work in the Legislative Committee." I asked him, "Why? You're a physicist." And he said, "I want to write the law on land." My jaw dropped. He went on: "I know the problems we need to solve to sign in this law. Put me in charge of this law in the committee." This was an absolutely amazing proposal, unconventional. I thought: Either he'll come up with something interesting or he'll mess up completely. I said, "Let's give it a try."[33]

In the summer of 1990, the country was on the verge of famine. This is not a metaphor or an exaggeration. Store shelves were empty. Even Moscow, traditionally better supplied than other big cities, had introduced a system of vouchers for goods in short supply. In Nemtsov's hometown of Gorky, the city deputies demanded that everyone except for emergency-care medical personnel, no matter their age, be let off work to harvest the crops to ensure that there would be food in the city. Riots over tobacco and vodka swept across Russia. Even in Moscow, people blocked the streets, demanding cigarettes. "The editorial office was flooded with calls from city residents who could not redeem their vouchers for meat products or sugar," wrote Gorky's newspaper *Leninskaya smena*. "'How long will this go on!' people are exclaiming, exhausted by their daily ordeal. Listening every day to a mass of reproaches, complaints and even threats, we feel the temperature of public indignation rising. If there is a delay, society will explode."[34]

Gorbachev and the Union government hesitated, but Yeltsin understood that they could not wait. They were already drafting reforms to allow the sale of land and other goods as well as codifying the legality of private property. Everything had to be done from scratch. For seventy-two years, the country had been without private property, and the only possible forms of farming were the *kolkhoz* (collective farm) and *sovkhoz* (state farm). The idea of transitioning to private land ownership seemed like a betrayal of socialism. It was just unheard of. Future agriculture minister Viktor Khlystun remembers Nemtsov's appearance at the June 1990 meeting of the working group on land reform. "He had a poor grasp of how land ownership was regulated, but he was very taken with the idea of multiple forms of ownership. He spoke briefly and powerfully. And he began to come regularly to meetings of the Agrarian Committee when land was discussed."[35]

Khlystun thought there should be cooperatives and farms in addition to private land ownership. To support Khlystun's efforts, Nemtsov began to promote the reform in his committee. Eventually the law was passed. But another question was on the agenda: who would implement it all? This is how Nemtsov met the economist Grigory Yavlinsky, who had already been working on a programme of reforms for several months and had just become deputy prime minister in the new Russian government. This would soon be called the 500 Days Programme.

Work on it was done at a dacha in a special state-owned settlement near Moscow called Arkhangelskoye. In the summer of 1990, Nemtsov and Raisa spent about a month in Arkhangelskoye. There, Nemtsov met Yavlinsky. "We were discussing, oddly enough, land reform," Nemtsov recalled. "There were a lot of other things related to the details of the 500 Days Programme—privatization strategy, de-monopolization of the market, releasing prices, creating an open economy, etc. [...] Yavlinsky and I even discussed appointing an agriculture minister, because I was working on land reform in the Legislative Committee. And then Viktor Khlystun was appointed. He was a very good minister."[36]

Yavlinsky's star was rising. By mid-1990, not one professional and ideologically open-minded economist had any doubts about what needed to be done. The programme of market reforms launched in Poland by the economist Leszek Balcerowicz served as a reference point. There might have been disagreement over details, but both the diagnosis and the essence of the economic therapy necessary for the country were obvious to all: price liberalization, financial stabilization, privatization. All this was in the 500 Days Programme, and, as Yegor Gaidar wrote, "One publicity innovation was absolutely brilliant—the break-down of what would be done by day."[37]

Initially Yavlinsky's programme was designed for 400 days. It ended up on Yeltsin's desk almost by accident in May 1990. Yavlinsky himself later claimed that someone had simply stolen it from the computer he used. One May afternoon he got a phone call from Yevgeny Yasin, an economics professor and colleague who was working in the Union government. Yasin said, "Yeltsin is reading out bits and pieces from your programme..." But in Yeltsin's telling it sounded like the reforms would last 500 days, not 400. Yavlinsky thought the culprit was Mikhail Bocharov, an economist and Yeltsin associate who was close to Gorbachev and who was also running for prime minister of Russia. Yavlinsky went to him. "Why are you deceiving Yeltsin?" he asked Bocharov, "This is a national programme. The only thing Russia's economy has registered on the books are dry cleaners and laundries... And it certainly can't succeed without raising prices." A few days later, Yeltsin was already waiting for Yavlinsky in his office. The arguments did not work on him. Listening to Yavlinsky's objections, he frowned and said: "You have to do it like I say: 500 days and for Russia. Go and write the text."[38]

With that, Yavlinsky made the meteoric rise from a Soviet state department head to deputy prime minister of the Russian Republic. But all the same the programme couldn't be carried out at the level of Russia. Without the inclusion of the Union levers of power, it was nothing but a fig leaf. The republics were still helpless compared to the Union. Then Yavlinsky realized that it should be a joint programme between the USSR and the Russian Republic, the leading republic in the Union. They had to bring the idea to Gorbachev.

But how could they convince Gorbachev to join forces with Yeltsin and convince Yeltsin to form an alliance with Gorbachev? First Yavlinsky flew to see Yeltsin, who was on holiday in Jūrmala, a resort on the Baltic Sea in the Republic of Latvia. As they strolled along the beach, Yavlinsky told him of his idea: create a working group of two governments to prepare a common reform, with Russia at the forefront of economic reform in the USSR. After hesitating, Yeltsin agreed. "So can I go to Gorbachev?" Yavlinsky asked. Yeltsin nodded.[39] It didn't take much to convince Gorbachev. Depressed by the defeats he had suffered at the Russian congress, he saw in Yavlinsky's programme a way out of this impasse. In addition, economic reforms—and cooperation with Yeltsin—brought him closer to his cherished goal: to keep the USSR from disintegrating. Gorbachev's biographer William Taubman relates that when Nikolai Petrakov, the economic adviser to the Soviet president, brought him a note summarizing Yavlinsky's programme, "Gorbachev, who seemed preoccupied, glanced at it quickly, then focused on it more carefully, and then suddenly came alive with an almost joyful grin."

"Where is this fellow?" he asked.
"At work," Petrakov replied.
"Where does he work? Get him here right away."[40]

Gorbachev was seriously interested in the 500 Days Programme. He met with Yavlinsky's team and forced almost all his ministers to meet with them, too. At one meeting after another, Gorbachev wanted to get down to details. But the Union cabinet, led by Prime Minister Nikolai Ryzhkov, rebelled against change. The Soviet bureaucracy simply could not entrust its future to thirty-year-old economists who talked about free-market prices and private property. These men were as determined as the leaders were. Ryzhkov arrived at one of these meetings in Arkhangelskoye—with a full motorcade as befitted the head of the Soviet cabinet—and he even brought lunch for all participants from the premier's special rations (a meal that young economists could only dream of in 1990). During the meeting, Andrei Vavilov, a twenty-eight-year-old researcher, the future deputy finance minister in Yegor Gaidar's government, recommended that Ryzhkov resign. Ryzhkov instantly stood up, left the room and drove off.

Despite Gorbachev's enthusiasm, the 500 Days Programme stood no chance. The old guard's way of thinking was simply incompatible with this programme of radical reform.

Negotiations and meetings went on for about a month. In the end Gorbachev gave up. He never dared to take any significant steps to change the economy. The 500 Days Programme was buried. Years later Gorbachev explained his refusal to Sergei Aleksashenko, one of the authors of the programme. "How could I trust you with the future of the country? You were so inexperienced, and I didn't know you at all."[41]

And so, perhaps the last chance to manage economic reform in the Soviet Union was lost. In October 1990, Yavlinsky resigned and left the Yeltsin government. "From that point until the autumn of 1991, there was no chance for any economically meaningful policy. A fierce power struggle began between the collapsing Union and Russia," wrote Gaidar.[42]

Yeltsin went on the attack again. "The biggest result of our work is the creation of a programme of radical economic reform," he said. "The initiative to develop it belongs to Russia. [...] But the situation in the republic is not improving. The main reason is the economic insecurity of our sovereignty."[43] Yeltsin knew what he was doing. He was starting to gear up for the elections again. He wanted to become president.

## Nemtsov goes abroad

Once Nemtsov became a people's deputy of the Russian Republic, he threw himself into political life. In light of his new position, the Radio Institute allocated him a room in the basement of one of its buildings. Fighting the Communist Party was still at the centre of the political battle, and work began on an anti-communist newspaper at Nemtsov's headquarters in Gorky. "We began to fight against Gorbachev and for Yeltsin," recalled Viktor Lysov, a close Nemtsov associate in those years. "We campaigned for him and supported everything he did." And in Moscow, the charming and sociable Nemtsov made hundreds of new acquaintances, from deputies to TV stars.

One of the people Nemtsov got to know well was the parliamentarian Viktor Aksyuchits. Seven years later, when Nemtsov came to Moscow as first deputy prime minister, Aksyuchits would become his adviser. When they met, Aksyuchits was primarily a religious activist, one of the founders of the Russian Christian Democratic Movement, but he was also one of Russia's first successful entrepreneurs. And it was thanks to Aksyuchits that in August 1990 Nemtsov went abroad for the first time in his life—to Paris, where Aksyuchits chaired a congress of young Christians and meetings with Russian émigrés.

In 1990 the contrast between grey, dark, half-starved Soviet reality and the world of the West was a profound cultural shock for anyone there for the first time. It was like stepping onto another planet. In his memoirs, Yeltsin's aide Lev Sukhanov recalled how shocked Yeltsin was when he walked through an ordinary supermarket in Houston during a visit to the United States in September 1989. It took Yeltsin a long time to come to his senses afterwards, when he was already on the plane, "sitting with his hands clasping his head", and then giving free rein to his emotions. "What have they done to our poor people?" he wailed. "It seems to me," Sukhanov wrote, "that after Houston […] Yeltsin's last pillar of Bolshevik consciousness finally collapsed."44*

The world of capitalism in its everyday incarnation was so much better—in every way—than Soviet life that it was very hard to put this into perspective. Nemtsov, of course, was not as sentimental as Yeltsin, but he, too, was amazed as he walked around Paris: the Champs-Elysées with its stores and boutiques, Montmartre with its street artists, and Rue Saint-Denis with its sex shops, stripteases and cheap variety shows. Aksyuchits, who in his youth as a sailor had been to European capitals, escorted Nemtsov around Paris as his more experienced senior comrade. "He held back his feelings," Aksyuchits recalled, "but it was obvious that he was shocked by all the incredible glamour."45 In his mind, the West was like a dream come true—a dream that could be brought to life in Russia, too, if Russia were free.

At that time in Nemtsov's mind, as in the minds of the overwhelming majority of democratically minded people, the concepts of "Yeltsin" and "freedom" were already almost synonymous. And this perception was reinforced as Gorbachev relied more and more on the hardline Communists in his entourage, and as the Soviet government became more and more firmly associated with political reaction. Perestroika discredited itself with new price increases and a monetary reform that was popularly called "Pavlovian" (after the new prime minister, Valentin Pavlov). The miners continued to strike. In January 1991, Moscow decided to use force in Lithuania, which had declared independence. Soviet tanks invaded Vilnius, and fourteen people were killed during the

---

\* Nemtsov retold a story he'd heard from the deputy Nikolai Travkin. Travkin described how he and Yeltsin had stopped at a supermarket during a trip to Sweden and Yeltsin "burst into tears right there in the store."

storming of the television centre (it is still unknown whether Gorbachev himself took part in making these decisions). From this point on, the democratic rallies in Moscow and other Russian cities were already distinctly anti-Gorbachev. Moreover, in Moscow, under the slogans "Today Lithuania. Tomorrow Russia. We Will Not Allow It!" and "Freedom Will Die with Us", hundreds of thousands of people took to the streets. Gorbachev even tried to ban rallies, but without success. In a television interview that was broadcast all over the Soviet Union, Yeltsin openly called for Gorbachev to resign.[46]

In this context, the All-Russian referendum of 17 March 1991 on instituting the office of the presidency in Russia was perceived as another step towards freedom. Nemtsov became one of about a hundred proxies for Yeltsin when he went to the polls. Nemtsov, a nationally known deputy who had already fulfilled at least two of his campaign promises—the city of Gorky had regained its historic name of Nizhny Novgorod and now allowed foreign visitors—was now campaigning for Yeltsin for the presidency. There was no doubt in Nemtsov's team that Yeltsin would win the election.

Surprisingly, even when Nemtsov was a parliamentarian and Yeltsin's confidant, he didn't think that politics would remain his vocation forever. He thought his political career was temporary—he'd continue to teach and his future lay in science. He wasn't dissembling or being coy when he said in an interview in May 1991: "A time came when it was hard to do science. Now our future and our fate lie in politics. I hope that in three or four years our scientific and artistic intelligentsia will step away from politics. They and other people will have an opportunity to work freely without interference. Our work—the work of the intelligentsia—in politics is not for ever."[47]

That's how they understood the situation at the time. People involved in politics didn't think it was serious or would last for long. "We thought we could work [in politics] for a while and then leave," Alexander Shokhin, one of Nemtsov's future government colleagues, later recalled.[48] Back then, in May 1991, neither Nemtsov nor others suspected that in a few months the Soviet Union would cease to exist and their lives would change for ever.

# CHAPTER 3

## 1991
## The Last Battle

### The first president

However paradoxical, Mikhail Gorbachev was accused of both having dictatorial tendencies and being weak, especially after the winter of 1991. More often he was accused of weakness. But Yeltsin strode towards the presidency of Russia in strong contrast to the indecisive Gorbachev and all Soviet officialdom. Gorbachev was afraid of reforms while Yeltsin was ready for them. Gorbachev zigzagged while Yeltsin made a beeline for democracy. The idea that the country's president must be strong and decisive arose from the political context, from the struggle between Yeltsin and Gorbachev. "The main paradox of Russia was that its state system had long been hobbling along on its own; no one was really running it," Yeltsin would write in his memoirs. "Russia has long lacked a truly authoritative leader."[1] The president should be a leader, the leader should be strong—these truths were self-evident.

Exactly one year after Russia's declaration of sovereignty was adopted, Yeltsin won the first round of presidential elections and became the first president of Russia. The inauguration was scheduled for 10 July. It was a truly monumental occasion: everything was a first. For the first time, a president elected by all the people was the head of Russia. For the first time, the president would take the oath of office before his people. For the first time, the government's responsibility to society would be stated aloud.

"For centuries in our country the government and the people have been at different poles [...]. For centuries, the state interest was placed above the individual," Yeltsin said at the ceremony. He was visibly nervous, but only once glanced at the text he held in his hand. "For the first time, the citizens of Russia have made their choice. They have chosen not only the president, but above all the path our country will follow. It is the path of democracy, the path of reforms, the path to renew human dignity."[2]

Over the rousing music of Glinka's 'Patriotic Song'—Russia's national anthem since November 1990—the familiar Russian republic flag was raised over the Kremlin building where Gorbachev had allocated Yeltsin a residence. This was an astonishing period in Russian history, although it didn't last for long. Two bears were in the same den, and two flags were flying over the Kremlin at the same time—the Union flag and the Russian flag. Neither at that moment nor later did Yeltsin have any doubts that he was destined to carry out a historic mission—to lead Russia through the storms of reform to true freedom.

## Gorbachev receives visitors

On a warm June day in 1991, Gavriil Popov, one of the leaders of the democratic movement who had just won the Moscow mayoral election, walked into the residence of the US Ambassador to the USSR. Sitting with Ambassador Jack Matlock at the table in his office, Popov exchanged pleasantries as he wrote something on a piece of paper. He knew that the residence was bugged by the KGB. He slid the note over to Matlock, which read: "*A coup is being organized to remove Gorbachev. We must get word to Boris Nikolayevich.*" Boris Nikolayevich Yeltsin, who had just been elected president, was in Washington, and in three hours he was to meet President Bush. Matlock wrote back: "*I'll send a message. But who is behind this?*" Popov picked up his pen again and wrote four names: Pavlov, the head of the Soviet government; Kryuchkov, the chairman of the KGB; Yazov, the defence minister; and Lukyanov, the chairman of the Supreme Soviet of the USSR.

That evening Matlock was in Gorbachev's office in the Kremlin, but he didn't pass on the names of the alleged conspirators. "How could the American ambassador credibly tell the chief of state of a power that until very recently had been an adversary that his prime minister, intelligence chief, minister of defence, and speaker of parliament were conspiring against him?"³* After listening to Matlock, Gorbachev grinned and assured him that everything was under control. And after the meeting he told his aide Chernyayev: "You know, Yevgeny Primakov [at that time a member of the USSR Security Council and one of Gorbachev's associates] said to me yesterday, 'You put too much trust in the KGB and your security detail. Do you trust them?' He replied, 'You, too? Another alarmist,'" Chernyayev recalled.⁴ Gorbachev was self-confident and an idealist. He could not believe that men whom he had personally appointed could raise their hand against him.†

There were other indications of the coming coup attempt. Actually, the reactionaries in the Communist Party had been on the attack since late 1990. For a while Gorbachev even played along with it, first because he was consumed by his battle with Yeltsin and second because he simply didn't know what else to do. After losing his last political campaign for the 500 Days Programme, he didn't know what to do next. "He had exhausted himself intellectually as a politician. He was tired," Chernyayev later wrote. "The era had overtaken him—the era that he had created himself."⁵ On the other hand, conservatives were invigorated. In January, the bloody coup attempt planned by KGB Chairman Vladimir Kryuchkov in Vilnius was, in fact, the first rehearsal for the Moscow coup.‡

---

\* Popov had his own sources in the KGB. One of the founders of the democratic movement, Yevgeny Savostyanov, wrote in his book *Democrat–Double Agent* that it was his idea to send Popov to Matlock; there was no other reliable way to get information to Washington. But Bush, instead of informing Yeltsin, called Gorbachev.

† After the coup attempt was over, Gorbachev told a news conference that he trusted Kryuchkov and Yazov most of all.

‡ The Republic of Lithuania declared independence from the Soviet Union on 11 March 1990 and began to disengage from the USSR, while the Soviet Union used economic, political and military pressure to keep the republic in the Union. In early January, Soviet special military units were sent to Lithuania, and on 10 January Gorbachev demanded a restoration of the constitution of the USSR in Lithuania and the revocation of all so-called anti-constitutional laws. On 11 January, Soviet military units began to seize key buildings, including the television centre. Fighting broke out and fourteen people were killed by the Soviet troops. The Soviet army, however, did not storm the parliament because of the crowds surrounding it. A muted stand-off continued for eight more months until the August coup attempt in Moscow.

Then Gorbachev received information prepared by the KGB that the Kremlin was to be stormed during large democratic rallies. Gorbachev believed this misinformation. He banned demonstrations and even agreed to bring troops into Moscow. Armoured personnel carriers and fifty thousand troops were brought into the capital, but later Gorbachev changed his mind and ordered the troops to be withdrawn.

The situation changed in mid-spring when Gorbachev began talks with Yeltsin and other leaders of the Union republics about a new Union treaty. These negotiations went down in history as the Novo-Ogaryovo Process, named for the luxurious governmental residence Novo-Ogaryovo on the Moscow River to the west of Moscow. The goal of the negotiations was to come up with a way to reformat the USSR: to give the Union another chance as a federation of independent states, delegating to the centre some specific functions, such as defence and currency issue. The Novo-Ogaryovo process marked a new truce between Gorbachev and Yeltsin, and now the reactionaries in the Union government were going against Gorbachev, not with him against Yeltsin and the democrats.

The first demands for Gorbachev's resignation were voiced at the plenum of the top leaders in the Communist Party in April. In June, at a session of the Supreme Soviet of the USSR, three days before Popov's visit to Matlock, the new Soviet prime minister, Pavlov, demanded, with insolence typical of him, that emergency presidential powers be granted to the government, which essentially meant taking them away from the president. Pavlov argued that Gorbachev had too much work. Pavlov's address to parliament came as a complete surprise to Gorbachev.

An hour later, Vladimir Kryuchkov stood on the same podium and told the deputies how American intelligence had infiltrated the Russian leadership decades ago. He was referring to Alexander Yakovlev, the architect of perestroika, whom Gorbachev had already relegated to the background. Yakovlev had studied at Columbia University in New York in the late 1950s and then served as Soviet ambassador to Canada. For the first time since perestroika began, at the highest levels of government there was talk of a Western-directed fifth column in power (in fifteen or so years' time, all state propaganda would be based on this idea) but most importantly, as William Taubman wrote in his biography of the

Soviet president, "One could hardly imagine a more brazen challenge to Gorbachev."[6]

Gorbachev didn't respond to this attack. No resignations followed. Gorbachev had already demonstrated his passivity and weakness so many times that his gatekeeper colleagues behaved like a pack of predators that smelled blood. The result was that ad-hoc conspiracies against both perestroika on the one hand and Yeltsin and Gorbachev on the other came to a head at the same time. In late July, *Sovetskaya Rossiya*, which had printed the Stalinist letter from Nina Andreyeva two years earlier, published 'A Word to the People', a proclamation that could be considered the manifesto of the future State Committee for Emergency Rule (and which was undersigned by some of its members). "How did it happen," the authors asked, "that we [...] let come to power people who do not love this country, who are servile to overseas patrons and seek their advice and blessing? [...] We must say 'no' to saboteurs and invaders!"

On the night of 29 to 30 July, Gorbachev, Yeltsin and Nursultan Nazarbayev, the president of Kazakhstan, met at Gorbachev's residence in Novo-Ogaryovo. The draft of the new Union treaty was ready, and the presidents decided to move up the signing from late September to 20 August. Yeltsin demanded that Gorbachev dismiss Pavlov, Yazov and Kryuchkov. Gorbachev agreed. To discuss this delicate personnel issue, the three leaders even went out on the balcony at the request of Yeltsin, who feared wiretaps. Yeltsin and Gorbachev insisted later that their conversation was recorded by the KGB and transmitted to Kryuchkov, who understood that he had to act without delay. However, the would-be conspirators didn't need wiretaps. "The text of the Union treaty alone was enough," wrote Ignaz Lozo, a German journalist who extensively investigated the coup, "for Kryuchkov, Yazov and Pavlov to clearly understand that if they signed it, they would largely or completely lose power."[7]\*

---

\* On Kryuchkov's orders, the KGB had been tapping phone conversations between Yeltsin and other Russian leaders for a long time, but it is impossible to say for certain that they listened in on the historic conversation on the balcony in Novo-Ogaryovo. Lozo believes that the suspicion they were being tapped was simply one of the many rumours circulating during the dramatic events of August 1991.

Vladimir Kryuchkov, the last head of the Soviet-era KGB, had worked as a prosecutor under Stalin. But the year that defined his world view was 1956. He was already a member of the diplomatic corps and worked as a secretary at the Soviet embassy in Budapest under Yury Andropov, who would go on to be chairman of the KGB and general secretary.* At the time, Andropov was the Soviet ambassador to Hungary and from then on became Kryuchkov's mentor, boss and lodestar. Andropov and Kryuchkov saw how Hungary rebelled against Communist rule in October 1956; how the Soviet army faced fierce resistance in the streets of Budapest; how, after Soviet then-leader Nikita Khrushchev ordered the withdrawal of troops from the city, Communists were massacred—they were hanged from trees; and how the Soviet army returned to Budapest and drowned the uprising in blood. Andropov and Kryuchkov saw that power rested on strength and fear, and what happens to that power when strength and fear are absent.

From the start, Gorbachev, who was himself one of Andropov's favourites and a protégé, saw Kryuchkov first and foremost as Andropov's assistant, someone who wasn't the brightest star in the sky but who would be obedient and serve him well. That's how fate elevated Kryuchkov in 1988, in the midst of perestroika, to the post for which the industrious but uneducated apparatchik—"the quiet old man with a steely gaze", as Yeltsin would call him in his memoirs—was clearly not well suited. Kryuchkov honestly supported Gorbachev, but he couldn't accept perestroika. With each passing day it became harder for him to remain loyal. By the spring of 1991, he was already one of the leaders of the conservative wing in Gorbachev's entourage, which sought by any and all means to reverse perestroika and regain control of the sprawling Soviet empire.

On 1 August, Yeltsin showed his hand. He announced that a new Union treaty would be signed on 20 August. On 2 August, Gorbachev officially confirmed it. There was no turning back: a new relationship between the centre and the republics would be a reality in the very

---

\* The general secretary of the Central Committee of the Communist Party of the Soviet Union was the *de facto* leader of the Soviet Union.

near future. On 4 August, Gorbachev flew to his Black Sea residence in Foros, Crimea, for a holiday. The following day, Kryuchkov gathered the future conspirators at a secret KGB residence in the neighbourhood of Yasenevo on the outskirts of Moscow. Kryuchkov led the conspiracy and devised the plan. They would fly to Gorbachev in Foros, give him the option of declaring a state of emergency in the country and, if he did not agree, "temporarily" hand over the presidential powers to Vice-President Gennady Yanayev.

On 18 August, at about 4.30 p.m., communication with the outside world was cut off at the presidential residence in Foros. Twenty minutes later Gorbachev was told that unexpected guests had arrived from Moscow. Frightened and taken aback, Gorbachev nevertheless refused to sign the decree on the state of emergency and sent them back to Moscow empty-handed. That very evening, Kryuchkov called the conspirators to the Kremlin. They officially formed the State Committee for Emergency Rule and decreed that the committee was the ruling body in the country. Preparations for introducing troops into Moscow began. Scripts for radio and television broadcast were hurriedly prepared overnight. At six o'clock the following morning, the decrees of the committee were read out in special news bulletins. A *coup d'état* had taken place in the Soviet Union.

## 1917 or 1964?

Nemtsov flew to Moscow on 18 August with his wife Raisa. They left their six-year-old daughter, Zhanna, in the village with her grandmother and were just passing through the capital on their way to Sochi. This was their traditional holiday spot, where Nemtsov would continue to practise his favourite new sport, surfing. Since Nemtsov was a parliamentarian, they stayed in the Rossiya Hotel right by the Kremlin walls. They checked into their room, unplugged their phones to keep from being woken up and went to bed. They were awakened by knocking on the door. Nemtsov's assistant Tatyana Grishina had reached a clerk on duty and asked him to pass on a message. Nemtsov immediately turned on the television. The ballet *Swan Lake* was on every channel.

On the morning of 19 August, time turned backwards. Columns of tanks rolled down empty Moscow avenues, bringing into the capital the grim, heavy, cold spirit of the Soviet past. The decrees from the State Committee for Emergency Rule stated that the transfer of Gorbachev's presidential powers to Vice-President Yanayev was "for health reasons." They spoke of the motherland being "in deadly peril", of the goal being to save the USSR, and they declared a state of emergency in Moscow, prohibiting rallies and demonstrations and instituting control of the media and a ban on the democratic press. Tanks on the streets of Moscow, *Swan Lake*, TV news anchors greeting viewers with a brief "Hello, comrades" before immediately reading decrees in a monotone... all this portended the horror of a return to totalitarianism. No one knew what was coming, but images of bloodshed and arrests loomed in the uncertainty. Once again, the shadow of the all-powerful KGB had fallen over the city.

Raisa Nemtsova was trembling with fear and almost sobbing as she walked with Boris from the hotel lift to the White House, where the Russian Supreme Soviet was in session. She did not know when she would see him again, or even if she would ever see him again.

At about the same time, the motorcade of the president and members of the Russian government had left nearby Arkhangelskoye for the White House. Yeltsin had flown in from Kazakhstan the night before. The first headquarters of the resistance to the State Committee appeared spontaneously around Yeltsin in the early morning hours at Arkhangelskoye and had produced an appeal to the citizens of Russia. As Yeltsin climbed into the car to go to the White House, his relatives, as his daughter Tatyana later recalled, were struck by the thought that they might be seeing him for the last time. Scenes like this—as if they were sending soldiers off to the front—were happening everywhere. "Masha [Maria Strugatskaya, Yegor Gaidar's wife] came out with the children to see me off to Moscow," Yegor Gaidar wrote about the morning of 19 August, "waving, with tears in her eyes, clearly not sure that we would meet again."[8]

"I didn't think about anything but how horrifying it was and wondered whether I would see my wife and children again," recalled Sergei Shakhrai. He, too, had been at Arkhangelskoye and also went from there to the White House. "My wife was on the steps. Women sense everything right away and were saying goodbye for the last time. But then there was the usual bustle of departure, which helps in stressful situations."[9]

The worst and more terrifying night—that of 20 to 21 of August—still lay ahead, but on the 19th it was already clear that something was awry. The conspirators were behaving strangely. First, they didn't arrest Yeltsin. As it would later turn out, a group of Alfa commandos—a special unit created under the KGB—had surrounded Yeltsin's dacha in Arkhangelskoye that night, but no arrest order was ever issued, and Yeltsin and his comrades-in-arms made their way peacefully to the White House. (In addition to Yeltsin, the conspirators had planned to detain sixty-eight other prominent democrats but didn't. During the three days of the coup, the KGB detained only four people.) Second, they never blocked or even turned off the phones in the White House. Third, the commanders of the military units entering Moscow clearly did not understand what was going on and what they were supposed to do.

The commander of the 106th Airborne Division, Major-General Alexander Lebed, was ordered to take a battalion under his command and "organize the protection and defence of the building of the Supreme Soviet of the Russian Republic." The battalion was to be met in the centre of Moscow. Lebed arrived at the White House alone, knowing nothing about what was happening in Moscow. He was astonished to see people building barricades around the building. Trolleybuses, cars, rebars and wooden planks were being used. Lebed had no idea what was going on. If this hadn't been arguably the most dramatic moment in Russian history in decades, his arrival might have made a good scene for a comedy. "I had the most confused thoughts swarming in my head," the general recalled. "I must say that, as I was leading the marching regiments, sitting in a communications car with no television set, I did not hear any statements from the State Committee or other leaders. The people who were building the barricades seemed to me to be simple, good people. If I was being ordered to protect the Supreme Soviet with my battalion's forces, then we would defend ourselves together with these people. Then a question naturally arose: against whom?"

After a while Lebed reached his battalion. That was on Kalinin Prospect (now renamed Novy Arbat), very close to the White House. The barricades were growing higher and becoming stronger. Those same "good and simple people" surrounded the armoured personnel carriers. The excited crowd shouted and jeered at the soldiers, but Lebed still didn't understand what was going on. He learnt about the State Committee in the White House, when he was taken to a meeting with Yeltsin.

"Yeltsin asked, 'What's your mission?' I reported, 'To protect and defend the Supreme Soviet building with the paratrooper battalion.' The president asked for clarification. 'On whose order?' I answered briefly: 'By order of Lieutenant General Grachev, Commander of Airborne Troops.' 'Who are you protecting and defending against?' Since I didn't know myself, I replied evasively: 'Who does a guard defend a building against? From any person or group of persons who threaten the post or the sentry.'"[10]

Actually, by then Yeltsin had already seized the initiative, and the State Committee had already suffered perhaps the worst blow—a moral defeat. Yeltsin had arrived at the White House unimpeded that morning and turned it into the headquarters of resistance. At noon he climbed atop a tank and read the handwritten address from Arkhangelskoye to the citizens of Russia. This scene and these words went down in history as his finest hour. "On the night of the eighteenth to the nineteenth of August 1991," he declaimed, "the legally elected president of the country was removed from power. No matter what the justification for his removal, this is a right-wing, reactionary, anti-constitutional coup." Yeltsin's speech was first heard by the hundreds of people gathered around. Then it was printed, copied and posted all over Moscow. More and more barricades went up. For the first time the Soviet authorities encountered popular resistance in the heart of the capital, and for the first time the people had a leader. "Perhaps never before did Yeltsin's legendary strength of will help him as much as it did during these hours," future aides to the Russian president would write in their book, *The Yeltsin Era*. "His quick action and determination had a demoralizing effect not only on the State Committee, but also on the rank and file."[11]

At first only the centre of Moscow heard anything about Yeltsin's speech. The rest of Russia continued to watch *Swan Lake* on TV and read the State Committee press releases.

That's why the second major symbolic victory over the coup conspirators was a simple question asked by Tatyana Malkina, a twenty-four-year-old journalist for *Nezavisimaya gazeta*, at a press conference late in the evening. The press conference was broadcast live, so the entire nation heard it. "Do you realize that tonight you carried out a *coup d'état*?" she asked. "Which comparison is the more apt—1917 or 1964 [i.e. when conspirators in the Politburo removed the head of state, Nikita Khrushchev]?"

This question, like most of the others asked at the press conference, had to be answered by the "headliner", Gennady Yanayev. Yanayev had learnt about the coup and his role in it only the night before, when Kryuchkov telephoned him and summoned him to the Kremlin. The vice-president of the USSR, formally the second person in the government, did not want to put himself in danger by disobeying the chairman of the KGB. The decree that made him president "in connection with Gorbachev's illness" had been written without him, and he didn't want to sign it. In fact, he'd personally called Gorbachev a few hours earlier since he was supposed to meet him at the airport the next day, and he knew that he was perfectly healthy. But the conspirators put pressure on Yanayev—reminding him that he was in the same boat with them—and Yanayev gave in. Now, the day after, he mumbled a barely intelligible reply to Malkina, but his words didn't matter. The important thing was the question itself, unthinkable in the world of the State Committee and KGB. The question instantly stripped the government of its lustre of victory, like in the fairy tale about the emperor with no clothes. Yanayev's slightly trembling hands, which the whole country also saw, soundlessly completed the picture.

## The road to the future

Nemtsov spent all three days in the White House. Raisa visited him there every day, and sometimes Nemtsov was able to call her at the hotel.

At the White House, life quickly settled into a routine. Everyone had something to do. Deputies telephoned their regions, trying to find out what was going on, passing on news from Moscow and rallying people against the conspirators. Nemtsov was doing this as well. Censorship had been instituted, and the independent press had been shut down. The White House even had its own radio station, which broadcast inside the building and to the people in the square, with the most famous journalists of the time on air: Bella Kurkova (the head of St Petersburg Television) and Alexander Lyubimov (one of the journalists of the groundbreaking talk show *Vzglyad*). "We really needed news from the regions," Lyubimov said. "We pretended that the whole country supported us. Nemtsov would come and tell us what was going on in Nizhny Novgorod."[12]

The country was frozen in anticipation, waiting to see who would emerge victorious from the standoff in Moscow. People took to the streets in major cities, but apart from Moscow, the only large-scale events were in St Petersburg, where the new mayor and one of the country's leading democratic politicians, Anatoly Sobchak, was calling for resistance. The struggle against the coup was playing out on a small patch in Moscow: the square in front of the White House and the few blocks around it.

The night of 19 to 20 August passed quietly. The group Democratic Russia decided to call everyone to a rally at the White House. Yeltsin was against it at first: he was afraid of detentions and bloodshed, but then he gave the go-ahead. At the same time, Moscow mayor Gavriil Popov wanted to hold a democratic rally near the Moscow city government building, known as the Mossovet. "We started calling people to both the White House and the Mossovet," said human-rights activist Lev Ponomaryov, then one of the leaders of Democratic Russia. "We decided that I would go to the Mossovet and bring people to the White House from there. And we did. Not only did the State Committee do nothing—we had a police escort with their lights flashing!"[13]

This may have been the most important rally in Russian history. On 19 August only a few thousand people had gathered in front of the White House, but the next day the crowd had swelled to between 150,000 and 200,000. "It was the crowd that made the biggest impression on me," Sergei Shakhrai recalled, "I was astonished by how they had come and blocked off the White House. It put everything in its place: it meant that we were doing the right thing. This was not just a rally for the sake of a rally. This was a rally around the building of the Supreme Soviet. It was a human shield around the symbol of democracy—the White House. And everyone knew perfectly well that the White House couldn't be protected. No number of human shields could defend the building if the armed forces attacked."[14]

Actually, it wasn't a rally. It was an unarmed people's militia. People poured in and stood in rows. Some brought sandwiches, some brought tea, and some brought paper for printing leaflets and proclamations. The people who came to the White House were ready for anything. Some deputies went outside and talked to the soldiers. Nemtsov and Aksyuchits went to Manezhnaya Square where a division of special forces, tanks and personnel carriers stood behind security barriers. "We showed our IDs and went through the checkpoints, walked from tank to tank and had heartfelt conversations with the guys," Aksyuchits said later. "We told them: if it comes down to it, you'll be shooting your brothers, sisters and fathers."[15]

While that was happening, a meeting was being held in the office of the Soviet deputy defence minister, Vladislav Achalov, on when and how to storm the White House. Kryuchkov wanted to schedule the assault for 4.00 a.m. General Lebed was also called to this meeting and reported that 100,000 people were standing near the White House, and that any military operation would end in mass bloodshed. At Achalov's request, he made a pencil sketch of something resembling a plan of attack. From the point of view of military strategy, the plan was a complete hackwork, but in the end it didn't matter: it seemed to vanish into thin air. The military looked at the plan, nodded and did nothing. No one wanted to take responsibility. "The State Committee fell hostage to disunity, indecision and the principle of collective responsibility," wrote Ignaz Lozo.[16]

At the very beginning of the coup, Kryuchkov made a cowardly mistake. He hadn't given the order to arrest Yeltsin because he hoped to negotiate with him. By the second day it was already too late: the State Committee had lost the initiative. The whole world was listening to every word Yeltsin said. Even the conspirators' censorship had failed: *Vremya*, the main evening news programme on nationwide Channel One, aired a long segment about the defence of the White House. The huge rally in front of the building paralysed the will of the military. Kryuchkov shifted decision-making onto the generals, but they failed to act. "Everything was passed on to the military, dumped on them, and it was all done verbally without any clear orders and without official documents," Achalov recalled later. "In the end, it was every man for himself."[17]

On the evening of 20 August, at the last meeting of the State Committee, Kryuchkov and Interior Minister Boris Pugo once again proposed dispersing the crowds in front of the White House and placing Yeltsin under house arrest. But once again, the idea just hung in the air. Once again, the conspirators made no decisions.

In the end, all they did was declare a curfew in Moscow. Defence Minister Yazov was against the use of force from the very beginning. He ordered night patrols of the city, and the military was ordered not to shoot and not to respond to provocations. The problem was that no one in the democratic camp knew anything about this order. To the contrary, rumours that there would be an assault had been leaking into the White House all evening, and everyone was preparing for an attack on the building.

The situation in and around the White House grew more and more anxious. People were lighting bonfires and continuing to build barricades. Yeltsin was calling state leaders. "Over those three days, he acted like a true Russian everyman," Nemtsov later recalled, "tough and brave—the way I imagine commanders behaved when they fought off attacks during the war." But, even then, Nemtsov noticed one of Yeltsin's most prominent traits—his mood swings. "He gave commands, sometimes ill-conceived, telling men what to do. And then he'd dissolve into a kind of melancholy only to come to again and begin to lead the defence."[18]

Chairman of the Russian Supreme Soviet Ruslan Khasbulatov warned the deputies about a possible assault and even offered to distribute weapons. "We have a well-organized defence," General Kobets, head of the White House defence, reported to the deputies. "Sixteen barricades, twelve of them at the first line of defence, 1,200 to 1,400 meters from the White House. We have 300 armed professional soldiers, and in addition Afghan war vets and 1,500 volunteers, mostly students..."[19]

After the coup attempt, a journalist from the magazine *Ogonyok* described that night: "The subject of Validol, an over-the-counter anti-anxiety drug, came up among the deputies. Someone realized that he had not eaten anything since morning and now it was the middle of the night; he was comforted by the information that it was better to take a bullet to the gut on an empty stomach. Various options were considered: they'd be arrested, they'd be put in barracks where they could continue their work... they'd be kicked out onto the street... 'Exactly 23 years ago,' said the deputy Viktor Sheinis, 'tanks entered Prague.' Boris Nemtsov shouted for men to join the troops..."[20]

But there was no assault. The tragic death of three people that night in the tunnel under Kalinin Prospect was caused by panic in the city and the anticipation of an assault. A platoon of armoured vehicles drove into the tunnel and found themselves surrounded by a barricade of trolleybuses and rebars. It wasn't even heading towards the White House, but the over-excited crowd didn't know that. At that moment how could Muscovites tell the difference between patrolling and storming? The crowd started throwing stones and Molotov cocktails at the armoured vehicles. Some people climbed onto the running board of the front vehicle and covered the windshield with a tarpaulin. Among them was twenty-three-year-old Dmitry Komar, who fell off and was crushed under the treads when the tank jerked back and forth to shake off the attackers. At the same time, the terrified mechanics began shooting in the air, trying to drive the crowd away, but one of the warning bullets ricocheted into forty-three-year-old Vladimir Usov, killing him. Twenty-eight-year-old Ilya Krichevsky was shot in the head, but how it happened remains unknown. Three days later the funeral procession would fill the entire city centre, Gorbachev would award Komar, Usov and Krichevsky the title Heroes of the Soviet Union—making them the last heroes of the USSR—and a year later Yeltsin would award them medals of Defenders of Free Russia.

Komar, Usov and Krichevsky died between midnight and 1.00 a.m. Shocked by this news, Yazov immediately gave the order to stop patrolling and to withdraw troops from the city at dawn. That was the State Committee's death sentence. During the night, Kryuchkov was still contemplating an assault, but the train had already left the station. He was still hoping for the best when, in the morning, Yazov's subordinates were coordinating the details of the troop withdrawal with the Moscow mayor's office. "If you stir up trouble, be sure you can answer for it," Yazov told the conspirators when they came to him to persuade the marshal to "go all the way."[21]

On 22 August Russia celebrated victory: the conspirators were arrested, Gorbachev returned to Moscow at night, and at noon the Russian tricolour, reborn, was raised over the White House. Triumphant Muscovites gathered by the walls of the White House. Nemtsov, wearing yellow trousers and a grey jacket, stood on the White House balcony not far from Yeltsin, looking out at this sea of people and cheering with everyone. This enormous, magical victory belonged to everyone. Those days and weeks were majestic and spiritually uplifting, a time when everything seemed possible. The forces of evil, which had long blanketed Russia, had fought their final battle and lost. They simply evaporated, vanished into thin air. The decrepit, corroded Communist dictatorship suddenly crumbled into dust, darkness dispersed, and the road to democracy and freedom became visible in the light of day. Ahead lay the road into the future.

# CHAPTER 4

**1991**

# A New Country

### A physicist and a priest talk to Yeltsin

By the end of September, Lev Ponomaryov and his allies in Democratic Russia were very angry. The Soviet dictatorship had collapsed, but there was much still to do, and they needed to work fast to achieve their goals. They had to put the coup conspirators on trial, ban the Communist Party, form a government and prepare for the upcoming elections.

But Yeltsin wasn't in Moscow. He'd gone off to his residence in Sochi and stayed there. Democratic Russia was the most powerful political force at the time. In 1990 it had organized the largest rallies in the country's history. Without its support, Yeltsin would not have won his key victory to head the Supreme Soviet of the Russian Republic. And now, Lev Ponomaryov and his associate, the priest Gleb Yakunin, were about to fly to Sochi to see Yeltsin and give him an ultimatum: if he didn't return to Moscow within a week, Democratic Russia would join the opposition.

Ponomaryov and Yakunin had one more mission: on behalf of Democratic Russia they were going to give Yeltsin their recommendation for prime minister. Ponomaryov had a Ph.D. in physics and Yakunin was a former dissident and advocate for religious rights who had spent five years in a Soviet prison camp. Not long ago, their opinion had counted for little. Now it was largely up to them to decide who would join the future government, and the candidates for prime minister were seeking their support. Ponomaryov remembers receiving a phone call from Alexander Rutskoi, the military officer Yeltsin had chosen to be vice-president. Rutskoi summoned him to his office. As he drew arrows and lines with chalk on the blackboard and peppered his speech with a slew of obscenities—as befitting a man of the military—he told them, "Don't think that all I learnt in the military academy was how to fly a plane. Democratic Russia ought to recommend me for the post of prime minister."[1]

Yegor Gaidar, along with his closest associate Anatoly Chubais, also came to see Ponomaryov. Gaidar, a thirty-five-year-old economist and grandson of the most famous Soviet children's writer of the 1930s, had been studying transition economies and reforms in the socialist countries for the past several years. He already had experience in preparing policy briefs for the Politburo (when Gorbachev took over in 1985) and for the Soviet government in the late 1980s, when he worked for the magazine *Kommunist*. Even at the fledgling seminars held by young economists in a resort near Leningrad back in 1986, a team of market economists had formed around Gaidar.

In 1990 Yegor Gaidar, a staunch liberal and clear-eyed believer in the market economy, became head of the Economic Institute that he had founded. And although Grigory Yavlinsky's star was shining more brightly at that moment, Gaidar was competing for the informal title of the country's leading new-style economist. Pyotr Aven, a veteran of Gaidar's economic circle and later a minister in his cabinet, recalled that in the spring of 1991 they saw themselves as the future cabinet. After all, someone had to save the economy, which was in the death throes of a collapsing state. "All across Eastern Europe, young economists were coming into government, and we presumptuously believed that there was no other team in Russia better than us," Aven recalled.[2] A few days before the coup attempt, Gaidar received an offer to become an economic adviser to the Russian president. Gaidar met with Gennady Burbulis, the secretary of state and Yeltsin's right-hand man, on 19 August in the White House. In mid-September, Gaidar and his associates had a commission from Burbulis and were already writing a programme of economic reforms. They stayed at one of the government dachas in Arkhangelskoye. "What was good about Gaidar's plan,"

Burbulis recalled later, "was that every idea in his document came with steps and instruments for implementation: law, decree, decree, law, directive. It was clear what was being proposed and how it would be implemented."[3]

When Gaidar and Chubais learnt that Ponomaryov was holding consultations with potential candidates and came to him for support, they already had something to show him. They persuaded him that they were ready to take on the responsibility. Ponomaryov was particularly impressed that Gaidar had a team and wasn't working on his own. "We discussed the matter at the Democratic Russia council," Ponomaryov recalled, "and decided that we would recommend Gaidar's team to Yeltsin. They were professionals who knew the modern European economy."[4]

Alexander Korzhakov, Yeltsin's security chief, met Ponomaryov and Yakunin at the gates of the presidential residence in Sochi. Yeltsin, accompanied by Burbulis, received them the next morning. Ponomaryov told Yeltsin: "On paper you can be the head of the cabinet, or Gennady here can. But in reality, let Gaidar head it up on your behalf."[5] Yeltsin paid attention. He paid even more attention to the ultimatum issued by Democratic Russia. A week later he returned to Moscow.

## Youth or experience?

The decision certainly wasn't made only in response to the demands of democratic activists. Yeltsin realized that they had to act decisively and make drastic changes to the economy. But Ponomaryov and Yakunin's recommendation of Gaidar carried weight. Yeltsin met with Gaidar in late October. The fiasco of the 500 Days Programme, which had been buried by the elderly Communist Party bureaucrats, had not yet been forgotten. But the Soviet Union was no more. Although its collapse had yet to be formalized by the Belovezh Accords in December, the Union effectively ceased to exist the day after the coup failed. With the central Union government gone, Russia could and indeed had to go forward on its own, a responsibility that fell to Yeltsin. He understood that compromise with the socialist order was no longer possible—they had to take the leap into capitalism. He believed in the free market. The academics and managers at Gosplan, the Soviet-era agency responsible for the entire country's economic planning and development, could not make such a leap. "Something had to be sacrificed—either youth or experience," Yeltsin told the deputies, justifying his choice of Gaidar.[6] He sacrificed experience. He bet on fresh minds that had not been corrupted by the bureaucratic groupthink of previous years. It was a thoughtful—or, in the case of Yeltsin, an emotional—choice, but in any case, a conscious one. He was certainly not dissembling when he announced the programme to the deputies of the congress and said it was the most important decision of his life. "Gaidar's professional concept coincided with my inner determination to go down the bumpy part of the road quickly," Yeltsin would write in his memoirs. "I could not make people wait again, delay such important decisions, such important processes for years to come. We had already decided to do it, so why wait?"[7]

Yeltsin delivered his historic speech launching economic reform at the Russian Congress on 28 October. He spoke of the "unique opportunity to stabilize the economic situation in a few months and begin the process of recovery." He said that prices would be freed this year—which meant immediately—and spoke of a deficit-free budget, privatization and other reforms. He said at first it would be hard, but by next autumn, in a year's time, the situation would stabilize and become easier. Many years later Gaidar explained that in their October meeting he didn't claim to Yeltsin that economic growth would begin in a year. Judging by the experience of Poland, that was impossible. He had said only that the problem of commodity shortages would be solved within a year.[8]

The Russian press immediately dubbed the Gaidar reforms "shock therapy." Reformers have always objected to this term, saying that people understood the "shock" in Gaidar's plan as the electric shock in a defibrillator used to save a person having a heart attack.

It was another grand moment in Russian history—grand in the sense of a transformation of enormous scale. With this, Russia changed its status, as it were, transforming itself from one of the republics of the Soviet Union into an independent, sovereign country, and one that saw itself as a democratic market economy and part of a civilized world community. Indeed, at the end of December, after the official death of the USSR, Russia's name would also be officially changed to the Russian Federation. This was Yeltsin's goal. "He was opting for a Russian state—self-standing, governable, and capable of modernization and normalization," Timothy Colton wrote in his Yeltsin biography. "To put it another way, he opted for nation-building over empire-saving."[9]

At the same congress, Yeltsin announced that he would lead the new cabinet in order to assume public responsibility for the reforms, and the deputies readily approved. Gaidar became deputy prime minister. He and his colleagues were put in charge of the entire economic bloc. Viktor Khlystun recalled that on 14 November, when the main appointments in the cabinet had already been made, he received a phone call from Gennady Burbulis.

"The president expects you tomorrow morning at nine-thirty."

"To discuss what? What should I prepare?"

"The topic is your appointment as minister of agriculture."

"Gennady," Khlystun protested, "I'm not an agronomist. My specialty is forms of land ownerships. I can't be agricultural minister."

"Tell all that to the president," Burbulis said.

Khlystun stayed up all night, trying to come up with arguments to explain his refusal to the president. With his arguments in his head, he went into Yeltsin's office in the Kremlin at 9.40 a.m. on 15 November. As Yeltsin stepped out from behind his desk and put out his hand for a handshake, he said warmly, "You need to work in a new capacity." Khlystun started to say he wasn't ready to take this post but didn't have time to finish his sentence. The president interrupted him. "Was I ready to be the president? We'll work and learn as we go. This isn't up for discussion. Here, read this." Yeltsin handed to Khlystun the signed decree of his appointment and looked at his watch. "In fifteen minutes, the session of the new cabinet will begin. Don't be late."

Yeltsin turned around and walked out of his office through the back door. Khlystun couldn't possibly make the meeting on time. The president was assembling the cabinet for its first, historical session in a conference hall in one of the Presidential Administration buildings outside the Kremlin. Khlystun couldn't walk there in fifteen minutes. When he did enter the hall, Yeltsin was already speaking. "Why are you late?" he asked in a threatening tone, and after his trademark pause added: "Some people here think that they are not ready to work in the cabinet. But let me make it clear: I'll decide who's ready and who's not."[10]

After reprimanding Khlystun, Yeltsin continued to address the new cabinet: "You and I have a great responsibility. Each of us is aware that we are entering a risk zone, that we are risking our political careers and reputations. But I am personally taking this step openly, directly and without hesitation, because Russia has tremendous potential, and I believe in Russia. And we must somehow convey this faith to the people. We will win a few months with this faith—maybe the most important months that we will have..."[11]

## Democracy or an iron fist?

The revolution started by Gorbachev had ended in conservative reaction and economic disaster. No one had any doubts that the reforms would be very painful. Gaidar told Yeltsin outright that he would soon have to fire him. Since then, historians and participants have wondered whether Russia could have made this sweeping historical change more easily. Could Russian democracy have become more stable?

One of the famous complaints about Yeltsin was what Lev Ponomaryov had told him in Sochi on behalf of Democratic Russia. After the coup failed, Yeltsin should have acted quickly on the wave of victory when the democrats' position seemed unshakable. Instead, he went to Sochi for almost a month. He should have pushed to adopt a new constitution, dissolved the congress and held new elections. Viktor Sheinis would later compare him to Napoleon—what if he'd gone to the Côte d'Azur after his victory at Austerlitz?[12] The more time that goes by, the more valid the criticism seems. Had he moved quickly, Russia might have been spared the terrible, fateful events of October 1993, when a civil war broke out in Russia and Yeltsin gave the order to fire on the Supreme Soviet building—and this time, unlike in August 1991, the order was carried out. Over the years it became clear that this was typical of Yeltsin. He'd hesitate and freeze in dramatic moments and then suddenly break out of his lethargy only when he had no choice. This character trait would play a significant role in Russian history several times.

What did Yeltsin do in Sochi? According to the press, he played tennis. Perhaps he drank. He was under enormous strain from the events of August, and he had been given enormous power—this time real power—and inherited insurmountable problems. What should he do with the Soviet Union? What should he do with Russia? How should reforms be carried out? Yeltsin would later admit that by putting off questions of Russia's political reorganization until a better time, he had missed a very important chance. "I probably made a mistake," he'd write, "by choosing my main line of attack on the economic front and leaving the playing field of state structure to constant compromises and political game-playing."[13]

The draft of the new constitution was almost ready when Yeltsin announced the economic reforms to congress. But neither Yeltsin nor Ruslan Khasbulatov, the chairman of the Supreme Soviet*—who was beginning to get a taste for his powerful new post—wanted to discuss it. So they tabled it. But that was not all. When Yeltsin declared economic reform to be the main priority with all other issues subordinated to it, he demanded a one-year moratorium on all elections in the country. "It is not possible to conduct full-scale election campaigns and comprehensive economic reforms at the same time," he declared. "It would ruin everything!"[14] At the same time, the president was granted extraordinary powers, albeit temporarily. He could appoint and remove members of the cabinet and future governors, and in economic matters his decrees had the status of law if they were not challenged by the Supreme Soviet.

The decisions of Yeltsin and his team were understandable. Who would dare to deregulate prices—something that could no longer be delayed—while simultaneously conducting dozens of local election campaigns? Would that have been wise? This was naturally one of the

---

\* At the time, the Russian legislative branch consisted of the Congress of People's Deputies, which during this period convened about three times a year, and its permanent working body, the Supreme Soviet of Russia. Ruslan Khasbulatov headed the Supreme Soviet.

main topics in the media. In November 1991 the novelist Alexander Gelman asked in an article in the newspaper *Moskovskie novosti*, then the main mouthpiece of the liberal intelligentsia: what would Yeltsin's greater power lead to? Wasn't it dangerous? "Are democracy and an iron fist compatible or incompatible—not just anywhere, not in general, but right now, here in Russia, in the current economic, political, psychological situation? Here's my response. A weak hand would destroy our democracy—or rather our potential democracy. This is a certainty, a given, beyond any doubt. The iron fist of power can turn itself inside out and also lead to dictatorship, but even so, it doesn't deprive us of the hope that after we pass through a phase of moderate authoritarianism, it will lead society to solid democratic ground."[15]

Of course, when discussing this transitional period of "moderate authoritarianism", Gelman didn't mean decades but rather the year or two of special powers that Yeltsin had requested from congress. Back then, the wheel of history was spinning so fast that it would have never occurred to anyone to think far ahead. True democracy was to come at the next stop. It seemed natural that it would take shape on its own, if one wanted it to, and if there was a trusted leader at the helm. "Some may object. Isn't this exactly what the coup conspirators said? They, too, spoke of strong state powers for the sake of democracy," Gelman continued. "So, what is the difference then? The difference is that people listened to them but did not believe a word they said, while people trust Yeltsin."[16]

This was true. Polls showed that people still trusted Yeltsin, and, in the autumn of 1991, when he had vanquished the coup conspirators, his rating was above fifty per cent.[17] Hopes and expectations were still pinned on him. During the coup new heroes had emerged, such as the democratic mayor of Leningrad, Anatoly Sobchak, and Vice-President Alexander Rutskoi, but Russia still had only one recognized leader: Boris Yeltsin. Gavriil Popov, one of the leaders of the democratic movement in those years, described the attitude of society towards Yeltsin in the summer and fall of 1991: "The people were not going to do the work themselves. Someone had to come and give them another life instead of the one that no longer suited them."[18] In the eyes of the Russian people, from the very beginning Yeltsin was not the leader of a broad democratic movement. He was the rebel who challenged the Communist Party. In the autumn of 1991, the only thing that had changed was that the rebel had won.

Throughout the tumultuous years of the late 1980s and early 1990s, Russian society did not express clearly articulated political leanings. The pro-democracy movements were strong in Moscow and the big cities, but even there they had weak organizational structures and internal contradictions. What is freedom? What is democracy? What is the market? Most people gave simple answers to these questions: "Everything will be fine once the Communist Party disappears. It's the Communist Party that prevents us from having freedom and prosperity." Even before the coup in the summer of 1991, pollsters at the Russian Public Opinion Research Centre registered that for sixty-nine per cent of the population, their hope for the rebirth of Russia was associated with the fact that "after seventy-four years in power, the Communist Party has thoroughly discredited itself."[19] As Nemtsov said more than twenty years later, at one of the protest rallies: "We were romantics then. We thought that if we could just defeat the conspirators, we'd have happiness, success, prosperity and plenty, and Russia would become the freest, happiest country..."[20]

And then the conspirators and the Communist Party disappeared. The country's leading political force, Democratic Russia, which brought Yeltsin to power, began to split into factions and interest groups immediately after the coup. As time went on, Yeltsin became less willing to take Democratic Russia into consideration. The unity of the deputies on the issue of Russia's sovereignty disappeared completely when it came to reforms. It is clear why this happened. If sovereignty was in everyone's interest—the new Russian elite wanted to displace the old Soviet-era elite—reforms did not have consistent support in society. Even before the reforms began, both voters and their elected representatives did not trust the architects of reform. This was clear from the polls: in December 1991, only twenty-eight per cent of Russians believed that the government would be able to carry out reforms, while forty-six per cent did not. (In neighbouring Ukraine, for example, the numbers were just the opposite: forty-one per cent optimists and only twenty-five per cent sceptics.)

## Boys in pink trousers

By the end of 1991, however, the economic situation was catastrophic. The Soviet Union was bankrupt. There was no gold reserve. There was no bread. As of 15 November, reserves of flour were enough for two days; the reserve norm was fifteen days. Lack of fodder led to pestilence in poultry farms and a reduction of livestock. In the Nizhny Novgorod region, where Nemtsov was about to be appointed governor, state sources reported that, "Meat products can only be purchased with vouchers,* and there aren't enough reserves for December. Milk appears in stores and is sold out in an hour. Butter is sold for vouchers—200 grams per person per month. There isn't enough food. You can't buy vegetable oil anywhere."[21] There wasn't famine, but there was a risk of famine. Minister for Agriculture Khlystun reported weekly on the food situation in the country to a special commission chaired by the president.

In September, as the president's representative in his region, Nemtsov summoned the heads of transportation depots to his office and demanded that they provide buses. Some of the harvest was left in the fields, and people with bags and sacks went on weekends to pick potatoes, cabbages, carrots and beetroots. When he became governor, Nemtsov almost immediately asked the military deployed in his region to set up field kitchens in the city to feed the hungry.

Nemtsov's second problem at the end of December was rioting over vodka and cigarettes. When people couldn't redeem their vodka vouchers and find cigarettes to buy, they blocked the streets. This is how Nemtsov described the situation in December 1991 in his region, which was fairly typical of the situation all over the country: "The picture was catastrophic. My wife got up to stand in line a four o'clock in the morning for milk so that my daughter Zhanna could have it for breakfast. Everyone had seventeen different produce vouchers, and men were on the streets turning over buses and demanding cigarettes. I worked as a

---

\* Citizens were issued vouchers allowing them to purchase certain amounts of food, oil, alcohol, soap, sugar, cigarettes and other goods every month. The items and amounts were determined by region.

dispatcher, not a governor: cigarettes here, milk there, bread over there. And that was with what we had. On top of it all, it was a cold winter, and the region was freezing."[22]

The new government had no time or room to manoeuvre, as Yegor Gaidar admitted: "The picture that emerged in detail confirmed the sad truth. We had no resources to mitigate the social price of launching a new economic system. It was impossible to postpone liberalization of the economy in order to introduce structural reforms slowly. Two or three more months of passivity and we would have an economic and political catastrophe, the collapse of the country and a civil war. I am sure of it."[23]

Yeltsin was the reformers' sole support. The new Russian elite did not see the need for economic liberalization. Congress was eager to give Yeltsin emergency powers to carry out reforms because it wanted to absolve itself of responsibility for them. And at the end of November the Supreme Soviet, headed by Ruslan Khasbulatov, was already rolling back presidential initiatives. "Three months after the failed coup, the situation in Russia obviously does not augur well for democratic forces," wrote *Moskovskie novosti*. "During this time, they have failed to create a stable social and political base for their government, and the credit of trust that the White House [i.e. the president and the cabinet] possessed not long ago is fading today, on the eve of the reforms. Society, tired of non-stop uncertainty and instability, instinctively reaches for a firm hand."[24]

A harbinger of the impending crisis in relations between the branches of power—a crisis that would end in armed confrontation in the streets of Moscow in two years' time—was the démarche of Vice-President Alexander Rutskoi. General Rutskoi hadn't got the post of prime minister that he wanted, and the position of vice-president provided no real power. On 30 November, he suddenly spoke out against the upcoming price deregulation and lashed out at the Gaidar team before they even began work. "They are boys in pink trousers, red shirts and yellow shoes," General Rutskoi taunted, threatening to resign if Yeltsin didn't heed him.[25] Russia was just taking its first steps forward, and consensus on the principles of the path that lay ahead had already dissipated in the cold autumn air.

## Nemtsov

In a 1992 interview Nemtsov described how he became governor: "If I think back on everything that led me to the office, I can say with no exaggeration that it was a chain of coincidences, out of which the right path, as you know, inevitably appears. [...] But it was all very unpredictable. Who could have predicted that there would be a coup? That I would leave for vacation on 18 August via Moscow and arrive on 19 August, and that I would have to defend the White House for three nights? Nobody could have foreseen it. But that's what happened."[26]

In fact, Nemtsov's presence at the White House during the coup attempt played a crucial role in his future. During those dramatic days, he was in regular contact with Yeltsin. The president and his staff were in the wing on the other side of the building from the deputies, and deputies were not allowed in. But Nemtsov was allowed in to see Yeltsin. He even helped check Yeltsin's office for bugs, and Yeltsin authorized him on behalf of the Supreme Soviet to negotiate with the military. "I had a paper," Nemtsov recalled, "that read: 'I have appointed Deputy Boris Nemtsov to represent the legally elected Supreme Soviet in the military units of the Ministry of Defence, the Interior Ministry and the KGB. [Signed:] Yeltsin.'"[27] Later, during the victory rally, they stood side by side on the balcony. Yeltsin no longer thought of Nemtsov as just a young supporter. They had stood together, shoulder to shoulder, defending the White House and freedom. Immediately after the coup attempt, Nemtsov was appointed representative of the president of Russia in the Nizhny Novgorod region.

The idea of presidential representatives in the regions had come up before the coup when Yeltsin was elected president of Russia in June 1991. These would be something like presidential commissars, who would defend the interests of the new Russian authorities within the old but still functioning Soviet structures and Communist Party regional councils.

The coup hastened the implementation of these plans. While Moscow and St Petersburg confronted the conspirators, the rest of Russia froze, waiting to see who would win. Two-thirds of local leaders did not support Yeltsin, and some openly pledged allegiance to the State Committee. There was an urgent need for new leadership in the Russian provinces, and at first Yeltsin and his administration planned to hold gubernatorial elections in the autumn. But even more quickly—literally on the day after the coup—Yeltsin had to send representatives to the local administrations. At that moment, governing the country was his number one problem. Growing separatism in the national republics within Russia, such as Tatarstan, was a serious source of concern. In the heat of the struggle with Yeltsin, Gorbachev had promised them broad autonomy, and in a brief period of time many regions had even voted for sovereignty. In the autumn of 1991, the possibility of Russia's disintegration was no empty threat. Two weeks after the coup, it happened in Chechnya. Supporters of General Dzhokhar Dudayev seized power in the republic, and a month and a half later they declared independence.

Alexander Minzhurenko, a democratic activist and deputy in the Congress of the USSR, headed the headquarters of resistance in the Siberian city of Omsk during the August coup attempt. During those three days, he was in close communication with the White House and printed and distributed decrees and leaflets that he received by fax. On 22 August he was already in Moscow and immediately learnt that Yeltsin would offer him the job of presidential representative in the Omsk region. At first, Minzhurenko hesitated—it wasn't immediately clear what a representative of the president of the Russian Republic would do—but later he agreed. Yeltsin summoned him. "Can't you see—the Union is falling apart," Yeltsin told Minzhurenko nervously, even irritably. "Russia will crumble if we sit by and do nothing. Right now, the local governments are all Communist. We will introduce elections, but all sorts of people will be elected, and the president will lose control. That's why I need my own loyal people in the provinces."[28]

The terms of reference for presidential representatives were written right there, in the next room, by hand. On 27 August, Minzhurenko, Nemtsov and a few others were again invited to Yeltsin's office and appointed presidential representatives in the regions. They were tasked with collecting complaints from citizens and monitoring the implementation of presidential decrees. "If they mess up, we'll remove them,"

Sergei Shakhrai told journalists at the time.²⁹ Yeltsin set another goal for them: to select worthy candidates who could win elections in their regions.

During the coup, Nizhny Novgorod regional leaders had supported the conspirators, not Yeltsin. They censored local newspapers—although the journalists rebelled and published newspapers with blank pages—and Alexander Sokolov, head of the regional Communist Party ruling body, held meetings with the chiefs of local law enforcement agencies to put down any expressions of mass discontent. After the coup, Sokolov was dismissed from his post, and the democratic members of the regional council simply sealed up the building of the Communist Party headquarters. The region was left without any leadership at all. "The question was: who would take charge?" Nikolai Ashin recalled. The democratic community was at a loss, but Ashin had no doubt—Nemtsov should be appointed.³⁰

By October, Nemtsov was ready to put his candidacy for governor forward. At the end of the month, Yeltsin summoned his representatives to hear their reports. By this time the Presidential Administration had already decided temporarily to replace the election of governors with appointments (which Yeltsin announced to congress on 28 October). At the meeting, Nemtsov started up a conversation with Minzhurenko.

"Who are you going to recommend for the post of head of the administration?" Nemtsov asked.

"I haven't decided on a candidate yet," Minzhurenko said.

"You ought to put your candidacy forward," continued Nemtsov.

"I'm already thinking about it."

"Come on, I'm a historian, an assistant professor. What kind of governor would I make? It's not a political job. It's managerial."

"You could keep your political functions," Nemtsov said, trying to persuade Minzhurenko, "and pick deputies responsible for specific areas. You'd oversee it all."

Minzhurenko hadn't thought about it like that, and Nemtsov's suggestion threw him off.

"Maybe he's right," he thought.³¹

Back in August, deputies of the Nizhny Novgorod regional council had sent Moscow recommendations for two candidates to head the administration. The democratic bloc had put forward Igor Petyashin, director of the local Institute of Communication Systems, and the Communists had recommended Ivan Sklyarov, head of the city of Arzamas.* Yeltsin's office even agreed to nominate Petyashin, but then Petyashin suddenly got cold feet and refused under the pretext that the election of the head of the administration had been replaced by appointment. "New candidates had to be nominated," the *Nizhegorodsky rabochy* newspaper wrote in October 1991. "At this point the idea came up putting forth the candidacy of Boris Nemtsov, the Russian president's representative in our region. After a day and a half of deliberation, he gave his consent. And he stated his readiness to work with Ivan Sklyarov."[32]

In October, at yet another meeting with Yeltsin, Nemtsov again tried very hard to convince Minzhurenko to run for governor. He didn't want to feel out of place as governor, and he felt more comfortable offering his own candidacy to Yeltsin alongside someone else. But Minzhurenko turned him down. He could not get out of his mind a recent call from the director of the local factory that produced cooking oil. The factory had run out of packing boxes, and the director threatened to stop shipping oil if the boxes were not delivered. "Why are you calling me?" Minzhurenko asked, genuinely puzzled. "Who else would I call?" the director said. "I always called the local Communist Party boss, and he called the cardboard factory and gave the director what for." The entire Soviet economic system was based on those "what fors." Minzhurenko was horrified at the prospect of devoting his life to solving problems like shortages of cardboard boxes.[33]

Nemtsov did not want to deal with boxes either. So, if appointed, he would offer the position of vice-governor to Communist Ivan Sklyarov. "Nemtsov was smart," Tatyana Grishina, his aide at the time recalled. "He knew he didn't understand administrative issues, and Sklyarov

---

* These councils were the highest authority in the regions, and the president could not ignore them. Therefore, the presidential decree issued after the coup stated that the candidacy for the post of the head of the administration had to be coordinated with the regional councils. In practice, however, this did not always happen.

was a manager. Besides, it was a compromise [with Nizhny Novgorod's elite]."³⁴ By offering to share power with the Communist Sklyarov, Nemtsov arranged for additional support in the regional council. Nemtsov came to the podium and said exactly that: He was a politician, Sklyarov would deal with the administrative issues, and together they would move mountains. The deputies liked the sound of that, and they recommended that Yeltsin appoint Nemtsov.

Many Nizhny Novgorod democrats, who were at the wellspring of the local democratic associations, were suspicious of Nemtsov. They considered him an upstart and an outsider. The local media began printing appeals not to appoint Nemtsov governor. In one article, a leader of the local branch of Democratic Russia ranted that not only was Nemtsov incompetent, but he had "entered into a coalition with the political and economic Communist Party elite, who had supported the State Committee for Emergency Rule." However, other activists stood up for Nemtsov, insisting that he was "capable of implementing decisively the president's policies and reforms."³⁵

In Moscow, people were also arguing about whether Nemtsov should be appointed governor. Sergei Shakhrai supported the appointment. "I said that he was certainly up to the job," Shakhrai recalled. "They knew him in the region—mostly in the city. He made up for his youth and lack of knowledge with natural instinct. I think that the phrase—'natural instinct'—was something the president understood and respected." (Some of Yeltsin's associates at the time believed that Yelena Bonner, Sakharov's widow, also urged Yeltsin to appoint Nemtsov.)

Yeltsin's associate Valery Makharadze, who would soon be the government's chief inspector, was against it. He listed Nemtsov's shortcomings: youth, lack of administrative experience, and—for some reason—insufficient knowledge of agriculture. But Shakhrai did not give up. "I had two arguments in Nemtsov's favour," he said. "I said it was primarily an industrial and defence-industry region. And that Nemtsov had written a draft law on land for my committee. Yeltsin was astonished. 'Boris? He wrote a law on the land?' I said 'Yes.' To be honest, Nemtsov wrote a law on the political aspects of land use, about reforming and transforming land ownership laws, not the subject of state power. But those two arguments worked."³⁶

A third argument probably also played a role: thirty-two-year-old Nemtsov was the most popular deputy in Nizhny Novgorod. According to opinion polls from October 1991, his approval rating was forty-two per cent, which was twice as high as that of his closest rival.[37] But regardless of who recommended the young Nizhny Novgorod deputy to Yeltsin, it was the president's decision. On 30 November, the president issued a decree appointing Nemtsov as head of the Nizhny Novgorod regional administration. According to Nemtsov, Yeltsin gave him these instructions: "In general, you're green, no life experience, and the region is very important. [...] I will put you in charge. I'll give you a three-month probation period. I will come and check up on you. If you fail, I'll pull you."[38]

The building of the Communist Party headquarters in Nizhny Novgorod was completely lifeless. There was no electricity and none of the elevators or telephones worked. The office of the local Communist Party chairman was on the fourth floor. In December 1991, Nemtsov moved in. "The local people have already begun to call the new fathers of the region [i.e. Nemtsov and Sklyarov] kamikazes," wrote the Nizhny Novgorod newspaper *Leninskaya smena*.[39] Grigory Yavlinsky, one of Nemtsov's close associates at the time, recalled that day: "He was sitting in the Communist Party headquarters, in the office of the regional Communist Party chairman. Everyone had gone off, and he was sitting there alone, wearing jeans and white socks, with his hair a total mess. And he asked me, 'So, what should I do?'"[40]

The old life was over: the road back to science was closed. Nemtsov was now part of the power structure. He was in politics for the long haul—maybe even for ever.

# PART 2

# CHAPTER 5

## 1992–93

## The Capital of Reform

### The mink-coat rally

"Two million—once! Two million—twice! Two million two hundred thousand. Two million four hundred thousand. Two million four hundred—once! Two million four hundred thousand—twice!" The auctioneer paused theatrically. "Two million four hundred thousand—sold!" The hammer fell.[1]

In the Soviet Union all prices were set by the government. The very concept of an auction was synonymous with capitalism and criminality. There was just about one professional auctioneer in the country, the legendary Arseny Lobanov, who had auctioned off horses for foreign currency since the 1960s. Now, at the first public auction, on 4 April 1992 in Nizhny Novgorod, he had sold a grocery store for 2.4 million roubles—or about $24,000.

Yegor Gaidar was in the hall, his face beaming with delight. He was watching his cherished dream come true: state property—shops with generic names like "Meat and Fish" or "Fruit and Vegetables", cafés, barbershops, dry-cleaners, and so on—that had been part of every Soviet person's life, was now moving into private hands. Equally pleased was Gaidar's colleague with bright red hair, thirty-six-year-old Anatoly Chubais, an economist from St Petersburg, one of the architects of Russian privatization who had recently been appointed head of the State Property Committee. "Just five months previously, [Gaidar and I] had been writing up all sorts of projects," Chubais later recalled, "and there we were as the government representatives overseeing their implementation. It was a happy moment."[2]

This auction launched privatization in Russia. On the block were only small businesses; the main privatization of large-scale industrial enterprises using vouchers would begin in July. The International Financial Corporation (IFC), a structure of the World Bank that helped organize the auctions, noted in its summer 1992 report that Nizhny Novgorod had been chosen as the test site for two reasons. First, it was a "typical Russian city", which meant that, if successful, the Nizhny Novgorod model could be replicated throughout Russia. Second, privatization was actively supported by local authorities, and "the experience of Czechoslovakia and Poland showed how important political support is for this type of privatization."[3] Both countries, especially Poland, served as examples of a successful transition from socialism to capitalism, and Polish, Czechoslovak and Hungarian experts participated in the Nizhny Novgorod experiment, underwritten by the IFC.

Nemtsov had been governor for only a month, but the Nizhny Novgorod region was already in pride of place. "Boris brought in experts from the World Bank's IFC and we got right down to work on privatization of small businesses. Their help was very useful," recalled Dmitry Bednyakov, then mayor of Nizhny Novgorod.[4] Preparations for privatization had begun in early January, when prices were deregulated and Yeltsin visited during his tour of cities on the Volga.

Yeltsin always said he was a man of the people. He was used to being loved by the people and, unlike other party bosses, he wasn't above going shopping and using public transportation. After a walk through a cold winter market, the president stopped without warning at a downtown grocer's. The shop was already well-stocked—the shelves had been replenished almost as soon as the prices were liberalized—but a kilogram of butter now cost 207 roubles, up from 3 roubles and 50 kopeks a month earlier. However, the Soviet price tag had in fact had nothing to do with reality, since by then shoppers couldn't find it anywhere; this was called "suppressed inflation."

Gaidar had assumed prices would jump by 200–300 per cent after the reform. He was almost right: In January, prices rose by a factor of

3.5 on average, but in the Nizhny Novgorod region the price of butter jumped even higher. The psychological effect was huge. Yeltsin flew to Nizhny Novgorod from Ulyanovsk, a coastal city downstream on the Volga, where butter, he was told, had jumped to 60 roubles. This might have been true. There were huge jumps in prices in the first or second week after prices were deregulated. The Ulyanovsk governor was an old-school Communist who was still trying to regulate prices while covering it up with smoke and mirrors. Nemtsov had done neither. In the store, as he later recalled, Yeltsin was attacked by "old ladies with string bags who wanted to kill him." This is one of Nemtsov's favourite stories:

> Someone shouted at Yeltsin, "Pensions are tiny, and butter has gone up to two hundred and seven roubles! In one week! That's more than fifty times higher!"
> "But there was no butter to buy before, and now there is."
> "It's better to use a voucher and buy a little. What's the point of having everything in shops when you can't buy it? A month's salary for a kilogram of butter!"
> Yeltsin turned to me.
> "Who set these barbaric prices?"
> Since I was young, I answered: "You did."
> "Me?!"
> "Yes, you! You signed the decree to deregulate prices and allow free trade. This is the result."[5]

Yeltsin, furious, reverted to the old-fashioned way of dealing with the problem. He ordered the director of the distribution centre to be fired, convinced that he had jacked up the price of butter. "Two hundred roubles per kilogram of butter is an outrage," Yeltsin said indignantly the same day at a meeting with workers. "It's a vestige of the old centrally controlled economic system."[6] These old ways continued only because the market players had not yet formed new relationships. The high price of butter was not Nemtsov's fault, and, strictly speaking, he did not have the authority to fire the store manager. Nemtsov said that the manager, whose name was Dokukin, met him halfway—agreeing to quit so he didn't cause problems for the promising young governor. Before leaving for Moscow, Yeltsin once again mentioned Dokukin. Nemtsov confirmed that he had been removed. Yeltsin only calmed down when he double-checked himself, calling from the car.[7]

At the very beginning of January 1992, Nemtsov was already one of Yeltsin's favourites and enjoyed his trust. "I believe that he'll follow the path of democracy. I certainly believe in his intelligence, his sense of responsibility and how active he is," Yeltsin said about Nemtsov before leaving the city. "His youth is not a disadvantage. Yes, his lack of production experience is telling, but this will disappear over the year. I think he's a good candidate for Nizhny Novgorod. And every day he will gain experience."[8] With this, Nemtsov was given a *carte blanche* for reform, and Nizhny Novgorod was destined to become a pioneer in small-scale privatization.

In the Soviet economy, a shop was merely showcase and a counter. Goods were sent to shops from the distribution centre that determined where the goods would go, their quantity and price. Before prices were deregulated, the man who ran the dairy distribution system ruled the dairy market. But if Dokukin had not quit, he would have lost his place soon enough anyway, because in a market economy the distribution centre didn't exist. When Gaidar and Chubais came with Nemtsov to the auction on 4 April, they had to fight their way into the hall through a crowd of protesters waving placards like "Gaidar, Don't Make Us Paupers!" and "Prices Sting and We Might, Too!" while chanting "Fire Them!"

The irony was that this anti-Gaidar rally was made up of the top Soviet trade administrators, who were hardly poor. "It was exasperating: the protest was clearly organized," Chubais recalled later. "These were well-dressed—even elegantly dressed—and well-fed people who were not living lives of deprivation."[9] These were mostly middle-aged women who headed food distribution centres, functionaries of the large Soviet food-supply system, masters of their universe who until very recently had been in control of the distribution of largesse. Nemtsov joked later that it had been an expensive French perfume rally. Later he told Gaidar, "If this is how the Soviet trade-sector bosses feel about our reforms, it means we're on the right track."[10]

The fears of the trade lobby were understandable, but they soon saw the advantages of the market economy. First, in Nizhny Novgorod privatization was done through compromise: the staffs of shops being privatized could buy them at a discount and pay in instalments. Second, the trade functionaries had money. "The ladies in mink coats quickly switched gears," recalled Pavel Chichagov, Nemtsov's associate at the time, "and started buying the shops themselves. Some resold, some closed them, but others began to develop them as businesses. In economics, this is called primitive accumulation of capital."[11]

In fact, the auction on 4 April was not the first in Nizhny Novgorod. In March, Bednyakov and Nemtsov had already held auctions, and at each of them dozens of lots were sold for very respectable prices for the time. And, judging by the excitement, Gaidar and Chubais could count on success. They needed it. Opposition to the reforms was growing, the political situation in Moscow was heating up, and in a few days another congress session would begin work, while a group of deputies led by Ruslan Khasbulatov were preparing, as Gaidar put it, "the first frontal attack on the reforms." Gaidar and Chubais needed a success story. Chubais said, "We needed to make some real progress before the congress, to send a signal out to the provinces, as it were. Then I found out from Nemtsov that he had a specific project—the first auction of city-owned stores and consumer service centres in modern Russian history. I did everything in my power to turn it into a political event, not just a run-of-the-mill commercial activity. Gaidar and I decided to go to Nizhny Novgorod."[12]

Their calculation paid off. "It was one of the few political victories we had in the early democratic period," Chubais later said.[13] The auctions in Nizhny Novgorod continued for another two years. "We sold off the entire service sector!" Bednyakov bragged.[14] The 4 April auction was a political victory not only for the government, but also for Nemtsov. Everyone was talking about the auction, and Nizhny Novgorod made international headlines for the first time since the release of Andrei Sakharov from exile in December 1986. *The Washington Post* wrote that Nizhny Novgorod looked more promising than Moscow and St Petersburg, which were bogged down in disputes over privatization methods.[15] The *Los Angeles Times* noted the political courage of young

Nizhny Novgorod leaders.[16] Nemtsov was taking his first steps towards international recognition—and towards his future status as the most popular governor in Russia.

## Nemtsov vs Gaidar

Yegor Gaidar was not interested in either money or comfort. He thought of his career as a mission, his purpose in life: to move the country away from the brink of the abyss and civil war and to put the Russian economy on a healthy, market-oriented path. He did not lie when he said that the days of his government—the first post-Soviet government— were numbered, and he did not regret it. Gaidar was ready to assume responsibility for unregulated—that is, high—prices and widespread poverty in Russia, even though this was really the price for the bankruptcy of the Soviet planned economy. Gaidar knew that the main thing he would need at the first stage was willpower. He would be bombarded with endless requests for money and would have to refuse them. Behind each of these requests, in one way or another, were real people, often profoundly unfortunate people—teachers, doctors, military personnel, scientists and pensioners who had nothing to live on. But economic laws are cruel and inexorable. It wouldn't help to turn on the press and print money. Money not secured by the growth of production and economic recovery depreciates, and it accelerates inflation, which then hits the wallets of the poor again. The monetarist Gaidar tried as hard as he could to restrain the growth of the money supply and make the country live within its means.

Nemtsov and Gaidar were allies, and they had much in common: a commitment to democracy and a market economy, a desire to see Russia become a modern European country, age, too, which was very important, and, finally, the fact that both were Yeltsin's protégés. But they moved in parallel, not as a united front. Gaidar and his associates were just settling into office. Although Nemtsov was younger, he was more experienced; he had entered politics considerably earlier and had already won elections. "Boris didn't grow up in our team," Chubais recalled. "He grew up independently of us."[17]

That's why Grigory Yavlinsky came to Nizhny Novgorod in the summer of 1992 at Nemtsov's invitation. The pair of them had known each other for two years. After Yeltsin opted for Gaidar and his plan, Yavlinsky had nowhere to put the plan he wrote—i.e. the 500 Days Programme—into practice. Already a well-known and popular politician, by the spring of 1992 he was in mild opposition to the government. Nemtsov held Yavlinsky in great respect, and after becoming governor Nemtsov always came to him for advice when he was in Moscow and eventually asked him to develop a reform programme for his region. Yavlinsky agreed. First of all, he wanted to work. Second, the research centre he had founded was in a difficult financial situation at the time: there were no contracts, and, consequently, there was no money coming in. There was so little money that Yavlinsky's team in Nizhny Novgorod worked for room and board. "They worked for food," Bednyakov recalled. "We put them up, fed them, and that was all. That was all they needed."[18]

At the regional level, there wasn't much scope for developing reforms. To the extent that it was possible, Yavlinsky and his team adapted their 500 Days Programme to conditions in Nizhny Novgorod to make the Nizhny Novgorod Prologue. Yavlinsky's team analysed economic statistics, proposed budgetary and tax manoeuvring (to find ways of providing financial support to employees in the public sector and government-owned businesses), developed the next stages of small-scale privatization (for example, that of freight transport) and came up with ways to reform public services and projects for targeted social assistance. An important component of the Nizhny Novgorod Prologue was the idea that reforms should be done by the local people themselves. "A lot must be done locally. And if the reforms that come from below are met and combined with the reforms from above, they'll be successful," Yavlinsky believed.[19] Yavlinsky and Bednyakov, who took part in the development of this idea, were especially proud of the simplified application system for registering private enterprises. "You go to the post office," Bednyakov recalled, "you take a form in two copies, fill it out, keep one, leave the other at the post office, and the post office sends it to the administration. If you don't receive a refusal in two weeks, your business is legal. That was it."[20]

One of Yavlinsky's key—and most attention-grabbing—ideas was the issuance of regional bonds, which were essentially local currency. The problem was that by mid-summer 1992, the state owed huge sums of money to both businesses and citizens. People weren't getting their salaries, businesses were not receiving money for their products. In this payment crisis, barter flourished, and money surrogates—coupons, bills of exchange and other paper obligations—sprang up like mushrooms after a spring rain.

Meanwhile, the government had an acute shortage of cash. Rising prices necessitated the issuance of new large-denomination banknotes. Gaidar ordered Goznak, the organization that printed banknotes, to do so. "However," Gaidar later recalled, "Khasbulatov summoned the head of Goznak almost immediately and gave him a dressing down: 'If you go and listen to Gaidar and his ilk, you'll cause inflation.'" In the tangled legislation of the time, it was not easy for the head of Goznak to figure out whose order was more important. After being reprimanded, the head of Goznak lay low. Work on the preparation of new banknotes was suspended.[21]

To deal with this acute cash shortage, businesses gave coupons and cheques to their workers instead of money, the workers took them to shops to buy goods, and businesses then covered the coupons by transferring non-cash equivalents to the shops. It wasn't just businesses that did this. With consent of the regional administration, even the Institute of Applied Physics in Nizhny Novgorod printed coupons.

Nemtsov had to solve somehow the problem of liquidity shortages: without money, workers would go on strike. "What can the governor and his team do," Nemtsov complained, "if the federal government won't give us cash? We already owe the population about five billion roubles in salaries. People's patience is running out, and there's no way to explain it other than the government's stupidity. Not paying salaries will ignite the already dangerous situation in the country [...]. Here I sharply disagree with the government."[22] Nemtsov took action. First, he filed a lawsuit against the government in the Constitutional Court.

And then he decided to issue *nemtsovki*—bonds issued by the regional government that could be used in lieu of money in shops. Later the shops would turn in the bonds and receive transfers into their bank accounts. "We figured out how to get collateral for the loans," Yavlinsky said. "It was very simple. We bought petroleum products and fuel. Fuel was going up in price because of inflation. And so we had collateral."[23]

Nemtsov's bonds were a great success. "As a result, regional bonds became a real competitor to Sberbank in attracting one of the cheapest credit resources—the population's savings," *Kommersant* wrote.[24] But in Moscow, Nemtsov's plan was not greeted with approval. This was natural: the federal government couldn't support the introduction of a local currency that tore a hole in the country's single economic space. "Gaidar almost killed me…" Nemtsov later admitted. "He even wanted to have me fired."[25]

*Nemtsovki* were never widely circulated. Moscow quickly sent the cash needed and the problem was solved. In other words, Nemtsov got his way. In the end, the *nemtsovki* were turned into fuel coupons for the regional fleet: they were issued to drivers, who used them to pay for fuel, and petrol stations then exchanged them for money. The idea was also to discourage local gangsters from robbing petrol stations.

This was not the only conflict between Nemtsov and Gaidar, although it was probably the most serious one. Like many other governors, Nemtsov refused to unfreeze fuel prices and tried to get the government to give him benefits, concessions, preferences or other financial perks, so that he could balance the regional budget. And, just like the others, Nemtsov got turned down. As his associate Chichagov recalled, "Nemtsov said, 'Yegor, you come here and sit here in my place.'"[26]

Sitting in Nemtsov's place meant, among other things, trying to solve the problems of the most ordinary and most often poor and unfortunate people who had nowhere to live, no access to medical treatment, and no money to buy the most basic necessities. Alexander Kotyusov, Nemtsov's aide and former student, recalled his first day at work in September 1992. On that day the governor received local citizens who had made an appointment in advance, usually about twenty people. "An old lady came in," Kotyusov said.

> They placed her documents on Nemtsov's desk. What was her problem? She had nowhere to live. She was from a village. Her husband was a drunkard, her son had epilepsy, her daughter was also seriously

ill. They had fifteen square meters of living space. She was on the waiting list for housing, her number was about one million, and so she was asking to be given an apartment out of turn as an exception. By "asking" I mean she fell on her knees and beat her head against the floor, weeping. Suddenly Nemtsov, in a dry voice, tells her: "All right now. Listen to me. Go out, calm down, come back in fifteen minutes. Or, if you're prepared to have a normal conversation, drink some water and continue. If not, leave." Later I asked him, "Did you really think that was appropriate? To talk so rudely with that woman?" He said, "I'm the governor. There are a lot of people like her. If I take every problem to heart, I won't be able to bear it. That doesn't mean that I don't sympathize with her situation."[27]

There really were a lot of elderly women like her. And Nemtsov did what he could.

If there was no other option, he turned to the businessmen who had supported him and asked for help. "Boris thought in terms of justice. An elderly woman came to see him," said Vladimir Sedov, a major Nizhny Novgorod entrepreneur and film producer, "and he called me. 'There's an old woman here. She needs an apartment.' We checked her situation and gave her an apartment. We knew we had to help Nemtsov."[28]

The relationship between Nemtsov and Gaidar was defined in those years by the difference of their powers and responsibilities. Nemtsov was responsible for his region; Gaidar, for the economy of the whole country. In 1992–93 Nemtsov actively criticized the government and Gaidar's tough economic policies, arguing that reforms were too radical and real life was more complicated than the plans invented in Moscow. Instead of "shock therapy", Nemtsov said the country needed "reforms without shock." On the four-question referendum to garner support for the Yeltsin government in April 1993, he left unanswered the question: "Do you support economic reforms?" even though Yeltsin's staff had campaigned strongly for a "yes" answer.

Many years later, Nemtsov said several times that he was ashamed of his many outbursts against the cabinet. In their disputes, Gaidar was certainly right, and he was wrong. But at the time, it was expedient for Nemtsov to keep his distance from the government. While the reformers were spending political capital, Nemtsov was earning it by virtue of his not being a member of their team. And besides, despite their frequent conflicts, Gaidar and Nemtsov treated each other with respect. Even the scandal with the *nemtsovki* did not permanently damage their relationship. Neither bore grudges, especially Nemtsov, and they had no trouble moving past their disagreements.

## Why you shouldn't take bribes

Nemtsov and Gaidar had one other quality in common: they had integrity. This helped them resolve tension and disagreements, since they each knew that the other wasn't motivated by personal interest.

In 1992 Gaidar had supported Nemtsov when he didn't want to permit raising the water level in a local reservoir. Later, Nemtsov described how Ivan Sklyarov—an experienced politician, who had once headed the city Communist Party—had advised him to bring Gaidar two large cans of black caviar and a three-litre bottle of vodka to thank him for his support. "I went into Gaidar's office and said, 'This is to thank you from all the residents of Nizhny Novgorod—caviar and vodka.' Gaidar was a very cultured man who generally didn't use foul language. But never in my life had I ever heard such a barrage of obscenities! He literally shoved me out the door."[29]

Corruption can cover a wide range of actions. What's the difference between a bribe and a gift given out of friendship? Where does a fair distribution of the public good end and nepotism begin? From his first days in office, Nemtsov was extremely scrupulous. His assistant at the time, Andrei Mladentsev, said that Nemtsov never said anything to businessmen that could be construed as a hint for a bribe to secure his support.

Nemtsov's scruples sometimes resulted in bad feeling among his colleagues. The businessman Igor Aronov, Nemtsov's friend since they studied together at the Radio Institute, told a story about once asking Nemtsov for help. While he was the head of Nemtsov's gubernatorial council of entrepreneurs, his car was stolen. The car had been provided to him as one of the leaders of the Nizhny Novgorod Fair, a new version of the historical market that before the 1917 Revolution accounted for nearly half of Russian export deals. Aronov asked Nemtsov to put in a good word for him at the factory so that the fair could buy him a new car at cost. Nemtsov refused outright. Aronov explained that the car was for business, not for him personally, and that the fair was not a private enterprise. "I would have signed," Nemtsov said, "if you weren't my friend." Aronov was furious over what he considered to be an offensive populist move.[30]

The businessman Artyom Tarasov was called the first Soviet millionaire in the press after making a large fortune just before the Soviet Union was dissolved. In 1993, a tender was announced in Nizhny Novgorod to implement mobile communications, and Tarasov and his partner decided to bribe Nemtsov in order to secure a lucrative contract. They were afraid to bribe the governor themselves, so they asked the TV personality Mikhail Borisov to accompany them to the negotiations. He agreed and, when Borisov was alone with Nemtsov, he put an envelope containing $5,000 in front of him. That was a lot of money at the time. According to Tarasov, Nemtsov looked at the envelope and suddenly asked, "Is this a bribe?"

"Yes," Borisov replied honestly as he slid the envelope towards Nemtsov.

"You know," Nemtsov said, sliding it back towards Borisov, "I like Tarasov, and I really could use the money. I'd like to take it, but I want a career in politics, so I have to be completely clean. Take the envelope back and tell Tarasov that if you win the tender honestly, then you'll get the contract. There's no other way. Don't let him be angry with me, OK?"[31]

Five thousand dollars was pennies compared to the temptations Nemtsov would face over the next couple of years. In Russia, the post of governor, which was directly linked to the distribution of property and state orders, was one of the most corrupt governmental posts. Several governors would become millionaires, and then billionaires, and the vast majority would secure for themselves large fortunes. Nemtsov only began to make real money—nothing close to a typical governor's wealth—after he left his position. His first comfortable living situation was a state-owned dacha near Nizhny Novgorod that he had been given use of as governor. "What kept me from taking bribes?" Nemtsov later wrote.

> I'll be honest: I was afraid I'd get caught. All sorts of things go through your head when you see a pile of money. Just imagine a table with a suitcase full of hundred-dollar bills. All my personal problems would have been solved with that kind of money. But I was also aware that with that kind of money life would change and there would be irresolvable conflicts [...]. Besides, taking a bribe is a huge risk for your reputation. The strange thing about bribes is that on the one hand, it's all very hush-hush, but on the other hand everyone knows about everyone else.[32]

For a long time, Nemtsov couldn't afford to buy a second suit. He didn't even have enough money to buy souvenirs when he was abroad. During his first trip to Paris and London in November 1993, Igor Maskayev, his assistant for international affairs, found himself in an uncomfortable situation. Before he joined Nemtsov in the civil service, he had worked in foreign business, so he was better off and better dressed. In Paris, Nemtsov spilt wine on his suit, and, when they flew to London, Maskayev sent the suit to the express cleaner at the hotel. Nemtsov was due to go to a reception with then-former prime minister Margaret Thatcher. Fifteen minutes before they were ready to leave for the reception, a British diplomat ran up to Maskayev in a panic. Nemtsov had not come downstairs. He was still in his room and there was some problem. There was no time to waste—one could not be late for tea with Mrs Thatcher!

Maskayev went to Nemtsov's room and found him in his underwear.
"Why aren't you dressed?" Maskayev asked, startled. "It's time to go."
"I have a problem."
"What problem?"
"The suit that you sent to be dry-cleaned hasn't been delivered."
"So put on another one!"
"That's my only suit!"[33]

Maskayev went to the diplomat. When it became clear that the meeting with Thatcher was at risk, the British Foreign Office did everything possible to help. A few minutes later an entire delegation led by the hotel manager came up to Nemtsov's room bearing his suit, fruit, champagne and apologies.

After becoming governor, Nemtsov immediately set about learning English, and in a couple of years he spoke it quite well. Public relations and fundraising for reform were an important part of his work from the start. He came back from that trip to London with £1.5 million in financial aid for agrarian reform.

## Merchants, traders and tennis tournaments

Nemtsov envisioned making the Nizhny Novgorod region a testing ground for agrarian reform. "I accepted his offer," Viktor Khlystun said.[34] Economists specializing in agrarian issues flocked to the region, and they soon developed the Nizhny Novgorod model of privatization of collectively owned farmland. Russia could not follow the same path as Eastern European countries and return land to its former owners; collectivization and the systematic extermination of the peasants had made that impossible. "In the end, we decided to do almost what Prime Minister Pyotr Stolypin did [i.e. with agrarian reform of 1905]. We decided to allocate shares to the people and let them decide what to do with them," wrote Vasily Uzun, head of the Agrarian Institute and one of the architects of the Nizhny Novgorod reforms.[35]

Employees of collective and state farms received shares that they could pool together to buy collective farmland and equipment at in-house tenders. The head of a small town two hundred kilometres from Nizhny Novgorod, Yury Lebedev (who would later become vice-governor) recalled telling people at a meeting at one of the state farms that this land was now their property. They could all buy the state farm together or they could withdraw from it and organize their own farm. "People didn't believe it. I remember one woman stood up and asked me, 'Are you saying that this is my land?' I said, 'Yes, it's your land.' 'I don't believe it,' she said."[36]

Nemtsov was in a hurry. The sooner all the collective farms were turned into private farms, the better. Khlystun persuaded him not to rush; if people weren't ready, nothing would work. He was right. The Nizhny Novgorod model had the catchy name ZERNO, which both meant "grain" and was the Russian abbreviation of Land Reform of the Nizhny Novgorod Region. In the first stages, ZERNO had good results: the private farms formed on collective farmlands turned out to be both more productive and more profitable.

But this worked when the best farmers or chairmen of collective farms were at the helm. In other places, reform efforts encountered some eternal Russian problems: drunkenness and a lack of initiative among the farmers; sabotage by government officials, who hid papers in safes and refused to explain farmers' rights and the purpose of these reforms; in-fighting among shareholders when dividing the profits from the harvest; and so on. Vyacheslav Bolyak, a vice-governor who later became the head of the town of Kstovo, said:

> [The Nizhny Novgorod model] was designed for leaders, experienced guys people would follow. I already knew that we didn't have that kind of leader in the Kstovo district. [...] Boris gave me a description of the programme. I sat down, read it and realized: if we tried to do this now, it would be a disaster. [...] I came to Nemtsov and said that ZERNO wouldn't work in our area. Boris immediately lost his temper. "It works everywhere, but it won't in your district? I'll fire you right now!" "Sure, go ahead and fire me. Who are you going to work with? Remember, you promised that you wouldn't get in my way." He got angry and then calmed down. And Kstovo didn't have ZERNO.[37]

The thirty-three-year-old governor was very energetic, but without managerial experience he inevitably made mistakes. For example, the city of Nizhny Novgorod was spread out on two sides of the Volga River. The public transportation system was in terrible shape, with rusty, old, unheated buses that packed in commuters like sardines during rush hour. The buses were falling apart, and the drivers were on strike. There was no money for salaries or new vehicles. The governor tried to solve the problem by reassigning buses from the factories and depots to run city routes. As a result, the transportation system stopped working altogether. Nemtsov was also criticized for disbanding building and construction schools, which eventually slowed the pace of development.

But on the whole, Nemtsov was successful both as a reformer and as governor. Nizhny Novgorod was turning into Russia's third major city, and it was easily the most progressive city of its time. Businesses wanted to move there. Nemtsov had revived pre-revolutionary Russia's most famous expo, the Nizhny Novgorod Fair, and investments were pouring into the region.

Foreigners were pouring in, too: journalists, businessmen and politicians. Three months before Margaret Thatcher invited Nemtsov to tea in her London home, the British politician, who had been popular in Russia since the Gorbachev era, visited Nizhny Novgorod. In her memoirs, she enthusiastically described their walk together along one of the city's main streets. She was quoted in the Russian press as having said: "It was impossible to imagine a greater contrast with the grey monotony of Moscow. One small shop stuck in my memory. It sold dairy products, and I'd never seen such a selection of cheeses anywhere else."[38] Six months later, Thatcher's successor, John Major, came to Nizhny Novgorod and even participated in the rehearsal of an auction to sell one of the collective farms.

That very street had begun to shine under Nemtsov. By mid-1993, shopfronts had been painted, and everywhere you looked there were summer cafés. In those days, it was an incredible breakthrough—virtually the first urban improvement project in the country. Historically a city of merchants and traders, Nizhny Novgorod flourished once again in the early 1990s. In the eyes of the public, it was a testing ground for economic reform and one of the centres of social life. The famous Russian film director Nikita Mikhalkov filmed *Burnt by the Sun* there and brought Hollywood stars to the city.

Nemtsov also organized tennis tournaments. Since Yeltsin played tennis, the sport quickly became fashionable, and ministers, businessmen and showbiz stars came to the city to play. The mayor of Samara, Oleg Sysuyev, met and befriended Nemtsov at one of those tournaments. "Nizhny Novgorod was a trendy place," Sysuyev recalled. "It was something of a model that we wanted to emulate. We saw the Nizhny Novgorod region as the frontrunner. Was it wealthy? I don't think so.

But Boris did everything he could to give a bit of European lustre to this Russian city."³⁹

Nizhny Novgorod also became known as "the land where journalists know no fear." The phrase was coined in 1994 by journalists from the city of Ulyanovsk, where the governor was the former head of the regional Communist Party. One day, when Nemtsov was late for a press conference, journalists were chatting among themselves, and the visiting journalists were asking the locals how they worked. Did the governor's office ask to see the questions beforehand? What were they allowed to ask about? Did they need accreditation in order to work with the regional administration? The Nizhny Novgorod journalists told them they could ask anything they wanted, and everyone was invited. "Just then Nemtsov rushed in, kissed the women journalists on the cheek, shook hands with the men, made a joke and went to the podium," the journalist Natalia Lisitsyna recalled. "After the press conference, someone from Ulyanovsk sighed with quiet envy, 'This is truly the land where journalists know no fear.'"⁴⁰

"I learnt from him how to work with the media," said Yury Lebedev. "I was trained in the old school. If my boss said a chipmunk was a bird, then it was a bird, and that was that. But suddenly you had to talk with journalists and answer tough questions. If you lied even once, they'd catch you and you'd look bad."⁴¹ Freedom of the press, the main achievement of perestroika, was still an integral part of the political landscape in the early 1990s. Photogenic and sociable, Nemtsov was good at using this freedom: journalists loved him, and he returned the favour. He never refused to comment; he answered questions on television just about every week, because he understood that this was to his advantage. And besides, he had no reason to control journalists—he had plenty of charisma and popularity.

Nemtsov also believed that the executive branch should not own media—unlike the legislative branch in those years, where they thought that media ownership was natural and normal. Shortly after the coup attempt, someone suggested that Nemtsov's administration should take control of the *Nizhny Novgorod Pravda* newspaper. Nemtsov refused.

Seven television channels were already operating in the region, and the number of newspapers had doubled. "Nizhny Novgorod region had one of the most powerful media markets at that time," the celebrated television host and producer Alexander Lyubimov recalled. "There was a large number of newspapers and television companies, and somehow they all managed to function."[42] Lyubimov, who was friends with Nemtsov, also came to Nizhny Novgorod for a few months to build a new independent television company. Nothing came of this venture, but it was a sign of how attractive the city had become to celebrities from Moscow.

In 1992, the reputation of Nizhny Novgorod as the capital of progressive trends quickly spread throughout the country. In September 1992, sixty Russian governors gathered in the city to discuss the future of reform—an unprecedented event for the provinces at the time. The president must have been pleased. His young protégé was not just coping: he was setting the bar higher.

The Moscow bureaucracy—and Nemtsov himself—learnt that Nemtsov was Yeltsin's favourite in April 1993, after Yeltsin confided to a foreign delegation at a Kremlin reception that he viewed him as his successor. The news quickly went viral in Moscow. "Boris believed it, and it helped him," said one of Yeltsin's aides at the time. "He became less cautious, because he knew Yeltsin had his back. He grew up faster in politics."

But meanwhile in Moscow, dark clouds had gathered over the reform process. The Gaidar cabinet was out.

# CHAPTER 6

## Winter 1992–Spring 1993
## Two Centres of Power

### Khasbulatov goes on the attack

Ruslan Khasbulatov owed his rise to the very top of the Russian government to his relationship with Boris Yeltsin. In the early 1970s they met in Sverdlovsk, when Khasbulatov was an instructor in propaganda techniques for the Komsomol and Yeltsin was just beginning to climb the Communist Party ladder. The second reason for his success was his nationality: he was a Chechen. At that time, the largest ethnic republics within Russia—Tatarstan and Bashkortostan—were in something of an opposition to the Soviet centre. By promoting a representative of non-titular nationality as his deputy, Yeltsin demonstrated that he was meeting the needs of the national autonomous republics in the country. And Khasbulatov was an intellectual, a university professor and a democrat, even if he wasn't a member of Yeltsin's team.

"Khasbulatov did not stand out in any way. He picked the winning lottery ticket when he was given a high position in the Soviet government," Viktor Sheinis wrote.[1] A year later, when Yeltsin became president, Khasbulatov—already known for his loyalty to Yeltsin—was the *de facto* head of the parliament and one the heroes of resistance during the coup attempt of 1991. Khasbulatov was one of the drafters of the historic appeal that Yeltsin had read out while standing on a tank in front of the White House, and then he led the resistance of deputies. In late October, Khasbulatov was elected chairman of the Supreme Soviet of the Russian parliament.

A methodical, patient, skilled government functionary and workaholic—first to arrive and last to leave—Khasbulatov soon realized that the opportunities of Russia's first parliament were almost unlimited, if only a person knew how to use them. It didn't take long for Yeltsin to notice that Khasbulatov passed populist laws at exactly the times when the president was not in Moscow. As head of the parliament, Khasbulatov set up the bureaucratic machine under him, and very soon deputies were standing in line for privileges or *per diems* for business trips. No important document would leave the parliament without his signature or nod of approval. He redistributed duties among his deputies in such a way that all significant issues were in the hands of the people loyal to him. In 1991–92, if the Russian congress and its working body, the Supreme Soviet, were temples of democracy, Ruslan Khasbulatov very quickly became the all-powerful high priest.

Many years later, Yegor Gaidar wrote that when he was working as an editor during perestroika, he had rejected Khasbulatov's scholarly articles because they were unoriginal.[2] A professor of economics, Khasbulatov must have hoped, like Vice-President Rutskoi, to head Yeltsin's first cabinet in the autumn of 1991, and he bore a grudge when he wasn't appointed. In November, when Gaidar was heading the government's economic bloc and there was a split in the parliament over market reforms, Khasbulatov sensed that Gaidar would make a convenient political target. Rutskoi was the first to attack Gaidar and his team, but Khasbulatov did not stay in the trenches for long. On 13 January 1992, the eleventh day of reforms, Khasbulatov went on the attack—not against the president but against the reforms and Gaidar—and suggested that Yeltsin "replace what is essentially a dysfunctional cabinet."[3] He added that if the president didn't do it, then parliament would. Yeltsin responded that the cabinet wasn't a glove to be taken on and off, and that he wouldn't dissolve it.

"Rivalry between the 'head of the Supreme Soviet' and the president may once again dominate political life, just like when [USSR Supreme Soviet Chairman Anatoly] Lukyanov had a complicated relationship with Gorbachev," commented *Kommersant* newspaper at the time.[4]

The prediction would come true. Soon a battle to the death between the branches of Russian power began—a battle that would end in less than two years with tanks firing at the Russian parliament in the White House.

## A creeping coup

Yegor Gaidar would later describe the April 1992 session of the Congress of People's Deputies as "the first frontal attack on reform."[5] The congress criticized his cabinet for days on end. The president's compromise proposals were rejected. The deputies, urged by Khasbulatov, passed a resolution giving the Supreme Soviet the right to enact a law on the cabinet and requiring the president to submit a nominee for prime minister within three months. At this point, the nominee wasn't important. What was important was that the executive branch was humiliated and hamstrung. "April 1992 is an echo of August 1991," wrote *Moskovskie novosti* at the time. "However paradoxical, the 'aggressively conformist majority' of the Russian congress appears to be the heir to the coup conspirators of 1991."[6]

Instead of pausing, Gaidar decided to escalate the situation: the entire cabinet resigned. This blackmail worked, and Gaidar emerged victorious from the first government crisis. The deputies, frightened that responsibility for the reforms would fall on them, gave their blessing—with reservations—for his team to continue working.

But this had been only a test battle. Khasbulatov moved his focus to Yeltsin. Their mutual hatred grew by the day. The country had just gone through over one personal conflict that largely determined the fate of the country—Yeltsin and Gorbachev—and here was another. This time it was hard to imagine two less similar people: one tall and handsome, the other short and thin. One was direct and impulsive, the other suspicious and wily. One cut to the chase, acting on instinct, while the other was cautious and cunning, calculating every step. One was a people's leader who won a mandate of trust in a direct election, the other—a master of bureaucratic intrigue.

During the April congress, Khasbulatov attacked the cabinet and demanded a personal meeting with Yeltsin. Yeltsin did not receive him, calling Khasbulatov "a double-dealer who would deceive him again."[7] As their enmity grew, the Presidential Administration would try to spite Khasbulatov in every possible way. For example, they cut telephone communications to the aeroplane he was in while speaking to the president of Uzbekistan, Islam Karimov.[8] Khasbulatov returned the favour. He spied on Yeltsin's supporters in the parliament, talked down to them and harassed them, and he insulted the president himself. In September 1993, while speaking in front of TV cameras, he even used the Russian gesture of tapping his neck to indicate that Yeltsin was making decisions while drunk.

However, as has so often happened in history, Khasbulatov's fight with Yeltsin was less a battle between two different characters and more a reflection of the balance of political power. The harder the reforms were and the weaker popular support for them, the more Khasbulatov's parliament attacked the cabinet and the president. In the absence of established and stable parliamentary parties—which, understandably, could not magically appear out of nowhere overnight—the conflict between Yeltsin and Khasbulatov turned into a conflict between branches of power. Or rather, to put it more accurately, the conflict between the president and the parliament rose to the personal level.

Constitutions of democratic states prescribe procedures to facilitate the peaceful resolution of political conflicts. But in 1992 Russia did not have that kind of constitution. The old, much-amended Brezhnev-era Soviet constitution violated the most basic principle of the democratic state system: the separation of the executive and legislative branches. It was amended to include the office of president, defined as the head of state and of the executive branch. But there was also an amendment that the Congress of People's Deputies had "the right to consider and decide on any issue within the jurisdiction of the Russian Federation." At the time it was passed, the amendment seemed like a victory for democracy, but now it was leading to a paralysis of power. "Any issue" meant any issue at all. Khasbulatov directed the deputies to pass laws on state subsidies to specific factories and sectors of the economy, as well as laws curtailing the rights of the president and his cabinet.

The pro-democratic press called this process "a creeping *coup d'état*." By April 1992, people were already wondering what Yeltsin would do when he was up against the wall. "We need not look far for examples," *Izvestiya* wrote at the time. "Gorbachev tried to use compromise to subdue the aggressive reactionary positions of the entrenched bureaucrats. Now they are pushing Yeltsin into a corner, forcing him to make a choice between democratic procedures and democratic reforms."[9]

In the spring of 1992, politicians discussed ways to resolve the situation peacefully through a referendum. But the right to call a referendum was also the prerogative of congress, and Khasbulatov knew he'd lose. Yeltsin's approval ratings were much higher than those of the deputies as a whole and of Khasbulatov personally. At the end of May, Yeltsin proposed holding a referendum on the question of a presidential system of governance during the transitional period. This was an attempted *coup d'état*, the deputies responded. The branches of power were in deadlock.

## Yeltsin sacrifices his queen

In January 1992, just as he was beginning his reforms, Yegor Gaidar optimistically gave himself and his cabinet two years. "Retirement by the end of next year," Gaidar said, "to deafening cries of popular indignation, but in accordance with democratic procedures." His resignation would not be a tragedy, he reasoned, if the cabinet were able to hit the key indicators: bring inflation under control and attain financial stabilization. "The surgery would be over, and it would be time to nurse the patient back to a full recovery," Gaidar continued, "and for that we need a more cooperative cabinet that would lower taxes, create prerequisites for economic growth and attract foreign capital. These are wonderful tasks, and I sincerely envy the people who will work on them."[10]

But his hopes were not realized. For the first three or four months, Gaidar and his team successfully restrained the growth of the money supply, but difficulties began in the spring. First, the miners demanded pay hikes. The miners were historically a powerful political force that had greatly helped Yeltsin in his struggle against Gorbachev and the Communist Party. Gaidar's protests were overruled, and they were given pay hikes. Yeltsin was counting on them again in his confrontation with the parliament.

Then state workers got a raise.[11] At that point, the parliament really got down to business, raising state outlays by eight per cent of GDP, which Gaidar, then acting prime minister, condemned as "the apotheosis of financial irresponsibility."[12] That summer the Central Bank, which was outside the cabinet's control, began printing money, which precipitated a non-payment crisis. "In terms of financial stabilization, the country was thrown back several months," recalled Andrei Nechayev, then economics minister. "Everything had to start all over again."[13]

At the end of August 1992, the rouble exchange rate collapsed, and a new round of inflation began: instead of the planned five per cent per month, by the autumn it was already twenty per cent. "We were clearly facing the threat of hyperinflation, a calamitous drop in the money supply and a reversal of the positive results of the reforms," Gaidar said.[14] The year of 1992 was the hardest year of reform in Russia, and the failure of fiscal policy led to a vicious circle: printing money led to higher prices; higher prices led to increased social tension; Yeltsin responded to social discontent by making concessions; the opposition became even more incensed; pressure on fiscal policy grew again.

Throughout that year, Yeltsin still hoped to reach an agreement with Khasbulatov and the Supreme Soviet. In late summer, his allies in parliament warned him that at the next session of congress, Khasbulatov would seek the cabinet's resignation. But Yeltsin was indecisive. He didn't agree to sacrifice Gaidar, but he gave up fellow democrats and market-oriented ministers, and he publicly criticized the cabinet. But, as Gaidar said before the December congress, "Appeasement of the aggressor is the worst policy."[15] In response, the deputies only raised the bar. They called for the president to be impeached. Gaidar's resignation was no longer enough for Khasbulatov. He planned to take over the country by cobbling the president and the cabinet with new amendments to the constitution.

The congress session opened on 1 December. For the first two days, nothing foretold the storm to come. But on the third day a fight broke out. "Help! Someone protect me from these people!" Khasbulatov shouted as several deputies from the democratic bloc rushed to the podium, protesting his sudden decision to make the vote on constitutional amendments a secret ballot. Deputies on the other side of the political spectrum responded to Khasbulatov's shouts for assistance, and a fight broke out.

There was good reason to fight. Khasbulatov wanted a vote to subordinate the executive branch to the congress, which would make the post of president a ceremonial position. A secret ballot vastly increased Khasbulatov's chances of victory. This was the day that anti-Yeltsin forces took control of parliament. "It turned out that the president's staunch supporters could not count on a 'fifty per cent plus one' vote. They couldn't even count on a 'thirty-three per cent plus one' one today," wrote *Moskovskie novosti*.[16]

The congress stopped a half-step away from a constitutional coup: the amendments were two votes short of passing. Only at this point did Yeltsin realize the gravity of the situation. However, his actions, as Viktor Sheinis later wrote, consisted of "a chain of mistakes, where one mistake leads to the next."[17] Yeltsin agreed to a deal. The deputies would be given the right to confirm the appointments of the foreign minister as well as the heads of all the security, military and law enforcement ministries. In return, Gaidar would be confirmed as prime minister. In the end, the constitutional amendment regarding ministers passed with flying colours, but the deputies voted Gaidar out.

The president's patience snapped, and he launched a counterattack. He decided to address the Russian citizens from the congress with a proposal to hold a referendum, while simultaneously calling on his loyal deputies to leave the congress so that there would not be a quorum.

When Sheinis and his colleagues learnt of Yeltsin's plan, they were certain it wouldn't work, and they tried to keep Yeltsin from announcing it. They even tried to get to the president and talk to him in person, but the guards wouldn't let them through. It was harder to get to Yeltsin than it had been a year ago. "We tried to explain that the fate of the parliament, and indeed the democratic process in Russia, depended on our meeting with the president before the session opened," Sheinis recalled. "We were told that Yeltsin hadn't arrived yet. We would be able to approach him only when he had taken his place in the presidium and Khasbulatov was opening the session. We stood behind him and spoke convincingly, we thought. Yeltsin didn't even look at us; he just frowned.

I don't think he said a word. He just gestured. A minute later he was already standing on the podium."[18]

Just as Sheinis expected, only a small number of deputies responded to Yeltsin's appeal, and it happened live, in front of the whole country. As described in the book *The Yeltsin Era*, written collectively by Yeltsin's closest associates, "It was a complete embarrassment, largely devaluing Yeltsin's strong performance. The president was at a loss."[19] After the first embarrassment, another occurred on the same day, 10 December, when Yeltsin arrived to speak at the Moskvich automotive plant. Instead of the customary ovation, the workers greeted him with tepid applause. "For Yeltsin this unsuccessful trip was a lesson and a breaking point in his outreach to the public. He realized that the stage of 'going to the people' had passed," wrote his former presidential aides.[20]

Khasbulatov responded to Yeltsin with a show of generosity. He announced that he was resigning, but only so that the deputies would ask him to stay on. Once again the question arose: the danger posed by the parliament, mainly by its speaker, was obvious, but what would happen if the president simply dissolved it? "As bad as the current parliament is," wrote *Izvestiya* commentator Otto Lacis, "taking away or curtailing its power is still highly undesirable and potentially dangerous for the development of democracy. Losses along the way will almost certainly outweigh gains, as our bitter historical experience shows. God forbid that we should ever live to see such a state of affairs in which the unrestrained *diktat* by some in the highest legislative bodies [i.e. Khasbulatov] would close off other paths forward."[21]

The December crisis was resolved with the help of the head of the Constitutional Court, Valery Zorkin. The anti-presidential amendments to the constitution would be suspended, and in April a referendum on a new constitution would be held. In return, the president agreed to propose to congress one of the first three candidates for prime minister from a list of candidates chosen in a straw vote. "We thought we'd managed to turn a defeat into at least an honourable draw," Gaidar later recalled. "All that remained was to decide on the candidates for prime minister."[22] But if Yeltsin had to make a deal, he had already decided to sacrifice Gaidar. Yeltsin was planning to nominate the reform-minded and liberal Vladimir Kadannikov, director of a large automotive factory, to the post of prime minister. But in his presentation before congress, Kadannikov was too obvious a supporter of Yeltsin, and did not make the cut. The results of the vote were:

- Yury Skokov, secretary of the Security Council and one of the leaders of the conservative wing in the president's entourage (637 votes);
- Viktor Chernomyrdin, former minister of the gas industry, now head of Gazprom (the state corporation that had been the Ministry of the Gas Industry prior to 1989) (621 votes);
- Yegor Gaidar (400 votes).

Yeltsin summoned Gaidar to tell him that he hadn't got enough votes. The choice was between Skokov and Chernomyrdin, and he asked Gaidar to recuse himself. Gaidar advised the president to opt for Chernomyrdin but refused to recuse himself. "It was painful to look at Yeltsin. It was obvious that the decision was not easy for him," he later wrote.[23] Chernomyrdin, who had promised an economy that would be an "orderly market not a street bazaar" to the deputies' applause, was confirmed as prime minister, while Gaidar went to hand over his portfolio. Thus ended his watch as head of Russian reforms, a watch that had lasted just over a year. In his struggle with congress, Yeltsin sacrificed a queen, but, as it would soon become clear, this sacrifice was ultimately pointless.

## Winds of civil war

On Saturday, 20 March 1993, at about 1.00 p.m., Sergei Filatov, head of Boris Yeltsin's administration, entered the office of Vice-President Alexander Rutskoi. Filatov was holding a draft presidential decree 'On the Activities of the Executive Branch Until the End of the Crisis in Power'. The decree did not explicitly mention dissolving congress, but its meaning was clear: Direct presidential rule would be introduced in Russia.

Rutskoi had long been at war with the cabinet, but he was still vice-president. After reading the text of the decree, he at first became angry and said he would not sign off on this piece of nonsense. But then he picked up a pencil and began to correct the text. Filatov took the decree with Rutskoi's notes and went to add the corrections. When he returned to the vice-president's office about an hour later, it was as if the vice-president had been replaced by another man. "Rutskoi took the draft of the decree he had corrected and began to erase everything he'd written," Filatov recalled. "When he had finished, he turned to us and said, 'I won't sign off on this, and I don't advise you to, either.'"[24]

By that time, the compromise reached the previous December had already fallen apart: the deputies reneged on their obligations. "It was the work of the Devil," Khasbulatov said to explain why the deputies had given up the right to choose the prime minister and agreed to a referendum. In early March, another congress was convened and made new amendments to the constitution, giving lawmakers additional rights, among them the right to revoke presidential decrees. All of Yeltsin's proposals, from the referendum to early elections, were eliminated. Yeltsin's advisers explained that the deputies were on the offensive, and that there was a high probability of another impeachment attempt at the next congress. Yeltsin was losing patience. How could he eliminate the diarchy that had become a personal threat?

On the president's desk was an analysis with three scenarios, prepared by the *siloviki*.[25]\* The first scenario was the least destructive and presupposed that an agreement on new elections would be reached with the parliamentary leadership. But once again, the government would have to sacrifice the reformers, and the future parliament would again be anti-Yeltsin.

In the second scenario no agreement would be reached. The president would secure the support of most of the regions and issue a decree to dissolve congress and hold new elections; congress would respond by holding a vote on impeachment. This would be unlikely to pass, but if it

---

\* *Silovik* is a term used to describe anyone empowered by law to use force against citizens—that is, people who head and work in the military, law enforcement and security ministries and organizations, as well as immigration control, the Justice Department, drug enforcement, intelligence gathering ministries and organizations, and the Federal Protective Service that guards officials.

did, it might lead to civil war. "In the worst case (if an attempt is made to resolve the situation by force)," the authors wrote, "Russia might completely collapse."

The third scenario described a blitzkrieg, essentially a coup: issue a decree to dissolve congress and then quickly seize the initiative—block the deputies and close the building so that congress was unable to convene. "On the whole," the note's authors continued, "this option of eliminating the imminent crisis of power, if properly executed, provides a quick and reliable way to hold early elections of the [new] legislative body."[26]

Yeltsin hesitated. He was torn between opposing impulses.

On the one hand, he sincerely wanted to go down in history as the founding father of democracy in Russia. On his desk lay another analysis, this one on the establishment of the Fifth Republic in France.[27] He, Yeltsin, could become the Russian Charles de Gaulle and usher in a new Russian constitution. But to do that he would have to negotiate with the leaders in parliament. On the other hand, he wanted to take another path that was more in keeping with his nature. He didn't want to unravel the knot slowly. He wanted to cut it once and for all.

In the end, that's what he decided to do. The draft decree introducing presidential rule—the one Filatov gave to Rutskoi for his signature—was written. He had already taped a television address to the nation, in which he said that he had signed the decree and was taking responsibility for the fate of the country. This was to be announced on the evening news followed by a reading of the text of the decree. The decree had been sent to the TV station by courier, but it had not yet been signed.

Five minutes before the broadcast, a command came from the Kremlin: the address goes on air, the decree does not. Yeltsin never signed the decree.[28] He swung his bat but didn't hit the ball. He continued to hesitate. He later wrote that, "Maybe for the first time in my life, I put a stop to a decision I had already made. No, I didn't hesitate. I paused. You could say that I stopped."[29]

By the evening of 20 March, Alexander Rutskoi and Valery Zorkin were already furious about the presidential address, which had just been broadcast all over the country. Rutskoi would say in early April that he would never be reconciled with the president. Both men joined Khasbulatov, who knew what to do next: convene congress and attack the weakened president.

Events were unfolding rapidly. Yeltsin suddenly appeared before congress with yet another conciliatory speech. But why would he make peace if he had almost declared war? There was also something strange about his appearance: "His hair was uncombed, he mumbled [...] but no one could prove that he was drunk," historian Oleg Moroz later said about the speech. "But why did he do anything that raised suspicions? After all, it was tantamount to political suicide: it happened right on the eve of the impeachment vote."[30] Yeltsin's press secretary Vyacheslav Kostikov later explained that the president was driving home from the tennis court and suddenly decided to make a friendly overture to the deputies. In any case, Yeltsin only aggravated the situation. His speech made the deputies furious. The first impeachment in Russian history became almost inevitable.

On the same day, Khasbulatov was about to go home, when suddenly Zorkin and Chernomyrdin appeared in his office. They promised to persuade Yeltsin to hold elections for president and parliament at the same time. Khasbulatov began to lean towards this option.[31] It is clear why. First, Khasbulatov realized that he would not be able to seize power from Yeltsin easily, and that impeachment would only provoke him into a counterattack. (Indeed, by the time the impeachment vote was held, Yeltsin would already be armed with the decree to dissolve congress, and his security service would have instructions to block deputies from entering the building and to cut off the electricity and sewage systems in the Congress Hall.)

Second, the impeachment would be a victory not for Khasbulatov, but for the irreconcilable opposition, which was gaining strength and attacking Yeltsin under radical slogans of Soviet imperial revival. Khasbulatov decided not to bring Yeltsin down, but gradually, step by step, to take his power from him. That is why, on the eve of the vote, the speaker even confessed to journalists that he was personally against impeachment. Mutual restraint slowed things down. Both sides were frightened by the prospect of the conflict entering an open and acute phase of war. That night, Yeltsin and Khasbulatov came to an agreement.

On the morning of 28 March, there was a draft resolution that provided a peaceful way out of the diarchy by holding presidential and parliamentary elections simultaneously in November 1993.

As soon as the compromise resolution was read from the rostrum, "to everybody's satisfaction", as Khasbulatov put it, the deputies lost their nerve: instead of impeaching the president, which they thought they had in their pocket, they were offered early elections. "This is a conspiracy behind the backs of the parliamentarians. It's time to get rid of both Yeltsin and Khasbulatov," the deputies shouted, and put both the impeachment motion and the question of the speaker's early resignation to a vote. Neither proposal passed—the impeachment failed by just a few dozen votes—but Khasbulatov, who was frightened by the unexpected turn of events, learnt his lesson well. For the first time, the deputies had put him in his place. That was the last time he took Yeltsin's side. "[From that moment on] Khasbulatov ceased to be independent," journalist Oleg Poptsov later wrote. "The speaker got a 'stern warning'. The following months showed that the plan was a success."[32]

While the deputies were voting on impeachment, Yeltsin was at a street rally of supporters in front of St Basil's Cathedral on Red Square. "Vic-tor-y!" the president chanted. "Vic-tor-y!" the crowd shouted back. In reality, this was not a victory, but a brief respite in a bitter power struggle. The last opportunity for peace had been lost, and the struggle would soon begin to take on the features of a civil war.

## Yes, yes, no, yes

The failure of impeachment meant that they had to come to an agreement. Congress finally agreed to a referendum. Four questions were formulated for the 26 April referendum:

1. Do you trust President Yeltsin?
2. Do you approve of the social policies pursued by the president and government since 1992?
3. Do you think early presidential elections are necessary?
4. Do you think early elections of people's deputies are necessary?

The deputies formulated the questions in a clever way. First of all, the question about confidence in the reforms was put in such a way that, as Gaidar later wrote, even he "could not easily answer such a question with a short, unambiguous 'yes' on the ballot: at the time there was no unified economic policy, just fights, victories, retreats."[33] If that was the reaction of the policy's creator, what could be expected from ordinary people who were unlikely to understand how inevitable major reforms were after seventy years of dead-end Soviet economic policies and then another five years of perestroika? Second, the deputies and the Constitutional Court decided that the answers to the third and fourth questions would be considered positive and binding if they were supported by the absolute majority of voters, not just a majority of those who voted. This was unattainable.

Sixty-four per cent of voters showed up for the referendum. Overall, the "yes, yes, no, yes" formula, which was promoted by Yeltsin's headquarters and the democratic forces, won. A total of 58.7% of voters said they supported the president; 53%—to everyone's surprise—supported the reforms; 31.7% were in favour of early presidential elections; and 43.1%—that is, a markedly higher number—supported early parliamentary elections.

Yeltsin had scored an undeniable moral victory. He was being threatened with impeachment, and yet now he had proof that he was more popular than the parliament and that the people approved of the reforms. How could he be impeached now? But the results of the referendum did not formally oblige anyone to do anything. And, as *Nezavisimaya gazeta* wrote the following day, "The results of the referendum, as predicted earlier, open the door to a range of interpretations by both sides."[34]

Nemtsov voted for an early presidential election, even though Yeltsin had campaigned against it, and, right up until the parliament was dissolved in September 1993, he would speak out for new elections of both the parliament and president. Yeltsin's favourite and a popular governor, Nemtsov saw from the referendum results that the people supported reforms and Yeltsin. And so, Nemtsov suggested that the first step should be to remove "from the government the opponents of reforms." "The president should immediately form a cabinet, preferably of like-minded people, or at least of people united by a specific goal, not by general talk about putting food on the table throughout the country [...]. And the next step should be a new constitution."³⁵

The president's team had aimed at adopting a new constitution in March, which turned out to be when Yeltsin almost dispersed congress. The proposal was a pro-presidential constitution. Yeltsin did not want to advance the constitution developed by the commission at congress. "No one wanted the draft of the constitutional commission that was a more or less satisfactory form of historical compromise," Viktor Sheinis wrote. "That is why the 'presidential' draft appeared—it was an axe meant to cut a way out of the constitutional–political crisis."³⁶

But there was one big problem with this project: time. In theory, a demoralized congress could adopt a pro-presidential constitution, but it had to be done quickly, on the wave of the referendum victory. A preliminary draft of the presidential version was published at the end of April. Yeltsin had hoped to have it ready by the end of May, but it would take at least two months to draft.

Meanwhile, the ranks of moderate opposition to Yeltsin in the parliament thinned; some came over to his side. But the referendum reinforced the split in the public. Compromise did not suit the irreconcilable opposition—the same group that had set the tone at congress, put Khasbulatov in his place and courted political supporters among the most deprived and desperate part of society. The core of this radical anti-Yeltsin coalition were the diehard Communists who had long fought against Yeltsin (and Gorbachev before him). This included some of the coup conspirators who had already recovered from their defeat in August 1991.

During this period, Gennady Zyuganov rose to prominence. He was the leader of the Communist Party who had not been one of the conspirators but signed the conspirators' manifesto, the famous 'Word to the People' published in the *Sovetskaya Rossiya* newspaper in July 1991. By the spring of 1993, ultra-leftist communist views had become intertwined with ultra-right nationalist views. Viewpoints merged, red flags were raised together with the black-yellow-and-white imperial flag, communist slogans were chanted with anti-Semitic ones. This is when the term "red and brown" came into circulation. It was no longer Khasbulatov who was at war with Yeltsin—it was the irreconcilable opposition that chose to escalate the fight against what it called "Yeltsin's occupation regime." It united under the banner of the National Salvation Front, and Khasbulatov was now a toy in its hands.

On the morning of 1 May, a Communist demonstration quickly turned into a riot. The city authorities prevented the demonstrators from entering the city centre. Led by the most active parliamentarians, several thousand people moved in the other direction, and by Gagarin Square on Leninsky Prospect they ran into trucks and lines of police who were completely unprepared for the attack by several hundred men armed with flagpoles and crowbars. A mass brawl broke out. Sticks and stones were thrown at the police. Two trucks were burnt. "The organizers threw the crowd into the lines of riot police. The authorities and law enforcement demonstrated inexcusable unprofessionalism," was the headline of *Nezavisimaya gazeta* two days later.[37]

A protester who was never identified broke through the line of OMON riot police and climbed into an empty truck cabin. The keys were in the ignition. He started the engine and reversed it into the police cordon. Police sergeant Vladimir Tolokneyev, aged twenty-five, was crushed between the truck and a car. When the crowd parted, he was found in a pool of blood with his skull fractured. He could not be saved. Yeltsin attended his funeral. The first blood had been shed in Moscow.

# CHAPTER 7

## Summer–Autumn 1993
## Breaking the Deadlock

### Ratifying the constitution

Two years had passed since the conspirators who attempted a coup had been defeated, and the dark spectre of Communist restoration seemed to have dissipated for ever. There was truly a victory of freedom, of a very real and absolute freedom, the kind that Russia had probably never had before, except for the brief interval between February and October 1917—and a freedom that Russia would lose again in a few years. But although freedom flourished, democracy didn't. Instead of democracy, there was a battle for power and a population that barely understood what was happening. The nation was waiting for a miracle, but the miracle did not happen. Political scientist Kirill Rogov later wrote about the bloody events of October 1993, noting that the fateful role was played "first of all by the absence of common institutional goals supported by the voters, a shared understanding of what social order would replace the Soviet model."[1]

People were not building a new life but rather adapting to a new reality and new rules: a market economy, free prices, privatization and private property, freedom of speech—almost absolute at the time—freedom of private life, the very idea that the state was no longer their boss. But at the same time, they were having to get used to poverty and loss of social status. Doctors and teachers became "shuttle traders", travelling to foreign countries to buy cheap goods and bringing them home to sell. Engineers and scientists tried to start businesses.

By mid-summer, Yeltsin's credibility had dropped again, but he was still considerably more popular than Khasbulatov and the deputies. The people did not want to revolt. "They grumble about the president, but there is no alternative yet," Yeltsin's adviser Leonid Smirnyagin told him in the summer of 1993. "The people have shown that they can live independently."[2] Opinion polls showed that people were tired of the diarchy, and they wanted violence and a civil war even less, but this will was expressed too passively for Yeltsin's team to translate it into a full-blown mandate of trust. As a result, the flywheel of the crisis unwound ever faster, and the calls to fight the Yeltsin regime grew louder and more aggressive.

At the end of July, the pro-democracy deputy Lev Ponomaryov realized that he needed to talk to the president, as he had done in September 1991. And, just like in September 1991, Yeltsin had disappeared again—he'd gone off to one of his residences (this time on Lake Valdai, not Sochi), again at a time when procrastination was tantamount to death. Ponomaryov was certain that disaster was coming. The Supreme Soviet was reversing reforms, trying to revoke presidential decrees—such as the most important decree on voucher privatization—and had passed an intentionally unrealistic deficit budget. This group of "Conspirators 2.0", as Ponomaryov and his team would call them at a press conference, needed to be stopped immediately. There was only one way to stop the *coup d'état*: elect a new parliament.

But how could these elections be held? The constitutional convention finished work on the draft constitution proposed by Yeltsin, transforming it into a viable draft that no longer enshrined a purely presidential system of governance. It was a constitution for a presidential republic, but it was a democratic constitution, based on a balance of power and electoral procedures. A modern bicameral parliament was to be a counterbalance to the president. "Some bias in favour of the executive power remained," Viktor Sheinis wrote, "but this was nothing compared to its exaggerated role in the [original] draft [...]. In the new draft, the parliament could dismiss the government, but the president could also, under certain, clearly stipulated conditions and restrictions, dissolve the parliament and call early elections."[3]

But having drafted the new constitution, Yeltsin and his supporters were faced with an unsolvable problem: how could it be adopted? At the time the only legitimate way to adopt it was to have it approved by congress, but the deputies would not vote it in. And when the Presidential Administration asked regional councils to approve the draft constitution—the first step before it would be put up for a vote at congress—Khasbulatov simply sent all the regional deputies on leave.[4] The legal route to elections was blocked once again.

And that was not all. In late July, at a meeting of the Communist, militantly nationalist and anti-Yeltsin National Salvation Front, the participants declared, "We have no choice: either we go on a serious offensive and overthrow the criminal regime, or we will lose Russia."[5] The opposition decided to abolish the presidency and transfer all power to the Soviets (councils). These slogans sounded so radical that even Communists distanced themselves from them. In fact, the irreconcilable opposition announced that it was time to take up armed resistance. "Everything was said openly," *Izvestiya* wrote, "the struggle to control the media; mass street demonstrations; efforts to organize a mass workers' movement; work in military units, law enforcement and security agencies. In a sign of the readiness to go on the offensive, they had even formed self-defence groups." And the newspaper added regretfully that "due to the inaction of the presidential structures, opponents of the president and cabinet feel they will succeed. If the president had carried out the will of the people after the referendum, no summer–autumn offensive would have been possible."[6] In early August, the director of the Parliamentary Centre, where radical oppositionists used to gather, would come to Yeltsin and tell him that the basement of his building had been turned into a fully fledged armoury.[7] It would also come out that deputies were again preparing to impeach Yeltsin at the next session of congress.

Against the backdrop of all these events, Lev Ponomaryov and his associates went to see the president. Before their arrival, they decided to warn Korzhakov, Yeltsin's head of security, so that he wouldn't turn the deputies back.

"Just like the last time, Korzhakov was inappropriately rude to me," Ponomaryov recalled. "He said, 'What are you muddying the waters for? Don't you have anything better to do?' Once again, I had to remind him that his only job was to announce our arrival. It was July, and hot. The three of us had to wait three hours for an audience."[8]

Finally, Ponomaryov and his comrades were led into a space like a gym changing room. Yeltsin appeared straight from the tennis court and shower in gym shorts. He was still wet and had a towel over his shoulder. The relationship between the president and Democratic Russia was not what it was in 1991, and Ponomaryov did not give Yeltsin an ultimatum. He simply told him what was going on and urged him to go back to Moscow. Yeltsin listened carefully to the visitors and said, "I'll be back in a week."[9]

And he was as good as his word. Back in Moscow on 10 August, Yeltsin told his advisers, "The unresolved issue of the constitution and elections is pushing us to use methods of force. We've decided on the timing. In August we'll get ready and go on the political offensive in September. But what exactly are we going to do? What should we do about the Supreme Soviet? They're just itching for a fight. I'm being pushed from all sides to use force. Crowds are already shouting: 'Dissolve it!'"[10]

Then Yeltsin spoke publicly. He intentionally chose 19 August, the anniversary of the coup attempt, as the date for his keynote speech. He went on the offensive under the slogan of August 1991: freedom and democracy for Russia. "I am faced with a choice," Yeltsin said, "either carry out the will of the people in support of reform or allow the Supreme Soviet to ignore the will of the people and destroy Russian statehood."[11]

He announced that parliamentary elections would be held at the end of November.

Could Yeltsin have held a new election without dissolving the Supreme Soviet?

Did he have a choice?

Many of his supporters then and afterwards believed that he did. There were two alternatives to Decree No. 1,400, which the president was soon to use to dissolve the parliament:

Option 1: Do nothing. Leave things as they are. Of course, that would have meant living on a powder keg for almost two more years, but they could try. Viktor Sheinis described this option as follows: "The confrontation between the authorities will persist until the spring of 1995 [when both the president and congress would be up for re-election] or until congress itself decides that its hour has passed. This means that the people will be living in a state of constant tension, constant conflict, the legislative branch's constant harassment of the executive branch, and a war between the president and the country's minority. That war of the minority is *de facto* being waged today by the majority in the Supreme Soviet, a majority that has completely lost all sense of reality."[12]

Option 2: Adopt a new constitution (or, alternatively, hold elections for a new parliament), bypassing congress. Pretend that congress and the Supreme Soviet simply do not exist. The public are likely to accept this. "Few people would stand up for the deputies. The majority of them have done much to discredit both the parliament and, alas, parliamentarianism," Sheinis wrote.[13] The problem was that only congress could declare a national referendum on the current constitution. The only other option was to hold a plebiscite, a vote without constitutional status. This was not flawless from a legal point of view, but what were the alternatives when the legal avenues were blocked?

However, the president spent the summer vacation in the company of his faithful and trigger-happy bodyguard Korzhakov and far from advisers searching for a peaceful way out of the situation. He returned from his vacation convinced that he no longer had the desire or the patience to untangle this Gordian knot. "In early September," Yeltsin later recalled. "I made my decision. Nobody knows about it. Even the people in my inner circle have no idea that I've made my decision in principle. Russia will never have this kind of parliament again."[14]

## Decree No. 1,400

In Nizhny Novgorod, by 7.00 p.m. on 21 September, the entire city's beau monde had gathered in the hall of the Nizhny Novgorod Philharmonic. It was an important, solemn moment: Nemtsov had already done a great deal to immortalize the name of Andrei Sakharov in Nizhny Novgorod; now he was opening an international music festival named in his honour. On this occasion, the city was welcoming the legendary musician Mstislav Rostropovich, another defender of Russian democracy (a photograph of Rostropovich sitting on a chair in the

White House with a Kalashnikov assault rifle during the coup was one of the symbols of the victory over the conspirators). Nemtsov stepped up to the stage to read his opening speech. Just then, out of the corner of his eye, he saw his old friend, the TV correspondent Nina Zvereva, making frantic hand signals. Something had happened, or she would not be bothering him at such a moment. Crumpling up his speech, Nemtsov quickly went down to her.

"What's happened?"

"In an hour, Yeltsin will announce the dissolution of the Supreme Soviet. I got a call from Moscow, from the station."

"That can't be," Nemtsov exclaimed, "I would have known!"[15]

"He was terribly angry. How could I know something that he didn't know—Yeltsin hadn't told him," Zvereva recalled later.[16] Nemtsov's displeasure was understandable: as Yeltsin's favourite, he expected to be informed of the decision in advance.

Many believe that Khasbulatov provoked Decree No. 1,400 and dissolution of the Supreme Soviet when he used that insulting gesture on 18 September on live television, implying that when Yeltsin was drinking, he could do anything, even dissolve parliament. But actually, everything had been decided by then. The draft decree was ready on 14 September. Initially, Yeltsin shared his plans with a very small circle of his closest allies.

When Filatov, head of Yeltsin's administration, saw the draft of the decree, he was horrified. First, the decree was unconstitutional, and second, there had been no preparation for it. They should have first gained the support of as many people as possible—in the regions, in the parliament itself—and only then taken action. Yeltsin did none of that. The only thing he was sure of was that the *siloviki* would support him. On 16 September, he went on a special visit to the Dzerzhinsky division of the Interior Ministry, which were stationed near Moscow. It was the president's second visit to an army unit in the last three weeks. The point was not to check the loyalty of the troops—Yeltsin didn't doubt their loyalty—but to show his power. Nevertheless, after listening to a report by Anatoly Kulikov, commander of the Interior Ministry troops, Yeltsin suddenly looked at him carefully and asked whether he would be able to carry out the orders of the defence minister. The Interior Ministry troops were part of the police force, not the army, and the unsuspecting Kulikov—who would play a major role in the events of 3–4 October—thought the president had simply misspoken.[17]

Yeltsin had planned to address the nation on Sunday, 19 September, but he was persuaded to postpone the announcement. First, the rumours that something would happen on Sunday had been leaked to the press. Rumours were circulating that the president would do something like announce early elections, while the day before Vice-President Rutskoi had explicitly stated that "the Kremlin authorities have prepared everything for the introduction of presidential rule." During those days the Kremlin cut Rutskoi's office off from the government communications network, and this naturally exacerbated tension. If Khasbulatov and Rutskoi had known that something was being prepared, then the White House, where the Supreme Soviet convened, would not have been empty on Sunday. It would have been turned into a headquarters of resistance, and the plan for the Interior Ministry troops to surround the empty building would have fallen through. Second, the 19th of the month suggested 19 August, the date when the coup attempt had begun in 1991. The date had already been immortalized as the birthday of democracy in Russia. Yeltsin agreed to move the date, but only by two days at the most.

The next day Yeltsin brought Yegor Gaidar back to the cabinet, although not as prime minister but as first deputy prime minister for economics. The reasoning was simple: when it's war—all hands on deck. When Gaidar came to Filatov on Sunday to collect his appointment decree, Filatov told him about the president's forthcoming speech, now scheduled for the following Tuesday. Gaidar was stunned: the timing couldn't be worse, the irreconcilable opposition was ready and waiting for an attack, Khasbulatov had intentionally insulted Yeltsin in front of the entire country, and it would be impossible to occupy the Supreme Soviet building and stop its work without violence. It would all end badly. "It would be more useful to wait, to keep Khasbulatov's team in suspense, to make them nervous," he told Filatov. Filatov agreed.[18]

But Yeltsin was unpersuaded. Even his close associate, Security Minister Mikhail Barsukov, one of the first people Yeltsin briefed on the details of the operation, couldn't convince him. On Sunday the

19th, Barsukov told Yeltsin and Defence Minister Grachev that "as a military man, I believe that we are not ready for an announcement about the decree" and said that the security agencies might not use violence if ordered.[19] At the last moment Yeltsin refused to meet with Gaidar. On Monday, 20 September, Prime Minister Chernomyrdin tried for a long time to persuade him to postpone his plan, also with no success. On the morning of 21 September, at a crucial meeting in the Kremlin, Yeltsin would not let Filatov speak. "Sit down," he said when he got up to state his views. "I know your point of view already." At 5.00 p.m. he recorded his address to the nation. "Let's take a farewell picture," the president joked after recording the broadcast. "If it doesn't work out, we'll be in jail together."[20]

When Nemtsov heard about the president's upcoming speech, he ran to the TV set. At 8.00 p.m. the TV channels broadcast the recorded message. "The last few days have definitively destroyed the hopes of restoring any constructive cooperation," Yeltsin said, "and people are working to weaken and ultimately remove the President." The adoption of a new constitution is blocked, he continued, and said that the deputies were twisting the government's arms, trampling the will of the people and pushing Russia to the edge of the abyss. Therefore, he said, he was terminating the authority of the deputies and setting the date of elections of a new parliament for 11–12 December. He said he was not looking for personal gain and was in favour of holding an early presidential election "at some point" after the new parliament begins its work.

"Now *Swan Lake* will be played," Nemtsov joked. Just half an hour later, he commented on Yeltsin's speech. "On a purely human level, I agree that we should hold early elections for both parliament and president. The only thing that bothers me is that the president did not specify a date for the presidential election. And, from a legal point of view, I regret to say that the way it was done was not in accordance with our legislation."[21]

Less than an hour after Yeltsin's address, all the leadership of Nizhny Novgorod region gathered at Nemtsov's office. The chairmen of the regional council and city council had already condemned Yeltsin's decree as unconstitutional. Nemtsov's associates would later say that he was frozen by indecision. "Nemtsov flinched," recalled Vladimir Sedov, a businessman in Nizhny Novgorod. "He didn't know whose side to take: Rutskoi and Khasbulatov's or Yeltsin's."[22] In any case, Nemtsov was operating under the assumption that Yeltsin had violated the constitution, and, if so, he would be removed from power. As vice-president, Rutskoi would take his place, and what would happen next was crucially important. Nemtsov rushed off to try to speak to Rutskoi. He couldn't find him, but he got through to his wife, Lyudmila. "Tell him what our position is, all of us," Nemtsov said into the phone. "Tomorrow he will be declared president. [...] Believe me, he will be declared president. You will be the first lady. [...] But not for long, I hope. And here's why. Tomorrow he should say, 'Yes, I am constitutionally the president. But for the sake of keeping the peace in the country—write this down exactly as I say it—I propose, distinguished people's deputies, that you immediately announce the date for presidential and parliamentary elections. And, until then, I pledge not to take any action to form a parallel government, security forces, etc.' Do you agree with me? You're so clever. We're not complete idiots out here in the provinces."[23]

Nemtsov and Rutskoi had a good relationship since the first session of the congress in 1990, and Nemtsov was not put off by the fact that Rutskoi was a more and more virulent opponent of the reforms and was gradually becoming a stance against Yeltsin. They belonged to different political camps, but this did not prevent them from getting along. Rutskoi was not devious like Khasbulatov; on the contrary, he was a rather guileless politician. For that reason, he was an obedient instrument in the hands of the opposition, and a very necessary one. He would be the lawful president after the impeachment. But at the same time, Rutskoi was outgoing and good-natured, and he had a sense of honour. Nemtsov respected him.

Their friendship went back several years. The last time Rutskoi had come to Nizhny Novgorod was in the spring of 1993. "You're the governor! Why are you dressed like a bum?!" Rutskoi asked when Nemtsov met him in a worn leather jacket. Rutskoi immediately called his wife, who worked with Valentin Yudashkin, the leading fashion designer of the time, and asked him to make "this curly-haired man" a decent coat. Rutskoi assured him that price was nothing to worry about—it would be "symbolic." But when Nemtsov came to pick up the coat, it turned out that it cost $200. "My salary at the time was maybe a hundred dollars. I had to borrow money from Yavlinsky," he wrote.[24]

And now, six months later, Nemtsov was looking for Rutskoi again. By evening he had reached him. "I beg you, you must act wisely," Nemtsov said. "If you start appointing ministers now, in the regions they'll start dismissing local leaders and appointing new ones, there will be dual power structures, army personnel will be split, this will happen everywhere. I can't believe you don't see this."

Nemtsov's associates were anxiously listening in on the conversation, waiting to see how it would end. "No," Nemtsov said as he hung up the phone. "It's no use. He told me, 'I've got one homeland. I'm going to fight to the end.'"[25] On 21 September, the Supreme Soviet removed Yeltsin from power and proclaimed Rutskoi president. The new president appointed his own heads of the security ministries. All the bridges were burnt.

## The Supreme Soviet musters a militia

October 1993 reflects the events of August 1991 in a fun-house mirror. The original image is reversed. The White House is once again a hotbed of resistance. People are once again coming to protect the building, although in smaller numbers. Barricades are being re-erected. But two years before, it was a revolt against the Communist Party leadership and the Soviet government, and now the demonstrators in front of the White House were standing under red banners and slogans reading "Long Live the Communist Party!" Two years before, General Vladislav Achalov sided with the conspirators and waited for the order of the defence minister to take the White House by storm. Now he was sitting inside and overseeing the defence of the building. Once again, he and Yeltsin were on opposite sides of the barricades, but now they had changed places.

The road to the deadlock was paved with many irreversible, inevitable steps and factors: the poverty that had befallen Russia; Khasbulatov's personal ambition; unfulfilled public expectations;

Yeltsin's impulsiveness, blunders and personnel mistakes; and, most importantly, the deeply held conviction that a step towards one's opponent is always a sign of weakness, and that any compromise is a defeat. Now Yeltsin was breaking through this impasse with Decree No. 1,400.

"We can still make one prediction," Yury Baturin, the president's legal adviser, said. "Although the president's decision is just in the highest legal sense of the word, it is still based on the belief that it is acceptable to sidestep the law. It is an unavoidable and very large price to pay for the positive things that we are attaining as a result of this decision, and it will most likely be paid not by us, but by our children and grandchildren—I do not know how many years from now."[26]

The course of events was instantly unpredictable. Decree No. 1,400 came like a bolt from the blue, but the deputies were ready for it. They remained in place in the White House, where food supplies and an ample arsenal of weapons were already prepared. According to Anatoly Kulikov, head of the Interior Ministry forces at the time, "we were talking about almost two thousand Kalashnikovs, four thousand Makarov pistols, thirty machine guns, and twelve sniper rifles."[27] *Kommersant* wrote that on the night of 22 September, "a large number of small arms and ammunition, including grenade launchers and machine guns, were secretly moved into the White House."[28] Shakhrai cited the more modest figure of 100 automatic rifles.[29] In any case, as noted by historian Oleg Moroz, "from the very beginning, everything was the worst-case scenario."[30]

After the decree was announced, they breathed a sigh of relief in the Kremlin. They had been truly afraid of rioting, but the country as a whole did not react to the news that the Supreme Soviet has been dissolved. Some regional councils declared Yeltsin's decree illegal—including the Nizhny Novgorod council. In Novosibirsk the local governor, a longtime enemy of Yeltsin, even said that criminal proceedings would be initiated against anyone in the region who obeyed Yeltsin's decrees and disobeyed newly proclaimed President Rutskoi. But that was the only case in the country. No one really wanted to support the Supreme Soviet. The West also supported Yeltsin. To show once again the peaceful nature of his intentions, one day after the decree, Yeltsin set the presidential election for June of the following year.

"From the very beginning, using force was deemed unacceptable and ruled out," said Sergei Filatov, head of the Presidential Administration. "No military forces were brought into Moscow specifically for the decree."[31] The plan in the Kremlin was simple: isolate the Supreme Soviet and wait for the deputies to gradually leave the building, and in the meantime prepare for the elections in December. A day after the decree, telephone service and electricity was cut off in the White House. Then the water and sewage systems were cut off, too, so that the stench from the toilets would make people leave the building as quickly as possible. It wasn't a bad idea. "When they turned off the water and sewage systems, it was really unbearable," one of the deputies later recalled.[32] But the water and sewer systems had to be turned on quite quickly when excrement began pouring into the Moscow River.

Nemtsov came to the Kremlin headquarters "on the side of common sense," Sergei Filatov recalled.[33] Nemtsov suggested that instead of trying to force the deputies out of the building, they should instead try to split the deputies by attracting some to Yeltsin's camp with various privileges, perks and material benefits. Filatov supported him. On 23 September, Yeltsin issued a decree promising lawmakers immunity, annual allowances, pensions, and even apartments. And the day before, 22 September, the president called Nemtsov and demanded that he dissolve the regional council in Nizhny Novgorod that had declared Yeltsin's actions illegal. Nemtsov refused. "I told him that I didn't dissolve the council and in fact thought it would be completely wrong to do so. We have been working constructively with the deputies. Our deputies are of various political stripes, but we are able to solve conflicts at the negotiating table, and this is the strength and effectiveness of the Nizhny Novgorod government. I considered it a matter of principle."[34] As Nemtsov recalled later, it was a difficult conversation. Yeltsin demanded unconditional support and didn't get it.[35] The relationship between them soured for a long time.

The decree on guarantees for the deputies did not help much: the number of deputies who switched sides was small, and their departure had no effect on the situation. In any case, the deputies did not have the quorum required by law. "Even from the standpoint of the law in force at the time," Viktor Sheinis wrote, "the decisions of the parliamentary majority that was dissipating before our eyes were no more legitimate than the Decree No. 1,400."[36] But nobody cared about that anymore. The deputies quickly passed a law against anyone who attempted a *coup d'état*, with criminal penalties up to and including the death penalty.

Far-left and far-right extremists, and simply men looking for a fight, rushed to the building to come to the aid of the implacable anti-Yeltsin deputies in the building. In the courtyard of the building, far-right groups such as Alexander Barkashov's Russian National Unity and Stanislav Terekhov's Union of Officers formed battle divisions. They also guarded Khasbulatov. "Even then I considered it a huge ideological mistake," Yury Voronin, Khasbulatov's associate and first deputy speaker, later recalled. "The men in Barkashov's organization were rabid anti-Semites. They wore Nazi uniforms with insignia that looked almost exactly like a swastika, regularly marched near the White House, and would raise their arms in a Nazi salute."[37]

There were always several hundred armed men on the square in front of the White House. Newspapers also wrote of "reservists" ready to stand under arms at the call from the White House. Cordoned off by two or three rows of unarmed policemen, within a day and a half the White House had become a paramilitary haven with its own militia. "The hope that the situation would dissipate by itself was fading day by day," Sheinis wrote, "and the Kremlin clearly had no idea what to do next."[38]

## "I have a bad feeling about this"

The first shots were fired in the evening of 23 September, when several fighters from the White House self-defence units attacked the headquarters of the Main Command of the United Armed Forces of the Commonwealth of Independent States (CIS) on Leningradsky Prospect. They disarmed the guards and broke in, then used an automatic weapon to shoot a police officer who was passing by and asked to see their documents. They were disarmed and arrested, but a stray bullet killed a sixty-three-year-old woman who had looked out her window in a nearby apartment block. The blockade of the White House was reinforced. The building was surrounded by a spiral of barbed wire and soldiers in bulletproof vests from the Dzerzhinsky Division, the same division that Yeltsin had visited not long before issuing Decree No. 1,400.

Members of the parliament who remained inside the building sat in the cold by candlelight—they'd run out of fuel and the diesel generator had stopped working. Khasbulatov and "President" Rutskoi occasionally gave a speech from the balcony. Militia armed with submachine guns sat outside the White House, in the entryways and on the steps. The situation was a powder keg. "It was intolerable. In the centre of a city of millions of people there was a building crammed with guns and political hacks who were furious that they would lose their powers. But there was no question of any sort of storming or seizure of the White House at that moment," Yeltsin later recalled.[39] Constitutional Court Chairman Valery Zorkin tried his hand at mediation. His proposal to end the deadlock was to hold simultaneous parliamentary and presidential elections, but, after the events of March, Yeltsin ignored Zorkin.

The Kremlin demanded that the deputies lay down their arms and vacate the building; the deputies demanded that the blockade be lifted and that Decree No. 1,400 be repealed. The tense confrontation in the centre of the city could not go on for long. The White House was running out of food and medicine. As the blockade intensified, the danger zone began to expand to neighbouring streets. Clashes between activists and police occurred throughout the neighbourhood. After demonstrators blocked the roadway near the Barrikadnaya metro station, another police officer was killed. "If there is no assault, in a few days everyone who sits in the White House will either have to surrender or resort to firearms," *Nezavisimaya gazeta* wrote on 29 September.[40]

The head of the Russian Orthodox Church, Patriarch Alexy II, offered some hope for compromise. The deputies appealed to him, and he agreed to become a mediator. Yeltsin received him on 30 September when representatives of the deputies and the Kremlin were negotiating among themselves. "From the very beginning, we proposed to divide the problem into two parts," Filatov recalled, "surrender of weapons and political solutions. We proposed discussing the political issues once the danger of an armed conflict was eliminated. They set a counter-condition: that the lights and phones in the White House be turned on."[41]

The Kremlin agreed to these demands. On the night of 1 October, the deputies confirmed that they had invested two parliamentarians—two influential deputies, Ramazan Abdulatipov and Veniamin Sokolov—with the authority to negotiate. The two signed so-called Protocol No. 1: the lights and telephones would be turned on in the White House, the deputies would surrender their weapons, and the Kremlin would break the siege. This was progress. Of course, the Kremlin was negotiating from a position of strength. But Khasbulatov, Rutskoi and their supporters could still get out of the situation without losing face and even pick up some political concessions. The zero-for-zero formula suggested by Valery Zorkin—rescinding both Decree No. 1,400 and the decisions made by the Supreme Soviet—didn't suit Yeltsin. But the idea of holding presidential and parliamentary elections simultaneously to end the crisis gained supporters. And Yeltsin finally agreed to it.* The patriarch was supposed to join the negotiations in the morning. He was publicly neutral, although at the beginning of the crisis he was more sympathetic to the deputies.

In the Kremlin, they thought they'd pulled it off. "There was no army in Moscow because we didn't think we would need it," Filatov said. "We signed the protocol and assumed that we had managed to reach an agreement."[42] At 2.40 a.m. on 1 October, the White House got back communications, water and electricity.

The next morning, however, when Filatov and Moscow's mayor, Yury Luzhkov, who together with Sergei Filatov represented the interests of the Kremlin, arrived at the Danilov Monastery, the White House parliamentarians did not show up at the appointed time. Abdulatipov finally arrived.

"Where's Sokolov?" Filatov asked, rushing over to him.

---

* In an interview, Sergei Shakhrai said that Filatov brought a letter to the Danilov Monastery and gave it to Supreme Soviet First Deputy Speaker Yury Voronin. It contained Yeltsin's consent to simultaneous elections in November, but nothing came of it.

"They didn't let him go," Abdulatipov replied, "and I've stopped only for a minute to tell you that we've been replaced."[43]

It came out later that, the night before, the hardliners inside the White House, led by the first vice-speaker, Yury Voronin, had taken control and called off the deal. Khasbulatov, who was now almost inconsequential, was forced to call back the two representatives. Soon Voronin came to the Danilov Monastery with new conditions: Yeltsin's side had to unblock the White House completely. The issue of weapons in the White House would be resolved later along with other political issues. After that, negotiations continued for two more days, but they didn't get anywhere. The deputies would not give up their weapons, but they demanded that the siege against them be lifted.

"By its actions the other side has made the situation more dangerous than it was yesterday," Luzhkov told the patriarch at the end of the second day of negotiations, 2 October. "Your Holiness, I ask you to take measures to reason with these people."[44] Both Filatov and Luzhkov already realized that the deputies were negotiating only to stall for time.

"On the second of October, events took a qualitative turn for the worse," Anatoly Kulikov, head of the Interior Ministry troops, later recalled. "In an unauthorized rally on nearby Smolenskaya Square, they were putting up barricades and making Molotov cocktails. There were clashes between the police and the protesters."[45]

"I have a bad feeling about this," Filatov told Yeltsin later that same evening.[46] His feelings did not deceive him. By that time, Voronin and the military leaders in the White House had already planned an uprising that would take the president, the security forces and the government by surprise the very next day.

## Moscow at war

Civil war broke out at two o'clock in the afternoon of 3 October. Several thousand demonstrators marched from Oktyabrskaya Square along the Garden Ring Road, the main thoroughfare around the city centre, calling out, "Defend the House of Soviets!" At the head of the march were men in body armour and shields. The police cordons on Krymsky

Bridge and Smolenskaya Square scattered instantly. Soon the armed protesters broke through the cordon around the White House. The first automatic rifle shots rang out. At 4.00 p.m. guerrillas armed with submachine guns rushed across the street from the White House to storm the city hall.

An hour later the city hall was taken, a red flag was hoisted over the building, and about 200 detained soldiers of the Interior Ministry troops were escorted to the White House as prisoners of war. Six people were killed, dozens wounded. Kulikov quickly withdrew the remaining police forces from Moscow since they were unarmed and could do nothing. "The only sensible way out seemed to be," he thought, "to arm them, give them armoured tanks and then bring them back to the city." But at that point the rioters were clearly gaining the upper hand, and the Interior Ministry troops were leaving the city. There was already euphoria in the White House. They expected a quick victory. Rutskoi called for the formation of detachments to storm the Ostankino television centre. Khasbulatov called to storm the Kremlin and arrest Yeltsin.

At that moment, Yeltsin was not in Moscow, just as he had not been there the day before. He would arrive in the Kremlin by helicopter only after 6.00 p.m. "The president's absence was not justified in any way, and I am certain that it played a tragic role," Kulikov later said. "If only because some generals from the armed forces blatantly shirked their duties, and society, which needed daily communication with the president, was suddenly shocked to discover how weak the highest power in the land was."[47]

By the evening of 3 October, the vacuum of power in Moscow was already palpable. If the rebels attacked the Kremlin, who would defend it? When Filatov arrived there, he found uncertainty and confusion. There were no guards. No one could find Defence Minister Pavel Grachev. No one knew what position the army would take. "Panic filled the corridors of the government buildings," Sheinis recalled. "It's all over!" government officials said when the scheduled cabinet meetings never began. "Within the hour we will all be slaughtered."

As will become clear later, the government did indeed falter at this point, and the decisive battle in the two-day war in Moscow was the fight for the Ostankino television centre. If the Vityaz squad of the police force hadn't reached the TV tower before the assault began, the rioters would have seized Ostankino and the nationwide Channel One. If they had broadcast on that channel, revelling in victory, their delight would have encouraged many people. In this situation, military men who were hesitating might have refused to support Yeltsin.

The fight for Ostankino began at 7.10 p.m. when a grenade launcher was fired at the window of the building, killing the Vityaz sergeant who was inside. The battle lasted several hours. At 7.30 p.m., as Channels One, Three and Four went off air, the country realized that the unrest in Moscow had taken a serious turn. Yeltsin had already signed a decree declaring a state of emergency, but he did not appear on air until the next morning. "There was no time for speeches," Yeltsin later explained. "I was trying to shake my combat generals out of a state of stress and paralysis. Despite all the assurances of the defence minister, I saw that the army was for some reason unable to launch a defence of Moscow immediately."[48]

Gaidar said afterwards that the situation in the Kremlin and the government administration buildings on Staraya Square on the evening of 3 October had reminded him of the last meeting of the provisional government in October 1917, when "tens of thousands of cultured, honest citizens of St Petersburg easily allowed a small group of extremists to seize power."[49] Time was passing, there was fighting in the streets, and the authorities were silent.

Gaidar had just returned to the cabinet and had nothing to do with events leading up to this day, but he was the first government official to go to the only television channel that was able to continue broadcasting. He called on Muscovites to rally at Mossovet, the Moscow city government building on Tverskaya Street, to defend Russian democracy. The channel was broadcasting from a studio far from Ostankino, so it continued to work, and politicians, businessmen and artists streamed into the studio. "Get these violent men off our streets, throw them out of our cities," Yavlinsky urged. The actress Liya Akhedzhakova pleaded, "My friends, wake up! Do not sleep! Tonight the fate of our unhappy Russia will be decided. Our poor homeland is in danger! Do not sleep! We are under a terrible threat. The Communists are coming back!"[50]

Mayor Yury Luzhkov and several big businessmen—Mikhail Khodorkovsky, Vladimir Gusinsky and Kakha Bendukidze—showed a will to fight. They had their own relatively small security services. As the night wore on, a few dozen of Gusinsky's security guards were ready to move on his order. Gaidar's appeal drew a large contingent of pro-democracy Muscovites to Mossovet, ready to defend Moscow. Meanwhile, the battle was still raging near Ostankino and inside the TV centre. The armed men from the White House seized the first two floors of the building; journalists, bystanders and armed militants were killed. Armoured personnel carriers, which came to the aid of Vityaz, shot wildly in all directions. The attack on the TV centre from the White House was finally repulsed, and around 9.00 p.m. the guerrillas began to retreat, but indiscriminate shelling continued for a long time. Towards midnight, it became clear that the uprising was dying out. At 1.00 a.m. Prime Minister Chernomyrdin appeared on air with assurances that the situation was under control.

"I've done all I could," Gaidar said late at night to the businessmen who had come to support him. "I'm going to go and get some sleep."

"Maybe you should leave the country?" Vladimir Gusinsky suggested.

"They'll find me wherever I am," Gaidar said with a wave as he went off.

In the Ministry of Defence, Grachev was waiting it out, citing neutrality: the army is outside politics, as military commanders in the Kremlin and Khasbulatov used to say. The memory of August 1991 and its main lesson was still too fresh: tanks in the capital were a crime against the people. All evening Yeltsin kept calling Grachev. Where was the army? Grachev kept mumbling something in reply. He kept saying that the army was coming, but no one did.

Finally, Yeltsin had to get into a car and be driven to the Ministry of Defence on the Arbat to talk to Grachev instead of receiving him in the Kremlin. Rumours were circulating in Moscow that some military units had sworn an oath to Rutskoi. Even before the hostilities, there were reports that military counter-intelligence and several state security departments were opposed to Yeltsin. And after the storming of city hall, the commander of a detachment of the Interior Ministry forces took the side of the White House. Only the police and Interior Ministry troops fought down the uprising all through the night.

## A bloody trail

By the night of 3 October, neither the military nor the president had any plan for what to do next. The initiative came from the head of the presidential guards, Alexander Korzhakov. Shortly before the meeting, his deputy, sabotage-operations specialist Gennady Zakharov, who had developed the plan to defend the White House in August 1991, presented him with three possible courses of action:

1. Under cover of night, a SWAT team, professionally trained for such actions, would enter the White House and capture the leaders of the rebellion. "This option would not work at dawn," Zakharov later recalled, "because the assaulting units would suffer heavy losses on their approach to the White House. But at night this option would result in the least number of casualties."

2. Seize the White House by the same special forces, but during the day, with the support of troops. "Make a big show of storming the White House, but don't enter. Make everyone believe it. Take captive the White House guards around the perimeter of the building. In the meantime, like in the first version, the special forces move in." This operation was also designed to be without bloodshed.

3. If the assault drags on and the White House defence is organized properly, tanks and artillery would surround the White House and open fire on the empty floors to sow panic among the defenders. Then the special forces would enter. Casualties could not be avoided.[51]

Everyone at the historic night meeting at the Ministry of Defence told the same story, including Yeltsin.[52] The meeting was chaired by Prime Minister Chernomyrdin. After asking for proposals, there was a long pause. Korzhakov then called Zakharov, and he proposed three options (although everyone at the meeting later recalled only the third). "When a real plan emerged, it was easier," Yeltsin wrote. "One could argue with it, disagree with it, clarify it, but there was already a point of reference."[53] Sergei Filatov described the scene that followed.

"I must admit that this plan [Option 3] made me uneasy. It didn't sound like many of the men in the White House would survive. When Chernomyrdin asked for proposals and remarks, the people present responded with silence." Only Pavel Grachev said very quietly, addressing the president:

"We need a written order."

"What?"[54]

"I'll send it to you," Yeltsin replied glumly after a pause and left. As Grachev later recalled, he never sent the written order, but the question of the army's participation had been resolved.[55] The first two options—the least violent—were quickly forgotten. It was too late, the special forces did not have time to approach at night, and the military and special forces had not been able to coordinate their actions. That night Yeltsin visited the headquarters of special forces' Alpha Group. When he asked if his order would be carried out, he was met with a sepulchral silence.

Historian Oleg Moroz described the scene. After Yeltsin left, the officers of special forces told their superiors directly that they would not carry out the order.[56] They only agreed when one of the businessmen brought them money.[57] The military did not arrive at the White House at 6.00 a.m. as ordered, also apparently because they needed persuasion. They were also promised bonuses. Grachev later denied rumours that the military had been paid.[58] His deputy, Georgy Kondratyev, who headed the operation, was circumspect: "I don't know which of the military got money. I will not speak about all of the military. I personally am a military man, I did not receive even a kopek, and I would not have taken even a kopek."[59]

The whole world watched what happened next in the centre of Moscow on the afternoon of 4 October in a live broadcast by CNN. By 7.00 a.m. there were armoured troop carriers and trucks with paratroopers in front of the White House. They were fired upon. It soon became clear that snipers from the White House defence squads were on the upper floors of both the White House and the city hall across the street, as well as other nearby houses. Veronika Kutsyllo, a *Kommersant* journalist who had been at the White House from the beginning of the crisis, wrote: "I was asleep on folding chairs in the cafeteria on the sixth floor when I was woken up at five minutes to seven on Monday. I started to hear machine-gun fire. I looked out: an armoured personnel carrier was next to the building, shooting at the barricades, the cars and the canvas tents where the parliament defenders had slept the night before. We could see people lying on the square, either wounded or dead. One of them was dragged by his arms towards the White House, leaving a bloody trail behind him on the square."[60]

The first tank salvo was fired at the White House at 10.03 a.m. That stopped the clock on the roof of the White House for ever. Pavel Grachev later described this historic moment. "I said: 'Men, see the rooflines? Count off. One, two, three, four, five, six, seven—see the seventh window? We think that's Khasbulatov's office, and the leaders are in there. We need to hit that window. Can you do it?' 'Minister, it's just shooting from a tank, no problem.' 'Do you have shells?' 'Live rounds?' 'What do you mean, live rounds? Are you nuts? Use dummies.'"[61]

Crowds of onlookers gathered on the embankments and on the bridge over the Moscow River, staring in astonishment at the black smoke enveloping the White House building. Whole families, sometimes with children, came to watch the assault, and many of them would soon be killed by sniper bullets—battlefield doctors would later attest that they'd been hit by intentional shots to the head, neck and heart. The military also returned fire at any movement and killed random bystanders, mistaking them for insurgents. Sometimes gunfire erupted around the building and in nearby alleys. In all, the tanks fired twelve rounds and ceased firing at 2.00 p.m., but the machine-gun and rifle fire lasted a long time. "You could see stretchers with the wounded and dead being carried through the corridor," Veronica Kutsyllo wrote. "It looked like there were more dead than wounded. One corpse lay for a long time near the lift inside. You could barely walk down the hall without encountering dark stains of fresh blood on the carpet."[62]

Around four o'clock Nemtsov came out of a meeting with Chernomyrdin and the governors and walked along Novy Arbat. "On Novy Arbat, snipers sent by Rutskoi and Khasbulatov sat on the high-rises and shot tracer bullets all over street."[63] But the dénouement was already close: an hour later Rutskoi surrendered, and by 6.00 p.m. the

White House had been taken. The special forces did not even have to storm it. Rutskoi and Khasbulatov were arrested. It was all over.

The number of those who died on 3–4 October is still unknown, and the criminal investigation of the uprising was never completed. The official list of the investigation by the prosecutor general's office contains the names of 147 people killed. Yevgeny Yurchenko, an activist with the human-rights organization Memorial, would investigate and give another figure: at least 250 dead.

On 7 October, the day of mourning and funerals, Yeltsin told his aides that he would visit all the cemeteries. "You won't have time to see all of them," they replied.[64]

## The lesser of two evils

When the smoke over the Supreme Soviet building cleared, Russia had become a different country. Not long before these events, Boris Yeltsin had gone to great lengths to avoid a war with the rebellious legislators. Now that he had used tanks to break out of the impasse in the system of Russian power, he was constrained only by his own ideas about how democracy in Russia should be structured. "On the morning of 5 October, [Yeltsin] had all the power in the country," Gaidar later wrote. "We had gone from the muck of diarchy into a *de facto* authoritarian regime. A good part of the population, tired of the diarchy and rising crime, dreaming of the restoration of normal order, would support it, or at least not actively oppose this new regime."[65]

Firing on the White House undid all the work to find compromise. Why share the fruits of your victory with your defeated opponent? Very soon Yeltsin would cancel his own decree on early presidential elections set for June 1994. The reasonable and democratic constitutional draft prepared in summer by the constitutional convention would be tweaked in favour of the president. First, Yeltsin would cross out the provision in the constitution concerning the direct election of deputies to the upper house of the future Russian parliament, the Federation Council. Second, he struck out the lower house's right to confirm the president's dissolution of the cabinet. Both of these amendments would come to play their historic role. The victory of Yeltsin's coalition over the nationalists and great-power activists, Sheinis wrote, "in terms of state and law, would be a victory of the executive over the legislative branch."[66]

The dark legacy of the events was that the conflict ended in bloodshed. The image of a parliament building engulfed in flames and black smoke would remain in people's memory for a long time. "The unwillingness to compromise in the name of calm, peaceful resolution is also one of the lessons of those bloody events," Nemtsov later said.[67] It wasn't only Yeltsin's triumph; it was the triumph of violence as the main argument in political disputes, and the conviction that the stakes in political confrontation are exceptionally high. If you lose, you lose everything: your position in society, your freedom, even your life. And that's the way it always is.

The democratic press wrote that the revolution in Russia, which began in the late 1980s, ended on 4 October 1993 with the victory of the lesser of two evils.

# CHAPTER 8

### 1993–95
# The Successor

## Stop stealing

Boris Vidyayev, the director of the Gorky Automobile Plant (known by the Russian acronym GAZ), could not have imagined in his worst nightmare that the head of the region where he reigned as king and god would be a thirty-two-year-old youngster from a scientific institute. GAZ was conceived and built in Stalin's first five-year plan as the Soviet answer to Detroit and had always been the epitome of socialist industrial success stories. Vidyayev was a model Soviet manager. He wasn't a Communist Party boss, but a strong Russian man who had gone up the ladder of the factory hierarchy, from foreman to director. He was highly respected at GAZ. Situated on the outskirts of Nizhny Novgorod, the No. 1 Soviet automobile plant was always a separate—and more prosperous—city with a population of 300,000. Vidyayev had ruled it since 1986.

Vidyayev had a tough break: the collapse of the centrally planned economy dealt GAZ a heavy blow. By the beginning of 1994, the situation of the plant was as bleak as in the rest of the Soviet automobile industry. Tens of thousands of unwanted Volga cars piled up in warehouses, and the factory assembly line had long ago switched to a single shift. Nevertheless, Vidyayev managed to keep the plant afloat. As Nizhny Novgorod sank into poverty, he set up a barter arrangement with China, and in return for cars the automobile plant employees wore warm Chinese down jackets and ate decent food in the work cafeterias. More importantly, amid the devastation that engulfed Russian industry, Vidyayev had launched the mass production of a new van called the Gazelle.

Nemtsov generally managed to avoid serious clashes with the industrial lobby—the so-called "red directors." As Oleg Sysuyev, then mayor of Samara, another city on the Volga, said, "Nemtsov had substance, which the directors could see, so they had business-like relations."[1] A man who was open, active and honest, Nemtsov immediately made a good impression on some of them. Others counted on his connections. Under the federal programme to convert Soviet defence plants to civilian needs, Nemtsov was working in Moscow to carve out considerable tax breaks and cheap loans for enterprises of the military–industrial complex. "On the whole, thanks to cooperation between the governor and the old and new figures in the local economy, the region was effectively managed," wrote political scientists Vladimir Gelman and Sharon Rivera. "In fact, in the mid-1990s, Nizhny Novgorod was ahead of many other Russian provinces in a number of indicators of management quality."[2]

However, not all local industrialists supported Nemtsov. Some did not accept the new policies. "Directors of defence enterprises were very wary of Nemtsov when he came in 1991," recalled Olga Smirnova, a journalist from Nizhny Novgorod and later Nemtsov's assistant. "The Association of Industrialists quietly resisted him. They had to get used to the idea that the policies weren't going to change and that they should participate in the life of the region."[3]

GAZ director Vidyayev led the opposition to Nemtsov. The conflict between them flared up as soon as Yeltsin put Nemtsov in charge of the region. Vidyayev was demonstratively disloyal. He pitted other directors against Nemtsov. He insisted on the autonomy of GAZ and tried to formalize the status of the plant as a city within a city, a state within a state. But most importantly, GAZ did not pay taxes. The money GAZ earned remained at the plant. This was a fifth of the regional budget, and the difference in living standards between the plant and the city continued to grow. "Vidyayev behaved demonstratively and brazenly like an oligarch, and he didn't pay any taxes into the regional budget at all,"

Nemtsov later recalled.[4] When the privatization programme reached the Nizhny Novgorod industry by the winter of 1994, the conflict spilt over.

The voucher privatization introduced in autumn 1992 was built from the very beginning on a compromise with the directors of plants and factories. Otherwise, it simply could not have been implemented. As Maxim Boiko, one of the people who developed the programme, admitted, "It was clear that privatization, and the entire reform programme in general, could not be carried out against the will of the directors."[5] In exchange for loyalty to the reforms, the government gave enterprises certain preferences in how they were privatized. In the case of GAZ, this meant that one-third of the plant's shares would be sold in an open auction and the rest would be distributed to the plant employees. Vidyayev, who enjoyed the unconditional support of the workers, would, like many Soviet directors, make the transition from top manager to owner—or, at least, the owner of a large enough percentage of shares that would allow him to manage the plant as his own property.

In those days it was common practice for plant directors to take control of large industrial assets in alliance with regional authorities. Nemtsov reasoned similarly that the closer the owner was to the plant, the lower the risk that he would close it down or lay off the workers. A democrat who believed that Russia should follow the Western path of development, Nemtsov held left-liberal views and advocated a socially oriented market economy. On the one hand, these views were dictated by his position as governor. On the other hand, he did not support pure economic liberalism, a position that he made clear: "American capitalism is worse than European capitalism."[6] In his view, the role of the state in relations with major businessmen was to protect the interests of the people. "I will never believe that you think about the people. You only think about surplus value," he once told his economic adviser Andrei Mladentsev when they were discussing consumer loans for telephones.[7] Nemtsov's views gradually transformed into an idea of "people's capitalism", which he would soon defend in the Russian political arena.

Nemtsov looked down on the Moscow bankers beginning to build their business empires as cynical, soulless businessmen. "It was difficult to convince him that buying shares was the legitimate right of people who held financial resources," recalled Mikhail Fridman, by that time an established banker, financier and oilman, and later one of the richest people in Russia and a close friend of Nemtsov.[8] In early 1995, Fridman and his partners ran into resistance from the Nizhny Novgorod regional administration when they tried to buy assets there. "It seemed strange," said Fridman, "because Nemtsov had a reputation as a liberal who supported the free market and healthy forms of privatization and business in the region. But for some reason he didn't like our participation. Either the directors of these plants told him something about us, or it was something else. At the time a lot of people believed that we were speculators, buying up assets for next to nothing. Nemtsov was probably responding to that, too."[9]

At stake was an important asset—an oil refinery in Kstovo. Fridman and his partners were sending their oil there, and so they wanted to buy the refinery and form a holding company (which is how vertically integrated oil companies began to appear in Russia). But to do so they needed Nemtsov's consent. They had every reason to count on his support. The crude-oil supply system had broken down, the refinery was in a very precarious state, and of course the local government ought to have been happy to see investors. Fridman and his partners flew in for negotiations. Due to bad weather, the flight was delayed, and they were an hour and a half late for the scheduled meeting. "We got in our cars and raced to the Kremlin in Nizhny Novgorod," Fridman said.

> Naturally, Nemtsov was in another meeting—it was journalists, like usual (he loved spending time with them)—a huge group of people. We could hear his powerful voice through the door as the three of us sat waiting nervously in the anteroom. I get it—we had to wait. It's our own fault for being late. After another hour or so, we were told, "The governor is ready to see you." We put on guilty expressions and finally went into the office. Boris didn't spend time on our apologies and got right down to business. "So, what brings you here? You want to steal my plant?" Actually, he was even less polite. "Listen: no stealing allowed here. Five hundred million dollars, and you can take the plant and do what you want with it. Is that clear? Any other questions?" That was in place of a hello. We were like, "Well, as you know, we'd like to say... and then... as well as..." You

know—apologetic babbling. He was like, "Don't you get it? I told you. You can't steal anything here. Five hundred million dollars on the barrel head, and that's it, goodbye. Take the plant. That's all the time I have. Our meeting is over."[10]

Half a billion dollars for a failing oil refinery? It sounded like he was making fun of them. Fridman was shocked that a young, educated, cultured governor with the image of a romantic reformer was suddenly delivering a tirade "in the best traditions of Soviet management", as Fridman put it. "We didn't even talk about any other issues. After that conversation it was no surprise that we had difficulties with shareholder rights at some enterprises in the Nizhny Novgorod region. I already realized that this would be the way things would go. That's how we met."[11]

But Nemtsov's main opponent in the upcoming privatization of GAZ was Vidyayev. Nemtsov could not have him removed, so there was no point objecting when the government suddenly decided to change the conditions of the auction. Instead of selling thirty per cent of the plant, they were offering the controlling stake. This was an unprecedented step in the young practice of Russian privatization. In December 1993, *Kommersant* wrote: "Voucher privatization has never seen such a victory. No less than a controlling block of shares in one of the country's biggest and most famous industrial enterprises was being sold for privatization vouchers."[12]

It quickly became clear why Vidyayev didn't object to large-scale privatization. After the privatization commission took in bids at the auction, they realized that GAZ was buying itself through front companies. In fact, GAZ was using the government loans meant to cover the company's debts to buy the vouchers that the front companies were using when they purchased GAZ shares.

This was nothing new. In various locations "red directors" had used the funds of their enterprises in order to gain control over them through voucher auctions. But formally it was illegal, and the unprecedented success of voucher privatization turned into an unprecedented scandal. Nemtsov flooded both Yeltsin and Prime Minister Chernomyrdin with letters demanding Vidyayev's removal, and a special government commission concluded that the auction results had to be annulled. "There has been a misuse of public funds, a gross violation of financial discipline," Nemtsov explained, "which has caused dire financial conditions at derivative plants. When GAZ was buying up vouchers, it had debts of twenty-five billion roubles, and many people have been left without means of livelihood."[13]

Nizhny Novgorod entrepreneur Yevgeny Korovkin managed one of the firms that bought vouchers for GAZ. He later recalled how Nemtsov engaged him as an intermediary since Nemtsov and Vidyayev could no longer communicate in person. "We talked half the night. Nemtsov pushed his idea of putting former GAZ top manager [and Vidyayev's predecessor] Nikolai Pugin back in charge. My job was to convince Vidyayev to lay down his arms with dignity. I was assigned this task, because, I knew better than anyone else how GAZ funds had been diverted for the auction."[14]

But Vidyayev wouldn't budge. He would not agree to any compromise. Pavel Chichagov, then Nemtsov's assistant, was present at their last conversation. The tension was so palpable that he was afraid the meeting would end in a fistfight. "Nemtsov said, 'Vidyayev, you have to resign.' And he replied, 'I don't plan to go anywhere.' I don't remember a more difficult conversation—it was a clash of Titans. Vidyayev is very tough. They did not come to blows, but we had the police there just in case."[15]

While this was going on, investigators were already working at the plant, the head of the country's tax police was in town, and the prosecutor's office got involved in the case. Vidyayev had to retreat. His front organizations were closed down. In April 1994, Nikolai Pugin was appointed chairman of the board of directors and president of the plant. Three months later, the first Gazelles came off the assembly line. These were Russia's most successful vehicles, the embodiment of small business and Nemtsov's "people's capitalism."

## People's capitalism

The reformers' victory over the Supreme Soviet came at a high price and in the end led to unexpected consequences. The results of the first election to the new Russian parliament in December 1993 were a shock to Yeltsin. "Russia, wake up! You've lost your mind," Yury Karyakin, a first-wave democrat, said on election night. No one expected Vladimir Zhirinovsky, an eccentric, right-wing populist who promised "a man for every woman and a cheap bottle of vodka for every man", to celebrate victory. Yegor Gaidar resigned again (his second term in office was short-lived), the reform camp fell apart, and the leaders of the democratic revolution of the early 1990s faded from the political scene.

Against the background of the defeated reform policies, Nemtsov's star shone more brightly. His popularity grew and his political career became a national phenomenon. "Nemtsov is the only representative of the young generation of politicians from the 1990s who managed to stay afloat and even increase his political capital," *Kommersant* wrote in summer 1994. "All his peers, the people's deputies of the Russian Federation, have either slunk off into the shadows or gone out with a bang."[16] While Russian citizens were still disappointed in the changes initiated by Yeltsin, the transformation of Nizhny Novgorod proved that the hopes for a European path for Russia had not been completely in vain.

There was poverty everywhere, and Nizhny Novgorod could not boast much wealth. But the region was not in the red, and other Russian regions continued to look up to it. It was a testing ground for new economic and social ideas. The second issue of *nemtsovki*—those regional loan bonds—turned out to be bigger and more successful than the first. While the country was experiencing the first wave of unrest when investors discovered they had invested their money in financial pyramids, Nemtsov had something to offer. "He used to say," Chichagov recalled, "'Don't put your money there; put it into reliable securities.'"[17] The regional administration was protecting people's money from inflation. People believed Nemtsov and queued up at 6.00 a.m. to buy bonds. "The country's first regional loan—the Nizhny Novgorod regional loan—came due on 1 January 1995, and I can proudly say that for the first time in the long Soviet and post-Soviet period, for the first time in this history, the state has not cheated its citizens," Nemtsov later said.[18]

As soon as Nemtsov started to hold meetings with citizens, he quickly realized that the three main problems in the region were housing, bad roads and telephones. How could they get housing construction off the ground and end the huge queue for apartments? They came up with the idea of a housing loan based on the *nemtsovki* model. People who were prepared to invest their own money could move forward in line; the government would receive the investments; and the people would get housing. The most expensive bond with a face value of one square metre was issued in the NB (Nemtsov, Boris) series. Tens of thousands of square metres of housing were constructed in the region.

Meanwhile, Nemtsov continued to live in a state-allocated dacha. In the summer of 1994, the regional parliament decided to give him an apartment. Nemtsov's answer to the deputies was:

> Dear deputies of the regional legislative assembly. I am grateful for the decision you made on 21 June 1994 on measures to improve my living conditions. You are probably right, and a two-room apartment on the ninth floor is not the best accommodation for the governor of the region and his family. I know that many people in Nizhny Novgorod do not believe I live in an apartment that size; they think houses and summer homes are being built for me all over the region. You know that this is not true, and apparently this is what is behind your decision to give me a nice, comfortable apartment. I am very grateful to you, but I cannot accept your offer. Unfortunately, a two-room apartment for a family of three is an unattainable dream for many people in Russia. And, as long as it is, I believe that a governor and a member of the Federation Council elected by the people should live like his or her constituents. It's especially important now, when many apartments are being sold at auctions, and people who have been on the waiting list for fifteen–twenty years and are in dire need of better housing conditions have practically no chance of getting a free apartment. As for me, I wasn't on the waiting list for an apartment, and I consider it unethical to get one for free.[19]

The region also began to solve the problem of its poor telephone system. In Nizhny Novgorod and other cities in the region, people had been waiting for years for a telephone line, but there wasn't funding for it. So, the region issued a telephone bond: anyone who wanted to put in a phone quickly bought the bonds and got a phone installed in less than six months. "The loan system is so effective," Nemtsov explained proudly, "and, most importantly, it makes the government and the people so interdependent that we might never give it up."[20]

In 1995 a programme of housing certificates for the military was also begun. "The problem was that, in Russia, when servicemen left active duty, all they got was a goodbye," Yury Lebedev, vice-governor at the time, explained. "They had nowhere to go. They didn't have apartments. So, Nemtsov and his comrades came up with a programme."[21] When Defence Minister Grachev came to Nizhny Novgorod for a tennis tournament, Nemtsov made him sign a declaration of intent. Nemtsov managed to get funding in Moscow, and demobilized officers of the 22 Army, who had been brought back from Germany in 1990 and stationed in the Nizhny Novgorod region, began receiving housing for their families. They could even choose their apartment. Nemtsov described how it was going. "People started coming up to these 'humiliated and insulted' servicemen and said, 'Here's an apartment for you.' 'I don't like that one—can we take this one?' 'Maybe this one is better?' They felt that they were really appreciated by their country."[22]

The regional budget paid for travel for war veterans. Nemtsov monetized the guarantees of free medication by converting them into pension increases—once again by wrangling federal funding. A million-rouble grant paid out of the regional budget for every new child born was called "Nemtsov's million." Privatized Soviet-era supply buildings at the railroad company, lumber mills and other industries were turned into private bakeries and shops. The proceeds went to road construction. "To make sure people knew, I wrote on each road: 'This road was built on funds from privatizing this or that industrial space,'" recalled Yury Lebedev.[23] Nemtsov had his own system for testing road quality: he'd get behind the wheel of a Volga car, a shot glass of vodka would be placed on the hood, and he'd start driving. If the vodka didn't spill, the city would authorize payment to the road contractors. Nemtsov did not drink much, but the spectacular stunt with a shot of vodka symbolized the popular nature of the road programme, and the five thousand kilometres of roads built under Nemtsov changed life in the region for the better.

This was a self-perpetuating process. Thanks to Nemtsov's actions, the region had become as a testing ground for reforms, and, as a result, his political capital and fame in the country had grown; that fame, in turn, helped Nemtsov to get the green light and funding for public programmes from federal agencies; consequently, people saw that the region was responding to their real needs, and Nemtsov's popularity continued to grow. Nemtsov's "people's capitalism" really existed, albeit in one single region of Russia. Nizhny Novgorod began to claim its rightful status as the country's third city after Moscow and St Petersburg. Despite their difficult lives, local residents had pride and hope that in the future life would be even better. But the better things got, the more people worried: every time Nemtsov met with his constituents, they asked, "You'll go to Moscow, won't you? You'll leave us..."[24]

## A vaccine against authoritarianism

Dmitry Bednyakov was a senior special investigator and a teacher at the Gorky Militia School, a highly experienced lawyer and a hard-core supporter of the market economy. In 1990 he had tried to convince the Supreme Soviet of the USSR to adopt Yavlinsky's 500 Days Programme. When Bednyakov was employed in early 1991 as a specialist in the Committee on Legislation, he met Nemtsov in the smoking room. Nemtsov was impressed that Police Major Bednyakov had already handed in his Communist Party card. It turned out that they were both from Nizhny Novgorod and had even lived in the same apartment building. By December 1991, when Nemtsov became governor, Bednyakov was already a specialist in privatization legislation. First, he helped Nemtsov in the regional administration, and then Nemtsov told him he ought to think about putting his name in for mayor of Nizhny Novgorod. "It was a professional dare," Bednyakov recalled. "The idea was: you wrote laws on privatization, on investment, on business registration—now see how it works in real life."[25]

With Nemtsov's help, Bednyakov became mayor of the city of Nizhny Novgorod, and the role he played in small-scale privatization there in 1992 was enormous, if not decisive. But relations between Nemtsov and Bednyakov soon became strained. As is often the case, each had his own idea about the source of the conflict. "Nemtsov got jealous of me," Bednyakov said. Nemtsov's associates at the time thought that Bednyakov had betrayed his colleague and patron. Many years later, Nemtsov levelled against Bednyakov the same accusation that he'd levelled against Vidyayev: that the city of Nizhny Novgorod was the main donor to the regional budget, and Bednyakov wanted to control the tax revenues. According to one version, the feud began in spring 1993 with a dispute over the land under Nizhny Novgorod businesses. The local entrepreneurs asked to privatize the land. Nemtsov was for it; Bednyakov resisted. Politically, the conflict between Nemtsov and Bednyakov fit into a typical pattern of the 1990s: almost everywhere the governor and the mayor of the regional capital were at war. They fought over resources, the tax base, the right to dispose of property and, ultimately, power.

Viktor Lysov, then head of the regional administration's public relations department, returned to work on 2 January 1994 after a two-week holiday. "I've announced elections," Nemtsov greeted him. "We're going to change the power structure in the city."[26] In the mayoral elections set for the end of March, Nemtsov supported Yevgeny Krestyaninov, chairman of the regional council. But Bednyakov had a good chance, too. He campaigned actively and was supported by almost the entire city media. And then Bednyakov made a powerful counter move: he put forward a new charter of Nizhny Novgorod for a city referendum and suggested that the referendum and elections be combined.

When Nemtsov saw the draft charter, he immediately saw that it effectively established the mayor's independence from the governor and gave the mayor advantage over the city legislature, following the example of the newly adopted Russian constitution. Like Vidyayev at GAZ, Bednyakov was pushing for the city's autonomy from the region. With the new city charter, the independence of the future mayor was close to absolute. The draft charter, Nemtsov said, was "essentially a declaration of municipal sovereignty."[27] The difference was that while GAZ was a factory, an economic enterprise, and simply broke the law when it didn't pay taxes, Nizhny Novgorod was a municipal centre, and the new constitution gave local governments greater powers.

When the election campaign began, the conflict quickly went public. Nemtsov demanded that the referendum be cancelled (citing the opinion of the Kremlin legal department) and insisted that Bednyakov was trying to consolidate his personal power. Bednyakov objected that he was not obliged to listen to the opinion of some Kremlin officials, and the referendum would take place. Nemtsov's supporters insisted that Bednyakov was undermining the unity of the city and the region. Bednyakov countered: the new charter complied with the constitution and the law. In the end, Nemtsov went to the regional council: why was the charter of the regional capital being adopted without the knowledge of the deputies? Let the deputies have their say. "The charter," the regional administration insisted, "gives bureaucrats unbridled power."[28] The deputies supported Nemtsov, decided to cancel the referendum and, based on their decision, the governor issued a decree—legally very controversial—cancelling the vote.

But the campaign for the election of the mayor continued. The political struggle got personal. Nemtsov suggested that Bednyakov was a nationalist and an anti-Semite. Bednyakov did lean towards the far right, and anti-Semitic leaflets against Nemtsov had once again appeared in the city. "He's a piece of shit!" was Nemtsov's estimation of Bednyakov in a conversation with Lysov.[29] But a few days before the election, after receiving the results of another poll, the regional administration saw that Bednyakov was winning. "Nemtsov was shocked and decided on a desperate move," Bednyakov said. "He stopped the election."[30] Thirty-two hours before voting began, Krestyaninov withdrew his candidacy. By law, a no-alternative election was impossible, and so the election was cancelled—an unprecedented case in Russian political history in the first half of the 1990s.

"It was a very important moment," Bednyakov said. "Boris showed by his own example what was possible: You could take the democracy you fought for and break it."[31]

Since there were no elections, Bednyakov remained mayor of the city, and on what would have been election day, Nemtsov told him, "I'm going to Moscow to get you fired." Yeltsin had just returned from another holiday in Sochi. Nemtsov waited in the reception room and approached Yeltsin with a draft presidential decree to dismiss the mayor of Nizhny Novgorod "for a gross violation of official duties." "Is he in your way?" Yeltsin quickly asked Nemtsov and immediately signed the decree. Bednyakov went to Moscow afterwards, but it was too late. At the gate, his mayoral ID card was taken away, and the guards wouldn't let him into the Kremlin.[32] He had lost.

Power corrupts, especially if it is accompanied by public success and popularity. Nemtsov was no exception. Later, he said that this is how he got vaccinated against authoritarianism at the very beginning of his career. The story with Bednyakov cost him dearly and was perhaps his most serious mistake. He quickly realized this. A few months later, in January 1995, Nemtsov said in an interview, "It was a mistake, a really big one. But I don't make the same mistakes twice, and I won't make it again in the same situation."[33]

## Russia's next president

Yeltsin might fly into a rage, and he could be deeply offended, but he didn't hold a grudge. Nemtsov, who liked to form his own opinions of people, thought that Yeltsin's character was in part due to his build. A big, healthy man of peasant stock from the Urals was, he believed, above spats and holding long grudges. After a few months, Yeltsin had forgiven Nemtsov for his disloyalty during the September 1993 events. Almost a year later, on 13 August 1994, the steamship *Russia*, taking the Yeltsin family on a cruise down the Volga, docked at the Nizhny Novgorod jetty.

It was a big event for the city. The president was once again visiting his favourite governor's fiefdom, even if for a short stop. The whole family followed Yeltsin down the gangplank: his wife Naina, his two daughters, Yelena and Tatyana, and his three grandchildren, Katya, Masha and Boris. "It was all very sincere and touching. It was obviously not for show," Nemtsov later recalled. "It was clear that Yeltsin was the family favourite, but at the same time the atmosphere within the family was quite free-spirited. Everyone teased him—his daughters and grandchildren." The visit was not at all political. Naina and her daughters went on a tour and to an orphanage, while Yeltsin and Nemtsov first went to the Nizhny Novgorod Fair (which under Nemtsov became the hallmark of the city) and then to a tennis tournament. The president and the governor ceremonially opened the competition by picking up their rackets and playing to a point. (Nemtsov hit a foul.) Then TV journalist Nina Zvereva was brought to Yeltsin. The city had been looking forward to the president's visit. Nemtsov had been governor for a while, and it was time to evaluate the interim results. Zvereva asked the most obvious question. The videos of the interview have survived and gone down in history.

"Two and a half years ago, you said that you believed in Boris Nemtsov even though he was a very young governor. Has your faith in him got stronger?"

"He has matured so much that he's ready to run for president."[34]

With that, Yeltsin had effectively named Nemtsov his successor. A few days later, at one of the next stops on his trip down the Volga, Yeltsin would tell reporters that Nemtsov was not planning to run in the next presidential election in 1996. It was an important disclaimer. Yeltsin was making it clear that he was thinking about a second term, but this didn't change the sense of his comments. His comments might have been light and casual, but this was Yeltsin's first public admission that he had big plans for Nemtsov—he was extending a hand of friendship, in a way. "After that, our relationship became... well, not exactly friendly, but much closer than before," Nemtsov later said. "We began to understand each other better."[35]

A month later, during a trip to America, Yeltsin would introduce Nemtsov to Bill Clinton as the next president of Russia. "I remember how Clinton reacted," Nemtsov recalled. "He asked, 'What do you do?' I said, 'I'm a governor.' 'How old were you when you became governor?' 'I was thirty-two.' Clinton smiled. 'I became governor of Arkansas when I was thirty-two.'"[36]

It was easy to understand Yeltsin's affinity for Nemtsov. He had an affinity for tall and powerful men like himself. Height mattered a great deal. And he was impressed by Nemtsov's character—his independence, self-confidence, even arrogance, the way he acted like an equal.

Yeltsin's daughter Tatyana Yumasheva said that the fact that her father had never had a son also played a role—he saw a kindred spirit in Nemtsov. Politically, Yeltsin was really Nemtsov's father: He had singled him out from among the other young Russian deputies, promoted him to governor and given him a chance in politics. Nemtsov later recalled: "He considered the question of a successor to be crucial, primarily for himself, personally, but he hadn't decided. He told me, 'I don't have a son, but you're like a son to me—in terms of height and even anthropology.'"[37] They had a lot in common ideologically, too. Both wanted freedom. Yeltsin also saw in Nemtsov the same populist that he proudly called himself a few years before.

By August 1994, Yeltsin had changed. He was no longer the strong-willed, determined leader who had led the movement to freedom and democracy in 1991. Two years of intense political wrangling had worn him down. He was haggard and heavier. It was then, in 1994, that the phrase "the president is working with documents" began to be used to explain the president's absences from the public. He was losing energy and focus. He had few allies or even supporters among the remaining democrats. "We need to return Yeltsin to Yeltsin," Gaidar said.[38] "It seemed to me at the time that he had already grown very old and lazy," Nemtsov recalled. "That is, if you are permitted to say such things about the tsar."[39] From the leader of the democratic revolution, he was turning into an autocrat—"the president of all the Russians." Non-governmental staff and security officers, primarily the ubiquitous head of the presidential guards, Alexander Korzhakov, were playing too big a role. The president's opinions and decisions depended more and more on what his courtiers whispered in his ear.

Yeltsin was always a drinker, but now his weakness for alcohol was being discussed in the international media. Two scandalous episodes that have gone down in history date from autumn 1994: Yeltsin conducting an orchestra in Berlin during the solemn march of the last Russian soldiers leaving Germany, and his failure to get off the plane three weeks later while flying from the United States to Shannon, Ireland, where the Irish prime minister and his wife were on the tarmac for an official visit. Nemtsov was just about the only person who dared to speak directly to Yeltsin about it. He was in Berlin with Yeltsin at the time, and he came and told him what he thought about it. Yeltsin didn't like it, but once again he didn't hold a grudge. "I remember a difficult conversation with Nemtsov, a straightforward, brave man," said Vyacheslav Kostikov, Yeltsin's press secretary at the time. "He let loose a raft of criticism at me.

'You're his aides—why didn't you do something? Why didn't you say something to him? Were you afraid you'd lose your jobs? Why didn't you speak to him directly? Maybe he needs help...'"[40] After Shannon, Nemtsov told Yeltsin, "You might sleep through Russia, too." This was truly impertinent, but Yeltsin forgave him for that as well.[41]

Yeltsin had only a vague idea of how to lead Russia forward, especially after the defeat of the democratic forces in the elections to the Duma (the lower house of the new Russian parliament) in December 1993. "He was used to making tremendous efforts of will and concentration, which would produce visible and rapid results," Kostikov later wrote. "Now he was faced with problems that took five, ten or even more years to solve."[42] This was discouraging. In these circumstances, Yeltsin was naturally drawn to the fortunate and successful Nemtsov, who had moved forward easily and naturally with reforms, and who had even become more popular in the process.

A few years later, when Nemtsov left for Moscow and Nizhny Novgorod lost its reformist energy to become an ordinary provincial city again, many Nizhny Novgorod residents would blame Nemtsov for their dashed hopes. He abandoned them and life did not get better.

It is hard to articulate how feasible it was to introduce a new way of life in one single region of Russia. But in the 1990s, the personality of the leader had a great influence on the mindset of the elites, even at the local level. This was shown by a study that was conducted in 1996 in Moscow, Nizhny Novgorod and Tatarstan by Sharon Rivera, an American expert on Russia, together with the Institute of Sociology of the Russian Academy of Sciences. Officials and legislators in Nizhny Novgorod turned out to be the most progressive. They were noticeably more willing than their colleagues in Kazan and Moscow to advocate pluralism, market competition, democratic and liberal values.[43]

At the same time, most of the Nizhny Novgorod elite had previously been Soviet Communist administrators who knew nothing of liberal values. All things being equal, they could have easily been in a different camp. When Communist Party leader Gennady Zyuganov arrived in Nizhny Novgorod before the 1996 presidential election, he and his entourage sat across the table from Nemtsov and his team. With the exception of Nemtsov, everyone at the table was about the same age and had similar biographies. They even looked alike. But they thought completely differently. Some were for private property and rapprochement with the West; others, for nationalization of industry and the country's "special path" forward.

# CHAPTER 9

### 1991–94
# Chechnya and the Unnecessary War

## Dudayev comes to power

It was the end of 1990. The workday was ending, and the Soviet defence minister, Marshal Dmitry Yazov, was about to go home when he was stopped by a call from the duty officer. "General, Dzhokhar Dudayev is here to see you," the duty officer reported. Yazov was surprised. "Who did you say?" He hadn't summoned anyone and was not expecting anyone. The duty officer clarified that Dzhokhar Dudayev, division commander of strategic aviation, insisted on speaking with him.

Yazov immediately called Yevgeny Shaposhnikov, his deputy and commander-in-chief of the air forces. "Did you send Dudayev to me? What does he want?" Shaposhnikov, who was on friendly terms with the general, was surprised: he knew nothing about the visit. A division commander does not drop in uninvited to the minister of defence; this was a gross violation of army discipline. He could be punished for it. Nevertheless, Yazov received him.

Major-General Dudayev was a trim and distinguished forty-six-year-old, with a telegraphic manner of speaking and moving. He began, "Comrade Minister, I request a transfer to my native Checheno-Ingushetia to head the republican military registration and enlistment office."

"Are you crazy?" Yazov asked, taken aback. "You're the commander of strategic aviation! This is ridiculous!"

"Soon important events will take place in Chechnya, presidential elections for the republic. I want to take part in them."

"What president? What elections? What are you talking about, General? Dismissed! Get out of here before I remove you from your post for your violation of discipline."[1]

Marshal Yazov decided that the major-general was simply not himself. Dudayev left, but soon elders from Chechnya appeared in Marshal Yazov's office with the same request: to appoint Dudayev as the military enlistment officer of Chechnya. Yazov refused again, but, to his surprise, Gorbachev, still president of the Soviet Union at the time, called him and urged him to agree to the elders' request. "I told him that it made no sense to send Dudayev there—he was a good division commander," Yazov later recalled. "The troops need him. Gorbachev continued to pressure me. 'Can't you find another good division commander?' The whole conversation made no sense. In the end we agreed to hand over Dudayev."[2]

Gorbachev had a reason to pressure Yazov and help the Chechen elders. In the heat of the struggle with his main adversary, Yeltsin, he was trying to enlist the support of the autonomous republics within Russia. In April 1990 the Supreme Soviet of the USSR passed a law extending autonomous republics in Russia the same status as the Union republics and granting them the right to decide their status within Russia and the USSR independently.* Yeltsin tried to take back this initiative with his famous expression in autumn 1990: "Take as much sovereignty as you can swallow." In other words, take all the autonomy you want, but remain part of Russia. The national republics within Russia seized the moment and adopted declarations of sovereignty. This was the situation at the end of November 1990, shortly before Dudayev came to see Yazov and just as the Congress of the Chechen People was about to be convened by the anti-Communist opposition in Chechnya.

---

\* The Law on Secession from the USSR read, in part: "In a Union republic which includes within its structure autonomous republics, autonomous oblasts, or autonomous okrugs, the referendum is held separately for each autonomous formation. The people of autonomous republics and autonomous formations retain the right to decide independently the question of remaining within the USSR or within the seceding Union republic, and also to raise the question of their own state-legal status."

At the time Chechnya was still part of the Checheno-Ingush Autonomous Republic—that is, one republic of Chechnya and Ingushetia, two kindred nations that had suffered equally under Stalin's repressions. In 1944 the Chechens and the Ingush were deported to Kazakhstan and then rehabilitated and reunited as an autonomous republic inside Russia (within the USSR). The republic's leader, Doku Zavgayev, the first Chechen in Soviet history to be appointed by Moscow as head the regional Communist Party, was enticed by Gorbachev's promises and envisioned himself as the head of an independent country. He supported demonstrations organized by the opposition, and at the November rally he spoke about the revival of the Chechen nation.

Two days later, with Zavgayev's tacit support, the Checheno-Ingush Supreme Soviet adopted a declaration of sovereignty. "Zavgayev's team thought that with this step they had killed at least two birds with one stone," Dzhabrail Gakayev, a Chechen historian and a democratic activist of those years, later wrote. "On the one hand, they deprived the opposition of their main trump card, but on the other, they could subtly manoeuvre between the Union and Russian centres of power, taking advantage of the growing discord between them. However, what seemed like Zavgayev's win–win policy suited neither the new Russian authorities nor Chechen national radicals eager to seize power."[3]

Dudayev attended the November Congress of the Chechen People almost by chance. He was just passing through Chechnya: he had been promoted to the rank of major-general, the first and only Chechen general in the Soviet army. He came to pay his respects to Zavgayev and to thank him, as Soviet etiquette demanded, for the promotion. He was invited to the congress as the guest of honour and pride of Chechnya by the leader of the recently formed oppositional Vainakh Democratic Party, Zelimkhan Yandarbiyev, a graduate of the Moscow Literary Institute and a little-known young poet.

As behoves the guest of honour, Dudayev took the floor. He was more emotional and militant than Zavgayev. He spoke of the two-hundred-year Russian oppression of Chechnya and the need to defend Chechnya's freedom and independence in every way, including by force if necessary. The speech polarized the audience: one part greeted his speech with thunderous applause, while the other rather demonstratively stood up and left. Chechen nationalists took note. At the time there were no vibrant leaders among the Chechen opposition, and the charismatic aviator general was perfectly suited to this role.

It was a time of national revolutions in the Soviet Union republics, including the Caucasus, Azerbaijan and Georgia. Soon after Dudayev's visit to Marshal Yazov, Moscow would send tanks to storm the TV centre in Vilnius, but Dudayev, whose strategic bomber division was stationed in the Estonian city of Tartu, would refuse a similar order to blockade the TV centre and parliament in Tallinn.

By March 1991, Dudayev acquiesced to the demands of the Chechen opposition. He abandoned his division and returned to Grozny as the leader of the national liberation movement in Chechnya and head of the National Congress of the Chechen People (NCCP). "Between May and August 1991, Dudayev and his followers were able to turn the Chechen executive committee into a smoothly functioning mechanism fighting for power," Gakayev wrote. "It became a centre for the radical extra-parliamentary opposition that was against the official authorities of Checheno-Ingushetia but did not yet have sufficient mass support."[4]

In the summer of 1991, most Chechens did not want Chechnya to secede from Russia. Grozny, the capital of Chechnya, was more than half Russian, and many Chechens looked down on Dudayev's radical followers. But Zavgayev was unlucky: Although he kept a low profile during the events of August 1991, he was associated with the coup organizers. The new Russian leadership regarded Zavgayev as a representative of the ruling Communist establishment.

Furthermore, Ruslan Khasbulatov, speaker of Russia's Supreme Soviet and hero in the fight against the coup conspirators, had a personal grudge against Zavgayev, who had been influential in Khasbulatov's failed bid for the rectorship of Grozny University. Khasbulatov largely determined Russia's policy towards Chechnya; he even threatened to bring Zavgayev to Moscow in an iron cage if he suppressed anti-Zavgayev rallies. Moscow was betting on Dudayev, and Zavgayev found himself completely helpless when the protest rally that began in Grozny during the attempted coup quickly evolved into a power grab.

On 22 August armed Dudayev supporters seized the TV centre, then the government building, and then demanded the resignation of Zavgayev. Zavgayev refused, and the deputies of the Chechen Supreme Soviet supported him. On 6 September the NCCP dispersed the Supreme Soviet. Like the Bolsheviks raiding the Constituent Assembly in 1917, armed men stormed the building where the Chechen deputies were in session and forced them to surrender their mandates. Zavgayev was led out through the back door, and his supporter Vitaly Kutsenko, the chairman of the city council, hid in his office. According to one version, when Kutsenko saw Dudayev's followers breaking the door down, he tried to escape through a second-storey window but fell to his death. Another version has it that he was thrown out of the window.* Five years later, when the Russian parliament began to debate the causes of the war in Chechnya, Zavgayev would say: "The war started when Vitaly Kutsenko was murdered in broad daylight."[5]

Of course, everyone in Moscow immediately realized that there had been an armed coup in Chechnya. Khasbulatov flew in from Moscow and formed a temporary governing council to rule over Checheno-Ingushetia until the elections. But the structure did not last more than a week. Dudayev dissolved the council and set presidential and parliamentary elections for late October. These elections were not deemed valid: the numerous anti-Dudayev opposition groups in Chechnya at the time did not recognize them; the turnout, according to some estimates, was ten to twelve per cent; ballots were distributed to anyone who wanted them; and everyone could vote as many times as they liked. On 27 October, Dudayev won the presidential election with eighty-five per cent of the vote and immediately announced that Chechnya was seceding from Russia. Journalist Musa Muradov was then editor-in-chief of the *Groznensky rabochy* newspaper. When the text of the new Chechen constitution was laid on his desk, he could see where the document

---

\* Maryam Vakhidova, Dudayev's assistant, claims that Kutsenko was so terrified of Dudayev's followers that he threw himself out of the window. In an interview with the author, she said that Yusup Soslambekov, an associate of Dudayev's and one of the leaders of the NCCP, tried to save Kutsenko by grabbing his leg, but was unable to hold him. Kutsenko fell and Soslambekov was left holding his shoe.

came from. In parts of the text Chechnya was called Sudan or Estonia, because the constitution had been hastily copied from those countries' documents. "Those are minor mistakes," Dudayev's emissaries told him. "We need to establish sovereignty as soon as possible. People are tired: they can't wait."[6]

It was only then that Moscow finally became convinced that Dudayev was no ally, but a serious problem. With Vice-President Rutskoi's encouragement, Yeltsin signed a decree declaring a state of emergency in Chechnya. This was Yeltsin's first mistake of many in dealing with Chechnya. When he turned to Gorbachev for help—the military was still under his command—Gorbachev refused to help his political foe. As a result, on 9 November, a plane carrying a few hundred poorly armed soldiers, who in any case could do nothing to contain the angry Chechens, flew into Chechnya to depose Dudayev.

The appearance of men in Soviet military uniforms instantly opened old wounds among the Chechens. The bloody crackdowns on independence rallies and actions in Baku, Tbilisi and Vilnius were still fresh in their minds. And the deeper trauma of their nation's deportation had never been healed—in fact, the Kremlin was not even aware of how deep it was and the extent to which it defined public consciousness. Rumours were circulating that Moscow was preparing a new deportation. From every corner of Chechnya people came to defend the presidential palace and, they thought, their freedom. But their help was not needed. Dudayev gave the order that the completely unthreatening Russian military detachment be given food and drink and then sent back home.

This was the rebel general's finest hour. His popularity skyrocketed. "They wanted to scare supporters of the Chechen national movement, but instead they came up against their fighting spirit," wrote ethnographer Emil Pain, who would later help to find a resolution to the Chechen crisis. "They tried to prevent the legitimization of Dudayev, but they turned him into a national hero [...]. They tried to support the anti-Dudayev opposition, but they ended up consolidating the various political forces against Moscow in Chechnya."[7]

Dzhokhar Dudayev became the master of the situation in Chechnya, when Russian statehood was not even legally formalized yet; the

Belovezh Accords were not ratified until a month later, on 12 December. A time bomb was laid under its foundation: the problem of Chechen independence.

## Khasbulatov at large

Alexei Kazannik, a deputy of the USSR congress and a law professor from the Siberian city of Omsk, became famous in the spring of 1989 at the First Congress. The Communist majority did not elect Yeltsin to the Supreme Soviet, so the democrat Kazannik ceded his mandate to him. Yeltsin did not forget this noble gesture, and in October 1993, after the firing on the White House, Kazannik was appointed prosecutor general.

He didn't hold the post for long. Almost the first thing the new prosecutor general had to deal with was amnesty. When the president told him that he was preparing an amnesty—the first in the history of modern Russia—Kazannik warned him that the newly elected parliament would most likely give amnesty to Khasbulatov, Rutskoi and other conspirators, who would then be released from prison. Yeltsin did not believe him, but Kazannik was right. In February 1994, the Duma passed a resolution to release the members of the Emergency Committee and other conspirators in the October events in Moscow.

Kazannik received the order to release them; at the same time, he received the president's resolution to keep them in prison. The president justified his resolution legally. But Kazannik was a man of principle who intended to abide by the law, regardless of his own opinion that the defenders of the White House were conspirators, and wanted to bring them to trial. He called Yeltsin and asked him to withdraw his resolution. "No," the president replied. The prosecutor general shrugged. He'd have to defy the president and release them. Kazannik resigned. But before doing so, he called Lefortovo and ordered that everyone be released. "I came out of prison," Rutskoi later recalled. "Who was the first person to call me? Nemtsov. He was governor; everything was fine. He invited me to visit him in Nizhny Novgorod—to come and relax.

I said, 'Yeltsin will cut your balls off.' He said, 'You're my friend. I don't care what anyone thinks of me.'"[8]

Ruslan Khasbulatov was also released. He wasn't invited to Nizhny Novgorod, but he had somewhere to go. Soon he was in Chechnya.

## In search of a new Kuwait

In the two and a half years that had passed since the coup on 6 September, the situation in Chechnya had become deplorable. The Russian government had other more pressing matters to deal with. For a while, Chechnya was forgotten, and when it gained *de facto* independence, the Dudayev republic plunged into a severe economic crisis and lawlessness.

Chechnya was drowning in weaponry. General Anatoly Kulikov, then commander of the North Caucasus Forces (he would later be transferred to Moscow and take part in the events of October 1993), later recalled how, in February 1992, men from Dudayev's guards showed up at the headquarters of one of his regiments in Grozny, disarmed the guards and seized the weapon depots. The next day the storehouses were looted and burnt. More or less the same thing happened with the property of the military units quartered in Chechnya. In an attempt to give the seizure of arms a semblance of legality, Moscow officially ordered the transfer of half the weapons in Chechnya to Dudayev— as had been done in other Union republics—but in reality Dudayev received more. Very soon you could buy smuggled Turkish cigarettes and any kind of firearm, from revolvers to mortar launchers, at the Grozny market.[9]

Chechnya became an enormous, semi-criminal, offshore territory, where Russian laws, the Russian banking system, and the Russian prosecutor's office did not operate. There were no customs and no border with Russia, and the local airport became a hub for smuggling. "I could be wrong," Sergei Shakhrai later said, "but I think almost all the first computers imported into our country were smuggled through Chechnya."[10] The city of Grozny was a major oil-refining hub, and so oil fraud began: Russia continued to pump oil to Grozny refineries, and Dudayev's men sold oil for fuel and heating abroad. Hundreds of billions of roubles were transferred from Russia to Chechnya through fraudulent bank advice notes—forged bank orders sent to cash settlement centres permitting cash payments. A Chechen businessman told businessman Artyom Tarasov—the man who had once tried to bribe Nemtsov—"Artyom, it's so easy! We write a piece of paper. It goes to the bank. We get two truckloads of cash and take it straight home to Grozny."[11]

Of course, without the involvement of Moscow officials and Russian criminals, these and similar illegal scams could not have succeeded. Dudayev himself was neither a corrupt man nor a gangster; he had one mission in life—to see an independent Chechnya. But as the British historian and journalist Anatol Lieven wrote in his book about the war in Chechnya, it did not matter much. Dudayev did nothing to stop the production of counterfeit money and fraudulent bank confirmations, the theft of oil from the pipeline that connected Baku and Novorossiysk via Chechen territory, or the robberies of Russian transit trains.[12] Local residents adapted to this new life as best they could; each businessman had two stamps: "one with the chicken and one with the wolf", in local slang. The "chicken" was the two-headed eagle from the Russian coat of arms, and the "wolf" was the Chechen coat of arms (it was said that Dudayev's Russian-born wife had copied it from an image of the wolf Akela in a popular Soviet edition of Rudyard Kipling's *The Jungle Book*). Regardless of what Dudayev meant by national sovereignty, in the legal and political sense his regime was a failed, non-functional state in which order had been replaced by anarchy and violence. Schools and clinics were closed; people were not receiving pensions or salaries; life had become unsafe; and Russians, increasingly harassed by Dudayev's radical supporters, had begun to leave. At that time, many of Dudayev's supporters moved from the mountain districts to Grozny, shocking local residents with their coarse behaviour.

Dudayev had promised a new Kuwait, but it did not materialize. The revolutionary euphoria quickly gave way to disappointment. By 1993 Dudayev no longer controlled parts of Chechnya, and the anti-Dudayev opposition, which advocated reunification with Russia, were emboldened by strong public support. As in Moscow, there was in Chechnya confrontation with the parliament, but if in Moscow the president pushed for a confidence-building referendum that was then blocked by the parliament, in Chechnya it was the other way around. Dudayev and his supporters understood that they would lose the referendum on Chechnya's relationship with Russia. So, in June 1993, on the eve of the referendum, the future most-wanted terrorist Shamil Basayev, then commander of the famous "Abkhaz" battalion,* the shock force of Dudayev's guards, rolled self-propelled artillery onto Grozny's central square and fired at the city council building that housed both the opposition headquarters and the electoral commission. "Several men in police uniforms burst out of the building, and Basayev's machine gunners fired at them," Musa Muradov recalled. "The policemen fell, bleeding heavily. They were finished off."[13] This massacre of the opposition did not enhance Dudayev's popularity. His authority was waning, so, starting in summer 1993, he began to push for a meeting with Yeltsin. In October 1993, he congratulated Yeltsin on his victory over the parliament.

An opportunity to come to an agreement seemed to appear in early 1994. Moscow made several concessions and signed a federative treaty with Tatarstan, which also insisted on sovereignty, refused to take part in elections and the referendum, and seriously considered introducing its own currency. The same model could be used for an agreement with Chechnya. In March, an agreement in principle was reached to bring Yeltsin and Dudayev together.

The only condition, according to Sergei Filatov, head of the Yeltsin administration at the time, was respect for the Russian president.[14] "I came home in the evening," Filatov recalled, "turned on the TV, and there was Dudayev, calling Yeltsin a dog."[15] By early summer, there was no chance for negotiations. They wouldn't have come to anything, in any case. Dudayev would not lower the bar on his demands. He was obsessed with the idea of sovereignty and would probably not have agreed to the Tatarstan option. During the war, he said in one of his

---

\* Basayev's battalion was called Abkhaz because it took part in the Georgian–Abkhaz war of 1992–93 on the side of the Abkhaz armed forces.

interviews that it was impossible in principle to negotiate a peaceful agreement with Russia. "If we had tried to solve the problem [...] with politics, with loyalty, with humility—I can assure you that we would have been cut off at the root. There would never be a Chechen nation or state again."[16] He seems to have come to this conviction as early as 1991, if not earlier.

His impeccable military bearing had always been combined with nervousness and a short temper. General and military pilot Pyotr Deinekin, then commander-in-chief of the Russian air forces, recalled a scene from Afghanistan. Dudayev, a model officer, snapped insolently when the general noted his untidy tie.[17] Later, he went so far as to accuse Russia of preparing an earthquake in Chechnya. He could answer a single question for ten minutes with clenched fists in anger, or he could suddenly get up and walk out during the conversation, leaving his interlocutor in complete bewilderment. Anatol Lieven, who met with Dudayev more than once, wrote that he often thought Dudayev was literally insane—"mentally unstable with clear clinical signs of paranoia and megalomania."[18]

## Khasbulatov is sidelined

Khasbulatov's star was rising in Chechnya as negotiations with Dudayev were breaking down. Chechnya celebrated when he was released from prison in February 1994 and greeted him as a hero. Here was a serious politician, a professor of economics, recently one of the top officials of state, who was repressed by Yeltsin. When Chechen society became disappointed in Dudayev, they pinned their hopes on Khasbulatov. Khasbulatov toured Chechnya and spoke at rallies before crowds of 200,000 to 300,000 people. He had no claim to power in Chechnya, at least not openly. He said that, after Moscow, the republican level was beneath him. But power was slipping out of Dudayev's hands, and Khasbulatov's "peacekeeping contingent" was naturally very attractive to anti-Dudayev forces.

Khasbulatov's rise in popularity did not please the anti-Dudayev opposition. They had been fighting Dudayev for years, and suddenly a "nobody" had flown in from Moscow and begun to skim the cream off their successes. Umar Avturkhanov, one of the leaders of the opposition and chairman of the Provisional Council of Chechnya, created in December 1993, controlled the northern lowland part of the republic and had long been pestering Moscow for money, military equipment and arms to overthrow Dudayev.

In Moscow, no one was ready to support Khasbulatov. Yeltsin and the entire government regarded him as an enemy. It was impossible even to mention his name in a conversation with the president.[19] In his memoirs, Yevgeny Savostyanov, then deputy head of the Federal Counter-Intelligence Service (known by the Russian abbreviation FSK; successor to the KGB and predecessor of the FSB), who was tasked with solving the problem of Chechnya, wrote: "I thought Avturkhanov's demonstrative distancing of himself from Khasbulatov spoke very much in his favour."[20] Khasbulatov was also not perceived as a serious player capable of turning the situation in Chechnya around. At the end of August, the *Kommersant* newspaper wrote: "It's not clear why Moscow didn't want to use Khasbulatov in the crisis in Chechnya—either because of memories of the confrontation between the White House and the Kremlin, or because they didn't understand the real situation in Chechnya. According to observers, the former dominated, but the latter may also be the case."[21]

If Moscow had done nothing at all, the Dudayev regime would, in all likelihood, have fallen on its own. "By autumn 1994, Khasbulatov's popularity was already so high that it seemed it needed to rise just a bit more and Dudayev's power would collapse," wrote Musa Muradov.[22] Several years later, Sergei Stepashin, then head of the FSK, who had taken part in discussions said, "Some people simply did not have the patience to wait until the Chechens resolved the issues among themselves. We really wanted to help, to push the process along..."[23] Khasbulatov was taken out of the running. A year later, in September 1995, Yeltsin would mention him again. "He has a high rating in Chechnya. Why should we remind him of his past? We should invite him in for a talk. Besides, I think he's got much smarter in the meantime."[24] But it would be too late.

## The obvious solution

In the summer of 1994, terrorist acts near the Chechen border—taking buses full of people as hostages—were not just commonplace: they were conducted on a schedule, the last Thursday of every month. Train robberies and railroad sabotage continued. The Kremlin studied videotapes of executions in Chechnya. Avturkhanov appealed to Yeltsin for help.

By early July, Yeltsin's advisers offered him several options ranging from recognition of Chechnya's independence to a military operation. They recommended supporting the pro-Russian opposition without directly participating in events, and Yeltsin agreed with them. "The time had come for Russia to intervene," Yeltsin later recalled. "The stages of the plan were as follows: gradually infiltrate anti-Dudayev sentiment and forces into Chechnya. Provide monetary assistance and, if necessary, specialists. Do everything so that the people drive Dudayev out."[25] The Kremlin was counting on Avturkhanov and his provisional council. By the middle of August, they had several dozen units of military equipment and more than $2 million. There was fighting in Chechnya. Civil war was heating up.

By early October, Dudayev's forces had suffered several defeats, and Moscow was already planning how to deal with Chechnya once Dudayev was gone. In the middle of the month, units of the provisional council almost took Grozny. After that, Moscow decided on a covert operation: reinforce the opposition units with Russian tanks, storm Grozny again and finally overthrow Dudayev. At the last of the general staff meetings, someone came up with the idea of sending Russian soldiers and officers in tanks. This was contrary to the decision not to intervene directly. Savostyanov protested but without success. "I had to say something, so I said it would be better to recruit people abroad. No, they objected, there was no need to complicate things, the decision had been made, and the work had already begun."[26] This is how several dozen untested Russian soldiers ended up inside combat vehicles storming Grozny on the morning of 26 November. The attempt to overthrow Dudayev was similar to the Bay of Pigs operation carried out by Washington in Cuba in April 1961, and it was just as big a failure. The timing of the attack was not coordinated; there was no air support; Dudayev was fully prepared for the attack and trapped his adversaries.

"I was told," recalled Anatoly Kulikov, by then commander-in-chief of the Internal Forces, "that Avturkhanov was practically pouring cognac into glasses, celebrating victory, when the insurgents began shooting tanks in the city streets. Their crews, consisting mainly of Russian soldiers, went into battle, but they were not supported by the opposition units. Some died and others surrendered. This was an idiotic scheme simply doomed to failure."[27]

For the next two days Russia was convulsed with shame. In TV reports from Grozny, the captured tank drivers confessed that they were Russian servicemen; Dudayev threatened to shoot them all if Russia did not recognize them; and Defence Minister Pavel Grachev continued to issue denials: "The armed forces are not involved [...]. There are a lot of mercenaries fighting on the side of Dudayev and on the side of the opposition." Besides, Grachev said in a phrase that would become famous, the problem of Chechnya could be resolved with one paratrooper regiment in two hours—meaning that had the regular army attacked Grozny the result would have been different.[28]

Defeat is always an orphan. For decades, both camps around Yeltsin, military and civil, would blame each other for unleashing the war. But we know what took place at the Security Council meeting on 29 November. The main speaker was the minister for ethnic affairs—meaning largely in the Caucasus—Nikolai Yegorov, one of Alexander Korzhakov's recent appointments. Yegorov, a supporter of the military operation, was called "our second Yermolov"—the Russian general who conquered the Caucasus in the nineteenth century. He said that seventy per cent of Chechens would support Russian troops. Everyone voted for the invasion. Only Grachev objected. It's the other way around, he said, "seventy per cent of Chechens would be against us." He proposed at least to postpone the start of the operation. "It would not be expedient to send troops, especially in December," he later explained. "If we are to send them, then only in the spring. And before then, we should pressure Chechnya economically. Then encircle Grozny and wait until the rebels surrender. In the rest of Chechnya, work with the population to get back to normal life."[29]

But Yeltsin had already made his decision. The solution was clear and just waiting to be implemented. On the one hand, he was aware of his moral duty to stop the lawlessness in Chechnya. On the other hand, he was pressured by political considerations—the need to respond in some way to the war-mongering Vladimir Zhirinovsky, who had just been elected to the parliament. As Alexander Cherkasov, an activist and a board member of Memorial, put it, the policy towards Chechnya was "an attempt to draw the electorate to their side by using the mottos of the opposition, an attempt to bring a wayward province back into the fold of the empire, to boost Yeltsin's falling ratings."[30]

By the end of November, Russian internal troops were already deployed along the Chechen border. The shameful rout of tanks in Grozny had been the last straw.

When Grachev spoke out against it at the session of the Security Council on 29 November, no one believed him—he had just told the entire country that they could take Grozny with one paratrooper regiment. Everyone in the room jumped on him. Prime Minister Chernomyrdin suggested that he resign for cowardice and ignorance of the situation. Andrei Kozyrev, then foreign minister, was also present at that meeting. "I knew Yeltsin well," Kozyrev said. "I could tell by the look on his face what he thought: Pasha [Grachev] doesn't want to take all the responsibility—he wants to sit this one out. No one took his warnings seriously,"[31] especially since no one was expecting a protracted war. The leaders in the Kremlin were set on a quick, surgical operation. No one could have imagined in November 1994 that Chechnya would become Russia's Vietnam and that the Russian army, successor to the mighty Soviet army, would not break Dudayev and bring Chechnya back under Moscow's control within a month at the most. At the end of the meeting, Yeltsin instructed Grachev to present a plan for sending troops within a week. Grachev asked for at least a month. "You've got ten days," Yeltsin snapped.

In Chechnya, people thought Dudayev was crazy when he went on television and used a pointer to show how the Chechen militia would blow up Russian tanks. It was ridiculous: what could a small republic do against the armed forces of a world superpower?

But on 12 December, the army entered Chechnya. The war, which would result in tens of thousands of casualties and change the future of the country, could not be stopped.

## A 3D movie about Stalingrad

In early January 1995, the human-rights activist Stanislav Dmitriyevsky, who had put up tents in the centre of Nizhny Novgorod in May 1988 to protest the destruction of the ancient square, and the entrepreneur Igor Kalyapin, one of the founders of the Nizhny Novgorod Society for Human Rights, decided to go to Chechnya. The war had been going on for a month. Kalyapin's friends who had returned from Chechnya told him that young conscripts were sitting in mud in the trenches, terrified and shooting in all directions. It was clear from the news and television reports—mainly on the independent NTV channel—that the blitzkrieg had failed, and the military could not be believed. During the storming of Grozny on the night of 1 January, the troops came up against fierce resistance. But it was hard to get a complete picture of what was happening. "I remember very clearly having an intuition that something very important was happening there," Dmitriyevsky recalled, "and that the fate of the country was being decided."[32] So they went.

On 16 January they drove from Ingushetia in an ambulance with medical personnel to Chechnya, where they were detained by Chechen militiamen. They spent two days in a Chechen village and then several days in Grozny. "I was in shock," Dmitriyevsky said. "We were right in the thick of it. It was like a 3D movie about Stalingrad. That's what it felt like the first day. By the second day it was terrifying."[33] The activists realized that the storming of Grozny on 31 December was a disaster and that the Russian forces in the city had been completely defeated. As General Lev Rokhlin, who commanded one of the attacking groups, would later say, "The operational plan developed by Grachev and [Chief of the General Staff] Kvashnin was in fact a plan for the troops to die."[34]

The defence of Grozny was led by Aslan Maskhadov, a Soviet-era colonel and commander of an artillery regiment. A talented military commander, he was put at the head of Dudayev's armed forces. The scenario of 26 November was repeated, only this time the number of dead soldiers rose to 1,500, and their bodies lay for weeks in the tattered streets of the city. By the time Dmitriyevsky and Kalyapin found themselves in Grozny, the Russian troops controlled about one-third of the city and were shelling other neighbourhoods with artillery fire.

The city—or rather the ruins of the city—would not be taken until the end of February. No one will ever know exactly how many civilians died in Grozny and later throughout Chechnya. (To illustrate this point, only in 2008 was a mass grave with the remains of some 800 people who died in the winter of 1995 discovered in the city.) In spring 1995, Interior Ministry troops swept the village of Samashki, killing at least 100 civilians, including women and children. This would become a major international scandal. Human rights activist Alexander Cherkasov described the massacre: "There are no gunshot marks on the houses, the houses were burnt down, people were killed. The corpses were burnt by static flamethrowers."[35] Human rights activists would later estimate that up to fifty thousand civilians and about six thousand Russian servicemen died in the first Chechen war.[36]

The war in Chechnya was unpopular even before it started, and it quickly became a fully fledged political, military and humanitarian disaster. In December several high-ranking generals, including the first deputy commander of the ground forces, General Eduard Vorobyov, refused to lead this poorly prepared and, in his opinion, extremely risky military operation. Both sides of the political spectrum protested the war. Both saw the war as an attack on the democratic order in Russia itself. "Nineteen ninety-five might be the year when market institutions, which are still unstable, will fall apart, a year that could deal an irreparable blow to democratic rights and civil liberties in Russia," Yegor Gaidar said immediately after the invasion.[37] Grigory Yavlinsky and other deputies had gone to Chechnya to rescue soldiers captured during the attempted storming of Grozny in November. Now he, too, spoke out against the war. Several members of parliament, led by the well-known Soviet dissident and human rights ombudsman Sergei Kovalyov, rushed to Chechnya and were in Grozny during the invasion, hiding in apartment building cellars and in Dudayev's palace. Their stories added to the picture of the tragedy—and the Chechen commanders skilfully used the deputies' peacekeeping mission for propaganda purposes. In January 1995, coffins began arriving in Russian regions, including in Nizhny Novgorod, and mothers from every region rushed to Chechnya to save their sons. Protests of the war engulfed the whole country during its forty-five days.

Dudayev's followers knew that Dmitriyevsky and Kalyapin were in Chechnya on a humanitarian human-rights mission. Shamil Basayev, whose name did not mean anything to either of them at the time, served them soup in the canteen and even helped them find one of the captives, who was later freed. The activists communicated with the captives, recorded their information and took notes from them to pass on to their relatives. In their presence, the captured Russian soldiers were treated well enough, but people were already being shot, and very soon, by spring, atrocities on both sides would become commonplace. Dmitriyevsky and Kalyapin sheltered from the bombings in the basement of the Church of the Archangel Michael in Grozny, together with the priest, Anatoly Chistousov. A year later, the priest was executed as a Russian intelligence agent.

Among the prisoners at Dudayev's headquarters, Dmitriyevsky and Kalyapin encountered more than the servicemen who had been captured during the recent storming of the compound. They also found men who had been kept in cellars in Grozny for more than a month, although they hadn't fired a single shot. These were officers of the Shumilovsky Regiment, which was stationed near Nizhny Novgorod. On 11 December the regiment was in Dagestan near the Chechen border to support the entry of General Rokhlin's tank corps into Chechnya, when suddenly the road the military was on was cut by a crowd of local residents. The women, children and old men threw themselves under the wheels of the armoured vehicles. The soldiers had orders not to open fire, but even if they had not given orders, they would not have fired. The soldiers were quickly surrounded. Fifty-eight people were taken prisoner by Chechen soldiers who had infiltrated the crowd. Seven officers and twelve soldiers were taken to Grozny's cellars the next day.

The Officers' House of the Nizhny Novgorod Garrison had already set up an information centre where people could ask about soldiers sent to Chechnya. The House of Architects housed the local non-governmental organization, the Committee of Soldiers' Mothers. Rumours were circulating in the city: on the border with Chechnya, soldiers were living in poor conditions and were undernourished. Nemtsov quickly came up with the idea to take humanitarian aid and provide moral support to the Shumilovsky Regiment. And at the end of January, Nemtsov called television journalist Nina Zvereva: "Want to fly to Chechnya with me? You have half a day to get ready." Nina Zvereva worked at one of the national television channels, which was important to Nemtsov. The popular governor hoped that the whole country would see him helping his hometown boys who had gone off to war.

The rumours turned out to be true. At the Shumilovsky Regiment base in Dagestan, Zvereva filmed the soldiers: painfully thin, cold, covered with lice. The eighteen- and nineteen-year-olds looked at most sixteen, and next to the Dudayev Guardsmen they looked like children. They were Interior Ministry troops, but by the mid-1990s the entire Russian army was like this. Zvereva was not present during Nemtsov's conversations with the military commanders, but she understood from fragments of phrases on the plane that they were talking about rescuing officers who had been taken prisoner in December. Nemtsov had spent only one day at the Chechen border in late January, half of which—all night—was spent negotiating with Chechen field commanders. It seems that he was working for the release of Battalion Commander Vitaly Seryogin and Major Vyacheslav Afonin. Dmitriyevsky and Kalyapin had met them in Grozny and brought Afonin's documents to Nizhny Novgorod.[38]

The negotiations did not go well. In the morning Nemtsov was very gloomy, Zvereva recalled, pacing from corner to corner and repeating: "It's all terrible, it's all terrible." The Chechens demanded money—the hostage trade was gradually gaining momentum—but Nemtsov didn't have it. By spring 1995, ransoming kidnapped hostages had turned into an informal state policy. In March, when Nemtsov would again fly to Chechnya, Anatoly Kulikov would say, "We are doing everything we can. We contacted the Chechen authorities about ransoming our soldiers. We don't care how much it costs."[39]

It wasn't only money. The Nizhny Novgorod journalist Andrei Belyaninov distinctly remembers that the prisoners were freed in exchange for new Volga cars from the GAZ plant.[40] It makes sense. In the absence of cash, Volgas were the only liquid asset Nemtsov had. Ransoming the prisoners became his constant concern. Some of them were released. Vitaly Seryogin would spend more than nine months in captivity. Vyacheslav Afonin's body would never be found.

Then, that same spring, Kalyapin recalled, Nemtsov had an idea: gather signatures of people against the war in Chechnya.[41]

# CHAPTER 10

## 1995–96
## Peacemaker

### Living on undeclared income

In the history of Nizhny Novgorod, Russia and Boris Nemtsov, businessman Andrei Klimentyev is a special case. Once Nemtsov's friend and adviser, he became his worst enemy. After Nemtsov was assassinated, Klimentyev said, "By rights I should have been the one to shoot him, but some nice guy got to it before me."[1]

That was more nasty bravado and hatred than a real threat. Klimentyev was behind bars four times in his life—the last time after Nemtsov's death—but for scams and theft, not as a gangster or murderer.

The first time Klimentyev went to prison was under Leonid Brezhnev. When Brezhnev was in power, the ruling establishment was a separate caste within Soviet society, with its own special goods, wealth and material comforts. Through connections and privilege, this lifestyle was passed down in families: children of party bosses, diplomats, factory directors and business executives of all kinds had access to goods unavailable to their peers. Both in Moscow and in the provinces, where it was even more noticeable, the "golden youth" wore American jeans, went out to restaurants and drank expensive champagne. As the famous underground rock musician Yury Shevchuk sang in those years:

Stand there gaping, and take off your hats,
There's Daddy's Volga, driven by rich-kid brats.

This was exactly the scene in the early 1980s on a downtown street in Nizhny Novgorod (then still called Gorky) as twenty-eight-year-old Andrei Klimentyev, a university drop-out and the son of the head of a company with a monopoly on all the farm-equipment repair in the region, drove an expensive and luxury-class Volga. "Friends in my circle lived like hussars in old Russia," he recalled. "Hussars rode horses, and we drove cars."[2]

Klimentyev was well-known around town. He owned a flat in a prestigious neighbourhood of Nizhny Novgorod. He also had a VCR—a great luxury at the time—and hosted pay-per-view parties showing Western movies that had not been released in the Soviet Union, such as *Rocky*, *Jaws* and *Emmanuelle*. He had noisy parties in his flat with girls who couldn't turn down a chance to ride in his Volga.

But most importantly, Klimentyev played cards.

While some Soviet children of the elite dabbled in black-market buying and selling, Andrei Klimentyev was a professional gambler. He was the life of the party, but he played for money. It was rumoured around town that he was a card shark and a cheat and that the games at his place were rigged. People said he used special equipment that could read the backs of cards, had plants among the players at the table, and even had enforcers in case there was trouble. Klimentyev played mostly against people passing through town, the kind of people with money who came to Nizhny Novgorod on business. "In those days there were two kinds of life," he wrote in his memoirs (where he denied cheating): "Soviet Communist life and the other life. I lived the other kind of life, where there were other kinds of people."[3]

In December 1982, Klimentyev and his brothers were caught, arrested and put behind bars. The KGB was in charge from the beginning, indicating that the case was considered an important one. Apparently, the Klimentyevs had been caught in a sweep launched under Brezhnev to combat "persons living on undeclared income", which affected part of the *nomenklatura*. "The Klimentyev brothers fit this definition perfectly," a Nizhny Novgorod newspaper wrote many years later, "because they didn't hide their wealth, while clearly not living off salaries or university stipends. And they were infamous in the city."[4] Klimentyev and his brothers were accused of gambling and "distributing pornography and films with ideologically harmful content."

Many years later, Klimentyev would say that he and Nemtsov had known each other well in the early 1980s. Nemtsov did know one of his brothers, Sergei, from the tennis courts. But, although the young Nemtsov might have been at one of Klimentyev's house parties, they were not friends. When Klimentyev was jailed, Nemtsov had just turned twenty-three years old.

Klimentyev was released in 1989. By that time everyone had Hollywood movies and erotica at home, his other misadventures were forgotten, and, against the backdrop of the general fight against Communist rule, his case almost looked like a form of rebellion against the KGB. By the beginning of the 1990s, Klimentyev was a successful businessman who had made a fortune selling Chinese consumer goods and computers. Loud, outspoken, a good speaker, and self-confident— also rumoured to have refused to cooperate with the authorities while in prison—Klimentyev stood out among Nizhny Novgorod's entrepreneurs. He and Nemtsov quickly hit it off, this time on the tennis court. One of their matches went down in history, when Klimentyev lost a million roubles to Nemtsov. "The experienced tennis player Nemtsov easily beat the novice Klimentyev and donated his million roubles in winnings to an orphanage," *Kommersant* wrote. "The businessman didn't seem particularly upset; he was sure that his contacts would help him earn it all back."[5]

Local businessmen respected Klimentyev and admired his ingenuity, and Nemtsov, who was counting on the development of small business, looked up to him as a mentor. "When you listen to Klimentyev, you get the feeling that this man doesn't doubt for a second what he is doing and how he's doing it, and he's sure he's the only one who could do it. His manner made a strong impression on Nemtsov," Nemtsov's aide Kotyusov said.[6] At the Nemtsovs' house, Klimentyev acted like he owned the place. Nemtsov's daughter Zhanna recalled that he would show up in the morning and walk into her parents' bedroom without knocking.

Soon Klimentyev would become the owner of a nightclub (with "the best girls in town", as every Nizhny Novgorod hotel advertised) and two large stores in Nizhny Novgorod. But he started as economic adviser under Nemtsov and pursued his own interests at the governor's meetings with businessmen and elsewhere. Nemtsov did not mind: He thought Klimentyev was a smart man and admired his tremendous energy. However, Klimentyev didn't respect boundaries and got involved in everything. "He literally kicked open the doors to the offices of the governor and the chairman of the regional council," Nizhny Novgorod politician Anatoly Kozeradsky later recalled. "I think Klimentyev got away with that behaviour because in the early 1990s he was already a rich man. He thought he could advise Nemtsov on what should be done next and what market-based approaches should be adopted."[7]

## The Navashino millions

Nemtsov believed that industrial assets should go into the hands of local businesspeople, and he wanted to entrust one of them with the task of revitalizing the shipyard in Navashino, a small river town about 100 miles from Nizhny. For Nemtsov, it was also very much a personal project. He loved the idea that boats and yachts built right there in Navashino would be cutting through the wide expanse of the Volga. There were, of course, strong economic and social benefits as well. The shipyard, like many defence industry factories, had stood idle, but new orders would provide jobs for an entire town. The shipyard was also seeking new customers in Russia and abroad and working on plans to produce a new cargo ship. "Klimentyev, who was hard-wired to make money, realized that this project was a real money-maker," Nizhny Novgorod journalist Andrei Belyaninov said later.[8]

Klimentyev, who by that time had business in Norway, ended up having three roles in the project. He was a customer who ordered new ships, he was a partner of the factory—one of his Norwegian companies had the contract to prepare the documentation—and he was a co-owner of the plant after buying some shares. "Klimentyev told Nemtsov, 'Don't worry, Boris, it will all work out,'" Nemtsov's assistant Olga Smirnova recalled.[9] The new ship was envisioned as "universal"; that is, a ship that could be moored or repaired at any port in the world. The Navashino plant couldn't handle such a huge project, so the inner workings of the ship would be made abroad.

State financing was needed for this ambitious project. The Ministry of Finance gave Klimentyev a loan for imports with personal guarantees from Governor Nemtsov, who strongly supported Klimentyev. The total amount of the loan was $30 million, and the first tranche issued in 1994 was $18 million.

And then it all became "a confusing story", which is how Nizhny Novgorod businessmen usually describe what happened at Navashino. Klimentyev blames Nemtsov, who had become his worst enemy, and insists that Nemtsov put him behind bars because he was afraid of his—that is, Klimentyev's—growing popularity and ambitions. Outside observers have pointed out that the businessman and plant were never given a chance to carry out the project and, consequently, to repay the loan. It all happened too quickly: the loan was issued in early 1994, and a year later Nemtsov was already at war with Klimentyev. By early 1995, part of the first tranche had been spent on workers' salaries—the factory had already started building the ship's frame—and the other part, two million dollars, was on deposit in NBD Bank, which was formed with help from the regional government as part of a state programme to convert military industries to civilian uses. Nemtsov appointed his young assistant Boris Brevnov as chairman of the board of NBD Bank. This was a violation of the loan agreement. The factory was to receive and use the loan, but Nemtsov apparently did not completely trust Klimentyev from the start. "It was largely thanks to Brevnov that Nemtsov did not lose his career over this," Smirnova recalled. "Brevnov was like a watchdog."[10]

The scandal broke out after Klimentyev came to the bank to collect the money. "Klimentyev burst into Brevnov's office, shouting, 'Where's my money?' And for an hour he threatened him with 'What I'll do to you, and to him,' and 'Who the hell do you think you are?'" the entrepreneur Vladimir Sedov said. "Brevnov recorded the conversation and brought it immediately to Nemtsov."[11] Brevnov didn't give Klimentyev the funds. "It's true that there were irregularities on the bank's part,"

Nemtsov later said at a press conference. "But the money is safe, and that's the most important thing."[12]

The Ministry of Finance, citing misuse of funds, froze the second tranche of the loan, and the governor started looking into the matter. It turned out that no equipment had ever been delivered to the plant and the documentation for construction of the ships had not been prepared in Norway, as stipulated in the contract, but in Nizhny Novgorod. Later it turned out that Klimentyev had spent a part of the funds to repair his nightclub and open a new supermarket. Then it came to light that he had invested the money in his other projects, in order to repay the loan faster, which, given the high inflation at the time, was plausible. Shipbuilding is a low turnover business with a long production cycle. "We hadn't even got to the deadline for the loan repayment, and I was already in jail, and so was the director of the plant," Klimentyev complained later.[13] But the funds were earmarked, and Nemtsov came to the conclusion that Klimentyev had simply decided to steal the money.

When Nemtsov learnt that some of the money had disappeared, he called Klimentyev in to discuss it. He later described their conversation. "Did you take the money?" he asked.

"Yes."

"Are you going to pay it back?"

"No, I won't."

"Here's what you need to do: return the money by selling the casino, your stores and so on. I'll give you a week to do it. If you don't, I'll pass this on to the authorities."

"You won't go public with this because it will hurt you, too," Klimentyev replied.[14]

Klimentyev seems to have really believed Nemtsov would not dare to make this story public. "He thought that the inevitable media hype and threat to my reputation would make me keep quiet," Nemtsov later explained. "He didn't understand that if I had to choose between a scandal and decency, I'd choose the latter. The hell with the scandal so long as I wasn't a part of it!"[15]

In January 1995, there was, indeed, a big scandal. Nemtsov formed a commission to audit how the funds had been spent, but he was immediately attacked by his enemies. It was hard to understand who had stolen what from whom, and somehow Nemtsov was caught up in a corruption scam. Klimentyev announced that he was going into politics and accused Nemtsov of wanting to eliminate a strong rival. He even called on Vladimir Zhirinovsky, who had recently been openly hostile to Nemtsov, to be his ally.

## Orange juice

Nemtsov and Zhirinovsky had good reason not to like each other. They were both flamboyant public politicians who found it easy to talk to people. But they were ideological opposites. The conflict between them began in summer 1994, when Zhirinovsky, then at the height of his political influence, arrived in Nizhny Novgorod. Dissatisfied with the reception he received, he promised to arrest Nemtsov and then burst into the empty governor's office with his guards, where he made himself at home for two hours. A month later, when the president was travelling down the Volga, Yeltsin asked Nemtsov to get Zhirinovsky off his tail—his boat was trailing the presidential steamship. Nemtsov released water in one of the locks to ground the boat with Zhirinovsky and his entourage for four hours.

A year later, in June 1995, Zhirinovsky returned to Nizhny Novgorod and, in one of his speeches, declared in his characteristic manner that the region had the highest number of syphilis patients in the country. This enraged Nemtsov. He decided to challenge Zhirinovsky to a TV debate. He called his friend and colleague Alexander Lyubimov, who hosted a talk show on nationwide Channel One. "I told him it was a strange topic for discussion—syphilis," Lyubimov recalled. "It was a political talk show on a national channel. I didn't mind, but the topic had to be expanded. We needed to put it in some context. I then called Zhirinovsky, and he agreed."[16]

Neither Nemtsov, nor Zhirinovsky, nor Lyubimov expected that their on-air meeting would take place in tragic circumstances. On 14 June 1995, a large group of Chechen fighters led by Shamil Basayev stormed the town of Budyonnovsk in the south of Russia, 150 kilometres from the Chechen border. After killing several dozen civilians, the guerrillas seized more than 1,500 people and holed up in the city hospital. The Chechen war had suddenly spilt over into Russian territory. Stunned and horrified, the whole country sat before their television screens. This was the first terrorist act in modern Russian history.

The attack was part of the war effort in Chechnya. By the end of May, Dudayev was close to military defeat. The Chechen units had been pushed up into the mountains, and Dudayev was losing one outpost after another. On 4 June, Russian troops captured the mountain village where Dudayev's headquarters were located. On 13 June, two other key mountain strongholds were taken. Defeat was inevitable. Moscow had even announced that parliamentary elections would be held in Chechnya in the coming autumn. Dudayev either had to surrender or find another way to turn the war around.

Shamil Basayev decided on a large-scale hostage-taking operation. The first attempts to storm the Budyonnovsk hospital to release the hostages was a failure. The guerrillas fired back and threw hostages out the windows. Thirty-three people were killed, mostly hostages and a few special-forces soldiers. (In the end, 150 people were killed.) Then a group of State Duma deputies, headed by Sergei Kovalyov, reached Prime Minister Viktor Chernomyrdin, who was in charge while Yeltsin was on his way to the G7 Summit.

Kovalyov and other deputies immediately rushed to Budyonnovsk. For two days they made calls to Basayev and Moscow, trying to arrange negotiations and the release of the hostages. They finally secured an agreement for a telephone conversation between Chernomyrdin and Basayev on the night of 19 June. The Russian prime minister's telephone conversation with Russia's most dangerous terrorist began with a phrase that went down in modern Russian history: "Shamil Basayev, speak up." They eventually agreed that Basayev's unit would be allowed back into Chechnya in exchange for the release of the hostages, a ceasefire and the start of peace talks. After taking some volunteers from among the hostages and some parliamentarians and journalists as human shields, the terrorists returned to Chechnya in the buses provided by the federal side. At home they were welcomed as heroes. There they released the hostages they had taken with them and disappeared. The intervention of the deputies and Chernomyrdin prevented another attempt at storming the hospital and saved the lives of hundreds of Russian civilians. Dudayev's followers got a taste of victory and the much-needed respite that would change the course of the Chechen war.

The famous TV debate between Nemtsov and Zhirinovsky ended with a scene that became one of the symbols of Russia in the 1990s: Zhirinovsky threw orange juice in Nemtsov's face and Nemtsov flung it back at him. The broadcast took place on 18 June when the fate of the hostages in Budyonnovsk was still unclear. The attempt at storming the hospital had already failed, and Chernomyrdin had just got involved. Naturally, the main topic of discussion was the terrorist attack.

"Persuasion is useless. There has to be an assault. Nothing else will work," Zhirinovsky said.

"Guns must not be used when children are standing in the windows. If they storm the building, Basayev will survive but innocent people will die. Where did you get these misanthropic ideas?" Nemtsov retorted.

"Gangsters only understand the language of force," Zhirinovsky insisted.

"I'm certain we can still negotiate. We need to agree to everything. Why don't we use these opportunities? Why do we listen to the madmen?" Nemtsov replied, nodding at Zhirinovsky.

Nemtsov grew increasingly annoyed over the course of the show and didn't hide it. Zhirinovsky lost control. He brought up the Navashino millions: "Where are the millions of dollars sent to the region?" But then he clearly thought the syphilis story was the winning argument. "What have you done as governor? Besides syphilis and criminals, what else have you got? Diphtheria, what else?"

Nemtsov had been waiting for this. He took Yavlinsky's suggestion and pulled out an American Playboy magazine with an interview with Zhirinovsky.[17] In the interview, the politician, known for his flamboyance, appeared even more provocative. Afterwards the interviewer confessed that although she was not physically afraid during the conversation, Zhirinovsky "definitely crossed the line" by trying to persuade her and the translator to have group sex with his guards, saying he "would join later."[18]

The interview made a big splash and was widely circulated in the international press, since in spring 1995 the whole world considered

Zhirinovsky one of the main contenders for the Russian presidency. Zhirinovsky, realizing that he had said too much in the interview, tried to change the topic. But Nemtsov would not let him. After quoting the part of the interview where Zhirinovsky says that he had slept with more than two hundred women, Nemtsov said a phrase he'd prepared ahead of time: "We'll cure you. Just two injections and you'll be fine." Then Zhirinovsky lost his temper and threw orange juice at Nemtsov, and Nemtsov responded likewise.

Against the backdrop of the tragedy unfolding at the time, it was inappropriate and ridiculous. But that was what public politics were like at the time: candid, loud, rude and sometimes crude.

The show was a huge success. The TV channel reran the programme several times, and the story was picked up by other media around the world. "I was even recognized in Austria because of this programme," Nemtsov later recalled.[19]

Klimentyev went on the run after the criminal case and the arrest of the Navashino shipyard director. He was detained in late October in Tashkent, Uzbekistan. Two days later he was sitting in a Nizhny Novgorod detention centre, threatening Nemtsov with more revelations. This did not bode well for Nemtsov. He was running for governor and did not need a public scandal.

## Political heavyweight

Who would give up their political power voluntarily? The first gubernatorial elections in Russia should have been held in 1991. But like all the other elections, they were first postponed for a year in order to carry out reforms. Then everyone was too busy with everything else: the standoff with the Supreme Soviet, then parliamentary elections that they lost, then the war in Chechnya. Given all this, the Yeltsin administration was understandably reluctant to open up yet another frontline in the political battle. Elections were held for some leaders of the national republics within Russia, such as Tatarstan, or in some cases as an exception. "Since we were in a political civil war, it would have been fatal to lose the right to appoint governors. It was clear that the 'reds' would win, and we'd all be in big trouble," Anatoly Chubais, then the first deputy prime minister in the cabinet, later described his position at the time.[20] This was also the reasoning in the Kremlin.

In the end, they postponed the planned shift from appointed positions to elections until 1996, when both parliamentary and presidential elections were to be held. But that plan failed thanks to the efforts of two regional leaders. "When I was still in the cabinet," Chubais recalled, "there were two troublesome governors who proposed abolishing appointments and introducing elections. One was Boris Nemtsov; the other was Eduard Rossel. I did everything in my power to stifle their initiative. I lost and Boris won."[21]

By that time, Eduard Rossel, who was governor of Yekaterinburg, the capital of Sverdlovsk region, had already paid the price for his ambitions. In 1993, when Yeltsin was battling with the Supreme Soviet and making concessions to the national republics, Rossel established the Urals Republic. It had its own constitution and national emblem. But when Yeltsin defeated the Supreme Soviet, there was no reason for him to tolerate this kind of separatism. Rossel was sacked and his republic was abolished.

But Rossel did not abandon his ambitious plans. In the spring of 1995, the regional parliament he led announced summer gubernatorial elections. Although the Kremlin was against them, Rossel had appealed to the Constitutional Court. His assistant, Alexander Levin, recalled later that when the chairman of the Constitutional Court, Vladimir Tumanov, saw the appeal, he called Yeltsin. "He said that he had studied the case of the Sverdlovsk regional gubernatorial elections and concluded that Rossel was absolutely right. For that reason, it shouldn't be brought to trial—the president would lose, and it would be embarrassing. Yeltsin heard all this and was silent for a long time. Then he asked Tumanov what he should do in the situation. 'Let them hold the elections,' Tumanov replied bluntly. That was the end of the conversation."[22]

Nemtsov had always been in favour of gubernatorial elections. He strongly objected in September 1994 when Yeltsin used a decree to postpone again the transition to direct elections of regional leaders and local parliaments. Yeltsin issued the decree even though a month earlier, on a trip to Nizhny Novgorod, he had promised that the region could choose its own governor. "This is a decree to create all-powerful governors, with one caveat: they are all appointed and removed by the president," Nemtsov said indignantly. "This is nuts! The fate of the entire nation cannot depend on one person!"[23]

Nemtsov had a personal interest in holding local elections. Yeltsin's rating was falling steadily, and, in late 1994–early 1995, it was impossible to predict who would win the next presidential elections. Nemtsov was popular and could count on support in his region. But he also believed that the transition to direct local elections at all levels would finally put an end to the Soviet past and make Russia a democratic country. "The inevitability of elections should always be hanging over the government along with the certainty that a politician's actions would be under the spotlight during the campaigns," Nemtsov said at the time. Local authorities should be accountable to the people, and that is only possible when they are elected. Besides, electing governors is a key element of stability in Russia, especially in the run-up to unpredictable political changes. What if a new president is elected and removes everyone from office? "To some extent the election of governors creates a system of security in our country and ensures smooth economic, political and social development."[24]

In the spring of 1995, a paragraph on the elections of all officials was added to the Nizhny Novgorod regional charter, and Nizhny Novgorod became the next region after Sverdlovsk where the president permitted gubernatorial elections by decree. By autumn, there would be fifteen such regions. Elections were scheduled to be held in parallel with the parliamentary elections in December.

Two months before the election, the press had no doubt that Nemtsov would win easily. That said, not everyone was happy with Nemtsov; only about fifty per cent of the region gave him a positive rating. The scandals of the past two years, disillusionment with reforms, poverty—prices had doubled in 1995 alone—and a growing nostalgia for the Soviet past were working against him.

But Nemtsov held a hand of trump cards. First, he was well-known nationwide and was increasingly talked about as the successor to Yeltsin. By the summer of 1995, the only regional political figure with higher ratings was Moscow's mayor, Yury Luzhkov. Second, he was young, sociable, charming and had his trademark self-confidence. And since Nemtsov had always been independent and never hesitated to argue with either Yeltsin or the cabinet, his rating was not directly affected by their failures. Third, Nemtsov was in power, and the incumbent always has an electoral advantage. The regional administrative machine worked for Nemtsov, and he could take credit for all the achievements in social policy—from housing for the military to regional pension supplements and greater access to telephone lines in people's homes. In television commercials, Nemtsov was portrayed as a man for everyone, an influential governor who would help defrauded investors and defend the interests of the people.

To some extent Nemtsov was just lucky. The Communists, led by Gennady Zyuganov, were quickly becoming a stronger political force, but they were busy with parliamentary elections and not looking for a strong candidate to run against him. As *Kommersant* wrote before the election, the search for a single opposition candidate had "failed to yield any noticeable results so far."[25]

Vyacheslav Rasteryayev, a businessman who headed a construction company, was the strongest candidate running against Nemtsov. One of the so-called "red directors" who had headed the Gorky Water and Sanitation Authority during the Soviet period and was now a very wealthy man, Rasteryayev was one of the breed of experienced old-school managers who were gradually beginning to dominate Russian politics. He considered Nemtsov a cipher who had obtained status and power by chance. He was supported by the anti-Nemtsov front among the heads of industry and sympathized with the Communists. During the election campaign, Rasteryayev harshly criticized Nemtsov as an upstart and dilettante and advocated for an end to regional payments to the federal budget.

But the Nemtsov coalition was more powerful, in part due to the support of local industrialists and entrepreneurs. He did everything to win, campaigning all over the region down to the last village. People gave him a hard time at campaign rallies in depressed areas, but he always had the women's vote and the majority of votes in urban areas.

Nemtsov won the election by an impressive margin, winning the first round with more than fifty-eight per cent of the vote. As political analysts Gelman and Rivera have noted, Nemtsov was perhaps the only regional leader who did not come from the Soviet *nomenklatura* and still managed to win a competitive gubernatorial election during a deep economic recession.[26] Nemtsov's result was particularly impressive against the backdrop of another demoralizing defeat for the Kremlin. This time, the Communists led by Zyuganov triumphed in the parliamentary elections, taking more than twice the votes given to the pro-Kremlin Our Home Is Russia bloc led by Prime Minister Chernomyrdin. The Democratic Choice of Russia reform party led by Yegor Gaidar did not pass the five-per-cent threshold required to get into the Duma.

Nemtsov had become a political heavyweight. He insisted that he had a programme of action, that he'd just been elected for a second term in office and would stay in Nizhny Novgorod. But the doors to big-league politics had swung open before him.

## A million signatures against the war

By January 1996, the situation in Chechnya was changing dramatically. The truce that the military and Dudayev had agreed to after the attack on Budyonnovsk had held up for only a couple of months. In October 1995, there was an assassination attempt on Anatoly Romanov, the commander of the United Group of Russian Federal Forces, when he was on his way to negotiate a peace settlement with Aslan Maskhadov. Soon fighting flared up again. Since December, Dudayev's forces had again taken one village after another, showing Russia and the whole world that the Russian troops were not in control of the republic. They even stormed and held Gudermes, the second largest city in Chechnya, for more than a week, inflicting huge losses on the federal forces. Coffins began to arrive back in Russia again; civilians in Chechnya were being killed in bombing raids; and in Moscow officials and military commanders did not know what to do next. A year had passed since the war began, but there was no end in sight.

In January 1996, Salman Raduyev, Dudayev's relative and close military associate, led a large group of men in an attack on the

Dagestani town of Kizlyar near the Chechen border. Like Basayev in Budyonnovsk, he seized a hospital and more than 1,500 hostages. This time federal troops closed the road to buses with terrorists and hostages, but Raduyev attacked the border village of Pervomaiskoye and turned it into a combat stronghold from which he was able to break through encirclement. Several dozen fighters escaped into Chechnya.

Once again, the Russian security forces demonstrated their helplessness. The general sense of humiliation was compounded when Yeltsin gave his version of how special forces stormed Raduyev's entrenched forces in Pervomaiskoye.

"We have thirty-eight snipers there, and each sniper has his own target. He watches the target all the time. When the target moves, he follows him with his eyes. Constantly."[27] Yeltsin demonstrated before the cameras, turning his body like a sniper. But anyone watching realized that Yeltsin clearly had no idea what was going on.

The hostage-taking in Kizlyar brought Chechnya back into the international spotlight. Meanwhile, the presidential election was about to be held, and it was already becoming clear that the key issue for voters was how and when the war would end. Both the military and the executive branch were harshly criticized in parliament. On 12 January, when the security forces were already negotiating with Raduyev in Pervomaiskoye, Yavlinsky sent the president his peace plan: release of hostages, peace talks, troop withdrawal and an internal Chechen referendum on the status of Chechnya. At about the same time, Nemtsov wrote an open letter to the president.

If Nemtsov had been appointed rather than elected governor, he might not have decided to do what he'd been thinking about for months: collect signatures from Nizhny Novgorod residents on an appeal to end the war. But now Nemtsov had his own legitimacy, and he decided to do it. "There was freedom," Nemtsov recalled, "I could have spoken out against the war publicly, even on central television. Yeltsin would have tolerated it. But I thought we should do it differently, with the help of the people, because, if people are protesting, we need to make their voices heard."[28] In his address to the president, Nemtsov did not propose specific mechanisms or actions to resolve the conflict. It was an appeal:

Blood has been shed and people have died in Chechnya for many months on end. For many months, like an open wound, Chechnya has been hurting all of Russia, which is losing its sons. In our region alone, forty-three families have already been touched by the pain of loss, but that is not yet a full count. The merciless hammer of war demands new victims. The repetition of the Budyonnovsk tragedy in Kizlyar is shameful evidence that we are all becoming hostages to an uncompromising military confrontation. Violence generated by violence only triggers rampant terrorism and barbarism. The bloodshed must be stopped. Without this, there can be no cessation of hostilities and no stable peace. We call on you, Mr President, to make every effort and take every measure to put an end to military action on both sides, for the lives of your fellow citizens and the honour of your country are more valuable. Let the starting point of the Chechen pacification be the last shot in this disastrous war for Russia.[29]

Without administrative support it would have been impossible to gather a million signatures in ten days. But even with that support it was a feat to collect such an enormous number of signatures in record time. Nemtsov described it as a civic movement: the press printed the signature sheets, people filled them out and sent them back to the media, volunteers went door-to-door and collected signatures on the street. "People really supported the idea of getting signatures," said Stanislav Dmitriyevsky. "Nobody forced anyone. The majority of residents wanted the war to end."[30]

On 29 January, hundreds of folders of signature sheets were loaded onto a truck and driven to the Spassky Tower of the Kremlin. Nemtsov went to see the president, carrying one of the many signature folders and a certificate from the regional archive certifying the number of signatures accepted for deposit. It was a political gesture that grabbed everyone's attention, perhaps the first of its kind in Nemtsov's career. Experimenting with reforms in one's own region was one thing, but it was another to intervene publicly in a national problem that the authorities seemed incapable of solving. If he had been able to collect signatures across the country instead of just in his region, he would have brought not a million, but forty million, Nemtsov told Yeltsin. "Yeltsin was shocked. 'I have one question for you: are these signatures for me or against me?' I replied: 'It depends on what you do. If you stop the war in Chechnya, then they are for you, if not, then they are against you.'"[31]

Nemtsov told other governors that thirty million signatures was a realistic number of signatures and urged them to continue his initiative. This would surely end the war. Before an election, it would have been impossible to ignore this kind of protest. Nemtsov was probably right, and more signatures could have been collected. As he said on television on the day of his meeting with Yeltsin, "The situation is very similar to the mid-1980s, when literally everyone hated the war in Afghanistan."[32]

Stopping the war, of course, did not mean solving the dire problem that Chechnya had become, and Nemtsov's appeal did not contain a recipe for its solution. No one had one at the time. The plan proposed by Nemtsov, Yavlinsky and other democratic politicians was to negotiate and withdraw in stages. The appeal to Yeltsin truly reflected the whole country's question: when would it end? The issue was less political than moral. As sociologists noted, "Not only did the war in Chechnya go against the democratic beliefs of Russians that were formed during the years of *perestroika* and Yeltsin's reforms, but also it was perceived by ordinary Russians as immoral. In spring 1996, Russians were saying, 'Our children are dying there'; 'mafia groups are fighting for territory'; 'generals are good for nothing.'"[33] Russian society was in total agreement: eighty-four per cent of Russian citizens agreed that "the Chechen problem" was the most important or one of the most important issues.[34] Nemtsov simply put the general feelings and thoughts of Russian citizens into a visual form. Not everyone was supportive. "You're young, curly-haired and stupid," one of Nemtsov's acquaintances, the famous film director Nikita Mikhalkov, said. "In Russian history, there has never been a single instance of a governor telling the tsar that he is fighting the wrong war. On the contrary, governors have always been subservient to their superiors. Then you show up and start throwing your weight around."[35]

Yeltsin was so fond of Nemtsov that he forgave him for the signatures. "He was thrown by it, but not irritated," Nemtsov said. "He suddenly realized how important the issue was."[36] But the Kremlin is a huge bureaucratic system, and Nemtsov's démarche could not go without consequences. "I think there's a lot of dissatisfaction in the president's inner circle," Nemtsov said on the day he met with Yeltsin.[37] The presidential election was coming up, Russia was aiming to join the G7, and suddenly there's the governor of Nizhny Novgorod with a million signatures against the war. "Of course, it was a blow," said Emil Pain, then a presidential adviser, who in late February 1996 chaired a working group to resolve the situation in Chechnya.[38] Korzhakov, the influential head of Yeltsin's security detail, even claimed later that Nemtsov had been crossed off the list of successors after that story. It was an exaggeration, but it showed that Nemtsov's gesture irritated many in the Kremlin, including Korzhakov.

After the signature incident, Nemtsov no longer received help from Moscow and had his direct phone line to the president cut off. "A man came from FAPSI [the Russian acronym for the Federal Communication Agency]," Nemtsov recalled later, "He pulled the plug of the special switchboard out of the socket and took the machine away."[39]

But relations with Yeltsin did not deteriorate. At a meeting in the Kremlin, the president said that he would go to Chechnya in person. Nemtsov asked to go along, and soon an opportunity presented itself.

## How to end the war in Chechnya

Yury Kudryavtsev, the chief designer at GAZ who had played a key role in the development of the famous Gazelle, was highly respected in Nizhny Novgorod. When he asked Vitaly Potapov, head of the regional police, to accept his youngest son Alexander in the elite police department for combating organized crime, Potapov strongly objected at first—the work was dangerous. But Kudryavtsev insisted, and Potapov could not refuse him. Soon, Senior Lieutenant Alexander Kudryavtsev, along with other officers of the Nizhny Novgorod Police Rapid Deployment Task Force (Russian abbreviation SOBR), went on a business trip to Chechnya. Ten days before the end of his mission, on 7 March 1996, there was a knock at the Kudryavtsev family's door. When Vera, Kudryavtsev's wife, saw Nikolai Pugin, the plant's director, she was delighted; she thought he'd come to wish her a happy Women's Day (8 March). Then two men in police uniforms appeared in the doorway:

Potapov and Ivan Kladnitsky, head of the Regional Organized Crime Unit. When she saw them, Vera knew what had happened. They barely had time to grab her before she fell to the floor in a faint.[40]

The war was raging once again. On the morning of 6 March, Dudayev's troops attacked Grozny. One group was led by Basayev. The Chechens marched into the city from three sides simultaneously, swiftly reaching the centre and blockading the Russian troops located there. The Nizhny Novgorod SOBR unit was in another part of the city. "The Kurgan soldiers came under fire," Ivan Kladnitsky recalled. "Many of the Perm units that came to their rescue were killed, so the troops from Nizhny Novgorod came to their aid."[41] When the detachment entered the square, the trap was sprung. Without support from tanks and helicopters, the Russian police units were doomed. They were fired on by grenade launchers and flamethrowers. The army did not arrive until evening, and its arrival only resulted in massive civilian casualties. The police units suffered thirty-seven casualties that day. Among the dead were Alexander Kudryavtsev and nine other men from Nizhny Novgorod.

Nizhny Novgorod was plunged into mourning. No building was large enough for the funeral ceremonies, so the coffins were placed on the central square for people to pay their respects. On 12 March, the sombre ceremony turned into a powerful anti-war rally, unlike anything the city had seen for several years. More than 100,000 people went to the square. On an improvised podium Nemtsov spoke to the crowd, saying that it seemed like Boris Yeltsin was surrounded by a wall of people who didn't want him to know what the citizens thought. "We have to force our leaders to end this war," he continued. "Yes, many people now want revenge, especially men in SOBR and OMON [the Special Purposes Mobile Unit, often used in crowd control]. But with the kind of commanders who are in charge in Chechnya, we're going to lose even more men. Dudayev's gangsters must be punished, but also the men who have led our most talented, most courageous, most valiant fellow countrymen to mass extermination."[42]

Dudayev's men captured Grozny easily, but they didn't hold it. Three days later they marched out of the city, just as calmly, taking dozens of civilians with them. The attack on Grozny was intended to demonstrate Dudayev's strength and the simple fact that no matter how long Russian troops had fought in Chechnya, they still did not control a single inch of Chechen land.

For the Chechens, the situation in spring 1996 was drastically different from that in May–June 1995, when Dudayev was defeated. Over the past year, his commanders had grown stronger, set up bases in the mountains, replenished arsenals and learnt the rules of semi-guerrilla warfare. The swift attack on Grozny proved that there were only two ways of stopping the war: by exterminating the entire republic or by withdrawing troops under certain conditions.

Yeltsin had no choice. If he wanted to be re-elected, he had to show that he had a plan for peace. Back in mid-February, when he was running for president, he admitted that the war in Chechnya had been a mistake and promised to end it soon. "In the near future, a path to a peace settlement will be found," he said in an address to the Federal Assembly. "We are ready for compromises on the issue of Chechnya's status within Russia, but not at the expense of the security of our citizens."[43] A working group headed by Emil Pain was even created to resolve the conflict in Chechnya. By mid-April there seemed to be a glimmer of hope. "Despite the continuing clashes in various parts of Chechnya, the prospect of renewed negotiations between Moscow and supporters of Dudayev is becoming increasingly realistic," wrote *Kommersant*.[44]

The prospect of negotiations became even more realistic after the assassination of Dzhokhar Dudayev. On 21 April, his car was hit by a homing missile while he was driving in a Chechen village and talking on his satellite phone. As Anatol Lieven wrote, Moscow's single definitive success during the war was that the "ruthless murder of Dudayev really did contribute to subsequent peace in Chechnya." The Chechen president, who was fundamentally incapable of compromise, would not have signed any agreements.[45] Besides, it was impossible to imagine Yeltsin sitting at the same table as Dudayev.

But negotiations with Moscow were very useful for Dudayev's replacement, Zelimkhan Yandarbiyev, the mediocre poet and nationalist who called Dudayev to the Chechen People's Congress in November 1990 and then became his right-hand man. Sitting down at the negotiating table with Yeltsin would dramatically raise his status among Chechens.

The talks between Yeltsin and Yandarbiyev in the Kremlin on 27 May 1996 went down in history partly as an example of Yeltsin's amazing flexibility, his ability to adapt to a situation and quickly change his plan. Yeltsin biographer Boris Minayev wrote that the plan had been for Yeltsin to enter the conference room last and sit at the head of the table, at which the two delegations, Chechen and Russian, were already sitting opposite each other. This way Prime Minister Chernomyrdin, who was sitting opposite Yandarbiyev, would be the negotiator for the Russian side and the president would seem to be receiving both of them.[46] But Yandarbiyev's plane was two hours late and the scenario fell apart: Yeltsin, Chernomyrdin and the rest of the Russian delegation entered the hall together. Archival video footage clearly shows Yeltsin in a harsh tone offering—indeed ordering—Yandarbiyev to take the seat prepared for him, but Yandarbiyev refuses: no, they must sit as equals.

"We're not equals," Yeltsin said as he sat at the head of the table. "Sit down!"

Yandarbiyev stood across from him. "Boris Nikolayevich, I'm not going to sit when you use that tone of voice with me."

"It's a normal tone of voice," Yeltsin said. "Be seated."

"Let's talk one-on-one."

"No, we aren't going to talk one-on-one."

Yandarbiyev moved towards the exit. Yeltsin said: "You are not leaving here."

Their dialogue carried on for several minutes.

"There is a document that must be signed, and it will be signed today," Yeltsin said.

"If we don't come to an agreement, no document will be signed," Yandarbiyev said, shrugging.

"What do you mean? We must stop the bloodshed. Enough is enough. We've fought enough. We fought enough."

At that moment Yeltsin suddenly complied with Yandarbiyev's demand and moved from the end of the table to the middle, and the ceasefire was signed. Yeltsin's sudden move to meet his opponent halfway was intentional. He needed to get Yandarbiyev's signature on the document at any cost. The next day he flew to Chechnya.

## The dove of peace

A few days before Yandarbiyev arrived in Moscow, the system for direct communication with Yeltsin was reinstalled in Nemtsov's office. "A man from FAPSI came again, brought the machine and plugged it into the socket. Five minutes later the phone rang, and Yeltsin asked, 'You're the dove of peace, aren't you? Will you come with me to Chechnya and make peace?'"[47]

Yandarbiyev and his team remained in Moscow to discuss details of the agreement signed the day before in the Kremlin. Although they stayed voluntarily, they were virtually hostages. From the point of view of propaganda, Yeltsin's sudden trip to Chechnya was a winning move. It made the negotiations in the Kremlin seem less humiliating.

Nemtsov liked to talk about the trip afterwards. First, it was an adventure to fly to Chechnya with the president. Second, and most importantly, it was a political victory. Yeltsin had taken him along as a recognized peacemaker. "He wanted to emphasize that he came in peace," Nemtsov later explained, "and I was popular in Chechnya because everyone knew that I had advocated putting an end to the war."[48]

Nemtsov was a useful ally for Yeltsin. On the one hand, he was against the war and sharply critical of the Moscow leadership, while on the other, no one could suspect him of being sympathetic to Dudayev and his commanders. "At the time, people against the war had different agendas," Emil Pain later recalled. He had been on the same flight with Yeltsin. "The notion of Russian interests was important to Nemtsov. He was not a radical. He was a liberal statesman."[49]

The flight was scheduled for 9.00 a.m. At 8.30 a.m. Nemtsov was on the runway when the first curious incident of the long day happened. Korzhakov, head of Yeltsin's security detail, and Mikhail Barsukov, director of the FSB, asked him to talk Yeltsin out of taking the trip. An agent had reported that Shamil Basayev was preparing an assassination attempt on Yeltsin. "Korzhakov says to me, 'Can you show the report to him?' I say, 'Why don't you show it to him—you're the head of security.' He says, 'He doesn't listen to us, but you're the favourite, the successor. You show him.'"[50]

The presidential motorcade pulled up to the runway at five minutes to nine o'clock. When Yeltsin asked why they weren't on the plane, Nemtsov showed him the document. "I said, 'Here's why.' He takes it, reads it and looks at me. 'Are you chickening out?' I say, 'How can you say that? We agreed to go.' He points at Korzhakov and Barsukov. 'Aha! They're the ones chickening out. Well, then. You get on the plane and these cowards can stay behind.'"[51]

In the end, the presidential plane landed in the town of Mozdok on the border with Chechnya, and from there eight identical helicopters—another precautionary measure—flew into Chechnya. They didn't go to Grozny. They made two stops near the capital and spoke to the Russian troops. "The war is over. You have defeated the insurgents. You have destroyed the gangs, although there are still a few running around." Yeltsin chose each word carefully. "But yesterday in Moscow I saw Yandarbiyev sign everything—a cessation of all military operations."[52] Right there, on a tank, the president signed an order to demobilize early troops who served in hot spots and a decree that would reduce the term of service to a year and a half by the year 2000.

Nemtsov was happy. His policy had succeeded. He was witnessing the president ending the war. "Nemtsov admired this bold operation," Pain recalled. "He grinned and nodded to the men around him and said, 'Now that's a tsar!'"[53] Nemtsov was often taken to task for his habit of calling Yeltsin tsar, but he wasn't being subservient. He would remind people that the 1993 constitution gave the president *de facto* tsarist powers.

No one really believed that the decree to shorten the period of military service and transition to a contract system that Yeltsin announced then would work. But many people wanted to believe that the war had ended in victory, albeit on points instead of a knockdown, as it were. "I was sure that I was standing at the dawning of a tremendously important historical event," Emil Pain recalled. "There hadn't been such a favourable situation for ending a war in a long time."[54]

In May federal forces occupied several Chechen villages. The mountain village of Bamut, the only Chechen resistance stronghold that had survived until spring 1995, was captured after fierce fighting with heavy casualties. When it was over, the military leaders reported a "radical change in the military situation."[55] Yandarbiyev's subsequent visit to Moscow also inspired optimism: since he went to Moscow, it meant he had to. In a few days, the new status quo would be confirmed by the agreements signed in Nazran, the capital of Ingushetia: the withdrawal of forces and the disarmament of Chechen detachments, a prisoner exchange, and free elections in the near future. As Yeltsin said when he flew to Chechnya, "The Chechen republic will be given maximum independence."

In the run-up to elections, Yeltsin needed a peace-treaty-like air.

But even if the war was stopped for reasons other than purely electoral considerations, could the Nazran peace agreement, which slightly favoured Moscow, hold? History would soon answer that question: no. "The people who did the negotiations had already poked holes in their lapels for the Nobel Peace Prize," said human-rights activist Alexander Cherkasov. "And suddenly, literally on the day after the results of the second round of the presidential elections were announced, on the tenth or eleventh of July 1996, the villages of Gekhi and Makhkety were shelled, and the entire peace process ground to a halt."[56] Intense fighting broke out, and aviation and artillery once again bombed Chechen villages. In response, bombs exploded in Moscow trolleybuses, and Yandarbiyev declared war until victory. The fragile peace collapsed within days.

On 6 August, the people of Grozny awoke again to a cannonade of grenade-launchers: Chechen units had re-entered the city just as they had done five months earlier. And once again it was a military disaster. Fighting went on for days, hundreds of Russian soldiers were killed, and the civilian population suffered heavy casualties from the shelling.

But this battle for Grozny was the last. Alexander Lebed, the same general who had helped Yeltsin in August 1991, signed a peace agreement with Aslan Maskhadov in the Dagestani border village of Khasavyurt on 30 August. This time the war really did come to an end. In fact, the Russian army surrendered. "From a purely military point of view, Russia capitulated," *Kommersant* wrote after the event. "From the human point of view, it has stopped the senseless bloodshed that has claimed over thirty thousand lives. Politically, it has brought the situation back to the pre-war status of November 1994."[57] So what had been achieved? What had they gained at the cost of tens of thousands of lives?

Later, the generals and others would accuse Lebed of betrayal. They believed the militants could have been driven out of Grozny again. "Lebed wanted the momentary glory of being a peacekeeper," recalled General Gennady Troshev, who commanded the Russian group in Chechnya at the time and was outraged by Lebed's behaviour. "It was like he was saying, 'No one has been able to solve the problem of Chechnya for almost two years, but I can do it.'"[58]

The Khasavyurt peace deal was made after the presidential election. For the sake of victory in the second round, Yeltsin made a deal with the popular General Lebed, who had run for president, too, and had taken third place in the first round. Lebed supported Yeltsin, was appointed secretary of the Security Council and began to try on the laurels of the victor in the Chechen war. Yeltsin was completely worn out, and Lebed hoped that he might soon replace him. Right after the election, Lebed sanctioned a resumption of hostilities, hoping for a spectacular blitzkrieg. But when he saw it would fail, he was just as quick to refashion himself as a peacekeeper.

The truth was that Russia had lost the war—militarily, first of all—although in August 1996 many generals lacked the courage to admit it. Both the army and Russian society were demoralized by the endless horror of war. They had lost the will to continue. It had to end. The political mistakes made in the autumn of 1994 would not only be measured in human lives. In three years, the sense of national humiliation from defeat in the war would determine to a large extent the future course of Russian history.

But the attack on Grozny and the Khasavyurt peace deal would take place in August. Weeks earlier, on 29 May, Yeltsin, Nemtsov and the *siloviki*, as well as Yeltsin's aides and entourage, celebrated the victorious end of the war at a military base on the outskirts of Grozny. The president's first and only visit to war-torn Chechnya was a success. Vodka and refreshments were on the table, and toast after toast was raised. Nemtsov liked to describe their flight back to Moscow.

> We were sitting [on the plane], and Yeltsin suddenly says, "Well now, we should celebrate our successful trip." I look around the cabin of the presidential plane and see that by each seat is a 0.75-litre

bottle of Yury Dolgoruky vodka and snacks to wash it down—the usual Soviet assortment of meat and fish appetizers. Yeltsin says, "I don't want to make you uncomfortable, so I'll propose two toasts. Toast number one is to Russia, and toast number two is to the president. You don't have to drink if you don't want to. I'll just announce 'toast number one' or 'toast number two.'" By the time we arrive at Vnukovo Airport in Moscow, I was seeing two presidents, everything was blurry, and I couldn't think straight or stand up.[59]

When the presidential plane landed, Yeltsin suddenly sent the drunken Nemtsov to the Ostankino television centre to talk about the trip on the news. Nemtsov tried to object that he wasn't sober and in no condition to speak on live TV. But Yeltsin wouldn't listen to him. In the dressing room at Ostankino, the television crew tried to bring Nemtsov to his senses, dunking his head in a sink filled with ice water. On air, he tried to keep it together, but his mother said later that he looked unwell.

After the broadcast, Nemtsov returned to Nizhny Novgorod. At six o'clock in the morning, the phone rang again.

It wakes me up. Furious, I pick up the phone and hear the steely voice of the Kremlin telephone operator: "The president of the Russian Federation, Boris Yeltsin, will speak to you." I wondered, "What's this all about?" I hear a voice I'd know anywhere. "I saw you on television yesterday. Good morning. You didn't look too bad." I asked, "Why did you send me there?" "Don't you remember what you said when I didn't get off the plane at the Shannon Airport? Should I remind you?" "Yes, I remember what I said." "Tell me what you said." "I said that you might sleep through Russia, too." "Yes, that's what you said, so I decided to see how you handled it. You didn't look too bad!"[60]

In late May 1996, Yeltsin could afford to laugh and make fun of his favourite. He was on the road to the election, and, now that he had made peace in Chechnya, he had a chance of winning.

# CHAPTER 11

## 1996
## Communism or Democracy

### Gaidar looks for a successor

The start of 1996 found Yegor Gaidar in poor spirits. He had left the government long ago, but now his entire life's work was about to be destroyed. In the December parliamentary elections, his party hadn't even cleared the five-per-cent threshold and was not represented in the Duma. But the real disaster lay ahead: victory of the Communists in the June presidential election seemed inevitable. The unexpectedly strong success in the parliamentary election boded well for Communist Party leader Gennady Zyuganov.

Gaidar had finally decided to break with Yeltsin. While this had few practical ramifications, it was a powerful symbolic gesture. Gaidar—Yeltsin's political partner, the man with whom he began to carry out market reforms in autumn 1991—was severing relations. Gaidar explained that the democrats had lost the battle for Yeltsin, and it was time to put the relationship behind them. "To be frank, the president of 1991 and the president of 1996 are two very different people. There was a huge struggle for these two different Yeltsins. I thought I should stay in the battle for as long as there was a chance of keeping the 1991 Yeltsin. Now there is no hope of that."[1]

Everyone knew what Gaidar meant. Even physically, the current Yeltsin bore little resemblance to the Yeltsin who won the election in 1990 and stood on a tank in August 1991. His face was wrinkled and puffy, his movements were stiff, and there was deep fatigue in his eyes and posture.

He could not point to any unqualified success. It was a free society, and Russia had leapt from socialism to capitalism, but it wasn't the capitalism people had dreamt of five years ago. There was no miracle. Worn out by poverty, society became increasingly irritated as citizens watched more enterprising people amass their first large capital. Corruption was everywhere. The government was a collection of disparate lobbying groups, Yeltsin appeared and disappeared from view, the *siloviki* set the tone in the Kremlin, and the influence of the head of the presidential security team, Alexander Korzhakov, had reached unprecedented levels.

Democrats had moved away from Yeltsin when the war in Chechnya began. In January 1996, the last major figures in the liberal camp left government service. Yeltsin dismissed his longtime ally Sergei Filatov as head of the Presidential Administration and replaced the pro-Western foreign minister, Andrei Kozyrev, with the Soviet-era functionary Yevgeny Primakov. Finally, the first deputy prime minister, Anatoly Chubais, whose name in the past two years had been associated with privatization and the course of reform in Russia, had been dismissed.\*
The hostage crisis in Kizlyar and the events in Pervomaiskoye were the last straw for Gaidar. The incompetent and helpless security services and Yeltsin's disjointed comments about the thirty-eight snipers were, as he put it later, "the culmination of Yeltsin's crisis of authority."[2]

Yeltsin was preparing to run for president again. He already had a campaign staff headed by Oleg Soskovets, the first deputy prime minister in charge of industry, an old-school official and minister for metallurgy under Gorbachev. But no one thought Yeltsin could be re-elected with a rating hovering around the five-per-cent mark. So, he began to reshuffle the government, getting rid of the "ballast" that the voters didn't like.

Gaidar searched for a way out of the situation. Yeltsin's decision to go to the polls, he explained, would be a gift to the Communists and make it impossible for the various democratic-leaning parties to nominate a candidate.

---

\* When Yeltsin dismissed Chubais, he even blamed him for the parliamentary election he had just lost. He believed that if Chubais hadn't been in government, the Our Home Is Russia party, headed by Prime Minister Chernomyrdin, would have won twice as many seats. This was the source of the memes and expression "Blame it on Chubais."

But who could defeat Zyuganov in 1996? The first option, Chernomyrdin, was immediately dropped. The prime minister, experienced in the ways of power, understood perfectly well that getting in the president's way was not the thing to do.

Gaidar and his fellow party members immediately thought of Grigory Yavlinsky, the most prominent figure in the democratic wing at the time. But Yavlinsky already had a reputation as being a hard man to come to an agreement with. Before the parliamentary elections, Gaidar and Yavlinsky seemed to have found a way to work together even though Yavlinsky had been a constant critic of Gaidar's reforms. They agreed that their parties would run as one bloc, and that Yavlinsky would run for president as the joint candidate from the democratic opposition. But the next day Yavlinsky changed his mind, and the deal collapsed.[3]

In the end, Gaidar's camp came up with the idea of nominating Nemtsov for president and offering Yavlinsky the opportunity to run with him as the future prime minister. "Nemtsov combines two qualities: he's a politician with practical experience, and he hasn't done anything wrong. This is almost a unique case: there is no other politician like him," Gaidar said.[4] But this was utopia: Yavlinsky went to the polls on his own and did not plan to make way for anyone else. Nemtsov already had presidential ambitions—he was, after all, Yeltsin's favourite to be his successor. He decided to test the waters for a possible nomination at a private meeting with Yeltsin. On 29 January, as he handed the president the signatures he had collected against the war in Chechnya, Nemtsov also gently tried to convince him that he should not run again for president. Alfred Kokh later recalled, "He told Yeltsin, 'The entire democratic community asked me to talk to you.' Yeltsin asked: 'About what?' Nemtsov said, 'About your very low rating. You have a six-per-cent rating.' Yeltsin said, 'That's a lie invented by enemies of Russia. I have a sixty-per-cent rating.' To which Nemtsov said, 'Where did you get that from?' Yeltsin replied, 'Here's the FAPSI poll.* I have a sixty-per-cent rating.'"[5]

---

\* FAPSI was a Kremlin secret service that had been engaged in media analysis and its own sociological surveys ever since the early 1990s. Its functions were later transferred to the FSB.

The topic was closed. It was impossible to dissuade Yeltsin. Nemtsov hurriedly stated that he had no plans to run and had not given his consent to be nominated. And on 15 February, Yeltsin arrived in his hometown of Yekaterinburg. "I am confident that I can lead the country through turmoil, anxiety and uncertainty." Yeltsin's hoarse voice broke into a falsetto. "And so, I've decided to run for president of Russia."[6]

## The birth of the oligarchs

In the mid-1990s, the bleak Soviet era was still fresh in everyone's mind. Only six or seven years had passed since the first private cafés, car dealerships, computer resale companies and cooperatives that produced "boiled" jeans had appeared. Some of these cooperatives and salons soon turned into private banks, and their owners—educated, enterprising and, most importantly, incredibly energetic—went from being poor Soviet citizens to millionaires. In the beginning of the 1990s, becoming a millionaire and then becoming a multimillionaire was like moving at supersonic speed over unimaginable space into another galaxy. By the age of thirty or thirty-five, people who had just been students, Komsomol members and low-level engineers had already hired private security guards, moved into mansions formerly occupied by members of the Communist Party elite, and were discovering a new world of Western bank accounts, villas on the Riviera, vacations on yachts and travel on private jets. By late 1994 and early 1995, they raised their ambitions even higher. They realized that they could rise to a qualitatively different level and join the world business elite—to grab fortune by the tail and hold on tight.

The expression "shares-for-loans auctions" was invented inside ONEXIM Bank, one of the largest commercial banks at the time, which had developed from a bank that serviced state import–export operations. The thirty-six-year-old head of ONEXIM Bank, Vladimir Potanin, championed the idea of the auctions. He was the only oligarch to come from a high-ranking *nomenklatura* family; his father was an official in the Foreign Trade system. Vladimir Potanin was in the same class as Brezhnev's grandson at MGIMO—the Moscow State Institute of International Relations, run by the Foreign Ministry, that was a kind of training institute for governmental officials.

Privatization in Russia had already taken place, more or less. Stores and barbershops had gone into private hands, and most industrial plants had been auctioned off with vouchers, but the biggest and best parts of the Soviet economy in the oil and metallurgy industries stood untouched. Actually, they weren't standing. They were hanging heavily around the neck of a state that was going through a protracted economic crisis. The industries were riddled with debt, did not pay taxes, and were withholding wages from their workers. "This was the hen that was laying golden eggs," Sergei Aleksashenko, an economist and former deputy chairman of the Central Bank, explained. "Only someone got the golden eggs, while the state got tax and wage debts."[7]

These and other systemically important enterprises were not run by the state but managed by the same "red directors" who more or less successfully blocked the state's attempts to gain control of large factories across the country.

In March 1995, Potanin offered the state a deal. Big businessmen would take on these potentially golden but currently troubled assets, along with their problems and debts. The state would remove from its balance sheet systemically important enterprises with tens of thousands of employees—enterprises that the government was unable to support or reform. For example, Norilsk Nickel, located in the Arctic Circle—an enterprise Potanin had his eye on—supported an entire city with a population of 150,000 people. The state couldn't work with the current management. Why not let new owners take them on? Leonid Nevzlin, Mikhail Khodorkovsky's partner, with whom, through a shares-for-loans auction, he bought the country's largest oil company, Yukos, later said, "Chubais set a condition [for participation in the auctions]—no conflicts with the current management."[8]

The government would get real money and cover the budget deficits. Overall, through these shares-for-loans auctions, the state budget took in about $800 million for the blocks of shares in twelve companies. This amount was ridiculously small in the context of the 2000s, but in 1995 it was equal to almost half a per cent of the country's GDP.

In the end, the deal proposed by Potanin suited all sides—big businessmen, various clans in the government and the managers of the companies being privatized. It did not suit the oppositional parliament, which blocked the privatization of oil companies. But nobody worried about that, since this prohibition was easy to bypass. In fact, the point of the shares-for-loans auctions was precisely to circumvent this ban: the auction offered an opportunity to give the government a loan and obtain shares as collateral, and if the loan was not repaid by the following year (1996), the collateral—i.e. the company shares—would become the property of the lender. The loan was fictitious. The government had no intention of repaying these loans, and it didn't even include them in the 1996 budget. The auctions were fictitious, too—not formally, but in reality. The bidders knew in advance who was bidding for what and who would get what. The winner was determined by the strength of his claim on the asset. Foreigners were not permitted to participate in these auctions, but that, too, was a formality, since they weren't interested in investing, given the high political risks.

"Everything about loans for shares was the opposite of what the reformers had once stood for," *The Washington Post* journalist David Hoffman wrote in his book, *The Oligarchs: Wealth and Power in the New Russia*.[9] Many years later, the dubious nature of these auctions was used by the state both as a propaganda bogeyman and as a pretext for attacking the rights and interests of specific businesses and economic freedom in general. But as Chubais later said, the auctions put an end to the struggle for the transition to private property in Russia, and the new owners were truly in charge of these companies. "Clearly, the method was dishonest," Chubais said, "but for thousands of company directors across the country, the fact that the director of Norilsk Nickel agreed to auction off his company had tectonic significance. For us, it was the long-awaited and real result of our work, and it truly created private property in Russia."[10]

However, shares-for-loans auctions alone were not enough to turn multimillionaires into billionaires, opening the way to the elite of world business. Russia had to stay the course. The future success of entrepreneurs depended directly on the state of affairs in the country. They needed guarantees that capitalism and private property would not be abolished in Russia.

The other interested party in the deal was the one who sanctioned it—Boris Yeltsin. Yeltsin had been hesitating to run for a second presidential term. Sergei Filatov recalled that in August 1995, the president was depressed and told him he wouldn't run; he was exhausted, in ill health and wasn't spending any time with his family.[11] Korzhakov spoke of Yeltsin's reluctance to run[12] as did Valentin Yumashev: "Yeltsin felt that the support he had in 1991 was gone. That made him uncomfortable. He didn't want to run."[13]

If the ruling party headed by Chernomyrdin had won the parliamentary election of December 1995, Yeltsin might have nominated Chernomyrdin as his successor. But after the party's resounding failure, that was no longer an option. From the outset, the business elite knew they'd support Yeltsin, and now they had an extra incentive. Gigantic industrial properties were to pass from the state to new owners after the elections in autumn 1996, and support for Yeltsin was part of the deal. The businessmen bailed him out by giving the budget almost all the money they had at the time. "In other words, they had us by the balls, and if we did something wrong, they'd leave and we'd be left without a pot to piss in," Khodorkovsky recalled.[14]

This is how the political, economic and ideological interests of the state and the captains of industry coincided and merged. "Loans for shares was the first phase in Yeltsin's re-election campaign," Hoffman wrote. "It was the weld between the tycoons and the Kremlin, the embrace of wealth and power."[15]

And with that, the Russian oligarchy was born. Soon it would take over the reins of government.

## The Davos pact

Yegor Gaidar wasn't the only one depressed by the Communists' resounding victory in December 1995. Others also doubted that Yeltsin could be re-elected for a second term, and, with each passing day, Zyuganov's victory seemed increasingly inevitable. But if Gaidar was looking for someone to replace Yeltsin, Boris Berezovsky had a different plan.

Berezovsky was an applied mathematician by education and engineer by profession with connections at the enormous automotive plant AvtoVAZ. In the late 1980s, he founded LogoVAZ, a car-trading company, quickly became rich, then by 1993 a millionaire, and seemed to be only getting richer. With access to the Kremlin and government offices, and with relationships with the most influential officials, by early 1995 Berezovsky controlled the Aeroflot airlines and ORT—Channel One, Russia's main nationwide television channel. In 1995, he was on his way to becoming an oil magnate, too. In one of the shares-for-loans auctions he and his partner Roman Abramovich bought the oil company Sibneft for $100 million.

But most importantly, unlike many other big businessmen, Berezovsky always had a keen interest in politics. A gambler and risk-taker by nature, he was full of ideas, and even in 1995 he probably envisaged himself as a kind of grey cardinal.

When Berezovsky arrived at the World Economic Forum in Davos in early February, he saw the international financial elite greeting Communist Party leader Zyuganov as the future president of Russia. Berezovsky realized that it was time to act. The first thing he did was to contact his worst enemy: Vladimir Gusinsky, a tycoon, banker, and owner of NTV, the most influential independent TV channel, which had set the bar for independent news broadcasting in the country. Yevgeny Kiselyov, then the head broadcaster at NTV, recalled that forum: "Back then, there was a terrible feud between various oligarchs, and in particular between Berezovsky and Gusinsky. And suddenly Gusinsky's nemesis comes up to me, takes me by the arm and says, 'Yevgeny, where can I find Gusinsky?' I said, 'Boris Abramovich, what's the problem? Do you need to talk to Gusinsky?' 'Yes, we need to talk. Tell him I'm looking for him.' I told Gusinsky, and later a somewhat puzzled and clearly dumbfounded Gusinsky said, 'If you can believe it, Berezovsky suggested that we all make a truce, unite and support Yeltsin. But frankly, I'm not sure he's re-electable.'"[16]

At the beginning of 1996, the country was still reeling from the near civil war of 1993. What form the restoration of socialism would take under President Zyuganov was impossible to foresee, but people who had adapted to the new life over the years saw the return of the

Communists as a very serious threat. As he strolled around Davos, Zyuganov assured the Western financial elite that there was no need to fear him: there would be no nationalization, no restrictions on freedoms, no repression of business, etc. Although, as Khodorkovsky later recalled, in a personal conversation there in Davos, Zyuganov had told him: "We—my team—will nationalize everything, but we won't waste 'personnel like you'. We'll appoint you director of a large national-industrial complex."[17]

Behind Zyuganov were the same intransigent hardline Communists who three years before had been planning repressions and arrests, who had staged a coup and brought the country to the brink of civil war. Would Zyuganov retain the radical wing of his party? No one wanted to see what that life would be. "There are two Zyuganovs: one for external use, and one for internal use," Chubais said. In Davos, Chubais read out excerpts from the Communist Party programme to foreigners at a specially assembled press conference to show that Zyuganov could not be trusted.[18]

Gusinsky understood all this. Zyuganov frightened him, too. But he did not want to support Yeltsin either. NTV was a truly independent television channel, with a lot of coverage of the war in Chechnya.

In Davos, it took Berezovsky several hours to convince him. "Well, all right," Gusinsky finally said. "But what do you need me for? You can call off the elections."[19] Rumours that Yeltsin's inner circle was discussing a scenario for disrupting the presidential elections had been circulating in Moscow since autumn and had even leaked to the press. At the end of January, Gaidar warned, "Many people are deluding themselves that if something happens, we can just call off the elections. These are very dangerous illusions."[20] Everyone understood that if the presidential elections were not held, it would lead to a serious political crisis and, in all likelihood, bloodshed. Even if a crisis were averted, Berezovsky told Gusinsky, the country would be under the control of Korzhakov and the *siloviki*. That's why there was only one option, Berezovsky insisted. And no matter how unlikely it seemed that Yeltsin would win, he had to. But that could only happen if the business community united and seized control of the campaign from the old-school Oleg Soskovets and the *siloviki* close to the president. Anatoly Chubais would be put in charge as organizer, and Igor Malashenko—a professional media manager, NTV director and Gusinsky's right arm—would be creative producer.

The next day in Davos, Berezovsky was already talking to Chubais. Unlike Gusinsky, Chubais didn't need persuading. Even though Yeltsin had just fired him, Chubais believed his mission was to help him be elected president again and stop Zyuganov. "I asked Chubais to join us," Berezovsky later explained. "All of us—the financial elite—trusted him."[21] Berezovsky then went to Khodorkovsky and even to Luzhkov.

With that, the so-called Davos Pact was concluded.

## Chubais is the bearer of bad news

The next task was far more difficult: Yeltsin had to be persuaded. By the middle of February, Valentin Yumashev had been thinking for weeks about who would be able to explain to Yeltsin that, if things continued as they were, he would lose the election. Who would explain to him how his election campaign looked from the outside? The memos Yeltsin's aides wrote to him about it went in the bin, and Yumashev was looking for someone on the outside, a respected and authoritative person Yeltsin would believe. But who? The musician Mstislav Rostropovich, perhaps? The famous theatre director Galina Volchek? One of his classmates? Yumashev was running through the list of well-known names in his head until he literally bumped into Yeltsin's thirty-six-year-old daughter, Tatyana Dyachenko, who lived in the same suburban housing estate in Arkhangelskoye as Yumashev.

That was it. She was the one. Indeed, she turned out to be "the one" for Yumashev. Soon they would be inseparable; journalists and the political crowd would call them "Tanya and Valya." In 2002 they would marry, and Tatyana would take Yumashev's name. Berezovsky was delighted by the idea. Yeltsin was impressed by the parallel with the French President Jacques Chirac, whose daughter worked as an adviser to her father. And so, Tatyana joined the campaign headquarters' staff.

After attending one of Soskovets's meetings, she was horrified. It was like someone giving a report at a Communist Party meeting in the Soviet past. This was no way to win a presidential election in 1996. It was clear that Soskovets's campaign team was losing the election. So, when Chubais returned from Davos, Tatyana met with him and asked what they should do.

They came up with the idea of the Analytical Group. It would be an alternative campaign headquarters uniting professionals—media managers, sociologists, political consultants. "At that time, the concept of 'campaign management techniques' was not commonplace," sociologist Alexander Oslon, head of the Public Opinion Foundation, who joined the Analytical Group, later recalled. "But common sense and common ideas about how elections are 'done' in the West led the initiators of the 'third way' to insist that elections can only be won if the campaign is treated as an informational project with a clearly defined objective: getting enough voters to vote for a certain candidate."[22] The Analytical Group's innovative idea at the time was that the campaign would not be run by officials but by specialists hired by them and that the client would implement their recommendations.

But how could the client be persuaded that this was the only way forward? Yeltsin had won his previous elections in 1990 and 1991 as a hero of the people, carried by a broad wave of hopes and aspirations. Now things were different. Yeltsin needed to be brought down to earth. They needed to convince him of the real state of affairs.

At the end of February, Yeltsin's first aide, Viktor Ilyushin, arranged a lunch for Yeltsin with businessmen and Chubais. First Chubais spoke, then Gusinsky, and the conversation was similar to the one Nemtsov had had with Yeltsin a month earlier. Chubais started with the bad news, telling Yeltsin that the situation was really tough and that his rating was five per cent. Yeltsin, displeased, sniggered that, of course, that wasn't true.

"Everything people around you say about your popularity is not true," Gusinsky said in support of Chubais.

Yeltsin did not like Gusinsky. Now he was looking at him with hatred. "How do you know what they tell me?"

"Because you are acting as if you have already won," Gusinsky answered.[23]

Yeltsin listened to Chubais and the businessmen, said nothing to them and left. According to Hoffman, after this meeting Berezovsky managed to have a word with the president in private. He used this opportunity to warn Yeltsin, just in case. The election cannot be cancelled—that would lead to a civil war. Yeltsin, again, said nothing. The next day, he ordered the establishment of a second, parallel headquarters headed by Chubais. The first headquarters, led by Soskovets, continued its work.

## Elections without a choice

Days and weeks passed, the election was approaching, and Gaidar was desperate. Yeltsin announced that he was running for president, but Gaidar was still trying to find a replacement for him—a democratic candidate who could defeat Zyuganov. The more he thought about it, the more he liked the idea of Nemtsov. In early March, he went to Nizhny Novgorod to try to persuade him personally. Nemtsov received Gaidar hospitably. They flew together in a helicopter to a small village in the west of the region, and Gaidar was once again impressed by Nemtsov's ease in talking with people.

"We all concluded that Boris Nemtsov was the most likely figure to bring together the democratic electorate," Gaidar told reporters, but there was no chance of him being nominated.[24] For Nemtsov, competing with Yeltsin was unthinkable: it was both politically stupid and unethical. In the evening, over dinner, when the topic was raised again, he refused again: it was too soon for him to aim for the presidency. "I distinctly remember him thanking Gaidar for his trust and saying he was like a half-grown, young potato that still needed to sit in the ground," said Viktor Yaroshenko, a Gaidar associate at the dinner. "Gaidar was very upset."[25]

But Nemtsov could not avoid the upcoming elections. The campaign had not yet really begun, but it was already raising questions that he had to answer both to himself and to journalists. How dangerous was Zyuganov? What would happen if the Communists won? Either because of his inherent self-confidence and optimism, or because Nemtsov was far from the epicentre and growing panic in Moscow—or perhaps for both reasons—he did not believe that if the Communists won (which in March seemed almost inevitable) it would be the end of the world.

"The law of the pendulum, which has already been tested in Eastern Europe and in the Baltic countries, shows that, in the Yeltsin–Zyuganov scenario, Zyuganov wins," Nemtsov said on national television.[26] "The Russian democratic system was already strong enough to withstand a Communist revanche," Nemtsov continued. He said the Communist ranks would split, the democratic opposition groups would unite, and the independent press could no longer be silenced. In addition, Russia had large debts, which meant that the West would also be able to put pressure on a Communist government, and this would be another deterrent. Finally, they could take out something of an insurance policy. "Given the prospect [of Zyuganov's victory], which seems absolutely realistic, and I would even say almost certain, today our president has an absolutely wonderful opportunity to protect Russia from cataclysm. He could introduce amendments to the constitution restricting the president's power."[27]

This was early March, when Chubais' Analytical Group was just being set up. The election campaign was still ahead, but even thinking that Zyuganov might win was already unacceptable, and voicing the possibility sounded almost traitorous. "We decided that we'd stop the worst from happening," Mikhail Khodorkovsky said. "In March 1996, for us the victory of the Communists was almost the same as death."[28] Mikhail Fridman, a banker and close acquaintance of Nemtsov's who had signed on to the Davos Pact, recalled that a month later the oligarchs working to re-elect Yeltsin gathered to sign an appeal to Yeltsin and Zyuganov, which later became known as the Letter of Thirteen:

> I remember very well that everyone was unequivocal: Yeltsin must win, or it would be all over for us. I'm far removed from politics, but I said, "I may have to express some cautious disagreement with what's being said here. I do think we personally will probably be worse off if Zyuganov wins. But in terms of the historical process, the country might very well be better off, because, if the opposition comes to power as a result of the vote, it will set a precedent for elections. That would be a major historical moment, a turning point in Russian

history." The response wasn't just cold: it was a blizzard. Naturally, I immediately shut up, sat quietly and didn't say another word."[29]

Nemtsov was pounced upon by the press, called a coward and a conformist who had defected to the Communists and was campaigning for Zyuganov. The kindest explanation was that he was profoundly mistaken. "Was his statement a sign that part of the Russian elite was moving from the ruling party to the camp of the likely winner of the upcoming election on 16 June?" *Kommersant* wrote.[30] Nemtsov was attacked so vehemently that he had to clarify that he didn't support the Communists, but "you have to be realistic and look to the future with dry eyes."[31]

What the idealist Nemtsov did not realize was that the Kremlin did not consider the possibility of defeat. As Chubais would say later when the election campaign began in earnest: "We simply don't have a Plan B." At the time, Nemtsov was not aware that the 1996 presidential election was not an election in the literal sense. The stakes were too high. The alternative was clear: either Zyuganov won, or democracy won. There was no alternative. Being realistic meant not preparing for a likely victory for Zyuganov but rejecting it outright.

By March, Yeltsin had a Plan B. On Sunday, 17 March, at 7.30 a.m. Anatoly Kulikov, the interior minister at the time, was awakened by a phone call. Alexander Korzhakov, head of the Presidential Security Service, was summoning him to the Kremlin to see the president at 11.00 a.m. At 10.57 a.m. he went into the president's office. Kulikov later recalled: "Yeltsin seemed agitated. He shook my hand and, without further ado, announced, 'I have decided to dissolve the State Duma. It has exceeded its authority. I will not tolerate it any longer. The Communist Party must be banned, and elections must be postponed.'"[32]

## Plan B

By the winter of 1996, Alexander Korzhakov had long been more than just the head of presidential security. Apart from Yeltsin's family,

Korzhakov was probably the person closest to him. He was Yeltsin's main comrade-in-arms, his eyes and ears, his closest adviser, the No. 1 figure in Yeltsin's Kremlin. "He was part of his life," Nemtsov said of him. "I think Yeltsin would begin to feel unwell as soon as he saw that Korzhakov wasn't around."[33] In autumn 1995, he ranked fourth among the most influential Russian politicians, coming after Luzhkov, Chernomyrdin and Yeltsin himself.

In the Kremlin, Korzhakov was a major proponent of cancelling the elections for two reasons. First, he genuinely did not understand why they were needed. "What elections? We didn't take power to give it away so easily!" he'd say.[34] Second, he was worried about his boss's health. In the second half of 1995, Yeltsin suffered three heart attacks, spent most of October and November in hospital, and an ambulance was added to his motorcade. How could he conduct an election campaign in such poor shape? And then, not only did the Communists win the Duma elections in December by an unexpectedly wide margin, but they took over the parliament. They promoted a member of their party to the speaker's chair and took control of a majority of the committees. The belief that it was impossible to deal with such an openly hostile parliament was another argument in favour of a military solution.

Yeltsin was also frightened by the way world leaders had greeted Zyuganov in Davos. As time went on, his rating did not improve, and an election victory was looking increasingly unlikely. In late February, Soskovets told one of the American consultants who had come to help run the campaign, "One of your tasks is to tell us a month before the vote to cancel the election if you see that we are losing."[35]

A good reason appeared in the middle of March, and Yeltsin referred to it in his conversation with Kulikov. The deputies had voted to cancel the Belovezh Accords that had secured the dissolution of the USSR in December 1991. In other words, the deputies had restored the USSR on paper. Of course, this pre-election propaganda move could not have practical consequences. But it was a *casus belli*.

Yeltsin listened to Korzhakov's entreaties. And then the idea of postponing the elections "at some point [...] became Yeltsin's idea", Hoffman believed.[36] It suited his temperament to cut the Gordian knot in one fell swoop, as he had already done two and a half years before. He would write in his memoirs: "I have to confess: I have always preferred simple solutions."[37]

Despite all his shortcomings—lack of education, penchant for alcohol, impulsiveness and so on—after Yeltsin became president, he had lived with a clear sense of his mission: to make Russia a normal, democratic country. Along the way, he had to navigate formidable obstacles and problems. Something was always going wrong, and Yeltsin was trapped in a sort of vicious circle: he made a mistake, sought to correct his mistake, again made a mistake, and the finish line disappeared over the horizon. Now he realized that he needed two more years: he would dissolve the Communist parliament, ban the Communist Party, postpone the presidential election, prepare his successor—perhaps even Nemtsov, who was still young and not yet ready—and retire with a sense of accomplishment. "I need two years," he repeated like a spell to Anatoly Kulikov when he entered his office. "I have made up my mind."[38]

Kulikov left after arranging to meet later that same day, closer to evening. The whole drama unfolded for just over a day. Soon Berezovsky, Chubais, Tatyana Dyachenko and Yumashev were frantically searching for a way out of the impasse. Berezovsky found out what was going on and told Gusinsky that they were in big trouble: there was a document on Yeltsin's desk cancelling the elections and declaring a state of emergency, and a military division had been put on alert. What should they do? To prevent a repeat of the events of September 1993 when the Duma leadership barricaded itself inside the parliament building, by 5.00 p.m. everyone inside the Duma building had been evacuated—ostensibly because of a bomb threat—and 150 special forces officers occupied the building.

The president's aides were tasked with drafting the decrees. In the meantime, Kulikov went back to Yeltsin, this time with the prosecutor general, Yury Skuratov, and the chairman of the Constitutional Court, Vladimir Tumanov. They agreed ahead of time to take a united position: dissolving parliament and cancelling the elections was categorically not an option. For a start, Kulikov was not at all sure that law enforcers in the regions would carry out his orders. He was already imagining a civil war. Yeltsin had just thrown out of the office his aides, who had also tried to dissuade him from the venture. He met Kulikov, Tumanov and Skuratov coldly and angrily. "It was clear: Yeltsin would not accept our objections," Kulikov recalled. "I only asked: 'Wouldn't you like to convene the Security Council to discuss this situation?' He exploded: 'Enough is enough, I've had enough advice… I don't intend to convene any Council.'"[39]

Soon, Anatoly Chubais was in Yeltsin's office. Tatyana Dyachenko had persuaded her father to see him. The conversation lasted for more than an hour. This was not 1993, Chubais explained, and going against the constitution was fraught with dire consequences; to ban the Communist Party was madness. "I found myself in a situation of absolute open confrontation [with Yeltsin]," Chubais recounted. "It was obvious that he just didn't want to see me, didn't want to talk to me, didn't want to discuss the subject, didn't want to listen to my arguments."[40]

Yeltsin did not like Chubais, but his political instincts told him he should listen to him. When he left his meeting with the president, Chubais walked in on the presidential aides tasked with drafting the presidential decree. "Listen up, guys. Whoever writes the decree is responsible for it, whether their name is on it or not," Chubais told them. "All that's left is the resignation letter. This is the death of the president's political career."[41]

Meanwhile, Gusinsky met Luzhkov at the airport on his return from a trip to Paris. Inviting the astonished mayor into his car, Gusinsky explained what was happening.

"Are you sure Yeltsin is going to win the election?" Luzhkov asked.

"No, but we'll do our best," said Gusinsky. "Is life under the dictatorship [of Korzhakov and the *siloviki*] any better?"[42]

Luzhkov promised to call the president the next morning. The day before, Yeltsin had left the Kremlin and ordered the text of the decree to be delivered to him by 11.00 p.m., but he never received it. Instead of the decree, his aides wrote a note for him. "There is virtually no legal justification for this extreme option," its first paragraph read.[43] The note was handed to Yeltsin the very next morning when he arrived at the Kremlin. A final meeting was scheduled for 6.00 a.m. Both Kulikov and Chernomyrdin again opposed the dissolution of the Duma. When the president issued an order not to seize the Duma building and Communist headquarters for the time being, Kulikov realized that the special operation was off. At the last moment, Yeltsin's political instincts told him to abandon the easiest scenario. Instead, he would have to go to the polls.

Neither the press nor the public knew anything. The management of NTV was aware of what was going on from Gusinsky and Berezovsky, but they remained silent. "We didn't have to involve the media," Berezovsky said.[44] All that was left of the attempted coup were brief news reports about a search for an explosive device inside the parliament building and "large-scale command-staff exercises of the internal affairs bodies and internal troops." Zyuganov had also issued a statement that the Kremlin was getting ready to take some sort of action. Deputies who went to work early on Monday morning ran into an armed cordon, but it was quickly lifted.

Berezovsky and Chubais had won their first real victory. Yeltsin now had only one option: Plan A. He was going to the polls.

## Choose or lose!

Despite all the difficulties, Russia had been a free country for about half a decade, beginning with the election of deputies to the First Congress in 1990. All Russian elections—at least at the federal level—were transparent, open and free from any kind of pressure, be it from the state or any other political player. In late March, Boris Yeltsin's election campaign began. It differed from all the previous campaigns by a new concept—the idea that they could make people believe something and convince them to vote "the right way."

For the first time, elections were conducted in Russia the way they were in the West: with campaign managers and political consultants, pollsters, journalists, actors and television stars. The campaigns had strategies and were designed to target various audiences. And there was another "first": the election campaign was designed to mobilize as many people as possible to fight against the return of Communism. Yeltsin's "coup" had failed, and there was no civil war in the streets of Russian cities. But in spring 1996, all of the country's media and information sources became a battlefield.

Everyone who had managed to achieve some success by then was afraid of the Communists. But neither did they love Yeltsin. To convince them to vote for the lesser of two evils—Yeltsin—they first had to change him, or rather change the image voters had of him. Over the last five years, in the public mind Yeltsin had become his opposite: not a brave fighter against the system, but another secretary general in a fur hat; not a national leader, but a high-ranking official totally disconnected from the people. Therefore, Yeltsin, Oslon later recalled, had to "appear in the election period in his original state, the way he'd been when he was the people's idol and embodied the hopes for renewal for tens of millions of people."[45]

Although he came from the same system as Communist Party members, Yeltsin had always been different from the majority of them. He had sharp intuition and a capacity for change. He had political flair. For the campaign strategists of the Analytical Group, he turned out to be a smart client and easy to work with. Almost the first thing they did was to place two photos in front of him, one from the early 1990s—Yeltsin surrounded by people—the other from his latest election trip: the president surrounded by officials and guards. Yeltsin understood instantly. He transformed himself before their eyes and began to speak in "human" language again. "It was like our folk-hero, Ilya Muromets, had shaken himself awake," Gaidar recalled.[46] Gaidar was no longer hesitating and had stopped searching for an alternative democratic candidate. He supported Yeltsin along with his party. "By voting for Yeltsin, we are supporting not his administration, but private property, a convertible rouble and civil society in Russia."[47]

Yeltsin's own incredibly active campaigning—he toured two dozen cities in two months—was combined with a massive multi-platform advertising campaign. Commercials with the slogan "I Believe! I Hope!" showed Yeltsin as a man from a simple peasant family, just like everyone else. Under the slogan "Choose with Your Heart", people similar to Zyuganov's typical voters—pensioners and the working class—spoke out for Yeltsin. They didn't want a return to the past, when matchbooks were rationed and people in the countryside were forced into collective farms.

Four years earlier, MTV in America had run the "Choose or Lose" campaign to get out the youth vote for the presidential elections. Towards the end of Yeltsin's campaign, pop stars were already campaigning for Yeltsin under the slogan "Choose or Lose." Many of them were doing so because they believed in it. "Either we keep our native son Yeltsin as president, or the Communists will come back," said Vladimir Shakhrin, leader of the Yekaterinburg band Chaif, one of the country's most famous rock groups. But the musicians were also getting unprecedented fees, up to tens of thousands of dollars. There was never any talk about meeting the legal limit of $3 million for the campaign; the project to get out the youth vote alone was more expensive.

"We will win to prevent a return to the days when Russia was considered an evil empire," Yeltsin said in speeches. "We will win the elections so that we can start living freely and with dignity, like all normal people live in normal countries."[48]

At no time in the past five years had the state so methodically paved the way for its candidate to win the election: ensuring the payment of salaries and pensions, publishing decrees to support various industries. "The treasury may not withstand the generosity of electoral promises," wrote the newspaper *Izvestiya*.[49] According to Hoffman, the campaign was also largely financed by public funds through semi-legal schemes. Businessmen involved in the campaign bought government bonds at a discount. "Yes, Yeltsin made active use of his administrative resources," his aides admitted. "But for what? To restore the image of an energetic president pushing for Russia's transformation. It's not like we were helping the big boss twist the arms of all the other bosses to make sure he got the result he wanted."[50]

Relations between Yeltsin's team and the media were similar to their relations with performers. Journalists were genuinely afraid that Zyuganov would win. They wanted to help Yeltsin get re-elected, and understandably so. "If we work strictly according to objective, professional, unbiased, non-partisan rules and Zyuganov wins tomorrow, we'll have dug our own grave," Igor Malashenko, head of NTV and then *de facto* head of Yeltsin's campaign staff, said in spring 1996. "If, to avoid this, we side with Yeltsin and start playing along with him, it means that the mass media have become a part of the Yeltsin regime. It means that mass media have turned into instruments of propaganda. Damned if you do, damned if you don't."[51]

This dilemma was resolved in favour of partiality. NTV changed its sharp criticism of the president to a more benign tone. At the same time, however, many journalists and editors were also being paid more money than they had ever seen before. In Moscow alone, in June 1996, *The Washington Post* estimated that the monthly bribes paid to journalists for pro-Yeltsin articles reached $100,000.[52] From mid-April onward, in almost every mailbox in the provinces was one of ten million weekly papers called *God Forbid*—a very expensive and very effective propaganda newspaper written by Moscow's best journalists that depicted the horrors of Communism, predicting executions, famine and civil war if Zyuganov won.

The closer the country came to election day, the tougher the anti-Communist propaganda became. Zyuganov's victory was associated with inevitable upheaval. In March Yeltsin's victory looked utopian. By 20 April, Yeltsin and Zyuganov had the same ratings. But, perhaps even more importantly, opinion polls showed growing confidence that Yeltsin would win the election. The turning point came in the first days of May, when Yeltsin overtook Zyuganov in the ratings. It was just by one per cent, but it was a milestone. Yeltsin would soon consolidate his already strong position with a ceasefire in Chechnya.

## A marriage of convenience

But a massive advertising campaign was not enough. Yeltsin needed allies. Chubais had been negotiating with Grigory Yavlinsky throughout the spring. It was a political bargain: in exchange for withdrawing his candidacy for president and backing Yeltsin, Yavlinsky, who was harshly critical of both the war in Chechnya and the shares-for-loans auctions, demanded a change of economic course and the formation of a new cabinet that he would head as prime minister. Yeltsin would later write: "I did not want to make a deal for the post of prime minister." In mid-May he summoned Yavlinsky to his office in the Kremlin. His final offer was the post of deputy prime minister. The decree had already been signed, and, if Yavlinsky had agreed, it would have been published immediately. But Yavlinsky refused.[53] The conversation with Yeltsin was difficult. He insisted that Yavlinsky must withdraw his candidacy and even threatened, "You will have problems." Yavlinsky once again refused—definitively—and stormed out of the president's office. Just as Yavlinsky was at the door, he heard Yeltsin say, "Come back." He turned around and approached the president again. "You know," Yeltsin said, giving Yavlinsky a sly look. "I would have done the same in your place."[54]

Yavlinsky's decision to stay in the running put Nemtsov on the spot. Who should he back in the presidential election? Yeltsin had brought him to power, and he owed his career to him. For the past four years, however, Yavlinsky had been his comrade-in-arms, his mentor in the world of big politics. In any tough situation, Nemtsov would run to Yavlinsky for advice. "I suspected that Nemtsov was more inclined to support Yavlinsky," said Viktor Lysov, then Nemtsov's assistant. "But by May it was already clear that it was either Yeltsin or Zyuganov."[55]

Like Gaidar, Nemtsov had to choose the lesser of two evils. In Russian presidential elections, if a candidate gets more than half of all votes cast, he wins in the first round; if not, the two leading candidates go on to the second round, and then whoever gets more votes wins. As the first round of elections was coming up, the support of a popular governor would help Yeltsin. Berezovsky asked Nemtsov to appear on television.

"You're going to vote for Yeltsin, and you're urging others to do so as well," the TV presenter challenged him on air. "Aren't you being a traitor to Yavlinsky, who helped you carry out the reforms in your region?"

"Yavlinsky is one of the most honest and most talented people I've met," Nemtsov replied. "But all the same, I want my vote to count. It is obvious to everyone that there will be two candidates in the second round: Zyuganov and Yeltsin. And if I vote for someone else, it means that my ballot will be thrown in the bin."[56]

Yavlinsky later explained why people should vote for him. If he took third place in the first round, he'd be in a better position to bargain with Yeltsin and even demand some changes in his position in return for Yavlinsky's support. So, a vote for him in the first round would not be lost. But Nemtsov had his counterarguments. It was crucial that Yeltsin beat Zyuganov in the first round to keep voters from becoming demoralized—and to make sure that the bureaucrats would continue to regard Yeltsin as president. So, "every vote that would ultimately be cast for Yeltsin has to be cast for Yeltsin right away."

"Is this how you resolve the classic contradiction between conscience and expediency?" the interviewer pressed. (The interviewer's name was Dmitry Kiselyov, and he would go on to become the face of Russian state propaganda.)

"I love my country, and I love Nizhny Novgorod very much. I don't want anything terrible to happen to my beloved city. I have made my choice as a citizen. An election is not about marrying the person you love. It is a marriage of convenience. And in a marriage of convenience, you shouldn't feel disgusted and ashamed during the honeymoon for making a mistake."[57]

This was a turning point in the relationship between Yavlinsky and Nemtsov. Their relationship never recovered.

Nemtsov started campaigning for Yeltsin. In those years Russia had a "red belt"—a stretch of about half the country where local power was in the hands of the Communists. There was no way for the people in the Kremlin to put pressure on them, but they noted which governors helped Yeltsin and which didn't. Nemtsov, however, could not imagine forbidding Zyuganov to meet with people. Yeltsin's daughter Tatyana said this made her father angry: "I remember Papa asking Nemtsov, 'Why is Zyuganov making so many appearances in Nizhny Novgorod during the election campaign? When he says something, it's always from Nizhny Novgorod.' Nemtsov said, 'It's the law. It's democracy. You can see that I'm for you, of course. I campaign for you. I do my best. But I give everybody a voice. Elections are elections.'"[58]

Yavlinsky failed to take third place and dictate his terms in no small part because the architect of Yeltsin's victory, Boris Berezovsky, had managed to find the president another ally: Alexander Lebed, who had decided to enter politics and run for office. The popular military man with a gravelly voice was an ambitious, brutal general who had refused to storm the White House during the August 1991 coup attempt. Lebed was an alternative to both democrats and Communists. This was the first time Russia voters saw a *silovik* who promised to restore order. It was hard to believe that he would support Yeltsin. But Berezovsky persuaded him. "Lebed was categorically against it, and Yeltsin didn't see him as his ally either, knowing that he was not an easy man," Valentin Yumashev said later. "All the same, Boris [Berezovsky] put it all together so that both Lebed and Yeltsin supported it."[59] After agreeing to the deal with Yeltsin, Lebed immediately received both money for an ad campaign and the green light from the central TV channels.

On 16 June, in the first round of the presidential election, Lebed received fifteen per cent of the votes. Zyuganov won thirty-two per cent, and Yeltsin thirty-five per cent. With Lebed's support, he was virtually certain of a second-round victory. On 18 June, Yeltsin dismissed the odious Defence Minister Grachev, appointed Lebed secretary of the Security Council with broad powers: in effect, he now oversaw the army. Lebed called on people to vote for Yeltsin. The next day Korzhakov launched a second coup attempt, this time not among the voters but in the Yeltsin camp.

## Xerox box

Alexander Korzhakov and FSB Director Mikhail Barsukov, his ally in the power structure, could see that they were losing influence over Yeltsin. He would owe his victory not to them, but to Berezovsky, Chubais, other businessmen and the Analytical Group. Yeltsin certainly did not fully understand how his election campaign was put together and financed. Coming from the Soviet system, he did not attach importance to money, and the material side of power did not interest him. In this sense, Korzhakov's plan was a good one. If he could show Yeltsin that officials were stealing money from the election campaign, he'd be furious.

Korzhakov and his team had already been relegated to the periphery, but they were still involved in the work of the election headquarters. Korzhakov's first deputy in the Security Service, General Georgy Rogozin, was deputy chief at the headquarters. Known for his fondness for the occult and parapsychology, Rogozin regularly sent out astrological forecasts to staff chiefs. For example, the forecast for 16 June, when the first round took place, was as follows:

Around 10.12 a.m. there is an increased likelihood that false information will be invented to harm the individual.

Around 12.36–3 p.m. there is a high probability that a person in authority will issue a secret order to prevent the individual or his supporters and allies from accessing truthful information.

Around 3 p.m. the individual will realize what is happening, and he will see that he is the victim of a secret plot. All this will lead to anger that he will not be able to control and that he may direct onto those around him, as well as a craving for alcohol. The individual may take secret actions to rectify the situation.[60]

Chubais, Malashenko and other campaign managers usually deleted these texts immediately, but they shouldn't have. It's clear from the quoted passage that Korzhakov's camp attached great importance to special operations. Yeltsin's election headquarters occupied three floors in the President Hotel, and each room was bugged. Korzhakov had surveillance on everyone involved. Korzhakov also knew that a great deal of cash had been raised for campaigning and that they were being financed from offshore accounts. He regularly reported to Yeltsin about embezzlement in the headquarters. "Finally, Yeltsin got tired of reading my documentation about theft, and he said to me, 'Catch someone in the act! Can't you catch anyone?'" he recalled.[61] What happened next was covered extensively in the press. Korzhakov organized an ambush, and on the evening of 19 June, FSB officers detained two important members of Yeltsin's campaign headquarters in a government building: Sergei Lisovsky, an advertising executive in charge of the campaign's youth project, "Choose or Lose", and Chubais' aide, Arkady Yevstafyev. Lisovsky was carrying a box filled with half a million dollars to pay performers. It was called a Xerox box in the press, but it was actually just a box that had held printer paper.

News of the arrest soon reached Berezovsky and Chubais. They met with other key figures at the LogoVAZ reception house where Berezovsky usually held meetings, threw parties and hosted guests. Korzhakov was clearly going for broke. Later Berezovsky claimed that snipers had appeared on the roofs around the building. Everyone was genuinely afraid that the building would be stormed and they'd all be arrested. Malashenko recalled: "Berezovsky and Gusinsky remained the calmest. Together with Chubais, they quickly counted up our resources: two TV channels; direct access to the president through Tanya [Dyachenko] and Valya [Yumashev]; and two heavyweights, Prime Minister Chernomyrdin and General Lebed. But we realized that Korzhakov was backed by real power—FSB special forces."[62]

Berezovsky called Dyachenko. Gusinsky and Malashenko were already giving orders to television newscasters to publicize the situation. "Are we supposed to wait for them to arrest everyone?" Berezovsky asked Yeltsin's daughter, who still didn't understand what was going on. Chubais got a call from Nemtsov. "It's a hot mess," Chubais recalled. "And then Boris calls me. 'Hi, where are you?' 'I'm at LogoVAZ.' 'What's going on?' 'Looks like we're fucked.' 'It's that bad?' 'It's that bad.' 'Got it. I'll be there in a minute.'"[63]

Nemtsov arrived fifteen minutes later. He wasn't close friends with everyone there, but he and Chubais were colleagues. And it was clear that something serious was going on. "Nemtsov couldn't do anything to help," Chubais said. "But he had to come. That's the way he was. He had to be with you when times got tough."[64] The situation looked so dangerous that Gusinsky's guards even suggested he get ready for a shoot-out. To everyone's relief, Dyachenko and Yumashev arrived; Korzhakov and Barsukov would not have dared to storm a room with the president's daughter.

Yeltsin went to bed believing that law enforcement officials had caught two crooks, that the thieves would go to jail and that everything was fine. Tatyana Dyachenko woke up her father and persuaded him to turn on the television. Just at that moment the NTV channel was presenting a very different version of events: law enforcement was organizing a coup. Yeltsin agreed to receive Chubais the next morning, but Dyachenko feared that he would simply not make it to the president's office: "Korzhakov was capable of anything and everything. So I simply made Chubais and Malashenko get into my car and drove them onto the Kremlin territory. No one would stop me. I escorted them to the corridor in front of the president's office. There was a post where they only let through people with special passes, people the secretary in the reception room knew about. And that meant that Korzhakov knew about them, too."[65]

Lisovsky and Yevstafyev were released that night. The incident turned into a huge scandal, and Korzhakov and Barsukov retreated. But a stand-off remained between Korzhakov and Barsukov on one side, and Berezovsky, Chubais and company on the other. Chubais's chances were slim: Korzhakov was one of Yeltsin's closest associates and a *de facto* family member. Malashenko remained in the waiting room, while Chubais was allowed in to see the president. Their conversation lasted twenty-five minutes: "When Chubais came out with a stony face and I had no idea what was said, my heart sank," Dyachenko recalled. "Then the secretary stepped away for a second, and Chubais quickly told us, 'It's OK!'"[66]

In less than an hour, Korzhakov, Barsukov and Deputy Prime Minister Oleg Soskovets (Chubais considered him one of the conspirators, since he was Korzhakov and Barsukov's "godfather" in the power structure) were dismissed from their posts. Chubais celebrated his victory, which was totally unexpected for everyone except Valentin Yumashev, who had whispered to his friends in the LogoVAZ club the night before: "He will fire them." Yumashev, who had known Yeltsin well for a long time, apparently sensed something the others didn't. Korzhakov had been working on a special operation to discredit Chubais's headquarters, but in the end, he was too late. After he won the first round, Yeltsin realized that he would win the second one. He understood perfectly well that businessmen, together with Chubais, had forged his victory and that Korzhakov was going to spoil it. "The 'box of money' is a traditional Soviet KGB entrapment," Chubais said at his victory press conference that same day, recalling how the KGB had planted currency on dissidents.[67] (Chubais seemed to imply that the money was planted on Lisovsky and Yevstafyev, which, of course, was not true.) How he had persuaded Yeltsin that morning that he was in the right is unknown, but reportedly this was one of his main arguments—that Korzhakov and Barsukov were reviving methods of the Soviet special services. Chubais cited other examples to prove his point. Yeltsin may have been poorly versed in the theory of democracy and parliamentarianism, but he had fervently and sincerely loathed the KGB ever since his Communist Party days in Sverdlovsk. For this reason, he was constantly taking apart, shaking up and reforming the Russian security services to keep them from becoming a real force in Russia.

That's what Chubais played on. His strong hatred of the Chekists coincided with political expediency. "It was then that I realized," Yeltsin would later write, "that Korzhakov had finally appropriated to himself the functions of both the prosecutor's office, the court, and really all the law enforcement agencies."[68] This is how the almighty head of Yeltsin's security, who considered himself the second most important person in the country, was banished from the Kremlin. The next day, his deputy Georgy Rogozin disappeared from the President Hotel with his team and astrological forecasts. As Chubais said, a new Yeltsin was on his way to the election.

## Democracy wins

Two days before the second round, presidential candidate Gennady Zyuganov came to the Ostankino television centre to address the voters as mandated by election law. But instead of a personal address, Zyuganov brought a ten-minute video clip that his campaign had made. In the video, Stanislav Govorukhin, a well-known and very popular film director and actor, and a strong Zyuganov supporter, made a series of accusations. He claimed that the results of the first round had been rigged, that Yeltsin couldn't win even in one region during the Soviet period, let alone the entire country now, that during his tenure in office Russia had become mired in crime and corruption, that the money "in the Xerox box" would be enough to pay salaries to workers at ten coal mines, that Chechen guerrillas voted for Yeltsin, and more. His delivery was far more convincing than Zyuganov and made a powerful impression.

Yeltsin's staff still had much to fear: victory was a long way off. Yeltsin could not bear the stress of the election campaign—endless trips around the country, speeches, dancing on stage and all the under-the-carpet battles in state structures. On 26 June, just a week before the second round, he had a heart attack, his fourth in a year. His final tour of the Russian cities had to be cancelled. He was slow to recover and had a hard time forming sentences. He was predicted to be well ahead of Zyuganov, but how would his absence in the final days of the election race affect the results? Pollsters also warned that there was a risk of losing their lead if Yeltsin's supporters, thinking the job was done, didn't vote in the second round.

The ORT television channel, which was functioning as a *de facto* branch of Yeltsin's campaign headquarters, had seen the tape of Govorukhin's address beforehand. A decision was made not to air it. The law guaranteed candidates five minutes of direct pre-election airtime. Knowing this, the Communists bought an extra five minutes to show their video. But the ORT management found an irregularity in the paperwork and blocked the payment. When Zyuganov and Govorukhin showed up at the station, ORT director Konstantin Ernst shrugged, saying that he could do nothing—unfortunately, the ten-minute tape hadn't been paid for. But, he said, Zyuganov had his allotted five minutes of live airtime to address the voters. Zyuganov, annoyed that he wasn't getting his way, was ready to leave the studio, but Govorukhin brought him back. "What are you doing? You'll lose the election!" But Ernst was adamant. Twice Govorukhin brought Zyuganov back. When Ernst said "no" categorically the third time and tapped his watch to indicate that the broadcast was about to start, Zyuganov indignantly turned around and walked out. "You just lost the presidential election," Govorukhin shouted after him.

Yeltsin was lucky to run against a candidate like Zyuganov. Zyuganov lacked the energy and charisma to attract voters, and he proved to be a cautious politician. He wanted to win, but at the same time he feared victory. He understood why the special forces had occupied the parliament building in March. He, too, probably heard rumours that there were boxes of weapons being stored in the President Hotel between the two rounds of voting. He'd been told that Korzhakov said no one would hand power over to the Communists. Korzhakov was ousted, but who could guarantee that his replacement wouldn't be the same?

Similar conversations were going on in the President Hotel. The Yeltsin team discussed what would happen if Zyuganov proclaimed himself president. Where would he go when he realized that he could not claim power in Moscow? To Krasnodar? Kemerovo? Novosibirsk? There were enough regions of Russia where the Communists were in power that would welcome him with open arms. Would the country split into red and white, as it had done almost a hundred years ago? Would civil war break out? These were not idle fantasies. When one of the oligarchs who supported Yeltsin was asked what he would do if Zyuganov won, he answered quite seriously: fund an armed resistance.

In the end, they didn't have to fight Zyuganov. After losing in the second round of elections by over thirteen per cent (fifty-three vs forty per cent), Zyuganov did not contest the election, either out of caution or because he realized that he had truly lost. Fifteen years later, another Russian president, Dmitry Medvedev, would utter a thought that has taken root in the corridors of power over the years: "Hardly anyone has any doubt who won the 1996 presidential election. It wasn't Boris Yeltsin." This is not true. Yeltsin won by manipulating public opinion, thanks to what sociologist Lev Gudkov called Russian society's readiness to succumb to "the influence of political manipulation", thanks to obvious support from the government and, finally, thanks to his own energy and willpower. He did not win by falsifying the results.

Experts in electoral statistics point out clear anomalies. In Kabardino-Balkaria, for example, in the first round Yeltsin and Zyuganov got almost the same number of votes, but in the second round Yeltsin got almost twice as many. A similar pattern was observed in Tatarstan and other national republics, mainly in the Caucasus. Valentin Mikhailov, an election history specialist, has said that the second round would have been quite different in these regions if the vote count had been honest. But, despite falsification at some local levels, there was no doubt about the figures overall. Zyuganov lost.[69]

The day after his re-election, President Yeltsin addressed the nation: "You have defended your right to choose. Now no one will take it away from you."[70] Against the backdrop of the dire problems Russia faced in the first half of the 1990s, his victory seemed like salvation. "The elections have taken place, and all the voters won," wrote Otto Lacis on the front page of *Izvestiya* that same day. "For the first time in the centuries-long history of the Russian state, the question of the transfer of power was decided by ballot, not by force."

Time would be needed to study the victory and draw conclusions, but "Russia was saved by the fact that protests about the danger posed by Zyuganov were stronger than protests about the mistakes made by Yeltsin."[71] And that meant that the reformers had to seize their lucky chance to achieve economic growth and finally turn Russia into a civilized and prosperous democratic country.

# PART 3

# CHAPTER 12

**1997**
# First Deputy Prime Minister Nemtsov

**Power vacuum**

On the morning of Sunday, 16 March 1997, Nemtsov's deputy, Yury Lebedev, woke up, washed his face, had breakfast and walked out of his dacha in Zelyony Gorod on the outskirts of Nizhny Novgorod. Nemtsov's dacha was next door. It was Nemtsov's sixth year as governor. Crises and problems were a thing of the past, the system for managing the region had been fine-tuned long ago. Nemtsov was in excellent form, and he knew the region like the back of his hand. The people of Nizhny Novgorod thought the world of him. His job was almost routine. He and his deputy took the weekends off and got a good night's sleep. Lebedev looked around the yard. Nemtsov was at home but apparently still asleep—his car was parked in its place, and the guard assigned to him was strolling nearby. Nemtsov, as governor, was entitled to state security. Lebedev went up to the guard to say hello. He asked him how things were going. Berezovsky had been at the governor's house yesterday, the guard said, and then Yeltsin's daughter had come.

Lebedev immediately knew something was up.

Yeltsin's victory was supposed to open a window of opportunity for the government, give a powerful new impetus for reform. But more than half a year had passed, and nothing had happened. Yeltsin had won the election and then disappeared. The victory over the Communists was largely pyrrhic: after a heart attack in June, Yeltsin could not perform his presidential duties. The inauguration on 9 August was conducted in half an hour, because he could hardly stand on his feet. Journalists were constantly asking, "Is Yeltsin alive?" They were told, "The president is working with documents." On 5 November he underwent heart surgery. The operation was successful, but Yeltsin soon caught a cold and came down with severe pneumonia. He would never again work at full capacity.

Yeltsin's victory changed the balance of power in his immediate entourage. Korzhakov and Barsukov were gone. For a time, General Lebed was the country's main *silovik*. When the Chechen war ended, his popularity grew, and while Yeltsin was seriously ill the general made no secret of his ambitions. He wanted to be president, and soon. In the autumn, Lebed changed from being an ally to being a serious problem for the Kremlin: a popular military man, who wanted to make a power grab and had units loyal to him. Lebed's resignation on 17 October was something of a special operation. As *Kommersant* wrote, "No sooner had the ink dried on the [resignation] decree than the offices in the Council of Ministers were promptly sealed."[1] Around 1.00 p.m. all communication lines—city, internal and government—were cut in the entire building complex on Staraya Square, where Lebed's office was located, and buses with special forces appeared in the courtyard.[2] As it turned out, these were unnecessary precautions; everything went smoothly.

The government became what the press would call "the board of directors of Russia, Inc.." Yeltsin was chairman, and the board members were the men who had made his election victory possible: Berezovsky, Gusinsky, other oligarchs, Chubais, Yumashev and Yeltsin's daughter Tatyana. They were all euphoric, enjoying their victory after an uphill battle. Now they could enjoy the fruits of their success.

Chubais did not return to his previous job, but became head of the Presidential Administration; because Yeltsin was rarely in the office, he was immediately called the regent. Berezovsky became deputy secretary of the Security Council. Yumashev was appointed presidential adviser for media relations. The president's daughter Tatyana did not need a title, but she was given the post of adviser to her father. However, the reshuffling did not solve the main problem in autumn 1996: instead of reforms, there was stagnation and a power vacuum.

The economic situation remained bleak. The stock market had soared in reaction to Yeltsin's re-election, but there was a severe budget crisis. In early 1996, budget revenues began to plummet because the government had loosened fiscal discipline before the election. But that was only half of the problem. That autumn the financial authorities found themselves powerless before the main taxpayers—big businesses—that were getting exemptions or simply did not pay taxes thanks to their connections. They decided themselves "how much to pay into the budget, and they don't even try to conceal their tax debt. They just don't pay it. Some of these tax avoiders have strong patronage," Deputy Finance Minister Sergei Shatalov complained at the time. For example, the Ministry of Finance complained that AvtoVAZ paid 0.3 per cent of what it owed in 1996, and this was typical.[3] In general, the state was failing in its main function—fiscal viability.

In October, Chubais created the Temporary Extraordinary Commission, which was responsible for tax collection. He had expected that the name of the commission, with its echo of the All-Russian Extraordinary Committee for Combatting Counter-Revolution and Sabotage—commonly called the Cheka, the forerunner of the NKVD and KGB—would be suitably intimidating. But taxpayers were not intimidated, and little came of it. Journalists made fun of the image of Chubais as a Chekist–Bolshevik in a leather jacket and holding a Nagan revolver.

In the absence of cash, the state and businesses increasingly used cross-cancellation of debts, barter, in-kind exchange of treasury bills and other surrogates, which, in turn, only worsened the situation for tax collection. The government had to close the hole in the budget by borrowing money, and the budget became increasingly dependent on foreign borrowing, backed by GKOs—government short-term bonds.

The cabinet formed after the election—again headed by Viktor Chernomyrdin—was not at all reformist. The tone was set by former Soviet functionaries, and the oligarchs, who had already managed to take possession of the oil companies and metallurgical plants they had won at shares-for-loans auctions, sent their own delegate, Vladimir Potanin, the banker and now majority owner of Norilsk Nickel, who headed the economic bloc with the rank of first deputy prime minister.

The idea was simple: big business helped Yeltsin in the elections, the course was set, we are building capitalism, so let business bring order to the economy.

It did not help. First, the other oligarchs became suspicious that Potanin was working for himself. Second, the oligarch Potanin was not fit to be a state official. He was annoyed and bored by bureaucratic red tape, and his enthusiasm waned quickly as the economic crisis dragged on. "Sergei, do I understand correctly that we can no longer spend a penny from the budget on anything other than debt servicing, and we don't even have enough money for that?" Potanin asked Sergei Dubinin, head of the Central Bank, at one of the meetings in the government. "Yes, that's right," Dubinin replied. "Nobody pays taxes."[4]

To make matters worse, starting in 1997 the price of oil had begun to fall. Businesses were shutting down, there was a wave of protests and strikes and miners were blocking roads again. There were more than half a million teachers on strike in January 1997 alone. "Letting those eight months slide have seriously complicated the situation," Gaidar said at the time. "But despite this, the egregious crisis situation, especially with regard to the budget, makes tough measures a vital necessity."[5]

In February, after an operation and illness, Yeltsin finally returned to the Kremlin. By this point, both he and the entire Russian "board of directors" realized that they needed to act urgently. On 6 March, Yeltsin delivered his address to the Federal Assembly. "We're spinning our wheels," he lamented. "In the early 1990s, Russia transitioned to a market economy and moved forward, but then it stalled and got lost along the way. It's time to get back on track." The president's voice sounded almost as forceful and optimistic as it had a few years ago. The market economy is a level playing field for all, and it is the job of the state to establish and enforce it, he said.

Since the main problems were in the economy, Chubais left the Kremlin and joined the cabinet the next day. It was a joint decision, recalled Sergei Zverev, then a top manager under Gusinsky: Berezovsky, Gusinsky, Fridman, Potanin, Khodorkovsky and other influential oligarchs were all in favour, and the decision was taken unanimously.[6] Yumashev became head of the Presidential Administration at Chubais's request.

The two main objectives of Boris Yeltsin's second term were obvious: to achieve economic growth and to hand over power to a successor—democratically, of course. And the two extra years that Yeltsin dreamt of in March 1996, when he wanted to cancel the election, were still needed. "The deadline for Yeltsin and Chubais is absolutely clear. Two years," wrote commentator Leonid Radzikhovsky in early 1997. "In 1999, a new presidential race will start. If stagnation continues until then, a populist like Lebed will become president, or one of the *nomenklatura* feudal lords will be elected and pour cement in the swamp we're living in to make it permanent."[7]

## Moving to Moscow

No one today can say for certain who in the Kremlin suggested bringing Nemtsov to Moscow, but the first to do so was probably Berezovsky, the most inventive politician among the oligarchs and Yeltsin's inner circle. He also had a gift for persuasion. Berezovsky came up with almost all the clever policy moves during that period. He paved the way for Yeltsin's second term. He conceived and implemented the electoral gambit with General Lebed. There is no doubt that Berezovsky considered himself the leader of Yeltsin's new team, the "collective Yeltsin" that was now shaping the political course.

Nemtsov had little understanding of political life in Moscow. He was acquainted with Berezovsky, but only in passing.

"We've made a decision," Nemtsov said Berezovsky told him when he got to Nizhny Novgorod. "You ought to be promoted."

"Who are 'we'?" Nemtsov asked.

"Well, a bunch of us made the decision and told Yeltsin. And he listened to us, naturally. To cut a long story short, we decided to appoint you."

"Who do you mean? Who exactly are you? I know that you're a businessman. You own LogoVAZ, Aeroflot and something else. Who are you, anyway? Why have you come here?"

"Don't you understand? I told you: we run the country."

"What does Yeltsin do?"

"He's technically in charge, but we're the ones who decide everything."

"Boris, you're going to end up in trouble. This story is going to end badly."⁸

The idea of bringing Nemtsov to Moscow seemed logical. He was one of the most popular governors in the country, a serious figure, a democrat—but without a trail of failures and setbacks—an associate of Yeltsin, yet independent and not afraid to cross him. Yeltsin needed an ally like that.

Anatoly Chubais, who had just been appointed first deputy prime minister, discussed it with Nemtsov when they met in Moscow. It was early March. After securing Chernomyrdin's consent, Chubais offered Nemtsov the post of deputy prime minister. Nemtsov refused and left for Nizhny Novgorod. Given his reputation and popularity, Nemtsov thought he should be prime minister. The post of deputy prime minister did not appeal to him: the political responsibility was immense, his leverage was limited, and the election was still a long way off. All his friends and acquaintances insisted that he shouldn't accept anything less than the post of prime minister. "I remember we were sitting around, discussing things," says Fridman, who was friends with Nemtsov at the time. "And I said to him, 'Is it true that you are going to take it?' And he said: 'No, it's just a rumour.' I said, 'You know, I don't think it's a good idea… You're a popular governor, young, promising… I think it's a very risky move…' Is it better to be the top man in the provinces or the second man in Rome, eh? It's a well-known dilemma. So, I tell him there's no point. Why do it? He listened to everything and said, 'Yes, I totally agree. I'm not going to Moscow.'"⁹

But Chubais would not take no for an answer. He proposed making Nemtsov the second first deputy prime minister. Yumashev, who had just headed up the Presidential Administration, even wrote a special memo to Yeltsin explaining why it was necessary. Nemtsov continued to be pressured from Moscow, but he still refused. Yumashev got involved ("Boris, children and women all over the country love you, we need you badly"), and even Chernomyrdin, who was not at all eager to have him in Moscow, added his support.¹⁰ But Nemtsov refused to move to Moscow. "He's so stubborn," Yeltsin would complain later. "He's a bit like me."¹¹ "Then Anatoly and I decided that we had a secret weapon, the closest person to Yeltsin," Yumashev said. "If Tatyana goes to see Boris, she can explain that it's essential not only for Chubais, not only for Chernomyrdin, and not only for the country, but also for Yeltsin, and that it's very important to create a team to move Russia forward."[12]

On the evening of Saturday, 15 March, Dyachenko set off by car for Nizhny Novgorod. She was already on her way when Yumashev called Nemtsov and told him this. At the same time, Berezovsky was trying to persuade Nemtsov. "You know what? I'll only talk to Yeltsin," Nemtsov told him.[13] When Berezovsky found out that the president's daughter was on her way to Nizhny Novgorod, he immediately disappeared. "What a rotten thing to do," Tatyana told Nemtsov when she arrived. "It's outrageous. He heard that my father had given me an assignment. And he came first to show that he was in charge."[14]

They talked for hours, and after her persuasion, recriminations and tears, Nemtsov gave in. "He later said he was convinced by my last argument," Tatyana said. "When I said, 'Boris, when you were having a hard time, Dad always helped you. And now he needs help. You have to do it. You can't refuse.'"[15] She left without his answer, but she already knew that Nemtsov would agree.

In the future, Nemtsov would say that moving to Moscow had been a major mistake in his life. "Could I have become the successor without moving to Moscow, without all the big government offices and fights with the oligarchs?" he wondered. "I probably could have. The beautiful position turned out to be a dead end."[16]

Of course, no one can say how his career would have turned out if he had turned down Yeltsin's request at the time. The romantic hopes and rapid career advancement of the early 1990s were over. People were nostalgic and on edge, humiliated that Russia was not playing a leading role in world affairs. In political life, calculations, connections and financial interests weighed more heavily than values, great ideas and luck. Now thoroughness and solidity were in favour. The winds of Russian history that carried Nemtsov to the top a few years ago had died down. Paradoxically, the defeat of communism in the 1996 election also struck a blow to democratic ideals. It was as if communism and democracy constituted a single ideological system, a struggle of opposites, and, if one lost its meaning, the other would collapse along with it. Where democrats had once been fighting the Communists, a new kind of politician was now making a stand: the experienced old-school manager.

Nemtsov could not refuse Yeltsin for personal reasons. "It's probably wrong for a politician to do that, but when a man—in fact, a friend—does it, it's wonderful," Fridman said.[17] But he couldn't turn him down for political reasons, too. By 1997, the democrats had a host of grievances against Yeltsin but were unable to form an alternative political force. And saying "no" to the president probably meant parting ways with him and being left out of the powerful coalition. "Offers were made that were impossible to refuse," Nemtsov later explained. "I simply don't know of a single example when the president personally asked something and was refused."[18]

There was also a third reason for agreeing to the move: Nemtsov was bored as governor. In the 1990s, more than half a decade was almost an eternity. Like any leader in power, Nemtsov had grown complacent in Nizhny Novgorod and felt constrained. "I was handling economic affairs at the time, and when Nemtsov would return from a trip to Moscow or America, I would tell him how many roads had been built, where a cowshed had burnt down and so on," Yury Lebedev said. "I could see that he was not interested. He had already outgrown the role of governor. Of course, he had to grow."[19] What Nemtsov really wanted was to take the risk and go to Moscow, to the centre, where everything was happening, because he was impatient and because his love of politics was stronger than his desire to have a brilliant but safe career. In the future this personality trait would rule his actions many times.

Nemtsov told his wife Raisa what Tatyana had said: the situation was very difficult, the government, unlike him, had very low credibility, and Yeltsin needed help. Around 9.00 p.m. he called Yury Lebedev and asked him to postpone a meeting for him on Monday—he had to go on a business trip to Moscow. Lebedev remembered their conversation clearly: "I said to him, 'Boris, I know they're going to transfer you to Moscow. Listen, I want to give you some advice: don't go. They'll eat you alive. Don't go. Wait a little longer.' He said to me, 'OK, calm down. I'm not going anywhere. I get it. I'll call you tomorrow.'"[20]

On the morning of Monday, 17 March, Nemtsov flew to Moscow. Lebedev held a staff meeting in his place, and in the afternoon he went into the governor's reception room. The television was on. "Well, this is a very interesting option," Yeltsin said from the screen. He was sitting in his office, clearly very pleased with himself. Nemtsov sat on his right. "Two young men, you and Chubais, in the cabinet. You will be putting together an equally fresh, young team. Starting off with a clean slate."

Two minutes later, journalists were already congratulating Nemtsov on his new position as first deputy prime minister. And in another minute, the phone rang in the reception room. "It's for you," the secretary said to Lebedev. Lebedev picked up the phone. It was Nemtsov.

"OK, calm down, I'll come back, I'll see you, I'll tell you everything. And you don't have to meet me at the airport."

"No," Lebedev replied. "You're now deputy prime minister. You have to be met at the airport."[21]

Nemtsov moved to Moscow alone, while Raisa and Zhanna stayed in Nizhny Novgorod. At first he lived with Alfred Kokh, who also had a post of deputy prime minister in the new cabinet. The two had become friends over the past couple of years. Kokh's eldest daughter moved in with his youngest to make room for Nemtsov. "My wife does his laundry—his underwear and socks and shirts," Kokh said. "And in the evenings, we go to a restaurant in the neighbourhood by ourselves, without any security detail."[22]

A month later, Nemtsov moved to a state dacha in Arkhangelskoye and lived there alone. Later, he'd be joined first by his mother, then Zhanna (though not for long—she couldn't stand the atmosphere in an elite Moscow school and would soon return to Nizhny), and finally Raisa. The dacha where Nemtsov lived had only the bare necessities and no one to take care of things. Fridman told the story of visiting Nemtsov in Arkhangelskoye one day. All there was in the house was a bottle of tequila given as a gift by some delegation, which of course they immediately drank.

## The charge of the cavalry

"The old sectoral industry approach is over," announced Prime Minister Chernomyrdin at his first cabinet meeting.[23] To his right was Chubais, and to his left was Nemtsov, both now first deputy prime ministers.

The formation of a new cabinet with two first deputy prime ministers was perhaps Yeltsin's strongest personnel decision since late 1991 when he had asked Gaidar's team to join the cabinet. In March 1997, Chubais was not yet forty-two and Nemtsov was only thirty-seven. But their ages didn't matter. Chernomyrdin was right—what mattered was that the sectoral approach was over.

Since Gaidar's time in the Yeltsin government, reformers had always been opposed by a powerful Soviet-era deputy prime minister who held the levers of national economic management. This happened without fail. In the previous cabinet, for example, First Deputy Prime Minister Vladimir Potanin was opposed by First Deputy Prime Minister Vladimir Kadannikov, head of AvtoVAZ (one of the industrialists the Ministry of Finance could not force to pay taxes). But now the levers of power in the government that controlled everything from macroeconomics to the real economy were held by like-minded people. Chubais was in charge of the economy and financial policy (he also headed the Ministry of Finance), while Nemtsov was in charge of natural monopolies, the housing and utilities sector, the entire social bloc and anti-monopoly regulation. In addition to the post of first deputy prime minister, he was soon given the portfolio of fuel and energy minister in the new cabinet. "It was a fantastic, unprecedented arrangement," said Chubais, "that opened up terrific opportunities for reform."[24]

Both first deputy prime ministers had direct access to the president, which was the most important power lever in Russia. Both brought their own teams. Chubais brought everyone: Alexei Kudrin, who became his deputy in the Ministry of Finance, and Alfred Kokh, who, as deputy prime minister, became head of the Ministry of Property. Nemtsov appointed the mayor of Samara, Oleg Sysuyev, as deputy prime minister for social affairs. Russia had a cabinet made up of young reformers—as Yumashev put it, "the most powerful team ever in government."

Two other young men rose up the ladder in the cabinet shuffle. Nemtsov appointed Sergei Kiriyenko, a thirty-four-year-old banker from Nizhny Novgorod, as his deputy in the Ministry of Fuel and Energy. And when Kudrin moved to the Ministry of Finance, a fairly low-level administrator named Vladimir Putin replaced him as head of the Government Accountability Office.

The programme of reforms for the next three years, which was supposed to achieve the final victory of capitalism in Russia, included everything from military reform to the introduction of private land ownership, adoption of a new tax code and restructuring of the natural monopolies. It was assumed even back then that Gazprom would lose its monopoly on the gas pipeline, that privatization would begin in the electricity sector and that private carriers would compete with each other on the railways. This programme promised economic growth of five per cent by 2000. The manifesto of the young reformers, published under the title 'Seven Main Tasks', was a set of the most urgent measures, from a transition to targeted social assistance to compulsory declaration of income by officials and a reduction of personnel in state organizations.

Nemtsov thought he had been given a mandate to implement his own platform to fight predatory capitalism. In one of his first interviews in Moscow he said, "The president and I talked in general about what he thinks the country needs right now. And in fact, there's not much choice: either predatory capitalism, or people's capitalism."[25]

Chubais objected to the term "predatory capitalism." He found it inaccurate and populist (big business passed through the mafia stage in 1993–94, he explained), but otherwise he and Nemtsov were on the same page. "I believed then and still believe now," Chubais said in an interview, "that the essence of the liberal concept is that the state has to be as tough as possible in spheres where no one else can fulfil those functions. No one else can do it because businessmen have their own private interests, but the state is driven by the interests of society as a whole."[26]

Nemtsov got Potanin's former office on the fourth floor of the White House. Chubais took the office opposite. Officials were quick to point out that Chubais had a cart full of papers on his desk every day, while Nemtsov's desk was empty except for a switchboard with direct access to the president, the prime minister and several colleagues in the government. Nemtsov may have become first deputy prime minister, but he never became a bureaucrat. He was very different from other Moscow officials. "He was and is not afraid to act—a rare quality for an official," economist and ex-finance minister Boris Fyodorov said of him, "especially in Russia."[27] Nemtsov viewed his position in the cabinet in the same way he viewed his position as governor: They were political positions. He was both the ideologue of reforms and their implementer. "Shortly after his appointment, Nemtsov, who was in charge of the economic bloc, was heading a meeting with the military on financing the Ministry of Defence," recalled Oleg Vyugin, then deputy minister for finance. "In response to a speech by one of the generals, Nemtsov suddenly said, 'Listen, it's very easy. Stop stealing. You just don't know when to stop.' The generals were shocked speechless. This was not just a deputy prime minister—there were rumours that he was Yeltsin's successor."[28]

The same thing happened in other meetings. Nemtsov's informal, defiant style became his calling card. He might interrupt a meeting with ministers in his office, for example, to step outside to talk to someone, only then to come back in and brag that he'd just turned down another request from Berezovsky. This style was entirely part of his character, but Nemtsov was also able to put it to political use. When he shocked generals with his impertinence, it was neither crazy nor weird, Vyugin said. It was deliberate. "It was the charge of the cavalry."[29] Now that he was a high-ranking official, Nemtsov's method became breaking bureaucratic conventions. He saw the state apparatus as the enemy, and the fight against bureaucracy became part of his political platform—for ever.

## Switch to a Russian car

Even if the young reformers felt like they were on suicide missions in the new government, they didn't look like pilots on their last flights. Nemtsov's popularity soared almost as soon as his career in Moscow began. "Nemtsov's appointment was extremely encouraging for Russians," sociologists in the Public Opinion Foundation noted in April 1997.[30] According to their polls, he had higher ratings of public confidence than both Luzhkov and General Lebed, who was retired but still on the political scene. During that summer, Nemtsov was beating Zyuganov even in rural areas where the Communists had historically been strong, and he was beating by a wide margin any opponent in the second round of hypothetical presidential elections. "The Nemtsov miracle took off," said Gleb Pavlovsky, then a political analyst close to the

Kremlin.[31] Yury Lebedev remembers staying with Nemtsov at his dacha in Arkhangelskoye around this time. At 8.00 a.m. they left for the White House. A press digest for Nemtsov was already in the car: "As we were driving along, Nemtsov reads it and says, 'Do you want to see what my rating is?' He holds up a piece of paper. I see forty-five per cent! I was gobsmacked. That was really something."[32]

One of the most popular governors seemed to have become the most popular politician in Russia. On the one hand, his move to Moscow played a role. The public saw Nemtsov as the future successor: if the authorities were staking their bet on him, it meant he was powerful and in the running. On the other hand, Nemtsov entered the government as a politician, and his ideas were popular. He came to power to fight corruption, to fight against the tie between the government and capital—predatory capitalism—and privileges enjoyed by bureaucrats. A year later, in an interview in March 1998, Nemtsov would clearly, though not explicitly, compare himself with Yeltsin in the late 1980s. "Yeltsin was rebelling against the state apparatus. He is a rebel by nature. They tried to destroy him, but they couldn't. Kamikazes don't always die instantly."[33] Yeltsin fought against bureaucracy and privilege, and now Nemtsov had taken up the baton. Once Yeltsin had been accused of populism: now Nemtsov was accused of it. He was united with the people who were against the establishment and trying to keep the reforms democratic.

As soon as he arrived in Moscow, Nemtsov proposed several measures to combat corruption in the government, such as the introduction of tenders for public procurement and requiring declarations of officials' expenses. But a cavalry charge would not frighten the ageing Moscow bureaucracy, and, as the fate of Nemtsov's first and perhaps most famous initiative—forcing officials to switch to Russian-made Volga cars—showed, he was, of course, naïve and did not have a good sense of the balance of power. Nemtsov's Kremlin-promoted executive order on using Russian cars was published on 1 April simultaneously with the reform programme, two weeks after the new cabinet was approved. The idea was simple. Given the huge budget deficit and wage arrears, officials should support the domestic automotive industry and not drive foreign cars.

"Officials were shocked," Yeltsin later wrote about the ban on driving Mercedes and Audis.[34] At first, he supported his protégé's plan and even set an example himself by riding in a locally made ZIL limousine. As was to be expected, the public was in favour. Nemtsov, a popular politician and an outsider in the Moscow system of power, was doing exactly what people wanted him to do. He was putting the government in its place, taking away one of its main status symbols—an expensive foreign car.

The press, however, greeted Nemtsov's proposal with scepticism. Journalists got out their calculators and figured that a Volga was three times cheaper than an Audi A6 and much cheaper than a Mercedes. And repairs cost half as much. But a Volga reconfigured for government officials with a Land Rover engine and Frigette air conditioning would be much more expensive in exploitation. An ordinary Volga off the assembly line usually has to be rebuilt in a year. The ostensible reason was "to save state funds and support domestic producers." But it was widely understood to mean "we'll help Nemtsov's automotive factory in Nizhny Novgorod" where they were produced. The idea that in the seventh year of building capitalism people should abandon its benefits and return to Soviet practices seemed absurd.

The bureaucrats began to resist immediately, even as the presidential decree was being signed. The Ministry of the Economy slammed the Volga idea as protectionist and anti-liberal. The Central Bank suddenly recalled that formally they were not civil servants and therefore the instruction to give up their foreign cars did not apply to them. The opposition in the Duma hooted that Nemtsov was just lobbying his local industry. Even Nemtsov's friend Oleg Sysuyev had to be persuaded to switch to a Volga: "Nemtsov said to me, 'If you, my closest friend, won't do it, then who will?' So I switched to a Volga. Thank God, it broke down very quickly."[35] Actually, Nemtsov himself would try to catch a ride with Chubais, especially when Yeltsin summoned them. And a favourite joke in the White House was the story of how Nemtsov's Volga broke down on the Rubyovo-Uspenskoye Highway—the road to government dachas—as he was going to a cabinet colleague's birthday party. The other guests roared with laughter as they passed him.

Members of the government were ordered to auction off their foreign cars. The auction, held in June outside Moscow, failed miserably.

According to one of the LogoVAZ managers who was present, the cars were in horrendous shape, "like after an explosion", and only suitable for spare parts, if that. "It was sabotage. Absolutely," one of the organizers later recalled.[36] After the second auction in October, the presidential decree was tweaked: officials were now allowed to "switch [to Volgas] as their cars wear out." In bureaucratic Russian, this meant they didn't ever have to switch to a Volga. And so, Nemtsov's most high-profile project in power suffered a high-profile failure.

## Luzhkov takes on the young reformers

At the auction of government-owned foreign cars in late June, Nemtsov was surprised to find dozens of journalists waiting for him. They tried to trip him up with questions like "Why are Volgas better than Mercedes?" "What's the point of this show?" "How much did the owners of the venue pay you?" Later it turned out that most of the reporters had been bussed in from Moscow early in the morning, escorted by traffic police. Their trip was organized by the government administrations of Moscow and the Moscow region.

During the five years of Yury Luzhkov's rule, Moscow, the most liberal, wealthiest, largest and generally the most important city in the country—the city where history was either made or not—had become a state within a state. The city had its own, separate form of citizenship: the right to live there was still only for those with a residence permit (*propiska*), which every Soviet citizen coveted. The *propiska* still existed for Moscow even though residence permits had been abolished by federal law and later by decision of the Constitutional Court. Moscow had its own privatization rules, which Luzhkov defended before Yeltsin, while intensely criticizing Gaidar's reforms and Chubais's privatization. In Moscow, Luzhkov had built a centralized system of power with a loyal parliament, controlled security forces, managed the courts, had a press loyal to him and big business that was personally oriented towards him. Analysts at the time talked about the "Luzhkov clan" as a separate powerful political and financial force. In the mayoral elections, which were held simultaneously with the presidential elections,

Luzhkov received almost ninety per cent of the votes. In Moscow, he was king.

"Chubais is a radical: I am a doer," Luzhkov said.[37] He was the embodiment of the new type of "experienced old-school economic managers." They didn't spout political talk like the liberal reformers; they simply got down to work. Not long before Nemtsov arrived in Moscow, he had called Luzhkov "a cautious politician who always pretends that he is an economic manager, the chief builder who is cleaning up Moscow. This image—completely good and so essential to Russia—makes Luzhkov look like a great governor against the background of the others."[38] At the time, Nemtsov and Luzhkov, both at the top of the country's most popular politicians, both influential governors who had just won elections, got along and were allies. In late 1996, the two of them created and headed a club of donor regions and even held a joint press conference. Nemtsov was flexible. He was a Western-oriented democrat who had no quarrel with anyone. He managed to be on good terms with supporters of Gaidar, the anti-Yeltsin Rutskoi and the old-school Luzhkov. He only competed with Luzhkov on the tennis court. Oleg Sysuyev recalls that, in 1995, he and Nemtsov played a doubles match against Luzhkov and his regular partner Yevgeny Panteleyev, Moscow's minister for industry and a good tennis player. Of the four of them, Luzhkov was the weakest player—he had only recently taken up the sport. "I was amazed that it was so important to Boris to beat Luzhkov. It wasn't just a game. And when I did try to play against Panteleyev, a strong player—it was more interesting that way—Boris growled in my ear: 'Hit them to Luzhkov.' He wanted us to win. I think they were already competing. Boris wanted to be better. Boris wanted to rise above Luzhkov."[39]

Luzhkov was the kind of person who paid attention to such things. He was also very competitive. In fact, there was a persistent rumour that the bad blood between Berezovsky and Luzhkov began when Berezovsky beat him at pool. But with Nemtsov's move to Moscow, everything changed. The competition on the tennis courts became a political battle.

By the end of 1996, when Yeltsin was clearly in poor health, Luzhkov already had grand ambitions. Being mayor wasn't a big enough job for him. His contribution to Yeltsin's presidential victory was enormous—the entire city had been plastered with flyers showing Yeltsin and Luzhkov shaking hands under the slogan "Muscovites Have Made Their Choice!" Now the mayor of Moscow was counting on reciprocal support. And not without reason. It was actively discussed, it was expected, it was written about in the press. Sergei Filatov, who had been the head of Yeltsin's administration, would say that Luzhkov was the best candidate for Yeltsin's successor.

The sudden appearance of Nemtsov and the young-reformer government upset Luzhkov's plans. Yeltsin didn't need him anymore. Nemtsov turned from a potential rival into an actual competitor. When he joined up with Chubais, he became an irreconcilable opponent of the Moscow mayor's. Luzhkov went on the attack against the young reformers: he accused them of disrupting a profitable relationship with Belarus, he attacked market reforms, and he called for privatization results to be annulled. He convinced Yeltsin to let him reform housing and utilities in Moscow according to his own plan, not Nemtsov's. He even overstepped his position to get involved in organizing presidential events in the capital. This began his rift with Yeltsin.

The relationship between Nemtsov and Luzhkov changed drastically and only got worse. Nemtsov tried to initiate an investigation into embezzlement during the construction of the Moscow Ring Road—unsuccessfully—and continued to make a show of being puzzled by the business success of Luzhkov's wife, Yelena Baturina, who somehow managed to win one municipal tender after another.

After having lived in the capital for almost three months, Nemtsov still hadn't got the elusive Moscow residency permit, which was needed so that his daughter Zhanna could go to school. When they'd meet, Luzhkov would nod, but nothing was done. The housing board rejected the first deputy prime minister of the Russian Federation due to the absence of some information in the application—a paper certifying where his wife had been in 1992–94. Nemtsov loved to tell a story about this. Yeltsin would ask from time to time, "How's it going with that residence permit?" Nemtsov would say, "No movement." Oleg Sysuyev said, "Luzhkov did not want to register Boris in Moscow for a long time. Nemtsov's wife, Raisa, was giving him a really hard time about it. One day he told Yeltsin about it."[40]

Nemtsov said that Yeltsin became furious and had his secretary put through a call to Luzhkov. When he was connected with Luzhkov, Yeltsin simply said, "Petty, Yury Mikhailovich. You're being very petty." And he hung up.

Then he explained what had happened to the puzzled Nemtsov. Luzhkov was an experienced bureaucrat, and he wanted to find out why the president was calling him. He first called the receptionist in the Kremlin and asked who was in the president's office. He was told it was Nemtsov. The next day Nemtsov got his Moscow residence permit.[41]

But on the whole, domestic difficulties and bureaucratic intrigues did not trouble Nemtsov. He was delighted with his new life. In the past Nemtsov had made Nizhny Novgorod a fashionable city and invited the stars of world politics there. But now he found himself in a place where not just Russian, but world history was being made. The first wave of interest in Russia had long since passed, but now the second wave had arrived. Communism had been defeated, Russia was accepted in the world, the last preparations for Russia to join the G7 were underway and all doors were open. It wasn't just the thought of the presidency. Nemtsov was enjoying the optimistic feeling that no matter how circumstances turned out, this highly successful thirty-seven-year-old politician had a bright future. This was the general mood of those months: optimism and faith that all the major difficulties were behind them, that the country was moving forward, that tomorrow would be better than today. "That was the happiest time in my life," Sysuyev recalled. "I was so lucky to work in that government."[42]

But life was also keeping everyone on their toes. "We were always living in 'emergency' mode. I think it was exactly the same with Boris," said Sergei Yastrzhembsky, Yeltsin's press secretary at the time. "We were practically never at home: we left very early in the morning so we could be in the office when the president came to the Kremlin. And he liked to wake up very early. At the end of the day, we would get home half-dead and climb into bed to recharge our batteries. It was like living in a pot of boiling water."[43]

## The first battle for Gazprom

Meanwhile, the country was in a full-blown fiscal disaster; the state did not have enough money to pay pensions and salaries. Yakov Urinson, then minister for the economy, described how, before Chubais and Nemtsov joined the government in early 1997, he had received reports about children fainting from hunger in some schools.[44]

How could they fill the state coffers and pay off wage arrears? Of the seven major tasks in the young reformers' programme, this task was, of course, number one. There were basically two solutions: either force large companies to pay taxes or carry out new privatizations. But in both cases, the young reformers had to deal with the heads of state-owned enterprises, the very same red directors who still successfully resisted the state's attempts to impose financial discipline on them.

By summer 1997, for example, the largest chronic debtor to the budget was the state-owned company with the long name Nizhnevartovskneftegaz, the main production enterprise at Samotlor. This was the largest oil field in Russia, dubbed "the Soviet Kuwait." Chubais reported to the cabinet as early as autumn 1995 that under the direction of Viktor Paly, a legendary oil baron who had managed oil production at Samotlor since Soviet times, the company was evading taxes but spending more than $4 million on business and tourist trips and at least $27 million on the construction of a sanatorium in Crimea.

In June 1997, Chubais and Nemtsov planned to privatize the Tyumen Oil Company, which included Nizhnevartovskneftegaz. In order to do so, they needed to remove Paly from his post as general director. The government issued a directive to remove him, but Paly used one of the favourite tricks to fight the state: the airport in Nizhnevartovsk refused to land the plane with the government emissary on board, citing bad weather. Two weeks later, Chubais and Nemtsov made a second attempt. This time their delegate made it safely. Chubais later described the scene as follows: "The government envoy gets on the plane, arrives, attends the meeting... and votes for Paly! Nemtsov is furious."

"Why the hell did you do that?"

"I'm sorry, but I want to live. I have a wife and daughter—she's a little girl. I don't need all this trouble!"

"I'll fire you."

"I know. But at least I'll be alive."[45]

In the era of mutual non-payment, tax defaulters had one main argument: everyone owes them money, too. This was the argument made by Rem Vyakhirev, head of Gazprom, the corporation that united the entire Soviet gas industry. And he was right. Gas consumers all over the country owed Gazprom an astronomical sum. The situation was similar in the electric-power and railway sectors. The reform of the natural monopolies was supposed to solve this problem. Breaking up Gazprom, the national energy system and the railways would lead to market competition in these sectors. In the end, everyone would benefit. Consumers would get lower tariffs, companies would earn money, and the state would receive taxes. Thanks to his influence over Yeltsin, Nemtsov succeeded in having the decree restructuring the natural monopolies passed. Later, he called it "one of the most important reform documents of the 1990s."[46]

However, the gas part of the decree was less extensive than the sections on electricity and the railroads. "For some reason, when reading the part [about gas], it was like the developers themselves didn't really believe in the reality of their idea," wrote Mikhail Berger, who was then an economic journalist. For several years, Gazprom had been successfully fending off reformers with the support of its former head, Prime Minister Chernomyrdin. That was why, Nemtsov admitted, the section on Gazprom in the decree was weak. Conferences on energy reforms had been held constantly since April, while Vyakhirev continued to argue, to the applause of deputies, that Gazprom was a national treasure and should not be split up. To solve the non-payment problem, he suggested printing money.

Nemtsov started looking into Gazprom's complicated governance structure. Two things became clear. First, thirty-five per cent of the state's shares had been transferred to Gazprom's management (Nemtsov claimed it was to Vyakhirev personally, but Vyakhirev always denied it). Second, Gazprom had an option to buy back thirty per cent of its shares from the government in two years at the nominal price, i.e. very cheaply.

## 1997: FIRST DEPUTY PRIME MINISTER NEMTSOV

In this case, Gazprom could be legally taken over by its managers in a similar way to what happened to Surgutneftegaz,* one of the country's largest oil companies.

"Did Gazprom executives expect to become its owners? Neither Vyakhirev nor Chernomyrdin gave a clear explanation," *Forbes* magazine wrote many years later.[47] This wasn't an idle question, and it was hard to imagine it actually happening, since Gazprom was not one of many oil companies, but a monopoly on the gas market.

Vyakhirev later showed journalists another trust deed which allowed the option to be bought back not at face value but "at a price agreed upon with the government." If this was the case, it meant the state still had leverage. But Nemtsov never saw this second document, if it existed at all. Nemtsov kicked up a fuss and went to Yeltsin, complaining that the state could lose Gazprom. He would not win the fight with Vyakhirev until December, when Yeltsin would personally force Gazprom's chairman to sign a new contract, this time without the buyback option. "Vyakhirev and Chernomyrdin fought for the right to buy it down to the bitter end," Nemtsov said. "But Yeltsin's resolution on the contract, which I received, decided everything. In it, the 'tsar' wrote: 'This is theft of Russia!'"[48]

However, this victory came at a high price for Nemtsov. Viktor Aksyuchits, Nemtsov's associate at the time and head of his advisory service, remembered that Chernomyrdin wouldn't allow Nemtsov to go to Germany for the presentation of his new book, and it was only after a phone call to Yeltsin that he was able to leave.[49] "Boris Nemtsov had a long, hard fight over that trust agreement. It completely destroyed his relationship with the prime minister and ruined his career in general," Gaidar recalled.[50] Nemtsov thought it cost him the post of first deputy prime minister.

---

\* The ownership structure of Surgutneftegaz is not transparent. The company's management is believed to hold a controlling stake in the company through a number of offshore companies and subsidiaries.

## The second battle for Gazprom

Chernomyrdin wasn't the only person Nemtsov had a falling out with. On 26 June 1997, Chernomyrdin was due to fly to China to discuss important business: supplying turbines to a giant hydroelectric plant on the Yangtze River as well as gas from the Far East and electricity from Siberia. Nemtsov had flown out two days earlier to prepare for the prime minister's visit. Boris Nadezhdin, Nemtsov's adviser in the cabinet and secretary of the Board of State Representatives to Natural Monopolies, which included Gazprom, was in his White House office. As usual, he had Nemtsov's facsimile signature and the board's seal with him; Nemtsov trusted Nadezhdin to handle minor matters himself. Then there was a knock on the door. One of Berezovsky's assistants came in and said, "We need to get some papers signed… Viktor Stepanovich [Chernomyrdin] has already approved them." Nadezhdin looked at the document he handed to him. It was a directive to elect Berezovsky as chairman of Gazprom's board of directors at the shareholders' meeting in a week's time. At the top was a large notation—"Approved"—and Chernomyrdin's signature. Completely stunned, Nadezhdin took the document and ran to call Nemtsov. "Boris, what should I do?"[51]

Nemtsov was aware that Berezovsky was after Gazprom; he'd heard it first from American billionaire George Soros. The financier, philosopher and philanthropist Soros had welcomed the fall of the Iron Curtain. He had high hopes for Russia. In the early 1990s, he had donated $100 million dollars in grants to scientists in order to save the Russian fundamental sciences. In 1996, at Davos, he didn't believe that Yeltsin could beat the Communists. Now, a year later, Soros was more optimistic. He genuinely wanted to help the young reformers, especially Nemtsov, whom he liked. And if he could make some money in the process, so much the better.

In early June, Berezovsky suggested to Soros that he invest a billion dollars in shares in Gazprom, which, in turn, would help him, Berezovsky, put Gazprom under his control. Alexander Goldfarb, then an aide to Soros (and later to Berezovsky), described the plan: "Once he gained control of the gas giant, he intended to modernize the company and turn it into a transparent corporation operating by Western standards. The demand for gas in Europe will inevitably grow, and Gazprom will become one of the most powerful companies in the world."[52]

In any case, the investment promised to bring in enormous profits down the line. A special law capped foreigners' holdings of Gazprom at thirty per cent, which created two markets for Gazprom shares—one for non-residents and one for Russian citizens. Investors knew that at some point the cap would be lifted, Gazprom stocks would instantly appreciate, and domestic shareholders would become very rich.

Soros agreed. Berezovsky flew him to Sochi on his private jet. There they met with Chernomyrdin. After discussions, Soros was prepared to invest $1 billion, and then $2 billion more later. "Berezovsky was glowing," Goldfarb recalled later.[53] He assured Soros that Chubais and Nemtsov supported his plan. Soros flew into Moscow and stopped by to see Nemtsov the next day. "This was the first he'd heard of it," Soros later recalled. "He replied, 'Over my dead body.'"[54] Nemtsov talked Soros out of it, telling him not to help Berezovsky take over Gazprom—this was exactly the kind of predatory capitalism that they, the reformers, were trying to fight. In the end, the confused billionaire gave up the idea of Gazprom but lent a billion dollars to the government so it could pay pensions on time.

Berezovsky was beside himself. "Did Soros really believe that clown Nemtsov? Doesn't he understand," he shouted, "that Nemtsov is playing the role of 'Chubais with a human face' for stupid foreigners? I was the one who came up with that role for him!"[55]

Berezovsky saw himself as the director in the theatre, where Nemtsov was expected to play himself—an honest liberal reformer. In Berezovsky's logic, the cabinet was just the executive body under the board of directors of Russia, Inc. And he had a blocking stake in the company. Berezovsky wasn't the only one who looked down on Nemtsov. Nemtsov was considered a fool, Candide, a naïve provincial who had never seen big money, never played for high stakes. But he thought of himself as the successor to the throne and came up with little games like putting officials in Volga cars and making them declare their income. This was the general opinion of Nemtsov in the board of directors of Russia, Inc. and among the entourage that serviced it. And suddenly this conceited simpleton gets in Berezovsky's way and ruins his plans!

Berezovsky talked to Nemtsov, but Nemtsov dug in his heels and refused. As chairman of the board of state representatives at Gazprom, Nemtsov was firmly opposed to Berezovsky's appointment as chairman of the board of directors. Unlike Chernomyrdin and Vyakhirev, who certainly did not want Berezovsky at the head of Gazprom but were afraid to tell him directly, Nemtsov was straightforward. He was Yeltsin's favourite—no one could touch him. While on a trip to China, he called Nadezhdin and told him to hide the paper in a safe and wait for his return. Nadezhdin did. About twenty-four hours later, to his great surprise, Nemtsov bumped into Berezovsky at the airport in Yichang, Central China, fifty kilometres from the dam.

"What do you want?" Nemtsov asked.

"Well, we didn't part on good terms. We need to resolve this issue."

"Boris, we've already resolved it. Full stop."

But Berezovsky was not ready to end it. The next day, in Beijing, the first thing he did was to go to Chernomyrdin, who had just flown in, and tell him that his deputy was ignoring his instructions. This was intolerable. "What can I do?" Chernomyrdin shrugged. "He's the successor."

Once again Berezovsky had not got what he wanted. Once again Nemtsov, whom he considered to be his creation, had stood in his way. At the end of the negotiations, he essentially told Nemtsov, "I will destroy you."[56] Three days later, news agencies reported that Gazprom's management had succeeded in maintaining the same balance of power in their favour on the board of directors. Berezovsky was outraged; his candidacy was not even considered.

Nemtsov had been in his new position for only three months but was already surrounded by powerful opponents. And the main battle—for Svyazinvest—was yet to come.

# CHAPTER 13

## 1997
## A Boat Going Over a Waterfall

### The Davos Pact falls apart

In the first half of the 1990s, the former theatre director Vladimir Gusinsky embarked on the path of the oligarch-to-be. First, he opened a small cooperative to make copper bracelets. Then he became a financial consultant, founded a bank, got into real-estate development and established close ties with Moscow's mayor, Yury Luzhkov. In 1993–94 Gusinsky's security service, the biggest in Moscow, even helped the city authorities in their fight against organized crime. When Gusinsky set up the NTV television channel in 1993 at the suggestion of Grigory Yavlinsky, he still saw himself as a real-estate developer and banker. Everything changed after a run-in with the Kremlin. In December of that year, in a security operation dubbed "Face Down in the Snow", Alexander Korzhakov ordered presidential guards to shove Gusinsky's security guards to the ground and even broke one of their ribs. Korzhakov later explained the purpose of the operation: "We had to show the guys who was boss."[1] Gusinsky, fearing arrest, went to London for almost six months. "In London, Gusinsky watched Sky television," recalled Igor Malashenko, "and returned to Moscow a different person."[2]

From then on, television was all Gusinsky thought about. After setting up NTV, he started an ambitious and very expensive project: NTV-Plus satellite television. He even launched his own communications satellite. Gusinsky was not interested in the shares-for-loans auctions. The oligarchs had agreed among themselves back in February 1996 that there would be no more of them. "Berezovsky asked me, 'But what about you?' Gusinsky recalled. I said, 'I'm good.'"[3]

"We discussed it," Malashenko said. "He told me, 'Everything they [participants in the auctions] do is criminal. They'll go to jail. I don't want to.' I asked him where he'd get the money to finance his plans. He said, 'Loans. Our capitalization will grow faster, so we will always be in the black.'"[4] The NTV-Plus financial plan was based on the belief that the economy would grow and that a powerful middle class would emerge. Gazprom provided funding: Gusinsky borrowed $40 million, a loan he would come to regret. In the end, he was not involved in privatization at all. He was the only oligarch who didn't get an award for his contribution to Yeltsin's electoral victory, apart from the nationwide broadcast television channel for NTV. "The oligarchs said it wasn't right," Malashenko recalled. "He's one of us and he got nothing. What do you want?"[5]

So, at the end of 1996, the state came up with the idea of forming a big telecom holding company based on Svyazinvest, which united dozens of regional telephone operators, and Rostelecom, which controlled long-distance and international telecommunications. The result was a huge monopoly structure—something like an oil pipeline, but in the telecommunications sector. This "new and improved" Svyazinvest desperately needed investment: the country's largely Soviet telecommunications systems were in a deplorable state. The state decided to auction off a blocking stake: twenty-five per cent plus one share. For Gusinsky, this would be a core asset. "The idea to privatize Svyazinvest came to [State Property Committee head Alfred] Kokh," Gusinsky explained. "This was a great project to bring together all the telecom operators. All we needed to do was to convince the military and the special services."[6]

The *siloviki* opposed the privatization of Svyazinvest, fearing that Western investors would gain access to secret communication lines. An informal letter of intent was signed in the Kremlin under Chubais, who still headed the Presidential Administration. The meeting where the letter was signed was attended by Gusinsky, Chubais and Kokh, as well as Potanin, then first deputy prime minister in charge of the economy. The participants decided to auction off Svyazinvest. Of course, it was clear to everyone present that the main contender was Gusinsky. They agreed, he recalled, on two simple rules: "One: whoever makes the highest bid wins. Two: no government participation."[7] By "government participation", they meant Potanin. Kokh recalled: "Gusinsky pointed directly at Potanin and said, 'Volodya, I think you shouldn't participate for a number of reasons, first and foremost because you are the first deputy prime minister.' And Potanin said, 'I agree. I'm not going to participate.' That was the end of it."[8]

The old shares-for-loans auctions were over. A year before, oil rigs and metallurgical factories had been sold on the cheap, but now Gusinsky was ready to pay real money for Svyazinvest. The starting price of Svyazinvest was $1.18 billion, more than the government received for all the assets sold at all the previous auctions put together. A strategic investor was needed. In one sense, the Svyazinvest auction was similar to the previous ones: the winner was determined in advance. Just as the bidders at shares-for-loans auctions had negotiated with the managers of the companies to be privatized a year before, Gusinsky now literally pulled together the asset himself, spending five months persuading the security services to agree to privatization (two years earlier, the security services had blocked the government's first attempt to privatize Svyazinvest). He found an investor, the Spanish telecommunications company Telefónica. The next meeting was held in May 1997, again in Chubais's office, but this time at the White House because Chubais was already first deputy prime minister. Gusinsky wanted to reconfirm the agreement. He brought Berezovsky. Although Berezovsky was not involved in the auction itself, he wanted to partner with Gusinsky when he won. And besides, the deal was extremely important politically, so Berezovsky insisted on being there. Potanin took part again, now not an official, but an oligarch. It was suddenly clear that the terms had changed. As one of the participants later described it, Gusinsky reminded everyone that Potanin was not involved. And why not? argued Chubais. The deal was that First Deputy Prime Minister Potanin would not participate. Now Potanin was no longer a cabinet member, and no one had the right to keep him from taking part.

The auction would be fair. The highest bidder would win. End of.[9] Gusinsky had not expected this response. He'd been sure they had a firm agreement, and, instead of an acquisition, he got a knife in the back. He was stunned.

Gusinsky came to his senses and started threatening. If Potanin took part in the auction, first Gusinsky would start looking for dirt on the young reformers. Second, he'd "take off the prohibition" about reporting on the young reformers on his television news channel. NTV had been showing the government in a positive way, but if they—Chubais, Kokh and their comrades—thought everyone was so happy with them, they had another thing coming.[10] This was a serious threat. By spring 1997, Malashenko recounted, Gusinsky had "showered money on his informational attack squad and started giving direct orders to NTV's news service."[11]

"I thought that we'd made enough tactical concessions," Chubais said to explain his actions in the Svyazinvest conflict, "and that we needed to made clear, transparent rules of the game, the same for everyone."[12] By this logic, the auctions had been a tactical alliance between the top leadership in the country and the oligarchs to counter the Communist threat. The Communists had been defeated, and now it was the oligarchs' turn. But by Gusinsky's—and Berezovsky's—logic, the sudden change in the rules of the game itself was a blatant violation of the rules of the game. Yes, the auction would be fair, but it violated previous agreements. They thought the fact that Potanin was no longer an official was just an excuse.

A year before, the oligarchs had asked Chubais to run Yeltsin's election campaign, because he had been on good terms with all the big businessmen, and because everyone trusted him. Now Berezovsky and Gusinsky thought that Chubais had formed an alliance with Potanin. They suspected that Chubais had decided to promote Potanin for the presidency, or, conversely, that Chubais decided to become president with Potanin's help. This was supported by the fact that Potanin had purchased two influential newspapers, *Izvestiya* and *Komsomolskaya pravda*, and everyone was discussing his political ambitions. Potanin had been very unhappy when he was removed from the cabinet, which he suspected had been done with Berezovsky's involvement. Berezovsky became suspicious when in May 1997 Potanin's organizations suddenly tried to buy out Sibneft, the oil company whose shares he had acquired at a shares-for-loans auction in late 1995 and considered his property.

By all indications, in spring 1997 the Davos Pact, which had ensured peace between the oligarchs and secured Yeltsin's election victory—the "oligarch collective farm", as it was then called—was already falling apart. "The equilibrium between Russia's largest financial and industrial groups has been shaken: the reality is that competition is becoming far more intense," *Kommersant* wrote in May.[13] The euphoria of the election victory had turned the winners' heads. Now everyone wanted everything all at once. Oligarchs once again fought among themselves for new pieces of property and political influence. Berezovsky and Gusinsky were particularly feared. They had control of the two main TV channels—weapons of mass destruction that had proved effective in the presidential elections. Giving them the telecommunication infrastructure would mean giving them total control over the media space. Alfred Kokh was unambiguous: "I, for instance, believe that it would be dangerous to let Gusinsky and Berezovsky even near Svyazinvest, because the industry is strongly linked to telecommunications, and they are very strong there as it is. If we give them Svyazinvest, they will turn out presidents every four years like pies at a bakery."[14]

Chubais seemed dissatisfied with the role of the billionaires' hired hand. After all, he created them, he opened the doors to spectacular prospects for them, not the other way around. And when Potanin also found an investor, George Soros, and wanted to take part in the auction, Chubais, as Malashenko said, "decided to defeat the [Berezovsky and Gusinsky] coalition and find a new source of support."[15] It was a question of who would dictate the rules of the game from now on: Chubais and his team or the union of Berezovsky and Gusinsky?

## The battle for Svyazinvest

"Svyazinvest was the last straw," Berezovsky later said. If it "hadn't been Svyazinvest, it would have been something else."[16] But in spring 1997,

Svyazinvest was the perfect *casus belli*: the concept of fair bidding was ideologically impeccable, and the higher Svyazinvest's price went, the easier it would be for the government to plug the holes in the budget. The political struggle immediately took on an ideological dimension. What is the place of big business in governing Russia? What is the role of the state in its relationship with business? A few months later, when much blood had already been shed in the battle for Svyazinvest, Nemtsov would talk about the choice Russia had to make among the three types of capitalism, two of which collided in the battle for Svyazinvest:

> What kind of capitalism does Russia need? Here is the choice right now. The first kind is *nomenklatura*–bureaucratic capitalism. The leader of this kind of capitalism is Luzhkov. The slogan of this kind of capitalism is: "All the Power, Property and Money Belong to the Bureaucracy." The second is oligarchic capitalism. Its leader is Berezovsky. All power, property, and money belong to a narrow group of corporations, companies and people, but not to the bureaucracy. [...] In my opinion, the optimal capitalism for Russia is people's capitalism. Administrative power should be in the hands of the people elected, and property and money should go to as many citizens as possible.[17]

Yumashev persuaded Chubais and Nemtsov not to rush, to let Gusinsky have Svyazinvest. "Let's get all the big businessmen together," he said. "If we need him, Yeltsin can be there. If not, the three of us will bring them together and say, 'This will be the last auction like we had in the past.' We know that the rules of the game need to be changed, but Gusinsky already took some steps, so this auction will be like the previous ones. We understand that Gusinsky must win."[18]

But Chubais wouldn't give in, insisting that the government must act quickly, here and now. If they moved ahead bit by bit, nothing would change. So, Chubais deliberately blew up the vestiges of harmony in the board of directors of Russia, Inc. by announcing new rules of the game for Gusinsky and Berezovsky. It was not just a declaration of new and more equitable rules. It was a declaration of war. But a legitimate question hung in the air: what next? Where would this war lead? "I said,

'If this happens, we won't have a government of young reformers in a month,'" Yumashev recalled. "Chubais and Nemtsov said that wouldn't be the case. On the contrary: we can use this example now to demonstrate our power and capabilities. If we can put this player in his place, it will be the most important way to strengthen our power. Afterwards it will be much easier to work."[19]

The auction was officially opened at the end of May. On 23 June, bids began to be collected, and the bids were scheduled to be opened and made public at 5.00 p.m. two days later. With the active help of investment banker Boris Jordan, Potanin's pool of investors included a number of foreign banks and George Soros, who decided to invest $1 billion in Svyazinvest. Potanin's plan was purely speculative. He acted as a portfolio investor in order to resell the asset to a strategic investor. Gusinsky, by contrast, was planning to develop Svyazinvest himself. He was going to the auction together with Telefónica, which was going to manage the company if they won their bid.

Gusinsky and Berezovsky did not give up hope that Chubais and Potanin would come to an agreement. Two days before the auction, on 23 July, when Potanin at last officially announced that he was taking part in the bid, the two oligarchs made another attempt to resolve the matter amicably. They flew to Saint-Tropez for a meeting with Potanin and Chubais. David Hoffman describes the meeting in detail. Chubais was adamant; the oligarchs threatened. "The final warning came from Berezovsky. 'In one day, you can't just break the system over your knee,' Berezovsky said. 'You are igniting a war. You don't want it, but it is going to happen.' 'Don't dictate conditions to the state,' Chubais replied, tersely." They left Saint-Tropez with nothing. Then Gusinsky tried to negotiate with Potanin himself. According to Hoffman, they met for the last time two hours before the auction and discussed the price, with Gusinsky saying that Potanin told him the amount of his bid. Just in case, Gusinsky decided to add another two hundred million dollars to his bid, but ran into an unexpected problem: Telefónica, his main partner in the deal, simply had no time to approve a new bid in the remaining hour and a half. Still, he reckoned he would win.[20]

On the morning of the auction day, Gusinsky's PR manager Sergei Zverev wrote a triumphant press release stating that the MOST Group

(Gusinsky's bank and companies) was pleased to have won the bid and was looking forward to developing Svyazinvest together with ONEXIM Bank, i.e. Potanin. Zverev said he'd clear the press release with Potanin and others. It was Friday. The next day Zverev was going on vacation. His kayaks were ready, and towards evening he went home to pack. He was completely relaxed and so sure of the auction results that he wasn't even waiting for them. Suddenly he got a call from Gusinsky.

"We lost."

"How'd that happen?"

"Just like that."[21]

"Potanin, who should have bid less, bid a little more and won. He cheated," claimed Pyotr Aven, a former minister in the Gaidar cabinet who was now part-owner of Alfa Bank.[22] But even if this were true, the auction itself really was fair. No one knew ahead of time who would win the tender—not Gusinsky, not Potanin, not Chubais. When the envelopes were opened with great ceremony at 5.00 p.m., it turned out that Telefónica and Gusinsky had offered $1.71 billion, whereas Soros and Potanin had offered $165 million more. In the history of Russian privatization, this was an absolute record. "And just like that," Zverev said, with little sense of irony, "we lost the country."[23]

## $100,000 for a book

Losing an asset after investing so much effort? Suffering such humiliation from Chubais? Gusinsky was furious. On the evening of 25 July, he and Malashenko were in Spain, in Sotogrande, where Gusinsky and his associates had some real estate. Malashenko took great pains to reassure him. "Just forget about it," he kept saying all evening. "Svyazinvest is gone, and the hell with it. There will be other opportunities. Of course, we will not forget Chubais. He really screwed us. But in a formal sense, everything was done correctly, wasn't it? Exactly. Let's not start a war over this. Let's forget it."[24]

Gusinsky cooled down and agreed with Malashenko: the hell with Svyazinvest. But they had forgotten about Berezovsky. Although Berezovsky had nothing to do with the auction, he would not give up.

He had his own score to settle with Potanin, Chubais and Nemtsov. Berezovsky went on the attack. At his instigation, the day after the auction, Channel One television anchor Sergei Dorenko—who would soon be considered the country's top TV hit man—accused Alfred Kokh, head of the State Property Committee, of selling a stake in Svyazinvest to people with questionable reputations: Jordan, Soros and Potanin. By that time, Nemtsov had already approved the results of the auction—they were no longer privatizing for free, so the highest bidder won—and so he, too, got his share of insults from Dorenko: "Nemtsov is twitching and fidgeting like a cockroach that has been sprayed with poison."[25]

That was on Saturday. On Monday, the country's leading bankers and Chubais gathered in Gusinsky's office to discuss the situation. "It was just like one of those movies you see on TV when all the heads of mafia groups get together—except it was a meeting of oligarchs," recalled Aven, who was present at the meeting. The only item on the agenda was how strong Potanin had got. Fridman voiced the bankers' position: no complaints about the bidding itself, but "one bank should not be allowed to take such a lead." Everyone was in favour of giving Svyazinvest to Gusinsky. "It ended in a scandal," Aven said. "Potanin said he would not give anything away. Chubais supported him, for the most part."[26]

Up until September, Berezovsky tried to resolve matters by lobbying for a new tender of Svyazinvest. He consulted with Yumashev and Dyachenko, who tried to persuade Chubais, but to no avail. At the same time, both Berezovsky's ORT and Gusinsky's NTV, along with newspapers owned by the oligarchs, came down hard on the cabinet. Kokh and Potanin, who had been denounced as conspirators and were the talk of television, where they were torn to pieces. The country was plunged into a political crisis.

A week after the auction, Nemtsov was the first victim of an attack in the press. Alexander Minkin, a close acquaintance of Gusinsky's, revealed that in May Nemtsov had received a fee of $100,000 for the publication of his book *A Provincial in Moscow* in Germany.[27] Minkin also published a transcript of a wiretap of Nemtsov's telephone conversation with Sergei Lisovsky, the publisher. In this conversation, also taking place in May, Nemtsov is angry. He had just pushed through Yeltsin's decree making it compulsory for officials to declare their incomes, and now he found himself in a ridiculous situation. He had not yet received the fee for the book, but if he published his tax declaration without the fee, he'd be accused of hiding his income. Nemtsov shouted at Lisovsky, "There will be an international scandal... This issue has become purely political... You're fucking setting me up!"

By the mid-1990s when Russians began to make serious money, officials found themselves in an absurd situation: their decisions were worth millions, if not tens of millions, of dollars, while they themselves received minuscule salaries. Ministers could not live the way they were supposed to live on their official salaries. For example, Nemtsov received a flat from the state (as his own property), a dacha, free transport, etc. But he could not maintain the same dacha on his deputy prime minister's salary. When his wife, Raisa, moved in with him from Nizhny Novgorod, she went to the Kremlin waving utility bills: how was she supposed to pay for them on Nemtsov's salary? The Nemtsovs couldn't afford to buy the clothes they needed: for receptions and official visits, Raisa borrowed outfits from a friend.

Nemtsov was scrupulous in these matters. He would not consider taking a supplement to his salary from businessmen, although this was already common practice for people in the higher echelons of state service. Nemtsov had signed a contract for the book *A Provincial in Moscow* with the Vagrius publishing house in January 1996, when he was still governor. It appeared on the shelves in early April when he was already in Moscow and the talk of the town. "I have a vivid memory of the fifth anniversary of the Vagrius publishing house at the Central House of Writers. It was the 15th of April, and Boris was the main star of the evening," Vladimir Grigoryev, one of the publishing house's founders, recalled.[28] And, of course, Nemtsov got excited when he learnt from Grigoryev that a Swiss company had offered to translate his book into several languages, publish it worldwide and pay Nemtsov a fee of $100,000 dollars. "They must be crazy over there," Grigoryev added.

It soon turned out that the "crazy guys" were from the Swiss company Trans Rail, which had effectively monopolized payments for international transport on Russian railways. The system was very simple: Trans Rail received currency from foreign companies for transit and paid domestic prices to the Russian railways. "That's what we get for being idiots,"

Chernomyrdin shrugged helplessly when Nemtsov dug up where the railways' transit revenue went and showed him his calculations. And now Trans Rail was offering Nemtsov $100,000 in royalties for his book. Of course, this was an unacceptable offer. "Let them publish the book, I won't take anything from them," Nemtsov told Grigoryev, "even though I could really use the money." To help Nemtsov, Grigoryev turned to Lisovsky, and together they got together the funds to pay Nemtsov the same fee.

That's what Minkin found out about. "We just wanted to support the young deputy prime minister," Grigoryev said, "so the oligarchs wouldn't get hold of him."[29]

## What is "dirt" anyway?

Ever since Berezovsky published Yeltsin's memoirs as a way of getting into the president's inner circle, it was clear that publishing a book could be a source of serious income and could also serve interests unrelated to book publishing. But Yeltsin was an international figure, and presidential memoirs are an established genre. For many officials, publishing a book became a convenient way to convert dirty money into clean cash that could then be declared as income and spent in peace. Aleksashenko, for example, said he had been offered a similar procedure when he worked for the Ministry of Finance back in 1995.

It was hard to criticize Nemtsov over his fee. In his article, Minkin accused Nemtsov of using his official position for personal gain, latching onto another of Nemtsov's lines from the wiretap: "I am the author of a decree that I can't fulfil myself. Now I have to ask Yeltsin to hold back the decree because of you." It couldn't hurt Nemtsov. But as a postscript to that wiretap, Minkin added just one phrase: "Deputy Prime Minister and Head of the Ministry of Property Alfred Kokh also received one hundred thousand dollars from a Swiss firm for some book about privatization in Russia."

Kokh found himself in a more difficult situation: not only was he not a nationally popular politician, but the Swiss firm that was ready to publish the manuscript was linked to Vladimir Potanin's ONEXIM Bank (a fact that would be revealed in autumn).

And so, Kokh fell as the first victim of the battle for Svyazinvest, which went down in history as the "war of the bankers."* Three days later Kokh went on leave, but before doing so he left a letter of resignation on Chubais's desk.

Yeltsin easily gave up Kokh, but he was not about to give up his deputy prime ministers and young reformers, nor was he about to cancel the results of the auction. "I'm tired of defending you," he snapped at Nemtsov at one of his meetings. But at the same time he told him: "They [the oligarchs] are nobodies. I don't know a thing about them. You are the government."[30] Since there was no dirt—compromising material—on Nemtsov, NTV chose to portray him as a dolt, playing up his informal, loose style of behaviour. For television viewers and newspaper readers, easy-going became lightweight, reckless became foolish, informal became talkative. NTV mocked him for the Volga decree, and footage of Nemtsov breaking diplomatic protocol to meet Heydar Aliyev, the president of Azerbaijan, in white trousers on the tarmac was shown on screen many times. The white-trouser incident had taken place back in July. During a terrible heat wave, Chernomyrdin suddenly called and ordered Nemtsov to meet Aliyev at the airport. Nemtsov wasn't wearing a suit that day. He went to the airport in what he was wearing at the time. "Why do you come to work dressed like that?" Yeltsin snarled at him on the phone.[31]

On ORT Dorenko took a simpler approach. Since Nemtsov always appeared everywhere with at least two women, NTV recalled Malashenko "instructing their cameramen to trim the frame so that there was just one girl."[32] Dorenko did the opposite. He had some women come on his show and pretend to be strippers who were allegedly summoned by Nemtsov and Potanin "not for aesthetic viewing, but for their own pleasure." "The strippers stripped naked in front of Nemtsov and Potanin on a specially built podium above the pool." Dorenko savoured every word in his trademark delivery. "Our colleague Yelena Eriksen has in her possession a videotape of Nemtsov frolicking with some lovelies. The lovelies and Nemtsov were without their swimming costumes."[33]

---

\* It was called "war of the bankers" because it was bankers who took part in the Svyazinvest bidding war.

After September, the war between the oligarchs and the government escalated again. Berezovsky lost any hope of reaching an agreement with Chubais and turned his bayonets—his journalists—on him personally. Berezovsky's *Nezavisimaya gazeta* published a text under the pseudonym Ulyan Kerzonov* entitled 'Chubais Seeks Total Control over Russia', accusing Chubais of an attempted coup.[34] The Bolshevik Chubais, the paper wrote, is promoting Potanin for president and keeping Nemtsov as a fallback in case something goes wrong. NTV immediately picked up the story.

Nemtsov and Chubais launched a counterattack. Rumours leaked to the press that they were going to approach the president with the idea of dismissing Berezovsky from the Security Council. But Berezovsky managed to get through to Yeltsin first, and the president made it clear before the cameras just before the meeting that he had no plans to dismiss Berezovsky. "The relationship between Berezovsky and Tatyana Dyachenko and between Berezovsky and Valentin Yumashev has gone from good to one of trust," *Kommersant* newspaper wrote at the time, "Berezovsky's position at ORT is stronger than ever."[35]

Yeltsin showed one of his main leadership traits: in difficult situations, he tried to keep balance between interest groups. In Russia, Inc. he was chairman of the board of directors rather than CEO, not so much the supreme ruler—the head of the executive branch—as the arbiter who maintained the balance of power among the elite. Once again, he was looking for a compromise. Yeltsin probably didn't know how the conflict over Svyazinvest had started, but apparently he was taking pains not to let either side claim victory.

In mid-September, Yeltsin made another attempt to resolve the matter peacefully. He met with the bankers for the first time since he had received them a year and a half earlier at the start of the election campaign. Gusinsky was seated directly opposite Yeltsin. Yeltsin had always disliked Gusinsky, and now he was at the centre of a political crisis.

"Are you the one spreading dirt about members of the government?" Yeltsin angrily asked Gusinsky.

---

\* According to Arkady Ostrovsky, Boris Berezovsky wrote it under the pseudonym Kerzonov.

"What is 'dirt'?" Gusinsky snapped back quickly. "Either it is the truth, and then it is a question for the cabinet members. Or it is a lie, in which case it's just a lie."[36]

Yeltsin did not continue the conversation. The meeting with the bankers went nowhere. "Some hoped that Yeltsin would put Gusinsky in his place," Yumashev recalled. "But at the end of the meeting Yeltsin said in general terms: 'I won't let anyone harm the cabinet. I beg you to be responsible. We all have to think together about the future of Russia.'"[37] In the end, a decision was made to place Khodorkovsky in the role of mediator between the parties. Khodorkovsky was in favour of a new tender, but Chubais again said no. Yeltsin, in his own words, felt his "back was up against the wall." At the same time, prosecutors were investigating Kokh's notorious book, while news agencies, quoting knowledgeable sources, were scaring up a new wave of dirt on the first two deputy prime ministers and their associates in the cabinet. The clouds were gathering, and it was obvious that a thunderstorm would soon break.

## "Top Secret: I pass the baton"

Throughout the endless conflicts among the Russian elite in 1997, everyone understood that no one would be knocked out of the game for good. There were real interests at stake, both political and financial; some would win and some would lose, but the game would go on. Journalists were divided into warring camps along purely corporate lines. The major media was in the hands of the oligarchs and had become propaganda mouthpieces, but there were a variety of players on the scene. Political life was still open and full of opportunities.

The efforts of the young reformers seemed to be bearing fruit. By October, they had much to boast about. "Russia is half a step away from the start of real economic growth," Chubais told parliamentarians.[38] For the first time in all the Yeltsin years, the Russian economy showed positive momentum. It was still weak—the GDP grew 1.4 per cent in 1997—but there was hope that they'd already hit bottom and were coming up. Tax collection was still poor, but the government paid off debts on pensions in the summer and settled accounts with the military by autumn, thanks to the sale of Svyazinvest. And by winter it had paid its debts to state employees. Oleg Sysuyev recalled: "By the end of 1997, before a New Year's reception at the Kremlin, Chubais reported to Yeltsin that the wage debts had been settled."[39]

The opposition majority in the Duma prevented the government from passing any of the newly proposed reforms, but the general course for reform remained unchanged. Inflation was near zero, Russia joined the London Club and the Paris Club.* It became a member of the G7, turning it into the G8. The stock market was growing, and even important social indicators, such as life expectancy and crime solving, were rising. At the end of October, Chubais already thought it was realistic to achieve 7–8 per cent growth over the next two to four years. Even in January, Nemtsov would still say with assurance that economic growth was "as inevitable as the sunrise" and the country could expect a 4–5 per cent increase in GDP.

Progress wasn't just seen in boring statistics. There were new films and new music, new clubs and new trends. Moscow, still garish and semi-Soviet, was nevertheless becoming a fashionable city. Change and a new rhythm was felt in everything. There were glimmers of light at the end of the tunnel. Russia would soon be back on track, and in the future there would be prosperity and a special, but worthy, place in the club of great powers. The path, though thorny, was clear: Russia saw itself as part of Europe and the modern West.

Nemtsov was still riding high. At the beginning of September, six months after his arrival in Moscow, pollsters at the Public Opinion Foundation found that in a hypothetical presidential election he "would have the best chance of reaching the second round and better chances than his rivals of getting more votes in the second round."[40] Nemtsov was still the favourite and the successor. On 10 October, as he was flying to France, Yeltsin made it clear for the first time that this was his last term, and he hoped to be succeeded by "a young, energetic and combative democrat."[41] Yes, the journalists nodded, a name that begins with "N."

---

\* Informal international institutions involved in settling external public debts. The Paris Club settles government debt to creditor countries, the London Club to private banks.

Just before his visit to France, Yeltsin had presented Nemtsov with a photograph of them together, signed "Top Secret: I pass the baton. Yeltsin." (When Nemtsov showed it to Chubais, Chubais advised him to hide it and not to show it to anyone.) Everyone saw how much he trusted and favoured Nemtsov. They were often together: Nemtsov accompanied him on trips—both around the country and abroad—talking almost as equals, without flattery or sycophancy. "Both were alike in some ways—even to some extent in appearance. Both were tall, imposing, independent," Yeltsin's daughter Tatyana said.[42]

Nemtsov was more direct than Yeltsin, but both were good-natured. Yeltsin liked to make fun of Nemtsov. During a visit to Sweden in December 1997, after champagne at the Swedish king's reception, Yeltsin joked that Nemtsov would make a good husband for Crown Princess Victoria and even tried to put them in the same carriage after dinner.

Another time, even before the trip to Sweden, Yeltsin took Nemtsov to Krasnoyarsk for an informal meeting with Japanese Prime Minister Ryutaro Hashimoto. After a boat ride on the Yenisei, Yeltsin, visibly tired, suddenly decided to return the Kuril Islands to Japan. This was a huge scandal. The problem of the Southern Kurils had been hanging over Russian–Japanese relations since the end of the Second World War, and it could not be resolved on the fly. Nemtsov and Yastrzhembsky literally jumped out of their chairs when they heard this, and Nemtsov almost knelt in front of Yeltsin later, begging him to change his mind. In the end, Yeltsin gave them the night to resolve the Kuril question. As he patted Nemtsov on the shoulder, he told Hashimoto, "The boys will think it over and propose options." Hashimoto immediately suggested involving the Japanese ambassador in the brainstorming, but Nemtsov and Yastrzhembsky tactfully declined the offer. "Everyone said goodnight," Yastrzhembsky recalls, "and I turn around and look at Boris. His eyes were huge, his mouth pursed, and he said, 'We're in big trouble. This is high treason. This is a violation of the Constitution.'"[43]

The next day, they gently put a stop to the Kuril story, largely thanks to Nemtsov's ability to reason with Yeltsin. In the words of Irina Khakamada, who began as a member of parliament and became one of the young reformers in the cabinet, Nemtsov was the only one who could "mirror" Yeltsin—that is, speak his language.

Khakamada tells a story about Nemtsov's special ability. In February 1998, Yeltsin was going to Italy, and Nemtsov pulled a lot of strings for Khakamada to fly to Rome with him and persuade him to support her small-business proposals. Everyone took their seats, Yeltsin boarded and made his way to his cabin, and Nemtsov immediately followed him. "He was very close to the president and could see him whenever he wished." After a while, Nemtsov came out of Yeltsin's office and called Khakamada to come in. "I go in and sit down," Khakamada said. "Yeltsin already had health problems, slow reactions, and so on. He leans forward, looking at me, and his eyes are like a boa constrictor. A very intense stare. I got flustered. Because there was nothing human in those eyes. But there wasn't anything inhuman either. It's just that I'm the rabbit and he's the boa constrictor. And the boa constrictor is staring at me, wondering whether to swallow me or not. I got nervous and started spewing out everything I'd learnt. 'In Italy, ninety to one hundred per cent of the economy is based on small business.' Pause. Then he says, 'I know!' I go on to say something else. Again he looks at me: 'I see.' I thought: 'Well, that's it, I'm finished.' At that moment Nemtsov realized that this wasn't going well. He sat down next to me and started looking at Yeltsin. At that moment his face became a copy of Yeltsin's. He bulged his eyes, leant forward, looked into his eyes and began to speak very slowly. 'Here's the portfolio. There are three agreements here. She wrote them all. We need them. We will sign them. Here is the folder.' His influence was enormous."

## Circling the wagons

In October, against the background of the growing banking war, Yeltsin had another fully fledged crisis with the parliament. The Duma, led by the Communists, rejected the draft budget and decided to hold a vote of no confidence in the cabinet. The Duma speaker, Gennady Seleznyov, explained that since the constitution didn't allow the Duma to hold a vote of no confidence in Chubais and Nemtsov separately, they had no choice but to vote on their confidence in the head of state, and those two "can just stick their hands in their pockets and do nothing but smile."[44]

The parliamentary crisis stretched on for a fortnight, but the main target of the opposition really wasn't Chubais and Nemtsov. It was Yeltsin. The Communists had already bounced back from their defeat in 1996. Sergei Dubinin, then governor of the Central Bank, recalled that in October and November 1997 the parliament had sensed that the president and his scandal-ridden cabinet were weak. The deputies sabotaged all the initiatives from the executive branch under the principle "the worse it is for them, the better it is for us."[45] The conflict with the Supreme Soviet of five years ago was rekindled, and the Communists again went to war with Yeltsin.

Under Yeltsin's new constitution, after a vote of no confidence in the cabinet, the president had the right either to dismiss the cabinet or to dissolve the Duma and call for new elections. While Nemtsov tried to dissuade Grigory Yavlinsky's faction from participating in the vote to no avail, Chernomyrdin and Chubais addressed the lawmakers, telling them that if they really wanted it, the cabinet was ready to resign. Yeltsin, who believed any talks with the Duma were humiliating, agreed to join the negotiations and was willing to meet it halfway on some issues. The parliament withdrew the vote of no confidence and promised to pass the budget in exchange for a number of major concessions, but the respite was short-lived. In November, the Duma once again blocked passage of the budget. There was no way to change the deputies' minds.

On another front, Nemtsov and Chubais had lost another battle back in early October, when Nemtsov together with Yeltsin inaugurated the Nizhny Novgorod Fair. A few days earlier, there had been press reports that the president was planning to make a historic statement. These rumours were close to the truth. Nemtsov had persuaded Chubais to co-write a letter to Yeltsin, urging him to announce with a great deal of fanfare a "New Deal for New Russia, comparable only to Roosevelt's New Deal." "We cannot allow," Nemtsov and Chubais wrote to the president,

> Russian capitalism, which has already got past its first "uncivilized" forms, to degenerate into an oligarchic form of capitalism that is against the interests of average people. The predatory capitalism in Russia must be replaced by a democratic, truly people's capitalism

that is beneficial to the majority of Russians. The few "new Russians" [i.e. the new class of rich Russians that appeared in the 1990s] should be replaced by a multimillion middle class. We understand people's capitalism for Russia as a society of equal opportunities, a society without obscene wealth and poverty; a society in which the main factor of stability is a broad middle class; a new economic and social order that benefits the vast majority of Russians; a society in which the interests of large, medium and small capital are balanced in such a way as to ensure steady economic growth.[46]

This would be a powerful symbolic gesture—Yeltsin declaring a platform of popular capitalism, and not just anywhere, but in and with Nemtsov's home region. He would be supporting the young reformers in their fight against the oligarchs and securing Nemtsov's status as his successor.

But this new course was never announced, and the text was buried in Kremlin offices. According to Viktor Aksyuchits, who helped Nemtsov write it, Yumashev persuaded Yeltsin to postpone the speech on the pretext that the time and place were badly chosen. Why now? Better to do in the New Year. Why in the provinces? Better to do in Moscow.[47] (Yumashev refutes this: first, there was no such speech and no plans for it; second, Nemtsov and Chubais had direct access to Yeltsin, and he could not have prevented them from giving him a letter even if he had wanted to.) In Nizhny Novgorod, Nemtsov had to make excuses to the reporters, telling them that nothing had been planned and it was all speculation. All that remained of the speech was Yeltsin's general thoughts about the middle class, which should be the basis of economic development.

But this story faded in comparison with the book scandal that erupted in November. On 27 October, on his way back from a business trip to London, Chubais told journalists on his plane that he and his associates in the government "as a group of private individuals have prepared a fundamental monograph" about Russian privatization. The journalists were puzzled. What was the book? What was it about? Chubais replied that they had wanted to publish it by the first of October, the fifth anniversary of privatization, but they were running late, and the book would be ready in a month or two. Chubais added that ninety-five per cent of the fee would go to a special fund for the protection of private property that was being established.⁴⁸

Chubais was playing ahead of the game in order to knock the trump cards out of his opponent's hands. He had two audiences: public opinion and President Yeltsin.

## The book scandal

On the evening of Tuesday, 4 November, Chubais and Nemtsov arrived at Yeltsin's residence in Gorki outside of Moscow. Chubais told Yeltsin that "a powerful attack is being prepared against the government." It was going to be a big political crisis. Nemtsov and Chubais again brought a draft decree for Berezovsky to resign as deputy secretary of the Security Council. They said that Berezovsky was using his position for his own interests, both business and political, as well as to fight the cabinet. The information war against the government must end. "If you remove Berezovsky from the Security Council, he will instantly cease to be important. No one will care about his opinion, and the conflict will end," Yeltsin later said the men told him.⁴⁹ Yeltsin first listened, then summoned Yumashev and asked his opinion. Yumashev didn't agree. He said that on the contrary, if Berezovsky was forced to resign, the conflict would escalate. Nemtsov again began to persuade Yeltsin. "I told him literally, 'You either get rid of me or Berezovsky. I won't work with him.' He said, 'Don't give me ultimatums. Where is the decision on Berezovsky?' I said, 'Here it is.' He took the paper, picked up a pen and crossed out the word 'decree'. My hair stood on end. I said, 'May I ask what you're doing?' He said, 'Why should I remove Berezovsky by decree?' I said, 'Why not?' 'Why is he so important that I have to remove him by decree? I'll dismiss him with a memorandum. Do you object?' And he wrote 'memorandum.'"⁵⁰

This was victory over Berezovsky. However, the young reformers did not savour their triumph for long. A few days later, the journalist Alexander Minkin explained the details of the book deal: Chubais, Kokh (again) and three more members of Chubais's team in the government and in the Kremlin received $90,000 each for the book. This was a total of $450,000 and, Minkin declared, clearly "a hidden form of bribery."[51] The money in question had been transferred to their accounts in MOST Bank—Gusinsky's bank—as early as the spring.

"If Mr. Chubais was simply seeking to get rich, he could easily have followed the well-trod path of cash payments and numbered Swiss accounts," *The New York Times* wrote right after the story broke.[52] According to the most widespread version, the "fees" were part of the informal payment for Chubais and his staff in the presidential election campaign. "The source of the money was an extra-budgetary fund set up for the 1996 elections by Chubais together with oligarchs, who contributed five million dollars," according to journalist Arkady Ostrovsky.[53] "First, it would have been impossible to explain. Second, the publishing house belonged to Potanin's ONEXIM Bank."

Chubais understood all this. The publishing rights for the book were handed over to the Foundation for the Protection of Private Property that had been created at the end of October. The publishing house Vagrius and its owner, Vladimir Grigoryev, were also called in to help. "They asked me to cover for them," Grigoryev said. "I told them, 'This book looks interesting. The history of privatization in Russia—I'm ready to work with it. There is a synopsis, there is a chapter outline. Great! In principle, a book like this could be worth this much money: reprivatization, a unique case in the world.'"[54] And in November, after Minkin's revelations, Vagrius announced that it would publish the book in Russia. The next day, Berezovsky was already waiting for Grigoryev at the LogoVAZ reception house. Gusinsky was also there. Grigoryev was supposed to say before the cameras that he had covered up for Chubais. Emotional and heated as always, Gusinsky met him with threats.

"Listen, this book is just business," Grigoryev said, trying to maintain his composure. "I am very interested. We're going to make a lot of money."

"What do you want? Do you want me to give you a couple of printing houses?" Berezovsky pressed. "Do you realize that you are wrecking the whole system?"

"You're the ones ruining it. I'm against the system," Grigoryev said, standing his ground.[55]

But the scandal was already too big. The Kremlin was eloquently silent, the TV channels tore the young reformers to pieces. Chubais publicly admitted the fee was excessive, but that did not help. His team couldn't hold out. Within a few days, all the authors of the future monograph lost their posts (except for Kokh who had resigned back in August). Chubais lost his post as finance minister. "This book is both a great folly and a great mistake," Nemtsov said, worried for his friends. "And when the opportunity arose, [some people] took full advantage of it."[56] Nemtsov, who had nothing to do with the scandal, was stripped of his position as minister for fuel and energy. Chubais and Nemtsov retained their positions as first deputy prime ministers, but it was little consolation: they had been thoroughly discredited.

The Communists celebrated their victory. First the resignation of Berezovsky, then the defeat of the liberals in the government. Their opponents were destroying each other in front of their very eyes. "I witnessed an amazing historical spectacle," George Soros later recalled. "People fighting in a boat that was about to be swept over a waterfall."[57]

And that's what happened. While the oligarchs and the cabinet were at war with each other, the Russian economy was hit by a disaster that threatened to wipe out all the achievements of the past year. It was like a shipwrecked sailor who had managed to make a raft out of planks and finally sees land on the horizon just as he is hit by an enormous wave. On 23 October, the Hong Kong stock market collapsed, and within days the world was plunged into financial crisis. Russia was not immune as investors were pulling out of all emerging markets. By December, Dubinin said that Russia was on the verge of default, using dollar injections to hold the rouble exchange rate down and cut interest rates on government bonds (meaning they were borrowing roubles on the market at ever higher interest rates). The economy was once again caught in a vicious circle: higher short-term borrowing rates required financial resources, but where could they get them when taxes were not collected—especially during the confrontation with the parliament, which refused to approve the budget. But even at the end of the year, no one in the cabinet was aware of the seriousness of the situation, and the young reformers believed that, in the end, the crisis would not affect Russia. Nothing could shake their confidence that the tide had turned and Russia would never return to the past. "Are you here for long?" the Communists had once asked Chubais. "For ever," Chubais replied.

## The demotion game

Nemtsov was not formally involved in the privatization of Svyazinvest, but he was also hurt by the whole affair. "Boris was hit hard and unfairly," Malashenko later recalled, "war is war."[58] Television promoted anti-Nemtsov stories from newspapers, and newspapers, in turn, published articles based on the television stories. Nemtsov's ratings "collapsed ominously", *Nezavisimaya gazeta* wrote in the autumn, referring to the Sunday-news wrap-up on NTV called *Itogi* (*Wrap-Up*), hosted by Yevgeny Kiselyov, the channel's lead journalist and one of its executives. "I have sinned. I am guilty," Kiselyov later said with regret. "I started to record meticulously how much Nemtsov's rating had fallen in a week in every *Wrap-Up* programme. And, in a sense, I got the multimillion audience of the show involved in a game of demotion."[59]

The two main TV channels in the country, ORT and NTV, both played the demotion game. Television discredited Nemtsov and then recorded his drop in ratings as the results of their work. "We are dealing with Nemtsov's first public crisis as a politician," noted the same Berezovsky-owned *Nezavisimaya gazeta*.[60] We are dealing with corrupt journalists, Nemtsov said in an interview in 1998: "In Moscow, all the journalists have sold out. They will do as they are told. They have sacrificed their freedom for money. Why should I be offended? They are given an order, and they carry it out. Starting with Dorenko [...]. The only way to change the situation is to make sure there are twenty times as many journalists. And publications. Then the voice of the tycoon will be drowned out by the chorus of other voices."[61]

In March 1997, Nemtsov arrived in Moscow as a star, Yeltsin's favourite and his successor. By early 1998, he had been effectively destroyed as a politician. He had acquiesced to the Kremlin's entreaties and gone to Moscow, but when he arrived, he received no support from the Kremlin. On the contrary, they thought that Nemtsov was in the way, out of control, pushing ahead, not listening to advice. In April, his approval rating was forty-five per cent; in November, it was twenty-six. "As for Boris Nemtsov, I don't think he has the slightest chance of becoming president of Russia," Boris Berezovsky pronounced on 5 November, the day Nemtsov resigned. "From afar he seemed attractive, but up close it's obvious that he is not yet ready to tackle the tasks that need to be done by the president of the vast country of Russia."[62]

Nemtsov's ratings continued to fall. He had no allies left. Yeltsin was not at his best. Chubais was healing wounds from the book scandal and thinking of ways out of the situation. Their duumvirate fell apart, and in March Chubais left government to head Unified Energy System (more commonly known as RAO UES).

"Unfortunately, the privatization of political power is a problem in Russia," Nemtsov explained in an interview to journalist Yevgeniya Albats exactly one year after his appointment as first deputy prime minister.[63] Albats remembered the interview well. She came to the White House and the two of them had a long talk. "His ratings had collapsed," Albats recalled, "and I asked him, 'How could this happen, Boris?' He said, 'I am who I am. I'm a free man, I don't need any image-makers.'"[64] Both Albats and Nemtsov realized that Nemtsov had lost the game in the cabinet, or almost lost it, and that a new stage was coming. Hopes for the presidency were becoming nothing but fantasy.

"How do you assess your chances? What's your base of support?" Albats asked.

"I have no clans, magnates or factions behind me," Nemtsov replied. "What support base could I have? Public opinion is essential. I need it to work. There's no point in trying to predict my ratings in the year 2000."

"But it doesn't seem like you see yourself in business. Don't you have any career aspirations? It's clear that you have to move somewhere else," Albats continued to press.

"What do you expect me to say?" Nemtsov asked and ended the interview.[65]

Nemtsov had nothing to say. He had no Plan B. When Yeltsin summoned him to Moscow, he promised that he would not dismiss him for two years. But how could Nemtsov move forward without popularity, without allies, without a team and surrounded by powerful opponents? He was still first deputy prime minister, but now he stood alone in the field.

On the same date—the anniversary of his year in the cabinet—Nemtsov made a grand gesture. He launched a personal campaign against oligarch capitalism. On his own, he publicly advocated for the new course that he and Chubais had hoped Yeltsin would announce in October. He didn't change the programme. The mainstay of development should be the middle class, not the oligarchs; power should be elected, not owned by a narrow group of entrepreneurs linked to the state bureaucracy. But Nemtsov was no longer counting on Yeltsin. "For some reason he invited me. He said, 'Let's go, we have to hold a press conference on the fight against the oligarchs,'" Khakamada recalled. "To be honest, I was stunned."[66]

Since the early 1990s, the merger of state and business in Russia had been through exclusive access to state resources, from tax breaks and budgetary funds to land and property. So-called authorized banks got access to state money, companies got access to subsidies from the budget, special oil exporters bought oil at a fixed domestic price and then sold it at the world price, and finally, through shares-for-loans auctions, specific businessmen got the country's largest and potentially most lucrative assets. The merging of business and state power could happen at any level, local or federal, but the foundation of oligarch capitalism was the same everywhere, Nemtsov said.

He gave an example. "I recently talked to the owner of a café on the Arbat [a central street in Moscow filled with restaurants, bars and shops]. It turns out that a lot of space on the Arbat formally belongs to city hall, but the properties are managed by a small group of businessmen who rent out those spaces for big money, paying the city hall only a small part of what they get from the tenant. And the person who told me this said that the scale of this shadow income is so enormous that any attempt to change the situation would end in tragedy for the person trying to change it."

He gave another example: "A village administration exempts a consumer co-operative from taxes, and the co-op finances the district mayor's election campaign. The mayor wins and gives the co-op even more benefits and money from the village budget."

The only difference, Nemtsov explained, was whether the main person in this tandem was a businessman or a state official. In the regions, the bureaucrats were usually in charge, but "at the federal level, financial and commodity magnates are usually in the driver's seat in the financial–bureaucratic tandem."[67]

It wasn't that government hadn't tried to unbundle the business–government nexus. It even managed to do something. The institution of special oil exporters was abolished; the first—albeit still very timid—steps were taken to get rid of so-called "authorized" banks; the first tenders for the distribution of budgetary funds were held. However, the government had failed at the Svyazinvest auction, the team of young reformers had collapsed, and reforms had ground to a halt. Left without allies within the government, Nemtsov now appealed directly to society. He formulated his campaign as a political one: "Only a broad social movement based on the middle class can influence which path towards democracy the country will take in the twenty-first century. It has enormous potential."[68]

Nemtsov was not planning to create a political party. It was an abstract—and ultimately unsuccessful—appeal. Nemtsov was talking into the void. The oligarchs did not come to his roundtable: Berezovsky was receiving medical treatment for a back injury after he fell from a snowmobile in the Swiss Alps; Fridman was on a business trip; Potanin pleaded ill, though he had been at work the day before. Chubais, who already had one foot in RAO UES, did not show up either. Journalists—mostly editors-in-chief of publications controlled by Berezovsky and Gusinsky—did not support Nemtsov. Some said that Russia was not ancient Greece and there were no oligarchs. Others said that Potanin was an oligarch, but Berezovsky was not. Others wanted to know how Chubais would fight against an oligarchic regime that he himself had established.

The round table was held on 18 March 1998. Three days later, Yeltsin summoned Prime Minister Viktor Chernomyrdin to his residence near Moscow and directed him to resign. A day later, Sergei Kiriyenko was appointed acting prime minister. This meant two things. First, the Kremlin was beginning to prepare for the presidential election. Second, Nemtsov was no longer the successor.

# CHAPTER 14

## 1998
## The Emperor's Last Journey

**Who killed the tsar?**

Around 2.00 a.m. on 17 July 1918, Yakov Yurovsky, commandant of the Chekists in the Urals, went up to the private rooms of Tsar Nicholas II and the imperial family and ordered them to pack up and go downstairs. The enemy was close, he said; there was unrest in Yekaterinburg, and so they would be moved to a safer place. It took about an hour for the family to get ready. Then the tsar, the tsarina, the four grand duchesses, the thirteen-year-old tsarevich, along with their doctor, lady-in-waiting, cook and servant, went downstairs—all anxious but unsuspecting. They were led to a basement room where Yurovsky announced that the Urals Council of Workers' Deputies had decreed their execution. "What? How? I don't understand," Nicholas managed to utter before being killed instantly (according to other testimonies, Yurovsky pronounced the sentence again and fired afterwards). The execution was excruciating. Not all of the prisoners were killed immediately; the bullets bounced off the corsets in which the poor grand duchesses had hidden their jewellery, and the executioners finished off the wounded with bayonets and shots to the head. It took thirty minutes to kill them all.

This terrible crime was falsified immediately. Lenin received a telegram a few hours later stating that only the tsar had been executed and the rest of the family was evacuated. The next encrypted telegram clarified that, "The entire family has suffered the same fate as the head. Officially, the family will be said to have perished during the evacuation." The Bolsheviks published news of the tsar's execution but did not admit to killing the entire family for several years, which gave credence to the myth of Anastasia's miraculous salvation.

The remains of the executed family and entourage disappeared, and no one knew what happened to them until 1979.* After two years of searching, the writer and film director Geli Ryabov and geologist and local historian Alexander Avdonin discovered them in Porosenkov Ravine, fifteen kilometres from Ekaterinburg. Ryabov had made films about the Soviet police and was friends with Brezhnev's interior minister, Nikolai Shchelokov, who first encouraged him to search and then secretly sanctioned the search: he gave Ryabov a pass to the special archive.† This is how Ryabov got in touch with Yakov Yurovsky's son, who gave him a note that his father had written indicating the burial place: nine bodies were buried and covered with railway ties in a roadside pit, and two more were burnt in a bonfire. At the time, however, Ryabov and Avdonin did not dare to tell anyone about their discovery, fearing that the remains they had found would be destroyed by the KGB. Only in spring 1989, at the height of perestroika, did Ryabov make his discovery public. It was a sensation. In August 1990, he and Avdonin reached out to Yeltsin, the newly elected head of the Russian Supreme Soviet. Yeltsin ordered a post-mortem examination. In July 1991, the remains of nine people were exhumed. In 1993, the general prosecutor's office opened a criminal investigation into the discovery of

---

\* In 1918 Nikolai Sokolov, an investigator for the Omsk District Court who investigated the case on behalf of Admiral Kolchak, established the murder of the imperial family after the White Army took Yekaterinburg. He soon discovered items of clothing and belongings near an abandoned mine called Ganina Yama. Yurovsky first wanted to dispose of the remains there but then changed his mind. Failing to find the bodies, Sokolov concluded that they had been destroyed by sulfuric acid and fire.

† In his memoirs, Geli Ryabov wrote that Shchelokov first spoke to him about the Romanovs and the Ipatiev House, where they had been held, when he sent him on a business trip to Yekaterinburg (then called Sverdlovsk) and was well aware that Ryabov was looking in the archives, although they did not discuss it.

the unidentified remains and assigned investigator Vladimir Solovyov to the case.

By autumn 1995, the investigation was largely completed: anthropological, historical and, most importantly, genetic tests were conducted to confirm that the exhumed remains were the Romanovs. Everything matched—from the burial place indicated by Yurovsky and facial structure to the unique mutation in the genetic code of the DNA of one of the skeletons, Nicholas II, that was identical to the DNA of his brother, Grand Duke Georgy Alexandrovich, who died at the age of twenty-eight and was buried in the Cathedral of Saints Peter and Paul. A comparison of genetic material with more distant relatives in European royal families also yielded positive results. As reported in the materials of the state commission on the burial of the royal remains, genetic research on the skeleton of Grand Duke Georgy Romanov "with 99.99999999 certainty confirmed that skeleton No. 4 from the Ekaterinburg burial site belonged to N.A. Romanov."[1]

The 26th of May 1996 was the hundredth anniversary of the accession of Nicholas II to the throne, and the ceremonial burial of the tsar's remains could be part of Yeltsin's presidential campaign. It was on Yeltsin's order that the Ipatiev House was demolished in 1977. The KGB and Politburo were frightened that the mansion might become a place of pilgrimage and noted increased activity of "anti-Soviet circles." "Not implement a Politburo decree? As the head of the region, I couldn't even imagine it," Yeltsin later recalled.[2] So for him it was personal: a chance to perform an act of penance. Besides, consigning the royal remains to earth would symbolize the restoration of the bonds of time and peace in the country after seventy years of Communist rule. That would have been useful for Yeltsin in the 1996 presidential elections.

But matters weren't so simple. In September 1995, Olga Kulikovskaya-Romanova, the widow of Tikhon Kulikovsky, the nephew of Nicholas II, was asked to give testimony at a session of the government commission on the identification and burial of the tsar's remains. Her husband, the closest relative of the tsar at the time, refused to give his blood for genetic analysis during his lifetime—he considered the Russian prosecutor's office to be the successor of the Cheka—but, before his death in 1993, he changed his mind and left a notary-certified blood sample behind. His widow carried out a genetic analysis and wanted to make the results public. Since the discovery of the remains, Kulikovskaya-Romanova had maintained that they were false, but investigator Solovyov was confident that she had now changed her mind. She had cited world-renowned scientists who had helped her with the expertise, including the highly respected Russian biologist Yevgeny Rogayev. There was no doubt in their expertise or in the fact that they would confirm the conclusions of the investigation.

Then Kulikovskaya-Romanova took the floor and tore these conclusions to pieces. She stated that, according to the expertise, her deceased husband was categorically not related to skeleton No. 4. This was blatantly untrue. On the contrary, the conclusions of the geneticists she held in her hands confirmed kinship. "A schemer with morbid ambitions," Viktor Aksyuchits called her. "That's where all [the problems] started."[3] Then Kulikovskaya-Romanova went to see Patriarch Alexy II, and, as a result, the patriarch and the Church Synod expressed doubts about the results of the state commission and sent an official letter requesting answers to an additional ten questions. The ninth question was an issue long debated in the church: was the murder of the Romanov family ritualistic in nature?

There were many Jews among the Bolsheviks. The murderer Yurovsky was a Jew, and so was Filipp Goloshchekin, the military commissar of the Urals who was directly involved in organizing the execution. The anti-Semitic version of the ritual murder of the royal family, fuelled by Bolshevik lies, spread rapidly among the Russian émigré community. They were the basis of a book by General Mikhail Diterikhs, one of the commanders of the White Army in the Civil War, which was published in 1922. In the West, many descendants of White émigrés believed in the ritual murder of the tsar. In Russia, nationalists, some of the church elite and even individual members of the government believed it, too. Diterikhs insisted that members of the royal family had had their heads cut off and preserved in alcohol, and that Goloshchekin had taken them to Moscow.[4] Like any conspiracy theory, the people who believed this version cited many pieces of evidence. Solovyov remembered how, in 1995, a member of the government commission, the famous artist Ilya Glazunov, had told him the same thing: they brought the head of the emperor to Lenin in a jar of alcohol. The conclusions of the investigation and the identification of the remains left no stone unturned in checking this obscurantist version, but, all the same, the Orthodox Church feared an internal schism on the issue and refused to accept the commission's conclusions.

In the end, the Kremlin had to abandon the idea of burying the royal family in the spring of 1996.

## Meeting with the patriarch

In April 1997, Solovyov was summoned to the Kremlin by Denis Molchanov, an administration official. Why was the work going so badly? Why aren't the remains being identified? There was no money for additional genetic research, Solovyov answered, and, besides, the commission's leadership had changed and the new head, Oleg Sysuyev, had yet to convene a single meeting. "It would be good to replace him." "With whom?" Solovyov thought about it and suggested Nemtsov: he had met Queen Elizabeth II, hosted representatives of the Romanov house in Nizhny Novgorod, and was a physicist by education, which was also important. "There is passion in his eyes; he could probably do it."[5] At this point Valentin Yumashev, the head of Yeltsin's administration, appeared in the room. With his consent, Molchanov first called Sysuyev, who was happy to relieve himself of this responsibility. He was responsible for the entire social benefits bloc and had no time for it. Let Boris do it. Molchanov called Nemtsov, who agreed without a moment's hesitation.

Nemtsov had been baptized in the Orthodox Church, and, although he was not a religious man, he considered himself a believer and attended church. He was godfather to his closest friend Valery Anikin's daughter, and they had a tradition of immersion in frigid water on Epiphany (in 2000 Anikin died in a car accident and later Nemtsov continued the tradition in his memory). He and Anikin also went to services, usually in some quiet, remote church. Nemtsov did not flaunt his faith. As governor, he initially did not get into the needs of the local diocese, but as Metropolitan Nikolai of Nizhny Novgorod later recalled, "He became convinced that it was necessary to revive the Russian Orthodox Church, and he provided the diocese with full support."[6] Nemtsov developed very good relations with the metropolitan and launched a programme to bring Nizhny Novgorod churches back to life, reopening one hundred and fifty restored churches. Nemtsov was very proud of the Order of St Daniel of Moscow that the Orthodox Church had bestowed upon him.

The offer to head the commission to bury the remains of the imperial family—an honourable and symbolic humanitarian mission—went straight to Nemtsov's heart. Nemtsov initially did not know all the details of the investigation's trials and tribulations, but his adviser Viktor Aksyuchits, a theologian, monarchist and co-founder of the Christian Democratic Movement, had known Geli Ryabov for a long time and had followed the entire situation. "Nemtsov summoned me," recalled Aksyuchits, "and said, look at this proposal I got. I told him to do it. I know a lot about this, and we can handle it. He nodded. 'Then you take charge.'"[7]

Nemtsov quickly got to the heart of the matter. All the technical work had already been done; there could be no doubt in the conclusions of the investigation. Nemtsov secured funding for additional testing, and investigator Solovyov ordered the DNA analysis from the Tikhon Kulikovsky-Romanov blood samples be redone by Yevgeny Rogayev, the biologist the widow had referred to. After this examination, the last doubts vanished (if they had ever existed): it was confirmed with ninety-nine per cent probability that there was a direct relationship between Kulikovsky-Romanov and the owner of skeleton No. 4.* The only question really unanswered at the time was the fate of the remains of the other two executed family members. After more work, the remains of the tsarevich and Grand Duchess Maria were found in the summer of 2007 in an old fire pit a few dozen metres from the main burial site. This

---

\* According to Aksyuchits, Kulikovskaya-Romanova had managed to persuade Rogayev to remain silent in September 1995 on the grounds that her husband's blood samples had not been obtained legitimately, which is why Rogayev did not refute her testimony to the commission. Being commissioned by the state, however, was another matter.

finding confirmed the overall picture and the accuracy of Yurovsky's testimony.

Nemtsov's task was neither scientific nor technical. It was political: to convince the leadership of the Orthodox Church to recognize the authenticity of the remains of the imperial family. An influential faction inside the Russian Orthodox Church, led by Metropolitan Yuvenaly, then chairman of the church's canonization commission and the second person in the hierarchy, and Metropolitan Kirill, the future patriarch, still opposed the recognition of the remains. Aksyuchits said this was purely a matter of in-fighting: if one group was in favour, the other had to be against. Radical nationalists perceived the appointment of Nemtsov as head of the commission as a continuation of the Jewish conspiracy. "He and I laughed about being a pair of 'Jewish Masons,'" Solovyov recalled, "but in fact it was very serious."[8]

On 15 January 1998, Nemtsov, Aksyuchits and Solovyov visited Patriarch Alexy II. The meeting lasted three and a half hours over tea and jam pies. "I reported and answered all their questions," Solovyov recalled, "and the patriarch said that he had no doubts whatsoever: The remains were authentic."[9] The patriarch asked them to tell the president that there would be no obstacles to the funeral on his part, and he and Nemtsov began to discuss when it would be best to do it. Nemtsov, fearing a storm in the conservative press, suggested pushing up the ceremony to Forgiveness Sunday in March (the last Sunday before Lent begins). The patriarch objected that the Church would not have time to prepare and suggested that it be held in July, on the 80th anniversary of the assassination of the Romanovs.

A week before the meeting with the patriarch, Nemtsov and Aksyuchits had attended the Christmas service in the Kazan Cathedral on Red Square in Moscow. Nemtsov learnt from the abbot that the famous Church of the Intercession of the Mother of God—known as St Basil's Cathedral for the holy man interred within—had never been returned to the church. Nemtsov came up with a plan: a gift for the patriarch. He was prepared to raise the question of transferring St Basil's Cathedral to the Church with the president and the cabinet.

"But it hasn't been restored," the patriarch said.

"We'll restore it," Nemtsov assured him.

"Maintenance will be expensive," Alexy II continued.

"We will ensure state financing to maintain the church as a monument of our history and culture."

The patriarch, however, was much more concerned about something else. In early February, Boris Yeltsin would fly to Rome, meet with the pope, and, quite possibly, invite the pope to visit Moscow. Such a visit requires an invitation from the patriarch, and he couldn't invite the pope, Alexy II explained to Nemtsov. But Yeltsin was stubborn, and this would all end in a scandal. Nemtsov told the patriarch that he'd be with Yeltsin in Rome and make sure that the pope would not be invited.[10]

The meeting ended with everyone happy. Nemtsov reported to both Yeltsin and Prime Minister Chernomyrdin that the patriarch was on side, a government commission officially confirmed the authenticity of the royal remains, and on 27 February the issue of the burial was brought before the cabinet. On the morning of that same day, Metropolitans Yuvenaly and Kirill stated at a press conference specially called for the occasion that "the Church cannot err", and that if Nicholas II was canonized, it would be a sin to worship false relics. The Synod could not explicitly recognize the authenticity of the remains and therefore asked to bury them in a symbolic, nameless tomb. It was a scandal. "Are you trying to make an idiot out of me?!" Chernomyrdin shouted at the metropolitans. "Couldn't you have warned me? We had an agreement with the patriarch, I convened the cabinet, and now this?!" In response, the metropolitans shrugged and nodded towards the Synod as if to say, "That's the way it is. That's their opinion."

## A crumpled repentance

Yeltsin attached great importance to burying the remains of the imperial family. He still sought to correct a historical injustice and atone for his personal guilt by finally burying the remains of the tsar and his family. "I think it tormented him," Naina Yeltsina later recalled.[11] But he did not want to go against the patriarchy. Yeltsin met with the patriarch twice; the latter referred to the position of the Synod and asked Yeltsin for one thing: not to mention the names of the deceased during the burial ceremony. The Church's opinion was supported by many members of the Romanov dynasty, Luzhkov and other politicians, not to mention the Communists. It appeared that the burial of Nicholas II would divide rather than unite society. The president refused to go to St Petersburg, where on 17 July, the anniversary of the execution, the remains of the Romanov would be interred in the imperial family tomb in the Peter and Paul Fortress.

That was not the only problem Nemtsov faced in organizing the funeral. In July 1998, the treasury was completely empty; there was no money for the tsar's burial. Two million dollars was needed to make essential repairs to the Cathedral of Saints Peter and Paul. "I called Mikhail Zadornov, who was finance minister at the time, and told him to allocate money from the contingency fund we had. The funeral of the last tsar is really a contingency," Nemtsov later recounted. "He said his account had been seized. It was a month before the default. I said, 'What am I supposed to do? We have to bury them no matter what.'"[12] Nemtsov went to the head of the Central Bank, Sergei Dubinin, who agreed. On his instructions, the Central Bank simply printed the money, although this was against all the rules. "The symbolic price of this funeral was too high," Dubinin said. "What would people think when they heard about the country's financial distress on such an occasion?"[13]

That problem was solved, but another remained: how could Yeltsin be persuaded to attend the ceremony and pay his respects? Nemtsov asked the publisher Vladimir Grigoryev, who suggested they ask Dmitry Likhachev, an academic and a historian of Russian literature who enjoyed unquestionable moral authority. Perhaps he would try to convince Yeltsin. And on the evening of 15 July, almost on the eve of the ceremony, Nemtsov called Likhachev. The next morning Likhachev had already called Yeltsin. Likhachev, Nemtsov recounted later, said to Yeltsin: "Things haven't gone well for you, but perhaps you'll go down in history as the president who paid tribute to both Russian history and to the tsar and his family."[14] Mstislav Rostropovich also called Yeltsin at Nemtsov's request. Yeltsin agreed. He even recorded a special TV address: "I consider this our generation's repentance before [the tsar]." For eighty years, the truth has been hidden from the people, it must finally be told, and he must be there, in St Petersburg, and take part in it. "That's the decent thing to do."[15] The funeral ceremony had to be rearranged at the last minute to account for the presence of the president.

From early morning on 17 July, the people of St Petersburg streamed onto the streets. It was quite majestic, as if the entire city had come out to pay their respects to the imperial family. All along the route that the hearse took from the airport, the streets were lined with people who threw flowers on the roadways. Queen Elizabeth II, who was related to the Romanovs, sent pipers from the Scottish Regiment. Yeltsin gave a heartfelt speech, and some of the fifty descendants of the imperial family who flew to St Petersburg could not listen to it without tears. "The truth must be told," Yeltsin said. "The massacre in Yekaterinburg was one of the most shameful pages of our history. By consigning to earth the remains of the innocent who were murdered, we want to atone for the sins of our ancestors. Those who have committed this atrocity and those who have justified it for decades are guilty. Everyone is guilty."[16] (This fragment was edited at the last minute. On the plane, Nemtsov crossed out the line in which Yeltsin spoke of his personal guilt, perhaps because he thought that was too much for a head of state.) By the very fact of his participation in the funeral, Yeltsin had gone into conflict with the Church, but he had obeyed the patriarch and, bowing his head before the "victims of ruthless murder", did not call them by name, as the priests laid the imperial family to rest, chanting, "Their names, O Lord, you know." The Lord on high would know who they were.

In the end, despite great efforts, it was not possible to achieve the common repentance and reconciliation that Yeltsin dreamt of—not even on a symbolic level. Many years later, when the burial place of Tsarevich Alexei and Grand Duchess Maria was discovered, the scandal surrounding the royal remains erupted again. Despite the obvious facts and evidence, the Russian Orthodox Church still refuses to recognize their authenticity at the time of this book's publication.[17]

# CHAPTER 15

## 1998
## The Point of No Return

### Kinder surprise

On the morning of Monday, 23 March 1998, Mikhail Krasnov, the Russian president's legal aide, came to work and saw the just-published text of the decree dismissing Prime Minister Chernomyrdin from his post. Krasnov could not believe what he was seeing. For one thing, the decree did not have his signature on it, but any important document had to be submitted to him for vetting before it was given to the president to sign. Moreover, the decree was impossible. Krasnov immediately called Ruslan Orekhov, head of the Kremlin's legal department: "'Why are you putting through decrees like this?' 'Oh, I thought you did,' Orekhov replied, puzzled."[1]

According to the decree, Yeltsin had dismissed the cabinet and appointed himself acting prime minister. This contradicted the constitution. The president cannot head the cabinet; he is the head of the entire state, not the executive branch of government. Krasnov promptly informed Valentin Yumashev, head of the Presidential Administration, of the mistake and prepared a new draft decree. In fact, he needed to prepare two decrees, since the law on the cabinet stipulated that only the deputy prime minister may act as prime minister. Therefore, the first decree appointed Sergei Kiriyenko as deputy prime minister, and the second—as acting prime minister.

Krasnov resigned soon after. The events of 23 March were another confirmation of an already-obvious fact: the decision-making centre in the Kremlin, headed by Yumashev and Tatyana Dyachenko, who had direct access to Yeltsin, had got stronger. "Gone was the time when our opinion mattered," Krasnov said.[2]

By early 1998, Tatyana Dyachenko had long ceased to be merely the president's daughter or even just his image adviser. "The resignation [of Chernomyrdin] made it obvious that Dyachenko was in charge of all key political issues," wrote *Kommersant*. "In fact, according to the Kremlin, now virtually no appointment is made until it is discussed with Tatyana."[3] The influence of Yumashev had also grown. He was so close to the president's family that when they said "family", they meant him—and Berezovsky, too.

In the past, Kremlin aides had functioned autonomously and were not subordinate to Yumashev. The first attempts to turn the Presidential Administration into a citadel of power had been made by Chubais after the presidential elections. Despite his dislike of desk jobs, by summer 1998 Yumashev had brought Chubais's model to its logical conclusion and put a top-down management structure in place in the administration. Out of this came the Kremlin that everyone now knows.

Gone were the days when Kremlin staff dreamt of the future: the problems of the present demanded their full attention. The treasury was empty, the governors were either disobedient or openly hostile, the leftist opposition had recovered from its defeat in 1996 and was plotting to bring down Yeltsin, and presidential elections were just two years away. The Kremlin was growing anxious about one thing: how could they ensure victory for Yeltsin's successor, and, more importantly, who would that successor be? Certainly not Chernomyrdin, Yeltsin finally decided, and dismissed him.

"According to people in the Presidential Administration with inside knowledge, it was she [Tatyana Dyachenko] who dealt the decisive blow by convincing Yeltsin that the supposedly trustworthy prime minister had dared to make a play for the top Kremlin office while the president was still alive," wrote *Kommersant*.[4] Chernomyrdin had retreated into the shadows when Chubais and Nemtsov joined the government. But the war between the young reformers and oligarchs had brought him back to the foreground. People began to talk about Chernomyrdin's presidential ambitions immediately after the February meeting at Davos, where he quipped, "My optimism is based on my profound knowledge of Russia." That might have been too cocky. This suspicion was reinforced after his trip to the US and a meeting with Vice-President Al Gore. And it was confirmed again by the airing of a new television programme, *A Conversation with the Prime Minister*. But, according to Yumashev, Yeltsin had already decided to remove Chernomyrdin back in January.[5]

Shortly before this took place, Yeltsin asked Sergei Dubinin, the governor of the Central Bank, to stay after one of his meetings to talk to him privately. It was a long discussion. The president wanted to know who could lead the country out of the crisis. Dubinin already knew from Gusinsky that he was a candidate to replace Chernomyrdin and that some of the oligarchs would help him become prime minister. All the same, he suggested that Yeltsin should keep Chernomyrdin on. "People are tired of an uncertain future. We need a break, a compromise. Nemtsov, Chubais and even I are outsiders to the deputies in the Duma." These answers clearly displeased Yeltsin. "He didn't want to negotiate with Zyuganov," Dubinin recalled. "He wanted to change the situation."[6]

At about the same time, Chernomyrdin called Yakov Urinson, the minister for the economy, with whom he had a warm relationship, and asked him to come out to his dacha: "Come right away. I've got a million questions, and I can't discuss them over the phone." At the dacha, Chernomyrdin told Urinson that he had visited Yeltsin the day before and tried to convince him that he did not aspire to become president.[7] But while he was prime minister he had hampered the Kremlin's attempts to find a successor. Yeltsin himself confirms this in his memoirs, describing how the prime minister, with whom he had worked side by side for six difficult years, viewed his resignation: "It was obvious that [Chernomyrdin] was not psychologically ready to leave his post. His face reflected a mixture of anger and depression. Loyal, decent, honest, intelligent Viktor Stepanovich. But not the president for the year 2000."[8]

According to Yumashev, he had prepared a list for Yeltsin with about ten candidates for prime minister. This list included Interior Minister

Sergei Stepashin, Railway Minister Nikolai Aksyonenko—both of whom would compete for the job of prime minister in the near future—and several governors. Nemtsov's name came up in the press among possible Kremlin candidates to replace Chernomyrdin, but he had no chance and everyone knew it. In his memoirs, Yeltsin didn't even mention Nemtsov when he described how he settled on Kiriyenko by process of elimination. Before Chernomyrdin left office, Yumashev brought business leaders together for a consultation: how would they feel about the appointment of Kiriyenko as prime minister? The oligarchs generally approved of the new candidate, and no one objected to Chernomyrdin's dismissal. As Berezovsky put it: "We probably chose Kiriyenko because we didn't know him as well as we knew the others." For the first time in new Russian history, the replacement of a prime minister was carried out like a political special operation: Despite all the rumours, the dismissal was sudden, and the successor was totally unexpected.

Kiriyenko, a thirty-five-year-old banker from Nizhny Novgorod, had been brought into the government by Nemtsov. Ten years earlier, in 1988, they had both appeared at the famous Nizhny Novgorod election rally, Nemtsov as a physicist and a celebrity, Kiriyenko as a young, progressive Komsomol leader. Five years later, Kiriyenko—by then a Nizhny Novgorod entrepreneur—joined Nemtsov's team, heading the newly established regional bank that held all the pension accounts. Nemtsov then appointed Kiriyenko director of the state-owned Norsi Oil refinery in the region after spending two days convincing Alfred Kokh, then head of the State Property Committee, to take Kiriyenko on despite his lack of experience.[9] In 1997, Nemtsov took Kiriyenko with him to Moscow where he became Nemtsov's first deputy in the Ministry of Fuel and Energy. Later, he was given the ministerial portfolio when Nemtsov was stripped of it in December 1997, this time overriding Chernomyrdin's objections that, again, Kiriyenko was too young and inexperienced.

A youthful—even young—official with the manner of a straight-A student (which he had been at university), Kiriyenko also met Yeltsin's definition of a successor that he'd expressed six months earlier: "A young, vigorous and combative democrat." And even if the new candidate for prime minister had untested democratic convictions—he was a functionary with no serious political standing—Kiriyenko was certainly a member of the young reformers' team. But as Yeltsin's biographer Timothy Colton notes, "More than Chubais and Nemtsov in 1997, Kiriyenko was Yeltsin's second-term Yegor Gaidar, a well-connected wunderkind who would accelerate change as the agent of an impatient president."[10]

Yeltsin had a wealth of experience and the skills to handle both staff and bureaucratic intrigue. He also had an excellent memory. His personnel decisions were mocked, but they often proved to be thoughtful and well-considered. Kiriyenko had known Yeltsin since the trip to Nizhny Novgorod in the summer of 1994, when the president said that Nemtsov was "ready to run for president." Kiriyenko, then thirty-two years old, was introduced to Yeltsin and impressed the president with his account of how to reform the country's financial system. "Afterwards Yeltsin said to Nemtsov, 'Let me take him off your hands,'" recalled Viktor Lysov, Nemtsov's aide at the time.[11] After that, Yeltsin had probably kept Kiriyenko in reserve, and now it was time to bring him into play.

It was a meteoric rise for Kiriyenko. On arriving in Moscow, he initially had a desk in the anteroom of Nemtsov's office. A year later, he was already a contender for the post of prime minister. "Nemtsov laughed nervously," Boris Nadezhdin recalled. "According to his logic, this was impossible. After all, no one had even consulted him. Of course he was offended."[12]

## Before the storm

In the new cabinet, Nemtsov was not even first deputy prime minister, but only one of the three deputy prime ministers, albeit with the right to stand in for Kiriyenko during his absence. "It was a very difficult period for Boris," Yevgeniya Albats recalls. "I remember asking him, 'Boris, how do you feel about Kiriyenko being prime minister?' He said, 'Well, you know, he is just a temporary figure.' Of course, he wasn't a temporary figure. Kiriyenko was a much more acceptable figure than Boris was."[13]

It took a month for Kiriyenko to be confirmed as prime minister. He was approved by the Duma only on the third and final vote, when, according to the constitution, rejection of the president's nominee stipulated a new Duma and new elections. There were also rumours in the press that some of the deputies had simply been bribed, and deputies spoke openly about "bribes to Zhirinovsky." Despite the successful third vote, there was a crisis in relations between parliament and the Kremlin. "We have a repeat of the 1993 situation, but with a much broader social and political base of everyone dissatisfied with the presidential course in parliament," *Nezavisimaya gazeta* wrote.[14]

The new cabinet was immediately dubbed the government of technocrats. Yegor Gaidar and the staff of his economic institute wrote the programme the cabinet was to implement. It was the second young reformer cabinet, and it immediately acted the same way, only more decisively. The budget cuts, anti-corruption measures and privatization proposed by Kiriyenko were not substantially different from what Chubais and Nemtsov had promoted a year before. The only difference was that the economic situation had worsened: oil, which hovered around nineteen dollars per barrel in 1997, continued to fall, never rising above fourteen dollars after February. In April, foreign investors dumped GKOs* and left Russia in droves.

Kiriyenko's team worked more smoothly than Chernomyrdin's cabinet. This was partly due to the crisis—no one had time to settle personal scores—but also because Kiriyenko was young, was not indebted to anyone and had one main interest: to succeed. Nemtsov could not hold a grudge against him for long, and he and Kiriyenko quickly established a good working relationship. In an interview in the summer, Nemtsov remarked that the new government had a "high level of qualifications and very little intrigue."

Nemtsov had changed, too. In the previous cabinet he had been almost a boy, fortune's darling and Yeltsin's favourite, known for his arrogance. In the new cabinet, he was a seasoned official. He had settled down; he had developed gravitas. Journalists picked up on this and

---

\* The government issued GKOs, short-term government bonds. They had to repay their face value within a certain period of time and sell them at a lower price on the free market. For an investor, the yield on a GKO is determined by the difference between the market purchase price and the value set by the government, a difference that reflects the market's view of the government's credibility as a borrower.

asked him, "Are you saying you haven't noticed any change? Political analysts think you're consciously changing your image."

"Is that right? How am I changing it? I'd like to know. I don't have an image maker."

"You're much calmer. You hardly ever make any big public statements. In cases like this, people say, 'He's operating in the shadows.' Have circumstances changed?"

"There's just more work."[15]

Kiriyenko and his deputy prime ministers barely had time to sit in their offices and put pictures of their wives and children on their desks before the miners' strike began. Right after the May holidays, miners and their families blocked the railway in Inta, a mining town 200 kilometres from Vorkuta in the Arctic Circle. In Vorkuta, a few dozen miners practically seized the city administration building together with the mayor, who immediately supported their demands. The next day the miners from Anzhero-Sudzhensk lay down on the tracks in Kuzbas in Western Siberia. They were instantly joined by miners in the Rostov region to the south. A railroad war began. Economic demands—the payment of wage arrears—were quickly replaced by political ones. The miners blocked the railways, completely cutting off the Far East, and demanded the dismissal of the cabinet and president.

On 1 May, the spring labour holiday, a party at the Government Reception House outside Moscow turned into a staff meeting: Kiriyenko, Nemtsov, Sysuyev and Urinson discussed what to do and who would go where to convince the striking miners to lift the railway blockade. Urinson was sent to Vorkuta, Sysuev to Kuzbas, and Nemtsov flew to Rostov in Southern Russia.

They managed to achieve an interim victory in the railroad war, but then the government did not really know what to do next. In public, members of the government were careful not to reveal how serious the situation was in the spring of 1998, partly because the market reacted with panic to any show of anxiety. One of the most important aggravating factors was investor distrust of the new cabinet. Chernomyrdin was well known in the West as an experienced and cautious reformer. After him, the young Kiriyenko was seen as a weak and inexperienced prime minister, incapable of pulling the country out of crisis.

On 7 May, just as the deputy prime ministers were deciding where to go to appease the striking miners, the governor of the Central Bank, Sergei Dubinin, admitted that the country was facing "a new major financial crisis." Investors responded by dumping more GKOs. GKO prices plummeted, forcing the Ministry of Finance to raise the yields of the next issue—that is, to dig themselves even deeper into debt.*

In May and June 1998, neither Kiriyenko nor Nemtsov realized how close the country was to the abyss. Kiriyenko lacked the knowledge and experience to respond appropriately to what was happening. In summer 1998, there was a story floating around the White House that he refused to meet with David Lipton, the US treasury's under-secretary for international affairs and the key figure working to secure IMF loans to Russia, because Lipton was just "a deputy minister." No one seemed to realize the true scale of the impending disaster. Yeltsin didn't when he announced to the nation on 14 August that there would be no devaluation. In the Ministry of Finance, they also thought they'd squeak by somehow. The Russian establishment believed that if things got too bad, the West would come to the rescue because Russia was too big to fail, too important a country to be left to the caprices of fate. This belief gave Russian officials a false sense of security.

## The GKO pyramid: how the financial system collapsed

Domestic borrowing, GKOs, began to be used rather widely in 1995. After "black Tuesday" in October 1994, when the rouble exchange rate suddenly fell by half, a decision was made to stop the currency emissions the Central Bank was conducting. Tax collection was still ineffective. So where was the money going to come from? Russia began to live in debt.

* Part of the debt on one issue (tranche) of GKOs is repaid by the government using funds borrowed in the next tranche. Accordingly, a sharp drop in market quotations forces the government to sell the next tranches at an even lower price in order to entice investors with high yields. And when the only source of repayment for the previous tranche is the proceeds of the next one, the GKOs become a pyramid scheme.

Then the financial system was hit hard by the presidential elections of 1996, when political interests became a factor in the economy. "On the one hand, the government's tax discipline fell to an all-time low. Before the elections, the government didn't want to quarrel with anyone and didn't demand that taxes be paid," Aleksashenko wrote. "On the other hand, the Ministry of Finance had to be miraculously resourceful and find sources to finance the budget."[16] The economy was gradually becoming dependent on the GKOs that the government was using to plug up the holes in the budget. GKOs were an effective tool that for the first time brought a huge influx of foreign money into the Russian financial market at the end of 1996.

The young reformers knew they could not live in debt for ever. Their idea was that low inflation and therefore affordable credit would help businesses to get back on their feet, and that clear rules of the game and financial stability would bring investment into the country. Economic growth would become a reality and gradually allow the government to repay its debts and replenish the budget. The idea was to grit their teeth, keep the exchange rate down, borrow and wait.

At the end of 1994, after "black Tuesday", the Central Bank approved a currency corridor—in other words, it promised that the rouble exchange rate would not go above or below certain figures.* This seemed to work. For one year, starting in mid-1997, inflation stood at an unbelievably low six per cent (a record that would not be beaten again until 2012). The economy showed signs of growth for the first time, confirming that the plan was working.

At the end of October, however, the Asian financial crisis began with the drop on the Hong Kong stock exchange. Investors began to withdraw from emerging markets, including Russia, and banks began to get rid of GKOs. In order to help the government in this situation

---

\* The rouble-to-dollar exchange rate reflects how many dollars can be bought for one rouble. A low rouble exchange rate is beneficial to exporters: they will sell their goods for foreign currency and buy a lot of roubles with it. A high rouble exchange rate is beneficial for importers: they increase their revenues from the sale of goods purchased in foreign currency. A stable or appreciating rouble rate is beneficial to foreign investors who want to be sure that their investments in the Russian market will bring them a profit in foreign currency.

and keep the GKO price quotations at an unrealistically high level, the Central Bank bought them itself—for roubles. At the same time the Central Bank also had to keep the (overvalued) rouble exchange rate within the currency corridor by selling dollars and increasing their supply in the market. These two tasks contradicted one another and formed a vicious circle: with one hand, the Central Bank was buying up GKOs and throwing roubles into the market, and with the other it would immediately buy them back using its currency reserves.

The situation was complicated by the fact that Western investors drew Russian banks into the GKO market. The investors sold the roubles they made from the sale of GKOs to Russian banks at a predetermined rate. For a while, foreigners hedged against the fall of the rouble and Russian banks earned good money until the devaluation led to bankruptcy. The country's banking system was held hostage to the currency corridor—the government's guarantees that the rouble wouldn't fall. Oleg Vyugin recalled Natalia Rayevskaya, head of Avtobank, telling him after the default: "We trusted the government. We behaved honestly."[17]

If the price of oil had held at a certain level, the young reformers' plan might have worked: the engine of economic growth would have kicked in and the government would have been able to pay its debts. But at the beginning of 1998, when budget revenues started to fall again in line with the oil price, the situation became dire. At the cost of losing its foreign currency reserves, the Central Bank was forced to maintain the already clearly overvalued rouble exchange rate. This could not go on for long.

In November 1997, as the economy neared default for the first time, Dubinin and Aleksashenko managed to convince Chubais and Chernomyrdin to raise the Central Bank's key interest rate, which reduced available credit and undid one of the government's economic policy achievements. They also convinced them to raise the minimum reserve requirements for banks. Both measures reduced the amount of free roubles on the market and, consequently, the pressure on the rouble, allowing the exchange rate to hold.

The financial storm was exacerbated by a political one—the fight between the Kremlin and the parliament. A month after Kiriyenko's confirmation in the Duma, the parliamentary opposition began preparing for his impeachment. The gloves were off: the parliamentarians were openly at war with Yeltsin once again.

At the end of 1997, the financial system held together by a miracle, according to Dubinin: investors returned, money trickled back into the GKO market, bond yields plummeted, and the Ministry of Finance exhaled. But no lessons were learnt. The factions in the government worked things out and divided their spheres of influence. Oligarchs—many of whom had a vested interest in preserving the currency corridor—continued their campaign against the young reformers. The Kremlin was consumed by in-fighting. The Ministry of Finance believed that the peak of the crisis was over and that they could continue along the razor's edge. The leadership of the Central Bank, which was probably the only group at the time aware that the country was sitting on a powder keg, proposed a slow release of control over the rouble. But the cabinet insisted on maintaining the currency corridor, and Dubinin backed down.

In March, the Central Bank once again prepared proposals to abandon the currency corridor, but suddenly Chernomyrdin was fired, and this was no longer the top agenda item. Dubinin and Aleksashenko were planning to go to Yeltsin and Kiriyenko with a proposal to switch over to a floating rouble exchange rate right after the May holidays. But by then it was already too late. The financial markets were once again in an uproar. Kiriyenko was unable to complete the privatization of Rosneft, the biggest piece of property at stake at the time. Negotiations with the IMF for a loan were going badly, miners were rioting on the tracks, and it was clear that the treasury would not get an influx of money. Investors began to panic again and shed GKOs. At the same time, the stock market was falling, which also put Russian banks in a very difficult position: the foreign currency loans they had received in the West were backed by blocks of Russian shares, and, as the value of the shares began to fall, margin calls began to ring out.* The banks couldn't hold on, and

---

\* A margin call is the contractual requirement of a lender for the holder of securities to increase the collateral for the loan due to a fall in the value of the shares pledged against it.

the first bankruptcies began. The newspapers controlled by Berezovsky were already openly at war with the Central Bank.

As Martin Gilman, an American economist who was the IMF representative to Russia at the time, wrote: "In retrospect, the dismissal of the Chernomyrdin government and the bruising battle with the new Duma to confirm a new and inexperienced team under the bright, affable, but hopelessly overwhelmed Kiriyenko—more than any other single factor—tested the patience as well as credulity of Russian and foreign investors alike, and pushed the debt dynamics beyond the point of no return. The resurgence of the financial crisis in May seems to have been directly linked to the political limbo and lack of concrete actions to correct the financial imbalances."[18]

## Default

The exit in the currency corridor slammed shut. The Central Bank could no longer manage devaluation. Any significant reduction in the value of the rouble would automatically lead to panic on the currency market. People would rush to buy dollars, the rouble would collapse, triggering a collapse of the entire banking system. Kiriyenko and his cabinet were powerless. As Nemtsov later said, "If Jesus Christ with his limitless power had been appointed prime minister of Russia in March 1998, the same thing would have happened—maybe not in August, but in September or October."[19]

By June the yield on GKOs was reaching an astronomical fifty per cent. This meant that a third of the next year's budget would have to be spent on interest payments to investors—an impossible burden even for a robust economy. Since June, the Ministry of Finance had refused time and again to place a new tranche of GKOs on the market. But since the treasury was empty, the ministry had to borrow money from the Central Bank and not pay it back. In effect, it was currency emission. These funds were immediately put on the foreign exchange market, which exerted pressure on the rouble exchange rate. The Central Bank fought with the Ministry of Finance, trying to force it to pay back the money it borrowed. Newspapers published leaks about squabbles within the finance leadership. Although there was general agreement in the cabinet, there was simply no single team to deal with the crisis.

Kiriyenko tried to reassure foreign investors, but it didn't help, and the government was still not able to replenish the budget from taxes. "The steps Kiriyenko has taken to cut spending and raise revenues are either totally ineffective or will produce results next year at best," *Kommersant* noted.[20] It was clear that only outside help in the form of international loans could save Russia's economy. Chubais was called in again as special negotiator with the IMF. Chubais flew to Washington, and, after very difficult negotiations, he came to an agreement in July that the IMF would lend Russia $22.7 billion.

In exchange for providing funds, the IMF demanded that a reform programme with budget cuts be passed through parliament, but the deputies made a big show of rejecting all reasonable bills. This is how Nemtsov described it:

> Yeltsin is at the helm of a locomotive. Chernomyrdin, the assistant driver, is next to him. When the train approaches the abyss, they jump off and put Kiriyenko in their place and say: "Start steering, dear comrade!" He sits down and sees the abyss. What should he do? Hit the brakes. This is the anti-crisis programme. It was supposed to do the following. First, to get rid of the burden and oppression of the inefficient, miserable, stinking oligarchic businesses that do not pay taxes, produce nothing, take currency abroad and bleed the country dry. Second, clean up the banks that have been working mostly for themselves and not serving their customers—and if they did serve them, they somehow always managed to cheat them. This programme was submitted to our wonderful, glorious State Duma in the summer [...]. And instead of voting for this programme, the deputies passed a law on beekeeping.[21]

Meanwhile, the negotiators also ran into obstacles in the Kremlin. When the Yeltsin administration blocked a cut in pensions, the IMF reduced the size of the first tranche from $5.6 billion to $4.8 billion. The authorities were relieved all the same—they got cash that they could use to maintain the rouble exchange rate and buy out the GKOs.

The markets initially reacted optimistically, GKO yields began to fall, and the stock market rose. But not for long. At a meeting in late July, Aleksashenko asked Kiriyenko how the government would pay the president's salary if all its tax revenues were used to service the debt and no more money could be borrowed. Kiriyenko answered: "We aren't able to collect taxes due. Suggest what we should do."

"As a result, the July outturn was truly catastrophic," Gilman wrote. "For the month as a whole, only 13.8 billion roubles of a total of 38.8 billion roubles in government bonds. Of that net 25 billion roubles, about 7 billion roubles was owed to the [Russian Central Bank] which while tantamount to an illegal extension of credit, was not reimbursed. But the remaining 18 billion roubles had to be paid from budget resources. As a consequence, large arrears were incurred, estimated at 15 billion roubles, including the entire month wage bill of almost 9 billion roubles due the power ministries."[22]

Although they were aware of the gravity of the situation, none of the responsible officials foretold a disaster in August. Everyone went on holiday. Chubais flew to Ireland. The Central Bank's governor, Dubinin, went on holiday to northern Italy. On the morning of 13 August, Dubinin went down for breakfast as usual at the hotel, poured himself a coffee, opened the *Financial Times* and saw an op-ed by George Soros. "The financial market crisis in Russia has entered a terminal stage," Soros wrote and suggested devaluing the rouble by fifteen to twenty-five per cent.[23] Dubinin finished his coffee and went to buy a ticket for the next flight to Moscow. "It became clear, first of all, that no one trusted Russia—not foreign funds and investors, nor our own population," Dubinin explained. "Second, it was obvious that the government was no longer able to service its public debt obligations without funds from the Central Bank."[24]

This day went down in history as "black Thursday." The stock market plummeted 6.5 per cent, yields on GKOs shot up to 160 per cent, and the nation rushed to buy foreign currency. This is what Dubinin realized would happen when he opened Soros's article: anyone with any savings at all would rush to sell their roubles. No central bank in the world can play against its own population. The next day, there were queues at currency exchange offices and Yeltsin's statement that there would not be any devaluation seemed to have only spurred the demand. The rouble fell by ten per cent.

Dubinin and Aleksashenko were with Kiriyenko at around 10.00 p.m. on Friday, 14 August. "Next week we'll announce that the rouble will have a floating rate," they said, "but you can choose whatever day would be most convenient."[25] No sooner had Kiriyenko thought about it than the finance minister, Mikhail Zadornov, walked into the office with the news that next Wednesday the ministry would be unable to pay investors for the GKOs that had been presented for redemption. The weekend was spent in discussions with the IMF, with Chubais and Gaidar negotiating on behalf of the government. Late on Saturday night, a meeting was held with the oligarchs. "They invited us all—all the big guys—and told us they were going to freeze foreign debt on Monday," Khodorkovsky recalled. "They wouldn't give us a new tranche. 'We can't pay; there are no options.' So that was that. We said, 'Why is this happening? You promised us there would be no devaluation.' Chubais answered: 'This is your punishment for trusting the state too much.'"[26]

Two options were discussed. The first one would lead to hyperinflation: to print as much money as necessary to redeem the GKOs—that is, to devaluate and not default. The second one was to declare a default, restructure the debt, but try to keep the rouble rate within acceptable limits. That is what they did. Later Kiriyenko said the plan was that the dollar, then worth about 6.3 roubles, "was supposed to jump to about 12 roubles, but then fall to 8.5 roubles."[27]

The default came as a complete surprise to Nemtsov. On Monday, 17 August, he learnt about it from agency reports. "Why didn't you bring the cabinet together, at least overnight, and explain the situation? The cabinet would have voted to default," he chided Dubinin two days later. "This way, you and Kiriyenko have put everything on yourselves." A few days later, Yumashev called Dubinin: "You know you have to leave, don't you?" Dubinin replied that, yes, he did, but he would not write his resignation letter alone. He did not want to take full responsibility for the default. It would be unfair.[28] A couple of days later, Yeltsin sacked Kiriyenko.

The cabinet could not hold out after the default. But Gaidar, Chubais and Nemtsov believed that Yeltsin had made a mistake in firing Kiriyenko. Chubais later said he had tried to persuade the people influencing the decision—meaning Yumashev and Dyachenko—but to no avail. In fact, Gaidar considered Kiriyenko's resignation a greater disaster than the default: it devalued the government's post-crisis bailout arrangements with the IMF, and the market players understood this very well. "After that, we watched the rouble fall four-fold, more capital flight and a rapid rise in inflation," Gaidar said.[29]

Kiriyenko himself recalled later that on 20 August Berezovsky came to him with a group of bankers. Berezovsky demanded a cash loan to bail out SBS-Agro Bank, one of the country's largest banks. Kiriyenko said no, at which point Berezovsky promised he would get him dismissed. "It was an honest, open fight between Berezovsky and our cabinet," Kiriyenko later said.[30] Nemtsov was not shy about expressing himself: "The nastiest thing was how Kiriyenko was removed. You don't know who called whom. Where Berezovsky was. How Tatyana Dyachenko behaved. How Valentin Yumashev behaved. How Yeltsin behaved. I think it was an abomination. And, on top of it all, it was completely stupid, a gigantic mistake, a cowardly decision."[31]

Kiriyenko's resignation put Yeltsin in a very tight spot. He now had to convince the deputies to approve a new candidate for prime minister.

After leaving the president with a decree announcing his resignation, Kiriyenko went to the White House. Nemtsov and other members of the cabinet also went—it was something of a going-away party. Late at night, Nemtsov and Kiriyenko took a bottle of vodka and went to Gorbaty Bridge near the White House, where the striking miners had been taking turns demonstrating for four months. The two decided to drink with them, but it was awkward, and it ended when someone stole the bottle or broke it on the street.

On the same day, people found out that Yeltsin was once again calling for Viktor Chernomyrdin to be prime minister. The next morning, Nemtsov wrote his resignation letter and took it to the Kremlin himself. "I thought that working with Chernomyrdin would not be meaningful or useful," he recalled. "I couldn't stand the thought of working in his new cabinet that was incapable of doing anything."[32] If Nemtsov had stayed in government, he would have been both humiliated and vulnerable. He and Chernomyrdin had not got along before, but now he would not be able to communicate with the president over the prime minister's head as he had done in the past.

## The end of Russia, Inc.

At first, the default paralysed the Kremlin. The government collapsed, the president was not in control. The financial crisis and the vacuum of power made prospects grim, and people were even imagining street riots. Panic-stricken officials whispered to journalists that they didn't know how to survive until the year 2000. Major politicians untainted by the default now had their eye on the post of prime minister, including Moscow's mayor, Yury Luzhkov, and the chairman of the Federation Council, Yegor Stroyev, who had been a top Communist Party official in Soviet times. Everyone realized that the next prime minister would be a step away from the presidency, and both candidates scared the Kremlin. Although Stroyev demonstrated loyalty, he was close to the Communists in both views and background. Luzhkov made no secret of his ambitions, but his relationship with Yeltsin was already tainted, and the Kremlin feared that as premier he might decide on some sort of *coup d'état* even before the presidential election. All things considered, Yeltsin decided to promote Chernomyrdin again.

Big business and the president's entourage supported this idea: the experienced and authoritative Chernomyrdin could handle the crisis, and Yeltsin would feel secure even after leaving the Kremlin. Right after dismissing Kiriyenko on 23 August, Yeltsin immediately called Chernomyrdin, whom he had fired just five months earlier. "He called me on Sunday," Chernomyrdin recalled. "And he said, 'I've made Kiriyenko resign and I'm asking you to join the cabinet. I want to apologize to you on television today.'"[33]

Chernomyrdin dissuaded Yeltsin from apologizing to the entire country, but he readily accepted the apology: he, too, understood that this was really about the future presidency. In fact, Yeltsin did not hide it. He announced publicly that he was nominating Chernomyrdin not only because the country was in great need of his stature and experience at that moment, but also because there was "one more important consideration behind this proposal—to ensure the succession of power in 2000." As *Kommersant* wrote, "At first, it was supposed that Yeltsin would explicitly name Chernomyrdin a presidential candidate, but at the last minute it was decided that Chernomyrdin had been already treated with more than enough courtesy."[34]

The Kremlin did not expect any problems with Chernomyrdin's confirmation, but the parliament unexpectedly rejected his candidacy twice, despite the fact that the Kremlin was ready to make major concessions and even shift the balance of power in the constitution in favour of the parliament. Luzhkov was in Chernomyrdin's way. Zyuganov, the leader of the opposition, said he preferred Luzhkov as prime minister. There was no doubt in the Kremlin that Luzhkov had already made a deal with the Communists and promised them a large reward for supporting his candidacy. The Kremlin split: some in the Presidential Administration defected to Luzhkov. Luzhkov's messengers assured Yumashev that after 2000 Yeltsin would be guaranteed security and the appropriate status. But all of this was to no avail: Luzhkov was unacceptable to the Yeltsin camp.

In April, the Duma had feared early elections, and so they had confirmed Kiriyenko as prime minister in the third vote. But they wouldn't do it again. After the default, early elections would be a godsend for the opposition. In addition, the parliamentarians were preparing a new impeachment vote, and, if successful, the Duma, according to the constitution, could not be dissolved. Any scenario seemed to lead to disastrous consequences, up to and including civil war. Against this backdrop, the rouble had already lost more than half its value as it fell below the levels promised by Kiriyenko.

To nominate Chernomyrdin a third time was madness. This was obvious to the officials, advisers and businessmen who gathered at Yumashev's dacha in early September. They held a rating vote to see who they should replace him with; each of them wrote three candidates on a piece of paper. In first place was Yury Maslyukov, a figure close to the Communists who had held high positions in the Communist Party during the twilight of the Soviet regime and had been first deputy prime minister in the Kiriyenko Cabinet. In second place was Yevgeny Primakov, who had also been a high official in the Communist leadership in the Soviet period and had been close to Gorbachev. He was former director of foreign intelligence and, for the past two years, minister for foreign affairs.

Yumashev came to Yevgeny Primakov immediately after the Duma failed to approve Chernomyrdin the first time around. But Primakov was not interested in becoming prime minister. He managed to turn down the offer several times before being summoned to the Kremlin on the eve of the Duma vote. They appealed to his sense of responsibility: the economy is in ruins, the cabinet is gone, Yeltsin is barely hanging on; if one more thing happens, everything will collapse. "I don't know what happened to me, but these words were so ingrained in my soul that I only reacted by asking, 'But why me?'" Primakov later recalled. "'Because your candidacy will be acceptable to the Duma and everyone else today, and because you can do the job.' I don't even remember who uttered the last phrase—Yumashev, Dyachenko or Shevchenko [Yeltsin's chief of protocol]. After I blurted out my consent, they started hugging me. Someone ran to tell the president."[35]

On 11 September 1998, Primakov received a record number of votes in support of his candidacy. The Communist Duma enthusiastically endorsed a prime minister who believed in government control of the economy and who was the personification of the *nomenklatura* revanche that was to follow the failed experiments of the reformers. Yeltsin was not only suffering public humiliation; he was losing control of his government.

And so, within a few weeks of August–September 1998, Russia, Inc.—built by Yeltsin and his associates with the enthusiastic participation of oligarchs—had collapsed. The prospect of the liberal reforms championed by Gaidar, Chubais, Nemtsov and then Kiriyenko had failed—or at least it looked that way. The default was not only an economic disaster; it was, more importantly, a sign of political bankruptcy. Yeltsin had lost. Demoralized, weakened and tired, less than two years before the presidential election, he was left with a powerful parliament that had just installed as prime minister someone who shared their views. They could already smell blood.

Failure always makes a person want to slam the door on painful memories. Nemtsov resigned the day after Kiryenko was ousted. The decision was emotional and quick—maybe too quick. Nemtsov had not been driven out. When Yeltsin offered Nemtsov the post of first deputy prime minister in March 1997, he had promised not to remove him for two years. And when he became prime minister, Primakov, at Yeltsin's request, called Nemtsov back in.

Nemtsov hesitated. His friends and associates already had positions. Chubais was in charge of the Russian energy industry, and Sysuyev was making arrangements for a transfer to the Presidential Administration. Both persuaded him to come back. Nemtsov thought about it, then refused. He left, without a new position to go to.

This was the end of Nemtsov's path to Russian power and his plans to be Yeltsin's successor. Russian history took a different turn.

# CHAPTER 16

### 1996–98
# Putin

## Teammate, colleague, fellow traveller

Anatoly Sobchak, the mayor of St Petersburg, and Boris Yeltsin did not get along. They met in the late 1980s, when Sobchak became one of the leaders of the democratic revolution. But their paths to politics were very different. Yeltsin came from the party *nomenklatura*, while Sobchak was a university professor and lawyer. Although Sobchak joined the Communist Party at the height of perestroika, he was the very image of a model democrat, an intellectual and brilliant orator who exposed the crimes of the Communist regime.

In August 1991, the victory over the coup conspirators was forged mainly in Moscow, but St Petersburg played a role, too. On 19 August, Sobchak went straight from Yeltsin's dacha outside Moscow back to his home in St Petersburg, where he led the fight. Vladimir Putin was already one of his key staff members at the time. "I personally remember the square in front of the Mariinsky Palace in St Petersburg in August 1991," said Alfred Kokh, who was chairman of one of the Leningrad district councils during the coup attempt and soon after a staffer in the St Petersburg mayor's office. "A crowd of people had gathered. Sobchak was speaking, and an enthusiastic Putin was standing next to him, helping his patron to make a revolution. At that moment he did not look like someone who thought that the greatest geopolitical catastrophe was taking place."*1

For the whole world, Sobchak was also the face of the New Russian Democracy, almost on a par with Yeltsin. He was known, respected and accepted in the West, and world leaders often visited St Petersburg. Yeltsin tolerated it but could not help but feel jealous. Sobchak was one of the developers of the so-called "presidential constitution", which formed the basis of the constitution adopted on 12 December 1993. He supported Yeltsin in October 1993, but over time their relationship worsened. An excellent speaker but an arrogant and irascible man in everyday life, Sobchak was a poor administrator, quick to quarrel and barely involved in the running of the city. He would even lecture Yeltsin in face-to-face meetings,[2] and couldn't be bothered to hide the fact that he had his eye on the presidency.

Sobchak trusted Putin, who was the first among equals of his three deputies. When Sobchak would go out of town, he'd even leave him blank forms with his signature. In those years, St Petersburg had its own way of doing things: it was half-capital, half-mob territory, but for all that—free.

In the second half of 1995, Yeltsin asked Sobchak for advice on whether to seek a second term. "I replied that, in my opinion, in his state of mind and mood, the best thing for Yeltsin personally and for the country would be to pick a reliable successor and not take part in the election himself," Sobchak recalled.[3] He suggested nominating Chernomyrdin. According to someone in St Petersburg politics at the time, Sobchak certainly did not expect Yeltsin to cede the throne to him, but he believed that he would have a good chance at the presidency after four years under Chernomyrdin.

Yeltsin was annoyed by this answer, and they soon quarrelled about the elections. Sobchak wanted to hold the mayoral elections at the same

---

\* In President Putin's address to the Federation Council on 25 April 2005, he said, "We first must admit that the break-up of the Soviet Union was the biggest geopolitical catastrophe of the century. It was a real trial for the Russian people. Tens of millions of our fellow Russians and citizens found themselves outside the borders of Russia's territory. And then the epidemic of disintegration came inside Russia, too."

time as the presidential elections, and Yeltsin was firmly against it. That was when the *siloviki* in Yeltsin's entourage—the head of his security service, Korzhakov, and the director of the FSB, Barsukov—opened hunting season on Sobchak. By an unprecedented joint order of the FSB, the Interior Ministry and the Prosecutor General's Office formed a group to "investigate bribe-taking by officials of the St Petersburg mayor's office." Korzhakov's protégé, Yury Skuratov, who had just been confirmed by the parliament as prosecutor general, jumped on the investigation. The case was political from start to finish: one of the law enforcement officers recalled how Barsukov asked him and his colleagues if they had any dirt on Sobchak. They came up with the so-called "apartment affair", investigating whether the four-room flat added on to Sobchak's apartment had been a bribe.

In June 1996, Sobchak lost the St Petersburg mayoral election unexpectedly and by a narrow margin—less than two per cent. Putin, the *de facto* second in command of the city, was deeply involved in his campaign, but Sobchak lost the election by his own doing—mostly overconfidence. Yeltsin had not been re-elected yet—the second round of the presidential election lay ahead—and the new mayor, Vladimir Yakovlev, had already removed Putin, Sobchak's closest ally, from the mayor's office. The presidential representative in St Petersburg at the time, Sergei Tsyplyayev, recalled that authorities in Moscow had asked Yakovlev to wait a month at least before asking for Putin's resignation, to see how things went. Yakovlev clenched his fists furiously and replied, "Five days at most."[4]

In autumn 1996, Putin moved to Moscow, where he took a position as a deputy to the head of the Presidential Administration in the Kremlin. He had worked with Chubais and Kudrin under Sobchak in St Petersburg, and they helped him get the Kremlin job. For anyone who knew Putin back in St Petersburg, this seemed completely normal. "I welcomed him to Moscow in 1996," Koch recalled. "I knew Putin personally. I had worked with him in the St Petersburg mayor's office. Of course, there was some apprehension since he was a retired KGB officer. But he was fine at the time: he supported both privatization and all of our reform efforts. He did not interfere with us at all. In this sense, he was not quite considered one of us, but he was a member of the team, a colleague, a fellow traveller."[5]

That minor job in the Presidential Administration was the start of Putin's meteoric career in the Kremlin.

## Save Sobchak

Both in St Petersburg and later in Moscow, Putin was a capable official. He did not court publicity but was not afraid of it. He didn't have a way with words and spoke in official, bureaucratic language, but he spoke clearly and was easy to understand. He was a reliable team player, a problem-solver who shared the ideological beliefs of the authorities at the time. He could explain what democracy and the peaceful transfer of power meant: state accountability. "It is only in a democratic system," he said in a rare interview in 1996, "that law enforcement officers know that tomorrow or in a year there may be a change of political leadership in the country, region or city, and they will be held accountable."[6] In the same interview Putin said, "It seems to us all—I will not hide it, sometimes it seems to me, too—that if we control things with a very firm hand, then we will all live better, more comfortably and more safely. But in actual fact this comfort will very quickly pass, because a firm hand will start to strangle us very quickly."[7] He made this statement during the hot pre-election spring of 1996, so, by "firm hand", Putin meant the Communists. Putin, like everyone else in the elite, believed that Zyuganov's victory would mean the defeat of democracy.

When Nemtsov moved to Moscow in March 1997 and the young reformers joined the government, Putin moved up one more step to head the Kremlin's main control department. This position was more prestigious and came with a spacious office in the Presidential Administration, but it had little influence. Putin's virtues were loyalty, practicality and the ability to inspire trust. "From the very beginning, he was just really very good at his job, brilliant at explaining things, although the control department was a rather ridiculous department with not much to do," recalled Valentin Yumashev, then head of the office of the president.[8]

Although Korzhakov and Barsukov had been fired in the summer of 1996 and Yeltsin was no longer concerned with Sobchak, the "apartment affair" continued to be investigated, now pushed along by Prosecutor

General Skuratov. In autumn 1997, the former mayor of St Petersburg was half a step away from being arrested.* On 3 October, he was taken to the prosecutor's office for questioning and might well have been arrested (house arrest was virtually guaranteed), but Sobchak's wife Lyudmila Narusova took him from there in an ambulance straight to the hospital—reportedly with Putin's help—where a cardiologist they knew, Yury Shevchenko, diagnosed Sobchak with a heart attack.

Both Chubais and Yumashev stood up for Sobchak, but the *siloviki* wouldn't listen, so Chubais persuaded Nemtsov, the only person he thought could influence Yeltsin at the time, to talk to him. Nemtsov made a special trip to Zavidovo, Yeltsin's country residence outside Moscow, to talk to the president and break a tacit rule by standing up for Sobchak. He said Sobchak was being harassed and was about to be arrested.

After a pause, Yeltsin frowned and asked, "Is he a crook?"

"Only the courts will decide whether he is a crook or not, but he is not so socially dangerous that he must be taken into custody."

"I don't want to interfere in the investigation," Yeltsin said, cutting off the discussion.

Half an hour later, Nemtsov returned to the subject of Sobchak. "The thing is, he might die."

"Why?"

"He is at high risk for a heart attack. He has very bad chest pain."[9] There was another painful pause. Then Yeltsin nodded: he agreed to call Skuratov. The head of his security team brought in a special communications system, dialled Skuratov and, in the presence of Yeltsin and Nemtsov, said, "Boris Nikolayevich asks me to tell you with regard to Sobchak: you don't beat a man when he's down."[10]

But that didn't end the situation either. Sobchak still had both a criminal case and a possible arrest hanging over him. Then Vladimir Putin took it upon himself to save Sobchak. First, he went to his current boss, Valentin Yumashev, and told him that his former boss was in great

---

* Skuratov probably continued to work on the case against Sobchak to pursue two objectives: to show Yeltsin that it had nothing to do with political expediency and to score political points in the fight against corruption.

danger and that he intended to get him out of the country. It was quite an audacious move, especially considering that Yeltsin did not much like Sobchak.

Putin planned to evacuate Sobchak directly from the hospital to Paris on 7 November. The cover-up operation to mislead the security detail watching him was the celebration of Sobchak's daughter Ksenia's sixteenth birthday on the same day. Following Putin's instructions, Narusova made very obvious preparations for the birthday celebration, such as going to the market to buy special treats. Putin taught Narusova to evade surveillance by entering a front door and leaving by the back door. The scene to place a phone call to Paris, also organized by Putin, was like something out of a John le Carré novel. Narusova went into the fitting rooms of the Trussardi boutique, ostensibly to try something on, then slipped out into the courtyard and ran to the back door of Air France. They were expecting her. There she made a call through to Paris to have an ambulance meet Sobchak at the airport on arrival. When that was taken care of, she returned by the back door to Trussardi. An air ambulance was sent from Finland to St Petersburg by Putin's friend, the entrepreneur Gennady Timchenko (who in about a dozen years would be a billionaire from oil trading). Sobchak was put in an ambulance and driven to the airport; Narusova followed. There was no travel ban, as it turned out: Sobchak and Narusova went through passport control and flew out of St Petersburg.

Whether Putin was guided by considerations of loyalty or by his own personal interests—the security services might have eventually got to Putin as they worked on the case against Sobchak—or, more likely, by both, Sobchak's successful evacuation to Paris had the effect Putin never expected. It made his reputation in the Kremlin and probably played the defining role in his subsequent career leap. In his memoirs, Yeltsin describes the "profound respect and gratitude" he felt for Putin after learning of his act. For Boris Yeltsin's entourage, this was a very important moment, recalls Gleb Pavlovsky, then one of the leading spin doctors doing work for the Kremlin: "I remember hearing, 'He is one of us. Really. He's tough.' We thought of ourselves the same way."[11]

## Our man in the FSB

Putin carried off the special operation to save Sobchak brilliantly: risking his own job, he first got a safe haven for him in the hospital and then he tricked the security services to evacuate him from the country—and all without breaking the law. This was what Pavlovsky meant when he called him tough—he could walk right along the edge of the law. The higher the stakes, the more these skills were valued. The Kremlin was used to living in a state of stress, going out of the frying pan and into the fire, fighting off attacks on several fronts at once, and living by the adage "If you live with wolves, you need to howl like a wolf." In this environment, there was no room for sentimentality. On the contrary, cunning, quick reactions and decisiveness were regarded as virtues.

For all that, political life was still public and open; values such as freedom of expression, democratic elections and political competition were still the guiding principles, and interference in elections by force was unthinkable. That was a red line that no one from Yeltsin's camp would have thought of crossing. But life was already grittier than in the idealistic visions of the early 1990s. Insider resources and political spin had begun to play an increasingly important role in the electoral process.

This kind of behaviour was familiar to Putin. In one of the most famous episodes in his autobiographical book *First Person*, published before his inauguration in May 2000, Putin recounted how in the late 1970s members of the Leningrad KGB would prevent a protest act by dissidents on the eve of a historical anniversary. "Instead of dispersing and arresting them, they would lay wreaths themselves. Western journalists and the diplomats would stand and watch for a while, yawn a couple of times, and go home. And when they left, the ropes would come down and anyone who wanted to protest could. But they wouldn't get any attention [...] the way they did things was covert. It was considered indecent to be too obvious."[12] Later, making sure that nothing was obvious and that he had "left no fingerprints" would become one of Putin's main formulas for power and, more broadly, for understanding what politics is all about.

At the end of March 1998, a major scandal erupted. The Nizhny Novgorod mayoral election was unexpectedly won by Andrei

Klimentyev, the businessman Nemtsov had accused of embezzling the loan to build the Navashino shipyard. Klimentyev had spent six months in prison. Nizhny Novgorod residents supported a candidate who had already been convicted twice—for the same reasons they'd supported Vladimir Zhirinovsky in the 1993 parliamentary elections. It was a protest vote: people would vote for the devil himself, so long as he was against the regime. Gleb Pavlovsky said that after Klimentyev had won, he saw—for the first and only time in his life—the Kremlin in a panic. The election results were immediately annulled, and Klimentyev was arrested again. For the first time, the Kremlin interfered crudely in an election, so strong was the fear of a convicted businessman who was outside the system winning an election.

The scandal cost Viktoria Mitina, Yumashev's deputy in charge of regional affairs, her position. She left her job in May, at which time Nizhny Novgorod was no longer the only hot spot on the country's map. Russia was again hit by a wave of miners' strikes. What Yumashev needed in Mitina's place was a tough, results-oriented official. Putin was promoted again. As first deputy head of the Presidential Administration, he was put in charge of one of the most important and sensitive areas at the end of May 1998—relations with the Russian regions. From this point on, Putin was Yumashev's right-hand man and one of the most influential officials in the Kremlin. And as first deputy, he already had dealings with Yeltsin.

Two months later, Putin was made director of the FSB and moved to the Lubyanka, the building in central Moscow that had served as headquarters to every incarnation of the Soviet secret police. Putin did not want to return to the FSB, even as director. He felt at home in the Kremlin and had no good memories of the Lubyanka. After serving as a low-level intelligence officer in the 1970s, he spent two years in the Academy of Foreign Intelligence but failed to get into the elite of the KGB—illicit intelligence work—and in 1985 he was sent to the KGB station in Dresden. The German weekly *Der Spiegel* wrote that he was still a low-ranking officer, mostly occupied with "sifting through an endless stream of applications to visit family in West Germany or searching for potential informants among foreign students at the University of Dresden."[13] In 1990, he returned to St Petersburg and joined the KGB personnel pool. After the failed coup in August 1991, he left the KGB at the modest rank of lieutenant colonel. In the KGB, resigning means completely breaking off the relationship.

It was only in his civilian service that he finally had a truly successful career. But there was nowhere to go. "There is nothing surprising in [Putin's] appointment," *Kommersant* newspaper wrote at the time. "The Kremlin had no choice. The Kremlin believes that during parliamentary, and especially presidential elections, the director of the FSB must be someone with indisputable loyalty to the president, preferably with a past in the KGB."[14] In Putin, Yeltsin had a chief of the FSB with whom he already had a personal relationship. Putin was also on excellent terms with both Yumashev and Tatyana Dyachenko, who both trusted him implicitly. In Yeltsin's inner circle, he was a member of the team. "When the question of appointing the head of the FSB came up, Chubais actively lobbied Vladimir Putin for the position," recalled Oleg Sysuyev, then working in the Kremlin, "and I asked Chubais why, since I didn't know Putin. 'He's one of us,' he replied."[15]

In the FSB, Putin had an advantage over his predecessors in that he understood how decisions were made in the Kremlin. His rank of lieutenant colonel was low for the head of the FSB—for that position, the rank of general was expected—but it was compensated for by the trust of the leadership. "I don't care about my rank," Putin said at the time. "If the president said, 'Be the first civilian security director,' I'd accept without a moment's hesitation."[16]

Putin's career had taken off like a rocket. He had gone from mid-level officialdom to being the director of the FSB in less than two years.

# CHAPTER 17

### 1998–99
## President 2000

### The new diarchy

In September 1998, Russia was not yet a truly parliamentary republic, but it was no longer a truly presidential republic. For the first—and only—time, the main checks and balances of Yeltsin's constitution came into effect. A president with an opposition prime minister—something commonplace in France, the source of these constitutional provisions—was suddenly an aspect of Russian political life. The new prime minister, Yevgeny Primakov, was backed by a Communist majority in the parliament. Against the backdrop of a weak and humiliated Kremlin, the head of the cabinet became an alternative centre of power.

The default drew a line under the era of the 1990s—economically, politically and perhaps even more importantly, psychologically. It was as if the excruciating marathon in pursuit of the future that had required incredible effort not only from Yeltsin and his elite but also from society as a whole had come to an end. The result was excruciating: real incomes fell, prices soared, savings disappeared. But there was also a chance to stop, take a breath and take stock. And then it quickly became clear that this was not the end of the world. In fact, the default had some positive aspects. Money that had previously been swirling around inside the debt pyramid went into the economy, and the fall of the rouble stimulated import substitution and local production.

The personal embodiment of this respite—then called "political stability"—was the elderly, sedate and level-headed Primakov, the exact opposite of the reformers and the alternative to Yeltsin's entire course of recent years. Yeltsin must have understood that, but since Primakov wasn't a Communist, Yeltsin could catch his breath, too. They came to an agreement. "The agreement was," Valentin Yumashev recounted, "that he and Yeltsin would work together until the end of his presidential term and look for the next president together. Naturally, Yeltsin would have the last word."[1] It was a compromise. Primakov was showing respect for Yeltsin. And Yeltsin apparently did not immediately rule out the possibility of nominating Primakov for the presidency.

They had at least one conversation on the subject in the autumn. Primakov said he had no plans to run for president. But by December, Primakov was consolidating his position. He had never been Yeltsin's protégé, but now he was not only independent, but he was also the most popular prime minister in Russian history. His government's level of public trust was well ahead of the administrations of both Kiriyenko and Chernomyrdin. Opinion polls gave him a clear lead over any opponent, and his excellent prospects were already apparent to all. Primakov's approval rating was climbing steadily: in September, thirty-two per cent; in November, forty-one per cent; and in February, forty-seven per cent.[2] By winter, it became clear that Primakov, who owed nothing to Yeltsin, was playing a political game separate from him and the Kremlin, and that he offered no guarantees—no political continuity, and no status quo for Yeltsin's elite.

Primakov was not a sophisticated politician and didn't give it a lot of thought. He reasoned simply, valued human relationships and friendship, and instinctively was committed to a different, older order. He complained to Yeltsin about being vilified in the press, and then complained to his confidants about Yeltsin himself: why does the president say one thing and then something else happens? He probably could not understand why his relations with the Kremlin were becoming more and more strained.

On the other hand, the Kremlin understood what was going on perfectly well. With Duma elections a year away and the presidential elections in eighteen months, Primakov's success encouraged the opposition. The imposing prime minister became a catalyst for anti-Yeltsin sentiment. Once again, the Communists clamoured for impeachment. The nationalists got their voices back, and anti-Semitic slurs were heard from the Duma from time to time. Yury Luzhkov, who had set his sights on the presidency, announced the creation of his own party called Fatherland and routed the Gaidar–Chubais group. Several key Kremlin officials had already moved under Luzhkov's banner. Governors were deciding whom to bet on: Primakov, Luzhkov or Zyuganov.

Threats of imminent reprisals against Yeltsin and his underlings became commonplace. Against this background, Primakov's promise that he would grant amnesty to prisoners to free up tens of thousands of prison cells for economic criminals—an idea that pleased Primakov so much that he repeated it constantly—certainly sounded menacing. It is not certain that Primakov was referring to anyone in particular, but the Communists, followed by Luzhkov, were glad to explain who he meant: the people responsible for the default, the architects of privatization, the people who made fortunes out of it, and so on—all the way up to Yeltsin. As Sergei Stepashin, then interior minister, put it, "Primakov scared the whole group with his statement that they should be put away for economic crimes, and, of course, they started to attack him from all sides."[3]

In his memoirs Primakov wrote that he was prompted "to send a signal of his intentions" to corrupt officials based on the memos he received in December from the heads of all security agencies, from the customs chief to the prosecutor general, which revealed to him the full extent of the corruption plaguing the country. The prosecutor general, Yury Skuratov, for example, wrote that criminals and businesses were spending "twenty to fifty per cent of their profits" on bribing officials.[4] But in addition to this note, Skuratov sent the prime minister another one, in which he asked him to sign off on a list he had compiled of well-known figures, ranging from nearly all the former cabinet ministers all the way up to some oligarchs and governors. In essence, the prosecutor general was asking for political sanction for arrests, and this was the list of people against whom he planned to initiate criminal proceedings. The list had already been seen by Dubinin, who quickly found his name on it. The political repercussions of these arrests were obvious: they would be the basis for Yeltsin's impeachment. Primakov, however, did not sign anything. Allegedly, he only cautiously replied to Skuratov: "Act if you have legitimate grounds."⁵

Skuratov began to act. In early January, he opened a criminal case against Berezovsky. Not long before, Berezovsky had been building up and taking down ministers and entire cabinets. Now he was the prey in a different kind of hunt. Berezovsky was openly at war with Primakov, and Skuratov could confidently count on the prime minister's support. In his memoirs, he describes their conversation: "I went to [Primakov] and said, 'I'm initiating a criminal case against Berezovsky.' 'In connection with what?' Primakov asked. 'In connection with the fact that Berezovsky is laundering Aeroflot's money in Swiss banks. I ask for your support, your political support first of all.' Then Primakov stated without a second's hesitation: 'You have my word!'"⁶

Berezovsky wasn't Skuratov's only target. By then he had already begun to investigate corruption in the Kremlin, including tens of millions of dollars in kickbacks allegedly paid to Pavel Borodin, head of the president's General Affairs Department by the Swiss firm Mabetex for a contract to renovate the Kremlin. The same case later alleged that Mabetex paid off credit cards belonging to both Yeltsin's daughters, according to company head Behgjet Pacolli.⁷

Whatever Skuratov's agenda, by winter he had become a battering ram in the hands of the large and varied anti-Yeltsin camp. He was used by the Communists to promote impeachment. Luzhkov, who had already been fighting openly with Yeltsin, supported him. And although he tried to remain neutral, Primakov sympathized. Whatever the true extent of corruption in the Kremlin—Pavel Borodin would spend several months in jail in Brooklyn on these charges two years later*—Yeltsin's entourage once again became convinced that a change of course directly threatened their security. Once again, as in 1996, the stakes in the political struggle were too high. Once again, they could not relinquish their power. Who could guarantee that after the electoral

---

\* Borodin was arrested in the US at the request of Swiss prosecutors, but a year later the criminal case against him was dropped; no charges were brought against members of Yeltsin's family in Russia or in Switzerland.

victory of Primakov or Luzhkov, or both of them together, that Yeltsin's team or Yeltsin himself would not find themselves on trial? Many years later, Alexander Voloshin, one of the architects of Putin's rise to power, would say, "If our opponents, Primakov and Luzhkov, had come to power, I think we would have been torn to pieces."[8]

The fight was not so much for democracy and reform as for personal security and freedom. At the very least, it was no longer possible to separate the two, as a blunt statement from Gleb Pavlovsky, then a Kremlin analyst, put it in spring 1999: "We view the 1999–2000 elections as a unified process to transfer state power to other hands, a process that would be safe for those representing the state—high-ranking civil servants—and those constitutional freedoms that have been established over the past decade."

## A man resembling the prosecutor general

A compromising film showing "a man resembling the prosecutor general" having sex with two women had been put aside. It had been brought to Pavel Borodin a year before events of spring 1999 by Nazir Khapsirokov, an opportunist, businessman and head administrator of the prosecutor's office. In the general prosecutor's office, people liked to quote him, saying: "I might not be in the top position, but I'm certainly not in second place." He framed Skuratov. The famous phrase "a man resembling the prosecutor general" was coined at one of the meetings in the Kremlin. Once again, they were skating on thin ice. Initially, the plan was to get dirt on Skuratov and force him to go quietly. And so they acted. In early February, Nikolai Bordyuzha, who replaced Yumashev as head of the Presidential Administration, summoned Skuratov to his office and showed him the video tape. Skuratov immediately wrote a letter of resignation for health reasons and checked himself into a hospital.

The Kremlin expected that Skuratov's resignation would end matters. But under the Yeltsin constitution, the prosecutor general was appointed and dismissed by representatives in the Federation Council. At that time, the upper house was represented by regional governors and the heads of regional councils. To the Kremlin's surprise, they refused to accept the prosecutor general's resignation and scheduled the vote for March. Seeing that there was still hope, Skuratov quickly changed his mind about leaving. Now he was saying that he was "ready to continue working." On 17 March, Yeltsin failed completely: only six out of one hundred fifty senators voted to dismiss the prosecutor general. Once again, the checks and balances laid down in the constitution had worked. Some senators did not want to condone the Kremlin's attempt at compromising an official (it was already known that there was a tape), while others were already at war with Yeltsin. As Luzhkov said, addressing the senators, "Today, colleagues, we will vote not for or against the prosecutor general's dismissal, but for the people we support in the country. Do we vote for the continuation of crime, or will we support the legal system being implemented, albeit not without mistakes and shortcomings, through the efforts of the prosecutor general?"[9]

On the same evening, state television aired the scandalous tape on orders from the Kremlin. The heads of television stations explained implausibly that it was being made public so that no one could blackmail Skuratov.[10] When the video of "a man resembling the prosecutor general" was aired, it was as if a bomb went off.

But not even that helped. Russia was sinking deeper and deeper into a political crisis. The press wrote that power was gone from the Kremlin, Yeltsin had nothing to lose but his office, and impeachment was expected within weeks, if not days.

Yeltsin was being attacked from all sides. And right at that moment the international crisis over Kosovo was heating up. After peace talks with Slobodan Milošević failed, NATO announced air strikes on Yugoslav territory on 23 March. The bombing had not yet begun, but Primakov, who caught the news in mid-air on his way to Washington, turned the plane around and flew home. This grandstanding gesture went down brilliantly with the public.

Against this troubled backdrop, Yeltsin made two of his most important personnel changes that spring: Yumashev's associate Alexander Voloshin became head of the office of the president, and Putin was promoted again, this time to secretary of the Security Council in addition to head of the FSB. The Security Council had a broad sphere of responsibility, up to and including foreign policy, and Putin now had an opportunity to speak publicly on international issues. This was another step towards neutralizing Primakov as the Kremlin worked to break his control over the agenda. The power struggle was entering a decisive stage.

In the struggle with Skuratov, Putin, as head of the FSB, was directly involved and actively assisted the Kremlin. At least twice he spoke with the prosecutor general personally. Once, in the beginning, he telephoned him and advised him to resign before it turned into a public scandal, and another time he spoke with him during the famous meeting between Yeltsin and Skuratov in the hospital where Yeltsin was being treated. The tape with the compromising material just shown on television was on the table, with Yevgeny Primakov and Vladimir Putin standing beside it. Yeltsin said, "I'm not going to work with you," and Skuratov started to justify himself by talking about the Mabetex case, but then Putin intervened: expert analysis showed that the tape was authentic, he told the president. It was there, in his hospital room, that Skuratov wrote his new letter of resignation.[11]

The new resignation had to be approved again by the parliament. Putin took on this task, too. He and his staff in the FSB persuaded the senators to accept Skuratov's resignation. Putin was cold-blooded. Someone who took part in the Kremlin meetings at the time recalled that attempts to persuade the senators by appealing to their statesmanship, made him smile. "What nonsense," Putin would say. "Let's find out what we have on them, and then we'll talk." On at least one occasion, the senators were brought together for a talk at a resort near Moscow. Voloshin, Oleg Sysuyev, who was then his deputy, and Putin went to meet with them. Sysuyev was the first to speak. Then Putin spoke. His main message was that it wasn't wise to quarrel with the Kremlin; good relations would always be useful.

But the second attempt to remove Skuratov also failed. The senators balked, and the Kremlin was not able to change their minds. As a result, a criminal case was launched against Skuratov—another special operation—and Yeltsin dismissed him by decree. It was not until a year later, when the war ended in a final victory for the Kremlin and Putin became president, that the Federation Council formally released Skuratov from his duties.

The strong resistance in the upper house made a strong impression on Yeltsin and his entourage. The Kremlin saw a systemic threat in this spontaneous revolt. "It is too dangerous for the country," Yeltsin later wrote in his book, "when governors, who ensure stability in the Russian provinces, get involved in political intrigues."[12]

Putin paid attention. Reform of the Federation Council became part of Putin's programme for the presidential election. As soon as he was sworn in as president in the summer of 2000, governors and regional parliamentary chairmen were removed from the upper house, and the president gained the right to dismiss regional leaders. The phrase "stop Russia from disintegrating" became part of the political lexicon. In four more years, direct gubernatorial elections in Russia were abolished altogether, and the federalism prescribed in the Russian constitution finally gave way to the so-called "power vertical" (the top-down command structure). In another fifteen years, under the new constitution, senators would lose the right to appoint and remove the prosecutor general altogether.

Meanwhile, Voloshin was revealing his character. He had seemed to be a shy, intelligent man who spoke softly with a slight stutter, as if from uncertainty. The senators would boo and heckle him when he took the podium once again to justify Skuratov's dismissal.

But actually, Voloshin was probably the most determined man in the president's entourage. He and Putin, who always attended Kremlin meetings, were in the vanguard of the Kremlin's counter-offensive. Voloshin had long maintained that they should just sack Primakov. He was a highly popular prime minister under a very unpopular president who might be impeached. With Primakov gone, the impeachment would blow over. The suggestion was provocative. The Communists openly warned that, if Primakov was fired, they'd get people to go out on the street. The argument against Voloshin's proposal was that dismissing Primakov would be like kicking a hornet's nest: it would only make the left-wing majority in the Duma even angrier. But Voloshin stood his ground. On the contrary, he insisted, Primakov's dismissal would demoralize the deputies, and the Kremlin could seize the initiative.

And that was what happened. On 12 May, the day before the impeachment vote, Yeltsin forced Primakov's resignation. It was a clear signal to the deputies: "Go ahead and take your chances." Voloshin was right: the impeachment failed on all counts. There was little more than half a year before the parliamentary elections and little more than a year before the presidential elections. The Kremlin went on the attack.

## In search of Stierlitz

The official version, formulated after the election, is that Yeltsin immediately bet on Putin and did not consider Sergei Stepashin as his successor at all. "It was still too early to push Putin. But someone had to fill in the gap—or give the impression of filling it. As a misdirection," he would later write in his memoirs.[13] The fact that Yeltsin did not discuss presidential prospects with Stepashin as he did with Primakov seems to support this version. The Kremlin staff did not receive any command to promote Stepashin as the successor either. Moreover, before Stepashin's appointment, Kremlin lawyers were even tasked to find out whether it would be possible to appoint a prime minister "for three months, for example." However, there is no doubt that in May–June 1999, Yeltsin and part of his entourage did not rule out moving Stepashin into the presidency. Stepashin himself says: "There was a chance."[14] Yevgeny Kiselyov, then a key figure at Gusinsky-owned NTV, remembers being called to the Kremlin in May along with another NTV boss, and "Voloshin asked right as we were walking in, 'Do you think Sergei Stepashin could become president? After being first appointed prime minister?'"[15]

Yeltsin's eight years in the Kremlin were hard on him. The path towards prosperity turned out to be winding and thorny. Yeltsin believed in freedom, but he groped his way towards it. He was an authoritarian leader and a man of power, often acting like a monarch, but instinctively refraining—sometimes by choice, sometimes allowing himself to be held back—from attacking Russia's nascent political institutions. He didn't get involved in matters of the cabinet, he tolerated attacks from the press and parliamentary opposition, and he trusted governors. One of Yeltsin's main problems was that he had no party of his own, and he did not fully understand what a political party was. Without party commitments, Yeltsin could break with allies along the way to suit the political situation.

His political alliances were short-lived. He quickly found himself out of step with the first-wave democrats. Then he sacrificed Gaidar. The *siloviki* first lost the war in Chechnya and then almost dragged him into the shady scheme of annulling elections and dissolving the Duma in 1996. He had bet on young reformers—Nemtsov, Chubais, Kiriyenko—who in his mind had plunged the country into an economic crisis. His second term as president began with a heart attack and turned into a succession of severe setbacks, from Khasavyurt to the default. Yeltsin was approaching the end of his presidency in bad shape: a sick and tired tsar, cursed by the population for all their misfortunes year after year. He was surrounded on all sides by enemies and ill-wishers, chief among them, the Communists and Luzhkov. Every statement and every step forward was a struggle. With heavy steps and slow reactions but a still impulsive nature, he looked like a heavy old bear.

At this point, his family—his daughter Tatyana and her husband, Valentin Yumashev, to whom Yeltsin already felt fatherly—took the place of a political party and comrades-in-arms and became a kind of political institution. Berezovsky was open about it at the time. "Berezovsky became the first politician," *Kommersant* wrote, "to lift the taboo on publicly naming the *de facto* leaders of the country: Tatyana Dyachenko, Valentin Yumashev and Alexander Voloshin, who had joined them. In his words, 'This group has taken responsibility for decision-making.'"[16] The press also discussed the role of the young businessman Roman Abramovich, Berezovsky's partner in the oil industry. Journalists passed around rumours that Abramovich's influence in the Kremlin was already greater than that of Berezovsky. Thanks to Korzhakov, who bore a grudge against Yeltsin and in late 1998 called Abramovich "the cashier of the family", a group of people became "the Family." As Yeltsin became disillusioned with his fellow travellers, his idea of the kind of person who should succeed him changed. Public opinion had also changed. Anti-Soviet politicians like Nemtsov were out of fashion. People were tired and irritated. They regarded the past decade as a succession of deceptions and failures instead of reforms and the stability they had dreamt of. Nostalgia and fear of the future became the dominant emotions. In the meantime, opinion polls and Primakov's popularity, which skyrocketed, suggested that a presidential candidate should be sought among officials from the military, security and managerial class with Soviet pedigrees.

On the eve of Yevgeny Primakov's resignation, *Kommersant-Vlast* magazine published a poll asking which movie character readers would vote for in a presidential election. The front-runners in the poll were all strong-willed characters associated with the strength of the state: the film portrayals of Peter the Great and Marshal Georgy Zhukov, who had led the USSR to victory in the Second World War, and the charming and brutal investigator Gleb Zheglov from the Soviet crime film *The Meeting Place Cannot Be Changed*. The magazine quoted sociologists as saying, "When it comes to the leader of the country, the majority of Russians would be happy with an aggressive leader, not a caring one. People prefer force and brutality, expecting these qualities will help establish order in Russia."[17] Yet the most popular choice was the Soviet spy Max Otto von Stierlitz, from Tatyana Lioznova's legendary Soviet TV series *Seventeen Moments of Spring*. In the series, Stierlitz—really the Soviet KGB officer Maxim Maximovich Isayev—is an intellectual and brave man who coldly works for the Soviet army's victory behind enemy lines. The magazine put the fictional Stierlitz on the cover with the caption "President 2000."

Gleb Pavlovsky recalled that he'd been surprised when Voloshin, discussing the poll results with him, suddenly asked: "What about Putin?"[18] Putin's CV did indeed superficially resemble the biography of Stierlitz, in that both had worked for the KGB in Germany. In May 1999, Putin's name had already appeared on at least one of the internal Kremlin shortlists. In an analytical note of 12 May to recipients in the Kremlin, Pavlovsky wrote: "The lack of a very strict calendar of political planning leads (unless a miracle happens) to inevitable loss for our candidate P." "P" was, of course, Putin.

And yet, in May a very different set of officials made it to the successor shortlist: Interior Minister Sergei Stepashin and Railway Minister Nikolai Aksyonenko. Stepashin, an officer but with a background supporting democracy, also fit the image of a man in the military or security services. He had served Yeltsin faithfully, headed the FSK, resigned after the terrorist attack in Budyonnovsk in 1995, but two years later returned to the government, first as minister for justice and then as interior minister. At the end of April 1999, he was promoted to first deputy prime minister. All this was emphasized at a meeting in the Kremlin in early May when Yeltsin rearranged the seating. "That's not the way to sit around the table! Stepashin is first deputy. Fix it," Yeltsin said with annoyance. He then ordered Stepashin to "change seats." Witnesses of the scene exchanged glances: Was he really going to replace Primakov soon?

Stepashin was both well-known at the federal level and had a good political reputation. But Yeltsin was not guided by polls. He instinctively thought that someone like himself should succeed him. And he thought that person would be Aksyonenko, a man like him and almost his age. Like Yeltsin, Aksyonenko had been born to a semi-literate rural family. Like Yeltsin, he had achieved everything on his own and climbed every level of the Soviet administrative ladder. And like Yeltsin, he possessed a certain *nomenklatura* integrity. The president liked Aksyonenko; in the implicit race for the successor, he was the clear favourite, supported by both Berezovsky and Abramovich. Even Stepashin was clear when Yeltsin made him change seats at that May meeting: Aksyonenko would succeed Primakov. Voloshin was against it. Aksyonenko as the country's president? He couldn't imagine it. Igor Malashenko formulated the same idea at about that time: "Aksyonenko won't be president of Russia!"[19]

Voloshin and Chubais supported Stepashin, and it was not clear who Yeltsin's candidate would be right up to the vote in the Duma. When parliament speaker Gennady Seleznev was given an order brought by courier to introduce Stepashin in the Duma, he uttered a phrase—later famous—that he'd washed his ears that morning and clearly remembered the president speaking to him about Aksyonenko. Stepashin later recounted what had happened. "Everything was decided literally during the night," he said. "As far as I know, it was Valentin Yumashev, Tatyana Dyachenko, someone else—I think Roman Abramovich—and definitely Anatoly Chubais, since he told me about it later. They were discussing options and considered (except Yumashev, I think) that the Duma might vote to approve Aksyonenko, which would aggravate the political situation again. So, my candidacy suddenly emerged [...]. Anyway, Chubais somehow convinced everyone that I'd be approved and Aksyonenko wouldn't be."[20]

"I am not Pinochet, my last name is Stepashin," was how the new candidate for prime minister reassured deputies in the Duma. The deputies were living in constant fear of being dismissed, and Stepashin was showing that he would not swing a sword. Parliament approved him as head of government with unexpected ease and by a large majority. But what appealed to the deputies—Stepashin's peaceful intentions and malleability—was immediately perceived as a serious problem in the Kremlin.

## Yeltsin makes a choice

In mid-June 1999, Valentin Yumashev and Tatyana Dyachenko visited the dacha of Igor Malashenko, director of the NTV television channel and number two man in the media empire of Vladimir Gusinsky. The Kremlin's relationship with Gusinsky was deteriorating. In the 1996 elections, Gusinsky had helped the president, but now he was refusing to do the same again. But Malashenko was still respected and valued in the Kremlin, and Dyachenko and Yumashev wanted to convince him of the merits of Putin as a successor. Malashenko explained to them that Putin was from the KGB. "For a person of my generation, the KGB," Malashenko said, "is no longer the Gulag or mass shootings. It's control. Total control. I think it's a disaster for the country."[21] Yumashev and Dyachenko said that he shouldn't be judged by his work record alone and suggested that Malashenko talk to Putin personally to get a more honest impression.

Soon afterwards, at Malashenko's request, the banker Pyotr Aven hosted a dinner at his dacha and invited Putin. Malashenko came with his wife, and Putin came with his daughters. There was the usual table conversation about nothing. "After three hours, I knew nothing about Putin, and I came to the conclusion that it was pointless to look for depth where there was none," Malashenko later recalled. During the meal, Malashenko's wife got a phone call from her daughter who was on her way to a summer language course in Ascott, near London. She had just landed at Heathrow and discovered that the course administration had not sent a car for her, so she was asking what to do: wait or take a taxi. Her parents advised her to take a taxi. When they returned to the table and told their guests what had happened, Putin said they'd given her the wrong advice: "You can never be sure it's really a taxi." "The next day I told Dyachenko and Yumashev, 'I'm definitely not on board,'" Malashenko recalled.[22]

But with or without Malashenko, the Kremlin had already bet on Putin, which meant that Stepashin's fate was sealed. He had been a potential successor for less than a month. In May, the formation of the government had been an agonizing race to see who could get to Yeltsin's Sochi residence first with his list of ministers. Aksyonenko, now first deputy prime minister, had demonstrated that he was more than a deputy prime minister; he was in fact the shadow head of the cabinet. The Kremlin expected Stepashin to distance himself from Luzhkov, but he didn't. He was expected to replace Rem Vyakhirev, the head of Gazprom, since he leant towards supporting Luzhkov and Primakov, but failed to do so.

The Yeltsin loyalist Stepashin embodied the desire for compromise. "He is generally quite a soft man, compromising and decent," Nemtsov later explained. "We [Chubais and I] were sure that Stepashin wouldn't make a mess of things. For Russia, a president like that would be a step forward."[23] But for the Kremlin, softness was synonymous with spinelessness, and compromise ended with the appointment of Primakov. Now the war was being fought to the victory, and the winner would take all.

At the beginning of July, the political struggle entered a particularly difficult phase. Luzhkov and Primakov joined forces. The information war was heating up: ORT, Berezovsky's TV channel, was flinging dirt on Luzhkov and his businesswoman wife, while Gusinsky's NTV was exposing the "Kremlin camarilla" headed by Roman Abramovich. Stepashin was supposed to help persuade Gusinsky to play on the Kremlin's side, but even these talks failed. It was clear that Stepashin's position was extremely precarious. The press discussed whether he would stay in his post or be replaced by Aksyonenko. "I don't understand why the Kremlin is pushing under an honest man. You'd think they'd have someone else in reserve," Nemtsov said.[24] At the beginning of July, it was unimaginable that Stepashin would be replaced by Putin. In *Nezavisimaya gazeta*'s rating of leading politicians, Putin was then ranked eighteenth—an eloquent testimony to perceptions of his influence.

However, inside the Kremlin walls it was an entirely different picture. According to Pavlovsky, "From inside the administration, tapping Putin looked like the natural choice."[25] Dyachenko, Yumashev and Voloshin saw him as a close associate and reliable partner: loyal, reasonable, calm, clear, tough, with knowledge of power, and with what they considered a wide range of experience—leadership roles in a huge city, the head of the FSB and, more recently, the Security Council. He was young and spoke the same language as them. To them, Putin had already proved in practice that he was a member of the team, that he had no other agenda than that of the Kremlin—most recently in the Skuratov case—and that he was ready to fight and could be relied upon. Besides all that, no one was more like the folk-hero Stierlitz. Primakov was also a counter-intelligence man by profession, and he had already redeemed himself in the eyes of society. Indeed, society had made it clear that they wanted someone like Primakov, and here was Putin, who looked like an updated version. With the help of his associates, Yeltsin finally made his choice. Not Stepashin, not Aksyonenko: Putin would become president.

On 22 July, Stepashin set off on a trip across Russia and then flew from Vladivostok to Seattle on 26 July. There his tour of America began. In Seattle, he was met by Under-Secretary of State Strobe Talbott: "Talbott told me, 'We have information that there are preparations to fire you.' I told him, 'Anything is possible.' I realized it could go either way."[26] Stepashin returned, and, early on the morning of 5 August, Yeltsin summoned him to his office. Voloshin was also summoned, and he brought in a resignation decree already printed out. Stepashin was mentally prepared for the conversation, but he couldn't help turning red. "The conversation began: 'I offer you the position of secretary of the Security Council.' I replied: 'Let's discuss it.' 'What happened? What are your criticisms?' Yeltsin asked Voloshin to step out, and the two of us talked for about an hour. Then he walked out of the office and left me alone. It was an interesting situation. I sat alone, looking at books.

Naturally, I didn't touch anything, God forbid. Then he came back and said: 'Keep working. I'll tear up the decree.'"[27]

This was not the first time this had happened. In his memoirs, Yevgeny Primakov provides a transcript of Yeltsin's telephone conversation with Nikolai Bordyuzha, Voloshin's predecessor as head of the Presidential Administration, when Yeltsin informed him that he was dismissing him but offering him the position of secretary of the Security Council. Bordyuzha refused. Yeltsin changed his mind on the fly and told Bordyuzha that he was ready to reverse his decision, but that same evening he signed a decree on his resignation.[28]

As a result, Yeltsin's half-fired Prime Minister Stepashin flew off to the Volga region to hold meetings while the press was already leaking reports that he was about to be shown the door. *Kommersant* wrote: "The candidates for the post of prime minister are, in descending order of likelihood, Vladimir Putin, Igor Ivanov (the foreign minister who is said to have recently been on friendly terms with Boris Berezovsky) and Nikolai Aksyonenko (considered a protégé of Kremlin minion Roman Abramovich)."[29] The newspaper was close to the truth, but in fact everything had already been decided. A few days before the meeting with Stepashin, Yeltsin had summoned one of the most influential regional leaders, the head of Tatarstan, Mintimer Shaimiyev, to talk him out of an electoral alliance with Luzhkov. Unable to convince him, he told him outright: "In a while, I will dismiss the Stepashin government, and Vladimir Vladimirovich Putin will become prime minister. And then he will be president. Anyway, that's all I wanted to tell you."[30] Shaimiyev could not believe what he was hearing.

Stepashin returned to Moscow at 3 a.m. on Sunday, 8 August. He was met off the plane by Chubais. Knowing that the decision about Putin had already been made, Chubais, who had fought for Stepashin to the bitter end, arranged an audience with Yeltsin for Monday. It was their last chance. Chubais was scheduled for 10–11 a.m. On Monday, 9 August, at about 7.30 a.m., Stepashin's telephone rang: the president was expecting him in fifteen minutes at his residence in Gorki. When he entered the office, Yeltsin, Putin, Aksyonenko and Voloshin were sitting at the table. Yeltsin thanked Stepashin for his work and dismissed him. He was allowed to sign a decree appointing Putin as first deputy prime minister so as not to repeat the Kiriyenko story. After learning the agenda for the upcoming meeting with Chubais, the president simply cancelled it because it was moot. A few hours later, Yeltsin announced that he was appointing Vladimir Putin as acting head of the cabinet and saw him as his successor as president.

Nemtsov learnt that Putin would be the successor just a couple of days before these events. His aide at the time, Boris Nadezhdin, heard about it at a meeting in the Kremlin. They were expecting Aksyonenko's appointment, and when it was announced that Putin would be acting prime minister, everyone nearly fell out of their chairs. Nemtsov, too, was dumbfounded. "Boris just couldn't understand how this had happened," Nadezhdin recalled. "He thought that the president of Russia should be a man of Yeltsin's physical scale or like himself: a tall, handsome, high-profile man liked by women. Putin was completely different."[31]

Indeed, Yeltsin's successor seemed the exact opposite of Nemtsov, from appearance to mannerisms, from habits to political biographies. Nemtsov was tall, stately, imposing, with thick black hair. Putin was small, with a quiet voice and thinning hair that was flaxen, almost colourless. Nemtsov was anti-Soviet from the start; Putin had worked for the KGB. Nemtsov made a career as a public politician from the start and could not live without media attention, while Putin had never participated in elections and shunned journalists. Nemtsov worked openly and would stop at nothing. Putin preferred to work in the shadows, behind the scenes. Informal, free, unbuttoned, Nemtsov was the antithesis of a bureaucrat. Putin was the opposite. Finally, Nemtsov was known to the whole country. Putin was known to no one.

That was the most important thing. Putin's presidential nomination came as a shock, primarily because it was inconceivable that such a role could be played by a person who was not well known outside of the small circle of government and security officials. According to polls when Putin was appointed acting prime minister, three-quarters of Russian citizens had not heard of him at all. For Nemtsov, Putin was still a boring Kremlin clerk he occasionally ran into at work, but about whom he had little to say. While working in the government, Nemtsov remembered Putin mostly through memos addressed to him. He remembered Putin as an aide to Sobchak, then serving Yeltsin faithfully, going to

Berezovsky's birthday parties, dissuading him and Chubais from going to war with Gusinsky and Berezovsky in 1997.

From Nemtsov's point of view, he lacked the most important thing—a political persona. For him, Putin was basically a nobody. Suddenly he was prime minister and a presidential candidate. It wasn't that Nemtsov was against it. He was just taken aback.

The deputies were also taken aback, but they approved Putin in the first vote, although not by as convincing a number of votes as they'd given Sergei Stepashin three months earlier. It was almost impossible to believe that Putin would win the presidential election soon. The press was already discussing the likelihood of extraordinary measures like cancelling the elections. They decided that if they did happen, perhaps they'd finally see in Putin the toughness and decisiveness that were praised by sources in the Kremlin—qualities that were lacking in Stepashin. But at that moment, no one really understood that a war had been going on in the country for a fortnight. It was even more difficult to imagine that this war would bring Putin into the Kremlin.

## Betting on the war

The second Chechen war began on Saturday, 7 August, two days before Stepashin's resignation. Approximately one thousand fighters led by Basayev and the Saudi Arabian Ibn al-Khattab attacked Dagestan from Chechnya and seized several villages in the mountainous border regions. However, the raid by Basayev and Khattab could not be considered an attack from outside Dagestan. Moscow had long been losing control over Dagestan, largely because the centre could not support the local authorities with subsidies.[32] Shariah law had been introduced in several villages, and in spring 1998 the Islamic Shura of Dagestan* declared an alliance with Basayev. In Dagestan there was military action several days before Basayev's raid—a rebellion of local Wahhabis—and Basayev and

---

\* The Islamic Shura of Dagestan emerged in early 1998 as a structure of Islamists calling for armed jihad. In April, Wahhabis from Chechnya and Dagestan met in Grozny, and Basayev set the goal of uniting Dagestan and Chechnya.

al-Khattab's units included not only Chechens and foreign mercenaries, but also many Dagestanis.[33] Stepashin managed to visit Dagestan before his resignation, and in his parting words to the cabinet on 9 August he said, "We might lose Dagestan."

This war was inevitable. In 1996, Russia signed the Khasavyurt Peace Agreement with Chechnya. Russian troops withdrew, and Chechnya became *de facto* independent. Destroyed and war-torn—Grozny resembled post-war Stalingrad—Chechnya had become a militarized den of mobsters. In January 1997, Aslan Maskhadov, Chechnya's defence minister under Dudayev, was elected president. The most moderate of the Chechen leaders, willing to negotiate with Moscow, and the only one with whom Moscow was prepared to talk, Maskhadov was forced from the outset to share power in Chechnya with field commanders.

For the field commanders, kidnapping and human-trafficking became their main source of income. Journalists were also kidnapped. One of the first of such cases, which received national and international attention, was the capture of an NTV film crew headed by Yelena Masyuk in May 1997; the journalists were rescued by Vladimir Gusinsky (allegedly with Berezovsky's help). Many hostages had their fingers shot off and video footage sent to their relatives, and sometimes these videos were shown on Russian television. Anyone without someone to provide a ransom was killed. Torture, murder and public executions became commonplace. Radical Chechen leaders like Basayev plotted to establish an Islamic caliphate free from "the Russian yoke", first in Chechnya and Dagestan. Secular laws and orders were giving way to Shariah. The Wahhabis were forming something like ISIS: an extraterritorial terrorist regime with religious fanatics at its head. Maskhadov lacked the strength and determination to stop them. The field commanders arranged shootings and terrorist attacks and made attempts on Maskhadov's life. Unable to resist their onslaught, Maskhadov retreated.

In December 1998, the world shuddered to learn of the killing of four engineers working in Grozny: three British and one New Zealander. They were beheaded and their severed heads were thrown on the road. Three months later, in March 1999, the audacious kidnapping of General Gennady Shpigun, a representative of the Russian Interior Ministry in Chechnya, brought relations with Russia to the brink of a new war. Terrorists had stopped the aircraft Shpigun was in, tossed him onto the tarmac and then driven away with him. His body was found only a year later. Stepashin later said that "a plan of active operations in Chechnya had been under development since March."[34] In April, the Russian–Chechen border was closed, and additional troops were redeployed to the border; in June and July, armed clashes became regular. In August, the war began.

The Chechens were driven out of Dagestan within two weeks. In late August, Russian warplanes bombed Chechen territory for the first time since 1996, striking villages near Grozny where Basayev and al-Khattab allegedly had bases. Then Basayev and al-Khattab moved the war into Russian territory, to Moscow. On the evening of 31 August, a bomb went off in a video arcade in the shopping centre Luzhkov had recently built under Manezhnaya Square. Everyone suspected Chechens. The field commanders had long been threatening terrorist attacks, and the day before, in Grozny, Basayev had again threatened Moscow with a jihad. The next day militants of the so-called Dagestan Liberation Army claimed responsibility for the attack. One person was killed.

But that was just the first volley. The second was in Buynaksk, Dagestan, on 4 September. A truck filled with explosives blew up next to a five-storey building where families of federal soldiers lived. Sixty-three people were killed. Then real terror came to Moscow. Within a few days, two very powerful explosions had shaken the south-eastern outskirts of the city, one after the other. On the night of 9 September, a bomb exploded exactly at midnight, just as people were going to bed, causing the collapse of two entrances in a long nine-storey apartment block. It looked as if sections of the building had been hacked out with an axe. Four days later, a brick apartment building in an adjacent district collapsed after a similar explosion in the basement. It happened at five o'clock in the morning, when the residents were fast asleep. Almost everyone was killed. These two terrorist attacks took the lives of 230 people.

The first blast was terrible. The second plunged Moscow into deep shock. And a day later, a terrorist attack following the same pattern as in Buynaksk—a truck bombing—destroyed two entrances of an apartment block, killing nineteen people in the southern city of Volgodonsk.

Terror engulfed the whole country, but especially Moscow. It felt as if the temperature had dropped or life was playing in slow motion. As people walked down streets, they began to look around them. Many refused to sleep at home. People organized night watches in their entrances. Everyone was waiting for the next attack, and no one knew where the terrorists would hit. They tried to work it out: if the explosion was first in the south-east, and the second in the south, did that mean that the terrorists were moving clockwise and that the next attack would be somewhere in the south-west? Throughout all this, one question hung in the air: would this fear and helplessness last for ever?

That week Prime Minister Putin addressed a joint session of both houses of parliament, the State Duma and the Federation Council. Putin hadn't said a word about sending troops into Chechnya; at that moment, he was proposing encircling Chechnya with a "sanitary cordon" and, if necessary, bombing the terrorist strongholds, ideally with Maskhadov's support. But it was already clear what his response would be: "They spoke to us in the language of brutality and force," Putin said, "and we will respond in kind."[35] The troops deployed to the border of Chechnya were reinforced with multiple rocket launchers. Anyone who remembered the bombing of Chechen villages was immediately wary. "I know who is really being bombed there," warned Ruslan Aushev, the concerned leader of Ingushetia, neighbouring Chechnya, "the fighters won't suffer."[36] Putin hesitated for a short time, and it soon became clear that the buffer zone was a preparation for an invasion. On 24 September, Putin uttered his famous outhouse line at a press conference: "We will chase down the terrorists everywhere: if they're at the airport, we'll take them out in the airport. If they're, forgive me, in the outhouse, we'll wipe them out there, too. That's it. It's decided." A week later, after several days of heavy bombing, Russian tanks rolled into Chechnya.

Politically, the decision to go to war paid off, even though it had been hard to predict. Before, public opinion was against the war. Now, the resolute actions on the Chechen front became a turning point in Putin's election campaign.

Public opinion flipped in the second half of September—after the terrorist attacks and the initial response. Putin's rating flew up. "People believed," wrote Emil Pain, "that the Chechen problem could be solved by force, and the whole country could be put in order with the 'iron hand' that Putin had suddenly embodied."[37] By the end of September, Putin was only behind Primakov and Zyuganov in the presidential race. In October, the number of people ready to vote for him more than doubled, from ten per cent to twenty-six per cent, and by mid-November the ratings of both Primakov and Zyuganov were already falling rapidly.[38] By December, Putin's victory in the presidential election was a foregone conclusion.

In this campaign for a successor, even though Putin was only confirmed as prime minister, he was the *de facto* president. Yeltsin gave him complete freedom to act and did not interfere. This pre-election scenario—a strong prime minister under an outgoing president—was "Primakov 2.0." According to Pavlovsky, the Kremlin seemed to have snatched it out of the hands of its political enemies.[39]

Later it became clear that the Primakov model was more than a scheme dreamt up by political advisers. It became the model of the future. Primakov was already old, Putin was still young, Yeltsin agreed with a heavy heart to accept Primakov but chose Putin to be his successor. For all that, the two candidates—or rather, their images in the public and the expectations associated with these images—had much in common. Most importantly, both were allies of Yeltsin but, paradoxically, of his antagonists, too. Primakov had directly shifted into opposition to Yeltsin while Putin had not, of course. But his platform, his electoral moves and his background were so different from Yeltsin's that they were essentially their opposite. The revolution had ended. Now, like Napoleon after the Directory, Putin was running for president under the slogan of strength and order. And the public, which saw him as a saviour from the hardships of Yeltsin's rule, gave Putin *carte blanche* to do whatever he wanted.

"Putin's great popularity, the trust in him and desire to support him in presidential elections [...] do not mean that Russians had a clear idea of the direction Putin would lead the country," wrote sociologists Alexander Oslon, Boris Doktorov and Yelena Petrenko. "On the contrary, most of the population had no idea where and how the country would go at the beginning of the new millennium. However, this did not influence the popularity of the new Prime Minister. Apparently, most of the country's population liked the way he behaved and what he said, and they believed that the person they liked so much simply could not lead the country in the wrong direction."[40]

# CHAPTER 18

### 1999–2000
## Successor 2.0

### How to form a political party

The decision-making in the Kremlin that would decide the future of Russia went on without Boris Nemtsov. He had left the government in 1998, a step that proved unexpectedly stressful. Nemtsov had arrived in Moscow in March 1997 and immediately occupied one of the top government posts. Although Nemtsov did not have everything done for him, he didn't think at all about daily expenses or the usual everyday problems, especially since he simply had no time. Suddenly that life was over. "It was a nightmare," Nemtsov recalled. "For example, when [after my resignation] my friend Anikin and I went to a café near the White House, I didn't understand half the menu. I literally didn't know what anything was. Of course, I'd been spending money. But going to a restaurant or a café and ordering something for myself? I couldn't remember the last time I did that."[1]

The question of what he'd do and how he'd make a living was, if not immediately critical, then very nearly so. After his work in the government, Nemtsov was left with only a flat in the centre of Moscow (the one where Luzhkov did not want to register him). He still had the fee for his book *A Provincial in Moscow*, or, rather, half of the fee. Of the $100,000 paid, $25,000 had gone to his editor and another $25,000 on taxes. But even $50,000 was a lot of money at the time. For people in Nemtsov's circle—people who didn't steal from the budget or have their own business—an income of a couple of thousand dollars a month was the most they could imagine.

But Nemtsov discovered he could earn even more by lecturing in the West. As he considered what to do, Harvard University tracked him down. In the autumn and winter of 1998, Nemtsov gave several lectures at Harvard on the state of affairs in Russia and earned more than $10,000. In addition to Harvard, he spoke in London and Paris, at universities in Germany and Denmark. This was enough money to support both himself, his family and his mother, who received a monthly pension of 418 roubles (about $26 at the time).

These freelance jobs solved the problem of making a living, at least temporarily. But that wasn't Nemtsov's biggest problem. He was only thirty-eight years old, an established public politician with an illustrious record, and he had been at the highest levels of power, one step away from the very top. So what next? His former associates in the Kremlin and in the White House now looked down on him. To the public, he was no longer a political heavyweight. He was a frivolous liberal, an all-talk-no-action guy who had failed to keep a single promise and brought the country into default. Nemtsov was not as worried about losing his status as he was about having to accept that he had already peaked in his career—at least for a while, if not for ever. Nemtsov was worried. His aide Alexander Kotyusov even thought he regretted not accepting the offer to stay in the government.

In the second half of September as Nemtsov was driving around Moscow in his new Volga—he bought his own after turning in his governmental car—his mobile phone rang. It was Yeltsin.

> He called and asked, "What are you doing?" I said, "I'm not doing anything. I'm in my car." "Well, stop by the Kremlin." So I did. Yeltsin said it was bad that we were not working together—it was wrong to part after working together for eight years. We must keep working together. I said, "Boris Nikolayevich, I will never work in government again, thank you." "Let's find a job for you," he said, "so you won't be in government, but your experience won't go to waste." So I said that I knew my way around governance on the regional level and could oversee local self-government, and that I didn't need to be paid for my work.[2]

And that's how Nemtsov became deputy chairman of the Presidential Council on Local Self-Governance. In fact, he was the *de facto* head since Yeltsin was nominally the chairman. But it didn't matter: the council was an unnecessary structure that just existed on paper. In gratitude for his faithful service, Nemtsov received a small sinecure. The only real benefit of the position was that he now at least had his own office, a title and a position that looked good on a business card.

His office was in an early-twentieth-century building on Ilyinka Street in the oldest part of Moscow. In Soviet times, it had housed the archive of the Communist Party Central Committee and was exactly the way you'd imagine a Soviet archive. Yeltsin's reforms had passed it by. There was a long, red carpet on a creaky wooden floor, dirty windows covered with heavy curtains, and a dusty desk with a lamp on its faded green-baize surface. Nemtsov's office consisted of a reception room and inner office. His secretary, Irina Korolyova, and assistant, Alexander Kotyusov, sat in the small visitors' anteroom. The desk was for Nemtsov. He didn't grace his new office very often. In his new position, he wrote something like an "economic miracle" programme for municipalities, but local government did not take up much of his time.

Nemtsov already knew what he had to do: form a political party. Towards the end of September 1998, as Primakov's new cabinet settled into their offices and the political landscape became clearer at least for the immediate future, the State Duma elections were the main upcoming event. All the political players intuitively understood that the parliamentary elections in December 1999 would have a decisive influence on the outcome of the presidential election, and the Kremlin's opponents had an obvious advantage. The Communists were coming down hard on Yeltsin. Yavlinsky and his Yabloko party had good prospects. General Lebed had already won the gubernatorial election in a part of Siberia and was planning to use that as a springboard to Moscow. And when Mayor Yury Luzhkov finally accepted that he would not become prime minister and that, in fact, he was now the Kremlin's main enemy, he also took up party-building.

By the end of September 1998, Nemtsov finally decided to run for the State Duma. Chubais gave him his complete backing. At the time, the idea of a broad liberal movement was not yet clearly articulated, although the Kremlin was encouraging former officials to go into politics. "You are a good politician," Valentin Yumashev, then head of Yeltsin's administration, told Irina Khakamada, who was in about the same position as Nemtsov and did not know what to do with herself. "You'll succeed."[3] Like Nemtsov, ex-prime minister Sergei Kiriyenko also wanted to build a party. Naturally, they did not plan to build up fully fledged political parties. For the time being, Nemtsov and Kiriyenko needed political structures to use in the pre-election horse-trading.

Nemtsov called his party Young Russia and called on his acquaintances to be the party activists. The party slogan was "Freedom, Order and Justice." Nadezhdin wrote the charter (and wrote almost a copy of it for Kiriyenko). "We started thinking about who could head party cells in the regions," Kotyusov said.[4] In some places, these party cells were a formality, a fiction, but in places where a local politician could be involved, they were real grass-roots party organizations. The base was Nizhny Novgorod. For 50,000 roubles (less than $2,000), friends who were designers came up with the logo, and everything that could be used to promote the party was used. This meant, first and foremost, connections and relationships. In Nizhny Novgorod, for example, the Young Russia brand held Olympic games for the local journalists who competed in a variety of sports, from volleyball and swimming to darts and tug-of-war. The grand prize was a locally made van bought with money from local businessmen who were longtime friends of Nemtsov's. This was how Nemtsov and his party got free PR.

But none of this helped much. By the end of November, Young Russia's rating was hovering around one per cent. It was clear that, as a separate political force, Nemtsov's movement would not go to the polls.

## A common grave

There had been talk of uniting the democrats in the past, but it never got off the ground. The failure of the 1995 parliamentary elections was still fresh in everyone's mind, and the default seemed to end all discussion. But the subject was raised again when a horrific political assassination rocked the country. On the night of 21 November 1998, assassins shot and killed Galina Starovoitova, a first-wave democrat and one of Russia's most famous politicians, in the entryway of her own house in central St Petersburg. Russia had become accustomed to assassination attempts on famous people, but Starovoitova, an associate of human-rights defender Andrei Sakharov, embodied the democratic ideals of the late 1980s and early 1990s. And she was a woman.

On 22 November, Nemtsov's meeting with the activists of Gaidar's Democratic Choice of Russia party turned into an evening in memory of Starovoitova, a spontaneous rally that brought together in one room figures who had not been seen together for some time, from Nemtsov and Chubais to the priest Gleb Yakunin and satirist Mikhail Zhvanetsky. The gathering begged the question of joining forces; there were calls to lock the democratic leaders in one room and not let them out, like Catholic cardinals in a papal election, until they agreed to run in the Duma elections as a united front. It was already clear that Kiriyenko, Chubais, Gaidar and Nemtsov had to come to an agreement first. A day later, all the Russian democratic politicians gathered at Starovoitova's funeral in the Alexander Nevsky Lavra in St Petersburg. It was there that substantive negotiations began.

Two days later, *Izvestiya* published an election manifesto signed not only by all four of them, but also by Khakamada, Sysuyev (who had already taken a job in the Kremlin) and even by several governors. "In response to the brazen invasion of gangsters into political life, in response to attempts to turn the country back to dictatorship and socialist distribution of benefits, in response to demands being made throughout the country for the unification of democratic forces, we, the undersigned, are starting work to form a new social and political association with a centre-right orientation."[5]

In December, news broke of a coalition that would unite Chubais, Nemtsov, Gaidar and ex-finance minister Boris Fyodorov under the new Right Cause brand. This is the first time the liberals called themselves the political right. During perestroika, the Communist Party's reactionaries were called right-wing, and left-wing democrats opposed them. But later political descriptives began to change in order to seem more logical from a historical point of view: Communists, who traditionally advocated a substantial role for the state in regulating the economy and wide extension of social benefits, were called left-wing.

In distinction to the traditional political compass in the West, the political system in Russia was more like a Möbius strip: the Communists—the left-wing forces—carried Orthodox Christian banners and turned out to be fiercely conservative. And since the economy was based on oil revenues, no one at all supported raising taxes. Typically for Russian history, the reference point was the attitude towards the West. Since the leftwingers who were pining for lost Soviet greatness became Slavophiles, the Westerners—Gaidar, Chubais, Nemtsov and their comrades-in-arms—became right-wingers. Since the mid-1990s, liberalism in Russia has ideologically belonged on the right-wing spectrum.

The press was sceptical about the idea of a right-wing bloc. Indeed, it was difficult at the time to believe in the right's electoral success: the phrase "Blame it on Chubais!" had already become an aphorism; Gaidar was called the author of "anti-people reforms"; Nemtsov had been discredited by Berezovsky and Gusinsky; and Kiriyenko, with whom they wanted to unite and whom Chubais called a possible coalition leader, bore the burden of default. "There was no guarantee of success at all," Chubais recalled. "The expert position was very sober: 'This is a common grave for all the architects of the default. Great idea, guys! Where's the lid for the coffin so we can hammer it down.' And their point of view had a certain validity."[6]

In the early spring of 1999, talks about creating a right-wing liberal bloc were already underway in Oleg Sysuyev's office at the Presidential Administration. He was a good friend and associate of Nemtsov and Chubais. Sysuyev convinced Yumashev and Dyachenko that they shouldn't push away Nemtsov or the right-wing; at that point Yeltsin had no other supporters in the coming elections. Chubais, Gaidar, Nemtsov and Kiriyenko took part in the talks with Yumashev and Dyachenko. Khakamada was also invited. But the coalition didn't hold. Kiriyenko decided not to rush, and Khakamada refused the fifth place offered to her on the party list. At the same time, it was clear that the potential right-wing bloc had voters. They just needed to find the right way to reach them.

Kiriyenko kept to himself, nodding politely to everyone, but not giving in to persuasion. Back in September, he had turned down several offers, including the post of first deputy prime minister and director of a state bank. Kiriyenko was counting on either an even higher position or a lucrative alliance. Khakamada also negotiated with everyone from Chubais to Luzhkov, eventually reaching an agreement with Gusinsky to support her in one of Moscow's constituencies before Nemtsov and Chubais finally persuaded her to join the right. Khakamada haggled—she wanted both one of the top spots on the list and a voice in decision-making. "Boris called me and said, 'Irina, congratulations. You've driven everyone completely nuts. You will be third on the list.' I said, 'That's not good enough for me.' 'What else do you want?' I said, 'I want to be in the leadership of the future party and the future faction.'"[7]

In this way, spring and summer were spent on negotiations with everyone that came to almost nothing. The enthusiasm at the beginning of winter had waned, and the sceptics were predicting even more loudly that the liberals would never come to an agreement and that everyone would lose. The key question was: will Right Cause unite with Kiriyenko's New Force, or will they go in two blocs and bury each other? The rather pompous Right Cause congress at the end of May—nine parties united to form a pre-election bloc—did not provide an answer. Nemtsov failed to persuade his friend Oleg Sysuyev, who had just left the Presidential Administration, to join Right Cause. The reason, again, was simple: money. Politics didn't provide an income, and none of them wanted to be kept by oligarchs. Nemtsov earned his money by lecturing in the West. Sysuyev didn't have that option. The former mayor of Samara, deputy prime minister and top executive in the Kremlin took a job in a bank and retired from politics for good.

By late spring, Luzhkov had formed his own political organization, and the governors of the most important regions were gathering their forces as they discussed an alliance with Luzhkov. "Today, right before our very eyes, the Russian liberals are losing even the slim chance they had after Primakov's resignation," *Kommersant* wrote at the end of May.[8] 'Our Cause Is Dead' was the title of a report on the right-wing congress.[9] In the Kremlin, no one was particularly interested in any of this. First, they understood that the right-wingers weren't going anywhere. Second, no one had time for them. At this point all the manoeuvring to choose the successor was entering the decisive phase. Pavlovsky recalled: "The Kremlin's attitude was simple: 'We don't care about anyone who isn't a presidential candidate. And anyone who is a presidential candidate is our opponent.'"[10]

Kiriyenko continued to play his own game and suddenly started attacking Luzhkov, even though he had just been negotiating with him. It soon became clear that he was running for mayor of Moscow (the mayoral elections were held at the same time as the parliamentary elections) and was launching an election campaign. It was a simple calculation: Kiriyenko had been in office for such a short period of time that no one perceived him as a serious politician. In order to get some bargaining power, he needed to flex his muscles. Kiriyenko's personal ratings were higher than those of Chubais and Nemtsov, but his New Force party was also still hovering at the bottom of party ratings with one or two per cent.

## SPS

When Yeltsin named Putin his successor, the Kremlin was surrounded on all sides. Despite the failure of impeachment, the Communists were not discouraged and formed a bloc with the nationalists. The Kremlin's attempts to prevent Luzhkov's alliance with influential governors collapsed. All Russia, a political movement led by Shaimiyev, had already united the heads of Russia's largest regions and republics and was now merging with Luzhkov's Fatherland party. They put Primakov in first place on their membership roll and firmly held the centre-left on the political axis. This was a powerful bid for victory—first in the parliamentary elections and then in the presidential elections. This was strongly supported by the August 1999 opinion polls. Communists did not inspire as much fear as before, but Luzhkov, Primakov, and the governors who joined them were the most serious contenders for power in Russia.

Attempts to create a centre-right bloc headed by the newly resigned Stepashin, which would have brought together right-wing politicians,

Viktor Chernomyrdin's Our Home Is Russia, and individual governors, also failed. When Stepashin brought this idea up to Chernomyrdin, Chernomyrdin, in his usual manner, told the right-wingers to get lost. And no wonder: Nemtsov and all those young reformers had been at Chernomyrdin's throat since he'd been prime minister. Stepashin eventually joined Yavlinsky and his Yabloko party.

Before Stepashin resigned, Chubais had got Kiriyenko's agreement in principle to head the right-wing bloc. Nemtsov and Khakamada were already travelling around the country with their "You Are Right" campaign. Nemtsov, Khakamada, activists and anyone who wanted to join them would walk with a huge Russian flag down the central avenue in a city to a local stadium, where a political rally would be followed by a concert featuring the famous rock bands of the time, including Chaif, Mashina Vremeni, Bravo and Sekret.

At the end of August, Kiriyenko, Nemtsov and Khakamada announced the formation of the Union of Right Forces (Russian abbreviation SPS). They were joined by other politicians, including several governors. The shadow leader of SPS was Chubais. The Kremlin viewed the new political alliance favourably, but with scepticism. Three and a half months before the election, the SPS rating was about one per cent.

This is when it became clear that the first task was to get right-wing politicians to come to an agreement among themselves. SPS brought together people who had rarely been able to sit at the same table before: first-wave democrats and former Komsomol functionaries, lawyers and farmers, intellectuals and even Cossacks. Tensions grew between activists in Yegor Gaidar's Democratic Choice of Russia—Russia's oldest democratic party—and the businessmen headed by Sergei Kiriyenko. Both groups wanted Russia to become a part of Europe, but the former were concerned with democratic values and the latter had a more pragmatic approach. This led to the first serious conflict. What should the campaign's slogans be? Gaidar supporters insisted that they should talk about the fight against Communism and nationalism, about democracy and human rights; the campaign managers brought along by Kiriyenko were categorically against it.

The leaders still could not come to an agreement. Nemtsov was jealous of Kiriyenko, Khakamada did not trust him, and Kiriyenko distanced himself from both of them. And each wanted to be at the top of the list. In early October, the campaign consultants hired by Kiriyenko, Pyotr Shchedrovitsky and Yefim Ostrovsky, took all three to a resort near Moscow for a few days. The consultants lectured them, talked to them about campaign objectives, trained them and role-played. From time to time, other members of the headquarters would come to these seminars and speak to them, too. "The goal was to agree at least for six months," recalled Pyotr Shchedrovitsky. "We had to get their personal issues out in the open and use them to discuss how they were going to deal with each other in the future."[11]

At the end of the training, Kiriyenko, Khakamada and Nemtsov formulated three questions for themselves.

(1) What do we each want if we win the election?

Kiriyenko said he wanted to be the leader of the faction. "I would like that role myself," Nemtsov said, "but I understand that Kiriyenko will have it. So I agree to the deputy speaker." Khakamada wanted to head one of the Duma committees.

(2) What will each of them do if they don't win, and how is each prepared to help the rest?

Kiriyenko said he would go run for governor of Nizhny Novgorod region and wanted to involve both Nemtsov and Khakamada in the campaign. "I know how to make money with lectures, and I am ready to teach you that," Nemtsov said. Khakamada said she knew how to do great PR and was willing to share both her experience and the PR activities.

(3) What would happen if someone left the Duma after winning?

Nemtsov and Khakamada already knew that Kiriyenko didn't want to be in the parliament; he hoped for a position in the executive branch, and his two partners expected that he'd be offered one. In that case, Nemtsov said, "I would become the leader of the faction." Khakamada demanded the post of deputy speaker. Everyone agreed.[12]

Kiriyenko, Nemtsov and Khakamada worked through the rest of the campaign without a single quarrel and never broke any of their agreements.

After debate and deliberations, SPS decided to base its campaign on the idea of a generational shift and went to the polls under the slogan:

"Young. Competent. Energetic." The idea of youth and innovation carried with it a message about the break with the Soviet past and the inevitability of change, about a new page in Russian history that would be happier and bring greater success. The campaign manager was Chubais. Gaidar headed the SPS list for Moscow—Kiriyenko was running for mayor at the same time—Valentin Zavadnikov, a colleague and associate of Chubais, led the headquarters, and several oligarchs, including Fridman, Khodorkovsky and Oleg Deripaska, gave money to the campaign.

And the campaign worked. "A New Generation—We Need Young People" billboards appeared all over the country. SPS commercials used quotes from ordinary Russians of all professions and ages: "At least they weren't in the Politburo"; "They're young and not senile"; "They speak clearly and answer questions honestly"; "I support a professional army, which means I support the right"; "The next century is a century of women: I vote for Khakamada." For all three, but especially for Nemtsov and Khakamada, the campaign turned into a concert tour of the country. At the same time, there were debates on television—a very comfortable milieu for both Nemtsov and Khakamada—and Kiriyenko, too, felt increasingly confident in front of the cameras. Each had their own main talking point: for Khakamada, it was a professional army; Nemtsov campaigned for "living like they do in Europe"; and Kiriyenko, the freshest face in the right-wing pantheon, embodied innovation and youthfulness. "SPS was going to be a middle-class party," recalled Khakamada, "liberal, but also socially oriented. This came from outside the big cities and from Nemtsov. As a former governor, he was not a pure monetarist. That is, we were not thinking about stupid populism, we did not want to lie—but still, we had great respect for people and understood that they had to be involved in the reforms and they had to like them."[13]

Despite his experience and love of public politics, Nemtsov was initially timid at rallies and concerts. He wasn't comfortable shouting slogans to crowds of thousands, and he didn't know how to dance to rock music. But this quickly passed, and at the debates and speeches in front of supporters he was once again like a fish in water, swept up by campaign adrenaline. Nemtsov, well aware of his success among women, used his charisma again: "We are not counting on just the young. We are counting on all independent people. We're counting on women, I must admit," he said in one of his interviews at a rally. "We are counting on intelligent people."[14] Work had become a joy again.

From October until the election, there was no more friction or scandal within SPS. They were a team: everyone was doing their own thing, and campaigning went smoothly. The mood in the campaign headquarters was cheerful and good-spirited. Regardless of how the political puzzle came together at the polls, in general things were already good and would be even better later. The right-wingers were in high spirits: they had travelled all over the country, from the Russian heartland to Siberia and back again. Surrounded by thousands of supporters at endless rallies across the country, they were beginning to believe in their own victory. "It was a fantastic feeling," recalled Khakamada. "We began to live in a world where we had already won. The campaign went smoothly. We had no problems at all."[15]

## Sessions of mass hypnosis

The Kremlin remembered about the Duma elections towards autumn. At that point, SPS was the only political association that supported Yeltsin and was ready to support his successor, but the party's chances of making it into the Duma seemed slim. What should they do? How could they successfully oppose Luzhkov and Primakov? At the end of August, Boris Berezovsky started travelling around the regions, trying to pull the governors loyal to the Kremlin into a new movement. He even came up with a name for it: the Interregional Unity Movement—or just Unity, although he abbreviated it in Russian to "Bear." He managed to win the support of several governors, although they were hardly the most powerful. But at first the Kremlin didn't believe in the success of the party and didn't want to have anything to do with them. The Gusinsky-owned newspaper *Segodnya* called it "Berezovsky's menagerie."[16]

In late September, thirty-nine governors signed a petition to form the Unity party, and in early October a Unity congress announced their first three candidates: that is, those who would work as the public faces of this hastily assembled pro-Kremlin political force. These three included

Emergency Situations Minister Sergei Shoigu, Olympic champion in Graeco-Roman wrestling Alexander Karelin, and Major-General Alexander Gurov, who in the early 1990s headed the department for combating organized crime. The press immediately called them a union of fighters and rescue workers. Shoigu was popular—he had an image as a rescuer who says little but does a lot—but not he, nor Karelin, nor Gurov had any experience in politics. Created out of nothing, with the help of political consultants and the government, Unity went into the elections with the slogan "Bringing Honest People to the Duma." The campaign did not fare well at first; its positive rating hovered around five per cent. Pavlovsky recalled that the campaign "amused our staff [Putin's HQ], and we laughed until we realized that the next Duma would be as hostile as the one under Yeltsin."[17]

Meanwhile, the Kremlin and Berezovsky launched an information campaign against Luzhkov and Primakov. TV journalist Sergei Dorenko, already renowned for his ability to destroy political careers on television—he had destroyed Nemtsov's rating after the privatization of Svyazinvest—was back in prime time on the Berezovsky-controlled ORT nationwide channel. Dorenko accused Luzhkov of murders, mafia connections and corruption. He filmed a bird's-eye view of his mansion outside the city in the pricey Rublyovka neighbourhood. But this was not the usual compromising material known as *kompromat*. This would make the information war against the young reformers look like an innocent prank.

In autumn 1999, a completely new type of propaganda appeared on the Russian airwaves, unlike anything that had ever been seen before. In the prime-time spot usually reserved for news shows, where the *Vremya* news programme had been broadcast for decades, instead of news the audience got a tangled mixture of satire and tabloid "investigations of scandals." Dorenko did not just denounce Luzhkov; he mocked and ridiculed him. He added moustaches, wigs and beards to his photograph on air and called him a pygmy. The question of whether or not to believe Dorenko was irrelevant. He wasn't after audience trust; his show was designed to hypnotize the viewers.

Primakov—Russia's most popular politician in September 1999—was portrayed as old and infirm. The propaganda message was that replacing a sick and old Yeltsin with a sick and old Primakov would be jumping out of the frying pan and into the fire. Primakov was associated with weakness and sickness: live on air, Dorenko relished close-ups of hip surgery—the same kind the former premier had undergone the previous summer.

At the beginning of October, Primakov and Luzhkov didn't take the ambitions of Unity seriously, and Gusinsky's NTV channel seemed to be as powerful a propaganda weapon as ORT. For every insult by Dorenko, NTV host Yevgeny Kiselyov would respond with another revelation of corruption and cover-up, and the term "family" became another word for "mafia."

Both sides used television propaganda in their coverage of the war in Chechnya, which had started again. Kremlin-controlled television insisted that under Putin's leadership the army was restoring order. NTV, with its slogan "News Is Our Profession", had earned both its popularity and its professional reputation for exposing the atrocities of the first Chechen war. It continued to pursue the same line, reporting on brutal security sweeps and sharply criticizing the military campaign.

The Kremlin's upper hand in the information war grew in step with Putin's growing credibility. During October, the ratings of the parties Unity and Fatherland–All Russia, the two parties of the authorities—those in office and those in opposition—began to move towards each other. The turning point came in November. After the first successes of the military operation in Chechnya under Putin's personal control, support both for him and for the war he was leading became overwhelming. At the beginning of the month, pollsters gave Unity six to eight per cent of the vote in the upcoming elections on 19 December. Polls gave Luzhkov's and Primakov's parties at least twice that, but Putin's position was undergoing a fundamental change. By mid-November he had become the front-runner in the presidential race. On 24 November, Putin announced before television cameras that Sergei Shoigu was his great friend and that, "as a citizen", he supported Unity. The rating of Unity immediately shot up like a helium balloon, and by early December the ratings of Unity and Fatherland–All Russia had switched places. Yury Luzhkov, the Kremlin's main enemy, seemed close to triumph when his hopes were dashed, and his allies among governors were concerned. Putin was not just on his way to the presidency with confidence, he could already count on something that Yeltsin and his cabinet never managed to achieve: majority support in the future parliament. Not only was Unity second only to the Communists in all the polls, but opinion polls also confidently predicted that Putin's other allies—SPS, led by Kiriyenko, Nemtsov and Khakamada—would pass the five per cent threshold and gain entry into the Duma.

## Putin to the Kremlin, Kiriyenko to the Duma

Like many democrats, Nemtsov was uncomfortable with Putin's past career in the KGB. What would Andrei Sakharov say about a president with this past? But at the time Nemtsov was less concerned about Putin being from the KGB and more worried—along with others in SPS—that Putin had a narrow outlook and that he might make mistakes while running Russia. "Boris told Tolya [Chubais]: you'll have trouble with him," said Valentin Zavadnikov, one of Chubais's associates and head of the SPS headquarters during the election. "But Chubais thought Putin could be educated and that it was possible to work with him."[18]

In any case, neither Chubais nor Nemtsov had a choice, and at the time there seemed to be many arguments in favour of Putin. First, purely political: Yeltsin's successor would continue his course. "Will is, perhaps, the main thing needed in Russia today," Chubais said at the time. "And Putin has the will to get things done. But most importantly, this trait in him is organically combined with an understanding and acceptance of basic human values: freedom, democracy, private property, human rights—everything that is called in the world liberal values. This is the key to success."[19]

Second, many people in Nemtsov's circle knew him—both from his work at the St Petersburg mayor's office and from his work in Moscow—and they had nothing bad to say about him. On the contrary, they only welcomed his move up on the career ladder. Everyone wanted to give Putin a chance. Journalist Yevgeniya Albats remembered Alexei Kudrin (Chubais's ally who had worked with Putin in the St Petersburg mayor's office) telling her then: "Zhenya, believe me, he's just like you and me."[20]

"Putin and I used to meet, drink beer, talk," Kokh recalled. "I thought he was an absolutely normal guy. And when he became director of the FSB and then a presidential candidate, it all seemed very positive to me."[21]

Finally, the right-wing needed Putin. It was a marriage not only of love but also of convenience. By the end of November, their position was already relatively stable—Chubais announced at the party conference on 18 November that there would be no problem overcoming the five-per-cent barrier—but the closer the right-wing candidates were to Putin, the better their results. This was the source of the slogan that the right-wing used in the December elections: "Putin to the Kremlin, Kiriyenko to the Duma."

Meanwhile, the idea of creating a buffer zone around Chechnya was abandoned in September. In mid-October, federal troops crossed the Terek River into the heart of Chechnya and moved further south, storming towns and villages and immediately encountering serious resistance. At the height of the pre-election campaign, the war entered its bloodiest phase, with the Russian army taking control of flatland Chechnya. After the September terrorist attacks, Russian citizens shared the goal of this war: to stop the gangsterism and terrorism coming out of Chechnya and to restore order in the country. But it was often impossible to separate the guerrillas from the civilians. Artillery fire and aircraft carpet-bombing destroyed entire towns and villages, and the military committed brutal security sweeps, violence and murder. Refugees streamed out of Chechnya. The war was turning into a punitive operation.

In November, Putin, still prime minister, launched a new slogan—the complete annihilation of the terrorists, and again he was supported by the public and the majority of deputies in the parliament (the same majority that recently tried to impeach Yeltsin, in part for unleashing the war in Chechnya in 1994). Criticism from the West grew by the day—the West demanded that Moscow negotiate with Aslan Maskhadov, the president of what was then the Chechen Republic of Ichkeria. The war was shaping the agenda, forcing politicians to make up their minds, and it became the central subject of both the election campaign and public debate.

At the end of November, SPS made a statement in support of the actions of the federal authorities in Chechnya. Chubais even declared that "the Russian army is being revived in Chechnya" and called Yavlinsky, who had also called for negotiations with Maskhadov, a traitor.[22] His words, of course, caused a ruckus in the party: they seemed unacceptable to the old democratic guard that had come in under Gaidar.

Nemtsov was sceptical about the idea of negotiations with Maskhadov: he thought the time when they could have been useful had already passed. Nemtsov supported the SPS party line. Furthermore, he agreed with it in many ways, although not as strongly as Chubais. First of all, Nemtsov recognized that unlike the first Chechen war, this time the troops were not betrayed by the political leadership. Second, Chechnya was part of Russia and terrorists in the country must be destroyed—"the only good terrorist is a dead terrorist"—and constitutional order must be restored. "But we have to keep in mind that there are women and children and old people there who have to live their lives," Nemtsov continued, "so when we are elected to the Duma, we'll move to adopt a programme of state support for refugees. There are more than two hundred thousand of them."[23]

Everyone who followed the election campaign knew who was in charge in SPS. Anatoly Chubais had a large office in the headquarters of the RIA Novosti news agency. He had joined Nemtsov, Kiriyenko, and Khakamada together in one political project and put other relatively influential people in secondary roles. He controlled the headquarters' financial expenditures, supervised the creative work and was in charge of liaison with the Kremlin. To get the slogan "Putin to the Kremlin, Kiriyenko to the Duma" on billboards and SPS campaign materials in December, Chubais needed Putin's approval—and he got it. He also lobbied for a face-to-face meeting between Putin and Kiriyenko a week before the election, a meeting that gave SPS a powerful last push.

By early December, there was a glow of success around Putin. His associates and supporters—the team in a broad sense—were anticipating future victory. The gloom was receding, dispelling before their eyes, and all problems seemed to have been overcome—almost magically. Life had changed for ever, and Russia would never again return to its dark past. After the four years of bitter struggle during Yeltsin's second term, prospects were opening up again, hopes were rising, and people were making plans for the future. Such sentiments prevailed both in the SPS headquarters, full of drive and optimism, and in the Presidential Administration, which was already working as Putin's campaign headquarters. A new time was coming—a time that would belong to a new generation of politicians, a generation of modern forty-five-year-olds like Putin, Chubais and Nemtsov. "Look at Luzhkov, look at Zyuganov, look at all the other leaders," Anatoly Chubais had said in an interview the previous summer. "They are good guys, but it's quite obvious that this is their last chance. Who will need them in 2004? Now make a mental experiment and imagine Nemtsov, Fyodorov, Khakamada, Kiriyenko and Gaidar in 2004."[24] The more likely Putin's victory was, the easier it was to imagine them in four years.

At the time, Nemtsov's answer to the question of whether or not he supported Putin was clear. Nemtsov was on board. "I believe that Russia must elect a new president, one who is honest, physically strong and responsible," Nemtsov said. "I am convinced that Vladimir Putin should be the next president. So long as some people whom I won't name don't tie his hands, I'm sure he has every chance of being voted in. At the very least, I will support him in every way possible."[25]

The British economist Robert Skidelsky remembers a dinner party in November 1999 at Margaret Thatcher's home in London. There were about ten or twelve guests. Nemtsov, sitting to the right of the hostess, persuaded her to speak in support of Putin. "You love to visit Russia, you are adored in Russia, and, if you support him, you will be received there like a queen," Nemtsov told her. Thinking for a moment, Thatcher replied: "No. I won't support him. He has a bad face. I don't believe him. Think of it as a woman's intuition. I don't think he would make a good [leader]."[26]

The last week is crucial for any election campaign. It is at this point that most undecided voters make their final choice. The basic rule of political campaigns is this: in an election, as in sport, you must be invested in winning from the start, but the finishing spurt is the key to success. The right wing needed a surge, and they got it. Putin pushed them to the red ribbon when he met Kiriyenko on Monday, 13 December, with just five days left until election day. Kiriyenko was to present Putin with the SPS economic reform programme, and Chubais insisted that the report be as thick as possible: the thicker it was, the more competent the right would look in television coverage. They even shoved some newspaper articles and SPS programme documents in to make it thicker. The result was a folio of about a thousand pages. "The document needs serious study, but some aspects are quite clear," Putin said in his boilerplate language, patting his hand on the thick book and repeating the SPS slogan almost verbatim, "especially the part about promoting young, energetic people to all levels of government, including the Duma."[27] One could not have dreamt of a better final spurt to the finish line.

## "I'm leaving. I did everything I could…"

On the next day, 14 December, Yeltsin told Putin that he wanted to resign ahead of his term end to make sure that Putin would run as acting president and that the elections would be held at the end of March instead of June.* The idea was simple: the acting president—already the president—would have a stronger starting position than his rivals. But in December additional arguments appeared: polls showed that Putin's rating was at its peak, and the sooner the election was held, the more certain it was that he would win. Four months before, no one had known anything about Putin; now the whole nation was relying on him. Who knew what would happen in six months' time? It was better to hurry and act right away.

As both Yeltsin and Putin recall, Putin told him at the time that he wasn't sure he was ready. This was their second conversation about the future. Their first talk, which took place before Stepashin's resignation, was left uncertain. According to Putin, while Yeltsin later called him the successor on nationwide television, he told Putin he was a "prime minister with excellent prospects."[28] It appeared that they began discussing

---

\*  Yeltsin mentions the date of 14 December in his memoirs. In early January, *Kommersant* and *Nezavisimaya gazeta* gave the different date of 22 December—clearly from the same source. If true, Yeltsin told Putin that he intended to leave early after the State Duma elections, not before them.

Putin's future presidency in earnest as early as December. Putin later said that when he became prime minister he had no other plans—"I thought I'd work for a year and that would be fine"[29]—but by then he had actually been in pre-election mode for several months.

It is hard to believe that during their conversation in December Putin was ready to reject the proposal made to him. It is more likely that he was being cautious, keeping in mind Yeltsin's propensity to test his supporters for loyalty (as he did with Putin's former boss, Anatoly Sobchak, in late 1995). Who knows what Yeltsin had in mind? At first, when his candidacy was being discussed, Putin did not aspire to be the successor. But he was immediately seduced by the comfort of his new life. According to the recollections of one of his colleagues at the time, as soon as he entered the prime minister's office, Putin asked how secure he thought his new position was, and, glancing around the room, answered his own question: "I'm not going to give this up." Other associates of Putin recalled that by autumn Putin had already acquired a taste for power and was keen to become president. Sergei Pugachyov, a businessman close to Putin at the time, said many years later that Putin was impressed by the level of social amenities he suddenly had access to: "Just imagine, he suffered a disastrous mayoral election, then there were all kinds of problems, his dacha burnt down—all kinds of bad luck. Suddenly he was brought here and told: 'Here's a palace [i.e. a new residence], here's the country. Don't deny yourself anything.'"[30]

On the eve of the Duma elections, sociological surveys showed a situation favourable to the Kremlin. The pro-Putin forces—Unity and SPS—would finally destroy the longstanding monopoly of the leftist forces in parliament. But reality surpassed expectations. With 23.3 per cent of the vote, the Unity movement lost only one per cent to the Communists. This meant that Russian Communism of the 1990s—an explosive mixture of homesickness for the Soviet past, nationalism, monarchism, Stalinism and paternalism—was fading away. Protest was disappearing: the boundaries were blurring in the so-called Red Belt in the south of Russia, which had historically voted for Communists. The Red Belt was now tilting towards support for Putin. The Union of Right Forces received 8.5 per cent, a victory the right could never have dreamt of only a month or two ago. Moreover, Nemtsov scored a double victory, winning by just over one per cent the election in single-mandate districts of Nizhny Novgorod, beating his longtime opponent and former head of GAZ, Boris Vidyayev. The fact that he ran by himself, not as part of a party list, made the victory all the sweeter. Most importantly, the Fatherland–All Russia bloc came only third with a modest 13.3 per cent: Luzhkov and Primakov suffered a resounding defeat and lost their presidential prospects. Both understood this very well: neither would run for the presidency after Yeltsin suddenly resigned on New Year's Eve and the Duma elections seamlessly flowed into the presidential campaign. Both would soon be sworn in before Putin and under his banner. The Kremlin showed strength and retained power in its hands.

To avoid publicity, the Kremlin dragged its feet until the last minute, and Yeltsin recorded his New Year's Eve address at 10.00 a.m. on 31 December. By that time, the formalities had been done. Yeltsin signed his resignation and gave Putin the "nuclear suitcase" (or, to be more exact, Putin was introduced to the officers with the suitcase). At noon in Moscow, Yeltsin's address was broadcast. It was obvious that Yeltsin had difficulty reading the text from the teleprompter; he sometimes stammered, and he was clearly very emotional. "I am leaving. I did everything I could," he said. He begged the people's forgiveness—for dashing their hopes, for not making the leap "from a grey, stagnant, totalitarian past into a bright, affluent, civilized future", something many, and he himself, had believed was possible. ("Strangely enough, after that, after I said it all, I felt better," Yeltsin later said.[31])

His second term was full of pain and anguish—literally and figuratively—and he did not carry his presidential burden to the finish line. The constitutional transfer of power was sacrificed to a political campaign scenario designed to help his successor be elected president before the new millennium. Yeltsin explained that he wanted the election to be held on schedule—it was "the most important precedent of a civilized voluntary transfer of power"—but after weighing the pros and cons, he "made another decision." And soon, in the same office, but at a different table, so that the TV picture was different from the previous one, Vladimir Putin was wishing Russians a Happy New Year. "Today I am entrusted with the duties of head of state," he said. "Freedom of speech, freedom of conscience, freedom of the media, property rights—these fundamental elements of a civilized society will be reliably protected by the state."

## Who is Mr Putin?

Less than a week after Yeltsin resigned, *The New York Times* published an op-ed entitled 'Russia's Best Bet'. Yes, Putin is not a liberal democrat, authors Boris Nemtsov and American political scientist Ian Bremmer agreed, and under his leadership Russia will not become France. Yes, before Yeltsin made Putin prime minister last August, hardly anyone knew him, and Unity simply didn't exist. But it is precisely because Putin was not known and was not responsible for the policies and mistakes of previous years, Nemtsov and Bremmer explained, that he managed to win people's support. But Putin was in favour of a market economy and limiting the influence of oligarchs. That is to say: the reformers were back, the Communists had lost, and Russia was finally on the right path to build a fully democratic political system in the future.[32]

Putin had a unique quality: it was easy to project any and all hopes and interests onto him. Social groups with diametrically different perceptions saw him as an ally. Liberals believed that he would be faithful to Yeltsin's words and course. Leftists hoped that he would reverse that course. Westernizers wanted Russia to be friends with America and Europe. Nationalists hoped that Russia would quarrel with them. The reformers expected market reforms to continue, the *siloviki* wanted an increase in the influence of the security services, the army wanted respect, and the elderly wanted higher pensions. As a result, Putin was ideologically elusive. Nothing could be said about him—and it was unclear what to expect from him next. That was the point of American journalist Trudy Rubin's famous question at the Davos Forum in February 2000—"Who is Mr Putin?"—which so discomfited the Russian delegation.

Of course, some of the Kremlin's actions began to alarm Nemtsov and other liberals. The first session of the new Duma in January 2000 led to scandal. The right-wingers were still celebrating their historic defeat of the Communists and the formation of a new centre-right majority in the Duma, when it suddenly turned out that there was no centre-right majority—at least when it came to sharing leadership positions in the parliamentary committees. The Unity faction and the Communists struck a deal that was immediately termed a collusion. They divided the leadership positions in the parliamentary committees among themselves, and the post of speaker went back to the Communists. SPS, Yabloko and Fatherland–All Russia were left with nothing. They got up and stormed out of the hall. The deal was especially incomprehensible to the liberals, because there seemed to have been no need for it. Why would the Kremlin make a deal with the left when it already had allies on the right? And where did this political cynicism come from? Under Yeltsin, who had just resigned, Nemtsov protested, such collusion between the Kremlin and the Communists was simply unthinkable. This was a key question: if Putin approved of this collusion, then he, Nemtsov, would not be able to support him.[33]

The Kremlin's plan was purely political manoeuvring invented by Voloshin and approved by Putin, meant to drive a wedge between the Communists on the one hand and Luzhkov and Primakov on the other. The right and Yabloko simply fell off the radar. It was not a big deal, the Kremlin reassured SPS leaders; when it came to economic reforms, the centre-right majority in the Duma would be restored automatically.

Another wake-up call was the scandal surrounding the disappearance of Radio Liberty journalist Andrei Babitsky in late January in Chechnya, a man known for his sympathies for the Chechen fighters, their struggle and their terrorist methods. Babitsky was detained by federal troops, then exchanged for Russian soldiers captured by Chechens, and then he disappeared. Journalists in Moscow did everything in their power to find him. "Never since the beginning of perestroika have the authorities allowed themselves such blatant lawlessness and cynicism in their actions against members of the media," they wrote in an open appeal to the authorities.[34] Babitsky was found, but not before Putin, in an interview to journalist Natalia Gevorkyan, had called him a traitor and explained that he himself had agreed to the exchange. "What if they had asked to shoot him?" Gevorkyan asked. "That is forbidden by internal regulations," Putin said, cutting her off.[35] "We have begun to have doubts," was Nemtsov's answer at the time when asked if SPS would continue to support Putin in the upcoming presidential election, "not because we have changed our position, but because we got to know Vladimir Putin better."[36] The human-rights faction in SPS had already openly opposed him, and Chubais had to persuade his allies not to give up his election slogan. The second part—"Kiriyenko to the Duma"— had been achieved, but now they had to carry out the first part—"Putin to the Kremlin."

There was no doubt that Yeltsin's successor would win; the only question was whether a second round would be necessary. It wasn't. Putin got almost fifty-three per cent of the votes. There is an episode in documentary filmmaker Vitaly Mansky's *Putin's Witnesses*, based on video chronicles of those days. It's the evening of 26 March, the preliminary election results have just been announced, and Putin's team is celebrating their victory. Valentin Yumashev, Tatyana Dyachenko, Anatoly Chubais, Gleb Pavlovsky, Putin's aide (and formal head of his campaign staff) Dmitry Medvedev, and other Putin associates from St Petersburg are in the room. Putin arrives at the headquarters as the *de facto* president-elect, with a glass in his hand, congratulates those present on their overall victory and leaves, while Nemtsov's voice booms out of the television set. It's NTV summing up the results of the election. "It would have been better for the country if there had been two rounds," says Nemtsov. "Before the second round, the favourite should have made commitments to the people, and we wouldn't be in the state of uncertainty that we are in now... We voted with our hearts, not knowing what awaits us tomorrow."[37]

Nemtsov and Khakamada voted for Yavlinsky, but that did not change the fact that the right-wingers were Putin's allies and supported him in the elections as both a political party and as a parliamentary faction. His victory was also their victory. They were waiting for positive changes in the country and had big plans. At the SPS congress in late May 2000, Chubais set political goals for the next election: fifty right-wing mayors nationwide, fifteen governorships and twenty per cent in the December 2003 Duma elections. The hall burst into applause.

# PART 4

# CHAPTER 19

## 2000–01
## First Blood

### A strong state

The defeat of the leftist forces and the election of Putin as president opened a window of opportunity for Russia that could not have been dreamt of even the year before. A team of Russia's best experts had been preparing a programme for the development of the country for the next ten years—this had been generally known since December, although Putin did not publicize it before the election. The programme was being curated by German Gref, a thirty-six-year-old associate of Putin and Chubais's from the St Petersburg mayor's office. He'd called himself "Chubais and Nemtsov's man" back in 1997, when they were at the height of their influence. In Putin's government he was minister for economic development. Alexei Kudrin, another official from the St Petersburg team of Putin and Chubais, became finance minister. And Andrei Illarionov, an economist known for his radical liberal views, was given a position in the Kremlin as a presidential aide (the media reported that Putin liked his proposal to drastically cut government spending).

The transformation that was being contemplated was breath-taking, analogous to the great reforms of Alexander II. Did the bureaucrat and strongman Putin look like a reformer? No, but neither did the conservative Alexander who took the path of liberal reform not because of his convictions, but out of necessity. Just as Alexander's reforms, by design, were to restore the Russian Empire, humiliated by its defeat in the Crimean War and aware of its backwardness, so Gref's programme was designed to transform Russia into a modern European country. Just as almost 150 years ago, it was intended to change the entire state. Within ten years, Russia would have a deficit-free budget and low taxes, private ownership of land, an independent judicial system and an accountable bureaucracy, a compact army and a professional, non-corrupt police force. It would be a state where the growth engine was a market economy, competition and a level playing field for all, where property rights were protected and businesses were unencumbered by a burdensome bureaucracy. And just as Alexander's allies in the country had believed in a strong supreme power that would conduct fundamental transformations and instil a will to change in the public, so the liberals under Putin went forward with the slogans of strengthening the state. The main task of government is to protect the public interest, and only a strong government could handle it.

There was nothing fundamentally new in these ideas; this was Nemtsov's "people's capitalism." Yeltsin had been talking about a strong state since early 1997, and Gref's programme was much the same as that of the young reformers' government. What was fundamentally new was, first, the balance of power—a pro-Putin majority in parliament and public support for the new president—and, second, the situation: the price of oil started to rise simultaneously with Putin's accession to power. By summer 2000, it was already approaching thirty dollars per barrel.

The new government did not put off reforms. With the support of the parliamentary majority, it brought public spending under control for the first time in many years. The thirteen per cent flat income tax, for which Gaidar had campaigned so hard, was quickly made law in June. This was revolutionary. With such a low income tax, there was no need to hide income, and Russia was becoming an attractive country for doing business. Tax cuts were also supposed to strengthen the state: taxes would be easier to collect, and the tax police would be more effective. A new land code and judicial reform were on the way, promising radical changes, such as the introduction of jury trials and *habeas corpus* (that is, the transfer of arrest warrants from investigators to courts).

Experts explained at the time that independent courts would counter local officials' arbitrary behaviour. "The weakening of state power is a crime against citizens and the state," wrote Gaidar's associate and one of the authors of Gref's program, Alexei Ulyukayev, in the liberals' manifesto 'Right Turn'.[1]

The liberals advocated a strong state authority, capable of performing functions that no one else could or should perform, such as collecting taxes, fighting crime, etc. The problem was that it was impossible to draw a clear line between strengthening the power of a particular individual, who sat in the Kremlin, and strengthening the power of the state as a whole. Putin's first reform, a reform of the federal system, hit this problem square on. The point of the reform was to short-circuit the power of governors.

It was pointed out, not without reason, that one of the sources of instability in the 1990s was the autocracy of governors, who became something like feudal lords and established their own order in the regions, "swallowing as much sovereignty" as they could. Legal enclaves emerged in the country that were essentially separate political regimes with their own laws, armies and courts; there were even attempts to introduce their own currency. Nemtsov cited the example of the residence permit—the *propiska*—still in force in Moscow, despite the Constitutional Court's decision outlawing it. "Another of Putin's tasks will be to set up a non-political mechanism for removing popularly elected governors and mayors from power," Nemtsov said. "Not for political reasons, but for actions that could be regulated by a court decision." For example, the president could initiate the removal of a mayor or governor, and the Supreme Court would rule on it. Then the state would work. "And now people ask me if we are in danger of a dictatorship," Nemtsov continued. "My answer: There cannot be a dictatorship in a messed-up, disorganized, privatized state."[2]

The Kremlin saw federal reform differently, believing that the levers should be in the hands of the president, not the courts. So, in the Kremlin they decided to remove governors from the upper house of parliament, to take away their immunity from prosecution and their right to influence the appointment of local police and special services chiefs. In addition, a presidential decree divided the country into seven districts, and seven presidential envoys would oversee compliance with federal law and represent the interests of the centre on the ground. On the one hand, these steps were logical. The Federation Council should be made up of professionals, governors should not feel that they have complete impunity, and it would be useful for the centre to have some control over local law enforcement since it was, as a rule, corrupt. On the other hand, it appeared as if the governors were being punished for their recent attempts to take some of the Kremlin's power, including their attacks on Skuratov, and the Kremlin was removing the levers of power from them.

Although Nemtsov had some objections to some aspects of the programme, his party, the Union of Right Forces, generally supported federal reform. Boris Berezovsky, however, unexpectedly strongly opposed it. In spring 2000, he moved to oppose Putin, even though he himself had just gone to great lengths to help elect him president. In an open letter to the president, he called his anti-governorship initiatives a blow to federalism and a step towards dictatorship.

Putin had another task that was certainly not straightforward: to unseat the oligarchs. The country needed to halt the merger of business and power that had marked the second half of the 1990s. Nemtsov had been at war with the oligarchs from his first day in government in 1997 and saw their omnipotence as a major threat to the country's development. And so, naturally, on this issue he and Putin were on the same page. But it remained to be seen what it meant in practice to remove the oligarchs from politics. The arrest of the television tycoon Vladimir Gusinsky on 13 June 2000 put this practice to the test.

## The game is on

After Yeltsin's victory in the 1996 elections, NTV co-founder Igor Malashenko was offered the post of head of the Presidential Administration. Malashenko refused. He decided that it would be more interesting and, more importantly, more profitable to create a huge private media holding. After all, if you didn't take bribes, there was no way to get rich if you were living on a state salary. After Yeltsin's victory, both he and Gusinsky were confident that their venture would be successful. The days were gone when the Presidential Security Service headed by Alexander Korzhakov could shove Gusinsky's guards face-down in the snow in the centre of Moscow and force Gusinsky to flee abroad. In 1996, Gusinsky had believed that his position was secure and that his troubles were over for good. "Now we will withstand any government," Malashenko recalled him saying.[3]

In November 1998, the first Russian private satellite was launched into space from Cape Canaveral in Florida, giving birth to NTV-Plus, an ambitious and very expensive project conceived by Gusinsky in late 1996. Gusinsky believed that he would finance NTV-Plus on credit: the Russian middle class would grow, everyone would install satellite dishes, and he would repay his debts and become a more powerful media magnate than the state. Gusinsky borrowed close to $1 billion, nearly half of it from Gazprom. He was on good terms with Gazprom, which had already bought a large stake in his media empire. "How will you pay back such a huge amount of money?" Malashenko asked him in the early days of the project. "The capitalization of our business will grow faster than the volume of loans, so we will always be in the black," Gusinsky replied.[4] Whether or not he was right in his calculations remained to be seen: the default ruined his plans, and the middle class was too busy surviving to think about satellite dishes.

Putin had not yet been declared Yeltsin's successor then, but the war between the Kremlin and Gusinsky had already spilt over onto television screens. Berezovsky and Gusinsky's paths diverged again. Gusinsky refused to play along with the Kremlin, and it was obvious that he was betting on Luzhkov and Primakov (although Gusinsky and Malashenko denied it later). Gusinsky remained confident and acted from a position of strength, which allowed him to turn down any demands and ultimatums. NTV was a highly successful television channel and an effective weapon in the information wars. He was convinced that the Kremlin had no choice but to negotiate.

Government officials and businesspeople were used to Gusinsky's aggressive style and frequent threats. This had already happened in the summer of 1999, when the deadline was coming up to repay a loan from the American EXIM Bank with a guarantee from the Russian

Ministry of Finance. The loan payment was $15 million. Gusinsky asked the government for the money; ORT had received $100 million in state aid after the default, but NTV hadn't got a thing. However, Mikhail Kasyanov, head of the Ministry of Finance, refused Gusinsky, even though Prime Minister Stepashin had supported it. Kasyanov later recalled how Gusinsky's media outlets immediately began to describe him as a bribe-taker, labelling him "Misha Two-Per-Cent" (allegedly Kasyanov's cut for the deals he approved).[5]

There was a reason Kasyanov, who would become prime minister in May 2000, didn't give Gusinsky money; Kasyanov was on the side of the Kremlin. The head of the Presidential Administration, Voloshin, explained the position simply and clearly: "Why should the state finance people who have declared war against it?"[6] NTV continued to air compromising material on Voloshin and members of Yeltsin's family, while ORT, run by Berezovsky, aired compromising material on Gusinsky. Voloshin demanded Kremlin support from Gusinsky, but Gusinsky refused. So the Kremlin team switched to more forceful methods. At the prompting of the Kremlin, tax inspections were launched in the Media-Most structures that included Gusinsky's media outlets. But Gusinsky was not discouraged: conflicts between factions in power were commonplace in the 1990s, and this was the natural habitat for oligarchs. This was nothing out of the ordinary. "Stepashin is a friend. Kasyanov is an enemy. Voloshin is an enemy. Luzhkov is a friend. Primakov is an ally. Yeltsin is above the fray. It's all a game," is how Yevgeny Kiselyov, then NTV's chief news anchor, described the political landscape in 1999.[7]

The situation changed in the autumn. The Kremlin had a candidate—Putin. While Dorenko was mocking Luzhkov and Primakov on ORT and singing the praises of Putin, NTV journalists were harshly criticizing the war in Chechnya, exposing misdeeds of Yeltsin's entourage and giving airtime to Luzhkov and Primakov, although Gusinsky's media openly supported presidential nominee Yavlinsky. But Gusinsky was still sure of himself. Oddly enough, he had a decent personal relationship with Putin. At the end of autumn, he was optimistic: everything was fine, he had meetings in the Kremlin, and sometimes he stopped in to see the successor.[8] Shortly after the Duma elections in December, however, Gusinsky angered Putin and was again cut off from the Kremlin.

Putin's victory was a foregone conclusion, and the balance of power had shifted.

Vladimir Putin began to settle into the Kremlin but was, naturally, nervous. He wasn't certain that his position was fully secure or his power assured. He owed his meteoric rise to certain people in Yeltsin's inner circle and probably believed that they could change their minds. Besides, by his own example, he realized the incredible power of television, which had transformed him from an unknown official into a head of state. Putin understood that he had to make everyone pay homage to him—above all the press. According to the recollections of eyewitnesses, even before Putin became president he was already telling his supporters that he would not allow the press to treat him the way journalists had treated Yeltsin. So, when two months before the presidential election Gusinsky had NTV pivot its criticism from Yeltsin's entourage to him personally, Putin was livid.

On 30 January 2000, at the height of the presidential campaign, another episode of the popular satirical show *Puppets* was broadcast. The show, modelled on a French television programme, used latex puppet figures of politicians. This time, the plot was based on a fairy tale by E.T.A. Hoffmann, *Little Zaches*, about a mean, wicked and ugly dwarf people see as a kind and charming creature. The dwarf was of course a Putin puppet, Berezovsky was his enchantress, and the enchantment was television. Nothing could have hurt Putin more. Kiselyov remembers that a friend of Gusinsky's wife, Yelena, called to tell her what her close friend, Putin's wife, Lyudmila, had said: Putin was beside himself, ranting and raving.

In March, one day before the election, NTV broadcast a programme about "Ryazan sugar." Right after the terrible apartment bombings in Moscow the previous September, residents of a house in Ryazan suddenly found a bag of white powder and something resembling a detonator in their basement. The FSB claimed it was a drill and the bags contained sugar. The authors of the NTV show questioned this version. After the announcement of the programme went out on NTV, Gusinsky received a call from the Kremlin: if the programme was broadcast, he would become an enemy of the state. The oligarch ignored this threat as well. Late on the evening of 26 March, NTV summed up the election results. "I don't know what will happen to NTV," Nemtsov said on the air, "after one of the reporters laid out his version of the bombings in Moscow and other cities. I think there is a real threat hanging over NTV."[9]

Kiselyov said that Gusinsky was given three conditions to fulfil after the elections: he had to leave the country, the Putin puppet had to be mothballed, and NTV news editors would have to attend weekly news briefings at the Kremlin. If those conditions were met, the channel would even receive a stabilization loan of $100 million.[10] But Gusinsky again refused. He was used to threats and he was not afraid of Putin. They had a lot in common. The two men were peers—Gusinsky is five days older than Putin—and both grew up on the street, one in the outskirts of Moscow, the other in Leningrad, where they learnt how to fight and give as good as they got. David Hoffman recounts in *Oligarchs* how the ten- or eleven-year-old Gusinsky was walking across a yard past some men who were drinking vodka and playing dominoes. When they called him a kike, Gusinsky flew into a rage, lunged at them with a metal pipe and terrified them.[11]

In the spring of 2000, Gusinsky still did not believe that the authorities were capable of destroying his media business or him personally. But he knew that the authorities had a powerful weapon against him—his huge debts. Having invested the borrowed funds in NTV-Plus, Gusinsky was now dependent on the goodwill of the Kremlin, the cabinet and the state banks.

At first, they decided to pounce on Gusinsky when he didn't expect it. On 11 May 2000, four days after Putin's inauguration, history repeated itself. Like six years before, masked gunmen appeared in the centre of Moscow at the office of Media-Most, this time to carry out a search. Gusinsky was not in the country at the time. Malashenko later found a bundle of bullets planted in his office in a desk drawer. Malashenko was not frightened: he went to Ostankino and assured the team: "Everything will be fine—we will survive without Gusinsky."[12]

A month later, on 13 June, Gusinsky was summoned to the prosecutor's office for questioning. The case concerned the privatization of one of the St Petersburg TV companies which Gusinsky had bought to start broadcasting in St Petersburg. The case was minor; Gusinsky was a witness, not the accused; and usually the investigators came to his office, but this time they asked him to come in so that they could perform a simple formality—take his final witness statement and close the case. An unsuspecting Gusinsky showed up before the investigators without any fear, and they charged him with complicity in a crime, handcuffed him and sent him to Butyrka prison.

## Three days in Butyrka

This was a shock. There was no doubt that Gusinsky had been seized and arrested on orders from the Kremlin, even though Putin made excuses from his trip to Madrid. He said he was "concerned about what is happening." "I tried to find the prosecutor general. I called him, [but] he was not in Moscow." The arrest of an oligarch—one of the most influential and famous oligarchs—had previously been unthinkable. "Gusinsky's arrest is a turning point in Russian history," *Kommersant* wrote in the aftermath. "The Yeltsin taboo on involving oligarchs in criminal cases is gone; Putin has reversed it."[13] On the same evening, the entire elite of Russian business gathered in the office of Alfa Group's Mikhail Fridman and Pyotr Aven to write an open letter to the prosecutor general, demanding that Gusinsky be released from prison. The next day, Chubais, Aven and others gave a press conference. "This is bad news," said Aven. "We are deeply troubled by the measures chosen by the prosecutor's office," Chubais said. "Trust in the authorities both at home and abroad has been undermined by the measures taken against Gusinsky."[14] SPS, Yabloko, as well as the Luzhkov and Primakov factions protested. Berezovsky, who had already joined the opposition, was furious. Sergei Dorenko, the same TV hit man who killed Luzhkov and Primakov on ORT, now said on air: "When the president talks about the dictatorship of the law, I am reminded of the dictatorship of the Stalinist constitution... A person may be humiliated and intimidated strictly according to the law, but in an absolutely illegal way."[15]

Gusinsky was released three days later, on 16 June. "It was clear from the very beginning that this was not a fight against crime and corruption, but a political act of reprisal," Nemtsov said the next day.

"It took a long time for the authorities to realize that they had made a foolish mistake, and, when they did realize it, they decided to pull back. Well done. But what was the point of the whole thing?"[16] In fact, not Nemtsov, nor Dorenko, nor anyone but those directly involved in the arrest and release of Gusinsky understood what was going on. They did not know that on 15 June Malashenko had flown to Moscow. After Gusinsky's arrest, he had followed Putin to Spain and given one press conference after another. When he got back to Moscow, Malashenko had gathered key Media-Most employees at Gusinsky's dacha and told them that he had received a phone call from Press Minister Mikhail Lesin. Lesin had explained that Gusinsky would be released in exchange for agreeing in principle to sell off all his media to Gazprom for $300 million. They had until evening to decide; if they said yes, negotiations would begin. Malashenko said he could not refuse such an offer. The following evening, Kiselyov's phone rang: "Gusinsky calls and says, 'They let me out. I'm standing in the street, and I don't even know where I am.' It took us about ten minutes to get to Butyrka."

Negotiations between Malashenko and Lesin over the sale of Gusinsky's media holding lasted a little over a month. Sometimes they would meet several times a day to discuss details, then Lesin would go to the Kremlin, come back, and the negotiations would continue. Sometimes they involved Alfred Kokh, whom Gazprom had just put in charge of Gazprom-Media, the company that managed the group's media assets. Gazprom-Media was to take over the NTV television channel and the Ekho Moskvy radio station, both owned by Gusinsky and popular since the early 1990s. At the end of July, the parties finally struck a deal, and at 5.00 p.m. on 26 July the prosecutor lifted the ban on Gusinsky's departure from the country.

His private jet was already waiting for him at Vnukovo-3 Airport. Gusinsky was nervous: what if they changed their mind at the top and would not let him out? What if they arrested him again? He needed a witness, an escort, someone he could rely on in the moment. So, he asked Nemtsov for help. Gusinsky and Malashenko picked up Nemtsov in Gusinsky's armoured Mercedes. It had been exactly three years since the results of the Svyazinvest tender had been announced, and Berezovsky and Gusinsky had pounced on the young reformers. Three years ago, the oligarchs had been the predators and Nemtsov the victim. Now, persecuted by the authorities, Gusinsky sought his support. Malashenko recalled that "the conversation in the car was nervously cheerful." At the border everything went smoothly, and Nemtsov waved to Gusinsky and Malashenko as they passed through passport control. There was no practical sense in Nemtsov's presence, but Nemtsov was the only one who covered for Gusinsky that day and escorted him into exile. Gusinsky would never return to Russia.

## Keeping the oligarchs at arm's length

Why did Nemtsov get along with Gusinsky? Why did he see him off? Nemtsov never bore a grudge. It was in his nature. He would forget about offences and conflicts, and the oligarchs didn't hold a grudge against Nemtsov either, because they knew he had no hidden agenda. Even after Putin came to power, Nemtsov turned out to be the only Russian politician who could get billionaires who wouldn't shake each other's hands to sit at the same table. Beginning in late 2001, every three months, Nemtsov, now the leader of SPS, would gather in a restaurant the oligarchs who provided funding for SPS to account for how the funds were spent. At a single table there would be Potanin, Khodorkovsky's partner Leonid Nevzlin, Fridman, and others who didn't get along.

In both the oligarchs' endless internecine strife and their relations with the state, there was no well-established unbreakable alliance, no pre-written script, no obvious outcome for everyone. It was a game. "Everyone wants to put someone in jail!" *Kommersant* wrote after Gusinsky's arrest. "Chubais wants to jail Korzhakov, Korzhakov wants to jail Gusinsky, all of them want to jail Potanin, Berezovsky and Abramovich want to see Chubais behind bars, and Gusinsky, Primakov and Luzhkov want to jail Berezovsky. It was the dream of every decent oligarch to put a fellow oligarch in jail. When you'd meet them in private, they'd tell you, 'I'll put him in jail!' But no one did. Why? Because that's how Yeltsin understood democracy."[17] With Putin's arrival, the rules of the game had changed. The gloves were off, and the punches weren't to the gut anymore: they were to the face.

The arrest and release of Gusinsky prompted Nemtsov to go to Putin. At the time, they had developed a good relationship, and Putin met one-on-one regularly with Nemtsov, who by then was leader of the SPS faction in the Duma. (In May, Kiriyenko* had moved from parliament to the Kremlin as presidential envoy to the Volga, and Nemtsov had taken his place.) "They were on a first-name basis," Khakamada recalled. "They discussed everything under the sun. Even lifestyle. Even personal life. How Nemtsov was fine, doing whatever he wanted. And how Putin wasn't doing as well because he was… [the president]."[18] Nemtsov urged Putin to meet with the oligarchs. He insisted that the authorities and big business should sign an agreement: "In this situation, where there is constant confrontation and misunderstanding between business and the country's leadership, there should be some kind of charter with the requirement that all the oligarchs would keep at arm's length from the authorities."[19] Nemtsov, who fought against oligarchic capitalism, had been impressed by the fact that Putin had no obligations to the oligarchs so he could deal with them. But with the arrest of Gusinsky, relations had become fraught. In addition to Gusinsky's arrest, the tax police had come for Vladimir Potanin and Vagit Alekperov, president of the Lukoil company. Distancing the oligarchs from power had to be done correctly. Putin agreed to meet with them.

This would be the legendary "kebab pact", when Putin and the oligarchs agreed on new rules of the game over shish kebab. The oligarchs would stay out of politics and pay taxes, and the government wouldn't revise the results of privatization.

Actually, there weren't any kebabs and there wasn't a pact. But it became immediately clear that the rules of the game were changing when Putin received the businessmen at the Kremlin on 28 July. There had never been a meeting like this before. Naturally, its agenda was set by the arrest of Gusinsky. As Oleg Sysuyev, who was then working at Alfa Bank, put it before the meeting, "The notion of 'arm's length'

---

\*   Fifteen years later Kiriyenko was appointed the first deputy chief of Putin's administration. Six more years later, in 2022, in this capacity he was responsible for Russianization of the territories of Ukraine captured and annexed by the Russian military.

began to sound like Siberia." But Putin was quick to dismiss the claims. He said business was to blame. After all, these businessmen "formed the state structures", and so, if any of the oligarchs wanted to complain, they "ought to look in the mirror."[20] The businessmen were assured that there would be no revision of the privatization results. They left the meeting with the understanding that the fate of Gusinsky did not threaten them directly: it was a special case. The businessman Kakha Bendukidze—who in four years would leave Russia for Georgia, never to return—recalled that Putin also asked the men present to contribute to a charity fund to support veterans of special services, and the oligarchs immediately stumped up tens of millions of dollars.[21]

Nemtsov was encouraged by the results of the meeting he organized. He said that "the stage of initial accumulation of capital in Russia [was] over" and "the principle of all businessmen keeping the same arm's length from the government [was] not a dream but reality."[22]

## Protocol No. 6

By that time Berezovsky had already announced that he was in opposition to Putin, so he was not invited to the Kremlin. Gusinsky wasn't invited either, but he had been out of the country for two days by then. The contract for the sale of Media-Most had been signed, and a sigh of relief was breathed in the Kremlin. But, even as he flew out of the country, Gusinsky was vacillating. He had not yet decided whether to comply with the contract. That's why Malashenko was leaving with him: should Gusinsky suddenly disavow his signature, there would be problems for Malashenko because he had negotiated the deal with Lesin. About a week later, Gusinsky gathered his team at his villa in Spain to discuss what to do: take the money and leave Russia for good or announce that the contract had been signed under pressure and fight on. At that point, the people around the table learnt that Gusinsky had an addendum to the contract, the so-called Protocol No. 6, which was signed by Lesin. It was a guarantee that Gusinsky and his partners would not be jailed or prevented from leaving the country. Lesin made a mistake. He granted Gusinsky's request to put these guarantees on paper, and now they confirmed that Gusinsky was being extorted to relinquish his company. In addition to this addendum, Gusinsky showed a videotape that he had recorded before signing the contract. On the tape he confirmed in the presence of his lawyers that everything he was about to sign would be signed under duress and would therefore be invalid. So now they faced a choice: surrender and get a pay-off or fight. The majority of those present voted for the money. Gusinsky thought about it and said, "No." He had listened to everyone, but he had the last word, and his last word was: "Fight."

All the same, Gusinsky was in no hurry to declare war. He was biding his time, wondering whether it was possible to smooth over relations with the Kremlin, at least to ascertain where Putin stood on the deal. An opportunity presented itself on 13 August at an informal meeting between Putin and the Kremlin press pool. Putin had flown to his Sochi residence for a few days, and the journalists had flown in to join him. Among them was NTV correspondent Alim Yusupov, who had the assignment of trying to start a conversation about Gusinsky. Yusupov asked outright if Putin was ready to talk to Gusinsky. Would he talk to the disgraced oligarch if he suddenly called? Putin shrugged his shoulders: if there's a phone, he's ready right now. Kiselyov described getting the call from Yusupov when he was behind the wheel of his car in the middle of an intersection and wanted to hang up. But Yusupov said that Putin was sitting right there, waiting for the call.[23] Ten minutes later, Gusinsky called Yusupov, who passed the phone to Putin. The conversation was brief:

PUTIN: Hello, Vladimir Alexandrovich.
GUSINSKY: Hello, Vladimir Vladimirovich. We should meet to talk.
PUTIN: Yes, of course.
GUSINSKY: How may I contact you?
PUTIN: Through the same channel.
GUSINSKY: Thank you. Goodbye.
PUTIN: Goodbye.[24]

Putin will always remember his Sochi holiday, but not because of Gusinsky's call. It was inextricably linked to his first major political crisis: the sinking of the *Kursk* submarine in the Barents Sea and the death of 118 crew members. By the time he met with journalists, the submarine had been submerged 108 metres below water for over a day, but neither journalists nor Putin himself realized the extent of the tragedy: Putin was told on the morning of the 13th that the boat was lying on the seabed and rescue operations were underway. On 14 August the disaster was reported publicly, but even then Putin did not cancel his holiday. He didn't respond for another full day. Twenty-three sailors remained alive for at least forty-eight hours after the explosion, but it was not known until the rescue operation began that most of the crew had died immediately. Putin continued his holiday, did nothing and refused international assistance while the submariners sent SOS signals from the bottom of the sea. This was a major blow to his reputation. And, of course, it was discussed on television. On 22 August, Putin flew to Vidyayevo, near Murmansk, to meet the widows and mothers of the sailors who had died.

He was angry, but not at those who had caused the disaster. "For me, the easiest thing would be to put someone in jail. Or to fire someone. But that would be unfair," he said. He was angry at the television channels that reported the sinking of the *Kursk*. He told the grief-stricken widows and mothers who packed into the auditorium of the Fleet Officers' Club that the owners of the TV channels "stole money, bought mass media and manipulated public opinion",[25] intentionally dramatizing the situation in order to keep stealing from the state.

The next day, Putin again hosted journalists for an informal talk, this time in the Kremlin and this time about the *Kursk*. Putin spoke again about how oligarchs had bankrupted the army and the navy. Alexei Venediktov, editor-in-chief of Ekho Moskvy, was the only representative of Gusinsky's media at the meeting. As the meeting drew to a close, Putin asked Venediktov to stay for a moment. When they were alone, Putin sat down next to him and put his hand on Venediktov's knee. "Lyosha," he said, using Venediktov's nickname, "I will never talk to Gusinsky again. After NTV lied and slandered us over the *Kursk*, that's it, we're done talking."[26]

On 2 September the ORT channel, which was still controlled by Boris Berezovsky but owned by the state, attacked Putin in a programme devoted to the *Kursk* tragedy. Dorenko bitterly denounced the inconsistencies in Putin's comments about the sinking and the rescue operation. The war that Berezovsky had declared on Putin in the spring had come to its logical conclusion. The oligarch who had played a key role in Yeltsin's re-election in 1996 and who seriously saw himself as the kingmaker and almost the shadow president could not accept being pushed out of power. In the spring he joined the opposition, and now he was going for broke. Dorenko knew this would be his last broadcast. And while he was on the air in Moscow, Putin had flown to New York and was being interviewed by Larry King. "What happened to the submarine?" King asked. Putin smirked and answered with a line that will be remembered for ever: "It sank."

To be absolutely fair, it was more of a nervous grimace than a smirk. Psychologically, Putin was still inside the crisis. He realized he had made a mistake. In those terrible days in August, he sensed his own weakness, not least at the meeting with the mothers and wives of the submariners. This was mainly because the press, still free at the time, actively discussed officials' lies and the contradictions in official versions of the *Kursk* sinking, as well as Putin's confused response. As the future would show, Putin fights down his feeling of weakness by launching a counterattack. To Larry King he said at the time: "It has become obvious that this situation has been used to shake the very institution of presidential power."[27] Even before his trip to America, Putin had talked to Berezovsky: the party was over; Berezovsky had to give back his stake in ORT; Putin would control ORT broadcasting from that time on. Berezovsky refused. Soon he would follow Gusinsky into political exile.

## A dispute between economic entities

It was not hard to get Dorenko off the air or to slap Berezovsky's hand, since he didn't own ORT television. But taking NTV away from Gusinsky proved to be more difficult. *À la guerre comme à la guerre*: in mid-September Gusinsky recanted his signature on the deal with Gazprom and made public Protocol No. 6. At the height of the scandal, Alfred Kokh, head of Gazprom's media assets, appeared holding promissory notes. If the debtor reneged on the deal, he had to repay his debts. Kokh insisted that he was not personally interested in controlling NTV. During another round, he even suggested that Gusinsky sell his shares in NTV and other NTV assets on the open market and pay the money back to Gazprom to close out the debt. But after all the scandals, no one in the West was willing to buy Media-Most's shares. Criminal proceedings were instituted against Gusinsky again, and he was even briefly arrested in Spain on an Interpol warrant.

In January 2001, after more scandals, broken settlements and countersuits, the network suddenly found a Western investor. Gusinsky got American media tycoon Ted Turner, the founder of CNN, interested in NTV. "The idea was that Turner would repay the debt to Credit Suisse First Boston, which was guaranteed by Gazprom, and for this he would get a blocking stake," recalled Kiselyov.[28] In this way, everyone could have their cake and eat it, too, and NTV's independence would be preserved. Turner approached Putin: he and his partners were willing to invest more than $300 million in NTV, but they needed a personal guarantee from Putin that the government wouldn't put pressure on the channel. Putin said that all investors in Russia are equally protected by law, so he couldn't give a special guarantee. Turner understood what it meant and abandoned the project. Meanwhile, the state was moving towards its goal. Gazprom filed for NTV's bankruptcy, the courts accepted the claim, and journalists were already being questioned by prosecutors.

So what was NTV? Was it an independent media outlet, an outpost of freedom of speech? Or was it a political company, a weapon in the hands of a once-powerful oligarch? And what was the war against NTV? A government crackdown or "a dispute between companies", as the Kremlin put it? Nemtsov had no clear answer to these questions. On the one hand, it was obvious that the state was destroying freedom of the press, he said. On the other hand, he agreed that Gazprom's financial claims were legitimate. "It is very difficult to understand what is more important for us: protecting property rights or protecting freedom of speech."[29] Nemtsov was friends with Kokh and believed that he wouldn't impose censorship when he was in charge of NTV.

It had been almost a year since the state had turned on Gusinsky. In the spring of 2001, Kokh was still bankrupting Media-Most. He was trying to keep the rebellious journalists in line: he was not fighting them, and there would be no censorship. Nemtsov supported him. He believed that by taking NTV away from Gusinsky, it would be possible to get NTV out of state control, which he thought was the most important thing. So, he supported Kokh's idea of installing Boris Jordan, an American investment banker of Russian ancestry, as NTV's general director. After all, a US citizen would not clamp down on freedom of speech in Russia. Nemtsov spoke about this on NTV live in early April, when the war was almost over. The forces were too unequal: Gusinsky had lost. Gazprom had finally obtained court decisions allowing it to take possession of Media-Most's shares and had already appointed Jordan as an anti-crisis manager and general director. A week before Kokh and Jordan would take over the studio with the police, Nemtsov and other guests—politicians and journalists—were in the NTV studio.

On air Nemtsov tried to persuade the NTV journalists not to leave after the takeover: "Most importantly, I believe that Gusinsky is a great businessman. He created a powerful company from scratch. He's fighting to the end, and I respect him for that. And I respect the management of NTV, which is also fighting to the end. But I don't want there to be a pile of ashes after today's broadcast. I am against this. This is about the fate of our country. I realize that we are all upset about this, but I'd like us to consider this question: is it good or bad for our country when journalists leave? It's terrible. We need to keep fighting. We need to stand together and defend our independent position. And I can assure you that an enormous number of people will help you in this."

Journalist Yevgeniya Albats was in the studio and replied, "Boris, you and I have known each other for a lifetime. We both remember when a sense of morality [...] made you, a physicist in Gorky, enter politics and led me to become a journalist. That's the way we were raised. We've all learnt the words 'pragmatism' and 'rational choice' in recent years. But there are some things that decent people don't do. Even though I really want to, I cannot agree with you. There is morality. And there is the belief that we have children and cannot get involved in anything vile and underhanded."[30]

After the defeat of NTV, some of the journalists led by Yevgeny Kiselyov left the channel. Others stayed. At the time they were probably strike-breakers, but soon that wouldn't matter. In predicting the independence of NTV's editorial policy, Nemtsov (like Kokh) was generally right. Jordan promised that if there was censorship at NTV, he would resign, and under his leadership the channel did have a relatively independent editorial policy. This was especially noticeable against the background of the censorship and propaganda that was rapidly getting worse at the other mainstream television channels. Gazprom did not intervene at first. Kokh had plans to sell NTV, a non-core asset for the gas corporation, to new owners, and Jordan had even found investors.

In September 2001, when the dust settled on the NTV bashing, Kokh came to see the new head of Gazprom. Rem Vyakhirev, who was appointed head of Gazprom in 1992 and who had sworn allegiance to the Luzhkov and Primakov camps during the tumultuous events of 1999, had been replaced a few months earlier by Alexei Miller, a thirty-nine-year-old official who had worked under Putin in the St Petersburg city hall's foreign-affairs committee. "That was the first bell," recalls Kokh, who knew Miller well from his college days, "The guy was carrying Putin's briefcase and greeting delegations, and suddenly he's the head of Gazprom."[31] It was clear that the main thing for Putin was to put someone absolutely loyal to him at the head of Gazprom.* And indeed, from then on Gazprom would become his personal fiefdom, the "commanding height" he held in the Russian economy and in Russian politics. At a meeting, Kokh, as head of Gazprom-Media, was supposed to bring Miller, now his boss, up to speed on the media assets taken from Gusinsky, their condition, and how best to sell them. But the meeting never took place. After waiting for ten hours in the reception room, Kokh left without saying a word. Three days later, he went to see Miller again, and this time he spent twelve hours in the reception room, again to no avail.[32] The next day, he tendered his resignation to Miller, and the plans to privatize NTV were soon abandoned. Putin had no intention of putting the powerful weapon of a nationwide television channel in the wrong hands.

---

\* Mikhail Kasyanov, then prime minister, later recalled that he objected to Miller's appointment as head of Gazprom because of his incompetence and that "during his first year at Gazprom, Miller did virtually nothing but learn."

A few months later, in February 2002, Kokh decided to run for senator. Governors and speakers of regional parliaments had already been kicked out of the Federation Council, and under the new procedure, regional governments, governors and legislative assemblies each delegated a representative to the Federation Council. Kokh was elected by the regional parliament of St Petersburg. On the same day, he was summoned to the Kremlin. "Why did you announce your candidacy without consulting us?" asked Viktor Ivanov. Ivanov was a former KGB colonel and St Petersburg city hall official who later joined Putin in the FSB and was now the first deputy head of the Presidential Administration, in charge of personnel matters. Kokh shrugged and said he didn't know that nomination to the Federation Council had to be coordinated with the Kremlin. Ivanov said that he would have to hand in his resignation letter. Kokh refused and left. His election to the parliament was soon challenged by the prosecutor's office: he had allegedly filed an incorrect income declaration, and the vote in the regional parliament had been conducted with a procedural violation. Hence, the Federation Council refused to confirm his credentials. "I went back to Ivanov," Kokh recalled, "and he said again, 'Hand in your resignation.' I said, 'I won't.'" The next day, his accountant was summoned for questioning.[33] At the end of March, a month after his confirmation as senator, Alfred Kokh asked the Leningrad regional parliament to withdraw his candidacy.

# CHAPTER 20

## 2002
## Nord-Ost

### Europe's last dictator

By the autumn of 2002, Belarusian President Alexander Lukashenko had fully earned the moniker "Europe's last dictator." He had been in power for eight years and had no plans to retire. In summer 1994, Lukashenko, a charismatic and unwavering leftist populist who had been a political officer in the military and director of a sovkhoz (state farm), managed to accomplish what neither Khasbulatov in 1993 nor Zyuganov in 1996 had been able to do in Russia. In 1994, he won the presidential election by a landslide and came to power under the slogans of pulling back on reforms, restoring socialism and reuniting with Russia. Repression and censorship were quickly introduced, and within a year Lukashenko had staged a *coup d'état*, gaining through a referendum the right to dissolve the parliament and zero out his presidential terms so he could run for office again. "It is already clear that there will be no parliament in Belarus, no elections, and the remnants of a free press will disappear. The country will be ruled by a presidential junta," wrote Vasil Bykov,[1] one of the most famous Soviet Belarusian writers who had once been a frontline war correspondent. He was a seer. Soon Lukashenko dissolved the parliament and established a police state in the country, where the secret police—still called the KGB in Belarus, just like in the old days—persecuted oppositionists and dissidents. Persecution is an understatement. The Lukashenko regime practised political assassination.

On the evening of 7 May 1999, unknown assailants abducted Yury Zakharenko, ex-minister for internal affairs. He was a popular general, highly respected by security officials, but considered by Lukashenko to be one of his main enemies. Less than six months later, in a similar fashion and almost in the city centre, Viktor Gonchar, perhaps the most influential Belarusian opposition figure, was pushed into a car as he was leaving a bathhouse. Along with him was his friend, entrepreneur Anatoly Krasovsky, who was also involved in politics and had been released from custody just three weeks earlier. Neither man was ever seen again. A year later, on 7 July 2000, journalist and cameraman Dmitry Zavadsky disappeared. And in 2001, two investigators of the Belarusian prosecutor's office, Dmitry Petrushkevich and Oleg Sluchek, escaped from Belarus to Poland and told sensational details about the "death squad" created by the Belarusian special services.*

Until Putin came along, Lukashenko had been campaigning hard to reunite with Russia. He had his eye on the tsarist crown and hoped to move into the Kremlin himself. In 1997, there was even a bit of a blow-up over his plans. A week before the Russia–Belarus Union Treaty was to be signed, Chubais, then the first deputy prime minister, suddenly noticed that the draft prepared in Minsk gave real power levers to Lukashenko and the Union parliament under his control. Chubais ran to the Kremlin, the treaty was rewritten, but Lukashenko was not discouraged. In 1999, he was in fact running his own election campaign in Russia. A good orator, he promoted the idea of the union of the two countries, which was then very popular, as a restoration of the USSR. In general, he looked good against the background of the lacklustre and dull Russian Communists, who arranged for him to receive ovations in the Duma. Lukashenko walked with an enfeebled Yeltsin through the Palace of Facets in the Kremlin, no doubt imagining himself in his place.

When Putin was elected, the balance of forces changed dramatically. Now the politically advantageous idea of the union of the two

---

\* In a December 2019 interview with Deutsche Welle, Yury Garavsky, a former member of the Belarusian special police (SOBR), described in minute detail how he was personally involved in the murders of Zakharenko, Gonchar and Krasovsky.

countries was promoted by Moscow, only in the Kremlin it was understood to mean, roughly speaking, Belarus's becoming a part of Russia. Lukashenko temporized. Verbally, he continued to support the forming of a union with Russia, but from the position of Belarusian sovereignty. This was the cause of the first conflict between Putin and him in spring 2002. "Don't put apples and oranges in one basket," Putin told him, meaning that Lukashenko should figure out what he wanted—to revive the USSR or just to have the power of veto over all the decisions made in Moscow while sitting in Minsk. Naturally, integration stalled, and the Kremlin encouraged the diplomatic approach that SPS and Nemtsov, as party leader, had towards Belarus: sharply criticizing Lukashenko and actively developing relations with the Belarusian opposition.

Russian liberals found themselves in an ambiguous position. They were opposed to the strengthening of censorship and increasing control over political life. In early spring 2002, Nemtsov said in a speech: "Journalists have learnt what they can and cannot do, governors are silent, senators are nearly all appointed by the Kremlin, pro-Kremlin factions control the Duma. There's no getting away from it."[2] Yury Luzhkov, Yevgeny Primakov and the governors who had opposed the Kremlin in 1999 gave up the fight; their parliamentary factions now voted as the Kremlin told them to. The Duma had become an arm of the Kremlin. United Russia, Putin's party, was formed in autumn 2001, and the entire Russian bureaucracy gradually merged into it. What distinguished it from the Communist Party was the absence of a Politburo and even minimal collective decision-making. All decisions were made in the Kremlin, and the party's *raison d'être* was to implement Putin's will in parliaments at every level, from regional to federal. Putin was building his "power vertical"—his personal power—and the party became its foundation. By early 2002, he had largely subjugated television and governors, and the country's legislative branch in its entirety.

"There is a crackdown on any kind of dissent in Russia," Nemtsov said.[3] Political analysts called this regime a managed democracy. Opposition voices and alternative viewpoints could be heard both in parliament and in newspapers, sometimes even on central TV channels, but they had no influence on events. Political scientist Valery Pribylovsky described managed democracy as freedoms "allowed to the extent that they do not violate the administrative oligarchy's monopoly on power."[4] The question was what came next and where it was leading. From the point of view of its ideologues, managed democracy was supposed to be a transitional stage on the way to real democracy and a full rapprochement of Russia with the Western world, as evidenced by both economic reforms and Putin's pro-Western policy. It was time to move into opposition, Nemtsov insisted. The rollback of freedoms was too obvious and disturbing, and the strengthening of authoritarian tendencies too visible. But the pragmatists among the liberals protested that it was all right, that Putin was one of them. And in the Kremlin, they turned a deaf ear to Nemtsov's criticism. Let him criticize—it's a democracy, after all, so long as his faction supports the government on the issues that are important to it. In spring 2002, SPS was even allocated two extra committee chairmen positions in the Duma, a sign of the Kremlin's confidence in the party.

A comparison with Belarus clearly showed the difference between a managed democracy and a dictatorship. At that historical moment, Russia and Belarus were in opposition. Russia was moving forward, towards a market economy and partnership with the civilized world. Belarus was rolling back, and Lukashenko was already considered an outcast in the West. The fate of the opposition in Belarus was fundamentally different: critics and opponents of Lukashenko were harassed and arrested. They were not allowed to participate in the elections, and, if they were allowed, the results were falsified.

## The return of the KGB

Nemtsov and Khakamada had a flight booked to Minsk for the morning of Wednesday, 23 October. They were flying to a conference organized by the Belarusian opposition, the United Civic Party and its leader Anatoly Lebedko. The Belarusian opposition had cooperated with Russian democrats since the mid-1990s; in 1999, Lebedko's party even sent its activists to help SPS in the Duma elections, and the parties had since held several conferences in both Minsk and Moscow. At 1.30 p.m. a Belarusian Airlines flight landed at Minsk airport. Apart from

Nemtsov, Khakamada and political scientist Sergei Markov, who was flying to the same conference, there was no one in the business class cabin. They were the first to disembark. As soon as they got off the plane, Belarusian KGB officers kept the rest of the passengers from getting off. They wanted Boris Nemtsov.

No one was more critical of the political regime in Belarus than Nemtsov, and he was not hesitant to express it. "He didn't just criticize the political and economic model in Belarus, he also expressed very harsh personal opinions about Lukashenko himself, and, of course, all this was laid out for Nemtsov," Lebedko recalled.[5] Nemtsov was well known in Belarus, and his appearances drew full houses. But, most importantly, Nemtsov constantly pressed on Lukashenko's sore spot: he kept bringing up the kidnappings and murders of his political opponents.

Two years had passed since the last assassination, but they continued to haunt Lukashenko. In the West, human-rights activists and politicians talked about them. In Russia it was most often Nemtsov. He had known Gonchar personally. And when relatives of the murdered Gonchar and Zavadsky came to Moscow, Nemtsov met them at the train station, organized a press conference for them in the Duma, initiated a joint appeal from several factions demanding that the killers be found quickly. Even Unity and the Communists signed the appeal. "Nemtsov took us to offices in the Duma and helped us a lot in Moscow," recalls Gonchar's widow, Zinaida Gonchar. "A report about it appeared on TV, and when I returned to Minsk, I started having major problems at the Academy of Sciences where I worked. In the end, I had to leave."[6]

Nemtsov had become a problem for Lukashenko. The Belarusian leader decided to act. Khakamada said, "Suddenly a windowless van, the kind they take convicts in, pulls right up to the stairs and men grabbed Nemtsov. Someone tells me, 'You can get on the bus. They'll take you to the conference.' I said, 'I'm not going anywhere! I'm his deputy. I won't give you Nemtsov just like that.' I ran up to him and said, 'Take me, too.' So we got in, and they drove away."[7]

Nemtsov, Khakamada and, since he was there, Markov were all taken away in a police van. Lukashenko was out for confrontation. Not the Russian Duma, nor the Foreign Ministry, nor the Kremlin could ignore the arrest of two high-ranking Russian political figures, the leader of a parliamentary faction and vice-speaker of the State Duma. It took a while for the detainees to understand what was happening. When they asked where they were being taken, Nemtsov and Khakamada were told that it wasn't their business. Finally, they got through by phone to Lebedko, and he explained that it was the KGB. Nemtsov had no experience of arrests. Lebedko did. Once, he had been dragged out of his own car, pulled into another car, handcuffed, his head wrapped in a jacket, pressed to the floor and driven away. "They drove for a long time, then led me somewhere and took off the jacket. I could see some kind of room. Only after a while some people came in, and I realized that it was the KGB basement near the Amerikanka [the KGB detention centre in the centre of Minsk], where I'd later be incarcerated for four months. That was when I physically felt fear. When they came and said that they were KGB officers, I was glad to see them."[8]

Nemtsov, Khakamada and Markov were driven around Minsk for about an hour without anyone saying anything about the purpose of the detention or where they were being taken. Their faces were not covered, and they were not handcuffed. When the cityscape gave way to fields and forests, Nemtsov and Khakamada decided that they were too important and that Lukashenko was thinking about the consequences. But all three were quite uncomfortable. Eventually they were brought to another airport, escorted into the VIP hall—just Nemtsov and Khakamada first, without Markov—and forced to buy return tickets to Moscow. Suddenly, people appeared in the lounge with a leather folder and asked Nemtsov if he had forgotten it in the car. Nemtsov said no. They turned to Khakamada with the same question. She also said no. All this was filmed on video. "And after that they said, 'Let's see what's inside,'" Khakamada said. "The camera pulls up to the table and starts filming. They open the folder. Inside are stacks of dollars and materials, and it says SPS in big letters. And then I understood what was going on. For the first time I saw what I had only read about in Solzhenitsyn's books. Now I saw how it was done in real life."[9] Nemtsov reached for the folder to check what was in it, but Khakamada stopped him just in time to keep him from leaving fingerprints on the folder. Khakamada said it was a dirty set-up and Nemtsov demanded a lawyer. Ten minutes later, they were put on a flight that had been held from departure since the morning and deported to Moscow. The Belarusian Foreign Ministry said there were no claims against Khakamada or Markov, but Nemtsov was deported in response to "repeated gross facts of interference in the internal affairs of Belarus aimed at undermining the state structure." KGB officers, the Belarusian Foreign Ministry continued, received an anonymous call that SPS Chairman Nemtsov was carrying a large sum of money and subversive literature for the opposition, and the officials seized them.[10]

This was going to turn into a major scandal. The Kremlin promised an appropriate response. The Russian Foreign Ministry expressed deep concern. This was the headline news on television until about 9.30 p.m. At that moment Olga Chernyak, a journalist for the Interfax news agency, called her newsroom. "We are at the Dubrovka Theatre Centre. There are terrorists in the hall," Chernyak said. War had come to Moscow.

## Terrorists at Dubrovka

*Nord-Ost*, a musical inspired by Broadway hits, had been running at the Dubrovka Theatre Centre for a year—once a day and twice on weekends—and was a real breakthrough for its time. There were complex dance numbers, expensive sets and a real bomber landing on the stage. So when a masked man with a submachine gun stepped onto the stage at the beginning of the second act and started shooting in the air, at first the audience thought it was part of the show.

Never before had terrorists taken hostages in Moscow. There were about a thousand people in the theatre, and many behaved calmly and heroically. The producer of *Nord-Ost*, Georgy Vasilyev, could have left the building unnoticed at the very beginning of the attack, but he stayed. It was his show, and he couldn't leave. Choreographer Sergei Lobankov gathered the children around him and looked after them throughout the three days of the siege. And Maria Shkolnikova, a physician with a speciality in paediatric cardiology, became the chief negotiator.

Maria had come to the performance together with her husband Vladimir, a demographer, and their fifteen-year-old son Maxim. A few hours after the siege began, her husband was the first hostage released in exchange for a promise to get them an interview on German television. "Right away, [the terrorists] asked if there were any doctors," Shkolnikova said right after her release. "I immediately raised my hand, said that I was a doctor, a specialist—one of the specialists in my profession, president of the Association of Paediatric Cardiologists of Russia, and as a doctor I helped people."[11] Shkolnikova did not only help the other hostages; she established contact with the terrorists and spoke on behalf of the hostages. In the midst of fear and panic, she exuded calmness and confidence. When the terrorists lost their tempers, she found the right words to defuse the situation. That's how she got them to listen to her.

The terrorists quickly laid out their demands to the hostages: the end of the war and the withdrawal of Russian troops from Chechnya. At first, they even insisted that the hostages call their friends and acquaintances and convey their demands to the authorities through them. But then Shkolnikova sensed that time was running out, the situation was heating up, but there was no progress. The situation headquarters had still not made contact with the terrorists and there were no negotiations for release of the hostages.

An hour and a half after the terrorists took over the Theatre Centre, around 11.00 p.m. on Wednesday, 23 October, Putin summoned the chief of the Federal Security Service, Nikolai Patrushev, Interior Minister Boris Gryzlov, his chief of staff Alexander Voloshin, and Prime Minister Mikhail Kasyanov. The security forces—Patrushev and Gryzlov—proposed taking the centre by storm. Kasyanov was against it. Putin asked questions and didn't articulate a position. The next morning, Putin sent Kasyanov in his place to the APEC summit in Mexico. Later, after the assault on the theatre, NTV would enrage the Kremlin by superimposing subtitles over the silent portion of the video footage of Putin's private meeting.

It was clear from the start that the government was seriously considering an assault. The hostage-taking in Budyonnovsk in 1995, Prime Minister Chernomyrdin's phone conversation with Basayev, Basayev's escape from right under the noses of the security services—all these events were in the public memory as symbols of the helplessness of the

Russian authorities. Putin could not allow a repeat of Budyonnovsk. Television was preparing the ground for an assault. "There will be no more Budyonnovsk and Khasavyurt, there will be no political agreement with gangsters and scum," journalist Mikhail Leontyev said on national television on the night when the theatre was taken, with little regard for the fate of the hostages. Negotiations had been ruled out.

In their monograph on the terrorist attack, Adam Dolnik and Richard Pilch, two of the world's leading experts on political violence and terrorism, pointed out the outrageous fact that the authorities made no use of trained professional negotiators at Dubrovka.[12] Terrorist leader Movsar Barayev was not contacted by anyone who could be considered an official representative of headquarters until a call came at 9.00 p.m. on Friday from General Viktor Kazantsev, the presidential envoy to the North Caucasus. He said he'd come the next day, Saturday, to Dubrovka and hold talks with them.

In fact, Kazantsev's call was a ruse. On Friday afternoon, the terrorists began to threaten the hostages, saying they'd shoot them if no one in authority contacted them. Kazantsev's call was to reassure the terrorists so that they wouldn't begin to harm the hostages beforehand. The terrorists were satisfied and encouraged by the call and waited for Kazantsev to arrive at 10.00 a.m. on Saturday morning. At 5.30 a.m. gas was piped into the theatre and the assault began.

An official spokesman for the headquarters would later state that the decision to storm the building was made after the terrorists had shot two hostages and a group of other hostages tried to escape. This was a lie. Sixteen years later, Vladimir Putin would justify his personal decision to storm the building with the information he had that the terrorists were planning to shoot hostages on Red Square the next day, but there is no evidence of this.\* Kazantsev's call removed the threat of hostage execution, although there is no evidence that the terrorists would have

---

\* The terrorists wanted the relatives of the hostages to hold an anti-war demonstration on Red Square, and the relatives tried to do so, but failed. The authorities prohibited them under the pretext of possible provocative actions. At a meeting with relatives, Valentina Matviyenko, then deputy prime minister for social affairs, bluntly explained the reason for the refusal: "We can't let Russia look weak." In any case, there is no confirmation of the plot described by Putin.

carried out their threat. In the materials of the criminal case on the Nord-Ost attack, there is an intercept of a telephone conversation that took place between Barayev and one of the Chechen leaders, Zelimkhan Yandarbiyev, on the night of Friday–Saturday. Barayev said: "We're keeping people here so that later they'll tell everyone what happened."

After Kazantsev's call, Barayev indicated that he wanted to end the event peacefully, without casualties. And Putin's statement is inconsistent with the fact that during the assault the terrorists did not detonate the bombs they had in their possession.

Dolnik and Pilch suggest that there was still a high degree of certainty that non-violent solutions were still possible on Friday evening. They determined this from several indicators. First, the terrorists had not carried out their threats. Second, they had not used execution of hostages as a deterrent.* Third, they refined, and essentially softened, their demands as they went along. In any case, Dolnik and Pilch believe the situation headquarters could have secured the release of at least some of the hostages before the assault without conceding anything of substance. There were possibilities, and more than one. But HQ didn't even consider them. "In most hostage-taking cases it is the authorities who try to stall for time to apply the standard negotiating method," write Dolnik and Pilch. "In Moscow the opposite happened, and as far as we can tell, the Russian leadership also pushed up its own deadline for negotiations."

Apparently, there were no professionals either in Putin's entourage or in the FSB who could suggest the right approach. But the main problem was the categorical attitude: no negotiations with terrorists, not about anything. Anna Andrianova, one of the hostages, recalled later that the terrorists were "really waiting for some official representative", but no one came. "It felt like we were buried before they even tried to save us in any way."[13]

---

\* The terrorists killed four people during the siege, but Dolnik and Pilch note that none of these killings were cold-blooded shootings to demonstrate the seriousness of their intentions. In two cases, they were in response to what they considered "irrational behaviour", and two other hostages died from accidental gunshot wounds.

Vladimir Putin saw the seizure of the Theatre Centre as a personal challenge. The official doctrine, entrenched since the beginning of the second Chechen war was that the "international terrorism" that had taken root in Chechnya and had come to Moscow was an unmanageable, otherworldly evil. No dialogue was possible in principle. During those three ill-fated days, any attempt by the hostages to broadcast the demands of the captors, let alone to see anything human in them or in their demands, was interpreted by the authorities as "Stockholm syndrome."

## Negotiating with Abubakar

Maria Shkolnikova quickly realized that it was up to the hostages to rescue themselves. Anna Andrianova and another hostage, Zhanna Tolstova, told the *Moskovskaya pravda* newspaper on Friday, the eve of the assault, that the picture painted by television was far from reality and "had Masha Shkolnikova not established contact [with the press], things would have ended much earlier due to inaction of our specialists." "The patience of these people may run out, and they will bring things to an end," hostages explained.[14] Movsar Barayev and his right-hand man, Abubakar, did not have a clear plan of what to do after they had captured the theatre. Shkolnikova's plan was to do everything in her power to stop the assault and to look for anyone the terrorists would be willing to talk with. As she formulated it in one of her conversations with journalists, "We need individuals who can influence policy in the state, fight for the liberation of Chechnya and whose opinion is important in the country."[15] For this reason, she spent the whole night of Wednesday–Thursday, as well as Thursday morning, broadcasting live on Ekho Moskvy radio and on REN TV. The terrorists mentioned Chechen deputy Aslambek Aslakhanov and the journalist Anna Politkovskaya. Politkovskaya was in America. Aslakhanov phoned Barayev, but the conversation did not go anywhere.

Then Shkolnikova mentioned Yavlinsky and Khakamada. It was 7.00 a.m. on Thursday. It turned out that Yavlinsky was far away, in the Siberian city of Tomsk. The hostages began to wonder who else they could involve and decided to call Nemtsov. "[The terrorists] agreed to negotiate with Nemtsov—not to negotiate, but to tell him their demands. Nemtsov, Yavlinsky and Khakamada are the people who provoke the least antipathy," Shkolnikova told REN TV live at 2.00 p.m. on Thursday, 24 October.

Chubais had been in contact with Putin since Thursday morning. He then got in touch with Nemtsov and Khakamada. According to Khakamada's recollection, he said: "Please don't comment, don't speak, don't initiate anything, no matter what. Everyone sits in their own office. Ira, you sit in the deputy speaker's office. Boris, you sit in your own office. And until HQ calls you, do not open your mouth."[16]

Khakamada soon received a phone call from Dmitry Lesnevsky, son of REN TV founder Irena Lesnevskaya, saying that her name was on the list given to the hostages: "Please go to Dubrovka and negotiate." The official representative, Sergei Yastrzhembsky, confirmed it. Nemtsov also went to Dubrovka. They were met by staff members as well as by Iosif Kobzon, one of Russia's most famous singers and a parliamentarian, near the Theatre Centre. By that time, Kobzon had already been in the building. He had come on his own initiative and was actually the first negotiator. He spoke to Abubakar. In consultation with headquarters, Kobzon offered him money, a plane and a helicopter. Abubakar refused everything and demanded an end to the war. "It's unthinkable," Kobzon replied, meaning it was unclear what that meant and how to achieve it. "At least stop the clean-up operations," Abubakar said. "That can be discussed," agreed Kobzon.[17] Abubakar eventually handed over to Kobzon three children and their mother and an Englishman. As the Polish journalist Andrzej Zaucha writes in his book *Moscow: Nord-Ost*, it was the terrorists' own idea of a goodwill gesture—handing over children and an Englishman to the first person who comes to negotiate. Kobzon begged them to release the woman: "What's the point of you having a mother without her children and me having children without their mother?"[18] Soon Kobzon called Abubakar back from the operational headquarters and told him that several other people wanted to talk to him, including Khakamada and Nemtsov. Kobzon later recalled "[Abubakar] said, 'Khakamada and Nemtsov can come.' 'Fine.' And I go down to the courtyard and said, 'Irina, Boris, you can come through.'

Irina says, 'I'm ready.' And Nemtsov says, 'I need to consult about this.' And he disappeared. Completely."[19]

This story would haunt Nemtsov for the rest of his life, especially since, after the theatre was stormed, Kobzon said that Nemtsov had simply run scared. Later, Nemtsov would explain that he stayed outside and negotiated with Abubakar on the phone because it was "President Putin's firm demand, direct and unambiguous",[20] but no one believed him. "It would have made sense if he had been invited in alone. Not great, but it would have made sense. But Kobzon and Khakamada were going inside, too. What kind of plan was it—they wouldn't mess things up, but he would have?" wrote Alexander Minkin, the same journalist who had published the dirt on Nemtsov and the other reformers in the summer of 1997.[21]

In fact, it was Vladislav Surkov, the Kremlin official in charge of domestic policy, who decided to make Nemtsov look like a coward in the aftermath of the siege. It was because of him that Nemtsov would be remembered later for refusing to go inside and for "letting a woman go in ahead of him."

But Nemtsov was telling the truth. According to Chubais, the order for Nemtsov to stay out of the building was to be strictly enforced, and Chubais told him so: "Boris, the prohibition is categorical. You are not to go in under any circumstances. Khakamada will go."[22] And so, Nemtsov did not go in. Later, he'd point out that Putin didn't let Luzhkov go in either. Years later, he admitted that it was one of the biggest mistakes of his life.

The question from the journalist Minkin, however, was not unwarranted: why didn't Putin let Nemtsov and Luzhkov go, while he gave everyone else a green light? Ten years later, Nemtsov explained why: so their political capital wouldn't go up. "Voloshin told me, 'Putin doesn't want your ratings going up,'" Nemtsov said. "The logic was that if either Luzhkov or Nemtsov went—that is, the mayor of Moscow or the former governor—and if, let's say, the hostages were released, then they'd be heroes. Right? They didn't want our success. That's what Voloshin told me."[23]

Voloshin refutes this. According to him, Nemtsov was probably banned from going inside over fears for his life: weighing the situation,

Putin might have decided that the terrorists posed a serious threat to Nemtsov, not Khakamada. But then why did Putin let Yavlinsky go inside the theatre when he flew in from Tomsk? What's the fundamental difference between Nemtsov and Yavlinsky in this situation? The question is worth asking, especially when you consider that Putin was in fact concerned that politicians might use the Nord-Ost situation for self-promotion. This is clear from his words to Yavlinsky three days after the theatre was stormed: "You, unlike many others, aren't making a private PR campaign out of it. For that, I thank you very much."[24]

There is little doubt that Putin's decision to keep Nemtsov away from the terrorists was not guided by general considerations but by his own attitude towards him. Relations between them had already deteriorated. Nemtsov constantly disagreed with Putin on a variety of subjects. He opposed local government reform. He condemned the crackdown on NTV. He criticized the Kremlin's policy in Chechnya. In autumn 2001, this led to their first public skirmish: Nemtsov called for negotiations with Maskhadov, and Putin advised him to "stop messing about on the country's political scene and give up his mandate as a deputy in the State Duma." "The president has apparently confused me with his subordinates," Nemtsov retorted harshly. "He didn't elect me, and it's not his place to remove me."[25] But for Putin, that was just empty noise. He did not believe in Nemtsov's subjectivity as a politician and saw him less as a political partner or even an ally than someone at the level of an aide. Nemtsov and his associates had got into the Duma thanks to him; they rode on him into parliament in 1999 like fleas on a dog. Nemtsov was always "other" to Putin: too loud, too open, too independent, too informal and, lately, increasingly irritating. So, it was simply not an option for Putin to let him interfere in a drama with such high stakes, a drama unfolding before the entire country and that personally touched Putin.

Chubais arranged with Putin for Nemtsov to negotiate with Abubakar by phone. It was not easy: Putin was not interested in negotiation; he was preparing an assault. Chubais realized this as early as Thursday afternoon: "I realized that preparations for an assault were underway. [My argument was that we should] keep doing [what we were doing] and negotiate at the same time. This was the right thing to do, at least to divert [the terrorists'] attention, but at best to get people out. It was very dramatic, but in the end [Putin] agreed and sanctioned Boris's talk with Abubakar."[26]

Yavlinsky also understood the situation. Having gone to Dubrovka late on Thursday night as soon as he flew in from Tomsk, Yavlinsky went straight to the Kremlin to see Voloshin to convey the terrorists' demands. Years later, he recalled: "But there was already another plan in the Kremlin. I didn't know what it was, but it was clear that it was quite different."[27]

Nemtsov spoke to Abubakar several times on Thursday and at least once on Friday evening. There is a transcript of the Friday conversation in the criminal case file. Nemtsov is trying to persuade Abubakar to release the children, fifteen ninth-grade students from a public school who came to the play with their teacher. Nemtsov gives a guarantee that Boris Jordan, director of NTV, will show the interview with Barayev that was recorded on Thursday and not aired, much to the anger of the terrorists. But Abubakar is no longer interested in the interview: "Let him show it or not—it makes no difference to us now." Nemtsov then returns to the option they discussed on Thursday: the terrorists release people in exchange for an end to fighting, killing and clean-up operations in Chechnya.

> NEMTSOV: Look, I can tell you this... You and I had agreed that if today was a peaceful day, you would gradually release children and women. You said that.
> ABUBAKAR: This wasn't a day of peace. There has not been a single day of peace so far in Chechnya.
> NEMTSOV: Today is a day of peace.
> ABUBAKAR: The process should have started... The process should have started. Nothing has been decided. The decision should also be in writing, and we should hear it announced on TV. The whole nation should hear.
> NEMTSOV: The president spoke today.
> ABUBAKAR: When it happens, everyone will know about it. And now you are—what do you call it?—what you said is not clear, it's all murky.

NEMTSOV: The president said on TV that he is ready.

ABUBAKAR: It's black, Boris. There's no light in this darkness.

NEMTSOV: Do you know why you can't see the light? Do you want me to tell you?

ABUBAKAR: Yes?

NEMTSOV: Because you have to be able to meet a person halfway. Do you understand? You have to be able to, you know?

ABUBAKAR: We are ready to make concessions. We are ready. But they have to be from all sides... when everyone is freed. All you say is free the hostages. There are four people, ten people, every person...

NEMTSOV: Today is a day of peace in Chechnya.

ABUBAKAR: Good.

NEMTSOV: There were no raids in Chechnya today. No one was killed there today in Chechnya. People lived peacefully in Chechnya today. You told me yourself that this is your main task. Today has been a peaceful day. Release the children. One day has passed. You have saved the lives of people in Chechnya today, whatever you might say.

ABUBAKAR: No, we are not going to release anyone. There are no children, the children have been released.

NEMTSOV: The ninth grade is still there.

ABUBAKAR: The little children, under eleven years old, have been released.

On Friday evening, when this conversation took place, Barayev and Abubakar were already highly agitated. Their main demand to end the war, conveyed through various intermediaries, from Kobzon to Anna Politkovskaya, was summed up as follows: Putin must declare his readiness to end the war by making contact with Maskhadov and withdraw his troops from one of the districts in Chechnya. Knowing that there would be no negotiations with Maskhadov, Nemtsov reminded Abubakar that he'd said he'd release the hostages in the event of a partial cessation of hostilities. This manoeuvre could have led to a positive result. But unfortunately, two hours before the last conversation, Abubakar learnt that on the morning of that day one of Barayev's relatives had been taken away by the federal military. (This is also in the criminal case file.) Abubakar tells Nemtsov about it.

NEMTSOV: And where is he, where was he taken?
ABUBAKAR: He had nothing to do with this, nothing to do with anything in the military, he has never even held a gun in his life, and yet they took him away. That's a fact. Now a relative just called from home.
NEMTSOV: Just a second, wait a second.
ABUBAKAR: They did plenty of things like this, even today.
NEMTSOV: No, wait, Abubakar, let's be clear, you and I agreed that...
ABUBAKAR: Agreed... agreed! We did not agree about anything. We were just talking. If the demands are met, we will see. The demands have not been met.
NEMTSOV: No, just a second!
ABUBAKAR: No commissioner of human rights... No one has come to us yet, they haven't even called us.
NEMTSOV: Who hasn't called?
ABUBAKAR: There has to be at least some person authorized by Putin to call us, you know?

The terrorists didn't release anyone else. Nemtsov followed Voloshin's instructions and handed Abubakar's phone number to an "authorized person", General Kazantsev. He telephoned half an hour later, set up a meeting for the next morning and asked for the children to be released. Abubakar again refused. And six hours later, the hostages saw a yellowish cloud appear from the ceiling and smelt a sweet odour: in the early hours of 26 October, the federal headquarters gave the order to release the gas. The assault was launched. The gas did not have an immediate effect, neither on the hostages, nor on their attackers. There is no doubt, Dolnik and Pilch write, that a significant number of terrorists remained conscious for quite some time and could have detonated the explosives planted throughout the hall, had they wanted to. There is no answer to the question of why the terrorists did not blow up the auditorium, and apparently there never will be one. As investigator Vladimir Kalchuk, who was in charge of the Nord-Ost case, later said: "We will never know."[28]

## Assault with poison gas

For three days the entire country had sat by their televisions and radios. In the hours immediately following the storming of the theatre, the incredible tension of the days gave way to a state of near-euphoria. People exhaled. The assault itself was carried out brilliantly by the FSB special forces. The terrorists had been killed. The building did not blow up. Most of the hostages survived; at first, it seemed that almost everyone was alive. It was a victory. The evil that had come to Moscow had been defeated. The triumph was not yet over when, at 6.00 p.m. on Saturday night, Nemtsov went live on Channel One. There was no clear picture yet of what had happened after the assault. The headquarters had already acknowledged the use of gas and put the death toll at sixty-seven. It was still a huge success.

Like everyone else, Nemtsov felt a sense of relief and victory. Like everyone else, he was proud of the prowess and professionalism of the special services. Like many, he wanted to support the government. At this moment, he was with Putin. (Putin even called him and thanked him for his masterful handling of the phone calls with Abubakar.) "Russia has survived as a state," Nemtsov said. "It was a moment of truth, and it is extremely important that President Putin did not give in and did not engage with them." He cited his last conversation with Abubakar as proof that by the evening of 25 October, the terrorists had become "completely uncooperative." His conclusion: Russia had shown the world how to defeat terrorism.[29] On the same day, Putin addressed the nation. "Terrorists have no future," he said, "but we do."

In the meantime, gruesome details had already begun to emerge. After capture and release came the third tragic act of the Dubrovka drama. The casualty figures rose, and, as people got a clearer picture of what had occurred and saw the image of lifeless bodies piled onto buses, the conclusion became more horrifying. These casualties had been avoidable. These people had died for nothing. They died without getting the antidote in time, choking on their own vomit, choking because their tongues were stuck in their mouths as they were crushed under piles of bodies in buses. They died because there had been a well-prepared operation to kill the terrorists but no operation to rescue the hostages. No one was in charge of the evacuation of the nine hundred hostages. The rescuers could not distinguish the dead from the living. There were no stretchers. There weren't enough vehicles, and the drivers of the buses that were there did not know where to take the victims. Hospitals had not been prepared for the influx of patients, all exhibiting the same symptoms. Doctors had not been prepared for poisoning. They did not know what to do; they had not been told the composition of the gas, and it would remain a mystery for ever.

As Dolnik and Pilch point out in their study, there is no rational explanation for the way the rescue operation was conducted. People continued to die, and a few days later a final figure appeared: 130 dead. Of these, only five had been killed before the assault: the rest were victims of the rescue operation itself.

How miraculous, how magical the deliverance had looked when the special forces stormed the hall—and how catastrophic the aftermath.

This seems to have been the moment—the sobering realization of the awful truth of Nord-Ost—that became the turning point in the relationship between Nemtsov and Putin. Nemtsov would later say bluntly: "I personally have only one story that describes Putin and explains why I became an oppositionist. It's the story of Nord-Ost."[30] Nemtsov and his faction proposed a parliamentary enquiry, but the Duma rejected the proposal. After that, SPS itself convened a public commission. The commission did not consider the question of the assault itself or political responsibility, and it came to politically correct conclusions: the assault was exemplary, the riot police worked professionally, but the operation to rescue the hostages was a failure. SPS placed the main blame on Moscow's chief medical officer, who was a member of the counter-terrorist headquarters but did not play a serious role. It is not known even with certainty that he was informed in time about the assault or the nature of the measures taken. In mid-November, Nemtsov, along with other leaders of parliamentary factions, was received by Putin. Nemtsov told him about the results of the investigation: "I came to Putin and said, 'Look, these people could have been saved. We are obliged to institute criminal proceedings for the criminal negligence of those who rescued them and punish them.' He said, 'Why?' I said, 'Why? So it won't happen again. He said, 'Well, we can't bring these people back, they're already dead... Why get people all worked up?'"[31]

Putin did not punish anyone. Of the officials responsible for everything that happened during those three terrible days in Moscow, the only official reprimanded was the policeman who gave the Chechen female suicide bomber a Moscow registration. However, there were consequences. It wasn't long before Putin was reprimanding NTV's general director, Boris Jordan, for allegedly showing live footage of the assault. That actually wasn't true, and Alexei Venediktov recalled later telling Putin as much.[32] Three months later, Jordan was fired; NTV would soon become a government mouthpiece like the other two central television channels. From then on, no one would be able to criticize Putin on television ever again.

Managed democracy failed the test of humanity in the Dubrovka tragedy, and Vladimir Putin for the first time clearly demonstrated one of his cardinal rules: the actions of the Kremlin are not subject to public scrutiny. And that was something Nemtsov could no longer accept. "After Nord-Ost, everything took off," Khakamada said. Instead of a recent ally, Nemtsov now saw Putin as his enemy. The feeling quickly became mutual.

## Visiting Akhmat Kadyrov

Akhmat Kadyrov was a brave and determined man. During the first Chechen war, he had declared jihad on Russia, but a lot had happened since then. When Russian troops entered Chechnya in October 1999, it was no coincidence that Kadyrov, then mufti of Chechnya, became their ally.

Kadyrov had declared war on the Wahhabis in 1997, when Chechnya had gained its independence and whole villages had come under the control of local field commanders. Many Chechens were unhappy about the shooting galleries under their windows, the bearded men with machine guns poking around, the thugs who came to Chechnya from Arab countries and behaved as if they owned the place. Akhmat Kadyrov was well aware of discontent. He spoke out openly and publicly. He demanded that the foreigners go home before they brought trouble to Chechnya. He urged the Chechen imams to unite against the increasing lawlessness and insisted that Maskhadov disband the armed groups.

Kadyrov put his life at risk, became inured to frequent assassination attempts, and became a very popular figure. When the moderate field commanders were frightened by the strength of Basayev and al-Khattab in 1999, they did not go to Maskhadov but to Kadyrov. If there had been free presidential elections in Chechnya in 1999, there is no question that he would have won.

When the war began, Kadyrov had no choice but to shake the hand extended to him from Moscow. But when the Kremlin quickly put him in charge of the local administration, his authority was shaken. Kadyrov went from being a popular leader to being a puppet, his position maintained by the bayonets of interventionists. Kadyrov took another risk: he openly protested the atrocities committed by the Russian military, but he could not stop the daily clean-up operations, shelling, kidnappings and arbitrary killings. By autumn 2002, the war had formally ended and the field commanders had come over to Kadyrov's side, but some areas were still under the control of the Chechen fighters, and clean-up operations and atrocities continued. The military had the real power. Funds sent to Chechnya were distributed through the commandant's offices, and temporary departments of internal affairs (known as VOVDs) were notorious for their brutality. The hostage-taking in Moscow untied the Kremlin's hands. In response to the Nord-Ost attacks, Moscow announced "harsh, targeted clean-up operations." The federal authorities still did what they wanted.

The Kremlin's plan to put in place a new constitution, elect a president and officially start a peaceful life in Chechnya had already been in place before the Nord-Ost attack. Even though the withdrawal of federal troops from Chechnya was suspended after the theatre siege, the Kremlin not only refused to abandon the plan, but redoubled its efforts to implement it—first a referendum on the new constitution in spring 2003, and then a presidential election six months later. Kadyrov was very nervous. On the one hand, he realized that he had no chance of winning a free election—he would lose by a big margin to Aslambek Aslakhanov, who had very public ambitions, as well as to the very popular Chechen businessman Malik Saidullayev, and many others. On the other hand, he was not at all sure that he was the one whom the Kremlin saw as president of Chechnya. Putin met with him, but gave him no guarantees, and Kadyrov's draft constitution, which proposed a ten-year residency requirement for the future president (disqualifying all viable contenders from the election) was rejected by Moscow out of hand. The press said that the Kremlin no longer needed Kadyrov. But the mufti did not give up. For this reason, when Aslakhanov suddenly announced at the end of November that a congress of the Chechen people would be held in Moscow on 16 December, Kadyrov immediately convened his own, alternative congress.

He decided to hold the event, called the Congress of the Peoples of the Chechen Republic, in his native city of Gudermes on 11 December, four days before Aslakhanov's. From the outset, it was clear that it would be a meeting of the Kadyrov clan, but the more respectable guests from Moscow, the better, and so official invitations were sent to the State Duma. The leaders of the other factions declined, but Nemtsov decided to go. He took his press secretary, Yelena Dikun, and three journalists with him.

The Gudermes administration hall could seat no more than two hundred people, so it was a stretch to call it a congress. Other than representatives of the Chechen diaspora who had flown in from Moscow, Nemtsov was the only guest from the capital. He stood out sharply in this stuffy room, packed to the brim with supporters of Kadyrov and surrounded on all sides by fierce-looking machine gunners in camouflage uniforms.

All the speeches came down to a simple idea: Chechnya must lead a peaceful life as part of Russia, and Akhmat Kadyrov must be its president. The text of the pre-written resolution was the same. Nemtsov was one of the last to speak, and the contrast between him and the others present was stark. Nemtsov said that the referendum and presidential elections should not be held at gunpoint, that there would be no peace in Chechnya without negotiations with the separatists, that not everyone with a weapon was necessarily a terrorist. And the longer Nemtsov spoke, the louder the comments from the hall. Kadyrov interrupted Nemtsov's speech several times to reassure the audience. He spoke in Chechen, and Nemtsov did not understand him. He said that "Nemtsov is our guest and deputy," that there was no harm in him and let him say what he wanted.

The congress ended, and Nemtsov went out into the courtyard. At that moment, a young man who looked like a fighter or a security guard, accompanied by several young men like him, approached him. "They had large assault rifles and bandoliers like revolutionary sailors. All of them had long beards," said journalist Alexander Ryklin, who had flown to Gudermes with Nemtsov at the time. "And [their leader] said something to Nemtsov. Harsh. It was an aggressive conversation. Boris said something in reply."[33] It was Akhmat Kadyrov's son Ramzan. He had just turned twenty-six and had been head of his father's security service since the beginning of the war. Ryklin did not hear the conversation, but other witnesses made out what Ramzan said to Nemtsov. He said that if he came to Gudermes again, he would kill him.

Neither Nemtsov, nor Akhmat Kadyrov, who quickly put his son in his place, nor any of the other witnesses to the scene, took the threat seriously. "There was no sense of serious danger," Ryklin recalled.[34] Nevertheless, Kadyrov advised Nemtsov to leave and gave him an armed escort. Of course, it wasn't Ramzan he feared. Akhmat Kadyrov was afraid of a provocation, including from the federal military forces. It was better to get Nemtsov out of harm's way. Lodging was found for him in a private house about an hour's drive from Gudermes, in neighbouring Ingushetia. The next day he flew to Moscow.

A referendum on the Chechen constitution was held in March 2003, and presidential elections took place on 5 October. Kadyrov's fears proved to be unfounded: the Kremlin backed him, and by election day he did not have any serious rivals. At the beginning of September, the well-known Chechen entrepreneur Khusein Dzhabrailov withdrew his candidacy. Then, two weeks before the election, Aslambek Aslakhanov stepped down. Malik Saidullayev was in trouble. At a meeting with Putin shortly before the election, he proposed to withdraw his candidacy if the Kremlin so wished, to which Putin replied, "May the best candidate win," and said he had promised Kadyrov nothing. As a result, Saidullayev was removed from the election through the courts. But even by ridding Kadyrov of strong competitors, the Kremlin would not have been able to ensure his victory, and the vote was a pure sham. In fact, Kadyrov lost even to the extra people registered especially for the election. However, at the end of the count, it was announced that he had received more than eighty per cent of the votes. From then on, his son was chief of security for the elected president of Chechnya.

# CHAPTER 21

## 2003
## The Other Russia

### The end of business the Russian way

By early 2003, one of the biggest problems for Mikhail Khodorkovsky, Russia's richest oligarch, was bribes. More specifically, the problem was cash bribes and contributions at the behest of the Kremlin.

The practice of big businessmen financing the Kremlin's needs, including by cash donations, was nothing new. After the parliamentary elections in December 1999, Khodorkovsky and his partners, as well as other oligarchs, were asked to contribute a certain amount of cash for the upcoming presidential election campaign. Khodorkovsky and his partners collected a bag of money and handed it to a uniformed emissary who came for it. Then the money was unexpectedly returned to them; it wasn't needed. The overwhelming victory in the parliamentary elections greatly reduced the cost of Putin's presidential campaign. But the practice continued, and when Putin moved to the Kremlin, his administration collected relatively equal tributes from all the oligarchs. Some of the money legally went to finance numerous Kremlin projects, from expertise on economic reforms to support for veterans' funds. The other part was still collected in cash, and Yukos, for example, had been giving the Presidential Administration about $5 million a year since 2001. In return, Yukos was promised two seats on the Kremlin party candidate list for the 2003 parliamentary elections.[1]

The problem was not that Khodorkovsky was unwilling to part with this money. In fact, he was willing to give more. The problem was giving cash. Since the early 2000s, Khodorkovsky had been trying to make his business conform to Western standards. Independent figures sat on the Yukos board of directors. Influential foreigners were invited to join the board. In two years, from 2000 through 2001, Yukos's vast assets were combined into a single share that was the basis of a powerful holding company. Khodorkovsky cut costs and improved auditing. He rushed the transition to international accounting, and, in the summer of 2002, Yukos was the first Russian company to disclose its ownership structure. The co-owners of Yukos became billionaires.

The reason for Khodorkovsky's success was far more than just the rise in oil prices that began in 1999. Yukos was also outpacing other oil companies in terms of financial results. A champion in corporate governance, Yukos became attractive to international investors, its shares quickly turned into blue chip stocks, and by 2002 the company was already overtaking Gazprom in capitalization. The era of "Russian-style business", as it had been in the 1990s—grey and murky, thriving on connections and corruption—was coming to an end. The era of integration into the global economy was dawning. Russian oligarchs had opened the door to the world, and Khodorkovsky led the way forward.

Yukos was becoming a global company, and Khodorkovsky was considering whether he should open his second headquarters in London or New York. He was eager to change the rules of the game. Moreover, he believed he had no choice. In summer 2002, some twenty per cent of Yukos shares were traded freely on world markets, mainly in American depository receipts. (Disclosure of the shareholding structure was necessary in order to gain access to the world market.) This meant that Yukos would have to abide by the American corporate code, which had just been tightened. Under the Sarbanes–Oxley Act, lying in financial reports was now punishable by ten to twenty years' imprisonment. "Basically, you certify that no one inside the company gives bribes," Khodorkovsky explained.[2]

This is how Khodorkovsky came to be at the forefront of the movement for transparent relations between the oil magnates and the state.

In 2002, he decided to limit out-of-pocket expenses to $10 million per year. A Yukos emissary went to the Kremlin for talks, informing Vladislav Surkov, deputy head of the Presidential Administration, that Khodorkovsky was ready to support Kremlin projects and would even raise his contributions, but with the new policy on transparency the company could not pay in cash. Surkov promised to tell his boss, and a week later came he back with the reply: "Tell Khodorkovsky not to show off and give cash like everyone else." He had to pay.[3]

Khodorkovsky was a player inside the system. He did not break the rules of the game. He did not rebel, he gave money when necessary, he coordinated big deals and projects with the Kremlin, and he asked for permission to support parties and deputies. But Khodorkovsky was not a typical oligarch. He did not buy himself aeroplanes or yachts and was even an extremely unpretentious dresser. He was not interested in material wealth for its own sake. After becoming the leader of Russian business and putting the best managers he could find at the head of his vast empire, he seemed to be trying on the behaviour of the great Western magnates of the twentieth century—the men who went down in history not just as moguls, but as visionaries and philanthropists. In December 2001, he set up Open Russia, Russia's first major Western-style educational organization.

At this time the oligarchs were thinking about how to legitimize in public opinion the results of the shares-for-loans auctions. Khodorkovsky came to Prime Minister Mikhail Kasyanov on behalf of all big business with the idea of levying a compensation tax on auction participants. "We wanted to start with $25 billion for everyone," Khodorkovsky recalls. "At the time, that was a lot. We knew they'd cite another figure, but we figured we'd come to an agreement."[4] (Kasyanov proposed the project to Putin, but Putin didn't greenlight it.) Khodorkovsky had already made arrangements with his partners that in 2008, the year he would turn forty-five, they would decorously leave the business and stop running Yukos. By then, Yukos would have ceased to be Yukos: Khodorkovsky and Abramovich planned to merge their companies, Yukos and Sibneft, into one of the world's largest oil concerns. The merger was to be followed by the sale of a large stake in the combined company to foreigners.

## New elite versus the old guard

The Yukos Affair, which determined the course of Russian history, can be traced back to a dispute between Khodorkovsky and Putin, or, more precisely, to Putin's dispute with Khodorkovsky, at the president's meeting with the oligarchs on 19 February 2003 in the Kremlin's St Catherine Hall. At this meeting, big business was going to talk about corruption and, in particular, about a scandalous purchase in the oil market that had just become public. The state company Rosneft had acquired the company Severnaya Neft for $600 million, although analysts estimated that it was not worth more than $350–60 million. According to rumours that made their way into the press, part of the sum overpaid by Rosneft was intended to finance parliamentary elections. "Officials summon oligarchs to the carpet and demand money for United Russia's election campaign," *Kommersant* wrote in December 2002. The amounts seemed enormous to business, and "the concerned oligarchs are allegedly running to complain about the exorbitant fees to Voloshin and Surkov."[5] The officials who levied the tribute on business were understood to be the so-called St Petersburg Chekists, led by Igor Sechin. Sechin, who had headed Putin's secretariat since the early 1990s, was always his closest subordinate, his loyal administrator or perhaps his valet, who followed him up the career ladder. For more than two years, Sechin had been deputy head of the Presidential Administration in charge of Putin's office, managing the president's schedule and determining what came across his desk. Putin was still surrounded by the old Yeltsin guard—Voloshin, Kasyanov and other officials and businessmen. But his personal minions, who were all somehow associated with the security services—Igor Sechin and Viktor Ivanov in the Kremlin, Nikolai Patrushev in the FSB, functionaries in the United Russia party and others—were also gaining more power. Known as "the St Petersburg Chekists", they were already part of the elite. Now they needed capital and resources, and their interests clashed with those of the old guard and the oligarchs who had made their fortunes in the 1990s. As Putin's obligations—as he understood them—to Yeltsin had come to an end, a conflict was brewing between the two camps in the Kremlin.

Khodorkovsky understood all this. The businessman Alexander Mamut was set to speak at the meeting with Putin, but he declined at the last minute and Khodorkovsky took his place. When he raised the issue of the purchase price of Severnaya Neft, which was about twice its estimated value, he was aware that he was entering into a battle with Sechin's faction. Khodorkovsky was doing this deliberately: for him, it was a fight for the country's course, not a fight with Putin. The content of Khodorkovsky's speech had been OK'ed by both Voloshin and his deputy, Dmitry Medvedev. Just before he was going to speak, Khodorkovsky once again asked Voloshin if he should bring up Severnaya Neft on camera. Voloshin went up to Putin to clarify. Putin nodded: yes, go ahead. Khodorkovsky did not break the rules of the game.

Putin began the meeting on a cordial and liberal note. Corruption, he said, was a serious problem, but instead of punishing people they should work to eliminate the basis for it. Here, he underlined, the interests of business and the state coincide. Alexei Mordashov, head of the major steel company Severstal, spoke after him. Then Khodorkovsky took the floor. He spoke about the oilmen's victory in getting equal access to the oil pipeline; this, he said, was how corruption could be reduced. He went on to point out how strange it was that there were two applicants for every place at the oil and gas institute, yet four or five for every one at the tax academy, when the tax officer's salary was on the average three times lower. Then Khodorkovsky said: "Everyone thinks that the Rosneft and Severnaya Neft deal was not completely transparent. The president of Rosneft is here; what does he say?"

Then Putin took the floor again. First, he defended future tax officials: "What you say is suggestive, but it's not right to have a presumption of guilt about students." Then he got to his main point. "The [Rosneft] board chairman should respond to what you said [about the Severnaya Neft deal], but some things are obvious. A state company wants to increase its reserves. And other companies, such as Yukos, have extremely large reserves. How it got such large reserves is a question that is part of the issue we are discussing today."

Participants of the meeting were taken aback by Putin's reaction: the head of a state-owned company was accused of corruption in the present, but the president responded by mentioning auctions that took place seven years ago. Neither Khodorkovsky, nor, apparently, Voloshin, nor even anyone else expected Putin to defend Rosneft's management. But Putin took Khodorkovsky's comment as a personal attack. In his book *All the Kremlin's Men*, journalist Mikhail Zygar wrote that, according to the banker Sergei Pugachyov—who the press at the time linked to the security services and Igor Sechin—immediately after the meeting Putin complained to him about Khodorkovsky: "And where did he get this Yukos, eh? After everything they've had a hand in, he accuses me of taking bribes? He's got some nerve, preaching to me in front of everyone."[6]

However unexpected Putin's retort may have been, no one at the meeting gave the scene much thought at the time. Journalists wrote that the oligarchs left the Kremlin satisfied. Talks to merge Yukos and Sibneft continued, unaffected by the pointed exchange in the Kremlin. Khodorkovsky was preparing to buy Sibneft from Abramovich for $3 billion, and in return Abramovich would receive a blocking stake in Yukos-Sibneft. Talks with foreigners were still ongoing. Two options were discussed: exchanging large blocks of shares in the future Yukos-Sibneft with Chevron or selling about ten per cent to ExxonMobil. In this way, the foreigners would gain access to Russian fields and a combined Yukos-Sibneft would gain access to Western technology. Putin was aware of these negotiations and approved them on one condition: that the Russian companies did not cede control.

On 22 April, Khodorkovsky and Abramovich officially announced the deal. Before they did, they had been to see Putin again, and he again gave his approval. That same evening, all the Russian oligarchs gathered in a Moscow restaurant. "Everyone supported us," recalls Khodorkovsky's partner Leonid Nevzlin. Big Russian capital was on the verge of achieving its primary objective: becoming a fully fledged member of the world economic system. The British company BP had just bought fifty per cent of the oil company TNK for $6.75 billion. Khodorkovsky and Abramovich were next to take off—they were going to conquer America.

## Liberals on the brink of failure

Grigory Yavlinsky and his Yabloko party had already teamed up once with reformers led by Yegor Gaidar. This was before the 1995 parliamentary elections, when Gaidar's Democratic Choice of Russia party had opposed Yeltsin over the war in Chechnya. "Objectively, the start of the Chechen war brought us closer [to Yavlinsky]," Gaidar later wrote.[7] Yavlinsky suggested that they go to the polls as a single bloc on one condition: that the democrats nominate him as their candidate in the 1996 presidential election. Gaidar agreed; they drank to victory. The next day, Yavlinsky changed his mind. "In the evening, I watched Yavlinsky's speech on TV and learnt there was not and could not be a coalition between Yabloko and our party," Gaidar recalled.[8] After that, Yavlinsky was always on his own and always opposed Yeltsin's government. In 1999, his faction even supported several points of impeachment against Yeltsin. Yavlinsky's relations with Putin were quite good: Yavlinsky did not retreat from democratic principles and criticized the political course, but he did not make personal attacks.

Meanwhile, relations between Yavlinsky and Chubais had been verging on mutual hatred for years. So, the idea of Khodorkovsky's partner Leonid Nevzlin to try once again to convince SPS and Yabloko to form an alliance had little chance of success. But the low ratings of both parties—it wasn't clear if SPS and Yabloko had enough support to get seats in the Duma—seemed to be pushing them closer together. And Yukos, one of the sponsors of SPS and the sole sponsor of Yabloko, was the natural intermediary between the two. Nemtsov was enthusiastic about the idea of joining forces and, according to Nevzlin, was even prepared to cede the top spot on the party list to Yavlinsky.[9] Nevzlin went further—he suggested that Khodorkovsky should head the future alliance; he'd be in first place, then Yavlinsky would be second and Nemtsov third. But Khodorkovsky immediately declined, citing his need to complete the deal between Yukos and Sibneft.

And so, in late autumn 2002, another attempt to form an alliance failed. Yavlinsky made it clear that Yabloko was ready to work with Khakamada and Nemtsov, but under no circumstances with Chubais. The democratic opposition charter that he proposed in December 2002 was specially written to make it impossible for people on the right to sign. It highlighted the "mistakes, and sometimes crimes, committed under slogans of democracy and reform by people who called themselves democrats and reformers." Khodorkovsky made a final attempt at unification in January 2003 after Chubais and Nemtsov asked him to talk to Yavlinsky. "He immediately bristled," Khodorkovsky recalled, "and asked, 'Are you making that a condition?' I said, 'No, I'm just asking.'"[10] Nemtsov then proposed a compromise: create two different factions in the Duma and sacrifice Chubais, who said he was ready to work behind the scenes. Negotiations were scheduled for 29 January. But the day before they were due to meet, Yavlinsky sent a formal reply to Nemtsov and Khakamada: "Unfortunately, your proposals are unacceptable to us."[11]

Could an SPS-Yabloko coalition have been viable? Even at the time sociologists doubted it. The Yabloko electorate, mostly intellectuals with a more leftist outlook, and the SPS electorate that was younger and better adapted to life in a market economy, were too far apart. "Our whole policy was built on the premise that we were against this type of reform," Yavlinsky explained. "They were the standard bearers of those reforms. Nemtsov was the political cover for the reforms, Khakamada—the personification, and Chubais—the producer."[12] In the end, the failed allies remained adversaries: negotiations continued but turned into pointless bickering in which both sides sought to discredit the other. "We proposed unification and got war instead," Chubais would say at the SPS congress in September 2003.[13] Meanwhile, Yavlinsky and his associates would suspect—not without reason—that the rightists were behind a negative PR campaign called "Yabloko without Yavlinsky" that had plastered Moscow with posters depicting the union of the apple (the image of Yabloko) and the Soviet hammer and sickle. Both parties only made things worse with their squabbling. Pollsters had explained that the ratings for Yabloko and SPS, two pro-Western, pro-European political forces, were correlated positively: when one rose, so did the other.

In short, whatever the leaders of SPS had in mind for this election, it all went wrong. The twenty per cent that Chubais had promised after their seemingly convincing victory in 1999 remained a dream. Under Nemtsov's leadership, the right did not earn any political capital. On the contrary: it lost support.

What had gone wrong?

In 1999, Nemtsov and his associates had an understandable slogan and programme. They were united—which voters saw as a plus—and they were eventually supported by Putin, who was already popular at the time. But things had changed. Sergei Kiriyenko had joined the government, becoming the presidential envoy to the Volga region; Chubais was head of the large, state-owned company RAO UES, so he was also in government; and Gaidar had retired from public politics but had the role of informal adviser to the government on reforms while still a deputy in the Duma. In the past, even human-rights activists and former Komsomol members coexisted in SPS. Now, some of the human-rights defenders had split off, and those who remained periodically chided Komsomol members for their friendship with the authorities. Nemtsov, even though supported by Chubais, lacked credibility within the party. He was considered a lightweight.

In 1999, it was clear what SPS was fighting for: a European path of development, political freedom and the reduced role of the state. But at that time, it was possible to live on slogans and promises: "Let us into the parliament and we'll make it happen." Now the winning idea was that the central government was the only force that could act as an agent of change.

The fate of the military reform that Nemtsov brought to Putin in autumn 2001 was a clear example of this. The reform was designed by experts at the Gaidar Institute. It envisaged the rapid transition to a contract army within three years, with compulsory conscription being reduced to six–eight months. Essentially, this short compulsory conscription was transformed into a school for training reservists. First, this solved the worst problem in the military—hazing—and second, it meant that a reservist could not be sent to war. Serving in the army was terrifying, and military service, as Yegor Gaidar put it, had become a kind of tax on the poor—young men who didn't go to college or couldn't bribe their way out of the draft at the military registration office.

Pollsters confirmed that society would welcome a shorter term of compulsory service. Putin agreed. He was persuaded, in part, by members of his cabinet that, if the two-year draft were not abolished, in a few years' time there would be no one to serve, because Russia was already heading into a sharp demographic decline.* He even wrote "I support it" on the resolution after a meeting with Nemtsov. The transition to a professional army and the reduction of conscript service also made it into the 2002 presidential address to the Federal Assembly. "Society needs reform, but the army needs it first of all," Putin said. However, the devil was in the details. The president was waiting for the results of an experiment being carried out near Pskov, where a division was being switched to contract service.

For Nemtsov, the popular military reform was almost the main electoral trump card. The right wing made a fully fledged bet on it, campaigning and holding rallies and concerts under the slogans "SPS for a Professional Army!" and "Military Reform Now!" In September 2002, Nemtsov flew to check on the experiment in Pskov. He tried to talk with the soldiers, but that didn't work. They didn't say a thing. To loosen them up, Nemtsov went over to the horizontal bar where he did twenty pull-ups, and the twenty-year-old conscripts did thirteen. When Nemtsov asked how much the contract soldiers were paid and saw the housing being built for them, he was beside himself. Their pay was so low that it wouldn't attract volunteers to the army nationwide, and the massive housing construction would have made the reform unsustainable for the budget. (Converting the existing barracks into dormitories for contract soldiers, which had been proposed by the Gaidar experts, was ten times cheaper.) Overall, the experiment discredited the reform. "You're doing it all wrong!" Nemtsov said angrily. "This is sabotage of military reform. I'm going to demand that [the head of the General Staff] resign."[14]

In the end, the military persuaded Putin not to rush the reform. "High-ranking officers are used to free labour," Yegor Gaidar explained in an interview with the author at the time. "Our colleagues at the

---

\* A demographic shortfall was predetermined by the sharp drop in the birth rate in the late 1980s and early 1990s. The transition to a contract army would have solved the problem of the inevitable drop in the number of young men of conscription age starting in the mid-1990s. Contract servicemen would serve in combat-ready units for three years or more.

Ministry of Defence say, 'If he's a contract soldier, you can't make him peel potatoes...'" Much of the recent discussions related to conscription was reminiscent of the situation in Russia just before serfdom was abolished. Back then, people would argue, "If I can't flog my serf, how am I going to run a farm?"[15]

Leonid Gozman, then adviser to Chubais and an SPS party official, was convinced that the open and forceful support for military reform by SPS set back the reform process.[16] The Kremlin did not want to give the liberals any electoral gifts. If the reform had been campaigned for quietly, behind the scenes, maybe it would have passed. In summer 2003, Putin put it this way: "I give credit to SPS, which is doing a lot [to develop military reform]," but the right wing was in the middle of an election campaign, so it wasn't worth listening to them.[17]

Soon the Gaidar–Nemtsov plan was buried once and for all, which had an adverse effect on the party. How can you go to the polls when you can't show the voter any concrete achievements? As pollsters in the Public Opinion Foundation noted, the accusation of empty rhetoric was one of the main reproaches against SPS. People said the rightists' words were "empty, unserious" and "just promises."[18]

## For or against Putin

The main difficulty, however, was something else. "The SPS leaders faced a systemic problem, which, in my opinion, they didn't really understand," recalled political strategist Yevgeny Malkin, whose team had worked with SPS since early 2002. "They lost their enemy."[19] In 1999, the adversaries of the SPS were the Communists, who were dragging Russia into the past. Four years later, there was no point in declaring war on the Communists—they had already lost. Meanwhile, from the first disagreements between Nemtsov and Putin to the 2003 election campaign, SPS was calling itself the constructive opposition to the government, supporting some decisions and opposing others. This electoral position was doomed to fail. Voters wanted a clear answer: was SPS for the government or against it? SPS could not answer this key question. There wasn't a trace of the team spirit that had so helped them in the

1999 elections. Part of the SPS parliamentary faction left to form a new party funded by Berezovsky, who had hardened his opposition (and had already left the country). The other part quickly realized that good relations with the Presidential Administration were more important, and they refocused on the Kremlin. Nemtsov criticized Putin many times, more harshly as time went on, but his criticism did not come across as the united political platform of the party. It was impossible to achieve unity. As the elections approached, the position of SPS became increasingly difficult. "We were totally broken down as we approached the 2003 campaign," Khakamada recalled. "I had already told Chubais bluntly: 'Stop playing around. We had hoped that Putin was a man who would move forward, but it's time to oppose him, with all due respect to the former Putin.' He looked at me very thoughtfully, but didn't reply."[20]

It was also difficult to go into opposition against Putin, because by this time he was already a very powerful opponent. With a trust rating of around seventy-five per cent, Putin dominated the country's political space unchallenged. Malkin described Putin as the saviour on whom the majority had pinned all their hopes (and television worked hard to reinforce this image). Any attack on him ricocheted back on his attackers. When the election campaign began, Nemtsov was persuaded that they shouldn't attack Putin. In April 2003, Nemtsov asked Alfred Kokh to head the campaign. Kokh agreed. "He showed Nemtsov a poll that said opposing Putin would deprive us of up to thirty per cent of the electorate," Chubais said. "It made a strong impression on Boris. Inwardly he was against it, but he still agreed—although with much more difficulty than in 1999."[21]

Surprisingly, however, supporting Putin did not draw more voters either. This was demonstrated back in April 2002, in local elections in Yekaterinburg, where SPS campaigned under the slogan "SPS is a Strategic Presidential Force." Nemtsov objected at the time but backed down so as not to start a fight. That campaign ended in total failure. "The result of the campaign was not the acquisition or even retention of votes, but a loss of votes," the party's political strategists wrote in their report. Pledges of allegiance to the government were not paying dividends. If Putin had backed SPS, as he did in December 1999, it probably would have helped. But now Putin was silent.

Malkin and his team suggested that the campaign be built in opposition to United Russia without attacking Putin personally. In about a decade, opposition figure Alexei Navalny would follow the same path, making the phrase "United Russia Is the Party of Crooks and Thieves" one of the most effective slogans in the history of Russian politics. Malkin had suggested a similar idea: "The Party of Bureaucrats and Russia's Enemies." "We are talking about a new class," he wrote in a memo to the SPS leadership, "which has privatized the state and is using it to redistribute the national wealth to its benefit." After reading these proposals carefully, Nemtsov still rejected them. The right refused to launch a massive attack on United Russia. "I knew the reason why," Malkin said, "It was Chubais. You can't attack the system when your party member is inside that system."[22] In addition, criticism of Putin's United Russia was dangerous, since it didn't please the Kremlin. Inside the Kremlin there was one simple rule: let the democratic forces fight among themselves all they want, but do not take votes away from the ruling party.

SPS could not resolve the question of whether to declare themselves the opposition or not. "Opposition to what?" Chubais asked his fellow party members at the congress in early September 2003. "Opposition to our reforms, opposition to our ideas, opposition to our colleagues now working in the government?"[23] Constrained by politics and without a fully articulated programme, the rightists were tempted to follow the same path that had already won them victory once before. As in 1999, they relied on soft-image advertising. The same concerts, rallies with the same rock bands, dancing and speeches from the stage, similar slogans, the same propaganda of liberal values, and the same message: the Union of Right Forces is the party of business and reform, the party of the middle class. The party went to the elections under the slogan "Choose Your Own Future."

But neither slogans nor concerts helped. Then to make things worse, they gave Chubais the third spot on its electoral list, replacing Kiriyenko, who had moved to the Kremlin. The top three on the campaign list were Nemtsov, Khakamada and Chubais. It was a very controversial and risky decision, since Chubais was strongly associated with the hardships of the 1990s. The meme "Blame it on Chubais" still had power. Chubais resisted at first, but Nemtsov and Kokh talked him into it: love is a step away from hate, they said, which means that the opposite is also true. (Later, Nemtsov admitted that this was a big mistake.) In the most famous campaign commercial, Nemtsov, Khakamada and Chubais are flying in a private jet with a huge "Russia" painted on it. They sit at a table in spacious white leather chairs, discussing something. "The idea was that we are honest, we are for the private economy, and that, if you do as we do, you too will have an aeroplane like this," Khakamada recalls. "But the reaction was, 'You sons of bitches! You've got your own plane!'"[24]

Oleg Sysuyev once came to an SPS campaign concert on Red Square in Moscow. As in 1999, Nemtsov and Khakamada were dancing on stage. "I immediately realized that they wouldn't get the votes," he said, "because Russia was living in a different reality. They didn't fully understand what Russia needed. I think that was their main problem."[25] Nevertheless, the right wing thought they had the victory in their pocket: by mid-October, SPS's approval rating was 5.3–5.5 per cent—enough to pass the legal threshold and get into parliament. "I pressured Surkov to give us more television airtime," said Kokh. "But Surkov said, 'What's your problem? Is money burning a hole in your pocket? Just sit tight. You won't get more than six per cent no matter what.'"[26]

## Attack on Khodorkovsky

On the afternoon of 2 July 2003, riot police wearing masks and carrying assault rifles burst into a ward in a military hospital near Moscow, where Khodorkovsky's partner Platon Lebedev was a patient. Two of them immediately blocked the balcony as a precaution. Lebedev was not even told which article of the criminal code he was being held under. "They will tell you there," the officer told him. "Why didn't we send Platon abroad? It's killing us," Leonid Nevzlin would later tell journalist Natalia Gevorkyan.[27] Nevzlin had information that Lebedev might be arrested. He needed to leave the country, but he arranged to go to the hospital for some tests and Nevzlin was persuaded it would be all right. The next day they came for Lebedev.

An hour and a half later, Lebedev was already being interrogated in the Investigative Committee. There, investigator Salavat Karimov—who would later be in charge of the Yukos investigation—told Lebedev that he was suspected of embezzling twenty per cent of Apatit, which had a monopoly on the production of raw materials for phosphate fertilizers. Yukos had indeed bought that stake in an investment competition in 1994. (Apatit's director—who was fired by Khodorkovsky after he bought the factory—would tell the court later that the investors had paid all the debts and that "the people at Apatit were happy and liked the way things were."[28]) Lebedev had nothing to do with the bidding to buy that stake, but by that time the prosecutor's office already had twelve volumes of evidence gathered over the many years of corporate competition between Apatit and another producer of phosphate fertilizers. Russian *Forbes* magazine would later write, "The case against Apatit was just lying on the surface [...]. When the law enforcement authorities started their investigation by looking at the compromising material in the press, they had enough to arrest Lebedev and Khodorkovsky and open cases against Yukos."[29]

On 3 July, after being held behind bars for twenty-four hours, Lebedev was charged. The next day, the US ambassador, Alexander Vershbow, hosted the annual 4 July reception. Of course, Khodorkovsky and his partners had been invited, and talk would surely have been of preparations for the merger of Yukos and Sibneft with one of the American oil giants.

"Do you realize what a scandal this will be? Think of the consequences of your actions," Lebedev told the investigators.

"You are trying to intimidate us," the investigators replied.

"Me?" Lebedev laughed glumly.

He still refused to answer Karimov's questions. It was impossible to make Lebedev testify in the case. He understood that this was war, that he was a hostage, and that it was certainly not Karimov who decided his fate.

Two weeks earlier, the arrest of Alexei Pichugin, the head of Yukos's economic security department, had not been seen by the company as something extraordinary. But the arrest of Lebedev was another matter. Although big business had got used to being attacked by law enforcement over the last two years, this was unprecedented. The fate of Gusinsky and Berezovsky showed that the Kremlin was ready to use the law enforcement system as a political weapon. In early 2002, the president of the Sibur petrochemical company, Yakov Goldovsky, was arrested in the waiting room of Gazprom CEO Alexei Miller. Control of Sibur soon reverted to its original owner, Gazprom. But Russian oligarchs—and Khodorkovsky was no exception—did not think it would happen to them. Recovering Gazprom's assets seemed a legitimate objective to everyone, and the Kremlin's fight with Gusinsky and Berezovsky was over control of the media. What did Khodorkovsky have to do with it? "We had nothing to do with the Kremlin," Leonid Nevzlin said. "We didn't owe them anything, and they didn't owe us anything."[30]

Khodorkovsky and his associates were not well acquainted with Putin and the St Petersburg team. "[For the new authorities,] we were outsiders in a number of ways: we were from Moscow, and we were from the 1990s," recalled Khodorkovsky's partner and former Yukos co-owner Vasily Shakhnovsky.[31] They were not close to the higher echelons of power, and they had few allies in the Kremlin and in the government. (Some sources attributed Khodorkovsky's interest in the Sibneft deal, in part, to his desire to use Abramovich's connections to establish closer ties with the Kremlin.) Few people were sympathetic to Yukos. The *siloviki* looked at Yukos with greed, rivals were jealous of the company's success, and many journalists at the time viewed Khodorkovsky as a cynical and tough oligarch.

Khodorkovsky had grand ambitions. He seemed to see himself as an influential figure in Russian politics. He planned to leave Yukos in 2008, which was also when Putin's second and legally last term in office would end. Managed democracy would reach an interim finish line. But what would be next? Khodorkovsky made no secret of the fact that he supported a parliamentary democracy. Wouldn't it make sense to shift the balance of power in Yeltsin's "presidential" constitution to the parliament? If Putin left office, there would be nothing untoward about this idea. Khodorkovsky insisted that he never plotted anything against Putin and considered his future solely "within the framework of the existing order." "This is how I saw my political career: I am very impressed by the work of the American congress as a [law-making] machine," he said. "My dream was to become chairman of a committee in the State Duma—say, the procedural committee—to fine-tune the mechanism. It's an interesting organizational challenge to turn the Duma into a congress."[32]

It is difficult to imagine that Khodorkovsky could be satisfied with this position, at least for long. "As early as 2004, a new government of the Russian Federation, controlled by and accountable to parliament, may be formed. Mikhail Khodorkovsky is considered a priority candidate to chair such a government formed in accordance with a new constitution," asserted a report published in late May by a certain think tank called the National Strategy Council on preparations for an "oligarchic coup in Russia."[33] The report was written by political strategist Stanislav Belkovsky, but the press at the time speculated that Igor Sechin and Rosneft head Sergei Bogdanchikov were behind it. Belkovsky cited Khodorkovsky as the "main ideologue" of the planned coup.

The rumours and suspicions on which Belkovsky's report was based came about in part because the four largest oil companies at the time—Yukos, Sibneft, Lukoil and TNK—had formed a powerful lobby in parliament. Yukos was clearly the front-runner. "The initiative came from us," Shakhnovsky confirmed.[34] The lobbyists were effective. In spring 2003, economic ministers German Gref and Alexei Kudrin complained to Putin that oil companies were thwarting their plans to change the extraction tax. Putin even voiced his discontent publicly in June. That spring, the oil lobby had also blocked an amendment that would have allowed the government to change the rate of export duties on fuel and lubricants. The amendment would have raised it during the sowing and harvesting season and lowered it off-season—and cut the export profit of oil companies. The Kremlin knew that Yukos was behind it. They even cited the payoffs. Lobbyists were allegedly paying deputies $15,000 a vote. At meetings in the Kremlin officials wailed, "What if the deputies were paid $150,000 each? They could buy a majority in the Duma! They could change the constitution!"[35]

This was a wild exaggeration. Oil companies only lobbied for their sectoral interests. But even if they did lobby for broader change, all the oil companies put together would not have been able to change the constitution; there wasn't any political basis to do so. Khodorkovsky took an interest in the elections and Yukos shareholders actively financed political parties (Yabloko in its entirety, SPS in part, United Russia like everyone else, and even the Communist Party*) as well as specific candidates in the oil regions. But all this was done in coordination with the Kremlin. In spring, during a face-to-face meeting, Putin asked Khodorkovsky to stop funding the Communists. "I said: 'I won't fund them,'" Khodorkovsky said. "'But it's one thing for me and another for the shareholders.' It didn't occur to me that they were giving money to the Communists, too. But he thought I was deceiving him.'"[36]

## Khodorkovsky's choice: compromise or jail

Belkovsky's paper seemed more like a public denunciation than a report. Formally, Khodorkovsky would be jailed for not paying taxes, but it is the version outlined in the report—Khodorkovsky as a conspirator, punished for attempting to seize power—that the Kremlin would put forward. In reality, however, the Belkovsky report served only as a cover-up for the attack on Yukos. The attack on the company began before the report was published and before the battles in the Duma. It began shortly after the meeting when Putin unexpectedly rebuked Khodorkovsky.

By the end of March, the Apatit case appeared to be back on the desk of the Prosecutor General, although just before that, Prosecutor General Ustinov had submitted a report to Putin that the prosecutor's office had not found fault with Apatit's privatization.[37] It was around this time that a group of FSB officers was formed to deal specifically with Yukos[38] and the tone of discussions in the Kremlin about Khodorkovsky changed. Until recently, Vladislav Surkov, who had worked for Khodorkovsky throughout the first half of the 1990s, had been speaking with him about returning to work at Yukos. Now at private Kremlin meetings Surkov was calling Yukos shareholders "kikes" and consistently demonstrating intense dislike of them.[39] (Anti-Semitism among the St Petersburg Chekists was commonplace, and it is likely that Surkov, an experienced

---

\* One of the Yukos stockholders, Sergei Muravlenko, who was a hereditary oilman and multimillionaire, ran for the Duma on the Communist Party ticket.

apparatchik, understood which way the wind was blowing and was imitating the words and intonations he had heard in conversations with more influential figures.)

At that February meeting with business leaders, the St Petersburg Chekists secured Putin's public support. They were victorious and began to fight even harder for Yukos assets. And when Putin personally approved the deal between Khodorkovsky and Abramovich in April and the subsequent sale of a stake in the combined company to American oil producers, he probably already knew that it would not happen. (Indirectly, this hypothesis is supported by the fact that Putin was unwilling in principle to allow Western shareholders into the Russian oil sector. He had approved the TNK–BP deal only because British Prime Minister Tony Blair had asked him to, and at the time Putin considered that relationship important.)

At Yukos they had to know that war had been declared against them, but even after Lebedev's arrest, they didn't imagine that this would be a battle to the death. There had been attacks on big business in the past. In the summer of 2000, for example, tax officials opened a criminal case against Vagit Alekperov, the head of Lukoil, the largest oil company at the time. He was accused of tax fraud and "false exports of oil products" worth half a billion dollars.* One of Alekperov's acquaintances believed that this was the response of the security forces and businesses associated with them to Alekperov's demand to be reimbursed the tens of millions of dollars he'd allegedly provided to finance the presidential elections. Alekperov went to the president. The criminal case was closed, but, according to the same acquaintance, Alekperov had to accept the loss of a large sum of money.

Fifteen years later, journalist Roman Shleinov studied documents from the archives of the Panamanian Mossack Fonseca law firm that provided offshore financial services and suggested in *Novaya gazeta* that Lukoil had managed to hold its position only because Alekperov hired someone who knew Putin well from his work in the KGB to head one of the offshore companies.[40]

---

\* False export is considered a form of tax evasion, as it allows the exporter to claim back the paid VAT tax without exporting the product.

At first it seemed that Yukos had been caught in a similar situation, and that this was another raid for personal gain concealed behind a scare story about Khodorkovsky's political ambitions. After arresting Lebedev, investigators summoned Khodorkovsky and Nevzlin, but both were released after questioning. Four weeks later, Nevzlin would leave—for ever, as it turned out—after Pichugin's lawyers had told him that their client had been injected with truth serum and forced to testify that Nevzlin had instructed him to kill people.* But until early to mid-September, Shakhnovsky said, there was a feeling that it was just a question of the price. "We'll make a deal and Platon will be released."[41] Khodorkovsky received an offer to pay an additional $280 million for the privatization of Apatit, an amount that appeared in the case file. "Admit it, pay it into the budget, and we'll turn a blind eye," Khodorkovsky said he was told. "I said, 'I don't mind paying, but who will say that's the end of it? I know only one person who can do that.' 'No,' they said, 'this is from Sechin.' By then, I had a good sense of Sechin. Tomorrow $300 million, then $5 billion, then there would be nothing left of me."[42] Khodorkovsky did not pay.

Intermediaries also came to Platon Lebedev in prison and told him, "Let's have civilized negotiations." "Only when I'm released," Lebedev replied. A meeting with Putin might have solved the crisis. According to Shakhnovsky, when he met the economy minister, German Gref, in a café after Lebedev's arrest, Gref, wanting to help, scribbled on a piece of paper: "Don't criticize Putin, go after [Prosecutor General] Ustinov," implying that Putin could still be counted on and shouldn't be alienated.[43] Khodorkovsky initially refused to ask for an audience with Putin, saying, "If the boss wants to see me, he can summon me." After a while, however, he was persuaded. He contacted Putin's secretariat and asked for a meeting, but it never took place.

In the autumn, compromising materials began to appear on Putin's desk. Khodorkovsky allegedly spoke at the same rally as Zyuganov.

---

\* In 2008, Pichugin testified in court that he was interrogated for six hours on 14 July 2003, and that before the interrogation he drank coffee, passed out and remembered nothing except that the questions "concerned Khodorkovsky, Kasyanov and the financial relations between them and Yukos."

There was a list of almost a hundred candidates he had supposedly sponsored in the election (the list was taken from Surkov's desk and was actually a list of candidates supported by various major companies, not just Yukos). In another report, Khodorkovsky was said to have gone to America to discuss with Vice-President Dick Cheney the possibility of turning Russia into a parliamentary republic that would give up its nuclear weapons.[44] Meanwhile, prosecutors were filing more and more criminal cases and new charges.

"There was a choice," Nevzlin recalled, "Either MBK [Khodorkovsky] would compromise or MBK would go to jail. The way he was behaving, it would be impossible to come to an agreement."[45] Khodorkovsky dug his heels in. He accepted the challenge. About a month before the climax, when passions were already at boiling point and Khodorkovsky's arrest was imminent, Mikhail Fridman happened to run into him in a Moscow restaurant. "I urged him to ease up, because I clearly understood that it could lead to very negative consequences," Fridman recalled. "I'm ready to go to jail," Khodorkovsky replied with a smile.[46] In early October, searches were already underway in the homes of Yukos co-owners, and journalists wondered which officials would dare to stand next to Khodorkovsky in front of TV cameras. Khodorkovsky was in Moscow at a major economic forum when investigators nearly stormed the Korallovo Lyceum for children from poor families, which was founded by Khodorkovsky and under the patronage of his parents. He was handed a note, silently left the forum and drove there. "I don't know what the investigation is trying to achieve by its actions," Khodorkovsky said. "But I state clearly that I will not become a political emigrant. If the goal is to put me in jail—well, with our laws as they are, it can't be ruled out."[47] Meanwhile, new wiretaps were laid on Putin's desk—probably showing that Khodorkovsky was speaking badly about him personally.

It is likely, however, that Putin did not have a clear plan for Khodorkovsky before he went on a tour of the country in October. Khodorkovsky flew from city to city, giving lectures, speaking to students, giving interviews to the local press—as if he weren't the target of the entire state machine. It was a direct challenge. From the Kremlin, it appeared that Khodorkovsky was campaigning. "I think it was then that the decision was finally made," said Shakhnovsky. Khodorkovsky became Putin's worst political enemy, and the raid became an operation to destroy Yukos.

What was driving Khodorkovsky then? On the one hand, he was prepared to be arrested, but he couldn't have imagined he'd be jailed for ten years. He couldn't have imagined that Yukos could be destroyed as a company. In those autumn days of 2003, it was hard to imagine the political show trial that the Yukos affair was about to become or the bankruptcy of a major oil company. Khodorkovsky had enemies and competitors, but he also had powerful allies—in the Kremlin, in the government, in business, in the West. He was counting on the support of President Bush. On the other hand, he made a conscious choice and accepted the challenge. He was completely unflappable. Calmly, confidently, with the same smile and, as usual, without a tie, wearing a jacket over a turtleneck, he said in one of his last interviews a few days before his arrest: "I don't care about money at all. I've started over many times, so that part doesn't bother me. If I thought it was impossible to build a normal democratic society in our country, I would have left long ago. But I believe it's possible. Simply, it has to start with someone who isn't afraid. I'm not afraid."[48]

Khodorkovsky was arrested in the early hours of Saturday, 25 October, when his plane, bound for Irkutsk from Nizhny Novgorod, stopped for refuelling in Novosibirsk.

## The collapse of SPS

On the morning of Saturday, 25 October, Anatoly Chubais arrived at the Hotel Baltschug in Moscow for a meeting of Russian and American businessmen. The meeting morphed into a council of the oligarchs, many of whom learnt in the hotel what happened to Khodorkovsky that morning. Everyone was shocked. While the discussion was going on, Chubais sat down to write a text. The statement from big business was harsh: "It's the businessmen who publicly disclosed their companies' finances and paid taxes transparently who will find themselves under the millstone [of the law-enforcement agencies]. [...] The authorities' gross mistakes have set the country back several years and undermined the credibility of their statements that the results of privatization would be not revised [...]. Only President Putin's clear and unequivocal position can reverse the situation." Some hesitated. "What if he is released tonight or tomorrow morning and we see him here?" Vladimir Potanin asked. Dmitry Zimin, owner of the telecommunications company VimpelCom, answered with another question: "What if they don't?"[49] In the end, everyone, including Potanin, signed. Chubais was assigned to read it. "I said, 'Are you guys sure it should be me, Putin's only appointee, who reads the document?'" Chubais recalled. "They told me, 'You'll do it better than anyone, and, besides, we respect you and are asking you to do this.' So I went to read it [in front of the cameras]."[50]

The oligarchs gathered at the Baltschug didn't yet know that Alexander Voloshin, the head of Presidential Administration, who had promised Khodorkovsky support and had learnt of his arrest on the news, had already resigned. In four days, Putin would accept his resignation. The fight between Sechin's group and Voloshin's group— between the St Petersburg Chekists and the Yeltsin family old guard— was over. Voloshin had lost, and, unlike the business leaders, he did not need to ask Putin any questions to clarify his situation. Nemtsov and Voloshin belonged to different camps, but now they found themselves on the same side of the barricades. "Voloshin's departure would mean a political U-turn towards the omnipotence of the security services," Nemtsov said.[51] Nemtsov immediately vouched for Khodorkovsky. He said Khodorkovsky should be released from prison on his own recognizance, which would require him to appear when summoned for questioning. This was, of course, ignored by the court and the prosecutor's office. At a meeting with ministers on Monday, Putin told Chubais and everyone else: "There will be no meetings, no negotiations about the law enforcement agencies [...]. I would ask you to stop all speculation and hysteria in this matter, and I ask the cabinet not to get involved in this discussion."[52]

With the exception of the war in Chechnya, this was the first time in almost three years of his presidency that Putin took a clear stance on a major political issue. There was more at stake than the fate of Khodorkovsky or Yukos. Putin would assert that Yukos was an isolated case, that there would be no revision of the privatization results.

Technically he was correct, but in reality the relationship between the state and private business had already been revised. The rules of the game had changed. "During the Yeltsin era, the bureaucracy was not involved in the redistribution of property. It distributed 'nobody's property', i.e. state property, in return for bribes—this is true, and everyone knows it," exiled Berezovsky had said after Lebedev was arrested. "But now the bureaucrats are convinced that private property is a long-term thing, so they have decided to take part in the redistribution process personally."[53]

The nature of corruption had changed. Previously, big businessmen used to bribe officials to make decisions in their favour. Now the officials themselves had gone into business and were resorting to state violence to do it.

By the time Khodorkovsky was arrested, the judiciary had long been overhauled: the reform of the courts took place in 2001. In addition to the inclusion of *habeas corpus* and wide introduction of jury trials, it changed the principles of the appointment of the judges. The president appointed—and even more importantly—reappointed chief justices, who exerted enormous leverage over judges. The judges also lost their immunity, to a large extent. At that time, these changes were in accordance with the idea of the strong state and were justified as necessary to constrain a corrupt judiciary. In reality, the Russian court system was embedded by 2003 in the Kremlin's "power vertical." And approval of judicial candidates by the security services had become customary.

During next months, the trials of Yukos owners and managers in dozens of criminal cases would show that the Russian courts had morphed into a ruthless punitive institution on the Kremlin's payroll. Informally, it would quickly be coined "Basmanny justice", in reference to the Basmanny District Court in Moscow, where trials of businesspeople, political activists, dissidents, suspected spies and anyone not fully supporting the government invariably end with a conviction and long jail term. It was in this court that the prosecutors cited the new *habeas corpus* law and would ask for arrest warrants in the Yukos case. Vladimir Pereverzin, one of the many prosecuted middle-ranked managers of Yukos, recalls how it worked in his memoir, *The Hostage*. When the forty-eight hours of his non-judicial detention were about to expire, he overheard a conversation between two investigators: "'We just have to warn the Fairy,' one said to the other. 'Yeah, I already let her know. It's all good,' the other replied. Later I found out that this is what they affectionately called the Basmanny Court chief justice."[54] Pereverzin would refuse to testify against Khodorkovsky and Lebedev or plead guilty. He would be sentenced to eleven years of jail.

In October 2003, the arrest of the country's richest and most successful businessman was a game-changer that altered the structure and the goals of the Russian government. The concept of managed democracy had been defeated, and with it the idea that the Russian political system was still moving, even if in a roundabout way, towards rapprochement with the developed world. "Khodorkovsky's arrest in 2003 was the line that separated Yeltsin-era Russia from Putin-era Russia," Natalia Gevorkyan wrote in her book.[55]

Khodorkovsky's arrest changed the course of the presidential election campaign. With just a month and a half before the election, the central issues were 1990s privatization and the fate of oligarchs. The question was posed in its most primitive form. Is it fair that they are so rich? Should they be punished? In campaign debates, Nemtsov defended Khodorkovsky. He said that whether or not Khodorkovsky was a thief should be decided by an open court: "We've got 'Basmanny justice' everywhere you look in Russia. We don't have an independent judiciary [...]. Why did they arrest Khodorkovsky—isn't it obvious?" he continued. "Because he is not subservient to the authorities. That's all there is to it."[56]

Opponents easily turned his talking points against him. Of course, they said, SPS is the party of big capital, Nemtsov, Khakamada and Chubais are just protecting their masters. Nemtsov and especially Chubais were hit by a wave of populism. "Don't make businessmen the enemies of the people. Let them pay salaries and create jobs," Nemtsov countered. He was answered: "You are not only the authors of the word 'oligarch'. You are the oligarchs' advocates."[57] For five years, Nemtsov had been fighting "gangster capitalism", and now he was accused of having created it.

"We should have been able to break the five-per-cent barrier," Kokh said, but after Khodorkovsky's arrest, censorship on the central TV channels interfered. "After Putin's 'stop the hysteria' speech, we were virtually kept off television for a month and a half."[58] On the night before the election, the popular television show *What? Where? When?* featuring Chubais and Khakamada was taken off-air, and a broadcast of a concert by the hit band Mashina Vremeni had cut from the performance the famous song 'New Turn', when the SPS leaders had come on stage with the musicians.

This censorship in the final weeks of the campaign may have influenced the vote, but in reality SPS had fallen victim to the shifting political agenda. "The essence of our positioning in this election was that we represented business, and business was the growing class that could lead Russia forward," Chubais explained. "When Khodorkovsky was arrested, it all came together: the oligarchs sponsor the SPS, SPS supports the oligarchs, and here they are on their idiotic plane to the West together [in the now-notorious campaign ad]. It was as if an atomic bomb had gone off."[59] The Yukos affair was still in its infancy, but it had already hit the liberals.

In the Kremlin, Vladislav Surkov was now in charge of elections. By the end of the election campaign period, he had already purged all Yukos-linked candidates from the United Russia list, and his concern was no longer whether or not SPS would make it into the Duma. He was worried instead about the sudden rise of the nationalist Motherland party, which he had just created.

Motherland had emerged almost by accident three months before the election. The nationalist politician Dmitry Rogozin, who was head of the parliamentary Foreign Affairs Committee, had grand ambitions. Since he was in Putin's good graces, he even hoped to become the leader of United Russia. In fact, at one of their meetings in early 2003, he said this directly to Putin. Putin replied, "We'll see," but he wouldn't give United Russia to Rogozin. At the very last moment, Surkov sent Rogozin to the aid of prominent leftist politician Sergei Glazyev.

The hastily cobbled-together campaign project was called Motherland. The Kremlin needed it to take votes away from the Communists. But Surkov did not expect that the project would be so successful. The charismatic populist Rogozin, skilfully playing on both xenophobia and envy of the rich, quickly popularized the new party.

The arrest of Khodorkovsky came in handy and served as a perfect illustration of the slogan—"Let's Return the Country's Wealth to the People"—that used by Motherland as its campaign motto.

At the height of the campaign, Rogozin seemed to be turbocharged. He applauded the arrest of Khodorkovsky and then demanded that Chubais be jailed. He didn't actually care at all about Chubais—he was just pandering to the voters. "The authorities are sly," Nemtsov said on this occasion. "They are deliberately stirring up class hatred and deliberately leading society towards division."[60] Towards the end of the campaign, liberals began to sound the alarm, urging their potential supporters to come to the polls if only to prevent a resurgence of nationalists. "Today the country is threatened by the Motherland party," Chubais said at the final press conference before the election, "There is no greater threat."[61] That didn't help either. Later, in the party's analysis of the reasons for the SPS defeat, it was noted: "What the Motherland bloc gained by fighting the oligarchs, SPS lost, especially in the final stage."

On election day, Nemtsov, Khakamada and Chubais still hoped to win. Khakamada later said that after the last debate Chubais went to the Kremlin and was told, "You supported Khodorkovsky, now reap what you sowed. You know the country you live in, you know that oligarchs are disliked, so you're going to get somewhere between 4.7 and 6 per cent of the vote. Tough it out however you can."[62] But the information board at the headquarters, on which the results of the local vote were to be posted, remained empty. The preliminary results announced at nine o'clock that evening left little hope. SPS had fallen more than one per cent short of the required five per cent. Towards one o'clock in the morning, as the votes were counted, all hope died. The verdict was in. Yabloko reached the finish line with a similar result. The democrats and liberals were out of the State Duma.

The defeat was an enormous blow to Nemtsov. He tried not to show it, and at 9 p.m. he came out to the meet the press along with Chubais and Khakamada. But he could not bring himself to go to the central television studios with them to discuss election results all night. He had not yet had that kind of experience in public politics. He had been through a lot—he'd been rejected as Yeltsin's successor; he'd left the cabinet without a job to go to—but he had never lost an election.

And now he'd lost twice—both as Boris Nemtsov and as leader of the liberal party. "I didn't cry," he wrote in his book *Confessions of a Rebel*, "but I drank. I drank a lot. I drank a lot more than I should have at my age. [...] It was galling, and I tried to drown my misery in vodka—the normal Russian way of self-medication. I drank at six in the morning, seven in the morning, and eight in the morning. Finally, around ten o'clock, I calmed down."[63]

His letter of resignation from the party leadership, written in advance in case of defeat, was in the party safe, but it was a mere formality. Without seats in the parliament, the Union of Right Forces wasn't a party anymore. This was the end of the line. That night Nemtsov had not yet foreseen all the consequences, but he could not help feeling that this was the kind of defeat that would make it difficult, if not impossible, to return to public politics.

## Putin's Russia

The weather was terrible. A blizzard had dropped an impenetrable wall of snow. The journey from Munich to Lech, an upscale ski resort in the Austrian Alps, took eight hours instead of the usual two and a half. It was early January 2004. Prime Minister Mikhail Kasyanov was spending the New Year holidays in Lech, skiing at the invitation of Austrian Chancellor Wolfgang Schüssel, and Nemtsov and Irina Korolyova (who was pregnant with their daughter Sonya) had come for just a day and a half. The drive took so long that Kasyanov didn't wait for them and went to bed. They would not talk until the next day.

Kasyanov explained later that he intended to resign after the presidential election scheduled for March 2004, but he probably realized that, if re-elected, Vladimir Putin would replace him. First of all, Putin had inherited Prime Minister Kasyanov from Yeltsin and his entourage. Second, the relationship between the two was becoming increasingly strained, and Putin had rejected Kasyanov's initiatives more than once. And finally, Kasyanov had condemned the arrest of Khodorkovsky on several occasions. Nemtsov saw all this, too. He had already resigned as SPS leader and was coming to Lech to persuade Kasyanov to lead the party. "He thought it would breathe new life into the party and neutralize the changing political situation," Kasyanov recalls. "Of course, we also discussed the course of the campaign."[64] They were walking and talking, followed by two security officers as required for the head of the cabinet.

Kasyanov turned Nemtsov down. What was the point of leading a party that had just been defeated in an election? He went back to Moscow, and a month later, on 18 February, Gazprom cut off gas supplies to Belarus. In response to the Belarusian refusal to create a joint state, Moscow hiked up the price of gas for Minsk. Lukashenko didn't sign a new contract, so Putin ordered Alexei Miller to turn the valve off. For the first time, Gazprom was cutting off gas to its neighbours. The next day, at a meeting in the Kremlin, Kasyanov objected: you can't cut off gas to the Belarusians; it's twenty-five degrees below zero. A highly irritated Putin quickly curtailed the meeting and left. He summoned the premier a few days later, on 24 February, and summarily dismissed him. It turned out that Putin suspected Kasyanov of conspiracy—arranging all of Putin's rivals in the presidential election to withdraw, so that the election would be disrupted and then Prime Minister Kasyanov would become acting president. Evidence included printouts of conversations between Kasyanov and Nemtsov in Lech. Nemtsov and Kasyanov discussed the election but never discussed the plan; transcripts of their conversations had been falsified.* On his way out of Putin's office after his resignation, Kasyanov bumped into Igor Sechin. "Thank you for teaching us how to run the country," Sechin told him. "Now we think we can do it ourselves. Don't think badly of us."[65]

The arrest of Russia's richest businessman only strengthened Putin's standing in society. He approached his second presidential term with an approval rating of eighty-six per cent and control over virtually the entire political sphere. He unified the fractured Russian bureaucracy

---

\* Kasyanov recounts this in his memoirs. Other sources also corroborate his account. Indirectly confirming Putin's belief in the conspiracy is the fact that in mid-February, Sergei Mironov, the speaker of the Federation Council who had been completely loyal to Putin since they worked together in St Petersburg, ran as a presidential candidate. He campaigned by calling everyone to vote for Putin.

under a single party brand; his administration controlled television, both houses of parliament and the judiciary. Governors were dependent on the Kremlin, and big business, terrified by the Yukos affair, toed the party line. In a year, Khodorkovsky and Lebedev would be sentenced to eight years, retrospectively accused of tax evasion by using preferential banking laws in other jurisdictions, and then Yukos itself would be broken up and nationalized.

The second Chechen war was officially brought to a victorious end. And then, on 1 September 2004, the worst terrorist attack in Russian history took place. A group of terrorists from Chechnya took more than a thousand hostages in a school in the North Ossetian town of Beslan: schoolchildren of all ages who had come with their parents to see the school-year opening ceremony. This time the terrorists were much harsher than they had been two years before in Moscow. They killed some of the male hostages and didn't give the rest food or water. The dénouement was even more tragic and bloody than in Moscow: 333 people, most of them children, were killed in the fire storm.

As in the aftermath of the Dubrovka tragedy, not a single official was punished, and the toothless parliamentary enquiry into the circumstances of what had happened was quietly approved by the upper house of parliament. This was intentionally done right before the New Year's holidays, so that the protests of the victims' relatives would go unnoticed. And, just as after Nord-Ost, a dramatic epilogue followed: in response to the attack, Putin cancelled gubernatorial elections. He had planned this for a long time and used the Beslan disaster as a pretext. With that, Russia was transformed from a federation to a unitary state, and Putin's system of one-man rule was complete.

# PART 5

# CHAPTER 22

## 2004
## Life on the Sidelines

### A solitary man

Vladimir Potanin and Mikhail Prokhorov, oligarchs and business partners, had bought the Luzhki resort near Moscow back in 1996. They spent a lot of time there, and over the years they had made it as comfortable as possible. Potanin loved peace and comfort. Prokhorov could not imagine life without sports, and so Luzhki was fitted with a basketball court, a football pitch, tennis courts, a swimming pool and a gym. Nearby was a ski slope, and, a stone's throw away, the Istra reservoir with water bikes and surfing. On weekends, guests at Luzhki often watched billionaire Prokhorov throw a ball through a hoop, while billionaire Potanin played dominoes or backgammon on a nearby bench.

Nemtsov moved into Luzhki with his former secretary, Irina Korolyova, and newborn Sonya in the summer of 2004. Potanin leased them—at a fraction of the official price, since Nemtsov was a friend—a small flat in one of the buildings: two rooms totalling about fifty square metres and a tiny cubbyhole of a kitchen. Nemtsov and his new family would live in that flat for eleven years. Nemtsov loved the place so much that he even wanted to build a house there and settle permanently. But fate would have it differently.

When he moved to Luzhki, Nemtsov began to exercise regularly, since all the facilities he needed were right at hand. Not a day went by without exercising. He even began to carry scales around with him. In general, he thought politics was "man's work" that couldn't be done without good health. He used to say: "A healthy politician means healthy thoughts and courageous deeds."[1] He and Prokhorov got to be friends through sports. "He liked windsurfing," Prokhorov recalls. "I liked water-biking more, but the two went together. Often in the evening or on weekends we would go to the Istra reservoir together, and gradually, over time, we became friends and started going out [on the sea] together."[2]

In October 2004, Nemtsov turned forty-five. He was no longer a young man who didn't have to think about the future. Nemtsov liked to flirt and have affairs; as Prokhorov said, "Nemtsov and I had another passion in common—girls."[3] But the image of him as an irrepressible, unbridled rabble-rouser incapable of serious relations was not true. He lived with two women, Raisa and Irina, for many years. "I left my first wife because I was tired of cheating on her. I had children with television journalist Katya [Yekaterina] Odintsova. Raisa found out about it. I could have made up a story, come up with something, but what was the point?" Nemtsov writes in *Confessions of a Rebel*. "To cut a long story short, the family fell apart."[4] By the summer of 2004, Nemtsov already had four children: Zhanna, who was almost an adult; eleven-year-old Anton, his first child with Odintsova, born in Nizhny Novgorod; Dina, born to Odintsova in 2002; and Sonya, born in May 2004.

Now that he was not serving in the parliament, Nemtsov found himself on his own. He had lost his illusions long ago and had no need to try to put himself in the place of others and compromise his principles. Although he was not yet an outcast, he was in something of a vacuum—without a cause, without a party, without like-minded people, without a team. His associates had fled the sinking ship: some to United Russia, some to the bureaucracy, some to business. In the past, Nemtsov would get in his car with his phone in his hand and talk the whole trip. Now the phone was silent, and the driver bought newspapers so that Nemtsov would have something to read on the drive. How could he build the next phase of his career? And what would a political career even be in these new conditions? How could he move forward alone, without status, without associates? What should he do?

In early 2004, Committee-2008 was founded. It was a kind of semi-dissident club that brought together a couple of dozen democratic politicians and journalists who had held prominent positions in the past but been relegated to the sidelines over the past two years. The idea originated in a conversation between Nemtsov and the journalist and writer Viktor Shenderovich, who had once hosted the programme *Puppets* on NTV. The popular satirical show inspired by *Les Guignols de l'info* and *Spitting Image*, with life-size latex caricatures of Russian politicians and public features had been axed and Shenderovich forced out. As journalist Alexander Ryklin put it, Committee-2008 appeared because Nemtsov was out of a job, but everyone knew him, and it was natural and logical to unite around him.[5]

The committee got its name because its goal was to elect a new president in 2008—not a presidential heir like Putin was in 2000, and not Putin if he suddenly decided to stay on for a third term. "The main result of the past four years has been the creation and strengthening of President Vladimir Putin's regime of personal power," the founding declaration of Committee-2008 argued.[6] Nemtsov formulated his main goal as creating "Russia after Putin as a democratic country."[7] But Nemtsov did not want to head the committee; he wanted the leader to be someone who had not been compromised by recent defeats. He and Shenderovich came up with the idea of asking world chess champion Garry Kasparov. He had a great reputation and was known all over the world. Kasparov was delighted. This great chess player, who inspired even people far removed from chess to root for him passionately during perestroika, had been politically active in the early 1990s. And now he was back in politics. With Committee-2008, Nemtsov had found at least something to do, but he had no illusions. Hard times had come, and they had to play a long game, to wait it out. "There was only one politician left in the country," he said. "The liberal movement had entered its dissident phase. We just had to get through it."[8]

## Who can go into politics?

Besides the question of his political career, Nemtsov had another problem: how could he support a family and all his children? Nemtsov started playing the stock market—in a few years, the Gazprom shares he bought would bring a solid income—but in any case, he needed a job with a good, stable income. He had friends and acquaintances in big business, but who would want to associate with a well-known oppositionist who was actively criticizing Vladimir Putin—now even more harshly than before?

"I was one of his closest friends at the time," recalled oligarch Mikhail Fridman. This was true: Fridman and Nemtsov met frequently, spent time together, holidayed, even went to lose weight together in European clinics. But from 2004 onward, Fridman began to distance himself from Nemtsov. He was well aware of the political situation: running a big business ruled out political ambition and even an articulated political position—anything but support for the government. "I told him frankly," Fridman recalled, "Boris, I know you. You won't be able to keep quiet. You are going to express your point of view. It will definitely be detrimental to my work. I can't afford that. And I must say that he reacted well, with integrity. There was not even a glimmer of resentment."[9]

It was true. Nemtsov did not hold a grudge against Fridman and still considered him a friend. Later, when times became very rough and their relationship was almost non-existent, Nemtsov would tell Irina, "If anything happens, call Fridman, he'll help." Nemtsov understood how the system worked. The informal restrictions imposed by the Kremlin meant that every player visible in society—be it a person, a company or an institution—had to exist and act within its public function without any deviation. All public activity had to be predictable—in other words, under control. A doctor should treat patients, a teacher should teach, an actor should perform, a businessman should do business, and so on. Only a politician could be in politics. Nemtsov wrote in his memoirs that Fridman couldn't do what he could do. Nemtsov could make harsh criticism. "But if, for example, Fridman or Potanin came out and said in a quiet voice, 'In my opinion, it's not quite right to express such obvious support for one of the candidates,' he'd face a prison sentence. Let me explain the thought process. [They think:] Nemtsov has not stolen anything, he doesn't have billions, we have not given him anything, he does not owe us anything. He makes a racket, but that's what his job is. What are you going to do about it? But businessmen—they've all embezzled something, so they ought to sit tight."[10]

Igor Linshits, a young businessman, was not as well versed in all these subtleties. He was head of the Neftyanoi concern, which, at the time he met Nemtsov, included a bank, an investment business in energy, petrochemicals and development, and even a pasta factory. Linshits had been friendly with Nemtsov since they met in 2001 through Fridman. He didn't have a subtle grasp of politics, but he could see that big business needed to be close to power in one way or another. Those were the rules. Linshits aspired to become a member of the club of big businessmen: he got to know officials, took part in political projects such as financing the TV-6 channel, where oligarchs unsuccessfully tried to re-assemble the NTV team that had been fired. He even wanted to be elected to the Duma as a delegate from the Communist Party. The press wrote at the time that one of the Communist Party sponsors owed Neftyanoi a large sum of money, and, in return for the payment, Linshits was offered a place on the party electoral list. However, the Communists did not get as many seats in the Duma as they had hoped—in the 2003 elections the Kremlin finally crushed the Communist Party—and Linshits did not get his parliamentary seat. On the other hand, by that time he was already on good terms with both Prime Minister Kasyanov and Nemtsov.

Khodorkovsky was jailed and Nemtsov was ousted from the parliament exactly at the time when the Russian economy was experiencing an unprecedented upturn. The price of oil rose, the economy grew by a record 7.4 per cent in 2003, and business entered a golden age. Millionaires were becoming multimillionaires and multimillionaires were becoming billionaires. While the middle class was buying cars and getting used to spending holidays abroad, the truly rich were buying property in Antibes and Forte dei Marmi and partying in Courchevel at Christmas. Linshits was one of them. By early 2004, he already had holdings in several major growth companies, including Mosinzhstroi, a major player in Moscow's construction market, and the newly emerged internet site Mail.ru.

Linshits didn't think he was taking a serious risk by hiring Nemtsov. In fact, he didn't give it much thought. He wanted to help his friend, and he was still drawn to politics. At Neftyanoi, Nemtsov was given the position of chairman of the board of directors. With responsibilities for public relations and government relations, he began to help Linshits develop the construction side of the business by introducing him to Moscow officials. Nemtsov became something of a developer. With his active involvement, Neftyanoi began building a huge business centre in Moscow.

Nemtsov once again had an office, a computer, a place for his secretary to sit and a space to hold meetings. Besides—and this was important—Linshits was paying him a good salary. There was nothing for him in politics: liberal ideas were unpopular, the political space was empty, gubernatorial elections were cancelled, and Putin's rating was sky-high. What option did he have but to make the most of his time? "My priorities have changed," Nemtsov said. "I have decided that in the next two years I will make money and acquire skills in applied economics."[11]

# CHAPTER 23

## 2004
## The Orange Revolution

### Ukraine at the crossroads

Ukrainian President Leonid Kuchma's reputation was ruined by what Ukrainians called the "cassette scandal." Journalist Georgy Gongadze, founder of the independent *Ukrainska pravda* newspaper, was kidnapped and murdered in September 2000. Two and a half months later, the leader of the Ukrainian Socialists, Oleksandr Moroz, stood at the speaker's rostrum in the Ukrainian parliament, the Verkhovna Rada, and played conversations recorded in the president's office in which Kuchma said the unruly journalist should be dealt with.

The conversations, recorded by Kuchma's former bodyguard Mykola Melnychenko (who later fled to America), were a bombshell. The voices of the president and his associates could not be misunderstood, and everything Ukrainians accused the government of—corruption, violence and censorship—was suddenly backed by irrefutable evidence. The tapes were sold on public squares, and street protests with the slogan "Ukraine without Kuchma" drew tens of thousands of people. In the eyes of Ukrainians, Kuchma had lost his legitimacy in late 2000–early 2001, and there was no way he could restore his credibility.

Kuchma was trying to keep the country under his control and ideally retain power, but that had suddenly become an equation with many unknowns. First, a popular protest movement was gaining strength as opposition leaders joined it one after another. Its standard bearer was

Viktor Yushchenko, a distinguished-looking forty-five-year-old financier and former head of the Ukrainian National Bank, a reformer and liberal, whom Kuchma had made prime minister in December 1999 to boost the failing economy—which Yushchenko had successfully done. "I'm leaving to come back," Yushchenko said when the Verkhovna Rada dismissed him in April 2001 at the behest of Kuchma and powerful oligarchs.[1] Now the vanguard of the opposition, the Our Ukraine party, had a leader and presidential candidate in the upcoming elections, and the protest movement became a fully fledged political force.

Second, relations with the West had taken a sharp turn for the worse. In the eyes of Washington and European capitals, Ukraine had changed from a promising young democracy with a place in the community of European nations to a corrupt autocracy where the authorities manipulated elections, suppressed freedom of speech, dispersed protests and most likely murdered journalists. Another problem was the country's clandestine arms trade. In one of Melnychenko's tapes, Kuchma can be heard agreeing to sell Kolchuga anti-missile radars to Iraq. In early 2002, this information reached Washington. The radars could pose a real threat to US and British fighter jets carrying out a UN resolution to patrol Iraqi airspace. The Kolchuga scandal meant there would not be a meeting with George Bush in November 2002 at the Ukraine–NATO summit in Prague that Kuchma had such high hopes for. The Ukrainian president had received the message from Washington that he was not welcome at the summit, but he came anyway. Summit leaders are always seated according to the English alphabet: Ukraine, United Kingdom, United States. To keep Kuchma from sitting next to President Bush and Prime Minister Blair, the protocol language of the summit was quickly changed to French. Kuchma had never been so badly treated in the West before. Only Belarusian dictator Alexander Lukashenko was treated worse: he was simply refused a visa to the Czech Republic.

And third, developments in Kyiv were closely monitored in Moscow. In 2002, the Kremlin's Foreign Policy Directorate even created a separate Ukrainian department that reported not to the head of the directorate, but directly to Vladislav Surkov, who had been in charge of domestic policy. The situation on the western borders concerned the Kremlin. The Baltic states had left for Europe and the accession of Belarus through the creation of a Union state had failed. This was when the Kremlin clearly articulated its goal of keeping Ukraine within its sphere of influence.[2]

Putin was personally concerned about Ukraine. At first, he wanted—and discussed with officials—how to get Ukraine to join the Eurasian Economic Community (EURASEC), the free trade zone that Russia established in 2001 together with Kazakhstan, Belarus, Kyrgyzstan and Tajikistan. At Putin's insistence, Ukraine was granted observer status in EURASEC. Then came the Common Economic Space (CES), the most important integration project for the Kremlin in the post-Soviet era, which would include a customs union between Russia, Belarus, Kazakhstan and Ukraine. The point of reference for the CES was the European Union. Without Ukraine, there was no point in it for the Kremlin. When Kuchma finally signed the declaration on Ukraine's accession to the CES in February 2003, Moscow celebrated a victory. Meanwhile, the announcement was greeted with surprise in Washington and the European capitals. How could Ukraine then join the European Union? But after Kuchma signed the declaration, he put a brake on the integration process. And he categorically refused to join the customs union.

Kuchma had been distrusted in Moscow ever since he issued a decree in 2002 confirming Ukraine's aspiration to join NATO, recalled Ukrainian political analyst Volodymyr Fesenko. Indeed, a year later NATO orientation was enshrined in the law on national security. The distrust in Moscow bordered on outright hostility. In the Kremlin they called Kuchma "a cunning Uke" who didn't keep his word and was now squirming because he'd got caught. After Kuchma, Putin needed a Ukrainian president who would make a clear move towards integration with Russia. Viktor Yushchenko, who joined the opposition, was unpalatable from the start. After Kuchma signed the documents for membership in the CES, Our Ukraine called for his impeachment.

At that time, in mid-2003, during the parliamentary election campaign in Russia, Chubais came up with the concept of a "liberal empire." The idea was that the Soviet Union should be replaced by another union, a liberal one based on the historical cultural community of the post-Soviet republics and with its centre in Moscow. Russia was too big to join the EU and NATO. "Instead," Chubais explained, "we need to see ourselves in a future great chain of Northern Hemisphere democracies": the US, Europe, Japan and Russia with its allies.[3] The utopian slogan of a "liberal empire" fit well with the ideology of the SPS: a strong and democratic Russia would be attractive to its neighbours and thus promote its political interests.

Reality, however, was different. In practice, as the publicist Kirill Rogov wrote during the Orange Revolution, "The Kremlin understands statehood in an archaic Eastern sense and sees its mission mainly in making a deal (preferably one that is not legal and therefore more reliable) with the ruling clans of the Union states that would guarantee their commitment to this type of statehood. The Kremlin would not be so much promoting Russian interests as exporting its political and economic model. Based on this logic, sharing the model meant sharing interests."[4] And that's how Ukraine became a battleground. The Kremlin needed a political regime in Ukraine that would be dependent on Moscow. The United States and Europe wanted to consolidate Western practices in Ukraine, and therefore also democracy. And so, the fight over Ukraine between Russia and the West turned into a fight over its system.

## Putin bets on Yanukovych

Ukraine had still not made it clear what it was: a post-Soviet autocracy, where power was either unchanging or inherited, or a European democracy, where the political opposition could come to power. Kuchma saw the ideal solution as a combination of the two. He dodged back and forth as best he could, trying to maintain the country's path to Europe that had been declared in the 1990s, while simultaneously trying to keep on good terms with a stronger Russia, which was annually subsidizing the Ukrainian economy with billions of dollars of discounted cheap gas. Russian oligarchs were actively moving into the Ukrainian market and setting up major companies and making the Ukrainian elite nervous. The Ukrainian elite was afraid the Russians would sideline them. A joke was going around Ukraine at the time: "What's the difference between a Ukrainian and a Russian oligarch? Ukrainians are just as full of themselves but not as rich." But it wasn't only Russian businessmen that looked down on Ukraine; the bureaucrats in Moscow did, too.

In 2002, Kuchma appointed Viktor Medvedchuk, a Kyiv oligarch and politician, to head his administration. At first, Putin knew nothing about him, but gradually Medvedchuk forged relations with both Dmitry Medvedev, when he replaced Voloshin as head of the Presidential Administration in the autumn of 2003, and Putin. The relationship turned from business to friendship, and in May 2004, at the start of the presidential campaign in Ukraine, Putin and Medvedev's wife became godparents to Medvedchuk's daughter Daria. By this point, Medvedchuk was more important to Moscow than his boss was.

The friendship between Putin and Medvedchuk may have warmed quickly thanks to their somewhat similar backgrounds. Medvedchuk had worked as a lawyer with the KGB during the Soviet era. They also shared some personality traits and mannerisms. Medvedchuk shared a liking for covert operations—he quickly gained fame in Ukraine as a grey cardinal—and he also had a reputation as a hell-raiser. Ambitious, tough, goal-oriented and very efficient, Medvedchuk always did what he said he'd do, and in the Kremlin they knew they could rely on him. In Kyiv he prepared constitutional reform for Kuchma. Kuchma had abandoned the idea of seeking a third term and was envisioning a redistribution of the power of the president, parliament and cabinet to preserve his role as arbiter of Ukrainian politics after the election. Medvedchuk's strong relationship with Moscow suited Kuchma, and he entrusted negotiations with Washington to his other aide, Serhiy Lyovochkin.

Medvedchuk shared with the Kremlin a common opponent: Yushchenko. Medvedchuk played a major role in Yushchenko's dismissal as prime minister, and in turn Yushchenko pushed for Medvedchuk's removal as deputy speaker of parliament. Yushchenko's Our Ukraine party constantly attacked him, recalling his unseemly role in the 1980 trial of the Ukrainian poet, dissident and nationalist Vasyl Stus, who had been arrested a second time for anti-Soviet activity.* At the beginning of the presidential race, Medvedchuk succeeded in spoiling Yushchenko's

---

* Medvedchuk was Stus's lawyer and pleaded guilty on his behalf, even though Stus rejected the plea. Stus died five years later in a camp in the Urals, and in 1989 his ashes were solemnly transported to Ukraine, where, in 2005, Yushchenko, already president, posthumously awarded him the title Hero of Ukraine.

cordial relations with Rinat Akhmetov, the main magnate in Donetsk and all of Eastern Ukraine, after realizing that their alliance would strengthen Yushchenko's presidential prospects. And when Yushchenko arrived in Donetsk in autumn 2003, he was met by a crowd organized by the local authorities at Medvedchuk's bidding that chanted "Shame!" and "No to Fascism!" There were many drunks in the crowd, and the area was plastered with posters of Yushchenko with a Hitler moustache raising his hand in a Nazi salute. It was the backdrop of the upcoming election campaign: in Eastern Ukraine, the election was held under the slogan of combating Ukrainian nationalism, which was equated to a Nazi threat, while in Western Ukraine, the voter in the east was portrayed as a drunken troublemaker from that same mob in Donetsk.

At the time, Kuchma had not yet named Viktor Yanukovych, the former Donetsk governor who had succeeded Yushchenko as prime minister, as his successor. Kuchma dragged his feet and never publicly announced his choice. Yanukovych's humiliating hiatus lasted so long that in April 2004, just days before his nomination, he threatened Kuchma in front of witnesses that he would pack his bags and return home to Donetsk. Kuchma did not like Yanukovych. Kuchma was, after all, a representative of the party *nomenklatura*. Yanukovych, who had been convicted twice for robbery and violence in his youth, was not on Kuchma's level. But the economic situation was in his favour: for the third year in a row the growth rate was above eight per cent. Most importantly, Yanukovych had rich backers: the Donetsk clan led by Akhmetov was ready to fund his presidential campaign.

Medvedchuk didn't like Yanukovych either, mostly because he wanted to be Kuchma's successor himself, but in the end the decision was made, and Kuchma pushed Yanukovych into the presidency. The Kremlin was reluctant to accept the choice: Moscow officials were not happy with Yanukovych either; they saw him as a provincial mafia boss, not a president. When talking to Yanukovych, Putin made little secret of his contempt. But there was no way around it. It was going to be Yanukovych, so they had to deal with him.

Attempts by Yushchenko's team to contact the Kremlin were cut off long before the campaign began. After Yushchenko left the post of prime minister and was considered the future president, he was never received on any official level in Moscow. Once, in late summer 2003, when Yushchenko planned to hold a conference with Russian politicians to show that he was not turning his back on Russia, his chief of staff, Roman Bessmertny, received confirmation that Yushchenko would be received in the Kremlin after all. Without the Kremlin's sanction, the conference could not take place.

Yushchenko and Bessmertny flew to Moscow, but nothing came of it. "The meetings never happened. We spent the whole day in a hotel and flew away with nothing," said Bessmertny. "We knew they were making a point."[5]

## Nemtsov bets on Yushchenko

Nemtsov had met Yushchenko in the mid-1990s, when he was governor and Yushchenko was the head of the Ukrainian National Bank. They had then crossed paths more than once when Nemtsov joined the cabinet. In 1997, the Ukrainian economist and reformer Viktor Pynzenyk founded the Reforms and Order party. He was called "the Ukrainian Gaidar": he carried out price liberalization and financial stabilization in Ukraine and was responsible for monetary reform, exit from the rouble zone, and the introduction of the hryvnia. In Russia, first Gaidar's party, the Democratic Choice of Russia, and then SPS became allies of Pynzenyk's party. "Nemtsov and I were in close communication through SPS," Pynzenyk said. "We had common views on reforms. We were two liberal parties."[6]

Later the Reforms and Order party merged with Our Ukraine. "I was more conservative, and they were more liberal," Yushchenko recalled. "I headed up the national-democratic aspects of our work and Vitya Pynzenyk headed the liberal course."[7] After SPS announced an alliance with Our Ukraine, SPS leaders hosted Yushchenko in Moscow. In November 2002, Nemtsov and Yushchenko signed a manifesto on cooperation in Kyiv. Nemtsov noted that not only did they share a commitment to democracy and a market economy, but they also "rejected the oligarchic regimes that were unfortunately being established in our countries."[8] Indeed, political analysts at the time described Yushchenko's struggle with Yanukovych as a confrontation between millionaires and billionaires: big business mostly supported Yanukovych, while small and medium-sized entrepreneurs sided with Yushchenko.

The political movement led by Yushchenko was based on a threefold platform: Ukrainian nationalism, economic liberalism and the goal of becoming a part of Europe. In Russia, a course to become a part of Europe was in conflict with nationalism, for obvious reasons: nationalism was sublimated to great-power statehood, and that conflicted with the choice to join the West. But in the western part of the Soviet empire, on the contrary, democratic movements were built on nationalism, and that was a natural way of joining the West—rejecting Soviet power and the Soviet past. Our Ukraine followed a well-trodden path.

As Nemtsov put it, "Yushchenko himself is a moderate, and, believe me, he has nothing to do with any nationalists,"[9] but the coalition he led included nationalists, including some who had fought for Ukrainian independence under Soviet rule. Yushchenko recalled how in early 2003 Nemtsov asked to be allowed to attend one of the meetings at the Our Ukraine headquarters. "We go in, and there are about fifteen people sitting around a big table. Boris sat near the window, I near the door, and to my right was Slava Stetsko, a unique woman, the leader of Ukrainian nationalists. Across from her was former Ukrainian foreign minister Hennadiy Udovenko. These were legendary figures who had long been flag bearers for the democratic national forces."[10]

Slava Stetsko fought the Poles in the 1930s, then became an activist in the Organization of Ukrainian Nationalists (OUN) and married Yaroslav Stetsko, Stepan Bandera's right-hand man. After her husband was arrested, she fled to Germany, where he was interned, and returned only in 1991 when Ukraine gained its independence. Russian propaganda has come to equate Bandera with Nazism, but, to the western part of Ukraine, Bandera was something like Che Guevara—a romantic hero from the past and a true patriot. Udovenko, on the other hand, had a diplomatic career in the Soviet Foreign Ministry, headed the Ukrainian Foreign Ministry in the mid-1990s and as minister signed the treaty on the status of the Black Sea Fleet with Russia before becoming one of the leaders of the national-democratic People's Movement of Ukraine. Both spoke Ukrainian; Stetsko did not know Russian at all. "And then Mrs

Stetsko," Yushchenko continued, "turned to Boris and tactfully said two or three respectful phrases about how we never advocate conflict with the Russian nation, with the Russian people. She spoke very much from the heart, and it was obvious that she had not prepared these words. I turned to Nemtsov. 'Boris, do you understand anything that Mrs Stetsko is saying?' Boris said, 'Be quiet, please, I understand everything.' It was very nice to see."[11]

## Two Ukraines

The first round of the presidential elections was scheduled for 31 October 2004. The election campaign was officially launched in July, and it was immediately clear that it was splitting Ukraine roughly in two. Cultural differences between the east and west of the country were evident in many ways. The people to the east often didn't speak Ukrainian at all and were either Russian or considered themselves Russian. For example, Yanukovych himself made two grammatical mistakes in the Ukrainian language when he registered as a presidential candidate with the Central Electoral Commission. Western Ukraine saw itself as European, sharing the same lifestyle as its neighbours—Poles, Slovaks and Hungarians—all the more so because the state borders in Western Ukraine had changed countless times over the past centuries. But neither under the first president, Leonid Kravchuk, nor under Kuchma, was the difference between east and west a social issue. The 2004 election exacerbated it.

This was a deliberate provocation by Yanukovych's headquarters in Donetsk, run by Andriy Klyuyev, a major local businessman and deputy prime minister in Yanukovych's cabinet. His campaign managers proposed the slogan "Let's Not Let Ukraine Be Divided into Three Sorts— 'Good West', 'Middling Centre' and 'Bad East'"—which was supposedly how Yushchenko's camp saw the future of Ukraine. Medvedchuk's adviser Mykhailo Pogrebinsky recalled how he tried to convince his boss this was a mistake that would alienate undecided voters. Medvedchuk shrugged and nodded towards Donetsk as if to say, "This isn't up to us, it's their decision."[12] The alternative was to position Yanukovych as a man of action who had brought about fantastic economic growth, but the more aggressive approach won out.

Ukraine could no longer sit on two chairs the way it had under Kuchma. Yanukovych represented the east with its coal mines, powerful economy that generated seventy per cent of the country's GDP, and desire to be closer to Russia. Yushchenko had almost total support in the west and symbolized the European choice. The support bases in their fiefdoms were unshakable; the battle was for the centre of the country. In the capital Yanukovych lost out at once. Although Kyiv was largely a Russian-speaking city, the capital backed Yushchenko. While Yanukovych's campaign managers portrayed Yushchenko as a Banderite and a fascist, who planned to eliminate the Russian language and sever relations with Russia, in Kyiv the outrage over Yanukovych's criminal record was reinforced by fear of the "men from Donetsk" who had earned a reputation as mafiosi and gangsters back in the 1990s. In addition, Yanukovych was Kuchma's protégé, and Kuchma had lost his credibility in Kyiv after the tapes scandal. Yanukovych should have distanced himself from Kuchma, one of his staffers later said, but he was afraid. Yushchenko, on the other hand, was the exact opposite of Yanukovych. He was not only anti-Kuchma; he had a reputation for being honest and cultured. And in addition: "He's a good-looking guy," said a political strategist who used to work in Ukraine. "Back then, every mother wanted a son like Yushchenko." All the same, by early autumn Viktor Yanukovych, a newcomer to the race, had caught up with Yushchenko in the polls. They were running almost neck and neck.

From the start, the men in the Kremlin made no secret of their preference for Yanukovych. Condoleezza Rice, then national security adviser to President Bush, recalled her arrival in Moscow in May 2004 in her memoirs. Putin showed her around his residence in Novo-Ogaryovo. "Within a few minutes Viktor Yanukovych emerged from a side room. 'Oh, please meet Viktor,' Putin said. 'He is a candidate for president of Ukraine.' I greeted the pro-Russian politician and took the message that Putin had intended: the United States should know that Moscow had a horse in the race to defend its interests."[13] Putin thought he was introducing a high-ranking US official to a future Ukrainian president. It was about this time that Putin first appeared in public with

Yanukovych as Kuchma's official successor and congratulated him on his economic successes. It wasn't just in the Kremlin that people believed someone could only become president of Ukraine after receiving the right to reign from Moscow: the same belief could be found in Kyiv, too.

The Kremlin's investment in Yanukovych was massive. Gazprom cut the price of gas for Ukraine from eighty to fifty dollars, and new tax deals between Putin and Kuchma subsidized the Ukrainian economy with another $800 million. These gifts allowed Yanukovych effectively to double Ukrainian pensions in September. Russian television became more and more aggressive in its campaigning for Yanukovych, and a brigade of Moscow spin doctors was sent to Kyiv.

Although in Washington they wanted Yushchenko to win, they decided not to support him publicly. In his memoirs, Steven Pifer, the former US ambassador to Kyiv who was at the time in charge of State Department policy on Russia and Ukraine, wrote that they "doubted that we understood enough about the Ukrainian electorate and how it might react if it believed the United States backed Yushchenko; any action on our part could well backfire and prompt an electoral backlash against him."[14] Washington focused on ensuring free and fair elections. They gave grants to the independent press, polling organizations and election-observer training programmes. And they pressured the Presidential Administration not to harass the opposition. Before the election, the State Department spent $65 million in Ukraine, and non-profit foundations received more than a million more from George Soros.[15] Some of the money went to train activists of the student organization *Pora!* (*It's time!*).

The presidential race was rife with scandals. Businessmen who supported the opposition were visited by tax inspectors, Yushchenko was constantly discredited and obstructed in every way, the main TV channels campaigned hard for Yanukovych and didn't give Yushchenko airtime. In the east, administrative resources were winning the day. Villagers said they couldn't even see a doctor without signing in support of Yanukovych's nomination. A scandal-ridden mayoral election in the westernmost town of Mukachevo was an indication of how the elections would be held in late November. The victory of the government candidate from a party close to Medvedchuk was blatantly falsified, and things got violent. "Mukachevo is a rehearsal," Yushchenko said. His camp expected fraud. Even the election of Sergei Kivalov, an Odesa businessman and politician with a police background, as Chairman of the Electoral Commission led to protest rallies in Kyiv. During the Orange Revolution he would be given a nickname that means "do the math" in Ukrainian and sounds like "faggot" in Russian. The opposition was working ahead of time to organize street protests against what were certain to be rigged elections.

## "Together we are many..."

The presidential election was an everything-goes fight from the start, but, even so, Yushchenko's poisoning in September shocked both the general public and the establishment. On 5 September, he became ill and was treated for a fortnight in Austria. At first, people made jokes about it: either he'd eaten something bad or he'd gone on a real bender. But after a while people stopped joking, and on 18 September, when Yushchenko appeared again in front of his supporters on Kyiv's Independence Square, the crowd gasped. Yushchenko was unrecognizable, as if he had gone to hell and back. His handsome face had turned grey, and his skin was covered with boils and a lumpy rash.* It was a turning point in the campaign. Suddenly it became clear that elections were war, and in a war people could be killed. When Ukrainians looked at the disfigured face of the opposition leader, they saw what the incumbent government was capable of. Yushchenko's popularity soared again.

Yushchenko's opponents responded to the mobilization of supporters by bringing out the big guns in Moscow. Vladimir Putin campaigned as actively for Yanukovych as if it were a Russian election, not a Ukrainian one. The plan was simple. Polls showed that Putin was the

---

\* In December 2004, Austrian doctors confirmed that Yushchenko had been poisoned with dioxin. Yushchenko's team claimed the Kremlin was behind the poisoning, but the exact circumstances could not be established. The investigation stalled, and in 2019 the Ukrainian military prosecutor's office said there was no evidence that Yushchenko had been deliberately poisoned.

most popular politician in Ukraine, and so all he had to do was channel his popularity to support a particular candidate, just as he had done so many times successfully at home. In late October, just before the election, Putin flew to Kyiv for an unprecedented three entire days to knock Yanukovych's opponent out of the race. First, he appeared on three Ukrainian TV channels at once in a programme was called 'Direct Line to Vladimir Putin'. This was an exact copy of *Direct Line*, the president's annual conversation with the Russian audience that was broadcast live but was always carefully rehearsed. Part of the show had always involved distributing largesse, so here Putin promised Ukrainians entry into Russia on their internal passports. Putin, his chief of staff Medvedev and Yanukovych had already hosted a ceremonial parade to mark the sixtieth anniversary of Ukraine's liberation from the Nazis. Both events had only one practical purpose: "In an unprecedented move," *Kommersant* wrote, "the Kremlin was not only clearly backing Prime Minister Viktor Yanukovych in the Ukrainian elections, but actually got involved in a presidential campaign in a foreign country."[16]

Kyiv had turned orange—the colour of revolution for change—even before the elections: orange flags were hung on balconies and windows, and orange ribbons appeared on every car, on sleeves, backpacks and bags. Although Yushchenko had won the first round, the official figures—39.8 per cent for Yushchenko and 39.3 per cent for Yanukovych—did not convince the Orange voters. The exit polls checked by Yushchenko's team showed a lead of about nine per cent. In another ploy, the Electoral Commission dragged its feet with the announcement of the results for over a week; the law banned campaigning until the announcement of the results, and so the authorities had an excuse to deny Yushchenko access to TV airtime, while Yanukovych was still appearing on the screen as head of state.

But these dirty tricks had little effect: Yushchenko and his team were already certain of victory. Yushchenko was supported not only by the popular "Orange princess" Yulia Tymoshenko, but also by Oleksandr Moroz, the socialist leader who came third in the first round, the same man whose revelations four years earlier had ended the political career of Leonid Kuchma. Yushchenko's election campaign was already approaching the finish line as a broad popular movement, joined by the most famous rock musicians, actors and athletes. The rap song 'Together We Are Many, We Cannot Be Defeated' by GreenJolly would soon become the anthem of the Orange Revolution.

The second round of voting was held on 21 November. Confident of his victory, Yushchenko urged people to take to the streets if the victory was stolen through widespread falsifications. Yanukovych's team also understood what was happening. "Two or three days before the second round, we were sure we would lose," recalled a staffer. "The prediction was that Yushchenko would win by a three- to four-per-cent margin." On 22 November, around 1.00 a.m., the first official results came in, although they were still preliminary. Yanukovych had fifty-one per cent, Yushchenko had forty-five per cent. At the same time, the exit poll that was carried out by the leading sociological services of Ukraine and Russia (financed by the American government) showed a different picture. These numbers were rapidly being spread around Kyiv: fifty-four per cent for Yushchenko, forty-three per cent for Yanukovych. In a month or so, Yushchenko would win what would be called the third round (a rerun of the second round) with almost exactly these results: fifty-two to forty-four.

A few days later, Yushchenko's ally Oleh Rybachuk made public wiretaps of phone conversations between Kivalov, Medvedchuk, Klyuyev and other Yanukovych campaign managers. The tapes, which the security services gave to Rybachuk, left no doubt about the falsifications. "There were several hours of tapes, but we publicized only about ten to fifteen minutes," Rybachuk recalled, "because we knew that to sow uncertainty in that camp, we just needed to show that there was overwhelming evidence of falsification. I remember the reaction when journalists at the press conference recognized the voices of the main speakers."[17]

In one excerpt a Yanukovych headquarter staffer named Levenets discusses the situation with an unknown person on election day:

LEVENETS: Greetings! So how are we doing?
UNKNOWN: It's not good. We're behind.
LEVENETS: What do you mean?
UNKNOWN: 48.37 for our opponent, 47.64 for us.

LEVENETS: That's at 6 p.m.
UNKNOWN: We agreed on a 3–3.5 per cent difference in our favour. We've got a table of results by region. We'll fax it to you in about fifteen to twenty minutes.

The official results would be announced in two days: Yanukovych won by a 2.8 per cent margin. But this only added fuel to the fire. In the early hours after the elections on Monday, 22 November, Independence Square filled with people. That was the beginning of the Orange Revolution.

## For your freedom and ours

"I believe we need a free and democratic Ukraine. I believe that we need a free and democratic Russia. And only together can we be prosperous and happy. We must stand together here today not only for your freedom, but for ours, too," Nemtsov said on the stage set up on the Maidan. He had never spoken to such a large crowd before.[18] There were about five hundred thousand people on the Maidan at that moment, and as far as the eye could see the square had turned into one solid orange wave.

Nemtsov had moved to Kyiv in mid-October, returning home only on the weekends. On 22 November, he went to the square. "The first time I brought him to the Maidan," Yushchenko recalled, "we were heading to the podium when he asked, 'Can I walk up to the people?' They were about five or six metres away from the stage."[19] Nemtsov was immediately taken in by the revolution.

Perhaps Nemtsov was carried away by the moment and didn't realize that he was repeating almost word-for-word the slogan—"For Our Freedom and Yours"—that seven dissidents had held up on Red Square on 25 August 1968 to protest Soviet troops in Czechoslovakia. In any case, his reference wasn't accidental. Just like the dissidents on Red Square, Nemtsov spoke for freedom and democracy in another country, but he was protesting a lack of freedom at home. And the fact that the Kremlin leadership had so actively intervened in the political struggle in Ukraine—although it did not go as far as tanks at the time—made the similarity even more resounding.

Immediately after the victory of the Orange Revolution, Nemtsov said in an interview that the people who run Russia believe in capitalism but do not believe in freedom and democracy.

> They believe that the Slavic world is not mature enough for freedom; the people need a shepherd who will drive the flock wherever he sees fit. Of course, this is not said aloud, but that's what they think at the top. And suddenly Ukraine says, "No! We choose democracy, freedom, human rights..." For the bearers of the authoritarian doctrine, this is a mighty blow. If everything works out in Ukraine, they will not be able to say that the Slavs are immune to democracy. So, when I'm asked today the most popular question here—after the Ukrainian elections will this be a win or a loss for Russia?—I answer: "It depends what kind of Russia it is. For a democratic Russia, it's a win."[20]

Nemtsov became a hero of Maidan. His speech was remembered forever in Kyiv. "What's more depraved than the union of a Chekist and a repeat offender?!" he exclaimed, and the square burst into approving laughter. It was a special and very important moment for him. Even though he was not a local, he spoke from a podium and a million hands applauded him.

The political crisis in Ukraine dragged on for a fortnight. Nemtsov came to Yushchenko's headquarters every evening and from there walked to the Maidan wearing an orange scarf. During those days, Kyivans came to love him as one of their own. Yushchenko said, "Nemtsov was practically carried onto the Maidan; he was everybody's favourite. When Nemtsov lost his expensive Brioni suit—he either left it in a taxi or somewhere else—everyone on the Maidan looked for it, and they quickly found it."

*Kommersant* journalist Valery Panyushkin described a scene in one of his reports from those days:

> At half past two, we went outside. A car came to pick us up, but there was a demonstration around the car, and there was also a

demonstration down the street, and there was also a demonstration on the Khreshchatyk, which lay in our way.

"Let's go on foot," I said, and we walked.

Every person we met tried to shake Boris Nemtsov's hand. There were about half a million of them. After about fifteen minutes, we finally crossed the Khreshchatyk and decided to take a taxi. Nemtsov raised his hand. The first car stopped. Four young women got out of the car, and one of them said, "You can take our taxi. Get in."

"Why are you giving up your cab?" Nemtsov asked.

"Because you're Nemtsov and you probably need to go to the Rada. Aren't you going to the Rada?"

"Well, yes, we're going to the Rada."

"Well, get in and go."[21]

For Yushchenko and the entire opposition camp, Nemtsov's presence on the Maidan was politically important. His impassioned speech on the square confirmed that not all of Russia was for Yanukovych. The day after Maidan began, Yushchenko took the presidential oath, first in the parliament building and then directly on the square. Nemtsov was afraid that the west would swear in Yushchenko, the east would swear in Yanukovych and the country would split in two. Yushchenko's oath did seem excessive. But later Nemtsov said that it played an important symbolic role showing the irreversibility of the Orange Revolution.

## Why was Maidan victorious?

Yushchenko advocated peaceful protest. He was ready for compromise and negotiated with Kuchma. Their interests coincided: Yushchenko agreed to carry out constitutional reform, which Kuchma had been nursing along for two years, and to share presidential powers. Nemtsov supported him in this. Ukraine was heading to join Europe, and in Europe—with the exception of France—power is in the hands of the parliaments, not presidents. "Boris and I didn't have much discussion about whether to move from a presidential to a parliamentary system," Yushchenko recalled. "I understood that my opponents would never accept me having the powers of President Kuchma. In our country, all the institutions had one surname—the president's surname. One person decided who would be prime minister, who would be a minister, who would be the head of the regional administration, not to mention the prosecutor's office, the Supreme Court, and so on. Besides, I knew that two-thirds of Ukrainians did not want to wake up in the morning and depend on the thoughts and actions of one man, whatever his last name."[22]

Tensions escalated throughout the week after the second round, both on the Maidan, where protesters feared an assault, in the offices of the Presidential Administration and at Kuchma's dacha in the very high-end Kyiv suburb of Koncha-Zaspa. At night, the three camps—Kuchma, Yanukovych and Yushchenko—negotiated among themselves. By day, the protest swept through Western and Central Ukraine, as far north as Kharkiv and as far east as Dnipro. Local administrations, students and journalists went on strike, with tens of thousands of people demonstrating in every major city. "I am very envious, but in a good way," Nemtsov said when he came straight from Maidan to REN TV, the only Russian TV channel that interviewed him at the time. "The Ukrainian people proved that they have dignity and pride and that they will fight for freedom and truth. This teaches us a lot. Usually Kyivans looked up to Moscow, but now many Russians will be looking to Ukraine."[23]

By the following weekend the crisis had reached a climax. Yanukovych, who had been declared the winner, was supported by Moscow. Putin congratulated him on his election immediately after the second round. Yanukovych and his men suggested that Kuchma declare a state of emergency and disperse the crowds that were blocking government buildings in central Kyiv. Kuchma refused to give the order. First, he realized that the security forces might not carry it out, second, he wanted to avoid bloodshed—especially since every day he was being pressured by the Americans and Europeans to find a peaceful solution to the crisis.

Yanukovych was not ready to take personal responsibility for a crackdown and possible casualties either. He kept silent when one of the army generals said at a meeting that Yanukovych's sanction would be sufficient to launch the operation. On 28 November, Yushchenko's associates told the American ambassador that a police unit was preparing to disperse crowds on the Maidan, according to information from the security forces. Yushchenko announced this right on the square and urged the protesters not to disperse under any circumstances. The same night, the US secretary of state, Colin Powell, tried to reach Kuchma, but he would not come to the phone. Eventually, he managed to reach Viktor Pinchuk, Kuchma's son-in-law and an oligarch who, unlike the Donetsk clan, maintained good relations with the Americans. Pinchuk soon returned the call, Steven Pifer recounts in his memoirs, and, referring to Medvedchuk's assurances, said there would be no crackdown.[24] Meanwhile, the Kremlin kept pushing Kuchma to empty the Maidan, or at least hand over power to Yanukovych as "the legitimately elected president."

On 1 December the crisis abated. Thanks to the efforts of the Polish president, Aleksander Kwaśniewski, and European Union representative Javier Solana, a declaration was signed to end the crisis, and Yushchenko and Yanukovych shook hands for the first time. The next day, Kuchma suddenly flew to Moscow, where he held talks with Putin at Vnukovo airport. Years later Kuchma admitted on the BBC that the Russian president had urged him to use force. "Putin is a tough man," Kuchma would say. "There were some hints, I guess you'd say. That's not a secret. But he never said right out, 'Bring tanks onto the square.'"[25] There is no question that Kuchma's peaceful stance was also influenced by the guarantees he received from Yushchenko that the new government would not persecute him. He also understood that if the military was brought in, Ukraine would find itself in international isolation, and nothing good awaited him. In the end, it was Kuchma who awarded victory to Yushchenko and prevented violence on the Maidan. No blood was shed.

On 3 December the Supreme Court of Ukraine ruled to rerun the second round of presidential elections. This was tantamount to recognizing Yushchenko as president. There was no doubt that he would win the third round, and he did. The Orange Revolution had won. Ordinary people took to the streets and defended their dignity and their future, throwing out the criminal and corrupt government themselves—that's how millions of Ukrainians, and indeed the whole world, saw the historic events of those days.

In January, after Yushchenko's official inauguration, Nemtsov was again stopped by Ukrainian journalists. He had just finished a game of tennis and was on his way to a restaurant. "This is a rarity," Nemtsov told them. "I was lucky enough to be involved in two revolutions, one after the other. In Moscow in 1991 and here in Kyiv today. I'm feeling a lot of emotions. A huge upsurge, the gigantic hopes of millions of people—and from that a sense of unity, solidarity, belief that everything will change for the better, the feeling of people's power."[26] Nemtsov was encouraged: he had seen with his own eyes an example of the victory of good over evil. "Since they succeeded, so will we," he said. At Yushchenko's inauguration at the Verkhovna Rada on 23 January, Nemtsov sat in the box of honour with friends and relatives of the newly elected president. After that, Ukraine would become almost a second home for him and an important part of his life.

# CHAPTER 24

## 2005–09
## The End of the Revolution

### A clean slate

In autumn 2005, Oleh Rybachuk, the head of President Yushchenko's administration, flew to Moscow. His counterpart in the Kremlin, Dmitry Medvedev, had arranged for him to meet with Putin. Rybachuk did not want to meet with Putin. He told Medvedev that since the two of them, both heads of their respective presidential administrations, were on good terms, they could handle matters themselves. But Medvedev insisted. The conversation between Rybachuk and Putin lasted about an hour and a half. Rybachuk told Putin about Maidan and election issues, in particular that after the polls closed the number of voters in the Donetsk region suddenly increased by 800,000. Both figures—before and after the polls closed—were included in the official reports of the electoral commission. "I said, 'This is obvious vote rigging.' He replied, 'I know everything—who, what and how.' He didn't believe the vote was rigged in Yanukovych's favour. I'd been in the epicentre. I started to explain to him how it all happened. He interrupted me halfway through. 'Come on, you're a smart man. I know it all, I was told who financed it, who set it up.' To him, my attempt to explain what had happened sounded simply absurd."[1]

Vladimir Putin had never faced a defeat like the one in Ukraine in November 2004. The Orange Revolution not only ruined his plans, it insulted and humiliated him, because he had invested all his political capital in Yanukovych's victory. In the past, the Kremlin had refused to accept Yushchenko's political agency and considered him an American puppet. The fact that his wife, an American of Ukrainian descent, had worked for both the State Department and the US Congress in the 1980s was evidence enough. Many people in the entourages of Kuchma, Yanukovych and Putin believed without question that in her youth she had been recruited by the CIA and got to know Yushchenko at the direction of the secret services. In other words, they believed that Yushchenko's entire political career was an American intelligence project. In Putin's view, he and Yanukovych didn't lose to Yushchenko and the half-million-strong crowd gathered on the Maidan. It was the US that had torn away from Russia a vital piece of the post-Soviet space. "Putin is furious that the US stole Ukraine," Vyacheslav Nikonov explained to the American ambassador in Moscow, Alexander Vershbow, over lunch in December 2004.[2] That rage was fuelled by a sense of betrayal and deceit. This was nothing new, but now the emotions were far more intense. As Nemtsov said around the same time, "Putin, unfortunately, is still unable to accept that Ukraine is an independent state."[3]

Three and a half years had passed since President Bush said he'd looked into President Putin's eyes and saw his soul during their first meeting at the Ljubljana summit. Putin had made an unexpectedly good impression on Bush, and so Russia and America started again with a clean slate. Three months later, on 9/11, after the attack on the World Trade Center in New York, Putin was the first world leader to call the American president to offer his condolences. He couldn't get through to Bush, so Condoleezza Rice picked up the call. She wrote that she told Putin, "...'the President is not able to take your call right now because he is being moved to another location. I wanted to let you know that American forces are going up on alert.' 'We already know, and we have cancelled our exercises and brought our alert levels down,' he said. 'Is there anything else we can do?' I thanked him, and for one brief moment the thought flashed through my head: *the Cold War really is over*."[4]

It was a turning point. On the one hand, Putin did not yet feel confident and wanted to be friends with the US. On the other hand, he seized the moment. By supporting America in the fight against al-Qaeda, Moscow legitimized its own military operation in Chechnya, portraying Chechnya one of the fronts in the great war on international terrorism. It was a good starting point to try to take relations with America to the next level—not only with America, but also with Western Europe. In those days, journalist Mikhail Zygar wrote, "Putin received every Western leader and foreign minister who paid a visit to Russia—and sat with them for far longer than protocol required."[5] He established excellent relations with Western European leaders: Tony Blair, Gerhard Schröder, Jacques Chirac and Silvio Berlusconi.

The Russian president made several generous concessions to the Americans. He persuaded his generals and intelligence officers to accept the temporary deployment of American military bases in the former Soviet republics of Central Asia, Kyrgyzstan and Uzbekistan. When the Americans told him they'd decided unilaterally to withdraw from the 1972 Anti-Ballistic Missile Treaty, he did not protest, even though it was humiliating for Russia. He was extremely invested in the alliance with America, and at first the Americans reciprocated. Alexander Vershbow, then US ambassador to Russia, recalled that in October 2001, during Putin's meeting with Bush on the sidelines of the APEC summit, Bush's advisers were drafting a common statement from both leaders about how Russia and the United States were becoming allies, not only in fighting a common enemy, but also in promoting shared values. "Russia is returning to the family of civilized nations. And it needs nothing but to have its voice heard, to be reckoned with, to have its national interests taken into account," Putin had said in Rome in May 2002, after the NATO–Russia Council was established.[6] As British journalist Angus Roxburgh wrote, Putin's speech made a huge impression on everyone, and George Robertson, then NATO Secretary General, remembered it for years.[7]

In May 2002, at the Moscow summit, Putin and Bush also signed the Strategic Offensive Reductions Treaty, symbolizing that Russia and the US had entered an era of harmony and friendship. "Putin is taking a risky but correct step," Nemtsov admitted in a conversation with the author, assessing the outcome of the summit. "Risky, because it contradicts the general mood of both the military and politicians in the country. Correct, because it is more advantageous for Russia to have America as a partner and an ally than as an enemy, and a lot of money and effort would have to be allocated to fight them."[8] This was the peak of westernization under Putin; after that, the thaw in relations between Russia and the West would turn frosty.

## The weakest go to the wall

When Putin spoke in Rome, he purposefully cited Russian interests. His alliance with the West was from the start built on rather shaky ground as a kind of business venture, a mutually beneficial exchange of information, services and favours. We supported you in the fight against al-Qaeda, you should support us in Chechnya; we agreed to your bases, you should meet us halfway on other issues. The Americans were naturally concerned with their own interests, not Russia's. On the one hand, American foreign policy was still largely following the concept advanced in 1999 by diplomat Thomas Graham Jr in an essay entitled 'World without Russia?' Graham suggested that after the 1998 default, Russia was weaker and was not staying on the path to democracy. "We are witnessing a geo-political and geo-economic shift of historic dimensions," Graham wrote, "one in which Russia will become less and less an actor in world affairs, while running the risk of becoming an object of competition among more advanced and dynamic powers."[9] On the other hand, the Americans did not think they had to return Russia's favours. For example, when the Americans were establishing a military base in Uzbekistan, they negotiated directly with the Uzbek leaders. "The Russians assumed that we were as business-minded as they were, and we assumed that they were doing this and that because it was in their interest and need," recalled Vershbow, "as was the case of closing the radar station in Cuba and a military base in Vietnam." Secretary of Defence Donald Rumsfeld put it bluntly: "The Russians have an interest in defeating terrorism, so why should we do anything in return?"[10] In addition, the Kremlin voiced requests reluctantly and vaguely. "As I recall," Vershbow said, "the Russians were too proud to ask for anything, so we had to guess what they wanted ourselves."[11]

At the time, however, senior US diplomat John Bolton conceded that the Bush administration could have probably got the discriminatory Jackson–Vanik amendment* repealed by congress if it had really wanted to do so.[12]

A harbinger of change between Bush and Putin was their conversation in May 2002, just as they were signing the nuclear treaty supplementary agreements and their friendship was at its warmest. In response to the US's raising of import duties on steel, Russia banned imports of American chicken legs, which were dubbed "Bush legs" in Russia. Putin told Bush that the US was deliberately exporting poor-quality chicken to Russia, and that chicken for US consumption was raised in one factory and chicken exported to Russia came from another. "Bush was astonished. 'Vladimir, you're wrong.' Putin refused to believe him. 'My people have told me this is true.' Bush was struck by the old-school Russian paranoia," writes American journalist Peter Baker.[13] Vershbow, who endured gruelling negotiations on the quality of "Bush legs" with the Russian Federal Consumer Protection Service (Rospotrebnadzor), explained that it was simply a question of demand for chicken parts in the US. Americans prefer white meat, so dark meat was exported to Russia as "a matter of taste, not quality."[14]

Soon Putin's unlikely analogies and counter-accusations against Bush and his administration would become commonplace. Bush would criticize the arrest of Khodorkovsky; Putin responded by citing the example of Enron (Enron executives had received long sentences for real financial fraud and the company had gone bankrupt). Bush pointed out the anti-democratic nature of the abolition of gubernatorial elections; Putin argued that the US president appoints the electoral college.†

---

\* The Jackson–Vanik amendment to the Trade Law of 1974 in the US imposed restrictions on trade with the USSR in response to Soviet obstruction of Jewish emigration. In 2002, George W. Bush tried to have the amendment repealed by congress but was not successful. The amendment was repealed only in 2012 with Russia's accession to the WTO, but it was immediately replaced by another sanctions law: the Magnitsky Act.

† The electoral college is formed by the states. Putin apparently meant that the electors confirm the winner after the presidential elections, but even in this case his comparison is flawed: their role is purely formal.

Bush criticized the clampdown on the free press in Russia; Putin cited the firing of TV host Dan Rather (Rather had revealed compromising material on George Bush Sr, but the documents turned out to be forgeries and CBS fired him). Bush later said that Putin wasn't well informed and added: "It's like arguing with an eighth grader with his facts wrong."[15]

Putin and the Western leaders pulled further and further apart. Putin stockpiled resentment. Over time, his collection of grievances evolved into a coherent foreign-policy doctrine: for a long time, the West had constantly deceived Russia, patronized it, humiliated and tormented it with double standards. Russia's patience finally burst. At the heart of this long list of grievances would be NATO's eastward expansion, which was in the Kremlin's view treacherous and in breach of agreement. Then, by the logic of self-fulfilling prophesy, tensions would escalate: the greater the sense of offence in the Kremlin, the more aggressive Russian foreign policy would become and the stronger the conviction in Western capitals that Russia should be contained. In fact, Western leaders never promised not to expand NATO.*

But even if the Kremlin thought otherwise, in late 2002, when seven countries—Slovenia, Slovakia, Romania, Bulgaria, Lithuania, Latvia and Estonia—were invited to join NATO (at that Prague summit where the organizers contrived to sideline Leonid Kuchma), the Kremlin voiced no displeasure. At the time, Russia was a NATO partner and had even suggested it might join the alliance. In March

---

* Vladimir Putin would later refer to promises made to Mikhail Gorbachev in February 1990 by US State Department chief James Baker: "The jurisdiction of NATO military forces will not extend an inch eastward." As historians have explained many times, these statements were made in the context of the German unification agenda and concerned the territory of East Germany. In any case, Baker was quick to retract his words as soon as he received the directive from Washington: they could discuss a ban on expansion eastward of military infrastructure, but NATO's jurisdiction would extend to the whole of Germany. As a result, the German Final Settlement Treaty, signed, among others by the Soviet Union on 12 September 1990, allowed a unified Germany to join NATO and thus expand NATO eastwards in exchange for the so-called nine assurances, including the limiting of Germany's military capabilities within NATO.

2000, as acting president, Putin suggested Russia could become a NATO member: "I don't see why not. I would not rule out such a possibility," he said in an interview on the BBC, "but I repeat—if and when Russia's views are taken into account as those of an equal partner."[16] Some two decades later, after the invasion in Ukraine, Putin recounted a unfavourable story in which he had asked NATO country leaders if Russia could join the alliance: "'Get out of here'—they wouldn't even consider it."[17] At around same time, in April 2022, Bill Clinton recalled how the US "left the door open for Russia's eventual membership in NATO", something he made clear to Yeltsin and later confirmed to his successor, Putin, during the short time when their presidencies overlapped.[18]

In 2003, the interests of the White House and the Kremlin diverged even more sharply over the war in Iraq. After weighing the pros and cons of Russian oil companies operating in Iraq, Putin decided it would be better to join the anti-war alliance with France and Germany. This was when the Yukos affair began and the phrase "values gap" began to appear in Washington's rhetoric.

But Putin did not believe in values. He believed that global politics were driven by mercantile interests and that everything else was a smokescreen. As the boundaries of his personal power rapidly expanded, he found it increasingly convenient to see the growing criticism from Washington as a malicious desire to drag Russia down and crush it. "The weakest go to the wall," Vladimir Putin would say on 4 September 2004, the day after the catastrophic storming of the Beslan school that had been seized by terrorists. "Some people want to skim off our cream, and other people help them by believing that Russia, as one of the world's biggest nuclear powers, is still a threat. Therefore, this threat has to be eliminated."[19] This was close to accusing the West of supporting terrorism. Three months later, the Orange Revolution in Kyiv provided him and his entourage with yet more supposedly "direct proof" of nefarious plans being hatched in Washington. The pieces of the puzzle came together: it was not the Ukrainian people who had overthrown a deceitful and corrupt government; it was the West, using Ukrainian nationalists, Banderites and Nazis, who had torn Ukraine away from Russia. And Russia was the next target.

## A pro bono adviser

Buoyed by the Orange Revolution, Nemtsov's spirits lifted. If he couldn't promote liberal European values in Russia, then he'd help Ukraine to do so. If he couldn't fulfil himself as a politician at home, then he'd do it in Ukraine. Yushchenko wanted to offer Nemtsov a position in his office, but he quickly discovered that hiring a citizen of another country was against the law. Then Nemtsov came up with a solution: he would become a freelance adviser to the Ukrainian president. He would help Ukraine attract Russian investments and generally work to improve Russian–Ukrainian relations. Thanks to Nemtsov, Yushchenko had a whole group of advisers in different fields and in different areas, and Nemtsov even convinced the World Bank to finance the advisory group's activities. Nemtsov worked pro bono.

Nemtsov was proud and pleased. He had found a way to convert his good relations with virtually all the major Russian businessmen into concrete business opportunities. And the project had an ideological underpinning: the more successful the Ukrainian economy, the more attractive its example would be to Russia. Yushchenko also expected to benefit from Nemtsov's appointment as his adviser. Relations between Moscow and Kyiv were palpably cold. In fact, Ukraine intended to withdraw from the CES. Yushchenko wanted to send a positive message to Russian business. In March, he hosted some prominent Russian oligarchs in Kyiv.

But Nemtsov immediately ran into difficulties in his new role. First, it turned out that Yushchenko was inaccessible. Even Yushchenko's closest assistants had poor access to him, let alone his freelance adviser. Second, political life in Ukraine quickly descended into chaos again. The cabinet was headed by the charismatic populist Yulia Tymoshenko. She froze gasoline and sugar prices, everyone feared a redistribution of property, and the investment climate began to deteriorate. Nemtsov spoke of the dangers of creeping nationalization, criticized Tymoshenko for populism, and called on Yushchenko to fire her. "As an adviser, my task was to fight for Tymoshenko's resignation," Nemtsov later recalled. "I told Yushchenko: 'Your economy was booming, but when you made Yulia prime minister, your economy started to collapse.

Fire her.' Yushchenko resisted for a long time, but eventually he fired her."[20]

The Orange Coalition that came to power soon split into factions, squabbling and bogged down in intrigue. While Tymoshenko feuded with Yushchenko, Petro Poroshenko, another key Maidan figure and secretary of the Ukrainian Security Council, feuded with Tymoshenko. Yushchenko could do nothing about it. Constitutional reform had stripped him of the expansive levers of power that President Kuchma had enjoyed. Yearning for freedom was not enough to bring a new life to Ukraine. Censorship and authoritarianism had been defeated, but corruption remained rampant, Freedom House noted in June 2005, and Yushchenko himself was reluctant to reform. "What gives hope is Yushchenko's gigantic enthusiasm and personal honesty," Nemtsov said. "Otherwise, [...] I believe there is more corruption in Ukraine than in Russia. And it is more malignant: a Russian official takes money and does something, while in Ukraine they take money and do nothing."[21]

Yushchenko had no team of his own. The aftereffects of the poisoning were still being felt. But most importantly, he did not understand his job. "We had an argument once," Oleh Rybachuk recalled. "He said: 'Listen, what should I do tomorrow, what should I do in a week, in a month, in a year? You have to tell me.' I thought to myself: 'I think you should have asked yourself that when you were running for president.' It was clear that he didn't have a goal for his presidency and therefore he didn't take responsibility. That's why his presidency was very chaotic, and he was very quickly dragged into a cat-and-mouse relationship with Tymoshenko."[22] In September 2005, Yushchenko dismissed Tymoshenko, and the democratic Orange Coalition fell apart. A few months later, the opposition, led by Viktor Yanukovych, won the parliamentary elections.

## It's not even a state

In Moscow, they were very pleased when the Orange Coalition collapsed. They began plotting revenge. Putin did not meet Rybachuk in

October 2005 in order to hear his opinion about the events on Maidan. He wanted to convey a very simple message to Yushchenko: if they did not agree on terms by January, he would cut off gas to Ukraine. "By 'agreement' they meant keeping the middleman—that is, the rules of the game that were in place under Kuchma," Rybachuk recalled.[23] This was certainly an issue to be considered, especially given that Gazprom had announced it would charge Ukraine not the $50 per 1,000 cubic metres of natural gas promised to Yanukovych, but the outrageous price of $220.

During the Kuchma era, the joke was that all the wealthy Ukrainians had made their fortunes on Russian gas. Russian gas was delivered by agents, and they—and apparently not only they—had made billions of dollars. Now Moscow proposed a similar scheme. There would be an intermediary between Gazprom and Naftogaz, Ukraine's gas transportation company. It would buy expensive gas from Russia and sell it to Ukraine at a reasonable price, which would be about $90 per 1,000 cubic metres. The price would be low because it was the cheap Turkmen and Kazakh gas supplied by RosUkrEnergo, the intermediary set up under Kuchma by Gazprom and some Ukrainians. This scheme was unprofitable for Gazprom: in summer 2005, Gazprom's minority shareholders claimed that the Russian monopoly would lose about $1 billion on Turkmen gas deliveries alone over two years. Why would Gazprom want to lose so much money? RosUkrEnergo would make good money. Rybachuk recalls conversations on the subject: "I started to ask what the profit would be, and I figured that it was about $500 million per quarter. I said [to our business partner in the Kremlin]: 'Two billion is our share per year?' 'Yes,' they said, 'you've got an election coming up, so this is in your interest. Now it's yours.' Can you imagine being told that? 'Here's two billion for a start. Do what you want with it.' I went to Yushchenko and said, 'If we go along with this scheme, it will corrupt our whole government.'"[24]

On 1 January, the Kremlin cut off Ukraine's gas, setting off a major international scandal. A few days later, Yushchenko agreed to the scheme that had been proposed. He called it a gas compromise. The names of the founders of RosUkrEnergo on the Ukrainian side remained secret, and only a year later did it emerge that it was Ukrainian billionaire Dmytro

Firtash, with whom Gazprom had done business under Kuchma. In Moscow, they were convinced that revolutions may come and revolutions may go; meanwhile, it was business as usual.

The Orange Revolution ran out of steam. The longer it went on, the more people felt cheated. Over three years Yushchenko's popularity gradually declined before finally collapsing. Soon Yanukovych returned to power, first becoming prime minister and later president. Moscow had always looked down on Ukraine and Ukrainian politicians and treated them with contempt. Developments after the Orange Revolution only served to reinforce the Kremlin's view that Ukraine was a weak, helpless state, a failed state with no national interest or strong power, no matter who occupied the highest office in Kyiv.

Putin came out of the Orange Revolution humiliated but also full of anger and determination. His growing imperial ambition needed arguments and easily found them. His disdain for Ukrainian statehood completed his belief that Russia had a birthright to dominate the post-Soviet space. In April 2005, he was explaining to Condoleezza Rice during her first visit to Russia as the US secretary of state that post-Soviet states "had taken their institutions and wealth from the Soviet Union. It was therefore not surprising that Moscow would have a 'continuing interest' in them."[25]

In March 2008, when the George W. Bush administration wanted to present a NATO membership action plan for Georgia and Ukraine at the upcoming NATO summit in Bucharest, the US ambassador to Moscow, William Burns, appeared before Putin to deliver his president's message: The rapprochement of Ukraine and Georgia with NATO would not threaten Russian interests. Burns recalled Putin's angry remarks. "Don't you know that Ukraine is not even a real country? One part of it really is East European, but the other is Russian."[26] Putin would soon tell Bush the same thing in Bucharest: Ukraine is not a state, and part of its territory was given to it by Russia.[27]

Nemtsov remained an adviser to Yushchenko until October 2006, when the Ukrainian president abolished the institution of freelance advisers. Nemtsov was effectively fired. He had not been able to have a meeting with Yushchenko since mid-summer when the political situation in Ukraine changed again and Yanukovych became prime minister.

In fact, Yushchenko was tired of Nemtsov, who was a nuisance to his entourage, and indeed to himself. "At some point, Yushchenko stopped communicating with Boris, because he would come and tell it like it was. He told Yushchenko he was wasting time, that he hadn't done this or that, that he should deal differently with oligarchs, and so on," said Ukrainian politician Ostap Semerak, who had maintained a close relationship with Nemtsov.[28]

Nemtsov told the press that he and Yushchenko remained friends, but of course he was very upset. As usual, however, Nemtsov did not hold a grudge against Yushchenko. But he didn't hide his disappointment with the Orange Revolution: "They have so discredited themselves, including Yushchenko," he said, "that they have a long way to crawl [towards democracy]." Nemtsov compared Yushchenko to Yeltsin: both were proponents of democracy and freedom of speech, both won on that wave, both failed to live up to expectations, and both quickly lost people's trust. But if Yeltsin's dream of a free Russia had been crushed, Yushchenko's dream of a free Ukraine was alive and well—that was the outcome of the Orange Revolution. Whatever happened next, and however difficult the path, Ukraine had made a strategic choice between authoritarianism and European democracy. And no one is questioning this choice, Nemtsov said in 2010 when Yanukovych became president of Ukraine.

In autumn 2004, Nemtsov had come to Kyiv as a disgraced politician, a former heavyweight pushed onto the sidelines of the political process in Russia. But for the Kremlin, the Orange Revolution divided the world into two camps: "He who is not with us is against us." Whoever supports Yushchenko is against Russia. And Nemtsov, no longer constrained by intra-party commitments and discipline, was increasingly critical of both the government as a whole and Putin personally. "Putinism is a velvet dictatorship," he said. Before long, he was a virtual pariah in Russia. He was bullied in propaganda and not allowed on national television.

In 2004, Mikhail Fridman could not risk offering Nemtsov a job, but they still spent time together. A year later, he had little contact with him. It wasn't just dangerous to hire Nemtsov; it was dangerous even to meet with him. Fridman broke with Nemtsov deliberately:

I understood that, if I kept the mode of communication with him that we had before he took up this clear, hardline opposition to the government, it would be impossible to convince anyone that I was not supporting him financially and not playing some kind of political game. No matter how many times I swore on whichever holy book that I was just friends with him because I liked going out to a restaurant with him in the evening, because his company was fun and interesting [...], no one would have believed me. And I realized that my association with him was becoming toxic to my business—my partners, colleagues and employees. That was a risk I could not take. I was forced to spend less time with a person who was really close and dear to me, who I thought and still think is smart, decent, honest and interesting. Unfortunately, I spent less time with him than I could have, not imagining that he had so little time left. I will regret that for the rest of my life.[29]

# CHAPTER 25

## 2005–08
## Sovereign Democracy

### Getting out the right youth vote

On the night of Sunday, 15 May 2005, Leninsky Prospect in Moscow was suddenly closed. Since the Soviet era, this major thoroughfare had been the route taken by international delegations between the airport and the Kremlin. That night, the right lanes of the highway from the city centre were completely closed to traffic. Local residents, including patients and their visitors in a hospital, were completely blocked from entering or leaving their courtyards. At night there was a mysterious sight: hundreds of young people—so young that they looked like teenagers—squatting on the wide asphalt pavement and carefully painting dotted white lines.

The next morning the people living on the prospect were awakened by the strains of the most famous song celebrating Victory Day, the defeat of Nazi Germany. Voices singing 'The scent of gunpowder was on the air this Victory Day...' burst out from specially installed loudspeakers. It was very strange. A week earlier, Russia had celebrated the fiftieth anniversary of the victory in what the Soviet Union calls the Great Patriotic War—that is, the Second World War—with great pomp and ceremony. The parade in Moscow was attended by more than fifty heads of state, including George W. Bush, Hu Jintao and almost all the leaders of Europe. There were solemn gatherings, fireworks and anthems.

Why were war songs being sung again? Had Groundhog Day come to Russia? The residents of the neighbourhood were even more surprised when they looked outside. They were used to mass events made to order by the state, but they'd never seen anything like this before. As far as the eye could see were thousands of young people in identical white T-shirts with red stars on the front and the words of the Russian national anthem on the back, standing in perfectly straight lines. Now they understood the purpose of those carefully drawn dotted lines. The young people were waving red-and-white flags and chanting, "Hurrah for the veterans!"

This was Nashi, the Kremlin's new, mass-scale youth project.

Recent events in Kyiv had strengthened the Kremlin's fears. The Orange Revolution was seen as a link in a chain of coups instigated by the West that were dress rehearsals for the next event, the main revolution: a coup in Russia. The Kremlin was convinced that the so-called "colour revolutions" that had taken place in the former Soviet republics were based on a single game plan that had been developed in the State Department and the CIA to overthrow unwanted regimes. Kremlin spin doctors avidly read '198 Methods of Nonviolent Action' by the American philosopher and activist Gene Sharp,* believing that they were holding their enemy's manual for overthrowing unwanted governments. But you fight fire with fire, or in this case you fight young people taking to the streets by sending out your own young people to take the streets. And you fight revolution-fomenting youth groups—such as Otpor in Serbia in 1998, Khmara in Georgia in 2003, and *Pora!* in Ukraine in 2004—with a youth group of your own creation. For Vladislav Surkov, by that time the Kremlin's chief ideologue, the time was right. Now he could implement on a completely different scale a plan he'd come up with a long while back.

At the beginning of Putin's presidency, the Kremlin was already considering how to counter what they called "the red–brown threat" (left-wing opposition). The leaders of radical nationalist and ultra-leftist movements were still young, charismatic, aggressive and attracted

---

* A catalogue of methods to oppose dictatorships compiled by Gene Sharp in his book *The Politics of Nonviolent Action* (1973).

relatively large crowds at their rallies. They'd been organizing street rallies since the early 1990s without any interference. In 2000, after a May Day rally, a day when the left-wing traditionally came out in force, a meeting was held in the Kremlin. At the meeting, the participants decided that organizations of Afghan veterans weren't the right groups to fight these radicals; they were afraid these organizations couldn't be controlled. They decided that they needed their own militant youth movement, and so Moving Together was born. Surkov entrusted it to Vasily Yakemenko, a young entrepreneur, producer and commentator from the working-class town of Lyubertsy outside Moscow.

Yakemenko had already made a name for himself in politics by then as a showman and black PR tricks manager on the Kremlin's payroll. In December 1999, at the height of the Kremlin's war against Primakov and Luzhkov, he suddenly appeared on television news as a music producer. He told a story about how men sent by Yevgeny Primakov had beaten up him and his musicians over a song they didn't like. In early 2000, Yakemenko hired some Moscow students to go onto the capital's main thoroughfare, Tverskaya Street, and pretend they were a rally of sex workers supporting Yury Skuratov who had famously been caught in a honey trap. When Surkov established himself in the Kremlin, he immediately invited Yakemenko to join him. But back in 2000 the FSB blocked his nomination, apparently because they thought his past was too questionable.

Yakemenko was an inspired planner of mass events who believed that the more outrageous and more obscene the behaviour, the more effective the event. "For a long time, I've wanted to create an organization to build character in young people," he once said.[1] But in the end, Moving Together is remembered not for its character-building but for its collaboration with fanatical groups, its pro-Putin rallies, and its fight against postmodernist writer Vladimir Sorokin. After the Bolshoi Theatre commissioned Sorokin to write the libretto for an opera, Moving Together activists set up a huge cardboard toilet bowl in front of the Bolshoi Theatre and threw tattered copies of the Sorokin's books into it while chanting that he was a pornographer. No one could miss the reference to Hitler Youth burning "un-German books" in Nazi Germany.

In the winter of 2005, Surkov and Yakemenko replaced Moving Together with Nashi (which means "our guys" or "people like us"). Ironically, the official name of the organization was the "Nashi" Anti-Fascist Movement. In reality, this was simply a rebranding. Moving Together, which Yakemenko himself described as a paramilitary organization, was too closely associated with Putin and harmed his reputation with their outrageous and aggressive acts. Nashi started its activities by paying students in Moscow dormitories or in technical schools outside the city to take part in the rally on Leninsky Prospect in May 2005.

This was not typical of Nashi. The activists who made up the core of Nashi had a different main objective: to make the lives of activists opposing Putin and the ruling party as miserable as possible, sometimes acting on the edge of the law, sometimes crossing the line. The structure of Nashi was built on an internal hierarchy and strict discipline. "Negative press accusing Moving Together of collaborating with street thugs taught Yakemenko the importance of the art of disguise," wrote journalist Ilya Barabanov. "When he set up Nashi a few years later, he put trusted comrades-in-arms from fanatical groups into staff positions but kept them out of visible roles."[2] But, in any case, the point was violence. Russian far-right journalist Yegor Kholmogorov, then close to the Kremlin, stated as much very clearly in the winter of 2004, immediately after the Orange victory in Ukraine: "Resistance [to the Orange Revolution in Russia] must be a guerrilla war and be violent or at least quasi-violent." The opposition, Kholmogorov explained, should be "pelted with eggs, vegetables, cakes, smoke bombs and firecrackers. Spray ice water on the crowd."[3] This is what Nashi focused on, modified to suit Yakemenko's fantasies, which seem to have mainly revolved around sexual imagery. One of his co-workers in the Kremlin described how Yakemenko once slipped a pornographic magazine into a colleague's briefcase. His co-worker went in to see his boss, and when he pulled papers out of his briefcase, the magazine fell out. In 2002, he proposed that the Free Generation Movement—another fledgling right-wing group the Kremlin was flirting with—should get a huge number of young people to march on to Red Square, turn their backs to the West and pull their pants down all at once. They usually threw eggs and tomatoes at street demonstrators, but sometimes they'd throw faeces as well. When Nemtsov came to speak in Ryazan a few years later in 2010, his car was covered with dildos. "It has been established that the funding for Nashi and others is provided by Surkov. It's from the Kremlin's slush fund. These groups report directly to him. The phalluses that the hooligans in Ryazan left yesterday are Surkov's phalluses. I should like to point out to Mr Surkov that phalluses are not fingernails. If you cut them off, they don't grow back," Nemtsov wrote in his blog.[4]

## A besieged fortress

In 2004, just after Beslan, Russian domestic politics entered a new phase. Liberals were added to the list of the regime's enemies. Official propaganda presented them as agents of the West bent on suppressing and destroying Russia. "Basically, a fifth column of left-wing and right-wing radicals has emerged in our besieged country," Surkov said in one of his programmatic interviews in autumn 2004. "Lemons and some apples are now growing on the same branch.* Fake liberals and real Nazis have more and more in common. They are supported by the same foreign sponsors and share the same hatred—for Putin's Russia. But, in actuality, they just hate Russia."[5]

By then, it really was "Putin's Russia." At the end of Putin's first presidential term, it was no longer anything like the previous Yeltsin-era Russia. As relations with the West deteriorated and Putin consolidated power and tightened his grip on political life, there was a need for a new state ideology. Where was the country headed?

And so, the doctrine of sovereign democracy that Vladislav Surkov proposed to Putin became reality. The so-called managed democracy of the early 2000s was conceived as a transitional stage towards conventional democracy, but sovereign democracy took a fundamentally different route. "We have nowhere to run but back home," Surkov said in another of his keynote speeches. As political scientist Kirill Rogov wrote, "If managed democracy was a little shy about its inferiority,

---

\* A play on words referring to Eduard Limonov, leader of the left-wing radical National Bolshevik Party, later banned, and the liberal Yabloko ("apple") party.

sovereign democracy decided to make it a point of pride. It declared that there is no such thing as real democracy."[6] Most importantly: Russia was not subject to rules devised in the West.

Sovereign democracy was not a fully fledged ideology. Rather, it was a kind of corporate press release, a crib sheet for explaining Russia's internal processes to the outside world. Why should all the power in the country be in Putin's hands? Because Russia is a unique power with traditions stretching back centuries, which has always, throughout its entire history, been forced to defend its millennia-old way of life against invaders. In November 2004, Putin told President Bush over lunch during the APEC summit in Santiago that Russia needed a form of government that was "in tune with Russian traditions."[7] "It's the ideology of a besieged fortress," Nemtsov explained. "'There are enemies and villains everywhere. Everyone wants to stifle a strong Russia, but just let them try—we'll show them.' That's what sovereign democracy is all about."[8] It offered nothing but opposition to the West and used images from the past instead of creating a vision of the future.

The Day of National Unity—the new name of the traditional November holidays—was another of Surkov's concepts. It no longer celebrated the October Revolution of 1917. It now commemorated the liberation of Moscow from the Poles in 1612. The Poles, of course, symbolized the West. In a new history textbook commissioned by Surkov in early 2007, the history of post-Soviet Russia was divided into three chapters: 'Perestroika', 'Russia after Perestroika' and 'Sovereign Democracy'. The publication of the textbook caused a commotion: for the first time since the Soviet era, Stalin was mentioned in a positive context in an official publication. But, most importantly, the point of reference was changing. Putin's Russia was not presented as a continuation of the Russia of the 1990s, but as a new and improved version of the Soviet regime: freer, more prosperous, more flexible and more modern. This was true for the textbook and for the whole concept of sovereign democracy.

From the Soviet past, Surkov also borrowed the traditional image of the internal enemy: the slanderer and mud-slinger who disagreed with the one true party line and promoted an enemy agenda within the country. In Soviet propaganda, sociologist Lev Gudkov wrote, "this imaginary character served as the reason for mass mobilization, demands for universal vigilance and readiness 'to fight back.'"[9] Surkov had studied for a year at the Moscow Institute of Culture and always wanted to appear to be a modern and progressive official. He had works by the poet Joseph Brodsky and writer Jorge Luis Borges on his bookshelves and a portrait of rapper Tupac Shakur on his desk. But, when it came down to it, Surkov was using a time-honoured political technique. In the words of the political commentator Alexander Morozov, "For Surkov's people, bashing liberals or National Bolsheviks was a PR game, not an affirmation of any system of values."[10]

At first, Nashi left Nemtsov alone. The Kremlin was haunted by the spectre of the Orange Revolution, so Mikhail Kasyanov became the first rogue politician in Russia and Nashi's first victim. When the former prime minister announced he was running for the presidency, he was the candidate most reminiscent of Viktor Yushchenko—at least on paper.

## The official who said "no" to Putin

A career bureaucrat who began his career way back in Gosplan, the Soviet planning ministry, Kasyanov was neither a dissident nor, unlike Nemtsov, a public politician. He ended up in the opposition by accident, simply for not accepting any of Putin's job offers.

In February 2004, Kasyanov was removed from his position as prime minister rather tactlessly. First, President Putin did not explain the reasons for his dismissal. Second, when he informed Kasyanov of his decision, he forgot that, under the Russian constitution, it is not the prime minister but the whole cabinet that resigns. But, despite all this, Putin had one firm rule: don't throw the people fired into the gutter. There was always a place for everyone in the system of power.

Putin first offered Kasyanov the post of secretary of the Security Council, but he refused. Then the Kremlin considered making him mayor of Moscow. Kasyanov would have said yes to that—the mayor of Moscow is historically the third highest position in the informal power hierarchy—but this clearly did not appeal to Putin, who was looking to give him a sinecure rather than a serious job. In summer 2004, Putin suggested that a new interstate bank be set up specifically for Kasyanov. The bank would be responsible for economic integration between the post-Soviet countries and Europe. Kasyanov was considering the offer when terrorists attacked the school in Beslan. He realized that times were changing radically, and would be for a long time, and so he refused again.

Putin's offers are not to be turned down. Kasyanov was the only senior official to say no to the boss. He was something of a hedonist and an aristocrat, and he held himself in high regard. If he agreed to the bank sinecure, he would have had to bow down to Putin, as it were. Kasyanov could not do it; he would have found it humiliating. In December, Putin summoned the former prime minister and reiterated his offer. "I said that I had considered the subject completely closed after our previous meeting in November and that I had already started my own consulting business," Kasyanov recalled in his memoirs. "Putin didn't try to persuade me and said, 'You know, if you get involved with opposition activities, I'll take you down.'"[11] Two months later, Kasyanov announced that he was entering politics on the same day that Putin was explaining to Bush at the Bratislava summit that appointing governors was essentially the same thing as the votes cast by the electoral college in the US presidential election.

In Putin's worldview, Kasyanov was not a traitor to him; he was indebted to Yeltsin for his position of prime minister, not Putin. But he had joined the opposition, so he had only himself to blame. Parliamentarian Alexander Khinshtein, a former journalist known for his connections in the security agencies and his publications of compromising materials (sanctioned "leaks"), initiated a criminal case against Kasyanov for illegally privatizing a dacha in 2003. The privatization of state-issued flats and dachas by top officials had been common practice since the 1990s, a kind of informal compensation for service. (Nemtsov, for example, became the owner of the flat Yury Luzhkov initially did not want him to be registered in.) But in for a penny, in for a pound. If you are in the opposition, don't take hand-outs from the state. A criminal case against Kasyanov was opened. At the same time, the press and parliamentarians called Kasyanov "Russia's Yushchenko" or a "US State Department stooge." In autumn 2005, Kasyanov announced that he would run for president in 2008.

## Nemtsov loses his job

In the early hours of 8 December 2005, three buses escorted by police cars with their flashers on pulled up to the offices of Neftyanoi on the Ring Road in the centre of Moscow. Investigators and about two dozen special-forces officers got out of the buses. They cordoned off the premises of the Neftyanoi Bank that was part of the concern. Searches began, and employees were only permitted to leave the building in the evening. Nemtsov was outraged: "There are no criminals in the bank," he said. "They could have come quietly and got all the documents they needed. Instead, they brought in special forces and locked people up in their rooms—they wouldn't even let them go to the bathroom."[12]

Nemtsov worked for the Neftyanoi concern and had nothing to do with the bank that so interested law enforcement. Within Linshits's business, it was a separate structure. Investigators had already been there a few months earlier, and Nemtsov had even met with Surkov at the time to find out what was going on and why. Whether Surkov helped is unknown—at the time he did not control the security forces as closely as he did later—but, in any case, the bank was left alone. This time Neftyanoi was searched at the same time as another bank called MDM, where the billionaire Alexander Mamut had been the chairman of the board of directors. *Kommersant* quoted a Neftyanoi employee that in this way "the authorities are warning Mamut and Nemtsov not to finance their friend Mikhail Kasyanov, who had recently announced his intention to form a democratic coalition."[13] The Kremlin suspected that a Russian Orange Revolution was being prepared and already had a leader as well as in-country sponsors.

During the search of the bank, a so-called slush-fund box was supposedly found: stamps, letterhead and documents that allegedly served as proof that the company was using cash. (Linshits later claimed that the stamps and papers had been planted during the search.) Nemtsov went to see Surkov again, and a week later he wrote his resignation letter. "They requested very insistently that I quit Neftyanoi," Nemtsov later recounted. "The problem wasn't even that I was criticizing Putin's policies, but that I dared to spend time with Kasyanov."[14] Linshits and Nemtsov thought that the resignation would dispel the clouds that had gathered over Linshits and his business. After all, they'd carried out the Kremlin's wishes, eliminated the political risks, and now there was nothing left to worry about.

Meanwhile, Kasyanov was working on his bid for the presidency. The plan was for him to first become the leader of a political party, but the Kremlin had tightened the laws on party activities, adding requirements that were now almost impossible to meet. Since it was impossible to create a party from scratch, Kasyanov began negotiations with the Democratic Party of Russia (DPR). The DPR had been well-known and active in the early 1990s but later lost momentum. However, it still had all the necessary documents and organizational structure.

When Kasyanov arrived at the party forum in Kursk, he was greeted by a crowd of teenagers with banners reading "Down with the Orange Mishka!" and "Kasyanov, Go Back to America!" The leader of the Nashi squad chanted into a megaphone, "Kasyanov, give back the dacha!" A teddy bear—called a *mishka*, which is also the nickname for Mikhail—with orange balloons was released into the air. Eggs and stones were thrown at Kasyanov, and scuffles broke out as the police looked on and did nothing. It was Nashi's first public act against the opposition. From then on, this kind of harassment, with slight variations, became routine for any politically unacceptable opposition groups—that is, those opposition groups the Kremlin would not let run in elections.

The congress where Kasyanov was to be elected leader of the DPR was scheduled for Saturday, 17 December. But when Kasyanov and his supporters arrived in the morning at the site where the congress was to be held, they were not allowed in. The guards were provided by a private security firm belonging to a Duma deputy, so the Kremlin didn't even have to send in their own. The only delegates allowed in were those who had been "corrupted" the day before by political strategist Andrei Bogdanov in agreement with the Kremlin. "Corrupted" was Bogdanov's word: for voting "the right way", delegates received $10,000 each. Kasyanov and his remaining supporters hurriedly found another hall on the outskirts of Moscow. Surkov sent his agent there disguised as an electrician. He walked around the room with a roll of electrical tape and a torch, supposedly checking the wiring but, in reality, reporting to the Kremlin on the Kasyanov conference. But they had nothing to worry about. Thanks to the bribed deputies, Kasyanov didn't have a chance.

After the unexpected search of Neftyanoi in December and the subsequent resignation of Nemtsov, Igor Linshits was understandably nervous. He breathed a sigh of relief—it looked like nothing really bad would happen—only after he had crossed through passport control at Vnukovo airport on 23 December and flew in a private jet to Courchevel, where a large company of oligarchs, celebrities and newsmakers were going to celebrate Christmas as usual. The nightclubs and restaurants of Courchevel had already stocked up on the best champagne, truffles and black caviar, and two weeks of noisy and merry holidays awaited Linshits. On 27 December, he had to return to Moscow for a day or two to hold a couple of meetings and to see his co-workers at a New Year's Eve party. Linshits drove to a small airport for private planes near Geneva, got into a jet and settled in his seat, when suddenly he noticed that there was no water on board. Just as they were starting take-off, he stopped the plane and got out to get a couple of bottles. Just then his mobile phone rang; it was his secretary, wanting to clarify some details about an upcoming corporate party. "Oh, yeah, I almost forgot," she added towards the end. "There's a summons that's been faxed to you from the prosecutor's office." Linshits hung up, turned around, got in his car and drove back to Courchevel. Two weeks later, the prosecutor's office put him on an international wanted list.

A month later in February 2006, the deputy Khinshtein who'd been dogging Kasyanov since the summer, held a press conference and declared that "the team of democrats in the service of the US President, namely Kasyanov, Nemtsov, and Linshits, are busy preparing an anti-constitutional coup."[15] Igor Linshits was outside Russia when he heard the charges. He'd be able to return to Russia only five years later, when the criminal case against him was closed for lack of evidence. Mikhail Kasyanov was left without a party. Nemtsov was out of a job.

## Energy superpower

It was a strange time. The Russian economy was still growing at unprecedented rates. The golden years had arrived, the blessed state of "stability." The default and oil at eight dollars a barrel still lingered in the memory as the price of oil was breaking through one psychological barrier after another: forty, fifty, sixty, seventy and, in early 2008, one hundred dollars per barrel. Gas and metal prices went up at the same time. During Putin's time in power, the Russian budget grew sevenfold. Everyone benefited from pieces of the oil pie. People didn't just live better— people lived better and better every day, every week, every month. On average, each Russian improved his or her wealth by ten per cent a year over the course of a few years. Shopping centres, car dealerships, fitness centres and restaurants sprouted like mushrooms in the cities. Banks handed out loans right and left—in 2006 every second Muscovite was already living on credit—and along with the rising oil price, consumer demand became the motor of economic growth. A consumer society had emerged. In 2006, Russia was already ahead of any other country in Europe in terms of retail turnover. Never before had the life of the average Russian citizen changed so rapidly: everything became more comfortable, better and of higher quality, from food to furniture, from washing powder to cars. The Russian middle class, which accounted for approximately one-fifth of the country's population, was undergoing a dramatic change in lifestyle for the better.

In the wake of the oil boom, Russia increasingly called itself an "energy superpower", continued to spoil relations with the rest of the world and quarrelled more aggressively with its neighbours. One scandal followed another. The year 2006 began with a gas clash with Kyiv, followed by a trade war with Poland, sanctions against Moldova and a powerful anti-Georgian campaign. Then, in November 2006, former Russian spy Alexander Litvinenko was poisoned with radioactive polonium in London, and the year 2007 began with a crisis in relations with Great Britain. In February 2007, Putin gave his famous Munich speech, after which Western politicians spoke for the first time about the prospect of a new fully fledged Cold War with Russia.* But it was as if all these diplomatic scandals were a mirage. Businesses paid no

---

\* Vladimir Putin's speech at the Munich Security Conference on 10 February 2007 is considered a watershed in Russian relations with the West. Putin sharply criticized the unipolar world order that was attempting "to teach Russia about democracy" and for the first time accused NATO of treacherous eastward expansion.

attention to them. Foreign investment in Russia hit new records in 2007, and ordinary people were more and more eager to enjoy the perks of Western life. In material, practical terms, the West was getting closer by the day.

The 1990s, with its political struggles, live television and interest in politics were a thing of the past. Public politics went out of fashion, gradually becoming as virtual as international diplomacy. Sociologists registered what they called "depoliticization." They noted, for example, an obvious change in perceptions of the function of television. In comparison with responses in 2000, the number of people who thought that television must inform decreased, and vice versa—the number of people who thought that the task of television was to entertain and educate increased. Human-rights activists and democrats of the first wave—people who didn't fit into the new reality, had lost money and influence and were repeating their boring, commonplace truths—were now increasingly looked down upon by journalists and the general public with scepticism, if not outright contempt.

Kicked to the kerb, Nemtsov looked like one of these losers. "You say understandable things," he was told on one of the television programmes of the time, "but think of how it looks from the outside. You're out of power, you lost the election, and now you're freely stating your populist criticism of the regime from your marginal space." Nemtsov was also out of fashion. Journalists regarded him as a simpleton and a womanizer. Many acquaintances from the old days shunned him and tried not to cross paths with him in restaurants. But Nemtsov was not embarrassed by any of this. He taught himself to be completely unperturbed. He went to high-society parties, spent time with women, exercised daily, mastered windsurfing and kitesurfing and was a founding member of the country's main annual windsurfing festival, the Russian Wave. The festival was popular entertainment for both the business elite and high society. "Someone had the nerve to snatch Boris Nemtsov's board right from under his nose, and he had to run to grab another, slowing both his start and the finish," reported a society rag about Russian Wave 2006, held on the Red Sea in Egypt. "Boris was annoyed and responded to this sagely, noting that this sport was 'even worse than politics.'"[16]

## Debating underground

Nemtsov was harshly critical of Putin and the regime he had built. "Many people think I am naïve," he said, "and I know that politics is considered to be a cynical and dirty business. I am reminded of this on a daily basis. But if there is an opportunity to tell the truth, you shouldn't reject the opportunity. I am willing to pay dearly to be a free man and speak the truth."[17] Nemtsov, like other oppositionists, was rarely invited to speak on national television anymore. The phrase pronounced by Duma Speaker Boris Gryzlov in late 2003, "Parliament is no place for discussions," had long since become a catchphrase.* Television was censored, and political discussion gradually moved to LiveJournal, the first fully fledged Russian-made social network. Bloggers became famous, and a blogging subculture emerged, along with clubs where bloggers met and held debates. Nemtsov came to one of these debates to argue with parliamentarian Dmitry Rogozin, the same nationalist who not so long ago had been a favourite of Putin's and wanted to lead his party, and had then crushed SPS as head of the Motherland Party.

Rogozin on stage with Nemtsov was no coincidence. After his triumphant results in the parliamentary elections in early 2005, Rogozin had led the charge against the monetization of retirement benefits. This reform—designed to replace the Soviet-era in-kind benefits, such as free use of public transportation for pensioners, with monetary compensations—caused a massive wave of discontent. The reform was so unpopular that it even hit Putin's ratings—the first time this had happened. Rogozin always wanted to have a closer relationship with Putin, but he got carried away in the wrong direction. He and a few other lawmakers went on a hunger strike in parliament to protest the reform. The Kremlin did not forgive him for that mistake. The Motherland Party, with its xenophobic and populist slogans, was first expelled from the Moscow parliamentary elections after it released a campaign video calling for "cleaning the rubbish [i.e. people from the Caucasus] out of Moscow." Then it was disqualified from all other elections, Rogozin was

---

\* Gryzlov's quote was in fact a little different, but this was the sense of it, and this is the way it has been remembered.

forced to resign, and finally the party itself was disbanded. By autumn 2006 Rogozin was still a deputy in the parliament, but he had lost everything else.

Around that same time, the already strained relations between Russia and Georgia sharply deteriorated. The Georgian president, Mikheil Saakashvili, expelled several Russian military personnel from the country, accusing them of espionage. The Russian authorities responded with an anti-Georgian campaign: flights were halted, Georgian businesses in Russia were faced with inspections, and Georgian citizens in Russia were deported *en masse*. The campaign overlapped with already strong xenophobic sentiments directed mainly against people from the Caucasus. In mid-October, when Nemtsov and Rogozin were debating each other, the campaign was in full swing.

The packed and smoky hall of the nightclub was chaotic. The host had to almost shout to introduce Nemtsov and Rogozin and explain what they'd be debating. "There are people walking in the streets of Moscow with 'I am Georgian' badges," said the host of the debate. "Nobody seems to be bothering them, but other Georgians are being harassed. They are detained, their restaurants are shut down, some casinos are closed. Some consider it ethnic cleansing. Others believe this is just an excessive implementation of a normal policy. Some are supporting Georgian tennis players at the Kremlin Cup tennis tournament on principle. And others are ready to go to war with Georgia tomorrow."[18]

Rogozin supported the anti-Georgian campaign. Nemtsov strongly condemned it. He said that the fight against crime should be conducted by the letter of the law and not for political expediency. "Should we not be friends with Armenians, should we fight against the Armenian [diaspora]?" he asked. He also said that under no circumstance should Russia annex South Ossetia and Abkhazia, two Georgian republics that did not recognize Georgian authority. "The whole world will perceive Russia as an aggressor," he said, "and it is not Georgia but our vast country that will be under blockade."

The moderator of the debate, a tall, stately, cheerful young man who was thirty years old, kept his neutrality. The audience knew him well as a popular blogger and aspiring politician who had staged noisy protests against infill development in Moscow. His name was Alexei Navalny.

It was his first meeting with Nemtsov. Navalny asked him, "You think Rogozin is dangerous, don't you? Before the election you said, 'God forbid Rogozin comes to power.' So should he be wiped out or not?" "He's already been wiped out," Nemtsov replied. "Don't you see? He's here with us. We're both young, both in good shape—he plays handball, I go windsurfing. And both of us were taken down, even though we're from different political camps. Because they are afraid of people with their own opinion, and it doesn't matter if you're a democrat or a nationalist patriot. I don't agree with Rogozin on many points, but I agreed with him about one thing—I was against it when his party was disqualified from elections everywhere. They've cleared the field to the point where now voices are only heard underground."[19]

## Yeltsin's death

On 23 April 2007, Yeltsin died of cardiac arrest. It happened unexpectedly. He was in the hospital for a planned procedure, and he was feeling well. On that day, his wife, Naina, was going to take him home. The day before, she had left him around midnight, and Yeltsin hurried her out: "You need to rest, it's late, and tomorrow I'll be home."[20] But in the morning he stood up abruptly and lost consciousness. His death came as a shock to the people close to him. He was doing well, and for seventy-six he looked much better than he had done on 31 December 1999, when he gave his last address to the public and handed the Kremlin over to Putin. Now that he was retired, he was coming back to life with each passing day, week and month. In his latest interviews, Yeltsin was in good spirits, vigorous, expressive and looking younger than he did at the end of his presidency.

The funeral for the first Russian president lasted three days. There had never been a funeral like this in Russia. It was a state funeral, but for the common people; it was democratic and yet grandly imperial. For three days, a long line stretched around the Christ the Savior Cathedral, where Yeltsin's body lay in state, and the line was made up of every kind of citizen: first-wave democrats and housewives, managers and students, businessmen and journalists. It was as if people were at last ready to forgive their former idol and hero after turning their backs on him, seemingly for ever, as the one responsible for all their troubles. Propaganda had long painted the 1990s as an era of hopeless anarchy and collapse, from which Vladimir Putin saved Russia, but Putin himself never said a bad word about Yeltsin. The president's solemn yet heartfelt speech was full of pride and reverence. He said Yeltsin "changed the face of power, he broke down the wall between society and the state [...] few people are bestowed with such a fate, to become free oneself and then lead millions."[21] Many years later, in his third decade of rule, Putin would no longer consider himself Yeltsin's successor, concluding that fate itself, divine providence, had brought him to the Russian throne. But back then, in 2007, it was important for him to consolidate tradition and, in doing so, to shore up the ideological foundation of his power: Yeltsin was Russia's first president; he was Russia's second.

Nemtsov was in London when Yeltsin died. He came to pay his respects to Yeltsin straight from the airport on the day of the funeral, early on the morning of 25 April. He did not receive a special invitation to the funeral like world leaders, governors and members of the government. He entered the cathedral with the crowd, bowed before Yeltsin and stood off to the side by the wall. Who was Yeltsin to him, the man who had, a long time ago, brought him into the high echelons of politics and wanted to make him his successor? The ties that had bound them together were probably not just political. "There was something so Freudian about this story, that he had no son and I had no father..." That was Nemtsov's comment to friends the day Yeltsin died.[22]

Nemtsov was outraged by Yeltsin's reclusiveness after his resignation: "The first president has a right to express his own position. Why did he relinquish that right?"[23] Indeed, in all the years of Putin's rule, Yeltsin sharply condemned only one decision—reinstating the melody of the Soviet national anthem in late 2000. Yeltsin, who saw his mission as ridding Russia of Communism, was categorically against it. "First under Stalin they sang the words, then Khrushchev came along and threw out the lines about 'the father of nations' but kept the melody," he said. "Under Brezhnev they changed something in the lyrics again. So now there will be new 'text' again? This is no joking matter."[24]

On other, extremely rare occasions when Yeltsin let it be known that he opposed the establishment of one-man rule and uniformity of opinion in the country, he expressed himself with great restraint. He withdrew from public life. In all the years after his resignation, he gave only a few interviews, and almost every time he emphasized that he would not publicly assess his successor. And as time went on, there was less chance to do so in person. Naina Yeltsin recalled that her husband's meetings with Putin "became more and more rare."[25]

It is possible that Yeltsin kept silent in order to protect his family from harm. That was the opinion of Mikhail Kasyanov, who maintained good relations with Yeltsin after his resignation (so good that Yeltsin let him know that he would have preferred him to be his successor rather than Putin).[26] Nemtsov also believed that there was an agreement between Yeltsin and Putin: in return for Yeltsin's not interfering, Putin would guarantee the safety of his family: "Otherwise, knowing Yeltsin's character, it's impossible to imagine why he kept quiet all this time"[27]—especially since in infrequent personal meetings with both with Nemtsov and Kasyanov, Yeltsin was, in their words, quite frank in his outrage at the increasing censorship and the abolishment of the election of governors.

But it's also possible that it was Yeltsin's decision, not a deal. There are different kinds of successors. Yeltsin never liked and could not like Putin the way he once liked Nemtsov. In 1999, when he found himself in extremely difficult political circumstances, he chose his successor out of necessity, not love. And he had then been constrained by this choice. What was the point of lecturing and bullying his successor now? He did the most important thing—he left on his own and handed over power in the country through elections, that is, democratically. Soon Putin would do the same, and he, Yeltsin, would go down in history—in fact, he already has—as the first Russian president of several, the founding father of the new Russia. He said so in an interview a few months before his death: "The main thing is that the country was freed from Communist dictatorship, the dictatorship of one party, and became a democratic country."[28]

Yeltsin's death caught Putin at the Kremlin door on his way out, less than a year until the end of his second term. But at that moment, just before he was to relinquish power, Putin was expanding his cult to an unprecedented scale.

## Putin's plan: the victory of Russia

In the December 2007 parliamentary elections, the SPS initially stood no chance. The new Operation Successor was entering a decisive phase. Vladimir Putin chose forty-two-year-old Dmitry Medvedev, the former head of his administration and first deputy prime minister since 2005, to be his successor. Putin knew Medvedev well from the early 1990s when he worked as a lawyer in the St Petersburg city hall.

As a result of the parliamentary and presidential elections, Putin was set to become the unquestionable national leader on whose moral authority the Russian state rested. Speaking from the rostrum of the United Russia congress, an ordinary worker of a provincial weaving factory—another typical image from Soviet political life, a delegate ready in the wings at all Communist Party congresses—pleaded for "something to be done to ensure that Vladimir Putin remains president after 2008."[29] United Russia went into the election with the slogan "Putin's Plan—Victory for Russia." In a film made especially for Putin's fifty-fifth birthday, the Oscar-winning filmmaker Nikita Mikhalkov portrayed him as the saviour of the nation, the man who had pulled Russia out of the horror that was the 1990s. In a nationwide performance directed by Vladislav Surkov, the entire country swore allegiance to the outgoing president, and any disagreement with him was interpreted as a betrayal of national interests.

But unlike Yeltsin, Putin was not going anywhere after his resignation. On the contrary, he was preparing an unprecedented experiment. He would leave the Kremlin but never let go of power. To achieve this, in May 2008, after the presidential election, he planned to become prime minister. In the parliamentary elections he was at the top of the United Russia electoral list. His party had to win a constitutional majority in parliament—two-thirds of the seats—just in case the successor had a sudden lapse. If he took a wrong step, the parliament could impeach him. This Plan B was devised at meetings in the Kremlin.

By that time, both gubernatorial elections and elections to the Duma from single-member districts had been cancelled.* That meant that the only way to be elected to the parliament was to be on the list of a political party and that future deputies would be under the Kremlin's control. But, at the same time, this meant that in order to have a constitutional majority, Putin's party had to win twice as many votes as all the other parties combined. In 1999, Putin helped SPS; in the next election, in 2003, he didn't care; now, four years later, there were simply no seats that could be given to the liberals: Putin's party, United Russia, now needed their mandates.

Nemtsov stepped down as leader of SPS at the beginning of 2004 and was soon replaced by a surprise candidate, the thirty-year-old vice-governor of Perm region, Nikita Belykh. He had nominated himself to lead the party and, in the end, managed to convince Chubais, Nemtsov and others to elect him. He was a fresh face, a successful politician in his own region, younger than even the young Nemtsov, and he had business experience. Best of all, he was from the provinces, which was also good for the party, since it had an image of being made up of Moscow snobs who were far removed from the life of common people.

So long as the rating of SPS, which was barely functioning after their 2003 defeat, was so low that it fluctuated within the range of a statistical error, the Kremlin simply didn't pay any attention to it. But in December 2006, under Belykh, SPS created a minor sensation in Belykh's hometown of Perm. SPS took second place in the elections, yielding only to United Russia, with sixteen per cent of the vote. This was a record—the party's best result in any election in its seven-year history. This was followed by several victories—less striking yet still impressive—in other regions. These successes were due in large part to

---

\* Since 1993, the lower house of the Russian parliament had been elected through a so-called mixed system. Half of the seats—225—were chosen in single-member electoral districts, and the other half by proportional representation from national party lists. In anticipation of the election of 2007, the single-member constituencies were abolished, and the entire Duma was elected from national party lists. This allowed the Kremlin to exercise better control over who exactly would become a deputy. After the controversial election of 2011, in which United Russia lost seats, the electoral system reverted to its pre-2007 formula.

a change in electoral tactics, which was the brainchild of Anton Bakov, a talented politician and political strategist from the Urals. Bakov proposed the concept of "finishing the building of capitalism." SPS went to the polls under leftist slogans such as demands for higher pensions and other social guarantees. Multiplied with Bakov's effective online political-marketing technology, these slogans brought about unprecedented results.

From the Kremlin's point of view, it was a gross violation of the rules of the game. The party of unpopular reforms had no right to use populist rhetoric. Second, and most importantly, it was a way for the right to take votes away from United Russia. Surkov wasn't the only one who realized this. "If SPS gets in the parliament, United Russia won't have enough votes for the [constitutional] quorum," Nemtsov said. "That's why the authorities are trying harder and harder to convince voters that no one but pro-Kremlin parties will get into the Duma."[30]

## Nemtsov, the outcast

Not far from Moscow's major hub of railway stations on Sakharov Prospect, where the largest protest rally in modern Russian history would take place in December 2011, is the office of Russia's foreign-economic-affairs bank, Vneshekonombank. There is an inconspicuous, unmarked door at the back, and in those years, if you entered through that door, you would meet Igor Putin, Vladimir Putin's cousin. This was the room that financed the Russian elections.

Making cash contributions to the Presidential Administration—what businessmen called "doing their homework"—had long been routine for big Russian business. But campaign finance practice was modified in 2007. Not only did the parties and their sponsors have to coordinate their cooperation with the Kremlin, but from now on campaign sponsors would have to bring cash to the Kremlin in shopping bags, which would be redistributed through that same door at the back of Vneshekonombank and under Surkov's firm control. "After the election," journalist Natalia Morar quoted political party administrators in *The New Times* magazine, "payments were made according to a schedule agreed upon ahead of time, such as every fortnight. The Presidential Administration dispersed money to political parties directly. This was the case with every political party with large budgets."[31]

At the start of the election campaign in the summer of 2007, several tens of millions of dollars* earmarked to finance the SPS campaign came to the Presidential Administration. However, the SPS never received a penny of it. "We were fed promises for several weeks, and then, in October, we were told that there would be no money," Morar quoted an SPS party official.[32] The Kremlin simply took away the SPS election fund, which had been largely financed by the Chubais-led RAO UES. Back in September, Putin publicly reprimanded Chubais, noting that the state, through him, was in fact "providing hidden support to this 'right-wing force', as it is called, the SPS."[33] This was a clear signal to Chubais to stay away from the SPS.

The campaign had to be run on the infinitesimal sum of money that SPS managed to get out of the Kremlin. When financing was cut off, it meant that the party had fallen from the category of "permitted opposition" to "enemy." Soon this was all made abundantly clear. The 1990s in general and the liberals in particular became the main target of the regime's election campaign. In November, in his keynote address, Vladimir Putin denounced "the people in the 1990s who used their high offices to serve the interests of oligarchic structures and squandered the national wealth to the detriment of society and the state." Putin said they'd corrupted the state, brought the country to default, and now they wanted to take revenge and restore the oligarchy. "They're about to take to the streets again. They've learnt a bit from Western specialists, they've practised on neighbouring republics, and now they're going to stir things up here."[34]

Thanks to the massive propaganda campaign that for years had been contrasting Putin-era stability with the "wild nineties", it was easy to identify the men in Putin's collective portrait: Gaidar, Chubais and especially Nemtsov, who was second after Nikita Belykh on the SPS election list. He had no claim to leadership; he was just called in to help.

---

\* *The New Times* magazine quoted the amount as $150 million. Another source put it at $70 million.

But as the most recognizable and public face on the right, he was the target of the propaganda machine's full force. "They should have retired to grow gooseberries at their country cottages, and Boris Nemtsov should have been a stripper in a nice bar," a United Russia functionary said in support of Putin's position. "But," he continued, "instead they've decided to criticize the current political course."[35] Despite the victories orchestrated by Bakov on the ground, the right-wing campaign was uninspired and piecemeal. In fact, the SPS ran three different and poorly connected campaigns. One, with a leftward slant, was launched by Belykh and Bakov. The second, more conformist, was run by the Chubais team. Finally, Nemtsov ran his own separate campaign. He was no longer campaigning for democracy and reform. These topics were off the agenda. Nemtsov protested the cult of Putin: "It is disgusting to look at the bureaucratic lackeys moulding another Leader of Nations," he said in one of his campaign commercials. "They must be stopped. Down with the cult of personality! Down with servility!"

Unlike in the last election, Nemtsov was now on his own. He did not toe the general party line—but in any case, there really wasn't one. "I've grown up a lot and now I see things differently from when I was governor and deputy prime minister," Nemtsov explained when launching his book *Confessions of a Rebel* (with its eye-catching subtitle, *Politics without Whoring*) which coincided with the start of the election campaign. "For example, now I believe that the main problem for Russia is not the right, the left or the centrists, but the cruelty, indifference, lies and cynicism [generated by the regime]." Why was no one held accountable for Beslan? Why were the hostages at Dubrovka killed? How did the president behave when the *Kursk* submarine sank?" The catastrophe, he continued, is that instead of quenching society's aggression, the Russian authorities "exploit it by inciting hatred for the rest of the world."[36]

When the election campaign began in September 2007, Nemtsov was considered an absolute outcast. From that moment on, he was permanently banned from mainstream national TV channels. He was no longer allowed to appear in any programme, even in the background. By that time, television already had a stop-list—Surkov's list of people not allowed on air. "I'm on that stop-list in an honourable second or third place," Nemtsov said at the time.[37]

During the election campaign, Nashi got the signal from the Kremlin to attack Nemtsov with aggressive catcalls. After that, not a single one of his public appearances took place without them. In his native Nizhny Novgorod, Nashi released a bad-smelling spray into the hall. They also handed out packets of noodles with plastic forks to the audience, calling them Nemtsov's promises—a crude illustration of a Russian slang expression, "to hang a noodle on someone's ear", which means to feed people a line. In Vladivostok, formaldehyde was spilt in the hall. In Rostov-on-Don, they went to a press conference dressed as Uncle Sam and covered themselves with fake dollars. In Krasnoyarsk, they poured liquid chocolate on Nemtsov. Another time in Krasnoyarsk they threw a big net over him with the label "Political Insect." The same thing happened in Kaluga, Voronezh and other cities all across the country. Nashi taunted Kasyanov with a rake—a play on an expression that means to make the same mistake over and over again—once even throwing one under the wheels of his car.

Meanwhile, right-wing campaign offices across the country were under fire. Walls, doors and windows of headquarters were pelted with manure. Millions of copies of campaign literature were confiscated and burnt. SPS candidates couldn't rent halls, they were not permitted to hold electoral events, they were routed by specially created spoiler parties, and fake SPS leaflets discrediting them were widely distributed. This time, the Kremlin waged a war to the death. The right-wingers were pushed out into the streets, the place where protest rallies were held by the officially banned nationalists and National Bolsheviks on the one hand, and by democratic activists led by Kasparov and Kasyanov on the other—as well as by aspiring politicians like Navalny and Yabloko youth leader Ilya Yashin.

The first violent crackdown in Moscow was on the March of Dissenters—as the rallies came to be called—in the spring of 2007.

Roughly two or three thousand protesters—the largest anti-Putin rally to date at the time—were cordoned off by riot police, but they broke through the cordon and marched from Pushkin Square along the boulevards in the centre of Moscow. The riot police used their batons, and about 250 people were detained. All the leaders of the march (except Kasyanov, who was protected by his guards) were also detained.

Unable to make themselves heard in any other way, the SPS joined the marches in the autumn. Nemtsov spoke for the first time at one of these marches in Moscow on 24 November 2007. "They're pulling one over on us when they say they defeated the oligarchs," he said from an improvised stage. "We were the ones who fought them. They were friends with them. We are for Russia and against corruption. We are for Russia and against lawlessness. We are for Russia and against Putin." Nemtsov even sang out a chant he made up: "Ole-ole-ole-ole, onward, Russia! Ole-ole-ole-ole, onward without Putin." The crowd began to pick it up. The demonstration was again dispersed by riot police, though not as violently as in April.

But another unprecedented event occurred. In the past, the detained leaders of the democratic opposition were quickly released. This time, Garry Kasparov, a presidential candidate known all over the world, was sentenced to five days of administrative detention. The next day, at the March of Dissenters in St Petersburg, police detained one of the leaders of the SPS, Leonid Gozman, and (unintentionally) broke his arm in the process. The day before, knowing that a violent crackdown was being prepared, a high-ranking official tried to dissuade Gozman from going to the rally, but it was too late: he had already announced that he was going, and he couldn't back out.

In the elections on 2 December, United Russia won the constitutional majority it was after. Later, independent observers determined that this was the first time an election had been won by massive fraud. The right-wing candidates got less than a percentage. The SPS was destroyed. Russia had changed from an imitation democracy to a Belarusian-style dictatorship. Nemtsov said, "A one-party dictatorship is being established in the country, and a man named Putin has emerged as the new dictator with the help of manipulation, deception and the secret services."[38]

Sovereign democracy had its moment of triumph. But, unlike in neighbouring Belarus, in a few months Russia would have a new president. In May 2008, Putin would cede his office in the Kremlin to Dmitry Medvedev.

# CHAPTER 26

## 2004–08
## Putin's Warrior

### Meeting near Argun

On 12 April 2008, in Gudermes, Chechnya's second largest city and the unofficial capital of its eastern region, a Hummer travelling at 180 kph (112 mph) and carrying two guards of the Chechen president Ramzan Kadyrov crashed into a car carrying two men from the Chechen East Battalion. The illustrious battalion was commanded by Sulim Yamadayev, a hero of both Chechen wars and a man who was not subordinate to Kadyrov.

Both East Battalion officers were killed instantly. Events quickly spun out of control and were soon like something out of *The Godfather*. The East Battalion believed that the fatal incident in Gudermes, the fiefdom of the Yamadayev brothers, was no accident. On 14 April, the day of the funeral, three of the four Yamadayev brothers were in Moscow. Only Badrudin, the youngest brother, who was known for his fiery temper, was at home in Gudermes. Sulim called Badrudin from Moscow and told him to go to the funeral. A conflict between Badrudin and Ramzan had been smouldering since 1999, when Ramzan made his usual run with a convoy of oil tankers to collect oil from a well that was controlled by Badrudin. But Aslan Maskhadov, the president of Chechnya at the time, had ordered that no oil should be given to anyone. A quarrel apparently then broke out between Badrudin and Ramzan.

At the funeral, emotions ran high. Badrudin stormed off, taking a couple of dozen men with him, and rushed off to meet Ramzan Kadyrov's motorcade. He reached Kadyrov near the town of Argun. Contrary to expectations, there was no shoot-out. Ramzan got out of the car, expressed his condolences, was affable, and even invited Badrudin in for tea. All in all, he settled the matter peacefully.

But on the same day, thousands of Kadyrov's guards appeared near Gudermes. They surrounded the East Battalion base and the Yamadayevs' house, demanding that Badrudin be handed over to them. The South and North Battalions were formed of men who had been guerilla fighters against the Russian military during the Second Chechen War but after the war had become loyal to Ramzan Kadyrov. It was a strange situation. The war had ended in victory for the federal government and their allies among the Chechens a long time ago, but here the federal government and allies found themselves once again surrounded by past enemies. "We have three heroes of Russia in our family, and for three days our house has been surrounded—and we don't even know who exactly they represent!" Sulim Yamadayev said in one of his most candid interviews. "But they are the men we fought. They are the men who fought against Russia and called us traitors!"[1]

With this, the final round of the struggle for power in Chechnya began.

The Yamadayev clan considered itself the equal of the Kadyrov clan. Sulim Yamadayev and his two elder brothers, Ruslan and Jabrail, were famous throughout Chechnya for their military victories. During the first Chechen war, the Yamadayev clan, like Akhmat Kadyrov, had sided with the insurgents who wanted independence from Russia. Ruslan Yamadayev was on good terms with Dudayev, and Sulim—then barely twenty years old—came to the aid of Shamil Basayev's forces twice when they were surrounded in the ruins of Grozny, saving them from certain death. However, the Yamadayevs switched sides and turned against the "bearded men"—conservative Wahhabis. "I had believed that Chechnya would be independent, that peace would come after the war [...] [but] I saw that people were being kidnapped and only the bandits were making money," Sulim Yamadayev later recalled.[2]

In 1997, the brothers joined forces with Akhmat Kadyrov, and soon afterwards they declared war on the Wahhabis. In effect, the

Yamadayevs' unit became the army of Kadyrov Sr. In July 1998, after a fierce battle, Sulim Yamadayev drove the Wahhabis out of Gudermes. As Akhmat Kadyrov later recalled, this was a missed chance to avoid a second war. Sulim could have pursued the "bearded men" and cleared all of Chechnya of them, and then Basayev would not have attacked Dagestan the following summer. But Maskhadov ordered a halt to the offensive, and Yamadayev complied.

In November 1999, Ruslan and Jabrail Yamadayev surrendered Gudermes without a fight to Gennady Troshev, commander of the Eastern Group of Federal Forces. The general would call them "unexpected allies" in his memoirs, and the bloodless capture of Gudermes will remain the main success of the Second Chechen War.

In her book *Chechnya Next to Us: The War Through a Woman's Eyes*, the journalist Olga Allenova describes the Yamadayev brothers as "representatives of one of the largest and noblest clans in the mountainous Benoy area, involved in absolutely everything: war, business and politics [...] the Yamadayevs have real power, real authority and real money in Chechnya."[3] Around the same time in 2000, the Chechen special forces under the leadership of one of the brothers, Jabrail Yamadayev, joined the federal forces. Three years later, Jabrail would be killed by a bomb planted by Basayev's troops, and Sulim would become head of the Chechen special forces. His unit would be officially called the East Special Forces Battalion of the Russian Ministry of Defence's GRU. Jabrail was the first of the three brothers to receive the title "hero of Russia" from President Putin, posthumously. The next to receive the title was his elder brother Ruslan, the most down-to-earth of the Yamadayevs; under Akhmat Kadyrov, he would become head of the Chechen United Russia party and, in 2003, representative of Chechnya in the Russian State Duma. Sulim would be the last one to be awarded by Putin, in 2005. The Yamadayevs felt their power. "Do you think you are playing me?" Ruslan challenged envoys from Moscow. "You aren't. I'm playing you."[4] The brothers had a claim to power in the republic, and the friction between the two clans—the Yamadayevs and the Kadyrovs—began under Kadyrov Sr, though at the time they were on the same side of the barricades.

## The strange death of Akhmat Kadyrov

The mystery of Akhmat Kadyrov's murder—the murder that changed everything—will probably never be solved. The popular theory that it was the work of Shamil Basayev has never seemed convincing.

The attack on Kadyrov during the 9 May 2004 Victory Day parade was like a shot from a sniper rifle. A shell-less bomb—plastic explosives in a plastic bottle—was embedded in the concrete grandstand of Grozny's Dinamo stadium directly under the Chechen president's chair. It killed him and Khusein Isayev, chairman of the republic's State Council and ripped the leg off General Valery Baranov, commander of the United Group of Federal Forces in the North Caucasus. Chechen guerrillas, nearly defeated and spent by 2004, were simply unable to prepare such a sophisticated attack. After the terrorist act, the official *Rossiyskaya gazeta* newspaper quoted sources in the Chechen special services as saying that Basayev and Maskhadov had let Kadyrov's relatives know that they were prepared to swear on the Koran that they had nothing to do with the murder.[5]

In theory, other influential Chechens could have been behind the assassination of Kadyrov, but in Chechnya there was little doubt that it was the work of the federal authorities. The federal troops had finished repairing the stands the day before the parade and checked the stadium before the celebrations on the day of the attack. Kadyrov's own security guards also checked the stands with sniffer dogs, but this kind of bomb can only be detected with special bomb-sniffing equipment. Later, people who wished Ramzan ill said that Ramzan had told a small circle that his father had been killed by the Russian special services. In summer 2005, the newspaper *Kommersant* quoted comments made by Ramzan Kadyrov to Chechen victims of a clean-up operation: "I have lost 220 people, all killed, and I lost my father," he said. "It makes no difference who did this. Whether they are in uniform or not, they're gangsters. They are criminals in uniform."[6]

Although Akhmat Kadyrov came to power in Chechnya with the help of federal troops, he certainly did not trust the Russian military or the Russian special services. By 2004, father and son Kadyrov had amassed their own army of six thousand men, mainly from former guerrillas, and Kadyrov Sr began to behave more independently after becoming president in October 2003. "I will not allow anyone to command the republic," he said immediately after his election.[7] His version of the agreement on the division of powers between Chechnya and the federal centre did not suit Moscow. His manner with Moscow emissaries became more and more confident, and along with that trust for him within Chechnya gradually grew. According to one version, Kadyrov was killed because of the tough stance he took on the issue of Chechen oil. During the war, oil theft became a criminal business that everyone was involved in, from the Russian military to the insurgents. Akhmat Kadyrov complained about the military both in meetings with Putin and publicly and demanded that Chechnya's oil revenues remain in the republic.

Akhmat Kadyrov constantly accused the military of crimes against civilians and demanded the withdrawal of federal troops from Chechnya. In his last interview, excerpts from which were shown on Russian national television the day after his death, Kadyrov said that not only was the First Chechen War an enormous mistake that Yeltsin made, but that "the Second Chechen War was unnecessary—overthrowing Maskhadov and removing Basayev was easy." By May 2004, Kadyrov had plenty of ill-wishers in the Kremlin, the army and the security services. Olga Allenova writes that in the spring of 2004 the conflict between Kadyrov and the military escalated to breaking point. "The Russian military saw the Chechen commanders who had fought against them now coming out of hiding to become heroes, and they were infuriated. Soon after, Kadyrov said that he was ready to accept Maskhadov and that he would persuade Putin to forgive him. That was his mistake. A month later he was killed. It was a strange death."[8]

## Putin's choice

Ramzan Kadyrov was in Moscow when he learnt of his father's death. On 7 May, they had both attended a reception at the Kremlin after Putin's inauguration for his second term in office. "My father insisted that I go with him [to the Kremlin]," the younger Kadyrov later recalled.

"He took me around to everyone he knew—politicians, officials, businessmen—saying, 'This is my son, Ramzan.' He introduced me to literally everyone who was there."[9] The next day Akhmat Kadyrov flew home, but he asked his son to stay in the capital. Ramzan stayed at the President Hotel in a room always reserved for his father. By 2004, an entire wing of the fifth floor was permanently reserved for the Chechen administration. Ramzan was there when he got news of his father's death. "Friends came over when I was still asleep and said, 'Ramzan, there's been an explosion in Grozny. But don't worry. Akhmat has been wounded in the leg and head. Everything will be all right,'" Ramzan said. "I didn't believe it. I knew that my father couldn't be wounded. He'd told me many times that his death would be instantaneous. I asked, 'What really happened?' And then they finally told me that my father was no longer with us."[10]

He was at the President Hotel when Putin's guards came for him. Ramzan was told to come down immediately, so he went as he was, in his tracksuit. In the car, he learnt he was being taken to see Putin. The footage from that meeting shows Putin first taking Ramzan's hand and then embracing him, unable to hold back his tears. Akhmat Kadyrov understood that he could be killed at any moment and had long been preparing Ramzan to become his successor. Ever since he became mufti in 1995, his son was always with him, and Kadyrov Sr coached him. "Kadyrov brought up his son as a prince and obviously turned a blind eye to the antics of the heir apparent," *Moskovsky komsomolets* wrote.[11] When Kadyrov Sr was appointed head of the Chechen administration, Ramzan was put in charge of security and had most of the responsibility for finances. He was his father's guard, his first adviser, his vizier.

Akhmat Kadyrov asked Putin to keep an eye on his son. By May 2004, it was obvious to everyone that Ramzan was the number-two man in Chechnya; all that kept him from the highest position was his youth. He became Chechnya's first deputy prime minister the day after his father was killed. "That meant one thing," Anna Politkovskaya wrote in *Novaya gazeta*, "Ramzan was now effectively the head of Chechnya. And this was Putin's choice alone."[12] The Kremlin promoted the Chechen interior minister, Alu Alkhanov, to the presidency, but in reality the power belonged to Kadyrov. Kadyrov was soon giving

Alkhanov orders in public, showing who was boss in Chechnya. As soon as Ramzan Kadyrov had his thirtieth birthday in October 2006, and was old enough to become president of Chechnya, Alkhanov resigned.

Soon it became clear that the transfer of leadership from Kadyrov Sr to Kadyrov Jr was a shift of great importance for Chechnya and Russia as a whole. The region that had been in the centre of Russian politics for the past decade was taken over by a very different kind of leader. Akhmat Kadyrov was an educated man; Ramzan Kadyrov had never studied beyond grade school and had seen nothing but violence and war around him since he was a child. People close to him, however, said that he was intelligent and had an excellent memory. "He remembers all the figures and details of how much everyone stole and what kickbacks everyone was receiving."[13] Kadyrov Sr was a politician; his son was a businessman and a strongman. Kadyrov Sr had authority; his son could only count on his guardsmen, who by that time were already hated by many Chechens. Kadyrov Jr "was not known as a talented military leader, or as a spiritual leader, or as an intellectual", *Moskovsky komsomolets* wrote. "His father's appointment made him powerful and strong."[14]

Kadyrov Sr made a forced alliance with Putin and was never fully loyal to the Kremlin. "He was a strong man who was not afraid to negotiate with the Kremlin despite the fact that all Chechnya called him a traitor," Allenova wrote. "And this inner strength emanating from him indicated that he would never become a puppet."[15] Actually, the word "puppet" didn't suit Ramzan Kadyrov either. Putin was more like a second father to him. Since the spring of 2004, Ramzan repeated constantly that Putin was the saviour of Chechnya and Russia, and that he was Putin's warrior. His father would never have expressed himself that way.

From the very beginning, the relationship between Ramzan Kadyrov and Putin was built on the personal loyalty of the new head of Chechnya. In a political sense, a contract was concluded between them: Kadyrov was given *carte blanche* to act inside Chechnya in return for his guarantee that the republic would be at peace. Ramzan Kadyrov always duly fulfilled his side of the contract and Moscow duly financed Chechnya, which got among the highest state subsidies of all the Russian regions. In addition, immediately after Akhmat Kadyrov's death, a foundation named after him was established in Chechnya. Journalists discovered many years later that under Ramzan Kadyrov the fund was financed not only by Chechen businesses, but also by public sector workers, who formally—voluntarily and involuntarily—contributed part of their salaries to it. The fund would become Kadyrov's personal treasury, which he would spend at his discretion, financing important construction projects, paying royalties for visiting stars and giving expensive gifts to celebrities—athletes, artists and public figures.

In March 2005, the federal special services killed Maskhadov. In July 2006, they killed Basayev, and a month later Putin ordered the withdrawal of troops from Chechnya. Peaceful life was coming to the republic, and the horrors of war were becoming a thing of the past. Palaces, fountains and one of the largest mosques in all Europe were built in the still-ruined capital city of Grozny. Relying on his guards and considerable financial resources, Kadyrov quickly turned Chechnya into a state within a state: He was a despot, no Russian laws were enforced, and only he had the right to punish and pardon.

## Visiting Ramzan

Anna Politkovskaya was not a reporter in the classic sense of the word. She was a human-rights journalist. Throughout much of the Second Chechen war, Politkovskaya travelled around Chechnya, writing mainly about the atrocities the federal military perpetrated on peaceful Chechens. She acted as a human-rights activist: she used her contacts to get people out of prisons and pits and saved people through her publications. Her articles about abductions, torture and killings in Chechnya regularly appeared at trials in the European Court of Human Rights in Strasbourg and were sometimes even the basis of criminal trials in Russian courts. Those were her greatest triumphs. No one had ever worked with such dedication in Chechnya, and she was a hero to Russian activists who worked on human-rights violations in Chechnya.

Politkovskaya was a sharp critic of Akhmat Kadyrov from the day he went over to the side of the federal forces. Ramzan came to her attention in 2003, when evidence began to surface—including through her own work—of the violence his guardsmen were inflicting. Politkovskaya was not shy about speaking out. She wrote that Kadyrov's guardsmen "behave in such a way that [...] it is unclear how exactly the guards of the 'acting president' [Akhmat Kadyrov] differ from gangsters and Wahhabis."[16] Immediately after Akhmat Kadyrov's death, she noted that the transfer of power in Chechnya to his son was the worst possible option, because "Ramzan is purely a man of war, and everyone in Chechnya knows that Ramzan is famous for being cruel and crude, and for his strong attraction to money from the state budget." "This is not just a mistake," she continued, "this is a tragedy that will only lead to more casualties."[17]

The only meeting between Kadyrov and Politkovskaya took place shortly after the death of Akhmat Kadyrov in late June 2004, when she was brought for an interview with Kadyrov at his base in his home village of Tsentoroy. The conversation did not go well. "You have come between the Chechens. You are the enemy. You are worse than Basayev," Kadyrov told her indignantly.[18] Politkovskaya did not come to Tsentoroy alone. She came with Natalia Estemirova, a journalist and human-rights activist from Grozny, who assisted Politkovskaya throughout the war years and became her constant companion. According to Estemirova, Politkovskaya and Kadyrov almost had to be pulled apart. But the next day was more frightening. Kadyrov summoned them again and brought out the Chechen man who had officially complained to the prosecutor's office and then told Politkovskaya that Ramzan had personally beaten him during the 2003 Chechen presidential election. He'd said that Ramzan had demanded that he plant a bomb in the home of one of his—that is, Ramzan's—father's rivals. Now this man stood before Politkovskaya and denied everything. "It was very frightening," Estemirova recalled. "The second visit was a big mistake."[19]

Politkovskaya continued to write about Kadyrov in the harshest of terms. This infuriated Kadyrov, who took great offence at any criticism directed at him. Two days before her death, Politkovskaya had called him a coward in a radio broadcast and said she dreamt of seeing him in the dock. By this point, however, Politkovskaya had already been under surveillance for several months. Her death sentence had been signed.

On Putin's birthday, 7 October 2006, Politkovskaya was murdered. The killer shot her three times in the chest and once in the head as she was getting out of the lift in the entrance hall of her house to get the groceries she had left in her car. Eight years later, the perpetrator and organizer of the murder, both from Chechnya, would be sentenced to life imprisonment—the organizer, who was never found, *in absentia*. A few days after the murder, Putin stood up for Kadyrov, saying that both he and the Chechen authorities were "more harmed by Politkovskaya's murder than by her articles."[20]

Three years later, on 15 July 2009, Estemirova was also murdered. Unidentified men kidnapped her in Grozny, shot her in the chest and head five times and dumped her body on a road in Ingushetia near the border with Chechnya. "Ramzan Kadyrov's impunity is based on Vladimir Putin's personal support," said Lyudmila Alekseyeva, head of the Moscow Helsinki Group at the time. "As long as he has that support, no one can touch a hair of his head, even if he kills us all."[21]

## An oath of fealty

In Chechnya, moving from illegal to legal status and back again was quick and easy. Yesterday's gangsters became policemen and patriots; any policeman or patriot could become a criminal at any time; any action of law enforcers could become an armed attack; and so on. Everything depended on how things were looked at and what was written in documents.

Movladi Baisarov was a former field commander under Maskhadov and later commander of the Chechen Gorets ("mountain men") detachment, a division subordinated to the FSB. He was indispensable to the FSB because he handled delicate requests. "For example, a general from Lubyanka comes to him and says, 'Movladi, some crooks cheated my wife and she lost money. Help me, my friend,'" *Novaya gazeta* wrote many years later.[22] But in 2006, Ramzan Kadyrov demanded that the Gorets detachment be moved under control of Chechen authorities, and Ramzan and Baisarov came into conflict. On 18 November, a month after Politkovskaya's murder, Baisarov was shot in broad daylight on Leninsky Prospect in Moscow as he was getting out of his car and heading into a restaurant. "Eyewitnesses say that after getting out of the car, Movladi Baisarov immediately walked towards a group of Chechens standing nearby," the *Kommersant* newspaper wrote. "The Chechens recognized the unshaven man in a black jacket as Baisarov, shouted something to him, and then grabbed Stechkin automatic pistols and opened fire."[23] The killers turned out to be a group of Chechen policemen led by Adam Delimkhanov, Kadyrov's right-hand man, who oversaw all of the Chechen security forces. Later, the newspapers wrote that his pistol was used to fire the last confirmation shot.[24] The shooting was officially registered as necessary action in response to resistance during an attempted detention.

By this point Ruslan Yamadayev understood that neither he nor his brother would have a quiet life in Chechnya. Not so long ago, he, one of the most influential Chechen leaders and a deputy in the Russian Duma, had been touted to become head of the republic after Akhmat Kadyrov's death. But his good relations with Ramzan Kadyrov were at an end, the East Battalion was in trouble, and a year later Yamadayev would be replaced in the State Duma by Adam Delimkhanov.

Ruslan expected that after the incident with Badrudin, Ramzan would launch an attack on the Vostok battalion and on his brother Sulim. That's exactly what happened. In the past Ramzan had called Sulim one of his comrades-in-arms. Now he accused him of abductions and killings and assigned his men to follow the Yamadayevs. If the brothers had sworn allegiance to Ramzan, they would have been spared, but they could not accept being in second place. Sulim Yamadayev's sin was being the only one in the republic not under Kadyrov's control, Ruslan explained.

The journalist Olga Allenova asked Sulim what Ramzan wanted.

"He wants me to leave."

"The battalion?"

"The battalion and Chechnya in general. Everything that is happening now is being done with one aim—to remove me. He drove Khalid [Ruslan's nickname] out of the Duma. He ousted Isa [the middle brother] from the Chechen parliament. Jabrail is dead. Only Sulim is left. When they surrounded Gudermes, the elders asked Ramzan to lift the cordon. He said: 'When the Yamadayevs and their families have left Chechnya, then I'll take down the cordon.'"

"Were those his exact words?"

"That's what I was told."[25]

In early August 2008, the Chechen prosecutor's office issued a search warrant for Sulim, but a few days later it became clear that there was no need to look for him. In the war between Russia and Georgia, the East Battalion, led by Yamadayev, was in the vanguard of Russian forces in an attack on Tskhinvali and had blockaded Georgian special forces in the mountains. Journalist Orkhan Dzhemal was there with him. He wrote in his report for *Russian Newsweek*:

> The journalists were more interested in the details of his relationship with Ramzan Kadyrov than in his exploits in the mountains.
>
> "Sulim, how come you're here, you're supposed to be arrested, you're a wanted man, aren't you?"
>
> Yamadayev got angry. "What arrest? I'm not hiding from anyone. Everyone understands that Kadyrov snapped his fingers at the prosecutors in his pocket, and they put me on a wanted list. Until 8 August I was in hospital in Moscow, and everyone knew where I was, if they wanted to arrest me. But they came to me and said: 'Sulim, the war has started, go and fight.'"[26]

A month later, on 24 September, Ruslan Yamadayev was shot dead in the centre of Moscow, a hundred metres from the White House, the new working residence of the newly promoted prime minister, Vladimir Putin. The armoured Mercedes carrying Yamadayev and his friend, the former Chechen military commandant General Sergei Kizyun, stopped at a traffic light, and Kizyun rolled down his window for a smoke. The car with the assassins stopped in the next lane. The killer got out, went to the open window, fired a few shots, got back in the car and drove off.

After another month, the East Battalion was disbanded. This could not have been done without approval from Moscow. "I don't know who at the top gave a direct command about me and East Battalion, but Ramzan Kadyrov, who invokes Vladimir Putin, is against me," Sulim said at the time.[27] He soon fled abroad, to the United Arab Emirates, and settled in Dubai. Although he knew there was an order for his assassination and tried to hide, he was killed there on 28 March 2009. A Dubai court sentenced to life imprisonment Ramzan Kadyrov's groom, the Iranian Mahdi Lornia, who lived in the UAE and looked after the Chechen president's horses, and put Adam Delimkhanov on an international wanted list. A Dubai police interrogator later told the court how Lornia confessed to him: shortly before the murder, Delimkhanov had flown to the UAE with a delegation from Chechnya and handed him a briefcase, ordering him to keep it until further notice; when he looked inside it, Lornia discovered a gold-plated pistol.[28]

The Russian special services must have known who killed the Yamadayev brothers and who ordered their murders. But there was an agreement between Vladimir Putin and Ramzan Kadyrov that Moscow would not interfere in internal Chechen affairs. It was a feudal agreement of the kind that in the Middle Ages suzerains used to make with their vassals: the leader of a mercenary army would take orders from the feudal lord and fight on his side, and in return the feudal lord would grant him patronage. Under that contract, Ramzan Kadyrov's power over Chechnya was indivisible and absolute.

# PART 6

# CHAPTER 27

## 2008–10

## The Thaw

### Better to be free than not

On the morning of 12 September 2007, three months before the Duma election and six months before the presidential election, Dmitry Medvedev's entourage was plunged into mourning: the newspaper *Vedomosti* reported that Sergei Ivanov, the former defence minister, would soon be appointed prime minister. This meant that Medvedev had lost the successor race initiated by Vladimir Putin. The news came as no surprise to anyone. As the contest entered its final phase, Ivanov raced ahead. First, Putin made him first deputy prime minister in February; second, Ivanov was considered Putin's chief foreign policy adviser, especially with regard to the United States; and third, beginning in the summer, Putin appeared in public with Ivanov markedly more often than with Medvedev. Finally, Ivanov outperformed Medvedev in opinion polls. Medvedev's aides were accepting condolences and considering how to rebuild their lives going forward.

The trick was that the succession race, if it existed, was only in Vladimir Putin's head. Everyone else—including Medvedev and Ivanov, who also did not know which of them would be Putin's successor in 2008—were part of a special cover-up operation designed to keep secret who would get the presidency from Putin until the very last minute. During the two years or more that this virtual contest had been going on, the outlines of the ideological struggle over the prospects for a post-Putin political course began to be clear. The *silovik* Ivanov, formerly at the FSB and resident spy in the foreign intelligence services, embodied the status quo—a continuation of the hard line in relations with the West and in domestic politics. Medvedev, on the other hand, was a young lawyer playing the role of "successor-liberal" and pursuing a softer line.

Far more important was the fact that they were both loyal to Putin and not associated with Kremlin factions. No one but Putin knows when he finally decided that Medvedev, not Ivanov, would run for president. One theory is that Ivanov lost out when he started to believe in his own prospects, jumped the gun and tried on the crown. In May 2007, for example, he held a press conference during which he was asked questions by journalists from various Russian cities via a live television link, a format all too reminiscent of the *Direct Line* events. In Soviet times, Ivanov was far more successful as a KGB officer than Putin. He was an intelligence officer, and he had a higher rank: colonel general. And Putin probably assumed that Dmitry Medvedev, with his background of a corporate lawyer with no real career and no connections to law enforcement, would be easier to control.

In any event, when Mikhail Fradkov, then prime minister, resigned on the morning of 12 September and everyone rushed to congratulate Ivanov, it was another bit of legerdemain. Viktor Zubkov, a member of Putin's inner circle and his old ally from the St Petersburg city hall, replaced Fradkov as prime minister. Zubkov was king for a day—a placeholder prime minister. At this moment, only Medvedev knew that in December, three months before the presidential election, he would be declared the successor and would immediately offer the post of prime minister to Putin. Thus began the brief "tandem" era in Russian politics, a time when there were hopes for change.

Medvedev was not like Putin. He was younger. He was not from the KGB. He seemed more open and modern. He also had a different personality. Even on a domestic, personal level, this difference was very noticeable. Putin was tsar, and by 2008 his domineering nature had eclipsed other normal human qualities. Even if you looked hard, you couldn't tell his likes and dislikes, what he enjoyed doing in his spare time, and so on. Medvedev lived a life more familiar to the man in the street. He used all kinds of digital devices and posted on social networks that were new at the time. He was a photographer, he liked hard rock, bright polo shirts and trainers, and he could even be seen dancing with his classmates at a reunion.

Medvedev's more liberal style was evident to all; business and the progressive elite applauded his slogan, "Better to Be Free Than Not Free." Sovereign democracy seemed to be a thing of the past, replaced by modernization and Medvedev's famous "four I's": institutions, infrastructure, innovation, investment. Year after year, for the past eight years, Vladimir Putin had been building autocracy. Now it was to give way to a modern state—at least in words.

More than the rhetoric changed. On the outskirts of Moscow in Skolkovo construction began on a huge centre for technological innovation, which, together with its campus, was to become the Russian equivalent of Silicon Valley. In less than a year, the relationship with the US was "reset", overcoming the poor relations with the West that had been exacerbated by the war with Georgia in August 2008 (in which Russia attacked a neighbouring country for the first time under the slogan of "peace enforcement"). Medvedev and Barack Obama signed a new treaty to reduce nuclear arsenals and jointly imposed sanctions against Iran. Preparations for Russia's accession to the WTO began in earnest. Medvedev broke the resistance of the *siloviki* and liberalized the criminal code: his amendments banned arrests under the so-called businessman's criminal code and reduced penalties for economic crimes. This was truly a major accomplishment, one of the most significant of Medvedev's period of "thaw." Vladimir Pereverzin, for example, the mid-level manager of Yukos who had refused to testify against Khodorkovsky and had been sentenced to eleven years, was released after a little over seven years thanks to the Medvedev amendments.

However, Medvedev's weakness and subordinate position was also quite evident. "Loyal, devoted, weak and obedient" was how Nemtsov described Medvedev in August 2008. This wasn't only the opinion of Nemtsov. All of Russia's elite knew that there would not be any profound changes forthcoming, since Prime Minister Putin hadn't gone anywhere; he was in control and most likely would return to the Kremlin. These suspicions were confirmed months after Medvedev was elected president when, in November 2008, he suddenly proposed amending the constitution to extend the presidential term from four to six years. Indeed, all of Medvedev's behaviour clearly testified to one thing: he tried not to upstage Putin or cross him. Medvedev saw his presidency as a task to be carried out, and preferably as well as possible.

Nonetheless, there were hopes for change with Medvedev. This was not because people thought he'd take firm hold of power and change the course of Russian history, but because of what seemed at the time to be the immutable qualities of Russian power. There was only one Cap of Monomakh, the crown worn by tsars, and it could not be placed on two heads. Whoever is in the Kremlin will take power into his hands, sooner or later. Medvedev would escape Putin's control. After all, the nature of presidential power is a matter of a single decree. "The Russian tradition is extremely simple," Nemtsov explained, "whoever is in the Kremlin is in charge. This is thousands of years old, and no one has ever changed it—no one! Putin decided to do it first, but it doesn't work that way. [...] Medvedev is ambitious, insanely ambitious, and he holds the top post in the state. [In Russia] the mindset is autocratic, so conflict is inevitable and will erupt sooner or later. It is systemic and does not even depend on personality."[1]

## The alliance of the wolf and the ram

Under Medvedev, the environment was not, however, more conducive for independent politicians. On the contrary, the situation got worse. There was now a clear-cut distinction between the loyal opposition—political parties that worked within the system and did not threaten the authorities—and the independent opposition, which would not be permitted to take part in elections. In fact, this opposition would be battled by any and all means. The SPS was to be completely destroyed. At first, election officials simply refused to register right-wing forces in any regional elections. Then the SPS got a bill: they were told they owed a huge sum of money. Later, in autumn 2008 under Medvedev, the SPS leaders received an offer from Surkov: the SPS would be liquidated, but they could have one third of the votes in a new right-wing party that would be controlled by the Kremlin. Nemtsov, "the informal leader of the SPS radical wing", as the press wrote at the time, had already suspended his membership in the party. Party head Nikita Belykh said he was against it and handed in his party membership card. Other party members such as Chubais, Gaidar and Gozman decided to accept the Kremlin's terms.

The decisions of the last "liquidation" congress of the SPS had been made in advance. All that remained was to present them to rank-and-file party members. Life is better than death, supporters of the union with the Kremlin said from the podium, adding that the situation in the country and the political course of the state could only be influenced from the inside. They made the case that it was useless to count on a revolution—the Kremlin was invincible—and if there were one, God forbid, its outcome would not please anyone. Yes, they said, the situation is difficult, but it's better to accept the Kremlin's offer. Otherwise, the party would be left to fade into the ranks of other marginalized and unsuccessful political associations. "The most painful thing a politician must do is to calmly assess reality, whatever it may be," said Chubais from the rostrum, "and so I ask myself a simple question: do I want to see Russia with a right-wing party or Russia without a right-wing party?"[2]

Boris Nemtsov had a different position that was unacceptable to the majority of party members. "Here sits Boris Nemtsov, a man with whom I have worked for fifteen years. But now we have different positions," Chubais continued. "I know his arguments; he knows mine. I understand that we have different opinions on the vote today. But that said, I will continue to respect Boris, because we went through war together, when—with no exaggeration—we thought we'd face either prison or death within five minutes."[3]

Nemtsov did not want to attend the congress at first—"What's the point if all the decisions have already been made?"—and no one expected him there. But at the last moment he decided to speak. He came, applied for reinstatement to the party so that he would have the right to speak, and then immediately asked for the podium. There was nothing wrong with compromise, he said, but there was no such thing as a compromise with the Boss. The wolf and the ram can only form an alliance when the wolf is sated and the ram does what the wolf wants. That was his first point. His second point was that a right-wing party under Kremlin control was doomed to fail. But his most important point was that liberalism and the current regime were incompatible in principle. "I do not agree with the majority on the question of joining the Kremlin project," he said.

> The SPS is the successor of Gaidar's party, Democratic Choice of Russia. The banners of both parties still bear the words "Freedom, Personal Property, Justice." The banners of Putin and Medvedev still bear the words "Censorship, Raiders, Basmanny Justice." So what do the government and our party have in common ideologically? I understood Chubais and many of you when economic reforms were introduced, when Gaidar's idea of a flat tax was accepted by the authorities. I understood when important laws on land and property rights were passed. I understand all that, but that was Putin's first four-year term, and now we have censorship, company raiders, "Basmanny Justice", international isolation and an extremely aggressive foreign policy.[4]

Nemtsov ended his speech with a proposal: if the party was not dissolved, he would take responsibility for it, including financial responsibility. But the fate of the SPS had already been decided.

Surkov would usually act in a different way. He would co-opt a party brand, then hand it over to loyal spin doctors and put his own people in charge. This time he didn't want to take control of the party, but to eliminate the brand itself. Otherwise, Surkov believed, the SPS would still attract democratic activists. This is why it had to be destroyed and a new political party established in its place. It was called Right Cause, also a familiar name: the future SPS party had begun its election campaign under that name in 1999.

## The new Russia, Inc.

Nemtsov had to reinstate his membership in the party in order to address the congress, because he had suspended it on the eve of the February 2008 presidential election. Nemtsov, together with Vladimir Milov, deputy energy minister, in the early 2000s and now a democratic activist, had published a pamphlet entitled 'Putin: Results', a journalistic analysis of the eight years of Putin's rule. Although the pamphlet only had a print run of five thousand copies, the report was circulated widely online and got noticed. Chubais was summoned to the Kremlin. "It was explained to him that the report was a bomb, a thing that would blow up the situation," *Kommersant* wrote at the time. After his conversation with Chubais,* Nemtsov moved the public presentation of the report to his personal office and announced the suspension of his membership in the party.[5]

Everyone, including Putin, had got used to Nemtsov's criticism over the past two or three years. Nemtsov and Milov wrote[6] that "the authoritarian-criminal regime formed in Russia during Vladimir Putin's years in power threatens the future of our country," but it is unlikely that the Kremlin was alarmed by this. The problem was different. Nemtsov and Milov, with facts and figures in hand, described in their report Russia's demographic crisis, the failure of pension reform, worsening inequality, the dependence of economic growth on oil prices, and the subordination of the judiciary to the Kremlin and the *siloviki*. "Instead of modernizing the country, the Putin regime has focused on redistributing property, missing an opportune moment for reform." But more importantly, they detailed how Vladimir Putin had been building "crony capitalism" over the years, with control of the biggest assets and financial flows going to his old friends. "Under the rhetoric of fighting the 'oligarch revanche'," the authors wrote, "there has been a rapid enrichment of a new, more powerful Putin oligarchy in Russia, at our expense and yours."[7]

There was a reason Vladimir Putin did not give the go-ahead to reform the gas industry in the early 2000s. "Gazprom was a champion for transferring crucial assets into the hands of mysterious 'third parties'," Nemtsov and Milov wrote. The first loss, they said, was the Sogaz insurance company, owned by Gazprom. In 2005, it was taken over by

---

\* In March 2022, after the full-scale invasion of Ukraine, Chubais left Russia and law enforcement officials in Moscow began investigating embezzlement in Rosnano, the state-owned nanotechnology venture that Chubais ran from 2011 to 2020.

the St Petersburg-based Rossiya Bank, whose largest shareholder was businessman Yury Kovalchuk. Kovalchuk had been a close associate of Putin's since the early 1990s and was one of the founders of the Ozero cooperative near St Petersburg in 1996. More than two years later, in December 2010, businessman Sergei Kolesnikov, who had fled to the West, revealed in an open letter to President Medvedev how his company had partnered with another of Putin's close associates to become a conduit for oligarch money collection back in 2000. An off-budget investment fund was established, part of which was used to build a palace for Putin near the Black Sea resort of Gelendzhik.[8] The *Financial Times* would soon write, again citing Kolesnikov, that another part of the money—the dividends generated by the investment fund—were used to buy shares in the charter capital of the Rossiya Bank by other close acquaintances of Putin.[9]

Nemtsov and Milov did not know these details at the time, but they did describe what happened next in the report. Thanks to the acquisition of Sogaz, the reserves of Gazprom's pension fund, Gazfond, were taken over by Rossiya Bank, and the money was soon used to "buy over fifty per cent of Gazprombank. By the end of 2007, it became the second largest bank in the country in size of assets after Sberbank."

In this way, asset by asset, brick by brick, a new edifice of Russian capitalism was being erected in the 2000s. Its beneficiaries, Putin's inner circle, formed a new class of billionaire oligarchs. Businessman Gennady Timchenko, the same one who helped Putin take Sobchak to France in autumn 1997, held a significant share of oil exports; the company of his judo partner Arkady Rotenberg became one of Gazprom's biggest contractors. Putin's friends did not just enter governmental and quasi-governmental business. They also entered politics. Nemtsov and Milov wrote that Kovalchuk now owned a gigantic private media holding company along with the long-suffering NTV television channel, and that his power "dwarf[ed] the power once held by Gusinsky and Berezovsky."[10]

In a few years, all the names of the owners and companies, the amounts of deals and other details would become widely known. But in early 2008, Nemtsov and Milov in their report drew the first collective portrait of the new Russia, Inc., which has held onto the reins of power ever since.

## Nemtsov out on the street

By the beginning of Medvedev's presidency, Nemtsov had nothing left of his former life—even his party headquarters building had to be sold. He learnt what it was to fail completely in elections and be the victim of constant harassment. In conventional terms, he couldn't fall any lower. After trying his hand at business, he returned to politics, but now, after the last debacle, he had no idea what to do next. Fortunately, he was temperamentally incapable of being discouraged for long, and his lifestyle did not change. He still alternated between politics and windsurfing, went to the gym, went to restaurants and had a busy social life. He suspended his SPS membership, attended the Russian Wave sports and music festival in Egypt and, after another conference of democratic forces, flew to Hawaii for the May holidays to go sailing.

Nemtsov parted ways with the SPS, but he no longer wanted to leave politics. He was now surrounded by a different set of people. He knew many of them, especially journalists, and had even worked with some of them in the past—for example, in Committee-2008 to ensure fair presidential elections—but, on the whole, it was an environment unfamiliar to him. These were young activists who had entered politics in the mid-2000s, older dissidents who had fought the Soviet regime back in the 1970s and first-wave democrats. Many of the people Nemtsov would be working with saw him as an outsider from the parallel universe of high-placed bureaucrats. "I didn't respect him at first," recalled democratic activist Nadezhda Mityushkina. "He was puzzled by us at first, and it took us a while to get used to him. He was also a person from outside our circle, with a different way of thinking and a different approach to things."[11]

Other activists thought the same thing. Nemtsov was helped by his communication skills and political experience. Their new democratic movement called Solidarity took its name from the Polish anti-communist resistance of the 1980s, which carried the hint that this new Solidarity could have the same mass appeal and influence. The main point of the political programme was the "peaceful dismantling of the Putin–Medvedev regime." Nemtsov and Kasparov were co-chairs, and the political strategy was formulated by Nemtsov. What could they do in a situation when they had no party, no headquarters and no chance of getting registered for elections? Nemtsov proposed three approaches: (1) furthering education—writing reports similar to 'Putin: Results'; (2) working the street—organizing rallies; (3) running in elections—to the extent that it would be possible. Their exposés proved quite effective. With access to television cut off, the report was at least one viable propaganda tool. In addition, the reports led to more activities: public appearances in the capitals, presentations in the regions, and so on.

Nemtsov thought that they should produce small reports with illustrations and graphs that could be read in a typical underground ride—something like a leaflet, only slightly longer. Activists, and even Nemtsov, handed them out in the metro. The report about Putin, published in a small edition, was the test case. They produced 200,000 copies of 'Luzhkov: Results' about Moscow's mayor, Yury Luzhkov, and corruption in Moscow. The print run was distributed in a fortnight, and another 100,000 copies were printed.

There was little or no scope for participation in the elections. Governors had been appointed, not elected, for a long time, and someone could only run for the parliament as a member of a political party. Stricter new legal requirements concerning the required number of party branches and so forth made it impossible to register a new party without the support of the Kremlin. There was only one option left: almost all major cities still had direct elections of mayors and heads of local government.

If Putin were still president, Surkov simply would not have allowed Nemtsov to participate in any elections. Why make trouble for himself? But now the question had to be cleared with Medvedev. In early March 2009, Surkov, first deputy head of the new Presidential Administration and still overseeing all domestic politics, told his boss that Nemtsov had decided to run for mayor of Sochi. Let him, Medvedev said. And with that, Nemtsov was allowed to run.

## The Sochi experiment

Sochi, the country's main resort on the Black Sea, a haven of Soviet luxury and the Russian Riviera, was once claimed by Stalin and his people's commissars for their summer homes. Later, in the 1970s and 1980s, box-like Soviet sanatoria sprang up along the coast, to be followed in the 2000s by the so-called luxury property and palaces of businessmen and top officials. Vladimir Putin took a liking to the presidential residence called Bocharov Ruchei and had it rebuilt to suit his needs.

In February, Nemtsov's assistant, Olga Shorina, showed him a letter sent to his address from Sochi activists inviting him to run in elections for mayor. Nemtsov was hesitant. On the one hand, he had been born in Sochi but moved away when he was still a child. On the other hand, he got immediately excited about the idea. And after Shorina flew to Sochi on a reconnaissance mission, the decision was made. On 12 March, the full political council of Solidarity flew to Sochi and unanimously supported Nemtsov's nomination. The election campaign kicked off.

But how to run a campaign in the new reality had to be figured out in practice. In the past, Nemtsov had had a party staff at his disposal, an office, political consultants—everything necessary to keep a well-oiled electoral machine up and running. Now he had nothing. He offered twenty-five-year-old activist Ilya Yashin, his associate, the job of chief of headquarters. "I was dumbfounded," Yashin recalled. "I couldn't imagine myself as a manager."[12] They had met in early 2008. Yashin was then one of the leaders of the youth faction in the Yabloko party and was already known for street activism, such as when he joined Yegor Gaidar's daughter Maria in 2006 to hang a banner from the bridge opposite the Kremlin that read, "Give the People Back the Elections, You Scumbags!" When Yashin and the radical wing of Yabloko wanted to make changes in the party's leadership, the party considered expelling him. "My phone rang," Yashin recalled. "'Hello, Ilya? It's Nemtsov. What's happening with you in Yabloko? Are they really going to expel you? What can I do for you?' That made a huge impression on me. A complete stranger, a major figure in both the opposition and the government, calls and asks how he can help me."[13]

Nemtsov and Yashin had the same view of politics, and Nemtsov was impressed by Yashin's courage. Now Nemtsov was inviting Yashin to come to Sochi with him. "I said to him, 'Of course, I have some idea about how elections are run, but I'm definitely not a professional,'" Yashin said later. "But he said to me: 'I understand everything. But you won't steal, and you won't be ideologically motivated. It couldn't be worse than that.'"[14] So Yashin flew to Sochi.

By 2009, Nemtsov was well off. He played the stock market and earned his first million dollars through, he said, investments in Gazprom. Since the autumn of 1998, when he bought shares in Gazprom, the company's market capitalization had risen a hundredfold.[15] He had other profitable stocks in his portfolio as well. Nemtsov's Sochi campaign was financed mainly with his own money, with some money from Kasparov and a few other sponsors. Friends would continue to help him with cash—secretly, so that the Kremlin would not find out about it—and he used his own money to pay for his political campaigns and the activities of Solidarity. Solidarity was almost entirely funded by Nemtsov and Kasparov.

The Sochi campaign did not require large sums of money. A small staff worked for little money—they were motivated by the idea—and they rented a private house in the city centre for the headquarters. It was off-season, so rent was cheap. And they hired a minivan to get around the city.

Nemtsov flew to Sochi in early March straight from another Russian Wave festival in Egypt. He was cheerful, chipper and deeply tanned. When he was introduced to the activists at the headquarters, nineteen-year-old Anastasia Faizullina gasped: "We're sitting, discussing something, suddenly Nemtsov walks in. My jaw dropped. I went up to Yashin later, asked: 'How old is he?' He said: 'Forty-nine.' I did not believe him. He was in great shape. Then I got used to it, of course."[16] The day would start with a breakfast of eggs, sausage and freshly squeezed orange juice. Then everyone would go to the gym in a nearby hotel. Nemtsov did not change his habits.

The Sochi campaign was an experiment. Nemtsov hadn't done anything like this since the 1990s. In the ten years since then, politicians had learnt that it was impossible to run a campaign without coverage on nationwide television channels. The Sochi campaign was fundamentally different. Nemtsov spent his days on the stump in commuter trains, beaches, public squares, apartment house courtyards and even going door to door. They organized four or five meetings a day, just the three of them: Nemtsov, Faizullina and a bodyguard (Kasparov sent his own when it quickly became clear that campaigning was not safe).

Propaganda on the central TV channels had long painted Nemtsov as a US State Department agent, an enemy and a traitor. People he met on the street in Sochi were generally friendly, but they did not always support Nemtsov. They blamed him for the default and other woes of the 1990s, remembered him for Yeltsin and his friendship with Chubais, making government officials travel in Volgas and speaking on the Maidan. But at almost every meeting Nemtsov left with gifts: a bottle of homemade Abkhazian wine and a bag of delicacies. "They give me ajika sauce, Abkhazian lemons and oranges, sulguni cheese, Korean-style carrots, tomatoes," Nemtsov said. "I don't take meat—it's Lent right now."[17]

Nemtsov campaigned at markets, gave toasts at an Armenian wedding attended by four hundred people and even took part in the city's downhill skiing competition. Once again, he was at ease, doing what he loved, and finding something to talk about with everyone—a pensioner, a housewife or a student. Roman Udot, an activist with Golos, an independent association of election observers, wrote about Nemtsov's performance in a Sochi sanatorium. "In [two and a half hours] the candidate did not sit down once. During this time, the candidate did not look at a single piece of paper. He was brilliant, mesmerizing—and he charmed and won people over before my eyes. Even though I had supported him, I couldn't have imagined it. I didn't think we still had any speakers like this."[18]

Because Putin had a residence in Sochi, local events were always closely watched from Moscow. But in 2007 Sochi won the right to host the 2014 Winter Olympics, and that victory was Putin's personal victory and his main project. A few years later he would tell how, back in the early 2000s, he "arrived in his Russian jeep" and chose the competition site himself. Over the next seven years, the Sochi megaproject would become the largest construction project in Europe; in the end, the Olympics construction cost more than $50 billion—an enormous sum that Nemtsov claimed exceeded the cost of building sports facilities at all previous Winter Olympics combined. Starting in 2007, Sochi attracted a lot of attention from journalists all over the world and from the Kremlin. Finally, according to the regulations of the Olympic Games, it was the mayor of the city chosen for the competition who was to host the Olympic torch relay at the close of the previous games and to inaugurate the games in his own city. This meant that the head of Sochi was going to be a political position, so the Kremlin got serious about the election of the mayor.

## Surkov's guys

Sochi residents were in two minds about the upcoming Olympics. On the one hand, they supported them overall: the games were prestigious, and the city would also benefit. On the other hand, they were afraid of the huge construction project. Construction of the port had already begun, trees had already been cut down, and people had already been evicted from Imereti Bay where the Olympic park would be built. Residents found the "metre for metre" program—a housing exchange that would give residents of Imereti Bay equivalent living space in other districts—unfair and were generally hostile to it. (Nemtsov suggested solving the problem by leaving the opening and closing ceremonies as well as all mountain sports in Sochi while moving ice hockey, skating and figure skating, which require separate stadiums, to Moscow or another site. The residents of Imereti Bay, of course, liked this plan.) In addition, the incumbent mayor, Anatoly Pakhomov, the former mayor of the resort city of Anapa, was an outsider in Sochi. In Sochi, residents thought of Pakhomov's nomination as an incursion of people from the neighbouring Kuban region who would set their sights on Sochi. And now, in order to ensure a convincing victory for their candidate, the Kremlin and the Kuban administration needed to neutralize Nemtsov.

To begin with, the nomination was simply turned into a farce. The former ballerina and socialite Anastasia Volochkova, the deputy Andrei Lugovoi, accused by Britain of murdering former KGB officer Alexander Litvinenko, and adult-film star Yelena Berkova were all nominated for mayor of Sochi. The idea was to make bad associations for Pakhomov's rivals. The press tried to discredit Nemtsov by calling the candidates "Berkova and others." Local TV in Sochi ran pieces claiming that Nemtsov had ruined industry in Nizhny Novgorod, associated with criminals, failed as deputy prime minister and therefore eliminated as the presidential successor, and finally protested against Russia on the Maidan. "Do you want a mayor like that?" television news asked. Another report claimed that Nemtsov's campaign was "financed by Americans" and that he'd pay them off "with Sochi land."

Even Putin got involved in the elections. He explained that the mayor of Sochi must be able to establish "business relations" with the Olympic construction site, with Moscow, and so on. "Foam is rising to the surface, and unfortunately it's toxic foam," Putin said. "I hope the people of Sochi will not allow anyone to use the Olympic project for ambitions that have nothing to do with the interests of the citizens."[19] This was covert campaigning for Pakhomov and against Nemtsov, his main rival. Sociologists had already established by then that affiliation with the authorities was an advantage in the eyes of voters, while being an oppositionist was a disadvantage. The Public Opinion Foundation wrote that, "Many respondents reason as follows: if you choose a candidate supported by the federal authorities, he will be able to 'cooperate successfully' with the centre, 'he will be supported, he will be helped'. And, if we choose the oppositionist Boris Nemtsov, then 'they will interfere with his work, and we won't benefit from that either, we don't need it!'"[20]

Two local radio stations at first agreed to take Nemtsov's ads, but soon called back and refused, explaining that the city administration prohibited them from airing them. Leaflets printed by Nemtsov's headquarters were confiscated. The leaflets read:

> They are turning Sochi into a Kuban village. I'll give the city back its federal status.
>
> They're raising utility rates. I will freeze utility rates.
>
> Their Olympic plan will destroy Sochi. My plan will save Sochi and the Olympics.
>
> They're kicking you out of your homes. I will provide you with decent housing.
>
> They are cutting down trees. I will plant them.*
>
> They're dumping sewage into the sea. I will implement the Clean Coast Programme.
>
> They are destroying our resort. I will preserve it.

---

\* "To plant" is also slang for "to put someone in jail."

The campaign turned into an endless stream of harassment and provocations. Nemtsov's headquarters suspected that someone local was spying on them. Pro-Kremlin activists followed Nemtsov everywhere and almost always knew his schedule in advance. One day some Koreans came to Nemtsov's house, supposedly to talk about the Olympics. It turned out that the meeting had been filmed on a hidden camera, and soon local television aired a story about Nemtsov offering the Korean delegation his help in moving the Olympics to Pyeongchang, Korea. After that, whenever Nemtsov met with voters, there were invariably some guys wearing "Korea 2014" T-shirts.

Soon the provocations turned violent. One local journalist, who interviewed Nemtsov for his campaign video, was punched in the face and told "working with Nemtsov is dangerous to your health." Just as Nemtsov was entering the headquarters before a press conference, someone distracted him and three teenagers jumped up behind him with bottles of Coke that they threw in his face. They then ran away. The bottles contained a mixture of Coca-Cola and ammonia, and a few drops hit Nemtsov in the eye. The provocateur who distracted Nemtsov was later identified as a member of Nashi from Ryazan. "These are Surkov's guys," Murat Akhedzhak, an election official, explained to Nemtsov at their only meeting.[21] Sometime later, Nemtsov also met with Surkov in Moscow. There was only one reason for the conversation, and the meeting ended with no result. Nemtsov demanded that the street violence be stopped; Surkov replied that he had nothing to do with it and had given no such instructions.

## Several ways to steal an election

In Sochi, poverty and luxury often live on neighbouring streets. Right in the middle of the city is electoral district 46–09: upscale restaurants, expensive hotels and spas rub shoulders with unassuming Soviet-era housing. When observers went to check on the family of a pensioner named Tamara, it turned out that her son, who had been marked as having voted, was unable to vote. He had been hurt in a car accident and was bedridden, living with his wife.

There are several basic types of fraud in Russian elections. The first is ballot stuffing. The second is the rewriting of the final numbers using falsified records: members of election commissions—often for money—sign blank forms, and the higher commissions simply write in the tallies they want. Observers at polling stations are shown the real tallies, and then the falsified tallies are sent on.

Other methods of falsification are practised in early voting and mobile voting. Early voting is very difficult to monitor. In most cases, civil servants, employees of budgetary agencies and large enterprises are brought in groups to polling stations and told directly who they should vote for. It is during early voting that so-called "carousels" are usually done. This is when a voter comes with a ballot already filled out, puts it in the ballot box, takes away a ballot given to him by the commission to pass it on to someone else, and so on.

Home voting in Russia is another opportunity for falsification. About six months before the elections, the social services give the electoral commissions lists of pensioners and people with disabilities. The elderly and disabled people are then persuaded one way or another to sign an application to vote at home. On the day of voting, a member of the electoral commission together with a policeman and a ballot box are sent to them, but there usually isn't enough room in the car for an observer. It is almost impossible to check afterwards who actually voted and how. Had the observers not reached Tamara, she would never have known that her son had voted in the elections.

In the Sochi mayoral elections, 31,000 people voted early—a figure unprecedented for those times, almost a quarter of all those who took part in the elections. A further twelve per cent voted at home. Observers then compared the results of early voting to regular voting at seventy-three polling stations in Sochi: with early voting Nemtsov's result fell more than threefold.

Nemtsov realized that he wouldn't be elected mayor of Sochi. He had fought to become Pakhomov's main rival, and he had succeeded in that. Right from the start, Nemtsov outpaced the other candidates by far. An outsider to federal-level politics, branded by propaganda as a loser and a buffoon, Nemtsov was struggling not so much with Pakhomov as with the entire Russian political machine that was working behind him. By the middle of the campaign, pollsters at his headquarters were giving Nemtsov about twenty per cent, a figure he himself did not seriously expect at first. Closer to the finish line, sociologists from the Public Opinion Foundation predicted the same number.[22] "It is not impossible that Nemtsov will make it to the second round, and in the second round his chances become much better," wrote Foundation specialists.[23]

Nemtsov's participation in the second round would be a failure for the Kremlin. The official, rigged result showed a complete victory for Pakhomov: 77 per cent for him and 13.6 per cent for Nemtsov. However, it appears that Nemtsov's second round was not stolen from him. The Golos association experts later concluded that Nemtsov probably got between 17 and 22 per cent of the vote, and this was not enough to get into the second round. But even the official result was valuable, especially against the backdrop of the one per cent received by SPS in December 2007. In Sochi, Nemtsov realized that he could stand up to the Kremlin, that he could still run for office, albeit under extreme conditions, and that he could still be in public politics—if only on the street.

## The end of the golden era

At one time the young businessman Georgy Boos voted for Democratic Choice, and he had gone to the Mossovet when in October 1993 Gaidar appealed to the public to oppose Rutskoi and Makashov. But when he entered politics in 1995 it was as an associate of Yury Luzhkov's. At the time, the Boos family firm—a large lighting company—was one of the major contractors for Moscow city hall. In the early 2000s, Boos was Nemtsov's neighbour in the Duma; they had both been deputy speakers of the parliament. But then their paths diverged. Nemtsov was booted from the Duma in December 2003; in 2005, Vladimir Putin sent Boos to govern Kaliningrad, a piece of East Prussia between Lithuania and Poland that had fallen to Russia after the Second World War. In Russia's westernmost region, where Europe is literally across the street, the political climate has always been mild. Boos went to Kaliningrad as a young reformer and Westerner. He didn't want to shake everything up but to build a fair and competitive playing field. But Boos was unlucky. In 2008, after several years of rapid growth, Russia was hit by an economic crisis.

Originating in the US mortgage-backed securities market in 2007, the economic crisis spread first through the US financial system, bankrupting some of the biggest investment banks and mortgage companies, then led to a global stock-market crash and plunging oil prices. In July 2008, the price of oil was hitting an all-time high of $143 per barrel, and Russia was swimming in petrodollars. By December, the price of oil was $33. After the price of oil fell, the rouble collapsed: in the first two months of 2009, the Russian currency fell by half. Margin calls started to ring out: large companies, which by that time had built up large external debt against their shares, suddenly found themselves on the verge of bankruptcy.

Even against the backdrop of the global crisis, the crash in Russia was deeper. It made clear that the success of the Russian economy in recent years, when it was growing at an average of seven per cent a year, was due mainly to the favourable commodity situation. With this, Putin's golden years came to an end. The price of oil went up again relatively quickly, but the Russian economy never returned to a sustainable growth trajectory.

The Kaliningrad region was hit particularly hard: separated from mainland Russia, it was extremely dependent on imports, which were now more expensive. In November 2009, the federal government sought out additional sources to patch the budget holes and decided to raise the transport tax. The transport tax is formed and collected in the regions and then transferred to the local budget. The regions have the right to set their own rates as they see fit, within the limits imposed by the tax code. Of course, the Ministry of Finance realized that governors would not take the initiative to increase the transport tax—who would want to make people angry? This is why Boos and the governors of neighbouring regions were brought together at a special meeting and warned that, if they did not raise the transport tax to the maximum, they would not receive additional budget subsidies.

Boos realized that he had no choice. He would be lost without the subsidies, so he gave the go-ahead, and on the same day the Kaliningrad legislature voted in favour. It was Friday evening, and by Monday Boos realized that he had been left hanging, along with several other governors who had gone along with the Ministry of Finance. All the other governors had refused. It became clear that no one would be punished, and Boos backed down, but it was too late. The people of Kaliningrad began to protest.

Konstantin Doroshok, one of the leaders of the protest movement in Kaliningrad, already knew Nemtsov. He had attended the Solidarity congress in St Petersburg in May 2009 with other activists. In 2007, he had gone from importing used cars (a typical profession in Kaliningrad) to being a social activist when thousands of Kaliningrad drivers, used-car importers like him, were suddenly served with papers for huge sums after the customs office retroactively recalculated the duties to be paid. At first, the protests were limited to picketing, but when Kaliningrad courts sided with customs, the outraged motorists decided to unite. "That's when," recalled Doroshok, "we realized that there was no justice for us, and we had to defend ourselves."[24] And so, in 2008, a public organization called Justice (in Russian, Spravedlivost) was formed in Kaliningrad. It was a kind of protest committee with Doroshok at its head. The activists began to look for allies and anyone else who, as Doroshok put it, "was also dissatisfied with the current government." They read Nemtsov and Milov's report 'Putin: Results' and started calling Solidarity.

In December 2009, the federal customs office created new problems for motorists: they virtually stopped the import of cars. Instead of dozens of cars a day, only a few were allowed through. There was a long queue at the border, people waited for days on end, and that December was particularly cold. The situation rapidly became very tense, the patience of motorists burst, and it ended with Doroshok and his companions blocking one of the checkpoints and not letting the customs officers out or in. On 12 December, Doroshok and his comrades led Kaliningrad residents to a protest rally. The motorists were joined by other groups of the discontented. Some protested the jump in utility tariffs, others the closure of a bankrupt hospital, and still others the cutting-down of trees in public gardens. In the end, seven thousand people took to the streets—a very large number for Kaliningrad—and political slogans were added to the economic ones. Protesters demanded

Boos's resignation. The rally was reported in the press, and activists from other regions streamed into the city. Something was happening in Russia's westernmost region.

## Get Putin out of office

Boos rushed to put out the fire. He returned the old transport-tax rate, negotiated with the customs officials and began to deal with the utility rates. Strictly speaking, only the transport tax was within his purview. Customs were outside his competence. The hospital had to be closed because it could not compete in the new system of insured medicine, and the number of patients dropped dramatically. And the city hall (with which Boos had a very strained relationship) was in charge of the municipal utility tariffs. But the public frustration was focused on Boos. He was not from Kaliningrad, but from Moscow, and was a representative of the central government. And if he was governor, he was responsible for everything.

The beginning of January was quiet. Boos was about to leave for Madeira on 23 January, his birthday, for a two-week holiday, when he was informed that another large rally was planned for 30 January, and that Boris Nemtsov would be coming specially from Moscow. Doroshok called Nemtsov, and his assistant Olga Shorina came to Kaliningrad to investigate. She returned to Moscow and told Nemtsov that he should go: "There will be a really cool rally."[25]

Boos called Nemtsov on the evening of Friday, 15 January, straight from the locker room after a hockey game. "Don't come," Boos said. Six years before, when Nemtsov had been booted out of the Duma and got involved in the Moscow construction business, Boos had helped him by persuading both Surkov and Luzhkov to leave him alone. Now he was expecting a favour in return. "I can't not come," Nemtsov replied. "I'm a politician. It is my job. But I won't say anything against you." Boos knew very well that if the protest grew, he would have problems with the Kremlin. He explained to Nemtsov that his very appearance in Kaliningrad would play against him, that he, Boos, was now doing in Kaliningrad what the liberals were fighting for, and that he was also abolishing the transport tax. Nemtsov told him that it wasn't just about the transport tax, but about unemployment, which had led to higher import duties on foreign cars, and the harsh censorship on Kaliningrad television. It's a political problem, Nemtsov said.

On the eve of his birthday, Boos flew to Moscow; President Medvedev had asked him to make a keynote speech at a meeting of the State Council, an advisory and generally toothless structure that the Kremlin had created for governors in 2000 after kicking them out of the upper house of parliament. The theme of the meeting—federalism and the development of the political system—was a topic Boos was deeply concerned with. In recent months, he'd had first-hand experience of the practical application of the principle of federalism as enshrined in the constitution. Boos had even planned to say that Russia should not be a monarchy and that centralization of power in Moscow would be detrimental to such a vast and diverse country, but the day before Medvedev had deleted the more acrimonious parts of his speech. All that remained were the general words that "the principles of political governance must be adequate to the multidimensional, ideological and cultural diversity of our society."[26]

After returning from Moscow to Kaliningrad, Boos spent several more days calming down public opinion, meeting with activists and deputies. On the eve of the rally, he thought he had succeeded. On the day of the rally, 30 January, it was very cold and snowing in Kaliningrad. The rally was supposed to begin at 11.00 a.m. Nemtsov had already flown in, and Boos sat and waited to see what would happen. On the hour, the square was empty. An hour later it was still empty. Boos relaxed, ordered the plane to get ready—he had just bought a nine-seater jet—and was soon on his way to the airport. Soon, the snowy wind had turned into an Atlantic breeze blowing outside the plane window as it headed right over the ocean for the Madeira landing strip. Just then Boos's mobile phone rang. It was Surkov: "What's going on there?" "Everything seemed fine when I left," Boos replied. "It's not now," Surkov said and hung up. His holiday was ruined after all. The next morning Boos flew back home.

Snow was falling, there was a strong wind, and it was very cold: In coastal Kaliningrad, -15 °C is much harder to bear than in Siberia.

According to one estimate, ten thousand people came out on the central square of Kaliningrad. By other estimates there were twelve thousand people. When Nemtsov stepped onto the stage, he couldn't believe his eyes. Moscow hadn't seen a demonstration of this size in twenty years, and for Kaliningrad this was just unbelievable. When Doroshok gave him the floor, there was applause but also boos. People of all political stripes, from democrats to communists, had gathered in the square, and not everyone was ready to welcome the Moscow opposition landing force. But there were only sounds of approval when Nemtsov said: "Why are there so many different banners on this square? Banners of the Communist Party, Yabloko, Solidarity? The flags of my friend Zhirinovsky, the guy I duelled with glasses of juice? Why? Because we're fed up with them! The church congregation takes after the priest, and Boos takes after Putin." Nemtsov continued: "Until we get rid of them in Moscow, there will be disgraceful practices in the provinces. Long live a free Russia without oligarchs and corrupt democrats! Get Putin out of office!" The demonstrators applauded.

In Moscow, the very existence of a demonstration of ten thousand people was a code-red emergency. But the Kremlin was even more concerned about the speed with which the protesters turned to anti-government slogans. The rally ended with demands for the recall of the 2004 gubernatorial elections, as well as for the resignation of Boos and, for the first time, Vladimir Putin. Very quickly someone coined the phrase Amber Revolution—Kaliningrad is the world's largest producer of amber—and emissaries from the Kremlin flew to Kaliningrad. Surkov initially forbade Boos to meet the protest leaders. He feared that if he bowed to the demands of the street, protests would spread to other regions. As a result, the protesters thought that the governor froze.

Things began to improve when the Kremlin gave the go-ahead and Boos was able to start negotiations with Doroshok and his associates. In spring, the governor set up a public council, and a working group that included activists was set up under each provincial minister, which gave them access to the work of the regional government. Boos became more accessible, and opposition and protest leaders were allowed on local television. "Boos before the rally and Boos after the rally are completely different people," Doroshok recalled.[27] The transport tax was abolished, and Boos sent to Moscow a raft of bills that the opposition supported.

On 31 January, the day after the rally in Kaliningrad and apparently under its influence, an unexpectedly large number of people—a couple of thousand people—turned out for another protest rally in Moscow. Those who came were dispersed, as usual, but everyone was talking about Kaliningrad. When Nemtsov returned to Moscow and was taken in a van by the police, even the militia asked him: "Were there really so many people there? Even more than here in Moscow?"

Soon Nemtsov and Kasparov were arguing over dinner whether it was possible to hold a protest in Moscow on the scale of Kaliningrad. Kasparov was sure that it was possible: the situation was heating up, there would be even more people. No, Nemtsov objected: maybe in the provinces, but Moscow was too rich and prosperous to protest. They made a bet over a case of good wine: Kasparov argued that a demonstration of 100,000 people would take place in Moscow as early as 2010, while Nemtsov argued that it wouldn't. Exactly one year later, in January 2011, Kasparov paid Nemtsov for the loss, and Nemtsov offered to extend the bet for another year on the same terms. Kasparov, with a chuckle, refused. Now he didn't believe in the possibility of mass demonstrations in Moscow either.

In August 2010, when Boos's gubernatorial term came to an end he was replaced by another governor. The opposition took credit for his resignation, but it was certainly not a victory. Boos's successor—this time, a local—convened the public council created by his predecessor three or four times and then stopped.

# CHAPTER 28

**2010**

**Arrest**

## New times

The rallies in Kaliningrad might have been the largest in the country, but they certainly weren't the only public protests. And the change wasn't the protest rallies, or rather it wasn't only the protest rallies. There was something new in the air, as if people had suddenly picked up a new scent. Things that no one had paid attention to before now outraged them, and much of that outrage was about corruption, the caste system, and officials making decisions outside the law. The rich and powerful were allowed to do anything and everything, while the rest of the population had to obey the law.

In the winter of 2010, in Moscow, a Mercedes driving a top manager of the major oil company Lukoil hit a Citroën. Two women, a doctor and her daughter-in-law, were in the car; both were killed. As conviction grew that the police were helping the Mercedes passenger evade responsibility, a powerful protest campaign began in Moscow and then spread across the country. People wrote about it in blogs, shared links, watched appeals for justice on YouTube, pasted stickers on their car windows that had the Lukoil logo crossed out and boycotted the company's petrol stations.

In the spring, there was another wave of outrage, this time when a new video went online, showing a Moscow driver describe how traffic police had made him and other drivers form a "human shield" on the highway to catch a criminal.

In the summer, a powerful outburst of protest was triggered by the beginning of logging in the town of Khimki, just outside the Moscow city limits, where the future Moscow–St Petersburg motorway was to be built. The protest quickly spread beyond Khimki. "The biggest problem in our country is cynicism. We are not enemies of the state. We're patriots. The enemies of the state are the corrupt bureaucracy," legendary rocker Yury Shevchuk said on Pushkin Square in Moscow.[1] He sang his famous song 'Motherland':

> They say she's ugly, but we don't care,
> We love her all the same, we swear,
> Even when she trusts the scum—
> And twists us all around her thumb...

And it seemed to echo his stadium concerts twenty years before when he heralded freedom to thousands and thousands of Soviet citizens.

Two months earlier, Shevchuk had appeared with other cultural figures at a meeting with Putin. Shevchuk began by telling how he had received a phone call before the meeting warning him not to ask sensitive questions. Putin then asked Shevchuk to introduce himself; Putin surely knew who Shevchuk was and was obviously trying to demean him.

"Yura Shevchuk, musician," the rock star replied. His answer flew all over the country. Two days after the Pushkin Square rally, U2 lead singer Bono performed at Luzhniki Stadium and called Shevchuk up on stage as if to make Putin see who Shevchuk was. The two of them sang 'Knockin' on Heaven's Door' together as the crowds roared. Soon after, Nemtsov tried to persuade Shevchuk to get more involved in politics, but the musician declined the offer.

In the autumn, horrifying news arrived in the capital from the south. In the village of Kushchevskaya, near the Black Sea, gangsters had murdered a local family, including small children, and twelve of their guests. The gangsters were linked to local law enforcement, and the word *Kushchevka* quickly became a catch phrase for mafia corruption and the merger of criminals and government officials. As Nemtsov said, "The police have turned into crooks."[2] The waves of anger provoked by these and many other similar news stories had no single source or organizers. They arose spontaneously.

Street protesters held one rally after another, but, despite changes in the public mood, these rallies rarely drew more than 1,500 people. Nemtsov, Milov, Kasyanov and Vladimir Ryzhkov (who had been a prominent political figure in the 1990s and was the last of this group to stay in the Duma until 2007) agreed to form a new democratic coalition. Soon after, in early December, the coalition was transformed into a political party called the People's Freedom Party, or PARNAS for short.

The longer the street rallies went on, the tougher the authorities cracked down. The Marches of Dissenters in 2007–08 morphed into a new protest called Strategy-31. On the 31st each month protesters came to the central Moscow Triumfalnaya Square to defend Article 31 of the Russian constitution, which guarantees people the right to peaceful assembly. The idea of fighting for one's rights—the right to assemble and the right to openly criticize the authorities—seemed to have reappeared from the Soviet era of dissent. The human-rights activist and former dissident Lyudmila Alekseyeva vividly remembered the day in 1965 when the first anti-Soviet demonstration was held on Pushkin Square in Moscow. The demonstration was organized by Alexander Yesenin-Volpin, a dissident mathematician and son of poet Sergei Yesenin, to demand a public trial for the arrested writers Andrei Sinyavsky and Yuly Daniel. Alekseyeva watched as Yesenin-Volpin barely had time to unfold the poster hidden under his coat and raise it above his head when KGB officers grabbed him, shoved him into a car and took him away. The poster read "Respect the Soviet Constitution"—a demand that would become one of the main slogans of the Soviet dissident movement.

Now, forty-five years later, the eighty-two-year-old Alekseyeva was in the square again, and with much the same slogan. Images of her arrest on 31 December 2009 were published all around the world: a very old woman in a fairy-tale Snow Maiden costume being detained by the police as they broke up a rally on Triumfalnaya Square. After that, Nemtsov, Yashin and their other Solidarity members started appearing on the square. The authorities continued to fight them. On Surkov's orders, protesters were not allowed onto the square, sometimes under the pretext of another rally or some construction work, but those who did come to rallies were rounded up and thrown into police vans. In May 2010, for example, almost two hundred people were arrested. Nemtsov was also regularly detained but quickly released.

Detentions and arrests were commonplace. Nemtsov never made it to the rally on Pushkin Square when Shevchuk performed to save Khimki Forest. It was 22 August, the anniversary of the victory over the attempted 1991 coup. He and other activists had been detained for trying to carry a Russian flag along Novy Arbat, a thoroughfare leading to the Kremlin.

The rules were being tightened day by day. Marching down the Arbat with a flag was a longstanding tradition that had been permitted just a couple of years earlier. But by 2009, Ilya Yashin got a head injury as he was being shoved in a police van. Nemtsov—who had been spared—came to the hospital to visit him, but now in 2010, Nemtsov was also detained. He wrote in his blog, "Can you imagine anything more barbaric than banning demonstrators from carrying the national flag through the streets of the capital on Flag Day? Can you imagine a country like that? Well, look no further."[3]

There was nothing the authorities could do about the protest flash mobs and outbursts of public ire. That's why they fought those they knew by sight—Nemtsov and his fellow opposition members. On 11 December, one of the fans of the Spartak football club was killed in a brawl with fans from the Caucasus. A few days later, when tens of thousands of football fans rioted on Manezhnaya Square, Surkov said that "the eleventh was inspired by the thirty-first", and put the blame on the liberals, who "keep making unsanctioned protests fashionable, and Nazis and lowlifes copy them."[4] Ramzan Kadyrov echoed that sentiment, blaming the pogrom on "the Kasyanovs and the Nemtsovs, who have prepared the ground for social uprisings."[5] The events concerned Kadyrov directly since the rioting in Moscow was openly anti-Caucasus.

## The Magnitsky Act

Vladimir Putin has always cared about who criticizes him and how they do it, and for that reason standards of acceptable criticism against him were quickly established, both in the press and in the political environment. Apart from the obvious unspoken prohibitions—for example, the taboo on discussing his and his family's private life—there was also a general rule: criticism should be as impersonal as possible, and the system as a whole should be criticized rather than its individual representatives, and certainly not Putin himself. Moreover, the criticism should not be harsh. On the one hand, this is common decency. On the other hand, it's easy to use it as an excuse for self-censorship.

Nemtsov constantly broke almost every taboo with one exception: He did not pry into Putin's private life because he was not interested in it. He branded the regime corrupt and thieving; he didn't choose his words carefully and easily slipped from the general to the personal. "We argued constantly about the style of his speeches," recalled Vladimir Ryzhkov. "You can't call your opponent terrible names. Boris did it all the time, unfortunately. He always had one argument: he's used to saying what he thinks; it's his nature—he says what he thinks."[6] All the troubles, all the evils of the Russian political system for Nemtsov were embodied in two people. The first was Putin. "The architect of this insane system has a very specific name," Nemtsov explained, "Vladimir Putin. And he has spawns all over the country. They are just like him, because, as they say, the congregation takes after the priest."[7]

The second person Nemtsov cited was Vladislav Surkov. Under President Putin, Surkov was a courtier, albeit a very powerful one. Starting in about 2003, he managed at arm's length both the law enforcement agencies and the courts, as far as domestic policy issues were concerned. But under Medvedev, Surkov's position changed fundamentally: He became the chief adviser, the vizier. He formulated the ideology of Medvedev's "thaw." He was in charge of modernization and patronized, for example, the construction of the Skolkovo innovation centre near Moscow. He played a major role in the reset with America and chaired the US–Russia Commission on Civil Society Development with Barack Obama's aide Michael McFaul. He oversaw all cultural policies and related budgets. And of course, as before, Surkov was in charge of all domestic policy.

Nashi was also in its heyday. Provocations and harassment of the opposition did not subside. A huge summer camp was built for Nashi on a picturesque spot in Western Russia on Lake Seliger. The president and the prime minister paid them visits, rock stars and well-known political analysts came to perform and talk, and the opposition was discredited there on a daily basis. For example, the camp had an installation of plastic heads on stakes with the faces of Nemtsov, Alekseyeva, Khodorkovsky and other opposition and human-rights activists, all wearing caps with fascist symbols and a huge banner with the words "You Are Not Welcome Here." "I believe that the entire political responsibility for the nature and direction of this kind of artistry lies not even with [Nashi head Vasily] Yakemenko—he's just obediently carrying out orders—but with his boss, Surkov," Nemtsov said. "As long as this gentleman is in charge of domestic politics in our country and travels freely around the world, we can't expect any changes."[8]

In late 2007, after Nemtsov had been harassed by Nashi activists for months, Nemtsov came up with the idea of convincing Western countries to impose personal sanctions against Surkov. Vladimir Kara-Murza,* a journalist and activist who was close to Nemtsov and his assistant in the Duma when he'd been a deputy, remembered the discussions. In mid-December, in Kasyanov's office, Nemtsov, Kasyanov and Bukovsky were discussing the upcoming presidential election. Kara-Murza recalled: "Boris began by saying how strange it was—these guys are flag-waving patriots who stand for sovereign democracy and trample on basic democratic values. But they love to make use of all the benefits and privileges of the democratic society that they hate so much."[9] And the classic example was Surkov "who travels to London every weekend." This was hypocrisy, he said, and it was time to bring it up in the West. These people should not be granted visas.

In November 2009, the terrible news came about Sergei Magnitsky, a thirty-seven-year-old corporate lawyer who had worked in Russia with investor Bill Browder and his Hermitage Fund. He had died in Moscow's Butyrka Prison. Browder settled in Russia in the 1990s, and

---

\* Kara-Murza was arrested in Moscow in 2022 on charges of disobeying police orders. While still in detention, charges of discrediting the military were added, followed by charges of treason. He was sentenced to twenty-five years in prison in April 2023, but released in a prisoner exchange in 2024.

his fund made a fortune investing in stocks of Russian companies, from Yukos to Gazprom. It was one of the largest in the country. Browder became notorious as an aggressive minority shareholder, willingly taking on the largest companies owned by the state or closely associated with them. He was expelled from the country in 2005, according to one version because he had enquired about the ownership structure of Surgutneftegaz, according to another because Igor Sechin had lobbied for him to be banned. Sechin was the head of Rosneft, which had received the oil assets of Yukos after the arrest of Khodorkovsky.[10]

In 2007, when he could no longer enter the country, Browder was gradually getting rid of his Russian assets when the police showed up at his Moscow office. During the raid, they confiscated the documents and stamps of the three Hermitage companies. By that time, these companies owned nothing, but, in 2006, they and the Hermitage investors had made about $1 billion after selling stock in Gazprom, which had soared in value when non-residents entered the market. Hermitage paid $230 million in income tax to the state budget for these deals. And, as Magnitsky found out, a few months after the investigators had visited, these three empty companies had been "stolen" and reregistered to unauthorized people as the nominal owners. Some supposed counterparties, Magnitsky discovered, had filed lawsuits against these companies, alleging that they owed them £1 billion, an amount equal to the profits they had earned in 2006. Moreover, the former Hermitage companies acquiesced to these lawsuits. And since they owed $1 billion, they did not make any profit. And, therefore, in late 2007 the budget refunded them the $230 million in tax they had paid. According to Browder, it "was the biggest tax refund in Russian history."[11] As Magnitsky discovered later, another investment fund, Renaissance Capital, "recovered"—that is, stole—$107 million in income tax from the budget through a similar scheme. In November 2008, Magnitsky explained all of this in great detail to a reporter from *Business Week* magazine and was arrested a few days after the article was published.[12]

In prison, Magnitsky was, to all intents and purposes, murdered: investigators and prison guards drove him to his death, thus silencing both the victim and the investigator of a crime that clearly involved high-level officials. Bill Browder tried to reach out to the US Congress while

Magnitsky was still alive and in prison. And after his death he redoubled his efforts. He transformed himself from investor to political lobbyist. As a result, in summer 2010, the first bill introducing sanctions—an entry ban and asset freeze—against several dozen Russian law-enforcement officials implicated in Magnitsky's death was introduced in both houses of the US Congress. It was called the Magnitsky Act.

In November 2010, a year after Magnitsky's death, Nemtsov flew to Washington. Kara-Murza, who had been living in the American capital for more than a year, arranged for him to meet with the bill's co-sponsors, Republican senator and former presidential candidate John McCain and Democratic senator Ben Cardin. "The initiative is good, but the law needs to be expanded to be used in the future," Nemtsov told them. "It should apply to everyone who violates human rights in Russia"[13]—above all to Surkov, who was responsible for "creating extremist youth organizations, running the Kremlin's black box and organizing fraudulent elections."[14] When Nemtsov flew back to Moscow, right at the airport the Nashi activists threw a huge butterfly net over his head. "The net at my house now is like a trophy," Nemtsov told *Kommersant* newspaper after the incident. "I'll put Surkov in it one day."[15]

In May 2011, McCain and Cardin submitted to congress a new, expanded version of the Magnitsky Act. "It was very important to Boris that the sanctions were personal," recalls Kara-Murza. "He said in every meeting: 'Leave the country alone, go after the bad guys.'"[16] After a year and a half of fighting with an American administration unwilling to spoil relations with Moscow, the congress passed the law in late 2012 when it also repealed the ill-fated Jackson–Vanik amendment. Nemtsov watched the vote live from the balcony of the US House of Representatives. When Russia becomes a democracy, Nemtsov said, he would press for the Magnitsky Act to be repealed, but, for now, it is the most pro-Russian law ever passed abroad.

## 'Putin: Results. Ten Years Later'

In summer 2010, Nemtsov published a sequel to his report on Putin, 'Putin: Results. Ten Years Later'. As Olga Shorina said, "The goal was to print a million copies."[17] The report began the same way, with a story about Putin's friends. "When we published the first version of the report 'Putin: Results', talk about Putin's powerful personal friends who wield billions, such as Timchenko, the Kovalchuk brothers, the Rotenberg brothers, was just a lot of rumours," Nemtsov and Milov wrote. "Now these people are officially on the list of billionaires."[18] They went on to talk about how they used state contracts to take part in major construction projects and build up personal property and assets; how the sons of businessmen close to Putin and high-ranking officials occupy top-management positions in state-owned companies and had stakes in large businesses. Once again, Solidarity activists and Nemtsov personally stood outside metro stations, handing out reports and giving presentations in the regions.

Trouble began immediately. In St Petersburg, 100,000 copies of the report were seized. Then another batch of pamphlets was sealed in a printing house near Smolensk. The activists who distributed the report were detained everywhere, and Nemtsov himself was detained twice. In late September, Gennady Timchenko filed a libel suit against Nemtsov and Milov, demanding compensation for moral damages for the offensive words that he was "nobody" before Putin came to power, as well as to refute the phrase that "there is reason to believe that all these Timchenkos [...] are nothing more than nominal owners of a large array of property, while the real beneficiary is Putin himself."[19] Nemtsov was convinced that, without Putin's knowledge, Timchenko could not have filed such a claim.[20]

It is no coincidence that Putin's close acquaintances were again the focus of Nemtsov and Milov's attention. Russia, Inc. was growing stronger by the day, and in the second year of Medvedev's presidency it was becoming increasingly clear that Putin had no plans to relinquish control. In August 2010, escorted by central-television cameras, Putin began a 300-kilometre trip across Siberia in a Russian car, which looked like the launch of his re-election campaign. In an interview in October, Nemtsov was asked how he assessed Medvedev's prospects for a second presidential term. One in ten, Nemtsov replied. Putin was likely to return. "Certainly for Russia, Putin's return to power is the worst-case scenario. Because he'll sit in the Kremlin until 2024. It's a stupid idea. It would be like Brezhnev 2.0, only worse, because there are more ways to steal and a much greedier and more cynical team, with none of the country's problems resolved and the obvious collapse of the state," he said. "Keeping Putin in power is the worst-case scenario for Russia, simply catastrophic. I pity the country—to sit under Putin's yoke for twenty-five years, well that's just... I ask all the people, even those loyal to Putin: how old will you be in 2024?" Nemtsov turned to the correspondent: "How old will you be?" "Forty years old," the reporter answered. "You will already be a middle-aged man. I will be sixty-four." "You'll be a pensioner..." "I don't think so," Nemtsov said. "I'm so healthy, I'll outlive them, I'm sure. That's my goal—both physically and politically."[21]

Nemtsov was indeed in great shape. He had just climbed Mount Elbrus together with Ilya Yashin and Alfred Kokh and planted at the top a Solidarity flag with the slogan "Russia without Putin." Psychologically, he was also in good shape: the Sochi campaign had given him confidence, and the street protesters—opposition not permitted by the state—had already recognized him as one of the leaders. Yes, the situation was difficult, and it was hard to move ahead, but Nemtsov made long-term plans and had not abandoned his presidential ambitions. All in good time. The road to true freedom is thorny and long. Nemtsov liked to cite the example of the Jews, who wandered in the desert for forty years: for Russia, the forty-year mark would be roughly 2024. "Being in the opposition is not very pleasant," Nemtsov said. "But you have to plan on running a marathon and keep telling yourself that your life is not a sprint. What's that expression? In Russia, you have to live a long life."[22]

## Talk with Vladimir Putin

Since Putin became president, there were only two ways for the public to talk with him: the big annual press conference and the call-in show *Direct Line*. The press conference attracts journalists from all over the country, but the hours-long performance has little to do with journalism. The journalists confess their love for Putin, invite him to visit, ask him to solve problems in their regions and criticize his enemies. *Direct Line* is the same, except that, instead of journalists, ordinary people from various parts of Russia ask Putin questions via teleconferencing.

Alexei Gromov began his career in the Kremlin under Yeltsin. He became Putin's press secretary and has remained his loyal assistant with the rank of deputy chief of staff to this day. In 2010, he was responsible for controlling the Kremlin press corps. While Vladislav Surkov dealt with ideology and public policy, Gromov was always directly responsible for propaganda. He conducted weekly briefings for television managers to make sure the television news hit the right points and censored criticism. In short, he shaped the entire news agenda. During the Soviet era, political censorship was an established governmental institution. It had its regulations, procedures, offices and staff. Putin's Russia replaced it with a flexible system of rules built on telephone calls, nods, hints, journalistic self-censorship and a close relationship of trust between the Kremlin and the mainstream media. The creator and curator of this system was Alexei Gromov.

The call-in shows have always been carefully rehearsed. Putin listens to the needs of ordinary people, personally solves their problems and punishes the guilty. Everyone who participates in the direct line is trained to learn by heart the questions they were given to ask. When Putin moved into the role of prime minister, they renamed them *Talks with Vladimir Putin*, but these were hardly two-way conversations. They were really monologues. Putin never allowed himself to be drawn into a discussion. At no meeting, at no briefing, and at no *Direct Line* could anyone object to anything Putin said or even ask for a clarification. Everything Putin said had to sound like the ultimate truth. The only exception was the extremely rare interviews with Western journalists, when the Kremlin could not dictate terms.

Mikhail Kasyanov recalled how Putin threatened him during their last conversation in December 2004, when he warned him not to dare go into opposition. "[He] added," Kasyanov wrote, "that in 1999, when I was finance minister, there were rumours about 'Misha-two-per-cent' going around Moscow. I responded, 'You know perfectly well that this is utter nonsense.' To which Putin said: 'People say that there is no smoke without fire. So keep that in mind.'"[23]

Putin did not forget his threat. Many years later, he was asked a question about Kasyanov on one of his *Direct Lines*. And Putin recounted how ministers Herman Gref and Alexei Kudrin had demanded that he fire Kasyanov because he was a crook. "You know," Putin went on, "he had a nickname before he came to the government: 'Misha-two-percent'. Because he was allegedly involved in some corrupt things. But because there was no proof of that, and because I thought this was all a matter of personal sympathies and antipathies, I let him serve out his term."[24] It was as if Putin himself had not accused Kasyanov of anything. But his story left the impression he intended—that Kasyanov was a bribe-taker.

Another *Talk with Vladimir Putin* took place on 16 December 2010. In the fifth hour of the live broadcast, the prime minister moved on to questions that he said he had selected himself and that were lying on the table in front of him. Looking at the piece of paper in front of him, Putin read out the question: "What do Nemtsov, Ryzhkov, Milov and so on really want?" And he answered it himself: "Money and power, what else do they want? In their time, in the 1990s, they made a lot of money, stole billions along with Berezovsky and the men now in prison we talked about earlier [i.e. Khodorkovsky]. They were pulled away from their feeding troughs, and now they've run out of money and want to go back to line their pockets. But I think that, if we let them do it, they won't confine themselves to a few billions—they will sell out all of Russia."

None of what Putin said was true. But the laws of the genre did not require veracity. For years, television propaganda had been telling viewers over and over again about the oligarchs and liberals who had looted the country. The ideology of Putin's stability was based on the myth of the turbulent 1990s, and Boris Nemtsov had been at the centre of this myth for years. Putin was reinforcing what people had heard on television almost every day.

The fact that the prime minister was repeating well-known facts was what his lawyer Yelena Zabralova later cited when Nemtsov, Ryzhkov and Milov sued for defamation, and, to their great surprise, the court accepted the suit for review. "For ten, fifteen, or twenty years, a man accepted what was said about him—that he embezzled money and committed crimes. He didn't care about his good name and didn't go to court, but now he's come to defend it," she said, citing not quotations from central television, but clippings from articles on websites that published compromising political material.[25] Let the defendant prove that his clients "stole billions", Nemtsov's lawyer Vadim Prokhorov demanded of the court. "And Putin's lawyer said," Ryzhkov recalls, "'Let's type in the names of Ryzhkov, Nemtsov, Milov, and see how much dirt there is about them.' To which our lawyer suggested typing 'Vladimir Putin' into the internet. And let's see how much dirt there is about him, that he stole billions of dollars. The judge scratched her head and said: 'It's true: if we type in everyone's name on internet, we won't ever find the truth.'"[26]

In the end, the court decided that Putin was simply retelling some general idea of the opposition. "The names Nemtsov, Ryzhkov and Milov," the judge ruled, "are not used as proper names, but solely to denote a particular class of political figures with a similar set of methods of political debate."[27]

## An act of personal revenge

On 31 December 2010, Nemtsov's daughter Zhanna and a friend suddenly realized that they had no plans for celebrating the New Year. "Let's celebrate together," Zhanna's father suggested. "Just go to Triumfalnaya Square in the early evening. I'll speak at a rally, and then we'll go and see in the New Year."[28] The mayor's office had given the opposition permission to hold the rally. Nemtsov arrived at the start, around 6.00 p.m., along with Zhanna. He chanted "Putin, resign!" and sharply criticized the new sentence announced three days earlier for Mikhail Khodorkovsky and Platon Lebedev: this time they were accused of stealing oil pumped by Yukos—that is, stealing from themselves—and they had another six years in prison added on to each of their sentences. Half an hour later, Nemtsov and Zhanna walked back through the police cordon towards their car parked on Tverskaya Street so they could go home and celebrate. Vladimir Ryzhkov walked along with them. When they came to the Tverskaya metro station, Nemtsov was suddenly surrounded by riot police who twisted his arms behind his back and dragged him into a paddy wagon without explanation. "We'll sort it out at the station," one of the policemen said when Ryzhkov asked, in outrage, what was going on.

Due to the New Year's holiday, Nemtsov was arraigned two days later, on 2 January. He was sentenced to fifteen days in custody. The court ruling stated that Nemtsov "refused to get in the van, resisted arrest, tried to break free, pushed police officers aside, shouted offensive language at them and tried to create a commotion among citizens nearby before being detained and taken to the police station."

In a complaint to the European Court of Human Rights, Nemtsov's lawyer would later state:

(1) For forty hours, from 31/12/2010 to 02/01/2011, Boris Nemtsov was held in inhuman conditions in a cage measuring 1.5 by 3 metres with a narrow wooden bench, a concrete floor and no windows. He was not provided with a mattress, bedding or even a place to sleep, and the walls were covered in health- and life-threatening plaster. [This embossed wall covering is called a "fur coat" in prison slang. According to the official version, the coat prevents inmates from writing on the walls; in reality, by preventing them from leaning against the wall, it harms inmates psychologically.]
(2) In the course of the court session on 2 January, Magistrate Judge Borovkova forbade Nemtsov to sit. Nemtsov, who had been held in unbearable conditions for two days and was physically and mentally exhausted, spent the entire court session, which lasted more than five hours, standing.
(3) The court refused to attach to the case three video recordings of Nemtsov's detention that were presented to the court and that refuted the version of the police officers who claimed that Nemtsov had not complied with their demands and resisted.

Administrative detention is served in special detention centres that are not prisons. This was a small two-storey building with bars on the windows and cells of varying sizes for up to twenty people. The toilet is simply a hole in the floor, separated from the cell by a low wall and a blanket or sheet instead of a door. The floor is wooden with furniture bolted to it: a table with a bench, bunks (some cells have bunkbeds) and stools, with shelves in the corner on the wall for food, tea and cigarettes. There are all kinds of people in detention centres, but there was no violence or the rigid rules of the penal zone.

Nemtsov spent thirteen days in the special detention centre. While he was there, pro-Kremlin activists directed by Yakemenko launched a campaign to convince the public that Nemtsov had been raped in his cell. They stood at the door of the detention centre with a poster of Nemtsov and the telephone number of the psychological support service for victims of violence in detention. They brought cages with roosters (prison slang for homosexuals) to the detention centre and tried, to no avail, to convince Nemtsov's cellmates who were released to give interviews about how he was raped in his cell and how he bribed the police. About halfway through his sentence, Nemtsov was placed in a cell with someone with a contagious form of tuberculosis, and Nemtsov had to undergo medical examinations after his release.

Putting a former first deputy prime minister and deputy speaker of the State Duma behind bars was unheard of. It had never happened before in modern Russia.* As Nemtsov himself later said, he was the only deputy prime minister to be arrested in Russia in the last fifty years.

No one knows who exactly came up with the idea of putting Nemtsov behind bars for a fortnight and what the reason was. But at the time it was already clear that the arrest could not have happened without sanction from on high. Nemtsov was probably being punished for everything at once: for Timchenko and the Rotenbergs, for his trip to Washington, for his numerous interviews. "He was absolutely certain," Ryzhkov recalled, "and I agree with him that they just wanted to punish him for his harsh criticism. 'What do you keep running on about? We're sick of it! Go to jail for fifteen days.' It was just an act of personal revenge."[29] Nemtsov believed that the order to arrest him came from Putin and Surkov who "wanted to frighten, demoralize and intimidate",

---

\* The arrests of coup conspirators in 1991 and Vice-President Alexander Rutskoi in 1993 were special cases in Russia's history.

he said upon his release. "In the end, they did not frighten, demoralize or intimidate."[30] Friends and comrades—both Fridman and Chubais—tried to help. Both knew Surkov well, both called him and urged him to release Nemtsov from custody. It was hopeless: they couldn't get him out before his time was up.

On the evening of 15 January, Nemtsov was released. It was Saturday. Zhanna met him to go to dinner together. It was the first time she had seen the activists trying to throw a big net over Nemtsov: "I wanted to run after them, but they ran away too quickly," she said.[31] Nemtsov was cheerful and courageous. "I will never leave. Putin can leave."[32] But the arrest made it clear that the rules of the game were changing. And the prospect did not bode well. After his arrest, Nemtsov finally gave in to the long-standing pleas of his close friends and relatives. He agreed to a protection detail.

# CHAPTER 29

## 2010–11
## The Rook and King Change Places

### Medvedev's show of ambition

No one but Vladimir Putin and Dmitry Medvedev know the exact terms of their agreement before the presidential election in 2008. But officials close to them understood the gist of their agreement as follows: in three or four years, close to the end of Medvedev's first presidential term, they would sit down to decide which of them should run for president. Even if Putin had already been planning his comeback in 2008—which is highly probable—he wouldn't have warned Medvedev about it in advance. This would have immediately humiliated Medvedev, and the tandem, as the joint government of Putin and Medvedev came to be called, needed to function smoothly. Everyone knew who was leading and who was being led in this tandem, but Medvedev proceeded on the assumption that if he made no serious mistakes and was loyal to Putin, he would have a chance of staying in the Kremlin after 2012.

Medvedev tried his best. He did not question Putin's authority, nor did he break the unwritten rules. He acted cautiously and was careful to ensure that the modernization he announced did not appear excessive to Putin. In the areas where Putin's interests were directly affected, Medvedev did not interfere at all. During the second Khodorkovsky and Lebedev trial, for example, Nemtsov personally asked Medvedev to get involved in the case. "That is outside my sphere of competence," the president replied.*

As it grew closer to the time to decide, however, tensions in the tandem inevitably became exacerbated. Medvedev was becoming increasingly ambitious. In summer 2010, he clashed with Yury Luzhkov. In response to criticism from the Kremlin, Luzhkov publicly attacked Medvedev and sought protection from Putin. How it began is not as important as how it ended: in October, Medvedev dismissed Luzhkov. Strictly speaking, by dismissing Luzhkov, Medvedev did not break the rules of the game. Luzhkov himself violated them when he publicly opposed Medvedev in his discussions with Putin, knowing that driving a wedge into the tandem was implicitly forbidden. But Luzhkov's dismissal was the first confirmation that Medvedev was capable of acting independently. "Before Luzhkov's dismissal, there had been a period of mild competition between Putin and Medvedev," Gleb Pavlovsky said, "but, after that, the atmosphere changed. Putin was stunned. And he naturally saw Luzhkov's dismissal as a kind of rehearsal."[1] This was all the more disconcerting, since Medvedev's confidence rating had caught up with Putin's that autumn. Moreover, internal opinion polls conducted at the request of the Kremlin recorded a marked increase in approval for Medvedev since the summer—even in the electoral groups on which Putin had traditionally relied: pensioners and military personnel.

---

* After receiving eight years in prison in his first conviction, Mikhail Khodorkovsky would have been released in 2011. In 2007, however, he and Platon Lebedev were indicted on new charges. Under these charges, transfer pricing—the accumulation of profits in an offshore trader for tax-optimization purposes, a standard practice for Russian oil companies—was interpreted as the theft of oil that Yukos subsidiaries had pumped out between 1998 and 2003, coupled with the legalization of the proceeds from it. The lawyers' objections were that Yukos had every right to give instructions to its subsidiaries; moreover, in the first Yukos case, the same transfer prices were presented by the prosecution as tax evasion. On 30 December 2010, the Khamovnichesky Court in Moscow sentenced Khodorkovsky and Lebedev to fourteen years imprisonment, with credit for time already served. In February 2011, Natalia Vasilyeva, assistant to the sentencing judge Viktor Danilkin, said in an interview that the judge had not written the verdict—the Moscow City Court had.

At the same time, Medvedev's reset in relations with the West peaked. The NATO–Russia summit in Lisbon in November 2010 was hailed by both sides as historic: the first time in two decades that Russia and NATO countries were able to come to serious agreements. In 2000, Putin's statement about Russia's possible membership in NATO sounded like a joke. Ten years later, as *Kommersant* wrote after the summit, "there has been a breakthrough in relations between the sides, after which the idea of Moscow joining the alliance no longer seems so fantastic."[2] The NATO concept approved at the summit noted that "Russia–NATO cooperation is of strategic importance" and that NATO and Russia should achieve "a true strategic partnership." Medvedev did not hide his satisfaction: it had been a negotiation of equals. At the same time, in Brussels, Berlin and other European capitals, the question of a visa-free regime with Russia was being seriously discussed. It all looked like a breakthrough.

All that remained was to agree on missile defence. There seemed to be a good chance of succeeding. Back at the beginning of the reset, as Obama was mending relations with Medvedev, the US president deliberately went one step closer to Moscow on the issue of deploying a missile defence in Europe. He abandoned the Bush administration's plans to deploy antimissile radars near Russia's borders. The ground-based systems were replaced with sea-based interceptors. At the time, their configuration precluded them from shooting down Russian intercontinental ballistic missiles aimed at America.

The problem was that Moscow wanted more: specifically, to include commitments on missile defence in the New START Treaty, the cornerstone of the reset. For Medvedev, this was a very important issue. Three years before, in his Munich speech, Putin had identified the West's assault on Russian interests as the main challenge facing the country. By securing concessions from Obama, Medvedev would prove to Putin and to all the hawks in the Russian elite that the reset bet had paid off. But Obama did not budge. The treaty, signed in April 2010, still made no mention of missile defence.

Medvedev then brought a radical new proposal to the NATO–Russia summit in Lisbon. Since Russia and NATO are partners, let them work together to defend themselves from the nuclear threat from Iran (and potentially from Pakistan, although this was not stated publicly). At the behest of the Russian military, Medvedev suggested dividing Europe into sectors: America and NATO would be responsible for one sector of missile defence and Russia for the other. Of course, Moscow could see that the proposal was unrealistic: NATO could not entrust the defence of a part of its territory to a country outside the alliance. Moscow planned to bargain. Although the initiative was rejected, the Medvedev camp noted that "the groundwork [was] done."[3] In fact, Obama and Medvedev agreed to continue to search for a solution, and there was hope that a compromise could be reached in time for the G8 Summit in Deauville in May 2011.

Medvedev was scoring points in this clandestine but increasingly obvious confrontation with Putin. As Arkady Dvorkovich, Medvedev's closest aide, said in an interview, "Anyone who looks closely at what Dmitry Medvedev is doing will realize that he wants to stay on for a second term and continue working on the goals he set in 2008."[4] There was an uneasy silence in the tandem: the president's and prime minister's offices had been at war with each other for a long time, and now they had stopped communicating. Putin had been expecting Medvedev to come to him to discuss the upcoming elections, but Medvedev never showed up. "One of Medvedev's aides suggested that he go to talk," Pavlovsky said. "The answer was, 'The president can't go to the prime minister to discuss elections.'" Putin's entourage already feared that Medvedev might dismiss him. When these concerns were brought to Putin's attention, he said irritably, as if doubtful, "He can't. He doesn't have the right to do it."[5]

Then civil war broke out in Libya.

## The fractured tandem

After the Arab Spring came to Tunisia and Egypt, it arrived in Libya and immediately became a disaster. In February 2011, an armed uprising started in the east of the country. By mid-March the death toll was in the hundreds, and Libyan dictator Muammar Gaddafi was preparing to storm the rebel stronghold city of Benghazi. The international community was considering intervention.

A few years later, *The New York Times* would detail how America got embroiled in the Libyan civil war. On 15 March 2011, the US representative to the UN, Susan Rice, told her French counterpart, Gérard Araud, "You are not going to drag us into your shitty war." At the time, the French were the main proponents of intervention, backed by the British. Paris and London demanded a UN resolution to establish a no-fly zone over Libya. Obama and the US military were against it. "Can I finish the two wars I'm already in before you guys go looking for a third one?" Defence Secretary Robert Gates said. But on the same day, 15 March, Obama gathered his team at the White House and Hillary Clinton, then secretary of state, spoke to them via video link. She had just met with President Sarkozy in Paris and explained that it was better to intervene in Libya than to stand on the sidelines. France and Britain would intervene in any case, and the rebels had support in the Arab world. Clinton convinced Obama to change his mind. The military, in turn, convinced him that a no-fly zone alone would not avoid a humanitarian catastrophe in Libya. That same evening, Susan Rice called an astonished Gérard Araud back: Washington would not only support its NATO allies but favoured a strong UN resolution that would authorize more serious forms of support for the rebels.[6]

It remained to convince the other members of the UN Security Council—Moscow and Beijing—not to veto the resolution. As soon as there was bloodshed in Libya, Medvedev sided with the international community and threatened Gaddafi with sanctions. When it came to the ill-fated UN resolution that sanctioned an armed intervention in Libya, the Russian Foreign Ministry proposed to veto it.[7] This was logical: Russia had always, even under Yeltsin, blocked international military interventions. Medvedev, on the other hand, was inclined to support the resolution, which he made clear to the US vice-president, Joe Biden, on his visit to Moscow in early March. As Michael McFaul, the Russia expert who held the post of senior presidential adviser in the Obama administration (and who came up with the idea of the reset), later wrote in his memoirs, he concluded that Medvedev had decided to allow a UN-sanctioned military intervention in Libya not because he had much faith in the mission's success, but rather because he sought to demonstrate to Obama his commitment to deepening cooperation between the United States and Russia."[8]

China's position played an important role. Beijing's agreement not to obstruct international military action strengthened Medvedev's position. Russia and China eventually abstained, and the UN Security Council approved Resolution 1973. The fact that the Russian ambassador to Libya was scandalously dismissed a few hours before the UN vote for—in the Kremlin's words—"not adequately representing Russia's interests in the Libyan conflict" indicates how tense the situation was in Moscow.[9]

It was not hard to fire the ambassador; it wasn't like trying to fire Putin. The resolution was passed on 17 March, and Putin must have known Medvedev's decision in advance. Like the missile-defence issue, it was discussed in the Russian Security Council with his participation. He also knew what Joe Biden had said in early March at a closed-door meeting with Russian human-rights activists and opposition figures in Moscow, which Nemtsov attended. Putin should not run for president in 2012. In this context, the reset had the hallmarks of a conspiracy in Putin's eyes.

Putin went in for a counterattack. On 19 March, the bombing of Libya began. A day later, during a visit to a metallurgical factory that looked like election campaigning, Putin was surrounded by workers. One of them had been told to ask about Libya. Putin trashed the UN resolution. "The whole thing reminds me of a medieval call for a crusade," Putin said caustically.[10] On the same day, Medvedev for the first time sharply rebuked the man who was his superior, or subordinate, or partner, or rival: "Comparisons with crusades are unacceptable."[11] This was a real scandal: the tandem was falling apart before everyone's eyes.

## 24 September

In May 2011, a small delegation of liberal lawmakers came to the Kremlin from the Duma. They weren't able to meet with Medvedev, but the delegation was received by Arkady Dvorkovich. The delegates told him that most of the A Just Russia faction in parliament supported

Medvedev and were even ready to stage a coup within the faction and the party so that Medvedev would have a base of support. But before they decided, they needed to understand Medvedev's intentions. Did he intend to seek a second term and perhaps even to dismiss Prime Minister Putin? Dvorkovich promised to pass everything on to his boss. A couple of days later, he came back with an answer: all this can only be discussed if United Russia's rating fell below thirty per cent.

That meant "no." In May 2011, according to public opinion polls, the rating of United Russia, led by Putin, was hovering around forty per cent, and there was no reason to expect it to fall. Soon afterwards, on 18 May, Medvedev arrived at Skolkovo to give his big annual press conference, a format he inherited from Putin along with the presidency. Everybody wanted to know only one thing from it: would Medvedev announce that he was running for a second term or not? Putin was waiting to hear, too: he began his scheduled meeting with the government only after the press conference had ended. Medvedev had dropped a hint: he might announce his candidacy, and perhaps even soon, but a press conference was not the format in which such things were announced, and, "in deciding who gets elected", he and his "like-minded colleague and political partner" Vladimir Putin would be guided by a "sense of responsibility before the country and its people."[12]

"There is no real grass-roots group supporting the president," *Nezavisimaya gazeta* wrote that day, assessing Medvedev's chances for a second term.[13] Medvedev was well aware of that. Over the past three years, he had deliberately done nothing to consolidate his supporters. By the end of his term, he didn't have a party of his own, and he didn't even have a team. He could still rely only on a few officials in his inner circle. And he certainly refused to support the liberal deputies who had offered to stage an intra-party revolt for him. Medvedev thought his best chance was to try to reach a direct agreement with Putin before the election. And that chance was vanishing before his eyes.

A week later, Medvedev met with Obama at the G8 summit. The day before, the American side had received Moscow's proposed missile-defence statement. Its contents were unknown, but, according to subsequent press reports, Moscow offered—apparently in a thinly disguised form—to limit strictly the number and speed of its interceptors in return for legal guarantees that ABMs in Europe would not be directed against Russia. The Obama administration was willing to offer political guarantees, but legal guarantees required congressional ratification. At the time, the congress was controlled by Republicans, who could not be convinced. Obama had to decline Moscow's proposed text, which he told Medvedev in Deauville. This was a blow for Medvedev. "It seemed to me that he had been led to believe that we already had signed off on the statement," McFaul recalled. "After the formal meeting, Obama and Medvedev stayed in the room to talk one-on-one for a few moments, while both Lavrov and Prikhodko cornered me to ask what had happened. They both were furious. As Lavrov explained, Medvedev had expended a lot of political capital to convince Putin and other hardliners in the Security Council to approve the statement. Now we were pulling back, and thereby undermining Medvedev internally."[14]

Medvedev sought to show Putin that the Americans were on the same page as Russia, but in the end the opposite was true, at least from Putin's point of view. The same could be said of Medvedev's position on Libya. It turned out that Putin was right to criticize the UN resolution: the NATO mission to protect civilians in Benghazi quickly evolved into a full-scale war with Gaddafi on the side of the rebels. (Later, after Gaddafi's brutal assassination and unsuccessful attempts to build a sustainable regime in Libya, the Libyan war would go down in history as a textbook example of the complete failure of Western humanitarian intervention.) Medvedev again lost out to Putin, who firmly believed that Russia's relations with the West, particularly the United States, were a zero-sum game: what was good for them was bad for Russia. In Deauville, Medvedev had no choice but to rebuke Obama for exceeding the mandate given by Resolution 1973. "I've never seen [Medvedev] so grim," McFaul recalled the meeting, "while he was talking [to Obama], sweat was dripping off him, not only because the room was hot, but because he probably realized that in his race for a second term, his special relationship with Obama was now not an advantage, but a problem. And he was right."[15]

Medvedev tried to keep his spirits up. At the St Petersburg Economic Forum in mid-June, he delivered what was essentially a presidential programme. He criticized state capitalism and called for large-scale privatization, promised an improved investment climate and decentralization, spoke of visa-free travel and judicial reform. This is how Medvedev pictured his second presidential term. "We can change the situation qualitatively in the next few years," he said. It was his swan song.

The historic conversation between Putin and Medvedev took place two months later, in late August, during their joint three-day fishing trip on the Volga near Astrakhan. Mikhail Zygar wrote that they discussed the events of the past year, including the situation in Libya. Putin explained his reasoning at length. "Medvedev had no reply."[16] He had no choice but to give in. They agreed that Putin would be president and Medvedev would become prime minister and the leader of United Russia. To soften the bitter pill, Putin promised Medvedev that he would be ready to hand over the presidency to him again in six or twelve years. "Medvedev came back from that fishing trip broken," says Gleb Pavlovsky. "You could see it in everything, right down to his gait."[17] A month later, on 24 September, at the United Russia congress in the Luzhniki sports arena, he announced that he and Putin would switch places. "Your applause," Medvedev said, "means I don't need to explain the authority Vladimir Putin enjoys."[18] It was a pitiful sight.

In defiance, Arkady Dvorkovich did not attend the congress. He sat in a café and watched what was happening on television. First, he tweeted: "It's better to play hockey at Luzhniki." Then: "Yeah, there's no reason to be happy." Then: "That's it, I'm switching to the sports channel." At that point, Medvedev called him and asked him to stop, reminding him that they still worked together in the government. Medvedev's thaw was over.

# CHAPTER 30

## 2007–11
## The Dude from Marino Who Reinvented Politics

### Be shocked if someone puts you down

In 2010, abstract democratic slogans sounded like an old broken record to the average Moscow hipster. Politics—all those parties, elections, divisions—had long been out of fashion. Professional politicians were considered losers from the past. A trend-setter in Moscow in the late aughts on the cover of the *Afisha* entertainment magazine might have been rapper Noize MC or TV presenter and socialite Ksenia Sobchak, daughter of Anatoly Sobchak, but certainly not Nemtsov, Kasyanov or Yavlinsky.

Moscow was becoming a more liveable city. Expensive and pretentious restaurants were now flanked by cosy coffee houses and burger joints, pedestrian streets were opened, and the first bicycle lanes became a symbol of the new trend—urban landscaping. Gorky Park, Moscow's main recreational area, had been transformed from a Soviet-era throwback with rusty rides and the unforgiving smell of bad kebabs into a modern European park. Life was buzzing, and Moscow's glossy magazines raved about the changes for the better since Luzhkov's scandalous dismissal. They were spearheaded by the new mayor, Sergei Sobyanin, once governor of Tyumen and then Putin's chief of staff in the Kremlin and in the White House. Nemtsov and his political associates were commonly referred to in this milieu as a "schizo-dem"—an offensive word for a democratic activist who had lost touch with reality and had gone mad fighting the regime.

This is not to say that there was no political life in Moscow, Russia's most liberal, most European city. There was, but talk of democracy did not resonate. Nobody was interested in changing the whole of Russia or overthrowing Putin. "Everything is set up in such a way that any statement by a public politician on even somewhat abstract topics is believed to be a cloud of specially released smokescreen for a trick, a deception, a cunning and dishonest intrigue," the journalist Yury Saprykin, one of its founders and ideologists wrote in *Afisha*.[1] A wide variety of civic activism grew up all over the country: from volunteerism to the fight against law-enforcement abuses, from local environmental movements to anti-corruption revelations. Interest was generated by those who were doing something concrete. "When the blogger Navalny," Saprykin said, "compared figures in the quarterly report of VTB Bank, he looked really good, but when he'd start talking about the ethnic issues or 'who to vote for in elections', it immediately sounded scripted and no one believed a single word."[2] Journalist Maria Eismont wrote: "In Russian society, there seems to be an emerging demand for a new type of modern hero: a simple citizen who publicly and boldly rejects the wooden authorities who are confident that they can do anything they want with complete impunity."[3]

That all changed on 24 September, when Putin and Medvedev announced that they would switch places. It was a bombshell. "I remember perfectly the moment when Medvedev looked happy as he offered his seat to Vladimir Vladimirovich. It was a hideous feeling. And I remember how I felt after they changed places. We opened Facebook and everyone there was like: 'We've been fucked over,'" recalled Ilya Krasilshchik, then twenty-four-year-old editor-in-chief of *Afisha*.[4]

Before they traded places, Moscow's young intelligentsia was already sceptical about Dmitry Medvedev, the "president with an iPhone." But they were even more sceptical about Putin: they had liked Medvedev's slogans about modernization and rapprochement with the West, and, most importantly, it seemed that there was a change in power at the top. And then it suddenly seemed to be a hoax: Putin and Medvedev had everyone fooled. The idea of small-scale projects and local, targeted progress, so dear to progressive Muscovites, lost its meaning. What good were bicycle lanes and iPads if Russia was not moving with the developed world, but in the opposite direction? "Is it worth improving the park if they won't let you improve Russia?" asked Saprykin in one of his columns in *Afisha*, where political commentary turned sharp after the Medvedev–Putin job trade.[5] Another trendy urban magazine, *Bolshoi gorod,* responded with a text on its cover that might have been a manifesto of political resistance in the country: "That's it! Be shocked if someone puts you down, stop being afraid, fight for your values, demand fair elections, and vote them both out."[6] But there was a dash of irony. At the end, the editors wrote, "Cheers!" Even as the *Bolshoi gorod* editors put forward what was essentially a political programme, they seemed to be afraid to sound too serious. Anything that seemed at all pretentious was still out of fashion among Moscow's progressive set.

Facebook, which was relatively new to Russia, was seething with anger. One of the main topics was the upcoming 4 December Duma elections. In the past, most discussions of the elections concluded that it was futile to try to fight. No one could see a winning strategy, since, no matter what you did, you came up against a brick wall: the loyal opposition that was permitted to run didn't rock the boat, protesters didn't have their own party, and there was no one to vote for. As Saprykin wrote even before the job switch at the top, "[Putin] somehow set it all up so that no matter what you try to do in the elections, it's all terrible anyway; no matter what you do, it's all your fault. If you didn't go to the polls, then you have nothing to complain about because you didn't use your opportunity to influence the country's fate. If you went to the polls, you have nothing to complain about because you chose these human robots. Thanks to this old guy [in the Kremlin], the word 'elections' has come to mean the absence of choice."[7] But the announced return of Putin and dashed hopes now called for a different approach. Alexei Navalny's suggestion to vote for any party but United Russia—which he called "the party of crooks and thieves"—was just the thing.

## Nationalism with a human face

The thirty-five-year-old politician Alexei Navalny stood apart. He wasn't like anyone else. He didn't fit in at any one point on the axis of political coordinates. Was Navalny on the left or the right? Liberal or conservative? Westernizer or nationalist? Over time it only became more difficult to be certain. This suited Navalny just fine. When a poll in the spring of 2013 showed that some people were put off by his nationalism, others by his liberalism, while still others were attracted to both, Navalny cited an old joke about a lion dividing the animals into smart and beautiful, and the monkey didn't know what to do—tear herself in half? He wrote on his blog: "I'm not going to 'tighten up nationalism' and 'turn down liberalism', or the other way around, in response to polls. My views are my views. They aren't a gas burner with a valve you can turn up or down."[8]

Navalny had sought to combine liberalism—or more precisely, democratic convictions—with nationalism since the very beginning of his career in the mid-2000s when he was simultaneously a member of the Yabloko party and was already thinking about founding a nationalist party or movement. Navalny began his speeches at rallies at the time with anti-oligarchic slogans—why are a bunch of oligarchs close to Putin robbing the country?—and then continued with anti-Caucasus slogans, which were gaining popularity in Moscow at the time. He quickly realized that there was a need for a new political party. Pyotr Miloserdov, a young right-wing activist in the Communist Party who was then in touch with Navalny, remembers how in June 2007, during one of the round tables, he suddenly received a text message from Navalny: "Let's create a healthy nationalist party." "It's a good idea, but we need resources," Miloserdov replied. "We'll find them," Navalny wrote to him.[9]

Both men understood "healthy nationalism" the same way. The liberal movement in Russia was dying out, while neo-imperialist and nationalist sentiment, on the contrary, was growing. Having lost their last Duma elections in late 2003, Nemtsov and Chubais embodied the failure of Russian Westernizing. The phrase "Russia is rising from its knees" was heard more often, and Putin was very popular. The Kremlin took up the imperial agenda and its course towards sovereign democracy. On the other flank, pogrom ideologues and skinheads swinging baseball bats fought for the rights of the Russian people. Navalny's understanding of "healthy nationalism" was supposed to both oppose the Kremlin and civilize the interests of Russians. "There is a specific agenda that people care about," Navalny later explained. "On that agenda is the large number of illegal migrants. It is a fact that Russia is in second place after the United States in the number of illegal migrants. It's a fact that the Caucasus, Chechnya in particular, has become a political, legal and financial offshore. Isn't that true? It's a fact. The enormous number of Russians who have remained outside the borders of Russia is also a fact. Russians are the largest divided nation in Europe; this fact is accepted and obvious to everyone. And so on."[10]

In 2007, the movement NAROD appeared; the name meant "people" (in the sense of ethnic group, nation) and was a Russian acronym for the National Association of the Russian Liberation Movement. Navalny was one of its leaders. "He said: 'Our first priority is to get rid of the discredited elements—the followers of Hitler, punks and crude pseudo-patriots—then get out of the marginalized ghetto of an insignificant insider's party and find support in the class of educated urbanites.'"[11]

NAROD called itself a national-democratic movement and sought to become part of a broad anti-Putin coalition along with the Westernizers. It seemed natural at the time: nationalist Dmitry Rogozin had stood on the Maidan during the Orange Revolution, and Nemtsov's associate Garry Kasparov had called for an alliance with Limonov's National Bolshevik Party, which advocated the revival of empire and the abolition of capitalism. Navalny was already on good terms with the new leader of the SPS, Nikita Belykh. (In 2009, Belykh was appointed governor of the Kirov region, and Navalny entered the civil service as his adviser.) When there was a debate over the NAROD programme, Navalny advocated a softer version of reprivatization—a revision of the shares-for-loans auctions—which would provide a mechanism for additional compensation from the owners. The movement's programme combined points about "creating conditions for the preservation and development of the Russian people", "a rational migration policy" and "the right to bear arms", along with recognition of the principles of separation of powers, elected judges and other demands to which Nemtsov would have subscribed.[12] Navalny was soon kicked out of the Yabloko party—formally for nationalism, but this happened at the very moment when he demanded Yavlinsky's dismissal after Yabloko failed in the parliamentary elections in 2007. Years later, Navalny explained that he was neither a nationalist in the literal sense of the word, nor a liberal, and he did not want to be seen as belonging to either camp: "I am a man of democratic and even liberal views, but on some issues—migration, for example—I am conservative. My manifesto is exactly that."[13]

Perhaps Navalny sincerely saw himself as both a liberal and a conservative at the same time, but NAROD was primarily a nationalist movement, and the propaganda videos that Navalny was then recording were even more chauvinistic. The problem was that the niche of nationalism "with a human face" that Navalny and his supporters were trying to occupy was not left empty by accident. Any far-right platform is always built on a simple and clear idea—the rejection of outsiders—and that is the message its supporters hear, no matter how hard the political leaders try to soften it by giving their programmes the gloss of a healthy and moderate conservatism.

NAROD lasted only a year and a half. Either Navalny realized that it wasn't to his liking and that the nationalist path was fraught with great costs for his career. Or maybe he was more interested in the practical rather than ideological aspects of politics. Tellingly, at Yabloko he headed the Committee for the Protection of Muscovites, which fought against illegal construction in the capital. As Miloserdov recalls, at some point Navalny simply "stopped picking up the phone" and "the movement dissolved by the tacit consent of the parties."[14]

Navalny would continue to go to "Russian Marches"—nationalist protest marches in Moscow—for years to come, explaining their necessity for the same reasons: the problem of migration, social stratification, the nationalists being forced out of politics, the privileged position of the Caucasus republics—and Chechnya in particular—and insisting that "the only way to make the Russian March look better is to go there yourself."[15]

## Politician No. 1

Very soon, in the spring of 2008, Navalny plunged headlong into another topic. He took up the fight against corruption. A lawyer by training, he came up with an ingenious move. Actually, he didn't come up with it himself; he borrowed it from business journalists. They would buy one share of the largest holding companies in order to gain access to shareholder meetings. "I thought about it," Navalny recalled, "and realized I had founded the Committee to Protect Muscovites because developers were taking away land, and these dudes are taking away money from the whole country. I went out and bought a share of every company."[16]

The difference between Navalny and journalists was that journalists jotted down information in notebooks and then wrote articles, while Navalny called press conferences and asked: where does the profit go? First, he flew to Surgut for a meeting of the Surgutneftegaz shareholders, then to a Rosneft shareholders meeting. His first target was Gennady Timchenko and his oil-trader Gunvor. On what grounds does a Swiss-registered intermediary company accumulate a substantial part of profits? Where are the documents? Soon this young politician was hitting state companies where it hurt. He was exposing financial machinations in billion-dollar contracts, suing and sometimes even winning. Under President Medvedev and his policy of modernization, Navalny was treated with respect, and he was even included in Sberbank's minority shareholders' committee.

It didn't stop there. Navalny proposed another utterly revolutionary concept. He invited anyone who wished to join the battle against corrupt officials. He invited readers of his blog to contribute funds to pay lawyers to challenge the results of unfair tenders. Within a week, he had collected a year's worth of funding. In effect, Navalny invented political crowdfunding, based on a sense of ownership of a common important cause.

This is how Navalny became the country's most notorious anti-corruption fighter. While not engaged in politics in the usual sense of the word, he became perhaps the most popular blogger, and, as the leading business daily *Vedomosti* wrote in recognizing him as "Man of the Year, 2009" in the "Private Person" category, he had "set a personal example by showing citizens how to protect their rights."[17] Now Navalny consciously stood apart from the nationalists, the liberals, Solidarity and Yabloko. He did not want to be associated with well-known opposition brands. He saw perfectly well how bored everyone was with the marginalized oppositionists and their tired slogans. He was reinventing the profession of politics.

Leonid Volkov, an IT specialist and political strategist who would soon become Navalny's right-hand man, remembered how he was attracted to Navalny when they first met in June 2010 at a conference of opposition forces "The *modus operandi* of any typical opposition politician or party back then was: 'Putin did something bad, let's release a statement.' Everyone was issuing statements on various topics. I had just finished working in business two weeks earlier, and I was very impressed by Alexei's business-like, project-oriented approach. He was completely different from everyone else. Everyone was operating in the usual paradigm, but Navalny said: 'Let's launch the RosPil project.' Even back then, he understood that every post, every text had to end with a call for joint action."[18] RosPil—a mash-up of *Ros-* ("Russia") and a slang term meaning "to siphon off funds"—was founded by Navalny in December 2010, after he had returned from six months as a visiting student at Yale University. The project monitored state purchases and how businesses misappropriated public funds.

By law, state contracts are awarded on the basis of public tenders, and RosPil activists looked for corrupt tenders on state procurement websites. RosPil was followed by RosYama—"Russian Potholes", public control of road quality—and RosVybory—"Russian Elections." Then came the crowd-funded Anti-Corruption Foundation (Russian abbreviation FBK), which was either a public anti-corruption project or a new kind of party. For Navalny, this was his political job: "I just decided from the beginning that I was going to be a politician who had a profession. I set up a foundation, I go to work at the foundation, and people work here, too."[19]

The FBK investigations that Navalny published on his blog, describing corruption in accessible language and, importantly, in a fun and entertaining way, raised his popularity to a new level. When *Kommersant* launched a project called the "virtual mayoral election in Moscow" in autumn 2010, Navalny won the online election by a whopping forty-five per cent of the vote. Nemtsov came in third place with twelve per cent, losing even to the "against everyone" option.

By the beginning of 2011, there was no doubt in Navalny's mind: he was the leader of political protest. And he was right. In Moscow, if not across the country, he was certainly the main opinion-maker. He was from a military family, had spent his childhood on military bases and did not graduate from prestigious high schools in Moscow; he was not part of the in-crowd and privileged class, but he was bold, witty and inventive. Navalny became a major political celebrity. All the glossy magazines wanted interviews and photo shoots. *Esquire* magazine put his portrait on the cover. "Am I the leader of the hipsters?" Navalny wondered about his new status. "I'm not sure. I'm more of a dude from Marino [a poor neighbourhood in south-eastern Moscow], who walks around in a coat with sneakers. But I will not wear glasses with hipster frames, and I'm happy to drink beer in places where hipsters wrinkle their noses and say, 'Eww.'"[20]

No one paid any attention to his rejections of these labels. In a country that rejected politics, he did not look like a typical politician. And that was exactly why he immediately became Politician No. 1.

# CHAPTER 31

## 2011
## Bolotnaya Square

### Boos heard all across Russia

In early October 2011, in a Moscow suburb, a group of opposition leaders debated what to do about the upcoming elections—elections without a choice—scheduled for 4 December and what they should call upon their supporters to do.

Garry Kasparov campaigned for a boycott. "The job of a responsible opposition is to prepare people for the coming changes. Boycotting polling stations on 4 December isn't all we're going to do. The elections on 4 December have nothing to do with us. We should be building our own alternative system and our own alternative bodies of governance. So what if it's all virtual? Remember that Peter the Great's toy soldiers eventually became his guards. But we have to get people used to the fact that we aren't taking part because our participation in this farce only helps the authorities."[1]

Nemtsov wanted them to write on the ballots. "It's no good participating in a farce, but a boycott is a passive form of protest," he said. "They won't know why you didn't come to the elections, why you didn't vote. Were you at home on the couch? Did you oversleep? Were you away?... We have to protest actively: go to the polls, make a big X on the ballot, write, 'Down with the party of crooks and thieves,' or whatever, and put the ballot into the ballot box. If millions of people do this, it will be like a rally in Triumfalnaya Square that is attended not by hundreds, but by hundreds and hundreds of thousands."²

Then Navalny came up with a new idea: vote for any party but United Russia. "We don't have a monopoly on the truth," he said.

> It's wrong to say that all the parties permitted by the government to take part are fakes and Kremlin puppets that we won't have anything to do with, and only our one and a half workers are in the right sect. Yes, all the current parties are under the influence of the Kremlin. Yes, they are all cowardly and brow-beaten, not in a position to stand up powerfully to a clique who has usurped power. They're afraid to get out from under their sofas and armchairs and say what we can say. We must help them do it! Yes, we will be taking the heat for these people, but by doing it we're building a new political space, a new political layout, which is called "we're all against them." All of us are against United Russia, which is the organizational and political base of this gang of crooks.³

Election analysis has consistently shown that boycotts and ballot defacement never produce politically tangible results—only a fraction of a per cent. But there was no easy way to verify if the idea Navalny proposed would work. How can one calculate the degree of protest in the votes cast for opposition parties permitted to run? The novelty lay in a more comfortable psychological effect: Navalny suggested that any vote cast against the ruling party should be considered a fully fledged protest.

In the end, Navalny won those debates with Kasparov and Nemtsov by a wide margin—not because he was more convincing, but because he was more popular. "Navalny's victory is further proof that people prefer action (albeit without any hope of result) to inaction," journalist and activist Maria Eismont wrote. "This is confirmed by the increasing number of volunteers who are ready to sign up as observers—not even because they support the opposition (few actually believe in it), but to make life harder for the fraudsters." As journalist Yekaterina Kronhaus wrote after the election, "For the first time on such a scale, ordinary people decided not to stay away from fraudulent elections, but to get involved in them: vote, observe and demand that their votes be counted correctly." Navalny was right. At the time, in early October, he could not yet understand how successful his tactics would be.

A month later, in early November, pollsters recorded a drop in United Russia's approval rating: from sixty per cent to fifty-one per cent among people who said they planned to vote. At the same time, Vladimir Putin's approval rating also dropped dramatically: over the previous year, polls showed that it had fallen from seventy per cent to sixty per cent, with half of this decline occurring in October.[4] This was very unusual. The ratings of the ruling party and its leader, pumped up with propaganda and campaigning, have always risen rather than fallen before elections. But this time the opposite occurred. This wasn't a coincidence. All the main opposition parties were seeing growing support, including the Communists, Zhirinovsky's party and even A Just Russia, which, according to polls in early November, had a fair chance of surpassing the seven-per-cent threshold necessary to enter the Duma. In Moscow, protest sentiment was particularly strong. Two weeks before the election, a packed house at the Olympic Stadium booed when Putin stepped into the ring to celebrate the victory of bare-knuckle fighter Fyodor Yemelyanenko. This was unprecedented. Putin had never been greeted by crowds this way before.

Experts did not expect such a change in the public mood. The main hypothesis, said sociologist Alexei Grazhdankin, was that "citizens finally realized the point of the job swap at the top" and that this "shameless act may have offended and demeaned voters."[5] In late October, pollsters from the Levada Center studied how public opinion responded to the end of Medvedev's presidency. The majority—almost seventy per cent—said they wanted economic reforms to continue; a similar number wanted to continue "developing mutually beneficial contacts with Western countries."[6] Neither of these was associated with Putin's return to the Kremlin: he made it clear that modernization was over and that under him everything would return to the way it was before Medvedev. There was no need to explain. Everyone had had more than a decade to determine Putin's priorities. He appealed to stability, the ideological foundation on which the regime had stood in the mid-aughts, but his speeches didn't get the audiences excited. It used to seem that Putin was always a success, that the wind was always blowing in his sails. Now, instead of being pushed forward by a tailwind, he was walking into a headwind.

## Karl Gauss versus United Russia

Nemtsov thought Navalny's tactics were misconceived. His own electoral experience—for example, in Sochi—told him that it was impossible to defeat United Russia. Election results would always be falsified. This was common knowledge: the elections would be rigged, and nothing could be done about it. Might makes right, after all. And there was every reason to think this was true. In Moscow, for example, two years earlier, the city elections were so scandalous that all three opposition factions slammed the doors and left the City Duma to protest the massive fraud. In 2009, *Russian Newsweek* correspondent Maria Zheleznova was a member of one of Moscow's electoral district commissions. She described her experience of vote counting.

> When we took off the ballots on top, we could see two thick stacks of ballots in tidy piles. They were lying flat, blue and pink stacks a centimetre or two thick each. The ballots could not have been lying like that if they were thrown into the ballot box one by one. Nobody even looked at them.
>
> "Esteemed committee members, esteemed chairman," I said, pointing at the piles. "Look at these two neat, thick piles of ballots on the table right in front of you!"
>
> "What piles?" said the woman next to me.
>
> "I don't see anything," said the chairman.
>
> "Come on, ladies, get back to work now," the woman next to me said.
>
> I had one more witness. "Do you see these piles of ballots?" I asked Andrei from the Communist Party. He looked at the neatly stacked piles and said nothing.[7]

Zheleznova saw a deal being carried out right in the open. The electoral commission members from opposition parties refused to record ballot-stuffing for ruling-party candidates. Later, Zheleznova compared the tallies written down at the polling station, which included the ballots falsified for United Russia that she saw, with the official results published by the Central Election Commission. Ballot-stuffing at the local level wasn't the end of the falsification. The official tallies from the local District Electoral Commission were changed on their way to the next level higher, the Territorial Electoral Commission (TEC). The official district commission tallies were changed so that the United Russia candidates had an even greater lead over opposition candidates. That was the source of the scandal: the opposition received less votes than had been promised.

In Moscow, bribery of commission members had been widespread since Mayor Luzhkov was in office. Each member of a district commission received 5,000 roubles (approximately $152). The heads of the TECs received 100,000 roubles (approximately $3,050). The money was distributed in envelopes through city councils and commissions, overseen by special officials. These and similar schemes worked throughout Russia for many years, according to a source close to the election process.

Election observers aren't the only people able to determine whether an election is fair or not. Mathematicians can, too. Elections produce a huge amount of data, which reveal general statistical patterns. A normal election turnout graph shows a Gaussian distribution, a bell curve that moves from the minimum number of polling stations with zero turnout upwards to the maximum number of stations with average turnout and then back down along the same trajectory, to the minimum number of stations with 100 per cent turnout. This is the pattern of turnout in European elections. In the Russian elections of the 1990s and early 2000s, the graphs did not deviate from the norm.

Sergei Shpilkin, a physicist fascinated by election statistics, analysed the 2007 Duma election results and was the first to spot an unnatural phenomenon: the right side of the sinusoid was curved upward, meaning that there were an unusually high number of polling places with high or very high turnout. This is a sign of manipulation. This has been the case in all elections since 2007, both parliamentary and presidential. "Official statistics show that in the 2000s, there was a significant distortion of at least one indicator—turnout—and this distortion gradually increased, reaching its peak in the 2008 presidential election," Andrei Buzin, head of Golos, an independent movement supporting voter rights, wrote in December 2012. "In the Duma elections, the highest level of falsified turnout was in 2007, not 2011, although it was the latter that sparked the protest movement for fair elections."[8]

Researchers then discovered another unique feature of Russian elections: the higher the turnout at a polling station, the higher the proportion of votes cast for United Russia or for a candidate from the government. That is, all the excess votes received at the polling stations with high turnout were always cast for one party. Theoretically, of course, one could imagine that United Russia voters were special: in some places they sat quietly, while in other places huge crowds of them came out to vote. But, as Shpilkin wrote, "if we put aside fantastic hypotheses, the most reasonable explanation for the behaviour of voters who vote for the government candidates seems to be that some of the votes for these candidates are the result of manipulation. This might be due to 'administrative pressure', like 'If you don't vote the right way, we'll cut off the gas (or not bring in wood, or close a store, or fire someone from work for cause).' Or it might be due to ballot-stuffing and fraud."[9] For example, after Shpilkin used a method to divide the votes cast for United Russia in the 2007 Duma elections into "normal" and "abnormal", he calculated that without fraud United Russia would have got 55.7 per cent of the votes, i.e. 278 seats, instead of the 64.3 per cent of the votes officially received, which garnered them 315 seats in the Duma. Without fraud United Russia would have had a simple majority, not a constitutional majority.

Preparations for the December 2011 elections were completed by the end of October. The Kremlin produced a table of indicators that had to be met. The table had three columns with figures for each region: (1) turnout; (2) United Russia; (3) Communist Party. These figures then went to regional officials charged with ensuring the result. As *Vedomosti* reported at the time, in mid-October 2011, the Kremlin set the goal of getting United Russia sixty-five per cent of the vote—that is, to repeat the result of the election four years earlier. Moscow was seen as a "strong" region that could help the ruling party. "Moscow's districts have already received instructions to ensure that United Russia gets at least sixty-five per cent of the vote," wrote *Vedomosti*, citing officials from city hall. "Otherwise, the district heads might lose their posts."[10]

In recent years, all the changes to electoral legislation had been designed to consolidate United Russia's dominant position and suppress alternatives: single-mandate district elections had been abolished, the threshold for parties had been raised, and the "against all" voting option had been removed. However, in November 2011, when United Russia's rating plummeted, it became clear that the government was turning into a hostage of its own rules of the game. Achieving sixty-five per cent was a pipe dream. A constitutional majority was out of the question.

The Kremlin accepted that their ratings had dropped. But they needed at least a simple majority—226 seats for United Russia. Since the beginning of the 2000s, the Kremlin's power base had controlled the parliament. The loss of a majority in the Duma, even in favour of the sanctioned and loyal opposition, meant a change of the political regime in the country. As Navalny said in his debates with Nemtsov and Kasparov, it would produce a completely different outcome. Nevertheless, as the election neared, pollsters made comforting predictions: they were confident that United Russia would reach the fifty-per-cent threshold. They were sure it would get fifty-five to fifty-six per cent of the votes.

## The night after the election

A week before the election, Nemtsov, Kasparov and other activists gathered at the Solidarity headquarters. They again discussed protest tactics: some, as usual, were in favour of a boycott, others wanted to deface ballots, and others still wanted to encourage votes for any party but United Russia. None of them considered this a serious argument. At the same time, they decided to apply to hold rallies in central Moscow, one on 5 December at Chistyye Prudy and, just in case, for one more on the 10th, on Revolution Square in the very centre of Moscow, next to Red Square. No one believed that these would be mass rallies. But the protesters thought that if 2,000–3,000 people came—it was election season, after all—it would be worth it. They applied to hold rallies of 300 people at each site, with the applications sent in by Solidarity activist Nadezhda Mityushkina and the Udaltsovs, a married couple.

Sergei Udaltsov, the great-grandson and worthy successor of the famous Bolshevik Ivan Udaltsov and the leader of the Left Front, was already a professional street protester by 2011. He had participated in the Marches of Dissenters started the Strategy-31 protests in 2009 and was used to being detained for several days. Because he was often detained along with Nemtsov, they had time in the paddy wagons to have ideological debates about what liberalism and leftist ideas were, and about how to combine the two in Russia and reconcile liberals and communists. When Udaltsov was locked up, Nemtsov, who respected him as an uncompromising and forceful protester, often visited him in the holding cell, bringing him food and other things, and even giving his family money.

Udaltsov was also planning to go to a protest on 4 December, election day, but, after being arrested so many times, he knew he was being watched. On 3 December, Udaltsov disguised himself in his wife's hat, glasses and someone else's jacket and went out into the street. Glancing around and not spotting any tail, he quickly got into the car of a friend who had been waiting for him. They drove to his friend's place, which had not seemed to be under surveillance. They weren't followed. They took all the necessary precautions. When they arrived, they even took the batteries out of their cell phones. Their plan was to get to Manezhnaya Square right by the Kremlin on election day, where an unsanctioned protest rally was scheduled for 2.00 p.m. Around 1.00 p.m. on 4 December, Udaltsov put on the same disguise of glasses and hat, and he and his friend went outside. Before they reached their car a few metres away, Udaltsov saw out of the corner of his eye four men jumping out of a parked car. Then everything happened very quickly: hands on the car bonnet, body search, arrest. The police told him afterwards that election day was a special case, and they were instructed to detain him for jaywalking and disobeying police orders, so he would just have to put up with it and not judge them too harshly. Under various far-fetched pretexts, one charge would spill over into another, and Udaltsov was not released until January 2012.

Otherwise, election day was relatively quiet in Moscow, apart from numerous reports of ballot stuffing and "carousel" voting. There were more violations than usual, because the number of observers was unprecedented, but everyone was so used to the violations that it's hard to assess the scale of them. There was one strange event: the Public Opinion Foundation, close to the Kremlin, published the results of their exit poll for Moscow at 3.00 p.m. (27.5 per cent for United Russia) and then did not publish any other exit poll results.

At 10.40 p.m., as the last polling stations closed, Putin and Medvedev went to the press. The exit polls published by that time for the country as a whole showed United Russia getting about fifty per cent. That suited them. "Real democracy in action," was Medvedev's explanation for the party's huge losses compared to previous elections, "but United Russia is still the leading force in Russian society."[11] On Monday morning, the results were published: United Russia got 49.5 per cent of the vote—that is, 238 parliamentary seats. It still had a majority in the Duma.

According to official figures, in Moscow, United Russia got 46.6 per cent. That was suspicious in itself, because in the Moscow region, for example, United Russia only got 32.5 per cent. Then, on Monday morning, details of the night's vote count began to pop up like mushrooms after the rain, thanks to observers and social networks, which were quickly broadcasting information. Muscovites saw a brutal battle between observers and electoral commissions. There were many accounts of observers being kicked out of polling stations and ballot boxes being swapped out. On the internet there were video clips showing ballot boxes already full before the opening of polling stations, chairmen of commissions marking empty ballots, and so on. A plethora of eyewitnesses told almost identical stories of district-commission chairs simply disappearing with bags of ballots.

"The counting has begun," wrote an observer at one of the polling stations in a western district of the city.

> During this count I managed to catch that A Just Russia party had three hundred and something votes and United Russia had 458... And then I saw the results sheet on the wall: A Just Russia had one hundred and something votes and United Russia had 506! This was

supposedly the results of the count I'd just heard. I asked for a recount of the ballots. I was told no. I started calling the A Just Russia headquarters. Then the chairman of the commission grabbed an unsealed bag of ballots from the table and, together with the secretary and some other commission members, left the room. An old man from the Communist Party followed them out, then came back and said they had driven off. Who cares about "carousels"? They plucked a figure out of the air, wrote it in, stole the bag of ballots and drove off!"[12]

"The elections were brazenly rigged," an observer from a central Moscow polling station wrote on Facebook. "Their certified results had nothing to do with reality. United Russia got 296 votes (twenty-six per cent), but in the official paperwork they wrote 888 votes, which means that they increased it threefold! The Communists got 367 votes; they wrote seventy-nine. The chairman of the commission and the secretary ran away from the polling station after the vote count."[13]

There were many such reports. The difference between the results at neighbouring polling stations was striking. At one polling station, United Russia got over seventy per cent, while at the neighbouring polling station it got at most twenty-five per cent. However, there weren't many polling sites with un-doctored results. Observers managed to find the final exit poll of the Public Opinion Foundation for Moscow, which had already been hidden in the archives (and then destroyed altogether), at 8.00 p.m. on 4 December: United Russia got 23.6 per cent. After the election, the Citizen Observer public initiative cited its calculations and stated that of the more than two million votes received by United Russia in Moscow, less than one million were real. Shpilkin would come to the same conclusion.[14]

"Putinism collapsed," Nemtsov commented on the morning of 5 December. "The booing at the Olympic Stadium was heard from Kamchatka to Kaliningrad. The whole country was booing. If [Putin] pretends that no one booed and everyone voted for him, then Putin as a politician and leader of the state is finished."[15]

The rally on Chistyye Prudy, announced by Solidarity and the Left Front, was scheduled for 7.00 p.m. Even the day before, on election day, no one was particularly interested in it. Nemtsov himself called activists, trying to get them out, explaining, "We don't want to look bad. We need a lot of people to come out." But that didn't have much effect. Ilya Yashin called Navalny: "Come on, Boris [Nemtsov] is asking for you." Navalny replied something like, "Stop bugging me with your Solidarity and your lousy rally—four gimps will come to it."[16]

That all changed on 5 December. "The formal organizer of the rally is Solidarity," wrote Navalny in his blog, "but that is now irrelevant. Whether you like it or not, you need to come. That goes for everyone. Nationalists, liberals, leftists, Greens, vegetarians, Martians. The party of crooks and thieves has stolen everyone's vote."[17]

## Dirty-boots rally

Dmitry Medvedev was in a good mood. He had come to terms with having to change jobs with Putin, and now the party he headed had won. On 5 December, his first working day after the elections, he and his aides celebrated the victory at his residence in Gorki outside Moscow. It was, after all, his victory, too. Time went by as they were drinking champagne and talking about nothing, until Medvedev was informed that an unexpectedly large number of people were meeting for a protest rally in the centre of Moscow. Shouldn't the interior minister be called, the president was asked. Medvedev brushed it aside: if it had been a serious matter, the minister would have called him himself.

The demonstration on Chistyye Prudy on 5 December, the largest protest rally in Moscow since 1993, went down in history as the "dirty-boots rally." One of the ponds that gave the area its name is set in a narrow park in the centre of a boulevard. There were too many people to fit on the sidewalks, so they moved to the snow-covered ground. After two hours of people milling around, the melted snow and earth turned into black slush. In the winter darkness, it was difficult to count how many people turned up, but there were at least seven thousand. The place for the rally had been fenced off in advance, but people did not fit inside and stood on either side of the barriers.

No March of Dissenters protest rally had ever drawn so many people. And the people were different this time, too. "There were students who had read about the rally on Twitter; there were people who had worked as election observers for the first time; and there were whole families with children. Many admitted it was the first time they'd come to a protest event," *Lenta.ru* wrote.[18] Navalny, who was late, practically stormed the barricades as he tried to get onstage.

Nemtsov was the first to speak. He had not felt such a surge of emotion for a very long time. For the past few years, he had been protesting almost by himself with just a handful of supporters, and suddenly thousands of people were standing and listening to him—and not just anywhere, but in Moscow. Even the day before, he couldn't have imagined it. "We were all dumbfounded," Vladimir Ryzhkov recalled.[19]

"They announced on their 'zombie TV channel' that they had 239 seats and 49.5 per cent of the vote," he called out over deafening whistles and shouts and then broke into his standard rallying cry. "Russia without Putin! Russia without Putin!"

"Russia without Putin!" the boulevard shouted back.

Nemtsov spoke, listened to a few speakers and left, so he did not see Navalny's speech and all that came after. This was Navalny's first big rally: he had never before spoken before such an enormous audience.

"They can call us micro-bloggers, social-network hamsters. Yes, I'm a network hamster," said Navalny, "and I'll bite the heads off those rats."

Having just threatened to bite everyone's head off, Navalny couldn't just go home; it would have looked bad. So he asked Ilya Yashin, who was leading the rally, to announce a march to the Central Electoral Commission (CEC) building. After some discussion—Ryzhkov was against it—Yashin took the stage and called for people to fold up their flags and posters and "take a walk." About 600 people followed him and Navalny. In the end, no more than fifty people made it to the CEC.

Dmitry Medvedev was still sipping champagne with his aides at his residence when the interior minister called him. He informed the president that there was unprecedented rioting on a street by the Lubyanka. Riot police were detaining people. No one had seen this kind of thing in Moscow before. The police were grabbing people and dragging them into police vans. They continued to pull people into the paddy wagons even after the crowd dispersed. Some three hundred people were detained, and dozens of those detained got five to fifteen days in detention. Of course, Navalny and Yashin got the maximum—fifteen days.

Yashin was already sitting in a police van when Nemtsov called. Why didn't anyone tell him they'd start marching? Because there was no plan, Yashin explained, and you shouldn't have gone off early to drink cognac with the girls. Nemtsov was ashamed that he had gone and everyone else had been detained. He would have joined the street march, too. He spent the rest of the evening outside the police station, trying to get the detainees out or at least to make their lives easier.

He was not the only one. Nadezhda Mityushkina, a Solidarity activist, had participated in all the rallies at Triumfalnaya Square and knew what had to be done. But she had never encountered this scale of detentions before: "We did not even know which police stations people were being taken to. A team sat up all night, calling every police station, asking if detainees had been brought in. Several cars drove around Moscow all night, and I was in one of them, delivering water, biscuits and sandwiches. We kept getting calls from people saying, 'Jeez, we found more people, and here's more.'"[20]

## How to make a revolution

Ilya Klishin, a twenty-four-year-old who worked in an advertising agency, escaped arrest that night only because he ran into a big department store and lost the riot policemen chasing him. Unlike many of his peers, Klishin was interested in politics even before Putin and Medvedev switched jobs and often attended the Strategy-31 rallies in Triumfalnaya Square—which was convenient because he rented a flat nearby. At the end of 2010, he started a blog together with a friend. Their idea was to combine politics with fashionable urban trends—that is, to write about politics like it was the hot topic in a glossy magazine. The blog, called *Epic Hero*, became quite successful. It was full of "correct" protest lookbooks, explained which kind of coffee—a Frappuccino or a coconut latte—from which coffee shop protesters should take to rallies, advised hipsters to write "Russia without Putin" in their Moleskins and encouraged them to become election observers, read the news, and so on.

On the evening of 6 December, the day after the rally at Chistyye Prudy, Klishin went to Triumfalnaya Square again. There, in this near-holy place, protesters began chaotically to fill the square after the previous day's rout on Chistyye Prudy. People had no plan, and the protest took the form of a neighbourhood walk until the police began to grab everyone indiscriminately as drivers angrily honked their horns and people shouted, "Putin is a thief!" and "Let's have new elections!" People were beaten and thrown into paddy wagons indiscriminately. Nemtsov was there, and this time was detained with the others. In all, about the same number of people were arrested as on the day before— around three hundred. These were unprecedented numbers. It was as if the city had declared war against its citizens.

On Triumfalnaya Square, Klishin learnt that one more rally was planned for 10 December, not just anywhere, but in the very centre of the city, on Revolution Square. Klishin was surprised: he had not heard anything about this rally. Returning home, he sat down to write the text. "The events of 5 and 6 December at Chistyye Prudy and Triumfalnaya Square," he wrote, "have shown that a new generation of protesters from the internet, from social media, from offices and universities has taken to the streets. There are a lot more of them. It is a citizens' protest over just one thing: election fraud. They have nothing to do with the old opposition, which for so long has been calling people to the streets and in the end was poorly prepared to coordinate action at the zero hour."[21]

Klishin also searched the internet, trying to find out what kind of rally was to be held on 10 December. He finally found the only link in a news article.

Udaltsov came up with the idea of filing an application for the 5 and 10 of December—just in case, as a backup. He was one of the applicants. Another radical opposition activist, Eduard Limonov, was also supposed to be an applicant, but he and Udaltsov had a falling out, and, at the last moment, Udaltsov wrote his wife in the application instead. (If Limonov had stayed as an applicant, the rally on Bolotnaya Square probably would not have happened: Limonov was firmly against the relocation.) The third applicant was Nadezhda Mityushkina. She picked up the signed permission from the mayor's office—also for three hundred people—on 6 December. And now Klishin found out about the rally, completely by accident.

Revolution Square? Wow, thought Klishin. He asked on Twitter who knew that there would be a rally in three days, right next to the Kremlin walls, permitted by the authorities? Nobody knew anything. Klishin then remembered that in his advertising job he often organized events on Facebook. Why not? He created an event for the rally on Revolution Square, then posted the link on his blog's social network and sent it to a few friends. It was two in the morning. He collapsed on his bed, exhausted, and fell asleep. He woke up in the morning when the phone rang. It was a call from a Canadian TV channel, and a voice with a strong accent asked: "Hello, are you the one organizing the revolution in Russia?"[22]

## Negotiations with the mayor's office

By the morning of 7 December, ten thousand people had already signed up for the rally through Klishin's Facebook event. When Ilya Krasilshchik, editor-in-chief of *Afisha*, noticed how quickly people were registering, he published an appeal on Facebook: (1) the rally should be specifically against fraud; (2) new people should speak, such as the rock singer Yury Shevchuk, popular writer Boris Akunin, and so on; and (3) "Many times more people should come than on Monday. It already seems possible."[23]

Krasilshchik was thrilled. He had no intention of going into politics or "overthrowing Putin", but he felt that his time had come—his time and the time of *Afisha* magazine, *Afisha*'s readers and all progressive Muscovites. "There was a feeling of soft power, and that peaceful Muscovites had evolved to the point of making peaceful protest to change things," Krasilshchik recalled.[24] He was already thinking about how to organize things better: it should be upbeat, fun and trendy, a big public event and not the usual dull political demonstration.

The 7th of December was a day of big business and big news. Thanks to Klishin's light touch, everyone was discussing the upcoming rally and what would happen. The idea was already going around that the colour of the rally should be white: white flowers, white balloons and white ribbons that could be tied to cars, purses and clothes to advertise the protest. Actually, white ribbons had been used for political protest since the autumn, but this time the idea went viral, popularized by the progressive—and uncensored—TV Rain channel, which had recently appeared on cable television.

By the afternoon of 7 December, the number of people registering on the Facebook page to go to the rally had exceeded fifteen thousand. It was around this time that Vladimir Kolokoltsev, head of the Moscow police, telephoned Alexei Venediktov, editor-in-chief of Ekho Moskvy radio station. Venediktov was more than the head of a popular Moscow radio station; he was an intermediary, a mediator. On the one hand, he had access to the Kremlin and communicated with officials; on the other hand, he communicated with the opposition and gave them airtime. "Can you stop by?" Kolokoltsev asked Venediktov. He was already beginning to realize what would happen. Venediktov arrived, and Kolokoltsev laid out a map of Moscow in front of him: "Here is Revolution Square. It cannot hold that many people. The protesters will inevitably push onto the streets, the police will push them back. That's already a conflict. What should we do?"[25]

Venediktov advised them to get in touch with the petitioners and the organizers, and then he left. In the meantime, the chat participants were discussing the format and location of the rally. What would happen if a crowd of many thousands came to Revolution Square, even though only three hundred people had been approved? On 7 December, disturbing news was already coming from the city hall: first, that Revolution Square would be closed for repairs, then that there would be no repairs but that more than three hundred protesters would not be allowed onto the square.

The only adult in the Facebook rally HQ with political experience since the 1990s was the well-known journalist Sergei Parkhomenko. "It occurred to me," Parkhomenko recalled, "that it was strange to discuss this without getting advice from the people who had been involved in politics all this time."[26] Parkhomenko personally knew the leaders of the recent political protests and had helped Nemtsov organize Committee-2008 back in 2004. HQ instructed Parkhomenko to get in touch. The next morning, when the Facebook event counter was already showing almost twenty-five thousand potential protesters, he explained over coffee to Nemtsov and Ryzhkov why so many people had come to the rally on 5 December, what was happening on Facebook, who the people organizing it all were, and where they came from.

Nemtsov was excited. He believed in the organizational power of Facebook right away and began to convince Ryzhkov that this was an important moment that had to be taken very seriously. He left for Nizhny Novgorod for a day, but before leaving he published an open letter to the mayor of Moscow demanding assurances of security for the protesters.

On Thursday, 8 December, people were beginning to panic. No one knew what would happen in two days. Would there be another crackdown and violence, but this time against tens of thousands of people? On the internet, people were gearing up for a fight. For the first time leaflets were circulating on social networks about what to pack in case of detention and how to protect yourself from being beaten.

The idea to move the rally to Bolotnaya Square across the river from the Kremlin came from the city hall. On 8 December, Mityushkina and Anastasia Udaltsova (whose husband was in custody) were summoned to the Department of Public Security, where they were told to move the rally to Bolotnaya. They argued with officials for several hours. Word got out about Bolotnaya, and a number of activists, including Limonov, immediately launched a determined protest: no, we can't give in, we have to stand our ground and push for Revolution Square.

The more the experienced activist Mityushkina considered the matter, the more she thought it made sense to accept the mayor's proposal. What would happen, she thought, when thousands of Muscovites, who had never been to a rally and had not been hardened in the battles at Triumfalnaya Square, came to Revolution Square? How would they all fit into the small space? How could they even ask these people to move, if they had to? There were no guarantees that the authorities would allow a stage and amplifiers to be set up. Besides, Revolution Square was a confined space, with nowhere to run and nowhere to hide. The whole thing could end badly, Mityushkina thought. Her only disagreement with the mayor's office concerned the people who would come to Revolution Square even if the rally was moved to Bolotnaya Square. Mityushkina insisted that these people should be given "safe passage" to Bolotnaya Square, but that was where the officials would not budge. This was no wonder: "safe passage" meant that thousands of protesters would be allowed right past the Kremlin walls.

Mityushkina eventually convinced Nemtsov, who was also involved in negotiations with the city hall, that Bolotnaya Square made more sense. But the city authorities would not agree to safe passage past the Kremlin. This meant that tens of thousands of protesters would show up at Revolution Square and inevitably find themselves in a stand-off with the police.

An agreement was finally reached a few hours later, when Ryzhkov got the consent of the Facebook rally HQ to contact the city hall again and explain what would happen. Ryzhkov and Parkhomenko went to the mayor's office, joined by Kolokoltsev. They agreed to move the main rally, but anyone who came to Revolution Square would be allowed to walk to Bolotnaya Square unimpeded. Then Venediktov was invited to join them. He showed up with a bottle of whisky to celebrate the agreement.

Towards the end of the meeting, Alexei Gromov, Putin's loyal deputy, suddenly appeared in the office. "Gromov came in and grunted, 'Well, what have you decided here?'" Ryzhkov later recalled.[27] Gromov's appearance at the city hall was no accident, of course. Normally, such matters would have been in Surkov's hands, but in December the Kremlin was in disarray. Bolotnaya happened just as there was a brief period of anarchy. Surkov, then Medvedev's right-hand man, had effectively stood down. Medvedev's team was packing up, and Putin's team had not yet moved in. The operational management of this crisis fell on Gromov's shoulders. The deputy mayor, Gorbenko, was coordinating actions with him and not the mayor. From the start, Gromov was in no mood to make concessions, but a compromise was reached because Kolokoltsev, the head of the Moscow police, was more flexible. Gromov's appearance was in itself symbolic: even if he had not entered the office, protest activists must have realized that they were engaging in a dialogue with the Kremlin *in absentia*.

Parkhomenko and Ryzhkov didn't stay for a drink. They wanted to get back to HQ as quickly as possible with the paper signed by Gorbenko about moving the rally to Bolotnaya with a permit for thirty thousand demonstrators. The document was addressed, on the one hand, to the applicants Mityushkina and Udaltsova and, on the other, to Nemtsov and Ryzhkov. Krasilshchik, Klishin and the others breathed a sigh of relief. The defeat that had seemed inevitable just a few hours ago was gone. The name of the Facebook event was immediately changed. it was now called "Rally for Fair Elections on Bolotnaya Square" (instead of "... on Revolution Square"). It was finalized the next day by Mityushkina. In Gorbenko's office, she received written guarantees that the people on Revolution Square would not be hindered and would be allowed to go to Bolotnaya Square and signed off on the changes. But by this time no one was paying much attention. Moscow was preparing for a large, peaceful rally on Bolotnaya Square.

## 10 December

As Moscow prepared, the number of participants who signed up on Facebook kept growing, but all the same, the number of people amazed everyone. On 10 December, 50,000–60,000 people came to Bolotnaya Square and a few thousand more came to Revolution Square, although no one knew what might happen. The day before, Nemtsov had urged Anastasia Udaltsova to be vigilant, as he thought there was a real risk of criminal arrests with prison sentences, not administrative detentions. He came to Revolution Square, just in case, and led the crowd of thousands to Bolotnaya Square in a kind of victory march.

The usual loudspeakers for rallies were set up on the stage, but they were not powerful enough to reach the enormous audience expected. But it didn't matter. Tens of thousands of people went to Bolotnaya, gripped by the same emotion, the same motivation and the feeling of unity, and this new and joyful feeling was much more important than being packed tight in a crowd. There was an element of wonder in it all. "Today is a very important day in my life," said the writer Boris Akunin from the stage. "I haven't seen Moscow like this for twenty years. Frankly, I thought I would never see it like this again." He was referring to the events of August 1991.

Official propaganda would immediately put the Bolotnaya Square movement on a par with the colour revolutions that had swept across the

Middle East and North Africa. Vladimir Putin would bluntly say that "it's a well-established scheme to destabilize society" that "didn't just happen on its own." And then he would recall the Orange Revolution in Kyiv and "some of our oppositionists" (referring to Nemtsov), who "were in Ukraine at the time" and now were "transferring this practice to Russian soil."[28]

But the Bolotnaya Square movement had little in common with the events of Maidan seven years earlier. It had no leader, no party in parliament, no presidential candidate of its own, and no hope for a change of power. Moscow rallied against mass election fraud, but it saw in this fraud something more systemic—the hypocrisy and deceit inherent in the authorities. In this sense, the events on Bolotnaya Square, although incomparable in scale, were indeed similar to those of August 1991, when Muscovites went out into the streets to protest Communism and the all-encompassing lies of the Soviet system. Like the demonstrations in August 1991, it was not a revolution or an attempt to overthrow the government, but a moral revolt against stagnation and humiliation. Whatever grievances people had against Gorbachev, when the coup conspirators removed him from power, they were turning the country back to the Soviet past. Whatever Medvedev may have been as president, Putin's return to the Kremlin dashed any hopes of seeing Russia as a civilized and modern country. And, like in 1991, people did not come out to Bolotnaya Square in December 2011 to defend their material interests. "We are here because we have dignity," Nemtsov said from the stage.

It wasn't just Nemtsov who spoke of dignity. "Something has happened," Ilya Krasilshchik wrote, "that made tens of thousands of successful people decide that self-esteem is more important than the ability to buy a refrigerator."[29] Indeed, sociologists later noted that in the winter of 2011–12, moderately well-off people turned out for the rallies in Moscow (although they were certainly not the rich people that the official propagandists claimed they were). Seventy per cent of those who took to the streets had a higher education. They did not intend to cause a riot and take the Kremlin by storm.

The strategy of the Bolotnaya Square movement was based on the idea that more and more people would come out into the Square each time. This was the only chance to force the authorities to meet the protesters' demands. Later, after the protests had been suppressed, Nemtsov and other activists would be accused of making a fatal mistake or even betrayal when they moved the rally from Revolution to Bolotnaya Square. They were said to have set up the Bolotnaya movement for defeat by doing what the authorities wanted and "draining the protest."

But from the very beginning, the goal of the Bolotnaya Square movement was to put peaceful pressure on the authorities. The movement was born out of the huge gap between social practices: dialogue, mutual respect and solidarity clashing with brutal, brash, authoritarian power. As this author wrote at the time, "Bolotnaya Square was the result of civil activism, which was already quite commonplace by then, and became a part of it. The movement was not just about rallies. It was simply that people finally noticed it on Bolotnaya Square."[30]

Ilya Krasilshchik, the editor-in-chief of *Afisha* who had been one of the main organizers of the rally on 10 December, returned home that evening and wrote on Facebook: "Today I saw the city of my dreams. It's full of all kinds of beautiful and cheerful people. It has polite police officers. It has people who feel that they are together and help each other. Even television is professional and objective [during Bolotnaya, television censorship was relaxed]. I did not know that the city could be like this… Soon it will happen again in a week or two. We will probably come out again. There will probably be more of us. And we will again see the city we want to live in."

The Bolotnaya Square movement's political demands were mainly to punish those responsible for election falsification and to hold parliamentary elections again (or, alternatively, to recount the votes). They didn't even have Putin's ouster on the agenda, although the protests were certainly directed against him personally. Alexei Navalny recalled his logic in those December days as wanting victory to come peacefully through elections. "The political regime will be transformed, and it will be easier for all of us. They'll let us go to the polls, we'll be able to create a political party. We'll keep coming forward, they'll keep retreating, retreating, retreating… and in the end we'll beat them."[31] Nemtsov expected that in the presidential elections in March 2012, Putin would not win in the first round and would not stay in power for long.

The Bolotnaya Square protesters were the vanguard of protest. According to pollsters, about half of Muscovites sympathized with them and their demands. Indeed, a lot of people watched with fascination to see how the confrontation between "the party of angry citizens" and the authorities would end. The so-called loyal opposition was inclined to support Bolotnaya. Six years ago, in 2004, A Just Russia leader Sergei Mironov had run for president while campaigning for Vladimir Putin. Now, along with other deputies, he was wearing a white ribbon on his lapel and rushing to speak at yet another rally. "You said you would never betray Putin," his comrades-in-arms reminded him. "But you can see that he is not in his right mind," Mironov replied.

The events of December 2011 also brought unexpected and unpleasant news for Nemtsov: he was not even close to being the most popular leader on Bolotnaya Square. He had not fully understood that ordinary people in Moscow were rejecting politicians as such, and he attributed his unpopularity to disappointment in the 1990s. An acquaintance in A Just Russia said Nemtsov told him, "For [the protesters on Bolotnaya Square], I'm a big shot from the 1990s, someone like Chubais and Gaidar, and that's a death sentence."

Nemtsov had to fight for a place in the rankings voted in by Facebook users in order to be among the speakers at the next big rally on 24 December on Sakharov Prospect. He came in fifteenth place and was able to speak (TV journalist Leonid Parfyonov came first). A year later, in October 2012, in the digital elections for the Opposition Coordinating Council, he would lose to someone distant from politics—the editor-in-chief of *Bolshoi gorod* magazine, Filipp Dzyadko. Sergei Parkhomenko and Navalny's young associate Lyubov Sobol (not to mention Navalny himself, who won by a wide margin) also got more votes.* Nemtsov was hurt, naturally.

---

\* The opposition founded the council in an attempt to form an elected body whose decisions would be legitimate in the eyes of protesters and the opposition not represented in the parliament. The elections took place online and the council was composed of forty-five members. Thirty were elected on a common list by popular vote, and five more from ideological curiae—left-wing, liberal and nationalist. The council lasted less than a year.

But the Bolotnaya Square movement was a powerful source of strength and energy for Nemtsov. He was once again doing what he loved and was at the epicentre of events. He did not become the leader of the protest, but he became its main organizer. Liberals, leftists, nationalists, hipsters (though perhaps less so)—all sought out Nemtsov as an intermediary. On 19 December, the tabloid *LifeNews* published compromising material: a large volume of wiretaps of Nemtsov's phone conversations. The wiretaps contained a lot of profanity and some insulting comments about other activists, but they could not seriously compromise Nemtsov. On the contrary, they showed that his intentions were sincere. What he said on the phone was consistent with what he said and did in public. And these wiretaps confirmed that Nemtsov did indeed play a key role in organizing the winter 2011–12 protests, whatever the issue—from where to put up the stage to how to compromise with nationalists and how the demands of the protest rallies should be formulated.

# CHAPTER 32

## 2012

## The Rout of the Bolotnaya Square Movement

### Let us die in Moscow

"The men in the Kremlin and the White House are there now because they have a television, some police and a couple of corrupt judges, but they don't have us—they don't have the source of power. We are the power here!" Alexei Navalny chanted, on stage after being released from his fifteen-day detention. "We are the power here!" shouted back at least 100,000 people who had come to Sakharov Prospect in Moscow on 24 December. This time the stage and speakers were as big as they needed to be so that Navalny could be seen and heard by everyone. After his speech, no one had any doubts that he was the leader of Bolotnaya Square. In winter 2011–12, there were many protests and one very large mass rally in Moscow, but it was the demonstration on 24 December that was the most powerful of the Moscow protests.

This happened during the short period of changeover in the government. Putin's team members—Sergei Ivanov, the head of his administration, and Vyacheslav Volodin, who had replaced Surkov as head of the political bloc—were already getting ready to move into the Kremlin offices allocated to them. Throughout December, the authorities thought and acted in different ways. Medvedev, still president, was ready to make concessions; Putin, about to be president, was not going to give an inch to the enemy from the very beginning. A few days after the Bolotnaya Square rally, during his *Direct Line* call-in show, he compared white ribbons to contraceptives and the protesters to Kipling's Bander-logs. Igor Kholmanskikh, a worker at a machine-building plant in Nizhny Tagil, came on the air with a speech written in Putin's office and rehearsed in advance: "I want to say something about these rallies. If our militia, or, as it is called now, the police, can't work and can't cope, then my men and I are ready to go out and defend our stability—within, of course, the framework of the law."[1]

Meanwhile, Surkov was finalizing the draft political reform that Medvedev had announced just before the rally on Sakharov Prospect: direct elections of governors and a new way to register political parties that changed the process from prohibitive to permissive (the new required minimum number of members would be only five hundred instead of the former forty thousand). Volodin and his aides learnt about this after the fact and were outraged. "We haven't even sat down at the negotiating table yet, and you're already giving up everything?" This was the mood at Putin's headquarters in late December, according to one of Putin's staffers.

Putin was thrown off by the first rallies—he did not expect events to take such a turn—but he quickly pulled himself together and had no intention of negotiating with the people on Bolotnaya Square. His old comrade, the ex-finance minister Alexei Kudrin, took it upon himself to mediate between Putin and the protesters. He came and spoke at the rally on 24 December, calling for a dialog with the authorities, warning, "Otherwise, there will be a revolution, and we will lose the chance for peaceful transformation that we have today." A few days later, Kudrin first met with the protest leaders in Ryzhkov's office, and then took the protesters' demands to Putin. Their main demand was for early elections. Kudrin took it very seriously. Nemtsov later said, "At the Sakharov Prospect rally, I asked him straight out: 'Lyosha, can you tell me honestly, were you sent here, or did you come on your own?' He replied, 'It's on me, I swear.' It turned out to be the absolute truth."[2]

Kudrin met with both the activists and Putin at least twice. After the New Year holidays, he returned to the Bolotnaya Square leaders with a definitive answer: "Guys, I can't do a thing." He said Putin formulated his position very simply: there is no one worth talking to on Bolotnaya

Square. Who is Navalny? A blogger? Who is Nemtsov? Who are any of them?

By mid-January, the power shift was over: Surkov had moved to the White House to serve in the government, Volodin had settled into the Kremlin, and Putin's election campaign was being designed in the spirit of Kholmanskikh's speech: counter-mobilization, street against street. Not only will we not negotiate, Volodin explained to Gennady Gudkov, one of the leaders of the protest movement; we will work specifically against you and target the Bolotnaya Square movement. None of the protesters' demands were ever met. Sovereign democracy returned: the Bolotnaya Square movement was essentially declared to be a movement against the people, the vanguard of hostile forces from the West attacking Russia. At counter-rallies organized by the government they called for a fight against the "orange plague." "The battle for Russia continues," Putin himself said from the stage at the Luzhniki Stadium a week before the presidential election, before ending his campaign speech with famous lines from a poem by Mikhail Lermontov:

> Let us die in Moscow, as our brothers died! We vowed to die,
> And we kept our oath of loyalty...[3]

This was a declaration of war. Protesters' expectation that their ranks would constantly grow turned out to be unjustified. Under pressure from the Kremlin, the loyal opposition withdrew from the protest and removed white ribbons from their lapels. Both Communist leader Gennady Zyuganov and A Just Russia leader Sergei Mironov were going to speak at the rally on 4 February, the last truly large demonstration of that winter. Zyuganov was the first to back out. Mironov changed his mind after him, despite the fact that a month and a half ago he had been pushing through the crowds to get onto Bolotnaya Square. Censorship was picking up again. In early February, Vladimir Pozner, a popular television host on Channel One, citing Putin's personal permission, promised to invite Nemtsov to his program, but Nemtsov was never allowed on air.

The authorities still tolerated large rallies in the city centre, but Putin was no longer going to make nice with the protesters. Even in

December, the Kremlin had considered tightening legislation on rallies. As the election campaign progressed, Putin's rating began to rise again. Now the Kremlin had a plan: re-elect Putin as president, after the inauguration completely get rid of Medvedev, and then really tighten the screws to put an end to discontent.

## Waiting for Maidan

On 4 May, Udaltsov, Navalny, Nemtsov, Kasparov and two or three other activists stood on Bolotnaya Square and discussed their plans for the rally set for 6 May and their overall strategy. Everyone agreed that the protest should be intensified; outrage over Putin's return to the Kremlin should be louder than usual. At the same time, everyone still considered only peaceful forms of protest. They eventually decided that the most sensible option was to stay at the rally site after it was over. They just disagreed about the details, Solidarity activist Sergei Davidis recalled later. Supporters of the soft option suggested holding the rally at the planned location, on Bolotnaya Square, and then staying there. Others, including Nemtsov and Navalny, believed that it would be better to move the rally and the stage onto the road leading to the Bolshoi Kamenny Bridge that crossed the Moscow River by the Kremlin. That would let them stay on the roadway when the rally ended. The next day, Udaltsov tried to coordinate the transfer of the stage from the public garden on Bolotnaya Square closer to the road, but he couldn't reach the officials in charge. The idea of moving the stage had to be abandoned.

Even during preparations, it was clear that this rally was not going as usual. First of all, the organizers got the final permission very late. Second, they only had three hours to set up the stage, which meant that they couldn't put up a large stage with powerful speakers. Third, there was a reason Udaltsov could not get through to anyone: unlike previous rallies, the mayor's office never informed the organizers who would be responsible for the event and avoided conversations. The atmosphere the day before was dark, full of gloomy forebodings. "Today I am NOT going to a protest rally for the first time since December,"

Ksenia Sobchak tweeted on the morning of 6 May.* She had been an active participant in previous rallies.

On the day of the rally, the cars bringing sound equipment were searched and not allowed to drive up to the stage. The police found two tents in the car and detained several activists. At the start of the march, a long queue formed in front of the metal detectors, as the police took more time searching the protesters. Eyewitnesses said they were looking for tents in particular.

Since 2004, the "orange threat" had been an obsession for the Kremlin. There were many tents on Maidan. Rumours that there would be tents on Bolotnaya Square, the slogan "Keep the Crook Out of the Kremlin" circulating on social networks, intelligence reports from the security services, and, finally, Putin's inauguration scheduled for the next day—all this made the Kremlin think that "Maidan"—that is, a protest leading to revolution—was being planned in Moscow. Not surprisingly, the pro-Kremlin press would later describe the events of the Bolotnaya Square rally as a failed coup attempt. And at that moment, the authorities perceived any departure from the agreed plan as an attempt at an armed insurgency. The police on Bolotnaya Square were not preparing for a peaceful demonstration. They were getting ready for an uprising.

## What really happened on 6 May

To everyone's surprise, the "March of Millions" lived up to its name more than the organizers had anticipated: tens of thousands of people came out to the rally. The procession on 6 May was supposed to start at 4.00 p.m. and end with a rally at 7.30 p.m. Parliamentarian Gennady

---

* Sobchak was probably aware of the protest leaders' plans to stay on the square after the rally, since that day she said the protest had become too radical: "We need to change people's consciousness without becoming radical extremists." The day after the rally was dispersed, she would write that she "knew in advance that the main goal would be to stand on the bridge, then break through the cordon and have a sit-in." But there is no evidence at all that there was a plan to break through the police cordon. In any case, it is not clear how they could have planned to break through barricades and have a sit-in at the same time.

Gudkov did not take part in organizing the rally. He was also not planning to stay for it. He had come into the city from his dacha together with his son Dmitry Gudkov, also a member of the parliament, and they planned to be back at their dacha by early evening. "We'll give support as citizens, stay for a bit in the crowd. I told my wife that we'll be home for shish kebabs—and told her to save two or three skewers for us. We'll be there by half past six."[4]

The Gudkovs were deputies and permitted to cross the police lines. When they arrived at Bolotnaya Square before the rally, they were stunned: they had never seen such a concentration of police forces. It was as if Moscow was preparing for an invasion by enemy troops. The Bolshoi Kamenny Bridge was blocked by two dense rows of riot police and vehicles. Later, in December 2013, the international commission that investigated the circumstances of the rout of demonstrators on Bolotnaya, wrote that eight thousand police officers had been posted in the Bolotnaya Square area alone that day. They were equipped with an extensive arsenal of riot-control equipment, from stun grenades and air guns to gas masks and truncheons. Separately, the report noted, a combat squad of 350 police officers, partly staffed by "officers with expertise in the martial arts", was there to seize "camouflaged organizers of actions that were not permitted along with other active participants."[5]

Bolotnaya Square is located on an island. On one side it is connected to the Kremlin by the Bolshoi Kamenny Bridge, where riot police and equipment were already massed; on the other side, it is connected to land by the Maly Kamenny Bridge. At first, nothing foreshadowed trouble. The turning point occurred at about 5.00 p.m., when the first columns of demonstrators came to the Maly Kamenny Bridge and walked into a police cordon right in front of them. The cordon left them a narrow corridor—no more than ten metres wide—to turn right and walk along the canal to the stage, but they could not enter Bolotnaya Square. In the plan agreed upon with the authorities—which was exactly the same route as the 4 February march and rally—there was to be no cordon in this spot. Bolotnaya Square was supposed to be open. But the fear of a repeat of Maidan was stronger than the agreement. All the protest leaders had long been under surveillance and their phones tapped. Of course, the security services knew that the organizers had agreed to stay after the rally on the roadway in front of the Bolshoi Kamenny Bridge. Nothing was to interfere with Putin's inauguration scheduled for the next day.

After conferring, Udaltsov, Navalny, Nemtsov, Yashin and the others declared a sit-in and defiantly sat on the sidewalk right in front of the police, demanding that the cordon be removed and that the rally participants be allowed to enter the square along the route agreed by the authorities. Gennady Gudkov remembered it well: "I was standing on the Maly Kamenny Bridge. Suddenly I see Nemtsov waving: 'Come here, to where we are. We decided not to go to the stage. Look at the narrow passage they set up. They won't let us pass. Come sit with us.'"[6]

Udaltsov and others urged everyone around them to sit down, and several dozen people followed them and sat down on the asphalt. Just then Alexei Mayorov, head of the security department at the mayor's office, ran up to Gudkov and asked him to come with him. As they walked towards the lines of OMON Gudkov told Mayorov that the corridor needed to be widened. Mayorov told him he'd talk to OMON and get back to him.

For the next half an hour, Gudkov father and son were negotiators between the demonstrators and the authorities. Soon a representative of the Moscow police department, Viktor Biryukov, approached. "I said to him, 'Listen, guys, you don't want problems,'" recalled Gudkov, "and he said, 'We won't touch them! Let them sit there. The weather is good, it's sunny and warm, no one will catch cold.' That is, he was joking a bit. I said, 'But it's better to move out of the way so they can start the rally.'"[7]

Videos caught what happened next. Gudkov began to discuss with Biryukov how to broaden the passage from the bridge to where the rally was being held. Because the path had narrowed so much, a big crowd of people was backed up along the route to the stage. Only half the number of metal detector frames agreed upon were set up.

At 5.30 p.m. Gudkov finally reached Deputy Mayor Alexander Gorbenko. "'OK,' Gudkov said, paraphrasing Gorbenko's words, 'we'll push the cordon back now. Just have them sign off on the change in the plans.' I went back, looking for the guys, but the crowd was already packed tightly. I yelled out their names, but they weren't there. And while I was calling them, it started..."[8]

Gudkov was probably late by only a couple of minutes. Just before 6.00 p.m. many people had to stand up just to keep from being crushed. The most committed demonstrators were still sitting, but they too would get up within three to five minutes: the pressure of the crowd was building inexorably.

"As one of the petitioners of the rally, I was ready to sign the proposed changes to the plan," Udaltsov recalled later. "We were sitting on the pavement. There were a lot of people, the atmosphere was tense, but everyone was positive and joking around. Suddenly I saw chaotic movement a little ahead on the left. People started jumping up, there was smoke—later we learnt it was from a torch—the crowd started pushing, we stood up and in the crush I lost sight of Nemtsov and Navalny..."[9] Gudkov claims that he saw a group of young men in hoodies who, according to his bodyguard, calmly passed through the cordons into the crowd, and then from inside started pushing people towards the OMON. Nemtsov was sure that these were provocateurs trained and instructed by special services. But it is impossible to say for sure. Perhaps everything happened by accident. At 5.55 p.m. the crowd broke through the cordon, pushed by the crowd behind them. The pressure was so great that people couldn't breathe; they were falling, screaming in pain and fear. Udaltsov tried to get a megaphone and shout something into the crowd, but he was simply swept away by the human wave. People around him fell to the asphalt. Nemtsov later said, "I found myself in a wild crush. I'm in good shape, it's really hard to run me over, but I could tell that it was really bad. People were falling in front of me, people were walking over them. I thought of Khodynka [where hundreds of people were trampled to death on the day of Nicholas II's coronation]. I suddenly saw that the guy who was standing next to me had turned completely blue, he was foaming at the mouth, and he said to me: 'Nemtsov, I'm going to die.' I realized that I just had to save him. It took all my strength to pull him out of there."[10]

The crowd was pushed forward and unintentionally broke through the police cordon. Both the demonstrators and the OMON were confused at this point. In another three minutes, when the riot police began to disperse the protesters, and some were already being grabbed and put into paddy wagons, a Molotov cocktail was thrown at the police. Video shows hooded and masked youths holding anarchist flags. At 6.00 p.m. the police began using their truncheons. Gudkov saw it all: "A bottle fell under the feet of an elderly man, and his shoes and pants caught fire. The crowd shrieked, the riot police rolled him to the ground and put out the fire. He got off with just a scare. That's what I saw. And then the brawling began."[11]

Navalny, Udaltsov and Nemtsov were detained about half an hour later near the stage, where they were trying to get people out of the crush. The equipment on the stage had already been turned off. Nemtsov grabbed a megaphone and climbed a tower for television filming. "They arrested Udaltsov. They arrested Navalny. They just detained a huge number of people. I beg you, don't disperse. Russia will be free," Nemtsov shouted, and with those words, three helmeted police officers dragged him down. He managed to shout, "We'll get through this!" before he was taken away. Two hours later, the demonstration was routed. The riot police were hitting left and right, and several dozen people were seriously injured. Six hundred and fifty participants in the rally were detained.

No one knows whether the situation was purposefully provoked that day, but it is likely that the brutal police crackdown was not planned in advance. Two powerful motivating factors collided: the Bolotnaya Square-movement leaders wanted to give an edge to the peaceful protest because the Kremlin was ignoring their demands; and, on the other side, the government wanted to be as tough as possible on the eve of Putin's inauguration.

Initially, the Kremlin planned to suppress the protests, first, by making it much harder to get permission to hold a rally, and second, by sharply increasing fines for organizing and participating in unsanctioned demonstrations. By 6 May, Volodin already had a package of bills on his desk that would raise these fines by multiples of hundreds. Right after the May holidays, a Duma deputy tweeted: "Get your *kesh* ready, *oppositionizers*", implying that they were paid by foreigners. The laws were passed at lightning speed.[12] (After that, the parliament came to be known as the "rabid printer" for the speed with which it produced one repressive law after another.) The rout on Bolotnaya Square came just in time. The arrests of the participants in the 6 May march on ridiculous and far-fetched charges would make any potential protester think twice. The arrests would quickly turn into criminal cases under one common name: the Bolotnaya Square case.

## At Ksenia Sobchak's apartment

Another rally was planned for 12 June. The day before, at seven o'clock in the morning, Ilya Yashin was awakened by the doorbell ringing. He was at the home of his girlfriend, Ksenia Sobchak.

Their first meeting was very romantic. It was on 24 December, at the rally on Sakharov Prospect. Sobchak was meant to be one of the last to speak. It was cold, she was freezing, and Yashin gave her his turn. Sobchak was already very famous at that time, both as a host of popular television shows and as a regular figure in high-society news. She was also interested in politics. That's why she invited Yashin to her programme on the MTV channel—in those days even MTV was discussing politics. After the broadcast, Yashin asked her out for coffee and soon their romance was the main gossip of the Bolotnaya Square movement. From then on, the two of them were together all the time: they protested together and gave interviews together. Nemtsov was worried about his friend and associate; he had heard that Putin viewed the affair as a way to make trouble. Putin had known Ksenia Sobchak since she was a little girl. She was the daughter of his boss, Anatoly Sobchak, the man to whom he owed his entry into politics and ultimately his incredible career leading to the Russian throne. Putin now believed that Sobchak was being used. He was convinced that they had deliberately muddled her and got her involved not only in the protest, but even in a relationship with Yashin—all to annoy him personally.

Ksenia thought it was the housekeeper and went to open the door. Yashin rolled over onto his other side and fell asleep again. But he quickly responded when he was poked with a blunt object and a rough male voice said, "Wake up." When Yashin opened his eyes and saw three policemen in helmets, body armour and holding automatic rifles, he first thought it was a prank. Ksenia could come up with a joke like this. But he realized it wasn't a prank when he was handed a search warrant as a suspect in organizing riots on 6 May. Yashin got dressed and asked, "Why did you look for me here? I'm not registered at this address."

"Intelligence information," the major replied.

The search was conducted by the book. The operatives turned everything upside down. Yashin, experienced in searches, managed to save only their cell phones, which he hid in the cat litter after asking permission to use the toilet. In a cupboard, operatives found a huge number of envelopes with cash—royalties for appearing at corporate events, one of the ways Sobchak earned money on the side. They totalled more than $1.5 million. For propaganda, this was perfect evidence that the opposition protests were financed from abroad. The investigators took the money with them.

Without Putin's authorization, the Investigative Committee would never have dared to barge into Ksenia Sobchak's home for a search in a criminal case that didn't even include her. (Investigators could have gone to Yashin's home as well. But the search in Sobchak's apartment was clearly intended as a signal addressed to her personally: stop associating with street protesters.) On the same day, Navalny and the Udaltsovs were searched. All were served with summonses for interrogation. The search at Navalny's place lasted twelve hours. "A large quantity of propaganda materials and literature with anti-state slogans, electronic databases and computers containing information relevant to the criminal case were seized. In addition, lists of people supporting their views—the so-called core group—were seized from the Udaltsovs," the Investigative Committee reported in a press release.[13] The operatives simply did not catch Nemtsov at home—he was at Kasyanov's dacha. He hid from the investigation, the Investigative Committee explained.

The next day there was a rally. It was a holiday—Russia Day. Twenty-two years earlier, on 12 June 1990, Nemtsov and other deputies of the First Congress of the Russian Republic (then still a part of the USSR) voted for the declaration of sovereignty. Twenty-two years ago, Russia was turning a new page, freeing itself from the totalitarian Soviet past, moving forward into the future, towards freedom. "Twenty-two years ago," Nemtsov said from the rally stage, "when I voted for a free Russia, I could not in my worst nightmare have imagined I would get a platoon of OMON armed to the teeth under the windows of my house. They're trying to scare us. They put two thousand people in paddy wagons after 6 May.* They're torturing our comrades. Even as we speak, they're torturing Navalny. They're torturing Yashin. They're torturing Sobchak. But we mustn't respond to their odious nastiness in kind. We must act properly, responsibly and peacefully."[14]

A policeman dressed smartly for the occasion of the Russia Day holiday handed Nemtsov a summons for interrogation right on the stage of the rally. And right from the rally, Nemtsov went to his home to be searched. He entered his apartment—already banded with a seal—accompanied by an investigator and three operatives. They were interested in money, telephones, computers and political literature.

"Boris Yefimovich, believe me, we don't want to tear through here like a hurricane," the investigator said, using the polite form of address. "After all, you are a well-known man, you worked in the government. I suggest that you voluntarily hand over the items of interest to the investigation, and we'll save each other time and nerves."

"Will you seize Thatcher's memoirs too?" Nemtsov joked.

The investigator did not take the piles of 'Putin: Results' reports or the $30,000 found in the safe. "It doesn't look like it's from the State Department," he said. Nemtsov even treated the operatives to cognac. "It's nice that you are so human," the investigator said. And one of the operatives took a picture with him before leaving. "I'll show it to my wife. She won't believe it."[15]

## The Bolotnaya Square case

It was a very tense moment. Yashin was summoned for questioning twice, and, on his way to the investigators for the second time, he was sure that the case would end in arrest and criminal charges. The day before, he had even discussed with Nemtsov the possibility of fleeing

---

\* After 6 May, police detained people taking part in spontaneous rallies in the city centre almost daily, mainly those on Chistyye Prudy near the monument to Kazakh poet and educator Abai Kunanbayev, where a spontaneous protest camp called "Occupy Abai" was formed.

the country. Two hundred investigators were working on the Bolotnaya Square case at that moment. The Kremlin's invented image of a quashed rebellion was now the cause for a large-scale criminal case.

In late June, the Investigative Committee named Navalny, Udaltsov, Yashin and Nemtsov as the main suspects. "Measures are being carried out to establish their role in organizing mass riots, as well as to identify the sources of funding for said events," a spokesman for the Investigative Committee said.[16] Sobchak tried to get the courts to have the cash seized from her returned, but at the court hearing investigators argued that the money could have been intended to finance the riots. "We were all pretty sure that we were going to jail," recalls Yashin.[17] By then, criminal cases had been filed against thirteen ordinary demonstrators.

Cases against protest leaders were brought one after another, on whatever grounds they could come up with. Nemtsov was charged with battery (in the winter he had taken the cell phone from a Nashi activist who had been harassing him and handed it over to the police). Navalny was charged with embezzlement, and since the end of July it had been forbidden for him to leave the country.* Garry Kasparov would be accused of biting a police officer, and a criminal case was hanging over the head of Gennady Gudkov. In September, his fellow deputies would strip him of his deputy mandate and expel him from the State Duma.

And then Putin suddenly backpedalled. He seemed to have decided that the protests had been neutralized and he could soften the blow. At the end of September, Sobchak got her money back, although she would later be punished—she was banned from hosting shows on the nationwide television channels. The scale and extent of the planned repressions was limited. The main figures in the Bolotnaya Square criminal case remained ordinary activists. By mid-October, seventeen people had been arrested. In November, a protester went to jail in the first real prison sentence in the Bolotnaya case.

The most famous arrestee was Udaltsov. He was accused of organizing riots on Bolotnaya Square, preparing mutinies and recruiting conspirators during his trips around Russia in the spring of 2012—all

---

\* The charges against Navalny were brought as part of the Kirovles case.

at the behest of foreign agents of influence. A criminal case was opened after the NTV television channel aired a compilation film, *Anatomy of Protest*, based on hidden camera footage of Georgian politician and "designer of colour revolutions" Givi Targamadze coaxing Udaltsov to overthrow the government in Russia. In actual fact, Udaltsov and Targamadze had discussed the possibility of starting a joint business to finance protest activities somehow. They were brought together by activist Konstantin Lebedev, who, it would later turn out, was recruited by the Russian security services and came to these meetings with a tape recorder hidden under his clothes. Shortly after the movie was shown, the third participant in these meetings, Udaltsov's associate Leonid Razvozzhayev, was kidnapped by Russian security services in Kyiv, where he had fled from persecution. Razvozzhayev signed a confession, but later retracted it, citing torture. "Torture is not new in recent history, but it is new in Russian politics," *Vedomosti* wrote at the time.[18] Udaltsov would first sign a paper, agreeing that he wouldn't leave the country, and then, in 2014, after lengthy proceedings, he was sentenced to four and a half years in prison.

And so, after four years of thaw and modernization, sovereign democracy was returning with Vladimir Putin, but in a much more severe form. Now it was full-blown reactionary politics. Unexpectedly faced with the first mass public protests of his political career, Putin was at first at a loss, but he quickly came to his senses and suppressed discontent by force.

# PART 7

# CHAPTER 33

## 2013
## Two Campaigns

### A special operation in Yaroslavl

The people of the ancient city of Yaroslavl, a town located about three hours north-east of Moscow, got to know Yevgeny Urlashov in the early 2000s when he joined the local progressive political faction. This group of active young deputies and their acid criticism of the mayor's office were not typical bureaucrats. Later, Urlashov joined the United Russia faction in the Yaroslavl city parliament, but he left it at the end of 2011. A few months later when the mayor, who had headed the city since the late 1980s, decided to step down, Urlashov surprised everyone by handily beating the former mayor's man, a rich local businessman.

The stars had aligned for him. The residents were outraged that once again everything was being decided for them. It wasn't enough that the former mayor had held the job for more than twenty-five years. On top of that, he wanted to force his chosen successor on them by first appointing him acting mayor. But to his credit, Urlashov ran a very successful election campaign under the slogan "I Will Give the City Back to the People." Day after day, week after week, month after month, he would walk around the courtyards of apartment buildings and talk with the residents. Local journalists wrote that he wouldn't stop until he wore out his shoes. And then, the winds of protest that were sweeping the country—the winds from the rout on Bolotnaya Square—were blowing at his back. United Russia was firmly associated with the nickname

Alexei Navalny had given it: "the party of crooks and thieves." And according to polls, half of the country agreed.

This was the start of a unique political phenomenon for Russia: a popular, independent politician, not affiliated with the *nomenklatura*, becoming the head of one of the largest cities in central Russia. Urlashov did not want to start a war with the city parliament or governor, and even less so with the Kremlin, but almost immediately the local elite began to take revenge by making his life difficult. One day the city parliamentarians reprimanded him, another day city workers didn't clear the snow, or they organized some other small disaster. By the summer of 2013, Urlashov was no longer running as an outsider, but as the leader of the opposition, at least at the regional level, aiming for his next victory in the regional parliamentary elections in September.

Urlashov also joined a party. After the Bolotnaya Square events of December 2011, Vladimir Putin needed a convenient sparring partner on the liberal flank in the March 2012 presidential elections to make his victory look more convincing. The Kremlin arranged for billionaire Mikhail Prokhorov to run. Prokhorov was surprisingly successful. He came in third place with eight per cent of the overall vote and twenty per cent of the Moscow vote. He even outpolled Putin in some parts of Moscow. On the wave of this success, Prokhorov founded a new liberal party called Civic Platform, registered with tacit permission from the Kremlin. It immediately attracted democratic activists, businessmen, and part of the liberally oriented establishment.

The party attracted democratic activists and entrepreneurs across the country who wanted to enter politics. In Yaroslavl, Urlashov headed the local branch. Even at the start of the election campaign it was clear that if he and his party mates were not stopped, United Russia would lose the election and control of the regional parliament. Urlashov was an excellent orator. He was the top politician in Yaroslavl, but his ambitions weren't limited to the city. Urlashov was not afraid to quote Navalny: "It's a party of corrupt people... Look how easily these words have stuck to them: 'the party of crooks and thieves'! They are mired in corruption, and they are afraid. They are cowards, they will try to block or remove other parties from the elections," Urlashov said on stage at a rally in Yaroslavl's central square on 19 June 2013. He reminded his audience that United Russia had invited him to join their party, but he refused and had been suffering from their retaliation ever since. "It's their last chance to hold on to the feeding trough and gorge themselves till it's coming out of their ears. How are they even going to go to the polls when half of them have foreign bank accounts? We'll check all their accounts..."[1] Thousands of people applauded Urlashov's every word. And when he announced that he was "picking up the gauntlet thrown down" before him and would run for governor, the square exploded into applause.

Two weeks later, late on the evening of 2 July, the car Urlashov was driving was suddenly blocked by a police car. Operatives jumped out, grabbed him, twisted his arms behind his back and drove him away. The next morning, he was charged with extorting large bribes, and a few weeks later Prokhorov's party was removed from elections in Yaroslavl. The special operation was run directly from the Kremlin; the risk of losing a crucial region three hours from Moscow was too great. Despite the lack of physical evidence in the case, the court handed down an unprecedentedly harsh sentence of twelve and a half years in prison.* Mayors in Russia have often been jailed, but never for so long.

## Nemtsov goes to the polls again

Nemtsov, Kasyanov and Ryzhkov found themselves in a privileged position for the autumn 2013 election campaign. The European Court of Human Rights had ruled that the dissolution of the Republican Party of Russia (RPR), which Ryzhkov had led since the mid-2000s, was illegal. The Russian authorities had to reregister it. Nemtsov and Kasyanov merged their PARNAS party with Ryzhkov's party and could now run in any regional parliamentary election. This was a stroke of luck in the early 2010s when the Kremlin had already crushed any opposition operating outside the system. Moreover, in the event of success in at least one regional election, the party would receive another major advantage: a

---

\* At the time this book went to print, Yevgeny Urlashov was still serving his sentence.

guaranteed right to participate in the 2016 Russian Parliamentary elections without the otherwise onerous mandatory collection of signatures. But where should they run?

Thanks to Urlashov, Yaroslavl had long stood out on the political map of the country. One spring day, long before the official start of the campaign, Vasily Tsependa, a Yaroslavl activist for RPR-PARNAS—the new name of the united party—called Vladimir Ryzhkov and said that they should run in the autumn elections. People were discontented, and RPR-PARNAS had a chance of winning. Tsependa explained that there were voters who resented the billionaire Prokhorov and wouldn't vote for Urlashov (this was before his arrest). People wanted real change, which meant there was a chance to reach the five-per-cent threshold.

Ryzhkov refused: he was going to go to the polls in his native Altai. He called Nemtsov, who lived next door to him. Soon Nemtsov was at his place, half-asleep and a bit bewildered, wearing his bathrobe and most likely his bedroom slippers. He asked what had happened. Ryzhkov explained. "Nemtsov replied, 'Are you nuts? Why the hell would we run in Yaroslavl?'"[2]

Nemtsov's reaction was understandable. He had at least been born in Sochi, where he'd run for mayor. But he had no ties to Yaroslavl. Besides, the people of Yaroslavl already had a recognized leader, Urlashov, and he had already teamed up with Prokhorov.

Nemtsov and Prokhorov were on friendly terms, but mostly on the sports field. They avoided talking about politics. "I would sometimes say to him, 'Boris, you say whatever you think,'" Prokhorov recalled. "'What kind of politician is that? In one sense, a politician says what people want to hear. That's a kind of professionalism. But you're a human-rights crusader. Politics is the art of the possible, of compromise. And you,' I told him, 'are a man of no compromise. If you're convinced of something right this minute, it's impossible to come to any agreement with you.' He would reply: 'You don't understand anything. Leave me alone.' So we agreed that we would never discuss politics."[3]

Nemtsov openly criticized Prokhorov when he compromised with the Kremlin—and encouraged him when he stopped being under their thumb—but this had no effect on their relationship. Nemtsov treated his friends differently.

But the elections in Yaroslavl continued to raise doubts. Why compete with Urlashov? Nemtsov's participation was discussed, but the RPR-PARNAS party was inclined to put the campaign in the hands of local activists. "We are not yet ready to name the leader on our party list," Ryzhkov told Yaroslavl journalists in late May.[4]

The arrest of Urlashov and the suspension of the Civic Platform from the race changed everything. Who could the disgruntled Yaroslavl citizens vote for now? Mikhail Prokhorov's party was out of the race. In fact, in less than two years, it would be taken over by the Kremlin and Prokhorov would leave politics; Putin would not tolerate any split within the elite. Nemtsov was still hesitant: if they lost in Yaroslavl, it would be his personal loss. Ilya Yashin went to Yaroslavl to speak at a rally in support of Urlashov and assess the situation. He wanted to find out how his arrest affected the mood of the voters. When he got to the rally, Yashin immediately sensed that the crowd was noticeably more radical than the local businessmen who were speaking. They were pressuring him to write Putin to sort things out and release Urlashov. "We can send petitions to Putin all we want," Yashin began, when it was his turn to speak, "but let's be honest here. Putin is responsible for the arrests. Putin created a system in which the opposition is jailed and beaten with clubs. And it is Putin who is the main thief in the country."[5]

The crowd applauded and chanted "Putin is a thief!"—a slogan that had been very popular on Bolotnaya Square. Yashin came down from the podium and drove out of the city, narrowly escaping arrest; the police had already been tailing him while he was speaking on the square. It was 16 July. From Yaroslavl, Yashin was on his way to Kirov, a city of half a million people almost a thousand kilometres north-east of Moscow, where he was supposed to meet Nemtsov. A day later, on 18 July, as the two of them drove from Kirov back to Moscow, he told Nemtsov that a campaign in Yaroslavl was perfectly feasible. Nemtsov then made up his mind: He would run for office again.

Their trip home from Kirov was grim. Both of them were depressed; they had just seen the local court sentence Alexei Navalny to five years in prison. The day before, Navalny had been officially registered as a candidate for RPR-PARNAS in the Moscow mayoral election. But on 18 July the judge read out the verdict of five years in jail and ordered that he be taken "into custody immediately." Navalny barely had time to hug his wife Yulia before bailiffs snapped the handcuffs on him and took him to the Kirov prison. Everyone was shocked. For the first time, Russia's opposition leader was being jailed for a long time on what were obviously trumped-up charges.

## How the Kremlin helped Navalny

On 4 October 2012, Putin was on his presidential jet, answering questions for a television show in honour of his sixtieth birthday. Putin's first answer to a question about Alexei Navalny was good-natured, even rather friendly. "Despite their sometimes boorish behaviour, I don't really mind [these young politicians] and very much hope that they might turn into serious people."[6] He did not call Navalny by his name—and he never would in a quirk that became more comical and mysterious as time went on. In any case, his answer contained two interesting points. First, Putin made it clear that he knew very well whom he was being asked about. Second, it was as if he was giving Navalny a kind of welcome, encouraging him, inviting him to cooperate: come on, boy, show us what you can do. "It's one thing to criticize something, even fair criticism," Putin said, "and another thing to propose a constructive agenda."[7] His words sounded like a hint: he, Putin, holds the door open, and if Navalny will play by the rules, there will be a place under the sun for him, too—even for Navalny, who only six months ago led the anti-Putin protest on Bolotnaya Square. This was when Putin redirected his repression of the Bolotnaya Square movement from the protest leaders to the rank-and-file activists.

Navalny was already firmly in place as the leader of the anti-Putin movement. Then, in October 2012, elections were held for the Coordinating Council of the opposition. A total of 170,000 people voted. Nemtsov came in 16th place. Navalny came in first place by a huge margin. Technically, everyone was equal on the Coordinating Council, but it was clear who the leader was. In January 2013, Navalny was asked about his plans: "There will be free elections and I'll fight to win."[8] In April, he answered clearly that he wanted to become president and change the country. But the presidential elections had just been held, and the next elections were still five years off.

Then suddenly another important electoral campaign began. Before leaving office, Dmitry Medvedev had reinstated the election of governors, and the Kremlin decided to hold the first mayoral election in Moscow in many years. They planned to make a show of not resorting to large-scale fraud to elect the current mayor, Sergei Sobyanin.

Sobyanin entered politics in the early 1990s. Once the mayor of Kogalym, the oil capital of Siberia, and then the head of the Siberian city of Tyumen, he worked with Putin in the early days of his presidency. He helped him carry out the first political reform: removing governors from the Federation Council. Before he was appointed mayor of Moscow in autumn 2010, Sobyanin worked for many years as Putin's chief of staff, first in the Kremlin and then in the cabinet. Like Putin, he was taken by surprise by the Bolotnaya Square protests.

Thanks to a huge injection of state money, for almost two years Moscow under Sobyanin had been changing markedly for the better. Parks and public spaces were improved; there were pedestrianized streets, new convenient buses and carsharing, reformed public-service centres, and so on. Sobyanin's rating in the city was rising, and Vyacheslav Volodin, who had replaced Vladislav Surkov in the Kremlin to head up domestic policy, believed that Sobyanin's convincing victory would put an end to the protest mood in Moscow. In early June, Sobyanin formally resigned. Putin immediately appointed him acting mayor and announced that there would be snap mayoral elections in three months. Navalny didn't hesitate. Of course, he would run in those elections.

But to run Navalny had to overcome two obstacles. First, he had to secure the support of a registered party. He didn't really have a choice: apart from RPR-PARNAS, no other party would nominate him. There was little enthusiasm within PARNAS, too, but Nemtsov came to his rescue. He enthusiastically supported Navalny's nomination and said he should run in the 2018 presidential elections. In the end, Nemtsov persuaded Kasyanov to support his candidacy, and Navalny became the mayoral candidate from PARNAS.

But the second obstacle seemed insurmountable. After Medvedev brought back gubernatorial elections at the height of the Bolotnaya

Square protests, Putin's team figured out how to get them under control. Even before Putin was sworn in as president, a so-called municipal filter had been introduced for the gubernatorial elections. Candidates had to collect signatures of support from the municipal deputies in the region where they were going to run. On paper, the filter added legitimacy to the candidate. In reality, the vast majority of the country's municipal deputies were members of United Russia, and that meant that the Kremlin was still in charge of deciding who could and could not be elected. Navalny's campaign immediately began looking for supporters in Moscow's municipalities, but there was no chance of collecting enough signatures.

And then the Kremlin unexpectedly came to Navalny's aid. Volodin looked at the poll numbers and thought: Navalny has no serious support, so why not let him run? It was not enough to end the Bolotnaya Square protests through repression—it should be crushed politically on the electoral playing field. Putin gave the OK, and Volodin first personally instructed United Russia to collect the signatures Navalny needed, then called the Central Electoral Commission and ordered his confirmation as a candidate. That's all it took. Navalny was officially registered as a mayoral candidate on 17 July. There were just under two months to go before election day.

## "Pack up and clear out"

It is still unclear how it came about that, with one hand, the authorities registered Navalny as a mayoral candidate and the very next day, with the other, put him in jail. According to one version of events, Volodin even asked to meet with Putin to warn him that the *siloviki* must be told not to put Navalny away; they needed him free. But he was too late. By the time Putin met with Volodin, the verdict had already been read out. According to another version, it was impossible to reach Putin, who was off fishing far from civilization in the taiga.

Meanwhile, the *siloviki* were serious. Back in April, when Investigative Committee spokesman Vladimir Markin was asked if Navalny was possibly the next Nelson Mandela, he laughed that of course he wasn't, because Mandela was in prison for fighting apartheid, not for financial fraud. As for the fight against corruption, he said that "even in prison many convicts write letters and statements fighting the flaws of the system."[9] Navalny would apparently fit right in.

The criminal case charging embezzlement from the state-owned Kirovles timber company, which had a *de facto* monopoly on logging in the Kirov region, first appeared in 2009. At that time, Navalny was adviser to the only true liberal holding office in the country, Nikita Belykh, who had been the leader of the SPS. In late 2008, he was appointed governor of the Kirov region by then-president Medvedev after the SPS had been dissolved. But at that time the case didn't get any further than an inquest; investigators couldn't find any evidence of wrongdoing. However, in May 2012, after the Bolotnaya Square crackdown, the Kirovles case was resurrected with Navalny as the prime defendant. The trial began in March 2013.

Back in 2009, Navalny's acquaintance Pyotr Ofitserov decided to start a business in Kirov trading in timber. Navalny and Ofitserov formed an intermediary firm that bought the timber cut by the first company and then sold it. The charge was that when Navalny and Ofitserov took the money for the timber sold by their intermediary firm, they had "stolen" it. Three years later, the European Court of Human Rights concluded that they were being charged with what were ordinary business practices. Even the Investigative Committee admitted that the case was political: the investigation was being conducted with a special zeal, they said, because Navalny was "taunting the authorities."[10]

The shock of the verdict, read out by a judge on 18 July, was all the greater because the judge had been friendly to the defendants throughout the trial and even laughed at Navalny's jokes. The day before Navalny had been registered as a candidate in the upcoming elections. *Lenta.ru* described the atmosphere in Kirov after the verdict: "Every third person in the courtroom and those waiting outside the courtroom cried. Posters appeared with only one word: 'Manezhnaya' [i.e. calls to go to Manezhnaya Square in the centre of Moscow to protest]."[11] Before the verdict, Nemtsov also didn't believe that Navalny would be jailed. "It's a reprisal," he said after Navalny and Ofitserov were taken to prison. "Now everything will depend on how people react to this decision. If we accept it, the repressions will continue."[12]

In the evening, Nemtsov and Yashin were on their way home, supporters of Navalny were gathering in central Moscow—about thirty thousand protesters would come to Manezhnaya Square that day—and dazed journalists who had arrived in Kirov for the trial were waiting for the train to Moscow in a restaurant near the station, which had become a favourite during the four months of the trial. Suddenly, Navalny's lawyers received a phone call from Henri Reznik, a well-known Moscow lawyer, advising them to appeal the court's verdict—not the verdict itself, but the preventive measure of detention, since the appeal had not yet been heard and the court decision had not entered into legal force. The lawyers twirled their fingers at their foreheads to indicate the insanity of trying to get the release of a defendant sentenced to a real term of imprisonment. This had never happened before in the history of Russian jurisprudence.

Imagine everyone's astonishment when, just twenty minutes before the train's departure, it turned out that the prosecutors had lodged the same complaint: they had done everything possible to put Navalny and Ofitserov behind bars, and now they wanted their jail time to be replaced with a pledge not to leave the country. What's more, their appeal hearing was scheduled for the very next day. The journalists ran to the station to turn in their train tickets.

The next morning, an unsuspecting Navalny was very surprised when someone came to his cell and said, "Pack up and clear out." Soon he was joking in court, demanding to see if the prosecutor had been replaced by his double, because his position had changed so dramatically in one day. The court let Navalny go free, to the applause of the journalists. They were utterly baffled: Navalny had just been jailed, and now he was being released. Navalny himself would later explain this unprecedented turnaround by the force of public pressure: if his supporters hadn't come out in the streets, he would have stayed in jail.

In reality, the system was obviously correcting a glitch it had caused. There was no doubt at all that Navalny had been released on Putin's say. Two weeks later, he indirectly admitted as much himself, noting that it seemed strange: one of the defendants gets a suspended sentence (the director of the timbering company who testified against Navalny and whose testimony was the basis of the case against him), while "the other one"—Putin still wouldn't call Navalny by his name—"gets five years in prison."[13]

The celebration of Navalny's release flowed smoothly first from the court to the restaurant, then to the train. The trip from Kirov back to Moscow turned from funereal to triumphant. At the train station in Moscow, Navalny was greeted by a crowd of supporters with shouts of "Hurrah!". The election campaign had not yet begun, but he was already entering it a winner.

## Vote for the opposition

From afar Nemtsov's campaign in Yaroslavl looked promising. But on the ground, the first poll yielded disappointing results. No one was going to vote for PARNAS or Nemtsov. Yaroslavl voters were sceptical about his nomination. First, he had a high negative rating. Nemtsov had been hounded and bad-mouthed on television for years. Second, no one knew anything about the party. Third, why had Nemtsov come here? What was he doing here? Fourth, he would leave just the way he came, and the region's problems would remain. With just over a month remaining until the vote, Nemtsov began to have doubts again. His enthusiasm waned, and he wondered if he should give up politics altogether. First, the defeat in Sochi—a rigged defeat, but a defeat all the same—and then the defeat of the Bolotnaya Square movement. He had been a governor, a first deputy prime minister, and deputy chairman of the Duma, and he probably wouldn't be able to get past the minimum voting threshold in Yaroslavl. This would probably be the end of the line.

Nemtsov was encouraged by Yashin, who once again headed his campaign headquarters as he had done in Sochi. They agreed that Nemtsov would postpone his plans to go to the sea for a summer vacation—it was August—and would instead essentially move to Yaroslavl, where they would work every day. Nemtsov had prepared a programme that covered everything from abolishing censorship at the regional level to mandatory audits of housing and utilities companies when housing tariffs were increased. But the main thing was to get walking around, if not the entire region, then at least its capital, where half of all voters lived. And, of course, he needed to convince people that if Nemtsov won, he would not leave. He'd stay to work in the region. They came up with the idea that, if Nemtsov won, he would buy a flat in Yaroslavl. If they elected him, Nemtsov said at meetings with voters, he would live and work here. Compared to the Sochi campaign, the pace had quickened. Nemtsov spent two or three days a week in Yaroslavl and several meetings a day—mostly in apartment complex courtyards. Come evening, he could barely walk.

Of course, there was a lot of interest in having a famous politician in the city. People sometimes asked him if he was Nemtsov or his son. But first Nemtsov had to dispel the image created over the years by state propaganda that he was a loser from the 1990s, a high-roller and playboy. "He arrives at the central market. There are people around him. There is a lot of scepticism towards him. But after he speaks for fifteen minutes they start smiling and accepting him," recalled Vasily Tsependa, a Yaroslavl-based PARNAS activist who later became Nemtsov's assistant.[14] Another local politician, Sergei Balabayev, was also running in the elections and ran into Nemtsov in a suburb. After the election, the two would become allies in the regional Duma. "On TV he is one man," says Balabayev, "but in person he turned out to be completely different. He is open, good-natured, not a snob at all. Easy to talk with. Maybe a little harsh in his statements for a provincial town, but a normal guy."[15]

Not everywhere, however, was Nemtsov greeted warmly. For example, workers in Rybinsk, the second-largest city in the region, famous for its aircraft engine plant, were stony-faced and called him a US State Department agent. But Nemtsov and Yashin were counting mainly on Yaroslavl itself. They built their campaign, first of all, on the slogan "Free Urlashov!" Nemtsov personally went to court to vouch for the arrested mayor and to bail him out. It was risky: no one knew if some dirt on Urlashov would suddenly turn up. The second basis of his campaign was fiscal federalism, a topic that was important to Nemtsov. This meant keeping taxes in the regional treasury and not sending them to the federal budget. Why did a donor region become a recipient region? Why is Moscow flush with money and Yaroslavl miserably poor? Because taxes go to the centre. Some taxes—at least excise taxes—should stay in the region. Third, the fight against corruption. Why is the Yaroslavl retail company that sets utility rates in the city registered in a Cypriot offshore company that transfers millions of roubles to support United Russia? As Nemtsov said before the election in one of his interviews (which the Investigative Committee immediately checked for extremism): "Our programme is very simple—the dismantling of Putin's regime at the regional level."[16]

Despite the small budget—Nemtsov paid for everything himself—he and Yashin organized this campaign better than the Sochi campaign five years earlier. On the one hand, they had experience, and surprisingly this time the campaign was operating on a legal playing field. After Bolotnaya Square, the Kremlin wanted to avoid scandals as much as possible. Yes, Nashi still pursued Nemtsov, and one of the scuffles—when Nemtsov was caught on film punching a troublemaker who threw an egg at him—almost ended in a lawsuit. But, on the whole, he had more opportunities to campaign in Yaroslavl. Nemtsov debated the region's leaders quite successfully. He had access to both outdoor advertising and the local press. Nemtsov's headquarters bought about twenty billboards in the city. His campaign billboard was his image with a slogan: "Vote for the Opposition!" "The owners of the outdoor advertising firm kept trying to get us to remove the word 'opposition' from the billboards. They called my campaign manager Ilya Yashin fifty times and he refused," Nemtsov said near the end of the campaign. "In the end, they said, 'Oh, the hell with it, we'll put them up.'"[17]

Several commercials were filmed. In one of them, Nemtsov drove a paver to lay asphalt on several metres of road to show that he could tackle one of the city's major problems. In another, he and his daughter Zhanna, who had come to Yaroslavl especially for the occasion, were filmed working out. First, they jogged around the stadium, and then Nemtsov twisted and turned on the horizontal bar. The idea was to contrast the strong, healthy, energetic Nemtsov with the clumsy bureaucrats in the local parliament. The ads must have been effective; towards the end of the campaign, when a PARNAS victory looked likely, Nemtsov would be denied access to television.

The ads in which they used sports and fitness had the slogan "Men, Stop Drinking."* Sports and healthy lifestyles later became one of the directions of Nemtsov's work in Yaroslavl. Later, he would donate his entire salary as deputy to build playgrounds with sports equipment near Yaroslavl's schools. When he and Zhanna were returning to Moscow on the train that day after being filmed for the video, Zhanna told Nemtsov he'd win the election; she could feel it.

Nemtsov was dismissive. "Come off it," he said.

"I'm sure of it," Zhanna insisted. She saw that the people in Yaroslavl had already warmed up to her father. She could smell victory.

"I haven't won an election in over ten years," Nemtsov said, still dismissive. To be exact, he hadn't won an election in almost fourteen years. His last victory was in December 1999.

"And now you're going to win," Zhanna insisted.

"I don't believe you."

"You'll see."[18]

## Navalny's triumph

"He really went around Yaroslavl's apartment-building courtyards, persuading grannies. It just seemed like nonsense, and I laughed at his campaign," Navalny later recalled. "You and your privatization and your white trousers, your Moscow face, newspapers and television saying that you have fifteen wives—you'll never get anywhere in the provinces."[19]

Navalny was expressing a common perception: Nemtsov was a hasbeen. Navalny even said that he'd asked Nemtsov not to help him in the Moscow elections—he thought his support would do more harm than good.

There had never been an election campaign like Navalny's in Russia before. It was like an American movie or television series. In 1996, Yeltsin and his staff had first enlisted the help of professional spin doctors and used Western experience, but it was an experiment, and spin

---

\* At first the slogan was "Russians, Stop Drinking", but Nemtsov decided to change it; after all, he was half-Jewish and not averse to a drink.

doctors were paid and put at the service of power. Now, seventeen years later, in an election in a huge city with millions of residents, Navalny had no resources other than his supporters: the experts who wrote his programme, the middle-class businessmen who were for him, the programmers who helped develop internet services, the volunteers who were on duty at campaign booths on the streets and distributed campaign flyers to doorways, the activists who put up stickers and posters and, finally, the ordinary Muscovites—and not only Muscovites—who financed it all: donations from individuals amounted to just under $3 million.

Like Nemtsov in Yaroslavl, Navalny seemed to belong to two worlds simultaneously. On the one hand, he was a hell-raiser on the internet and an enemy of the regime against whom several criminal cases had already been filed. He was banned from federal television channels (the only exception being television debates that he could not be legally prevented from attending)—a man the head of state refused to call by name. On the other hand, he was a registered candidate and, therefore, a legitimate opposition candidate, and people could openly campaign for and support him. For the first time, campaign booths appeared on the streets of Moscow—more than a hundred campaign mini-headquarters, where volunteers passed out brochures and leaflets. Car owners put "For Navalny" stickers on their rear windows. In the metro cars, next to the signs that read, "Don't lean on the doors", his stickers appeared with his slogan: "Don't lie and don't steal." For the first time, an online geotag programme was developed to unite Navalny's supporters and to let them see allies among their apartment-block neighbours. "It's hard for me to imagine the Sobyanin headquarters gathering crowds of people eager to work for their candidate twenty-four hours a day, without getting anything in return; Navalny's headquarters is made up of people exactly like that," wrote publicist Yury Saprykin.[20] Fuelled by public enthusiasm, Navalny's campaign machine had been in full swing since mid-June. And after he was magically released from jail in Kirov and returned victoriously to Moscow, the machine began to work double time.

It was truly a unique campaign. No one had ever done anything like this before, and after the election it would no longer be possible. The Kremlin would soon tighten the screws. Navalny's election programme, which was drawn up with the help of specialists, predictably focused on the fight against corruption and the decentralization of power, since this was an enormous city where elected municipal agencies had lost real power a long time ago. But it was clear to all his supporters that the fight was not about finding the right managerial solutions for Moscow, but about the right to participate in politics. The main point of Navalny's election programme was Navalny himself: a candidate of the people who challenged the authorities and the bureaucracy. Whichever way you looked at it, he was the exact opposite of both his rival Sergei Sobyanin and his boss Vladimir Putin. They were on the cusp of old age; he was young. They were dour; he was upbeat. They spoke in dry official language; he joked and spoke like a regular guy. They wore Loro Piana and Kiton; he wore Tommy Hilfiger and Uniqlo. They lived in luxury mansions in the exclusive suburb slangily called Rublyovka, behind fences and surrounded by security guards; his flat was in a very ordinary Moscow city neighbourhood. He had a family and children, and he didn't hide them; on the contrary, he was proud of them. "I was born and raised in Moscow, and I want my children to dream of living here," Navalny's wife Yulia said the first time she went on stage at a political rally during the Moscow campaign. "And I want to see a mayor who is not afraid to tell the truth. I want to see a mayor for whom I'm ready to go out into the streets and hand out leaflets."[21]

Finally, Putin and Sobyanin spoke from TV screens, but Navalny went out to the people. In all, he held about a hundred meetings with Muscovites, mostly in the suburbs and commuter districts. Meetings with Nemtsov in Yaroslavl were attended by a few dozen people at best, while meetings with Navalny in Moscow were attended by up to three or four hundred. "I imagined my ideal candidate," Navalny told voters. "What would I want him to do? I told myself: I want my candidate to come to my house, set up a stage, or just climb on a chair and answer my questions. I became that candidate: I go and answer questions."[22]

Towards the end of the campaign, after a meeting that was essentially a rally attended by several thousand people, Navalny was detained but quickly released. The Kremlin's directive to defeat Navalny at the ballot box, not by force, was still in effect.

Initially, the Kremlin expected Navalny to get five to eight per cent of the vote. Before his verdict in Kirov, pollsters had quoted roughly those figures. But after Navalny was released from jail, his approval ratings rose every week, and, before the election, pollsters were predicting twenty per cent.[23] The reality, however, surpassed all expectations: Sobyanin narrowly avoided a second round (Navalny insisted that the second round was stolen from him), while his rival got over twenty-seven per cent of the votes. In some districts—in the city centre and in the southwest, where a large proportion of the residents are middle class and the intelligentsia—he almost matched Sobyanin. In some districts, he even did better. Experts later attributed this result to an unexpectedly low turnout—voters loyal to the authorities did not go to the polls—but it did not change the essence of the matter: never before under Putin had the opposition achieved such success.

The Kremlin's plan was thwarted. The Kremlin candidate, supported by all the resources of the state—administrative, financial, with the status of head of the city and with Putin's vocal support on more than one occasion—should have torn this opposition blogger to shreds, but almost the opposite happened. It turned out that when the vote count was relatively honest, Navalny did not fail. He may not have won the election, but he certainly won a moral victory. The election in Moscow proved that Navalny was neither an upstart nor some nameless "internet blogger." He was a leader people followed, and he had enormous support.

## Second wind

In Yaroslavl, Nemtsov was not expecting the kind of results Navalny had in Moscow. He wasn't nearly as popular, and the arrest of Urlashov had turned people against politics in general. The feeling was that since anyone the authorities didn't want would be removed or jailed, what was the point of trying? Nothing would change. "Of course, I tried to inspire people, and I had some success, but still, there was not the kind of mobilization of turn-out that there was under Urlashov," Nemtsov said.[24] Shortly before the vote, polls showed that the PARNAS, led by Nemtsov, was teetering on the edge of the five-per cent barrier in the regional parliamentary elections.

But in the end, Zhanna was right: Nemtsov won. And he probably won with a better lead than the official result showed. On election day, exit polls showed that Nemtsov and PARNAS had about eight per cent of the vote, so it got in the parliament with points to spare. On the night of 10 September, during the vote count, their result dropped from 10 per cent to 5.15 per cent. The next day Nemtsov would claim that at least two of the three mandates he had won had been stolen from the party. Nevertheless, Nemtsov's campaign triumphed. The PARNAS party had its own deputy in the Yaroslavl Regional Duma: Boris Nemtsov.

Never before under Putin had any of the president's overt opponents won an election at this level. Nemtsov was the first—and remains, at the time of this book's publication, the last. Of course, the Kremlin was relatively lenient in allowing him to be elected, but it was a victory in its own right. It was a precedent. Another precedent was that the former first deputy prime minister of the cabinet was running for the post of an ordinary provincial deputy—an unheard-of story in Russian politics. Being the Yaroslavl deputy brought no privileges. Nemtsov did not even have his own faction—he was his own faction, although allies quickly appeared—but he said: "I don't need any title. My title is Boris Nemtsov. That's quite enough."[25]

It really was enough. Nemtsov would quickly become Yaroslavl's most popular man, and local politics would become part of his life. Within a week he would, as promised, buy a fifty-square-metre, two-room flat in central Yaroslavl. In December, he would have a house-warming party and take up his deputy's duties, not only because he promised his constituents but also because he missed working with people. Being an opposition street activist in Russia was exhausting and very monotonous: rally–report–post on LiveJournal or Facebook; rally–report–post again, *ad infinitum*.

Nemtsov would be busy: in the regional parliament, he would become a member of two committees at once—budget and law—and would begin to take part in parliamentary sessions, make speeches and promote legislation. Just like twenty years ago, elderly women would once again crowd the door of his office, hoping that he would help them. No one could compete with him in the local parliament, not in energy, nor in oratorial skills, nor in competence, especially in matters of federal agenda. The local deputy corps would change over the course of Nemtsov's year or so in office, even in their appearance: deputies began to attend meetings with their neckties loose or even without them, with their shirts unbuttoned or even in jeans like Nemtsov. There would be more freedom in the Yaroslavl Duma.

"We certainly don't have people who are so free, who call a spade a spade and make public what officials are doing," said Olga Vakhrina, his assistant in Yaroslavl.[26] The whole city watched in fascination as Nemtsov put officials in their place. Armed with numbers and statistics, he would argue with the local finance minister. "It was hard to deal with him: he just talked and made reference to the substance of an issue," said Balabayev. "He had mastered the subjects, whether it was about excise taxes, housing and utilities tariffs or noxious transportation emissions. The deputy governors always sweated when he opposed them, although he never belittled them—he understood their place in the decision-making system. He became the driver of local politics. You could say he woke it up."[27]

Nemtsov introduced a draft law on mandatory audits of companies in the housing and utilities sector when they raised tariffs—the bill he discussed while campaigning—but he couldn't get it passed. On the other hand, he discovered that the regional budget had overpriced medicines for cancer patients. He would expose a classic case of corruption and—amazingly—get one of the governor's deputies in charge of health care to resign. He proved that the deputy had secured big contracts for his wife's firm to supply drugs to local hospitals. "Nemtsov kept pestering me, telling me, 'Here are the materials, help us fight corruption, write about it,'" Navalny said later. "He got totally immersed in provincial politics, which any normal politician in any normal country should be doing. Every person in the country knows him, and he goes to a session of the Yaroslavl Duma. It was really cool."[28]

Normal political activity was just beginning. The victory in Yaroslavl had another important result: now Nemtsov and his party could go to the federal parliamentary elections without collecting signatures—that is, with a guarantee that they could register their party list. This meant that Nemtsov was now free to run in the autumn 2016 elections. At the very least, he could no longer be prevented from running in those elections. Nemtsov did not hesitate for a minute; of course, he would run for the State Duma from Yaroslavl. It would quickly become clear that he was likely to win, provided he was not obstructed; he quickly became very popular in the city. Psychologically, this victory was a huge relief: Nemtsov had finally broken his losing streak and had achieved political reincarnation. He proved to everyone, but above all to himself, that he wasn't a hopeless failure but a successful incumbent politician. He was still one of the leaders of the opposition, he was still against Putin, and he had finally got his second wind. Now he knew how to win.

# CHAPTER 34

## 2013–14
## Euromaidan

### Searching for the spiritual ties that bind

A year and a half had passed since Vladimir Putin returned to the Kremlin. For thirteen years he had ruled Russia, and the main issue of his rule—the problem of power—had finally been resolved. No one could now challenge his leadership, especially since part of the *nomenklatura*, frightened by Medvedev's thaw and what lay ahead, applauded his return and supported a tightening of the screws. In summer 2012, the rubber-stamp parliament passed laws stipulating huge fines for violating the rules of conduct at rallies, extrajudicial censorship of the internet and the concept of a "foreign agent" to be applied to disloyal non-profit organizations. At the same time, the US congress passed the Magnitsky Act sanctioning Russian official responsible for the death of Sergei Magnitsky in 2009. In return, the Russian government banned Americans from adopting Russian children. This ban was so heartless and outrageous—why punish innocent children and deny them a family because of sanctions imposed in Washington?—that even some members of the government spoke out against it. There was a rally in Moscow (Nemtsov was one of the organizers), and at Putin's regular annual press conference, Moscow journalists asked him just that.

There are different paths to despotism. Some tyrants come to power on a wave of fanaticism and then clamp down on their nations and unleash horrific wars for the sake of some "higher goal." Others come to power by chance. Putin was neither a cruel, ruthless autocrat who took pleasure in watching his enemies suffer (unlike Alexander Lukashenko in neighbouring Belarus), nor a fanatical tyrant ready to suppress everyone for some lofty cause. He simply believed that there was a reason the Cap of Monomakh fit him so well. The country needed him, which meant that he needed power; he had no other motive. Power and control became his programme, and repression was an instrument, not an end in itself. In the past, he could do without prohibitive laws and arrests, but now he believed they were an unavoidable necessity. Just as the era of Tsar Nicholas I's reaction began with the Decembrists' uprising,* so the vector of the country's development after Putin's return was predetermined by the Bolotnaya Square protests.

Putin became a guardian, a seeker of spiritual ties to bind the nation, and then a restorer of the empire not out of the dictates of his soul or the call of his heart, but for other reasons. First, he was carried along by the current. It was the path of least resistance in a country that, by the time of his accession, was carrying the great weight of resentment against the outside world for hopes dashed, for the fact that Russia had not turned into a prosperous democracy like the countries of the West. Putin built his political capital on these grievances, and the longer the propaganda was used, the more it fanned feelings of frustration and humiliation.

In 2011 a new oil boom began. Oil prices reached historic highs and only strengthened the high self-regard of Putin and his circle. As the political scientist Kirill Rogov wrote, the shock of the 2008 crisis was replaced by a new self-confidence, the banner of which was the idea of self-sufficiency and a national evening of the score.[1] From Putin's point of view, agents of external forces were on Bolotnaya Square, and now the central element of his political doctrine was confrontation with the West. Anti-Americanism became a religion. Any decisions by the authorities were now explained as a struggle for national sovereignty. Putin put an end to the discussion about Russia's special path:

---

\* The Decembrists were a group of liberal aristocratic military officers who rebelled against the tsar in December 1825 when the autocratic Nicholas I assumed the throne after the sudden death of his brother, Tsar Alexander I. In the end, five Decembrist leaders were executed, and the rest were exiled to Siberia.

"Attempts to civilize Russia from the outside were not accepted by the absolute majority of our people, because the desire for independence, for spiritual, ideological, foreign-policy sovereignty is an integral part of our national character."[2]

And since Putin was confronting America and more broadly the West, Russia had to appear to be a fortress of spiritual values against the backdrop of the multiculturalism flourishing in the West. Putin declared himself a conservative, a guardian of the traditional values of family, stalwart morality, Orthodox Christianity, and so on. "Russian society is clearly lacking spiritual bonds," he said from the Kremlin podium in December 2012.[3]

Second, Putin was mesmerized by omnipotence. He developed delusions of grandeur. All leaders are bronzed in one way or another, and in Russia they experience what Nikita Khrushchev's daughter, Rada Adzhubei, called "leaving the earth." After five years, she said, the head of state loses his sense of reality. She saw it happen to her father: "No one can resist the hypnotic power of the system [...]. At some stage you start to believe that you are the smartest man on earth, that without you everything will collapse, that only your decisions are right, that everyone loves you [...]. I saw it happen step by step."[4]

In the end Khrushchev ruled the country for eight years and was removed by his comrades in the Politburo, who feared his Thaw. There is no threat of Putin resigning. Unlike the Soviet leaders who built a collegial system of government, he has subordinated all state institutions to himself. And, from the very beginning, United Russia, Putin's party, resembled the Communist Party of the Soviet Union only outwardly—with the roar of applause at party congresses—but it did not decide anything. It only ensured his control over the country's political system.

Putin expanded his power methodically, dismantling the state institutions he inherited from Yeltsin step by step. His megalomania grew much stronger as he was soon totally unrestrained in his decisions. The longer he ruled, the more he was willing to believe in his own exceptionalism. According to one version, the turning point was February 2007, when Putin blew apart the world order in his Munich speech.[5] For the first time he challenged the West and was not rebuffed. It was then that he began to accept his true ambitions. He wanted to determine the fate of the world on an equal footing with world leaders. He was cramped in the corner that the West had put him in.

This is how public frustration—resentment of the world outside the borders, fanned by propaganda—was transformed into a programme of action. Putin saw himself as Russia. And later events only convinced him that he was right. When he returned to the presidency in 2012 after Medvedev's Thaw, Putin already saw himself as the country's saviour. While he was away from the Kremlin, Russia's ship veered off course and almost sank, but he returned, righted the wheel and set the country's course towards new victories.

In the past, Putin had shown some interest in church affairs and considered himself a Christian. In May 2012, a service in the Kremlin's Cathedral of the Annunciation, the sixteenth-century family chapel of Russian tsars, was held after Putin's presidential inauguration. Patriarch Kirill blessed his third presidential term as if he were anointing him to the throne. By then, the women from the punk band Pussy Riot were already in jail. In February 2012, on the eve of the presidential election, they had appeared in Moscow's main church, Christ the Saviour Cathedral, with musical instruments and the song 'Mary Mother of God, Drive Away Putin'. When Putin learnt of this, he was beside himself. He gave the go-ahead for the arrest and the verdict. "They were right to get two years in prison," he explained. "It's wrong to undermine the foundations of morality."[6] And then he ordered penalties for "insulting the feelings of believers" be included in the criminal code.

In the Christ the Saviour Cathedral, Pussy Riot was protesting the active inclusion of the Orthodox Church in Putin's election campaign. Putin and the Church were moving towards each other, and he was demonstrating his religious piety more often. This is how his megalomania manifested itself: Putin placed himself in a system of historical coordinates. His rule seemed to continue Russia's centuries-old traditional path. It made it easier for him to explain to himself why he had become the sole ruler of a huge country. The desire to inscribe himself in the historical pantheon was combined with a kind of religious mysticism. "As a Chekist at the beginning of his presidency, he regarded power pragmatically, but he eventually perceived a mystical dimension," said religious scholar and public-church activist Sergei Chapnin. "And certainly it's a huge country with huge resources. There must be a reason why he received it all, and no one really disputes it."[7]

Russia is not a religious country. However, sociological surveys registered an increase in homophobic attitudes in society, so homophobia became the main focus of the struggle for traditional values. The law banning homosexual propaganda among children adopted in summer 2013 was a political ploy. At first, the law included the word "homosexualism" from the Soviet criminal code, which had negative connotations, but then it was changed to "non-traditional sexual relationships." The idea was to ramp up propaganda on a hot-button topic to distract society from dissatisfaction with the government. The supposed concern for children concealed the real goal: to make homophobia official Russian policy. In addition, as sociologist Masha Plotko wrote, "homophobic propaganda also exploits widespread anti-Americanism and anti-Western sentiment in public opinion. America and gays are linked in mass consciousness and presented as a 'new-fangled' evil."[8]

The new law sparked protests all over the world and, much more worrying for Putin, it threatened his most important achievement, his main construction project, his calling card—the Sochi Winter Olympics. The February 2014 games were months away, but a world-wide campaign to boycott the games had already begun. Homophobia was completely at odds with the Olympic spirit and the Olympic charter. Putin could not allow the Olympics to be disrupted after he had invested so much energy and money in them. A mega-project on a scale comparable to the most ambitious plans of the Soviet government, the Sochi Olympics were to be the pinnacle of Putin's world fame, a symbol of the greatness of the Russia he had built. Putin had offered many assurances that there was no threat to athletes in Sochi, that there was no discrimination against gays in Russia, and that even he was acquainted with "some people like that." He attached such importance to the Olympics that, on the eve of the games in December, he even relented to Angela Merkel's pleas and released his foe Mikhail Khodorkovsky ten years after his arrest. He sent him straight from prison to Berlin by the same route that dissident author Alexander Solzhenitsyn, arrested for treason, took when he was deported from the USSR forty years earlier.

Although preparation to welcome famous guests to Sochi was somewhat nerve-wracking, all the bustling to get ready was rather pleasant, too. There was no reason for Putin to worry. The Bolotnaya Square movement had been stifled, protests had been crushed, there was no internal opposition, and everything was under control. The sluggish machine of state, which under Medvedev had set out on the road to modernization, had turned back. Like the king in poet Alexander Pushkin children's tale, Putin could at last hear the rooster crowing the all-clear sign: "Cock-a-doodle-do, reign abed in comfort and just enjoy the view."

And yet something was clearly going wrong. It was like a car with bad petrol in the tank: it could drive along the highway, but with so much sputtering, knocking and jerking that it seemed it might stall at any second.

First, there was the problem of Putin's rating. It had not risen since he returned to the Kremlin. In 2008, Putin left the Kremlin at the zenith of his popularity, basking in the respect and esteem of his fellow citizens. His return to the presidency was marked by being booed at Olympic Stadium. His rating was falling, and although in absolute numbers it was still high, by November 2013 it reached its lowest level since the beginning of the 2000s. Putin's rating was the tip of a melting iceberg: people were becoming more disappointed in the model of the regime he had built. Belief in the vertical power structure was declining, while assessments of the level of corruption were rising. Dissenters were chased off the streets of Moscow, but the public still saw the men in power as "crooks and thieves." The success of Navalny in Moscow and Nemtsov in Yaroslavl (and the victory of independent politician Yevgeny Roizman as mayor of Yekaterinburg, the third largest city in the country) was clear evidence of this.

Second, unlike the 2000s with economic growth that was unprecedented in Russian history, record oil prices were no longer helping. The Russian economy went from crisis to stagnation. Experts explained that the economic model based on domestic demand had run out of steam and now needed new systemic conditions for growth: trust from investors, guarantees of fair and open competition, strong institutions, and so on. But all this was unattainable under Putin's autocracy. The path forward was clearly in crisis. What could be done? How could the negative trend, especially in public opinion, be reversed to his favour?

Putin had a plan. In October 2011, he came up with a new idea to found the Eurasian Union, something like the European Union but in the post-Soviet space. Putin's ambitions had grown. The customs union, which he had been trying to create since the early 2000s, was now just a step along the way to a confederation of post-Soviet states with a common foreign and defence policy. The Eurasian Union would be something like the union treaty that Gorbachev had wanted to replace the collapsing USSR with in 1991. "We propose a model for a powerful supranational association capable of becoming one of the poles of the modern world," Putin declared.[9] Sceptics scoffed: a new version of empire centred in Moscow was utopian; what neighbour would agree to share its sovereignty? But Putin was not joking. This was how he saw his third term. He had returned to the Kremlin as a unifier of lands who would realize his people's dream of recreating a single state in place of the Soviet Union.

Of course, great difficulties lay ahead on the path chosen by the ambitious Russian ruler. The Eurasian Union project faced the same obstacle as the creation of the common economic space had done ten years before—it was unthinkable without Ukraine. History was going around in circles.

## Yanukovych goes to Europe

Vladimir Putin never liked Viktor Yanukovych, not before he abandoned his run for power in November 2004, and certainly not afterwards. When Yulia Tymoshenko came back to power as Prime Minister in 2007, Putin supported her. But in 2013, the Donetsk clan won over all the forces on the pro-Russian flank of Ukrainian politics and there was no one to support but Yanukovych. Yanukovych put Tymoshenko in prison, formally for abuse of power for signing extremely unprofitable gas contracts with Russia (at gas prices higher than those European countries paid), but in reality to get rid of his most dangerous rival.

Having won the presidential election in 2010 against a background of disenchantment with the Orange Revolution, Yanukovych had no intention of sharing his power with anyone. He cancelled constitutional reforms, returned vast powers to himself as president, handed over the largest media outlets to oligarchs close to him and control of the government and state finances to members of his family. Huge sums of money disappeared from the budget. Independent businesses across the country came under pressure from the Donetsk clans. As the Ukrainian magazine *Novoye vremya* would later write, "The period of almost four years that Yanukovych was at the helm of the country went down in history as a time of unprecedented plunder."[10]

Yet, surprisingly, it was Yanukovych who did more for Ukraine's European integration than his predecessors. "Ironically, Yanukovych, deeply anti-European in mentality, was better suited to the role of European steward than anyone else," wrote Ukrainian journalist Serhiy Rakhmanin. "The incumbent head of state was able to 'organize' officials, oligarchs and the 'anti-Western electorate'."[11] In the end, Yanukovych got citizens on board with the idea of moving towards Europe.

The Ukrainian president believed that his rear flank in the East was covered because he met Moscow's demands. Ukraine refused to join NATO, the Russian Black Sea Fleet had a lease in Sevastopol for another twenty-five years, and in 2012 Yanukovych had kept his promise to Medvedev. Despite violent outcry from the opposition, he had pushed through the Rada a law giving a special status to the Russian language used in Eastern Ukraine. Now Yanukovych was on his way to Europe.

By 2013, the political declarations of rapprochement with Europe had been signed, and the ratification of the substantive part was on the agenda—the association agreement with the European Union that included a visa-free regime and Ukraine's membership in the European free-trade area. This was a crucial step for membership in the EU.

Of course, Yanukovych did not want to join Europe because he believed in democracy and had suddenly been magically transformed into a Westerner. He wanted to give the opposition something to lose before the 2015 presidential election. The course towards European integration was a done deal in Ukraine. Even many big businessmen in Eastern Ukraine, which was closely linked to Russia, supported it. Yanukovych's position was becoming increasingly vulnerable. The high levels of corruption and nepotism were causing popular resentment, and the economy continued to decline. Ukraine, which had been a poor country, had not recovered from the 2008 crisis. By the spring of 2013, polls showed that Yanukovych would lose the election to almost any of the leaders of Ukraine's motley opposition. Of course, the Kremlin could help prop him up with gas discounts and loans, but Yanukovych understood that if he turned his back on Europe, he would never hold on to power.

Putin could never agree to Ukrainian integration with Europe. After he returned to the Kremlin, Yanukovych received a new demand from Moscow to join the customs union, which was conceived as the first step on the Kremlin's path into the future. The demand was increasingly insistent. Yanukovych manoeuvred, offering to take observer status for Ukraine in the customs union without giving up European integration. But the closer he got to the November summit, when Ukraine was supposed to sign the association agreement with the European Union, the more obvious it became that he couldn't sit on the fence much longer. He had to decide: Russia or Europe?

Yanukovych made his choice: Europe. He was still the Kremlin's strongest pro-Russian candidate in the upcoming 2015 elections. And Angela Merkel and François Hollande would stand up for him. Kremlin officials also understood that it was dangerous to push Yanukovych over the edge. They might go too far, and 2004 would repeat itself. However, it was not unreasonable for Moscow to expect that Europe, in the end, would not sign anything with Yanukovych, since he was not ready to meet the Europeans' key condition—releasing Yulia Tymoshenko from prison. Indeed, back in the summer of 2013, neither Merkel nor Hollande was ready to sign an agreement with Yanukovych.

However, at the end of July, when Putin came to Ukraine to celebrate the 1,025th anniversary of the acceptance of Christianity in ancient Rus, the situation had changed. Putin, inspired by the occasion, stressed that Holy Russia united Russia, Belarus and Ukraine. His entire visit was scandalous from the diplomatic point of view. Putin spent fifteen minutes negotiating with Yanukovych and then spent two days, first in

Kyiv and then in Crimea, with his ever-present trusted associate and confidant Viktor Medvedchuk. Both Medvedchuk and Putin's adviser in charge of the customs union, Sergei Glazyev, made their position clear: European integration would lead to Ukraine's loss of sovereignty and economic catastrophe. As Kyiv's *Zerkalo nedeli* newspaper later wrote, the so-called Glazyev–Medvedchuk plan, entitled 'On a set of measures to involve Ukraine in the Eurasian integration process', was put on Putin's desk back in June, along with a digest of stories on the main Ukrainian TV channels about "how bad the customs union is and how good Ukraine will be after joining the association with the EU."[12] In August, the Glazyev–Medvedchuk plan would be leaked to the Ukrainian press and be a bombshell.

Problems at the Ukrainian–Russian customs offices began at the end of July. By August, events were racing ahead. Russia blocked all Ukrainian imports in the hope that that when Ukrainian businessmen wouldn't have access to the Russian market, they would pressure the cabinet not to sign the free-trade agreement with the EU. In fact, the opposite happened. Anti-Russian sentiments soared in Ukraine, in Kyiv the customs union was called "a backwoods project", and Yanukovych's rating even rose in the face of confrontation with Moscow. Once again, he fled to Brussels for support, where now he was welcomed warmly. In the European Union, the balance of power had changed. The position of those who promoted European–Ukrainian integration as a political project to block Russia had grown stronger.

Resultantly, the idea of European integration with Ukraine got a powerful new impetus, and all that was left was to agree on the fate of Tymoshenko. Yanukovych did not openly agree to her release, but behind closed doors—both with her and with Merkel and Hollande— it was agreed that after signing the agreement he would release Tymoshenko for treatment at the Charité clinic in Berlin.[13] An indirect confirmation of this agreement is the fact that Tymoshenko would later call on the opposition from prison to vote for European integration, despite the fact that the Rada had failed to pass any initiative for her release. The final obstacle to the signing of the Ukraine–EU agreement had been removed. Yanukovych was to cross the last t's at the summit in Vilnius on 29 November.

## How the war started in Kyiv

No one knows for sure, and no one may ever know, what exactly Putin said to Yanukovych in Moscow on 9 November during their last meeting before the events of Euromaidan. It was the only meeting the Kremlin didn't officially announce and didn't comment on afterwards. Something was clearly going on. "Apparently the situation is truly very serious," *Kommersant* reported the day after. "What did they discuss? [...] Something has changed in this story [of Ukraine signing the agreement with the EU]. [...] And there can be only one reason for it: Yanukovych has realized what might happen to his country."[14] Three weeks later, at the summit in Vilnius, TV cameras captured Yanukovych explaining to an exasperated Merkel why he walked away from signing the agreement: "I want you to hear me. I have been alone for three and a half years, one-on-one in a very uneven playing field with a strong Russia."[15] A few years later, Ukrainian politician Hennadiy Moskal would cite a person in Yanukovych's inner circle and say that Putin had threatened him with the loss of all Eastern Ukraine. "Putin said, 'Russia will never share a border with the EU and NATO... As soon as you try to sign something, I will take away Crimea and the Donetsk, Luhansk, Kharkiv, Mykolaiv, Odesa and Zaporizhzhia regions...' [Yanukovych] turned white and gathered his advisers. There were four people there. One of them told me about it. [Yanukovych] was so scared that he didn't want to join Europe, or NATO, or sign the association agreement."[16]

When Yanukovych came back from the meeting, he explained to his close associates that his sudden turnaround was for economic reasons. On 21 November, a week before the summit, the Ukrainian government publicly announced that European integration was on hold. That evening Kyivan journalist Mustafa Nayyem tweeted, "All right then, time to get serious... Who's ready to go out on the Maidan before midnight tonight...?"

That was the beginning of the Ukrainian Euromaidan, which in three months would end with Yanukovych fleeing the country. It would go down in history as the Revolution of Dignity and, unlike the events of nine years before, it would culminate in a genuine popular uprising. "Euromaidan in 2013 was fundamentally different from the

Orange Revolution of 2004. Euromaidan had no leader, but it had a self-organizing network of grassroots volunteers and universal demands instead of narrowly partisan ones," write the authors of the book *The Turning Point Years: Pages of the Ukrainian Revolution*. "The main driving forces of the protest in the first days were the students at Ukrainian universities."[17]

Nothing good awaited Yanukovych in the long run, but Euromaidan could have ended without casualties and without such a rapid change of power. It most likely would have run out of steam only to be revived again closer to the presidential election. But on the night of 30 November, the Berkut (Ukrainian special forces) went out on the Maidan and severely beat up several hundred students. The next day, half a million people came out onto Kyiv's central square. A week after the clashes in the city centre and another wave of violence, barricades appeared on Maidan and self-defence groups were being formed. The largest rally took place on 8 December: about 650,000 people came to the square. The Berkut and *titushky*, young people hired by the authorities to provoke and attack the opposition, again attempted to disperse people from the Maidan.

Even at this point, however, all was not lost for the Ukrainian government. Hundreds of thousands of people greeted the New Year on the Maidan singing the national anthem, but then the protests gradually began to run down. After spending a month on the street, activists did not know what to do next. On Yanukovych's desk was a compromise prepared by his advisers: change the cabinet, carry out constitutional reform—revert to a parliamentary republic—announce that the current president will not run for a second term in the 2015 elections.

But the Kremlin was no longer seeking compromise. On 17 December, Yanukovych brought back from Moscow a $15 billion loan (or rather, the promise of a loan and its first tranche) and a thirty-percent discount on gas—a concession that had been unthinkable in the past. But along with the carrot came the stick. Vladislav Surkov, Putin's aide, was now the Kremlin envoy in charge of the fight against the Maidan protests. Beginning in December, he flew to Kyiv almost weekly and held meetings with the Yanukovych administration. He demanded that the Maidan be emptied. And after the New Year and Christmas holidays he brought to Kyiv eleven bills that went down in history as the "dictatorial laws." The Rada passed them on 16 January in an instant, with a simple show of hands and no debate. These were essentially the same laws that had made the Russian parliament a rubber-stamp body: the same censorship, the same fines and arrests for rallies, criminal liability for extremism and for slander, even the same "foreign agent" label for opposition-minded public organizations.

But unlike in Russia, in Ukraine these laws lasted two weeks and became the last, fatal mistake in the fight against the Maidan movement—the point of no return. They brought the confrontation to a point where reconciliation was no longer possible. The radical part of the Maidan, ignoring the opposition leaders who tried to reason with them, broke through the cordons, set fire to police buses and threw Molotov cocktails at the security forces. War broke out in central Kyiv.

"Throughout its years of independence, Ukraine has prided itself on its ability to resolve its societal conflicts, of which there have been many, almost without any bloodshed. On 19 January 2014 that record was broken, and hundreds of people were seriously injured," wrote the authors of *The Turning Point Years*.[18] On 22 January, the Maidan learnt of the first dead. In two more days, the uprising had spread first to regions in Western Ukraine and then to the centre of the country. The compromises Yanukovych offered were too late every time: what would have suited the Maidan a week earlier was now unacceptable. By mid-February it was clear that the dénouement was near. "The confrontation had already lasted for three months and could not continue in the same format," wrote journalist Sonya Koshkina.[19]

## Coup or revolution?

On the morning of 18 February, frustrated by fruitless negotiations with Yanukovych, Maidan activists moved to storm the Rada while the Berkut special police were issued live ammunition. And so began the events of the last three bloodiest days of the revolution.

The protesters suffered most of their casualties on 20 February from the Berkut troops and the snipers shooting from windows (the investigation would never be able to determine who they were). After the victory, a memorial and an alley of Heroes of the Heavenly Hundred appeared next to the Maidan. Two dozen law enforcement officers were also killed, some of them shot. By the morning of 21 February, Yanukovych, European mediators and Vladimir Lukin, Moscow's representative, had prepared a peace agreement: a new constitution, a new government, and early elections. Lukin sent a wire to the Kremlin, saying that the agreement would let them manage the situation and keep the pro-Russian faction in the Rada for the time being. The agreement was scheduled to be signed at three o'clock at the presidential administration, but in the end Lukin did not attend; he was stopped at the entrance by a call from the Russian foreign minister, Sergei Lavrov.

On the night of 22 February, Yanukovych flew to Kharkiv, where his supporters were in power. The new plan that had been cobbled together and then coordinated with Moscow was apparently for Yanukovych to settle in Kharkiv, where a Kremlin-backed congress of deputies from south-eastern Ukraine was to take place (Russian deputies, senators and political advisers were already in Kharkiv). At the time, Putin still hoped that Yanukovych would at least be able to hold on to power in south-eastern Ukraine and then possibly take back control of Kyiv as well. But that plan collapsed, too. Yanukovych didn't show up at the congress, and, apparently fearing arrest, fled Kharkiv for Donetsk. When Donetsk border guards stopped his plane before he could fly to Russia (although Yanukovych had not been arrested by the Ukrainians), he took a roundabout route to Crimea the same day. In Crimea he was met by Russian marines. A day later, a Russian military boat dropped him off in the Russian port of Novorossiysk. "I will say it openly—he asked to be driven away to Russia, which we did," Putin would later say.[20]

In Kyiv, the war was over by the time Yanukovych fled to Kharkiv. The agreement signed by Yanukovych and the Ukrainian opposition was already outdated before it was signed: on the afternoon of the same day, the Berkut had already left Kyiv. By evening, there were no security forces left in the government quarter. When the leaders of the opposition parties—Vitali Klitschko, Arseniy Yatsenyuk and Oleh Tyahnybok—appeared with the news of the truce agreement on the

Maidan where the dead were being buried, they were booed. The revolution had succeeded. There was no one and nothing to negotiate.

From the very beginning, Putin's plan was to frame these events as a *coup d'état*, supported and in fact orchestrated by the West. In December 2017, *The Washington Post* leaked a classified report by GRU, Russia's military spy agency. According to the report, "Starting the day after Yanukovych's fall, the military spies created a slew of fake personas on the social media platforms of Facebook and its Russian equivalent VKontakte [...]. The personas were meant to represent ordinary people from across Ukraine who were disillusioned with opposition protests at Kiev's central square, called Maidan."[21] Years later, Putin would cite the *coup d'état* in Ukraine as the ideological basis of his 2022 invasion of Ukraine.

But there was never a *coup d'état* in Ukraine. European leaders, though they contributed to the tensions between Yanukovych and the Kremlin in the autumn, tried—unsuccessfully—to cool the Maidan fervour from the moment people took to the streets. Russian propaganda would see direct evidence of American interference in the cookies and cakes that the US assistant secretary of state, Victoria Nuland, handed out on Maidan on 11 December—launching the popular "State Department cookies" meme—but just that day Nuland had disagreed with the demand for Yanukovych's resignation and urged opposition leaders to prepare for the 2015 presidential election. And on 21 February, the Polish foreign minister, Radosław Sikorski, pleaded with the Maidan council to sign the agreement with Yanukovych. But all their efforts failed as they were dealing with a truly leaderless popular uprising.

There is no doubt that by the time Yanukovych was evacuated, the annexation of Crimea had already been planned. Preparations had been made in advance: Surkov brought the speaker of the local parliament, Vladimir Konstantinov, to Moscow in December. Then Putin paused. On 23 February, the Olympic Games in Sochi were coming to an end, and he did not want to spoil the party. On the night of 27 February, Russian paratroopers in unmarked uniforms quickly rounded up the Crimean authorities and blockaded the Ukrainian military stationed on the peninsula without firing a single shot. Russian flags were raised over the parliament and government buildings. By 4 March, when Putin first spoke at length about the situation in Ukraine and said that the annexation of Crimea to Russia was "not under consideration", the issue had already been resolved, Mikhail Zygar wrote.[22] On 16 March, Crimea voted in a referendum almost unanimously to become part of Russia. The voting, however, was organized in much the same way as the Chechen elections of autumn 1991, when Dudayev seized power and declared himself president. On 18 March, it was finalized.

Less than a month later, war broke out in Donbas in Eastern Ukraine. Moscow initially supported the local militias against the new Kyiv government but then sent its troops to their aid in the summer when they foresaw the militia's inevitable defeat. As would be seen in 2022, no one in 2014 had correctly predicted how Putin would respond to the Euromaidan victory. Annexation of foreign territory? A bloody war that would claim thousands of lives? In Europe, in the twenty-first century? Such a thing was impossible to imagine. By the summer, Russia would be expelled from the G8 and slapped with sanctions.

And with that, the Russia that had been born with a vote for independence on 12 June 1990 ceased to exist. The page of history had been turned.

# CHAPTER 35

## 2014
## Russia after Crimea

### Second arrest

Nemtsov, like virtually everyone, foresaw neither the annexation of Crimea nor the war. Even at the very beginning of the events, as soon as he learnt that the Berkut had dispersed the students on Maidan with brutal force, he immediately suggested to Nadezhda Mityushkina that they take to the streets to support the students. "What kind of protest—a handcuff demonstration or solo picketing?" Mityushkina asked, meaning a demonstration that would get them detained or a one-person picket that wouldn't. At the time, no one had been detained for standing alone holding a sign. In the end, they decided to hold up a banner together, that is, to have a handcuff demonstration. Nemtsov had a train ticket to Yaroslavl for 7.00 p.m. Mityushkina was worried. "Well, keep in mind that you might miss your train," she wrote.

"So the f what? I'll take a later train. There's another at ten."

"OK, see you tomorrow."

"It's just wrong to stay silent."[1]

The next day, 2 December, Nemtsov and several activists were already unfurling a banner that read "Ukraine, we are with you" in front of the Ukrainian embassy in Moscow. "First of all, I consider Ukraine to be a very close, friendly country," Nemtsov explained to journalists. "Second, I am sure that if democracy triumphs in Ukraine, it will happen in Russia sooner or later, too."[2]

Everyone, including Nemtsov, was immediately detained. But the law-enforcement officers did not mistreat them. Nemtsov was released from the police station as a regional deputy without even a charge sheet being written up. During the Euromaidan demonstrations, he was unable to get to his beloved Kyiv, which had become his hometown over the years: Ukrainian security had simply banned him from entering the country while Yanukovych was in power. On 23 February, Nemtsov managed to lay flowers at the Ukrainian embassy in memory of those killed on the Maidan. That very evening, paintings by great artists of the Russian Empire and Soviet Union—Kazimir Malevich, Marc Chagall, Wassily Kandinsky—came to life at the Fisht Olympic Stadium in Sochi to an audience that included Putin and his guests, who had arrived for the closing ceremony of the Olympics. The Olympic flame was extinguished.

When Crimea was annexed, Nemtsov found himself behind bars. Over the three winter months, things in Russia had changed, and this time his status as a deputy did not help him. The day after the closing of the Olympics, on 24 February, a Moscow court passed sentences in the Bolotnaya Square case: ordinary activists, who were the main protagonists, received prison sentences of two, three or four years. Hundreds of people—including Nemtsov—marched to the courthouse in support of the prisoners, where police pushed them into vans one by one. They didn't touch Nemtsov then. But in the evening, Navalny called for everyone to protest on Tverskaya Street in the city centre. Nemtsov, Navalny, Yashin and Mityushkina were all sought out and detained.

"They're letting me go now," Nemtsov explained to Yashin in the bus. "I'm a deputy, so they can't detain me without the prosecutor's sanction."[3] Yashin shook his head in response. Later, when Nemtsov was held, he said, "This is an order from Putin personally. I'm a thousand per cent sure."[4] At the police station, they were immediately taken to the anteroom next to the cells, popularly called the "monkey cage." The experienced Mityushkina knew right away that they wouldn't be released that night. A few hours later, they were asked to go into the cells. So Nemtsov and Navalny spent the night together in the same cell, awaiting trial. The next day, Nemtsov would get ten days in jail, Navalny seven.

As Navalny later recalled, that night in the cell, 25 February, was probably when he had his longest conversation with Nemtsov.

> I said, "Boris, you've got this big problem. You're a great man, you understand everything. But the 1990s are hanging over you"—his meeting an official at the airport wearing white trousers, and privatization, which he was not involved in, but which everyone blamed him for. Nemtsov was blamed for all the problems of the Yeltsin government. I said, "Let's think what to do about it." But he had already realized that nothing could be done about it. Each time period is associated with certain people. You can't erase time, and you can't erase the people. He was a man of the 1990s. If you took Nemtsov out, it would be like the 1990s didn't exist for us. It's impossible to do. He was very well aware of that. He was still a relatively young politician with a lot of potential. He wanted to do it all. But he epitomized the 1990s, and that was a problem in the politics of the day. That's why I really appreciated what he did in the Yaroslavl region.[5]

In the morning, Nemtsov stripped off his shirt and started doing push-ups right in the monkey cage, coaxing Navalny to do them as well, and then started joking around with the police officers. He spent the next nine days in an isolation cell in the north of Moscow. Navalny was there, too, but they were in separate cells because "politicians are always separated." The detention centre had just been renovated and was considered exemplary; the cells were spacious and not overcrowded; the toilet was even behind a door. He could receive as many parcels as he wanted from whomever he wanted. In general, Nemtsov lacked for nothing other than a shower, which detainees could take once a week. He read Vasily Aksenov's novel *Island of Crimea* and exercised with his cellmates—four guys arrested for drunken driving.

This was his second arrest, and despite the relatively bearable conditions, it was difficult for him. According to Mityushkina, who was in a nearby cell, Nemtsov kept up a good front but looked very tired. He was fifty-four years old, and he felt his age. A habit of lunch-time drinks led to liver surgery and a switch from cognac to wine. His back hurt, even more in the cell since the bed was too short for him. Most importantly, the very thought of being behind bars was unbearable. When asked what he wanted apart from a shower, he replied: "I want my freedom."[6] He understood quite clearly that he couldn't withstand imprisonment. And he was not prepared to sacrifice his lifestyle for politics—he was who he was, and he wouldn't change. But he was not prepared to sacrifice his freedom either.

## Crimean euphoria

Nemtsov was outraged. The annexation of Crimea by armed men came as a double shock to him. First, it shattered his notion of how the world was supposed to work. Armed men annexing part of a neighbouring country? It was unthinkable. Nemtsov was a deputy when Russia adopted its declaration of sovereignty. He was a governor when Yeltsin signed the Budapest Memorandum with the leaders of the UK and the US in December 1994, guaranteeing the inviolability of Ukraine's borders in exchange for Ukraine giving up its nuclear capacity. (Nemtsov was still in jail when Putin explained that there had been a coup in Ukraine, which meant that it was now a new state, and hence Russia's obligations to it were void.) Second, it was personally painful. Over the last ten years, ever since Nemtsov had come out on the Maidan in an orange scarf in November 2004, Ukraine had become his second home, a place he cared deeply about. He often visited and was well known there. He appeared on local TV, and Ukrainians loved him. He had friends there, a small business in Ukrainian real estate and even a serious romance: he would date model Anna Duritskaya for two years, and they regularly flew to see each other—he to Kyiv, she to Moscow.

Both the seizure of Crimea and the war that soon broke out in Donbas—a war between Russia and Ukraine—were without exaggeration personal disasters for Nemtsov. These he could not forgive Putin. He wanted to act. On 2 March, while still in detention, he wrote in his blog:

> Putin has declared a fratricidal war on Ukraine. This bloody madness of the delusional Chekist will cost Russia and Ukraine dearly:

young men killed on both sides again, grieving mothers and wives, orphaned children. An empty Crimea, where no one will go. Billions, tens of billions of roubles taken away from the elderly and children and thrown into the furnace of war, and then even more money to support the thieving regime of Crimea. It's as if he can't hold on to power otherwise. The ghoul needs war. He needs people's blood. International isolation, impoverishment of the people, repression awaits Russia. God, why are we cursed like this? How much longer can we stand all this?!7

The next day, Nemtsov called for an anti-war march. When he was released a few days later, he explained why the annexation of Crimea was politically criminal. It violated international obligations undertaken by Moscow; it was illegal and "no one in the world except Putin and Maputo Island" will recognize the results of the referendum in Crimea or its annexation to Russia, not even Kazakhstan or Belarus. Annexation is economically dangerous because it inevitably leads to sanctions and will push Russia out of international markets.8 Nemtsov was right on all counts: only a few countries—Venezuela, Cuba, Nicaragua, Syria and Sudan—would recognize Crimea as Russian, while harsh Western sanctions against Russian energy, major state companies and banks would come as a surprise to the Kremlin.

Nemtsov already knew that his arguments would fall on deaf ears. He said that the imperial euphoria of Putin's Russia from the annexation of Crimea was like a drug: "No one who is high wants to hear arguments. They don't want to think rationally."9

It's unlikely that Putin expected the overwhelming positive public response to the annexation of Crimea. Over the course of March, his approval rating soared, jumping by twenty per cent in four weeks, reaching eighty-six per cent by the end of the month. At the same time, confidence in the government in general and patriotic sentiment soared, and what sociologists and political scientists would call "a Crimean consensus" emerged. Russian society suddenly came together in a monolith. "The significant bloc of people who recently openly and unequivocally condemned the activities of Vladimir Putin has actually ceased to exist as a nationwide phenomenon," publicist Sergei Shelin said in April

2014. "It's clearly not for ever, but the speed at which this segment of the population melted away is, to be polite, dumbfounding."[10]

Nemtsov had gone to jail in one country and been released ten days later in another. Support for Putin was now unconditional. Considerations that the acquisition of Crimea would undermine the Russian economy and would have to be paid for literally out of one's own wallets were dashed by a growing sense of pride in the country. Because the euphoria was not at one hundred per cent, Crimea split yesterday's allies, dividing families and friendships. Along with the melting of protest sentiments, the Russian opposition—the structure that had taken shape during the Bolotnaya protests and other rallies, as a result of the Coordinating Council and so on—also collapsed. Opposition figures were once again turning into renegades.

The monolith held and grew. The sharp uptick in fighting on the Ukrainian front, which essentially began in December, led to a new mobilization. Unanimous votes in parliament became the norm. Censorship intensified: independent media outlets changed their editorial boards and editorial policies under pressure from the Kremlin; the TV Rain channel, which achieved public recognition with its live broadcasts from Bolotnaya Square, was kicked off the cable networks. Those who disagreed with the annexation of Crimea and the war in Donbas were declared a fifth column. In April, a billboard with a portrait of Nemtsov and the text "Aliens among us" was put up in central Moscow on the famous street Novy Arbat. "The opposition is now occupying a niche that was occupied by dissidents in Soviet times," Nemtsov said in April. "It's very hard to be in the minority when the majority is aggressive, zombified, intoxicated by such grandiose successes, rising from their knees, fighting the national traitors, etc."[11]

Nemtsov's detention in late February was a harbinger of new times. The Bolotnaya Square case trials that led to his arrest went on throughout the winter. One by one, the defendants were put under arrest, and the judicial convict mill seemed unstoppable. As it continued, everyone was asking: who's next? Nemtsov was a witness. In December he testified in court: the rally on Bolotnaya Square on 6 May 2012 was peaceful, he insisted; there was no rioting, and the police had caused the crush of people themselves.

On 15 March, tens of thousands of people marched in Moscow in an anti-war rally. Nemtsov led the march, holding up a huge banner that read "Hands off Ukraine!" The day before, Konstantin Lebedev, the same provocateur recruited by the secret services, testified in court that the clashes with the police on Bolotnaya Square on 6 May were provoked by Nemtsov, Navalny and other opposition activists when they announced a sit-in. Like in summer 2012, Nemtsov could become a defendant at any moment. Another couple of days later, through a journalist acquaintance, word reached Nemtsov. The decision had been made—he was next.

## To emigrate or not?

"We're going to Israel," Nemtsov told Irina Korolyova, his common-law wife. "For a while. For at least a month."

"But how would that work, Boris? Sonya goes to school."

"Right. Sonya goes to school, and you come and go."

This conversation took place in the third week of March. A few days later, Nemtsov left, and Irina stayed in Russia. She went to Nizhny Novgorod to collect documents for Israeli citizenship. Since Nemtsov's mother was Jewish, he was entitled to an Israeli passport. Irina had a difficult time: Nemtsov's mother did not have the necessary papers on hand, and the two of them had to go to the archives to restore her Jewish ancestry. Meanwhile, Nemtsov was staying in a hotel in Tel Aviv. After a week, Irina came to visit and began to look for a long-term rental in the more affordable suburbs.

Nemtsov faced a dilemma. Going back most likely meant going to jail. Nemtsov did not want to go to prison. He was no longer young, and if he was imprisoned for five or six years, he would be an old man when he got out. But if he took Israeli citizenship, that would put an end to his plans to run in the parliamentary elections in 2016 and his participation in politics at all (if it were at all possible). Staying in Israel meant quitting the game. Nemtsov tried to convince himself that he could do good abroad. He could set up a foundation and promote democratic values. He could write his memoirs—he certainly had rich material. Or he could even open his own kitesurfing station. These thoughts were comforting: emigration was not the end of the world. Three months ago, Mikhail Khodorkovsky had begun to make a new life abroad. Alfred Kokh, a friend of Nemtsov's, had just left Russia for Germany to escape prosecution. Another friend, Igor Linshits, had not been back to Russia in almost a decade. Vladimir Gusinsky hadn't been in Russia for even longer, and they met regularly when Nemtsov visited Israel. He was in the same boat. Life went on for each of them—why should it end for him?

But Nemtsov still couldn't make the decision to emigrate. He took a short break, and on the advice of a doctor he knew, he went to a hospital near Tel Aviv to have the bags under his eyes removed. The simple operation was excruciating: his eyes hurt for a week, the stitches were infected for a long time, and he wore dark glasses for the next six months. The operation delayed the decision, but sooner or later it had to be made. Nemtsov continued to hesitate, but rumours of his departure compelled him to make a choice.

The rumours were started by Ksenia Sobchak: "Nemtsov is in Israel. And to avoid prosecution he probably won't return to Russia," she tweeted in mid-April.[12] This was very unpleasant for Nemtsov, who didn't like a young woman insinuating that he was getting cold feet. When he flew to Moscow at the end of April, the first thing he did was to post a photo of himself in front of Domodedovo airport on Facebook with the caption "Specially for Ksenia Sobchak." Deep down, Nemtsov realized that it would be difficult for him to undo all of his old life. He couldn't just slam the door—he wanted to go back to Russia. In his internal conversation, he needed an argument that would give him confidence. He needed someone to lean on. "I remember vividly when Nemtsov suddenly called and said, 'I need to meet with Bukovsky, can you arrange it?'" recalled Vladimir Kara-Murza.[13]

Vladimir Bukovsky was a legendary dissident who had spent a total of twelve years in Soviet prisons and penal psychiatric institutions. Nemtsov met him in 2002 during one of his trips to Britain, where Bukovsky had lived since the mid-seventies after the Soviet leadership exchanged him for Chilean Communist leader Luis Corvalán. When Bukovsky was arrested again in the spring of 1971, *Pravda* mocked him as "a malicious hooligan engaged in anti-Soviet activities." One of the most famous Soviet rhymes immortalized the exchange of men:

> They exchanged a hooligan
> For the commie Luis Corvalán.
> Let's go and bring back a whore,
> And send Brezhnev to another shore.

At their first meeting in 2002, Nemtsov and Bukovsky drank six bottles of wine, and the former dissident convinced the then-deputy and party leader that it was impossible to be in the semi-opposition. You couldn't oppose the government, for example, and still support President Putin. Bukovsky was a man known for his strength of spirit, a symbol of an uncompromising struggle against the regime for Nemtsov. In 2008, Nemtsov invited him to join Solidarity. Nemtsov said: "We have almost no unquestionable moral authority left in our country. This is a terrible problem—it's a tragedy. Thank God there is Bukovsky."[14] Elderly and unwell, Bukovsky often went to Israel for medical treatments; he arrived that spring, and Nemtsov, together with Irina and his daughter Sonya, went to visit him by the Dead Sea.

If there are omens, this was one of them. The trip from Tel Aviv to the Dead Sea was a nightmare: it took three hours instead of two in the sweltering heat, and the taxi driver drove so wildly they thought they would crash. The scruffy elderly dissident with uncombed hair and dirty clothes made a bad impression on Irina. Nemtsov sent Irina and Sonya off for a swim. He didn't want Irina to be there when they spoke, since she would start screaming that they couldn't go back because Nemtsov would be jailed in Russia. The conversation lasted about fifteen or twenty minutes.

"We were discussing whether he would be jailed for the Bolotnaya Square case," Bukovsky later recalled, "and he asked me if he should go back or not. I said, 'I'm sorry, but it's your decision.' And then he did, from my point of view, a dishonest thing. He asked: 'What would you do?' I said, 'Look, what are you comparing? These are different things. I don't have a family. You have three or four. And so on. Well, I'd go.' Besides, I told him that if he stayed here, he'd go crazy in six months—he's so used to being mixed up in Russian opposition politics. It's like an addict trying to get off drugs. He said, 'I'll go.'"[15]

On the way back, Nemtsov told Irina, "Pack our bags, we're going back to Russia." Israeli citizenship was put on hold. Nemtsov was on his way home, knowing that he would most likely be imprisoned.

But after his conversation with Bukovsky, he decided that he didn't care. He had already lived a rich and full life, enough for several lifetimes. If he went to prison, so be it. He was going home.

## A couple of words in Kyiv

Towards the end of April, Donbas and the Ukrainian east were heading for war. Prompted by Moscow, as abundant evidence would later show, armed rebels seized power in the two largest cities in the region, Donetsk and Luhansk, hoisted Russian flags and proclaimed independence from Kyiv. In an effort to crush separatist sentiment, the new Kyiv government sent in military units, but they hit against an extremely harsh reaction from Moscow. Putin called it "a punitive operation against its own people",[16] and the Russian army conducted threatening manoeuvres near the border. It became increasingly clear that Moscow was prepared to make every effort to prevent Kyiv from regaining control of Donetsk and Luhansk.

Putin's ambitions were not limited to Crimea and Donbas. He began to promote the idea of Novorossiya ("New Russia"), what he called the Russian lands from Kharkiv to Odesa that Russia supposedly once "gifted" to Ukraine. Putin's stated intent, which Ukrainian politician Hennadiy Moskal described after Euromaidan, to break off the entire eastern part of Ukraine was never an idle threat. According to Moscow's plan, the fire of separatism would engulf all of Ukraine to the east of the Dnipro River. The Kremlin had been commissioning opinion polls since the early 2010s, and the results showed that there was no separatism in Eastern Ukraine or even in Crimea. Their polls showed that Crimean residents didn't see "Ukrainianization" as the main threat; they considered the predominance of "people from Donetsk" as the problem. But the ease with which Crimea was seized convinced Putin otherwise, and

Viktor Medvedchuk, his main confidant in Ukraine, assured him that the eastern regions would rise up against the "Euromaidan rulers."

This was the origin of the Novorossiya project on the territory from Kharkiv to Odesa: a plan to split Ukraine through local power grabs. Over the next few years, Ukrainian hackers would break into the emails between Putin's ideologue, Vladislav Surkov, and one of his aides, and their correspondence proved that the Kremlin was actively directing insubordination of the regional capitals of Eastern Ukraine to the new leaders in Kyiv. Moscow was allocating large sums of money to that end.

At the end of April, Nemtsov flew to Moscow via Kyiv, just in time for a congress organized in part by Khodorkovsky. The congress was supposed to demonstrate the unity of the Russian and Ukrainian intelligentsia and passed a resolution that "Russia and Ukraine have stepped up to the dangerous line of a real war, and the peoples of our countries are plunged into confrontation against their will."[17]

"It's a question of whether or not Ukraine will survive and, if it does survive, in what form? I think the basic priority is to preserve Ukraine," Nemtsov told the congress.[18] He supported Ukraine heart and soul. He understood that Ukraine was heterogeneous and proposed making Russian a second state language, an idea that wasn't greeted enthusiastically in Ukraine, especially then. But Nemtsov stuck to his point: "Ukraine is as much a Russian-language-speaking country as Russia is, and, by joining together its people, Ukraine would find it easier to resist aggression from Moscow."[19] Like ten years ago, he believed that a free and independent Ukraine was the guarantee of freedom in Russia. And this freedom had an enemy—Putin. "Putin needs to dismember Ukraine, Putin needs to recreate an empire, Putin needs to enslave peoples, Putin needs to rule for ever: in fact, that's why he started all this," Nemtsov said.[20]

Nemtsov saw pure demagogy in Putin's ideas and words. He insisted that Putin didn't care about the interests of the Russians in Donetsk. "He can't do anything about the economy, so he needs a war."[21] He saw Putin as a tyrant who exploited the basest instincts of the Russian people, held power through lies and violence and was ready to sacrifice peace with Ukraine and Ukraine itself on the altar of his omnipotence. "This scoundrel, instead of dealing with Russia and solving our Russian problems, has decided to teach you how to live," Nemtsov said indignantly on a TV show on Ukrainian television. "It's infuriating!"[22] After the seizure of Crimea, he sincerely believed that Putin had gone mad with a sense of his own omnipotence and said so directly, even at rallies.

Nemtsov always said what he thought. He never spared words. This was especially true in Kyiv, and the more Nemtsov spoke, the angrier he got. On the sidelines of the congress, when asked by a Ukrainian reporter about the Ukrainian presidential elections scheduled for May and who Putin would vote for, Nemtsov couldn't help himself. "Vladimir Putin would vote for Yanukovych," he said. "He's fucking crazy, is Vladimir Putin, just so you understand."[23]

Nemtsov quickly realized that he had said too much and tried to joke about it: "If you quote me, they'll pull your license," he said. He didn't know that the interview was being broadcast live. However, no one paid much attention to his words then, in April. Life seemed to be returning to normal. As soon as Nemtsov got back to Moscow, he immediately went to Yaroslavl to a meeting of the local parliament. The threatening rumours were not confirmed: new defendants in the Bolotnaya Square case did not appear, Nemtsov was not arrested. Putin was preoccupied with events abroad and didn't have time for domestic repressions.

## "They can put me in jail, but they won't kill me..."

"Aren't you afraid of being killed?"

"No. I'm not a traitor or an enemy. I am an oppositionist, and I protest openly. I don't hide anything."[24]

When Nemtsov returned from Israel, in one of his interviews he was asked a question that his friends had also asked more than once. The answer was the same. They can arrest him, they can put him in jail, they can harass and persecute him all they want, but Putin will not kill him. He, Nemtsov, is an open and honest opponent for Putin, he is a public politician, he is in full view. Moreover, Putin owes him a debt of gratitude and remembers—Nemtsov repeatedly cited this argument in private conversations—how in 1998 he, then deputy prime minister, helped Putin, then newly appointed FSB chief, to strengthen his authority in the security services. At his request, he provided service flats for FSB officers. And Putin even reminded him of this himself when they last saw each other in 2002. No, they won't kill him. "Putin only takes out people who betray him," Nemtsov continued his response. "Since I've never had anything to do with the Chekists or Putin's 'Ozero Cooperative' [a group of friends connected politically and financially], let alone betrayed anyone, he won't kill me. The worst they can do is try to put me in prison."[25]

It would soon become clear that the threat did not necessarily have to come from the Kremlin, the FSB or Putin personally. The annexation of Crimea and especially the escalating war in Donbas heated up Russian society. The so-called Russian Spring mobilized nationalists and imperialists of all stripes and was a magnet for everyone who wanted to swing a sword (just as the White House in Moscow had been the same kind of magnet more than twenty years earlier in the autumn of 1993). Volunteers went to Donbas, and, when they returned, they came out at pro-government rallies under the slogan of a battle against the fifth column. They had already shot people, and no one knew what would come into their heads.

And then there was Ramzan Kadyrov.

In March, when Crimea was annexed, Kadyrov was raring to go into battle: he was ready to leave immediately for Ukraine; he was Putin's warrior, he would fight for him anywhere and against anyone and everyone. At the end of May, information about Chechen mercenaries fighting alongside the rebels in Donbas and dying there was leaked to the press. They are volunteers, Kadyrov shrugged, it's not like he can stop them. "Do you believe it?" Nemtsov, furious, asked on his Facebook page. "A fly doesn't enter Chechnya without Kadyrov's permission. And sending a squad of thugs to Donetsk without Ramzan's knowledge is impossible to imagine."[26] And why were they allowed across the border, armed to the teeth? The answer is obvious: because it is being done centrally, with Putin's knowledge and consent. Nemtsov even sent enquiries to the FSB and the Investigative Committee: why have no criminal cases been opened for illegal border crossing and arms smuggling? "If no cases have been opened, it means that it's Kadyrov's special forces and Chechen Interior Ministry troops," he explained.[27]

In late May, pro-Kremlin activists suddenly pulled out Nemtsov's profanity-laced remark from a month ago about Putin and demanded that he be prosecuted for insulting the president. The first outcry came from an eccentric woman named Rina Naumova-Davis. "I demand action," she wrote on her blog in early June. "Stop letting a cowardly thief and traitor to the motherland remain a deputy! For all his anti-Russian actions and statements, I demand that he be brought to justice!"[28] It was hardly a coincidence that Naumova-Davis and her husband, who also signed the complaint, were from Chechnya. At least in August, when the case of Nemtsov's verbal abuse went to the Moscow Magistrates Court, she wrote that "Nemtsov also repeatedly insulted the head of the Chechen Republic, Ramzan Kadyrov, in his statements."[29] This doesn't necessarily mean that the lawsuit against Nemtsov was instigated by Kadyrov or his entourage, but it does suggest that Kadyrov's entourage began to pay attention to that unfortunate phrase, probably right after Nemtsov had begun to write about Kadyrov's volunteers in Donbas.

However, the criminal case was never brought because the accusation was inconsequential: the tape with Nemtsov's remark was even sent for forensic examination, experts deciphered the supposed swear word as "crazy" and "strange", and the investigators concluded that there was nothing to investigate. By the end of the summer, Nemtsov's lawyer, Vadim Prokhorov, said that the problem had gone away, and he and Nemtsov stopped holding their breath.

## How to stop the war

In summer 2014, the situation on the front changed radically. On 17 July, the world finally realized that war was raging in Ukraine. On that day, a Boeing passenger jet flying from Amsterdam to Kuala Lumpur was shot down over Donbas, killing all 298 people on board. There had been nothing of this scale in a long time. After years of investigation, the court would finally reach its verdict. The airliner was shot down by insurgents using a Buk anti-aircraft system, which had been transferred to Donbas from a specific Russian military unit. The Buk could not have crossed the border without the authorization of the Russian military command. When the rebels got the anti-aircraft gun, they decided to try it out and mistakenly targeted it: they thought they were shooting down a Ukrainian air force aircraft. In November 2022, two Russians, Igor Girkin, the leader of the Donbas separatists at the time, and Sergei Dubinsky, former GRU general, were sentenced *in absentia* by a Dutch court to life in prison.[30]

There was a reason the Russian anti-aircraft system had appeared near Donetsk. In June, with the election of Ukraine's new president—a Maidan-era businessman and politician, Petro Poroshenko—the Ukrainian army had launched a full-scale offensive to the east, taking back city after city, village after village, from the separatists. Russia was increasingly involved in the fighting, sending sabotage teams, volunteers and military equipment across the border. But this was not enough. By early August, the Ukrainians had encircled Luhansk and reached the outskirts of Donetsk. After another two weeks, the war was virtually over: the insurgents were close to defeat. The Ukrainian army only had to block the last asphalt highway connecting Donetsk with the Russian border in the town of Ilovaisk, and Kyiv would regain control of Donbas.

Putin could not allow this to happen. Elite Russian units entered Ukraine. The Ukrainian offensive collapsed when more than two thousand Ukrainian soldiers were surrounded near Ilovaisk. Hundreds of soldiers died and hundreds more were captured. The defeat in Ilovaisk forced Poroshenko to sign the first peace memorandum. And with that it became definitively clear that Donbas was not returning to Kyiv's control, at least not on Ukraine's terms.

Wars are not without casualties. The Pskov newspaper *Pskovskaya guberniya* was the first to report on the deaths of Russian soldiers on Ukrainian territory. It published a report from the funeral of two Pskov paratroopers and soon after learnt that dozens of Russian soldiers had died under artillery fire during the hostilities. The funerals were held in secret, but the paper's publisher, local parliamentary deputy Lev Shlosberg, found out about them. "What war did these young men die in, and for whose sake?" he wrote. "Why is the Russian state silent, and how long does it hope to hide what is utterly impossible to hide?"[31]

Shlosberg said that the families of the victims were under pressure to keep quiet about what had happened. A few days later, Shlosberg was badly beaten and ended up in hospital, and journalists who had come to the cemetery to confirm his words were also attacked by unknown assailants. In Russia, the war with Ukraine continued as a war against the truth about the war.

"I don't want people to die. I don't want Russians to die, I don't want Ukrainians to die," Nemtsov said. "I don't want there to be refugees… I consider Putin's war against Ukraine a crime, a true crime."[32]

State propaganda did not just hide the truth about the losses. On Russian television, the war against Ukraine was a virtual TV sequel to the Second World War, in which the Western-directed reincarnation of the Third Reich—"fascists" and "followers of Bandera"—wanted to conquer the Russian Donbas and from there conquer Russia. At the same time, opinion polls showed that Russian citizens were not ready and did not want to send their children to the front to fight in a real war. So, Nemtsov reasoned, they had to hear the truth. "I believe that a powerful and mass anti-war movement will stop the war," he said.[33] It would stop it as it did in 1996, when he brought Yeltsin a million signatures against the war in Chechnya. The war would end when the people demanded it.

It was then that Nemtsov had the idea of writing a report on the war, putting out a huge print run and distributing it. He was a regional parliamentary deputy like Lev Shlosberg. In a month or two, he would come to his assistant Olga Shorina and, fearing they were being bugged, write her a note: the relatives of the dead soldiers from the Yaroslavl region had contacted him and he had to look into it. This was the start of the work on the report 'Putin: War' that Nemtsov's friends and associates would finish after he was assassinated.

The second obvious step was a massive demonstration. Protesting on the street without permission from the authorities was becoming increasingly dangerous. Over the summer, a new article was added to the criminal code—the third time in six months a misdemeanour for taking part in an unsanctioned rally was changed to a felony. Now, instead of being kept in local detention for ten to fifteen days, a demonstrator could face several years in prison. For Nemtsov, this changed everything.

"We can't lose people. Get everyone you can off the streets," he told his associates.

He got permission for the Peace March, the anti-war march he had planned for 21 September. Here the risk was different—it was political. Protest sentiment had been suppressed by a powerful patriotic wave. How many people would be ready to take to the streets under the slogans "No to War with Ukraine!" and "Putin, Stop Lying and Stop Making War!"? But unexpectedly the Moscow boulevards were filled with people: fifty thousand people showed up for the demonstration. Nemtsov was very happy.

"I am a patriot of my country. I am against the war. I don't want our wives and mothers to cry," Nemtsov said at the march. "Putin is a sick man. He is a mentally ill man. But he is not just a sick man. He is a cynical and mean sick man. He wants to rule us for ever. Until Russia dies. He is heading for dictatorship: concentration camps, political prisoners. Do we need that, tell me?"

"No!" the crowd shouted back.[34]

## Putin for ever

As Russia slipped deeper and deeper into international isolation, it was becoming a different country. The Boeing crash and the invasion of Eastern Ukraine led to a new round of sanctions against state banks, oil and defence companies. Investment was banned in entire sectors of the economy. Western companies began to wind down business in Russia. The Kremlin responded to the sanctions with countersanctions, which made for even greater isolation. The sanctions caused capital flight and cut off access to Western loans for major corporations like Rosneft. At the same time, the price of oil fell. Against this backdrop, the rouble collapsed at the end of the year. The price of oil would rebound, but it didn't change the main issue: the regime was continuing to change not only politically, but also economically. Oil prices could not ensure growth in a closed, state-run, corrupt economic system.

The Western world's attitude towards Vladimir Putin had been changing. The European and US press presented him as the world's leading despot. At the G20 summit in Brisbane, Australia, in November, world leaders gave Putin the cold shoulder, and he sat alone at the dinner table. Domestically, on the other hand, Putin's cult rose to new heights. Vyacheslav Volodin, the curator of domestic policy at the time, put it this way: "There is Putin, and so there is Russia. If there is no Putin, there is no Russia."[35]

After Crimea and Donbas, Nemtsov had no doubt: Putin himself would never give up power. He can't leave his post or he'd have to answer for everything, from Nord-Ost and Beslan to the criminal scams in Gazprom and the war with Ukraine. "Therefore," Nemtsov said, "Putin will cling to power indefinitely."[36] But he still believed in his forty-year marathon theory that he had developed in the early 2000s: the Russian people would walk towards freedom for forty years and would find it around the end of Putin's fourth term. The Crimean consensus would disintegrate as the Russian economy began to pay for the war, for Crimea and Donbas, for the sanctions imposed by the West. The dictatorship would collapse, and, if not in 2018, then in 2024 Putin would have to relinquish power, pressured by the mass disappointment in him and his policies. This was why, Nemtsov reasoned, they had to keep fighting: go out on the streets, stay in politics, get elected to parliament in the upcoming elections and tell the truth about the war. That is why they had to publish a million copies of a report on what was really happening in Ukraine. People's minds were being poisoned by state propaganda, and Nemtsov lobbied intensively to have propagandists, top managers and key mainstream TV channels placed on Western sanctions lists.

In November, Nemtsov made another attempt to unite the democratic opposition. He announced the formation of a coalition called For a European Choice. There is a party of Chinese Choice, he explained, led by Vladimir Putin. It was for isolating Russia from the West and turning it into a resource province of China: "It is the party of war, international isolation, repression, censorship, corruption and theft."[37] And to fight it, all the country's progressive forces, left and right, from liberals to moderate nationalists opposed to war with Ukraine, must unite under the flag of the European choice. "I don't need to be in charge, I'm happy being the moderator," Nemtsov said.[38] He had just turned fifty-five, and at his age he had experience and a reputation, an ability to talk and negotiate and seek compromise. In a documentary film directed by Zosya Rodkevich, which captures the last two years of his life, he says: "Life taught me that. I used to be so uncompromising—I would say that everything and everyone around was wrong. Now it's different."[39] Nemtsov was already clearly aware of his mission in Russian politics. He would let Alexei Navalny, the leader of the opposition, go for the presidency while he, Nemtsov, would build a broad democratic front. There was no one else to do this.

Alas, by then there was almost no one to unite. "Are you all alone, then?" Nemtsov was asked in an interview that dark, difficult autumn.[40] Only a few of those who had taken the stage on Bolotnaya Square three years earlier remained in Russia. Everyone else had left. Navalny was denied the opportunity to protest—when Euromaidan won in Kyiv, he was put under house arrest in Moscow. Party comrades squabbled among themselves. Nemtsov still had his loyalists Ilya Yashin and his assistant Olga Shorina by his side. Five wealthy acquaintances were still helping him with money secretly, so that the Kremlin would not find out. He spent the money on organizing speeches and conferences, party and electoral activities. But the struggle was getting harder every day. In 2013, during the campaign in Yaroslavl, pressure on Nemtsov had not gone beyond petty provocations. In December 2014, Nemtsov and Yashin formed a headquarters for the 2016 Duma elections, and it became clear that the campaign would be fundamentally different. Activists were being detained and even beaten, and when Nemtsov began to organize a rally in Yaroslavl in December, the shed where the campaign newspapers were stored was set on fire with a Molotov cocktail.

On the one hand, over the past three years since Putin had returned to the Kremlin, Nemtsov's life had gone the way he wanted. He was doing well: he had a job he loved—politics—and he had proven to everyone with his victory in Yaroslavl that he was still one of the country's opposition leaders. He acted openly and freely, said what he thought—sometimes laughing when he purposely cursed Putin in telephone conversations. He let the FSB hear it and didn't regret it at all. And he lived his life at his own pleasure: several times a year he went to

Rhodes, Mauritius, Munich or Tel-Aviv. He had affairs and didn't worry about the tabloids because he didn't hide anything.

On the other hand, how much longer could he keep up the fight? In the spring of 2013, Nemtsov arrived in Minsk at the invitation of the local opposition, the first time since 2002 when Lukashenko expelled him from the country. Nothing had changed. He saw the same faces, only much older, the same harassment and arrests, and the same hopeless ennui ahead. Does Russia have the same fate? Is this the future for him and his comrades? "My philosophy is almost Tibetan: I have to outlive it [i.e. the regime]," Nemtsov said in the film by Zosya Rodkevich. But the longer it went on, the harder it became. It became especially difficult when the war in Donbas began. After his return from Israel, Nemtsov's life was tense and unsettling.

Changing circumstances were changing his life. He had already realized that sooner or later he'd have to leave his beloved home, a modest two-room flat in Luzhki, the recreation centre near Moscow where he had moved ten years ago with Irina and newborn daughter Sonya. He was comfortable there: he could go to the gym, a restaurant, and could walk around in shorts and slippers. Luzhki now belonged to Potanin; his relationship with Nemtsov, once amicable, had soured in recent years. Potanin socialized with important Kremlin officials who came to Luzhki, and over time they had less interest in seeing Nemtsov. Sometimes he would hide in his flat, trying not to cross paths with his political enemies.

"We're moving out," Nemtsov told Irina on 27 December 2014, when he received a bill for double the previous rent: the discount he had enjoyed for ten years was no longer valid. Nemtsov did not want to own property. He would say that property makes an oppositionist vulnerable. But back in late 2010, he bought Irina and Sonya a small plot of land in a cottage community near Luzhki, and Irina had been quietly building a house. They moved in and welcomed the new year in their new home.

# CHAPTER 36

### 27 February 2015

## More than the viceroy of Chechnya

"We say to the world: we are Vladimir Putin's combat troops!" Ramzan Kadyrov's voice echoed through the stadium in Grozny where his father had been killed ten years before. "We will find the enemy of Russia in his lair, wherever he may be. Long live our leader, Vladimir Putin! Allahu Akbar!"

"Allahu Akbar!" the packed stadium shouted back.[1] It was a striking and frightening spectacle: twenty thousand combat soldiers with automatic rifles swearing allegiance to Kadyrov and Putin.

A few years later, one of the men of Kadyrov's regiment who fled Chechnya would reveal that the weapons held by the Chechen policemen at the stadium on that day, 28 December 2014, were not loaded. Kadyrov, who always feared attempts on his life and trusted no one but his inner circle, would only permit his guards and one particular police squad to carry loaded weapons.[2] But that did not spoil the picture: Kadyrov was showing the country and the world his personal army, ready to carry out his every order.

The image reflected reality. Over the years, Kadyrov had come into his own. In the past, influential Chechens had been involved in criminal disputes: they intimidated businessmen, used force to extort money from debtors and settled disputes worth millions of dollars. Under Kadyrov, important businessmen sought out the services of Chechen intermediaries. He was like an oligarch, too. He and his entourage copied the lifestyle of Arab sheikhs with palaces, business jets, exotic sports cars and thoroughbred horses. In 2011 the Dubai police withdrew an international search warrant for Adam Delimkhanov, which had been issued in connection with a murder. But by summer 2014, Delimkhanov—still a member of the State Duma and Kadyrov's right-hand man and the second man in Chechnya—was under US sanctions for links to crime bosses Washington called "the Brothers' Circle."[3]

Kadyrov was becoming more than the all-powerful viceroy of Chechnya. During the demonstrations on Bolotnaya Square, there were even rumours floating around Moscow that Kadyrov's guards were stationed in the city just in case Putin needed help to quell the protests. These rumours appeared because Kadyrov's guards were, in fact, spending a great deal of time in Moscow, and the fifth floor of the President Hotel was still the capital's informal residence for the Chechen elite. *Novaya gazeta* wrote that "only privileged members of the Chechen power structures walk the corridors of the VIP hotel on Yakimanka Street. But tactical groups of Chechen law enforcers rotate in and out of Moscow; they work for a few months, and then there's a change of shifts. They usually rent flats on the outskirts of the city, and their task is to carry out particularly sensitive orders—kidnappings, killings and extortion."[4]

In Chechnya, Kadyrov had turned the republic into an outpost of ultraconservative Islam. Russian secular laws were barely enforced due to strict religious censorship. Religious pressure helped Kadyrov to keep Chechnya under control. His guards flew to Syria and Libya, and he was already a powerful player in the Middle East, helping Putin forge contacts with the Persian Gulf monarchies. Human-rights activists regularly reported on violent repressions and extrajudicial killings in Chechnya. A few years later, policemen from Kadyrov's regiment who took part in these operations and then fled abroad would describe how Kadyrov's security forces carried out counter-terrorist operations. "The easiest thing to do was to abduct someone, keep him in the basement until his beard grew in, and then take him to the forest, kill him and call him a [religious] insurgent."[5] In December 2014, when Kadyrov swore he'd expel the families of militants from Chechnya and tear their houses 'down to the foundations', human-rights activist Igor Kalyapin—the same man from Nizhny Novgorod who had gone to Grozny in January 1995 when federal troops stormed the city—sent a query to the Prosecutor General's Office and to the Investigative Committee, asking whether collective responsibility contradicted Russian law. In response, Chechen police officers simply burnt down the Grozny office of the Kalyapin-led Committee against Torture. "In Chechnya, I am in charge of protecting human rights," Ramzan Kadyrov wrote on Instagram.[6] He felt both his power and Putin's support, and the war in Donbas was his finest hour. He showed off his triumph by gathering thousands of fighters at Grozny's stadium on New Year's Eve.

## Je suis Charlie

The French left-wing satirical weekly *Charlie Hebdo* was repeatedly threatened for its caustic cartoons of Islam and the Prophet Muhammad. On 7 January 2015, two terrorists who called themselves followers of al-Qaeda burst into the newspaper's Paris offices with assault rifles. Shouting "Allahu Akbar!" they fired on the staff. For France, the *Charlie Hebdo* shooting was like 9/11 in the US. A wave of solidarity with French journalists surged across the world, and the hashtag *"Je suis Charlie"* (I am Charlie) immediately became one of the most popular tweets in the history of Twitter. On 11 January, two million Parisians took to the streets to honour the victims. Moscow officially condemned the terrorist attack, and Sergei Lavrov even joined the march, which was attended by dozens of world leaders.

Meanwhile, the Russian authorities were championing fundamentalist and anti-European positions and insisting that religious feelings took precedent over freedom of speech. The Paris attack once again put the Kremlin and liberals on opposite sides of the barricades. The journalists were provocateurs who had no one to blame by themselves, pro-Kremlin political analysts argued.

Nemtsov was not on the sidelines of the debate. He stated that there was no justification for terrorist acts, and that journalists cannot be compared to murderers, however scathing their work. "To stop religious terrorism, we must fight for a secular state, that is, for the separation of the mosque from the government," he wrote. "Islam is a young religion, now in the Middle Ages, and ahead there lies a long struggle to defeat the Islamic inquisition."[7]

Kadyrov also made a pronouncement. The Paris attack gave him an opportunity once again to declare emphatically his ambitions as not just the leader of Chechnya, but a leader of world Islam and the guardian of traditional values. All those who supported *Charlie Hebdo* were his personal enemies, Kadyrov said. He made a direct threat against Mikhail Khodorkovsky, who had called upon Russian journalists to reprint the cartoons in protest of terrorism: "I am sure," Kadyrov wrote on his Instagram feed, "that in his beloved Switzerland [where Khodorkovsky was living at the time] there will be thousands of law-abiding citizens who will bring this fugitive criminal to justice."[8] Kadyrov also threatened the editor-in-chief of Ekho Moskvy, Alexei Venediktov, for conducting a poll among its listeners to decide whether or not cartoons of the prophet should be published. But for some reason Kadyrov did not react in any public way to Nemtsov's harsh statement.

Kadyrov assembled a huge rally in defence of his "beloved Prophet Muhammad." Schools, shops and cafés were closed in Grozny, and hundreds of thousands of people were bussed in from all over Chechnya and the neighbouring republics. Kadyrov was demonstrating that he was not only a bulwark of fundamentalism and the struggle against Western values, but also the leader of the entire North Caucasus.

Not long after, towards the end of February, Zhanna and Raisa decided to take a trip to Yaroslavl. Zhanna called her father. "Can we stay at your flat?"

"Let's go together," Nemtsov suggested. "I'll stay there for a day and then I'll have to leave, but you stay as long as you want."[9]

They went together. On the train, Zhanna sensed that something was bothering her father: "My father was apathetic, which was not like him at all. Tired and apathetic. He was tired not physically, but mentally, due to the constant pressure on him."[10]

In Yaroslavl, they went their separate ways. Nemtsov went about his business, and Zhanna and Raisa strolled around the city. Towards evening they met by chance in the city centre. "I don't have time to have dinner with you," Nemtsov told them. "I have to catch my train back and I still have things to do. Let's get together in Moscow!"[11] It was the last time they saw him alive.

In Yaroslavl, Nemtsov stopped in at the local studio of the Ekho Moskvy radio station, which he often did when he was in town. The head of Yaroslavl's Ekho, journalist Lyudmila Shabuyeva, remembered the day well. She was a little late and when she walked into the office, she saw Nemtsov sitting alone, gloomy and in complete darkness. Shabuyeva had never seen Nemtsov like that. She switched on a light.

"What's wrong?" Shabuyeva asked. "Why are you upset?"

"I'm getting death threats," Nemtsov answered.

Shabuyeva dismissed the threat. "What's new? Someone always wants to kill you."

"Not like this," Nemtsov said, and told her he was getting threats by text message.[12]

He was genuinely alarmed. He showed Shabuyeva a text message on his phone: "Jackal, I will kill you." On 16 February, Nemtsov posted another message he'd got on Facebook. It read: "Nemtsov is a national traitor! Shoot the traitor!" Alexei Venediktov would later tell the court that when Nemtsov came to Ekho Moskvy on the evening of 27 February—about four hours before the murder—he complained about the growing stream of threats over *Charlie Hebdo*. "Those were his words: 'Kadyrov and his followers.'" Zaur Dadayev, the assassin who shot Nemtsov on Moskvoretsky Bridge, would also point to *Charlie Hebdo* as the reason for the attack. He said that Nemtsov allegedly "approved of the cartoons and wanted to publish them in the Russian Federation." Kadyrov would also refer to the cartoons, saying that Dadayev, a deeply religious man, was "shocked by the comments in support of printing of the cartoons."[13]

It's clear why Kadyrov brought up *Charlie Hebdo* right after Dadayev and his accomplices were arrested. He was presenting the attack as a religious fanatic's outburst and claiming that the murderer arranged the contract killing himself. But that was not true. By the time the terrorists broke into the *Charlie Hebdo* newsroom in Paris, plans for Nemtsov's assassination had already been underway for several months.

## How Nemtsov and Navalny organized the Spring March

In the last month before his death, Nemtsov was working on two projects that were very important to him. First, he was one of the organizers of the Spring March, which he and Alexei Navalny had begun planning in late January. They had scheduled it for 1 March, in Russia considered the first day of spring. The date fell on a Sunday that year. Calling it the Spring March had symbolic meaning. The long cold winter was over, the sun was shining, and spring would raise everyone's spirits and give them strength of will. Warmth would conquer cold, good would conquer evil—the idea was to hold a positive, optimistic street event—or at least as much as it was possible in the winter of 2015. Nemtsov and Navalny announced the march together.

Perhaps for the first time in recent years, the Spring March combined two agendas, economic and political. The economic agenda was dictated by the crisis: the collapse of oil prices and the rouble that had caused incomes to plummet. "The idea of the march is simple," Navalny explained, "the men in the Kremlin have failed and will continue to fail. They had fifteen years and three trillion dollars from the sale of our natural resources [and failed]."[14]

The political agenda was set by the war in Donbas. For Nemtsov, it was a matter of principle for the anti-crisis march also to be anti-war. At the end of January, the fragile truce in Eastern Ukraine had collapsed. Fighting had started again. The scenario of August 2014 was repeated: the rebels first fought through and occupied Donetsk airport and then, supported by the Russian army, they launched a large-scale offensive. The Ukrainian forces were caught in a trap in the town of Debaltseve, the largest railway junction linking Luhansk with Donetsk.

The death toll was again in the hundreds. Ukraine was losing the war. By early February, when new peace talks began, the fate of Debaltseve had been decided, and with it the fate of Donbas. From that moment on, Moscow insisted that Eastern Ukraine should receive a special constitutional status within Ukraine, allowing it—or, rather, the Kremlin, which controlled Donbas—to block key Ukrainian governmental decisions.

Nemtsov, Navalny and their associates applied for permission to hold the march just after the Minsk Agreements were signed. No one believed they would hold. "Nobody has faith that the ceasefire will last," Nemtsov wrote on Facebook.[15] He believed that Donbas was lost and suggested building a wall between these territories and the rest of the country. On 15 February, he and Navalny split up and went to different metro stations to hand out leaflets about the march. Navalny was quickly detained; he had immediately begun tweeting, which made it easy for the security agencies to spot his location and order the police to detain him. But Nemtsov and his associates posted photos and videos of themselves handing out leaflets only after they had returned home, and no one touched them in the metro stations. "People were surprised that I have an annual metro pass," Nemtsov wrote on Facebook, "and they promised to come on 1 March."[16]

The authorities refused to issue a permit to hold the rally in the centre of Moscow. They suggested Marino instead. Navalny came to see Nemtsov and discuss what they should do. Should they agree or not? Some of the oppositionists were against it, calling it an insulting, unacceptable proposal. Besides, who would trek all the way out to Marino? But Navalny and Nemtsov decided that it was tactically better to agree; the authorities expected them to refuse, so, if they accepted the proposal, the rally would be permitted, and they would have another week and a half to campaign. "They wanted to trap us," Nemtsov said later at a press conference, "to offer us an option that we were certain to refuse, and so we agreed."[17]

"Well, people live there, don't they? In fact, I've lived in Marino for seventeen years, and it's perfectly fine," Navalny wrote on his blog. "We'll hold the anti-crisis march in a heavily populated area. It's going to be a people's march."[18] Nemtsov also saw the political rally in the city outskirts as a cause for optimism. It reminded him of the late 1980s, when huge rallies for democracy in Moscow were held outside the city centre, in Luzhniki Stadium, when Russians suddenly felt what freedom was, when every day there was more and more of it, and in the end the authorities were powerless against it. That would be the start of a new cycle.

That day, 18 February, would be the last time that Nemtsov and Navalny would meet. The next day, Navalny was jailed for fifteen days for handing out leaflets in the metro. He was not even permitted to attend Nemtsov's funeral.

Another, even more important project for Nemtsov was the report on the war in Ukraine that he'd decided to prepare the previous autumn. He had worked on it intensively since the beginning of 2015, spurred on by the fighting in Debaltseve and the zinc coffins that were being shipped home to Russia. Numbers of military casualties were strictly hidden. To avoid the scandals of the previous August, the Russian military command first sent contract servicemen into the reserves and then called them up and sent them to the war zone. Exactly twenty years ago, Nemtsov had flown to Chechnya for the first time, inspired by the powerful movement of soldiers' mothers back home in Nizhny Novgorod, who were willing to do anything to find their missing sons. Now the families of fallen soldiers, bribed and intimidated by the authorities, were often the ones who impeded the investigation into their deaths. Lev Shlosberg had described it, and Nemtsov heard about it, too. It would be written in the report 'Putin: War', which was published after Nemtsov's death. Relatives of the deceased received three million roubles as compensation but had to sign a non-disclosure agreement under threat of criminal prosecution. (The report would be written and published thanks to the efforts of Ilya Yashin, but many of Nemtsov's writings would be taken by the investigators during the search and disappear for ever.)

The report also contained a statistic: at least seventy Russian soldiers had died in the Donbas in January–February 2015. Seventeen of them were paratroopers from the town of Ivanovo, 300 kilometres from Moscow. When he got this information, Nemtsov planned a trip to Ivanovo. The relatives of the dead soldiers were afraid to speak in public, but Nemtsov was confident that, by coming to them, he would convince them to tell him where their sons were buried. We need evidence, he said; that's the only way to expose the authorities.

Nemtsov planned to go to Ivanovo in the next few days. The protest march was scheduled for Sunday. And on Monday, 2 March, he and Olga Shorina were to begin writing the text of the report. "We agreed that he would come to my office and we would start," Shorina recalled. "It was time to begin. We had a stack of papers, printouts. We'd sit down, he'd dictate, I'd take notes and mark what else needed to be found."[19]

## 27 February

By the time Nemtsov got up on the morning of 27 February to meet Anna Duritskaya's flight from Kyiv, the entire team of assassins from Chechnya was already gathered in Moscow.

Beslan Shavanov had been the last to arrive in Moscow the day before. Dadayev and Shavanov served together in the North Battalion stationed in Grozny. The North soldiers frequently travelled to Moscow, provided security for Kadyrov's associates and helped them with business—forcing businessmen to pay their debts.

The men in the group were united by tight bonds of friendship and family. The battalion was commanded by Alibek Delimkhanov, the brother of Adam Delimkhanov. Ruslan Geremeyev was his deputy. Geremeyev also came from a powerful family: Kadyrov had sent his uncle Suleiman Geremeyev to represent Chechnya in the upper house of the Russian parliament. Adam Delimkhanov was also Ruslan Geremeyev's distant uncle. Geremeyev and Zaur Dadayev were friends and prominent members of Kadyrov's Guard, both decorated with the Order of Courage in 2010. But Geremeyev was senior in rank, and of all the persons involved in the Nemtsov murder case he was the closest to Kadyrov and his entourage. At Kadyrov's inaugurations and other celebrations in Grozny he was always in the front row. And, as the telephone billing records would later show, Adam Delimkhanov—or someone using his phone—called him on the day of the murder.[20]

Ruslan Geremeyev was the leader of the group that was staying in two flats in two different buildings on Veyernaya Street in western Moscow: one flat had been bought; the other was rented. As one of the key witnesses, Zarina Isoyeva, the housekeeper who cooked and cleaned both flats, would testify in court, Ruslan Geremeyev was in charge: he hired her, he paid her, in February 2015 he threatened to break her legs if she said anything, and he was feared by the others.[21]

Ruslan Mukhudinov drove Isoyeva to buy groceries. His background was different: he was a former businessman who had lived in Moscow for a long time and rarely visited Chechnya. "His circle of acquaintances was not people from the security services, but the Chechen intelligentsia: teachers, singers and social media specialists," the independent media outlet *Mediazona* wrote in one of its investigations.[22] Financial problems forced him to go to work with Ruslan Geremeyev, and he was also registered as a solider with the North Battalion. Under Geremeyev he was both driver and legal representative. In September 2014, he was tasked with buying and renting the flats on Veyernaya, buying plane tickets for the assassins and taking them to the airport after the assassination. Geremeyev's brother Artur Geremeyev was his second driver, and the flat was registered in his name. In October 2014, they bought a cheap car, and Zaur Dadayev began to trail Nemtsov.

Nemtsov's plan for the evening was to give an interview on Ekho Moskvy and then have dinner with Duritskaya. Preparations for the march were also in full swing: Navalny was in jail, so Nemtsov was making arrangements with Navalny's right-hand man, Leonid Volkov. By 4.00 p.m. in the afternoon, the final versions of the slogans for the march had finally been approved: "Putin Is Crisis" and "Putin Is War." It was agreed that the leaders of the march would carry the tricolour Russian flag.

Nemtsov also needed to resolve a problem with Ekho Moskvy. The radio station had received money for advertising the march but at the last minute had decided not to run the ads. Alexei Venediktov said the managers of Ekho Moskvy at Gazprom had banned them: along with the war came censorship.

Nemtsov spent the day in his flat across the Moscow River on Ordynka Street. Just before 7.00 p.m. he published a call for a march on his blog. He persuaded people to come to Marino. "It is not the place that matters to us, but our demands at the march," Nemtsov wrote, "and I assure you that we will be heard from Marino better than the demands of solitary picketers in central Moscow."[23] He sent Duritskaya to a spa in his car and walked to the radio station. At 8.00 p.m. he was already on air, talking about the march and their demands. A new round of economic crises had been triggered by the war, Nemtsov said, but one of its underlying causes was the inefficiency of the economic model adopted in Russia, which was based on state control and oil exports. It was a deadlock. "There is only one way out of this deadlock—they must go," Nemtsov continued. "There must be new elections."[24]

"Why is the national flag at the head of the march?" host Ksenia Larina asked Nemtsov. "I think this is the first time the opposition is planning to use the national flag as the main flag, isn't it?"

"For me personally, Ksenia, the flag is a symbol of freedom," Nemtsov answered. "I defended the White House in 1991 under the tricolour flag. When we defeated the junta, the real junta—the State Committee for Emergency Rule—this tricolour flag flew over the White House. This flag is very important to me; it's the symbol of freedom. And I don't really understand why our symbol of freedom should be given to those villains."[25]

Indeed, the tricolour, which had replaced the red flag with its hammer and sickle in August 1991, was almost the only reminder that Russia in February 2015 was the same country that it was twenty-five years earlier when the shackles of Soviet power fell, seemingly for ever. The flag seemed to have subtly changed over the years, becoming the requisite background for any event that required the solemnity of statehood. In fact, the flag was fought over: demonstrators with Russian flags were deliberately seized at all unsanctioned street rallies, and Nemtsov was even detained several times when he and others staged processions with the tricolour on 22 August, Russian Flag Day and the anniversary of the victory over the attempted coup of 1991.

Nemtsov finished at 9.00 p.m., went home and then joined Duritskaya for dinner. They agreed to meet at the Bosco Café in GUM overlooking Red Square because Duritskaya had planned to go shopping beforehand. As she recalled later, Nemtsov joked that it was risky to have dinner before the march right in front of the Kremlin.

Outside GUM, Nemtsov was followed by Beslan Shavanov and Anzor Gubashev, another accomplice to the assassination, who worked as a security guard in a Moscow shop. Anzor Gubashev and his younger brother Shadid had moved to the Moscow suburbs many years earlier; they were Dadayev's second cousins and came from the same village.

Shadid had also been following Nemtsov since October, sometimes spending the night in a flat on Veyernaya Street. On 26 February, he met Shavanov, who had flown in from Grozny, at the airport.

When Shavanov and Gubashev followed Nemtsov that evening, Dadayev was somewhere nearby. Although Gubashev's and Dadayev's confused testimonies during interrogation after their arrest were not credible with regard to the organization of the attempt, motives and accomplices, they seem to have described the immediate murder scene correctly. Later both confirmed their words during a reconstruction at the crime scene. Anzor Gubashev said that at about 10.00 p.m. he was watching Nemtsov's house on Ordynka and was about to leave when he saw Nemtsov drive off in a car. He and Shavanov followed, saw Nemtsov get out of the car and go into GUM. Shavanov lost Nemtsov but then saw him with Duritskaya in the window—they were sitting at a table with a view of Red Square—and went back to the car.

"We had dinner," Duritskaya later recounted. "And since I'm lazy, I suggested we go home in the car with the driver who was waiting for us by GUM. But Boris was always trying to stay in shape. And he often liked to walk after a late-night dinner. I rarely argued with him. So we walked."[26]

They left the café and walked towards the Bolshoi Moskvoretsky Bridge off Red Square, which led to Ordynka on the other side of the river. The walk home would take fifteen to twenty minutes.

After about half an hour, as the killers were walking back to GUM they literally ran into Nemtsov and Duritskaya by Lobnoye Mesto, an ancient, raised podium on Red Square where the tsar's decrees were once read. Realizing that they were not catching a taxi but going home on foot, the killers decided to act. Gubashev and Shavanov got into the car. Gubashev took the wheel, Shavanov got in the back seat, while Dadayev reached under the seat and pulled out a pistol with a silencer and one of the telephones used in the preparation for the murder. They followed Nemtsov and Duritskaya. The Bolshoi Moskvoretsky Bridge was empty. Then Dadayev called Shavanov and said they shouldn't trail him home; they should kill him right there on the bridge. Gubashev and Shavanov caught up with him in their car and drove slightly behind him. It was 11.31 p.m. Dadayev approached Nemtsov before he reached the middle of the bridge and shot him three times in the back from a distance of about five metres. Nemtsov fell but tried to get up. He was still alive. Dadayev fired three more times. Of those six bullets, four reached their target: the first hit Nemtsov in the neck and ricocheted into his head, the second hit a lung, breaking two ribs, the third hit his heart and the fourth hit his liver and stomach.

When you see someone killed right in front of you, the brain instinctively refuses to believe it. As Duritskaya later recalled, she first thought it was some kind of cruel joke: firecrackers exploding under her feet, Nemtsov simply wounded in the leg. She asked him what to do, but he could no longer speak. Not a minute or two passed before Nemtsov stopped breathing. A snow plough drove past. "What's the number for an ambulance?" Duritskaya managed to ask the driver and then called. The ambulance and police arrived on the bridge very quickly.

Ilya Yashin was one of the first to arrive on the scene; at midnight he was already on the bridge. Next was Nemtsov's loyal assistant Olga Shorina. Police officers and doctors were swirling around Nemtsov. He was still lying face up on the pavement with his eyes open. When Zhanna and Raisa arrived, there were already many people on the bridge. There was weeping, journalists clicking their cameras, and the police cordoning off the pedestrian part of the bridge. Flowers were already lying at the murder scene. "We were in a strange state that cannot be described in words," Zhanna later recalled, "because there simply aren't words for it."[27]

## Heroes don't die

There are tragedies that are imprinted in the memory so that you always remember the moment and circumstances when you heard about it. Everyone's list is different, but Nemtsov's death is on many of those lists in Russia. The news of his death struck people to the heart, as if they'd lost someone close to them. On the night of 28 February, some wept at home, others went to the Bolshoi Moskvoretsky Bridge, others drank vodka. Grief took different forms, but it was widespread and shared. The realization of the scale of the loss was instantaneous and yet unexpected: Nemtsov had a reputation as an honest and reckless politician, but before his death no one would have thought of him as a hero or symbol. Nemtsov's life was always on display: rallies and struggles with Putin, public appearances and arrests, wives and children, affairs and kitesurfing. But it suddenly became clear that his lifestyle was inseparable from his identity as a politician. "He was too free a man," said Oleg Sysuyev.[28] Nemtsov and freedom, Nemtsov and the struggle for freedom became synonymous once he was gone. "My father would have been very surprised if he had found out that for a certain group of people he had become an unquestionable moral authority," Zhanna Nemtsova later said. "He certainly didn't dream of it. He wasn't a righteous man, to put it bluntly. He always said so. Nevertheless, thanks to his destiny, he became one."[29]

On Sunday, 1 March, the Spring March turned into a march of remembrance, and this time the authorities were quick to agree on a route. Tens of thousands of people marched through the city centre and across the Bolshoi Moskvoretsky Bridge. Hundreds of tricolours flew over the crowd, as if Nemtsov had a hand in organizing this rally, too. "Heroes don't die. These bullets hit each of us," read the text on the huge banner at the head of the march. A letter was added to the end of Nemtsov's first name, Boris, making another word—the command "Fight." That would for ever change the word's meaning. From now on, it would be both a political slogan and a tribute to Nemtsov.

Zhanna, Raisa and Nemtsov's mother walked in the march with everyone else. His mother walked the entire route. In two days, she would be eighty-seven years old. She buried her son on her birthday. On 3 March, the ceremony to pay respects went on for hours at the Sakharov Centre: Moscow had not seen such a long queue before a coffin since April 2007 when Yeltsin was buried.

A mountain of flowers appeared on the Bolshoi Moskvoretsky Bridge, which was given a second name: Nemtsov Bridge. People continued to bring flowers, portraits and candles, and a spontaneous memorial was formed on the bridge. The fight against the memorial began in a few days. First it was destroyed by pro-Kremlin troublemakers and then by the city's municipal services. After that, supporters had the idea of making a national memorial that would be guarded from vandals by volunteer activists around the clock, seven days a week. Volunteers were regularly attacked and arrested, but others immediately took their places. The memorial was cleared hundreds of times, and each time it was rebuilt.

## Political solution

After killing Nemtsov, Dadayev, Shavanov and Gubashev split up. Dadayev got in the car, rode a few hundred metres and then got out. Gubashev and Shavanov quickly abandoned the car in an alley in the city centre. All three then met again and went to 46 Veyernaya Street, where Ruslan Geremeyev was waiting for them. The younger Gubashev would later tell investigators that Dadayev asked him to go to Veyernaya, where the three killers told him that they had shot "that American scum and bitch Nemtsov" (he would also say that Dadayev had been smoking hashish).[30]

The next day Mukhudinov drove Gubashev and Shavanov to the airport, and they flew to Grozny. In the evening Artur Geremeyev left for Chechnya by car, and on 1 March Dadayev and Ruslan Geremeyev also left. Mukhudinov brought them to Vnukovo, checked them in and put them on a flight. The police database of information on everyone travelling through Russia would later show that they sat next to each other on the plane. On the night of 3 March, the younger Gubashev left for Chechnya by car. Mukhudinov flew out of Moscow on the afternoon of 3 March. Apparently, his task was to clean up all the loose ends: hand over the keys to the rented flat, get the rest of the accomplices out of Moscow, and so on.

Nemtsov's murder was solved faster than any other political murder ever committed in Russia before. Intelligence—primarily phone calls in the murder area—quickly led the FSB first to Veyernaya Street and then to the President Hotel, where the same phone numbers had been noted several times before. On 1 March, operatives found the car abandoned in central Moscow. The next day, the head of the FSB, Alexander Bortnikov, was already in Putin's office with a report. "The gist of the report," *Novaya gazeta* later wrote, "was that the perpetrators were a group of Chechen law-enforcement officers from the Interior Ministry's North Battalion, presumably under the leadership of Deputy Battalion Commander Ruslan Geremeyev."[31]

An FSB special forces unit flew to neighbouring Ingushetia. On 5 March, Dadayev was arrested by the Ingush Drug Control Service near Nazran, Ingushetia, but for a completely different reason: he was buying drugs. The arrest of a prominent soldier in the North Battalion without Kadyrov's authorization, especially in neighbouring Ingushetia, was a slap in the face to Chechnya. Chechnya immediately began to work on getting Dadayev released, but before they succeeded, federal special forces arrived in the police station, snatched him up and took him to Moscow. The Gubashev brothers were also arrested in Ingushetia: they had been in Chechnya, but, *Novaya gazeta* wrote, after learning about the arrest of Dadayev they went to his home, and there they were arrested.[32]

Shavanov was to be arrested in Grozny. While the special forces were preparing to storm the flat where he was hiding, one of the high-ranking Chechen security officers came in and shot him dead. In court, Anzor Gubashev would say the investigator had told him that's what had happened. Officially, Shavanov blew himself up with a grenade. At first, the investigation was led by Igor Krasnov, an experienced professional called Wolfhound in the law enforcement system for his tenacity: once he got his teeth into someone, he would not let go. Although he was still young, he was already famous for investigating the high-profile political murders committed by the nationalist group BORN in the late 2000s. It was he who led the first interrogations of both Dadayev and Anzor Shavanov, and he who got both men to confess.

"I don't understand one thing," Dadayev's sister said in mid-March. "He flew to Moscow with his commander and came back with his commander. Why is no one talking about the commander now?"[33] This question should have been addressed first and foremost to Dadayev himself. At the interrogation with Krasnov, he pointedly refused a lawyer and took the blame on himself. He didn't mention Geremeyev and said he did it because of *Charlie Hebdo*, apparently because he expected to go home to Chechnya soon and be free. He had good reason to think so. The Chechen authorities would transfer people who were important to them to serve their sentences in the republic. But often they did not serve out their sentences at all. In 2013, there was a major scandal when one of the photos on Ramzan Kadyrov's Instagram showed him with a Chechen who was supposed to be in prison for a murder he'd committed three years earlier in Moscow.

Krasnov, to his credit, did not release Dadayev and Shavanov on their own recognizance or put them under house arrest. And he took measures to locate Ruslan Geremeyev. The first attempt to arrest Geremeyev and Mukhudinov was made on 7 March in a village in northern Chechnya, near the Dagestan border where their houses were located. Neither man was found. A few days later, Geremeyev was already at Adam Delimkhanov's palace in his native village of Dzhalka in the northern part of Chechnya. But, as *Novaya gazeta* wrote, Delimkhanov, Senator Suleiman Geremeyev and Ramzan Kadyrov were there, and the village was cordoned off by members of the North Battalion.[34]

A messenger from Moscow was sent to Dzhalka—Viktor Zolotov, the commander of the Internal Forces who had been a security guard for Sobchak and a close associate of Putin's when he worked in St Petersburg. At that time Zolotov was considered an intermediary between the St Petersburg city hall and the criminal world, and then, many years later, between Putin and Kadyrov. Zolotov brought the news that the FSB and investigators were after Ruslan Geremeyev. This was apparently perceived as instructions to hide Geremeyev. By the end of March, he was no longer in Chechnya. According to *Novaya gazeta* he may have gone to Dubai as a groom for Kadyrov's horses under an assumed identity. Mukhudinov disappeared, too—he just vanished into thin air.

At the beginning of the investigation, the FSB and the investigators understood that the reason for the surveillance and the murder was the obscene word that Nemtsov uttered against Putin on 26 April in Kyiv. Ramzan Kadyrov undoubtedly had his own score to settle with Nemtsov, but the point of a demonstrative assassination of Putin's most famous and most unrelenting political opponent was to present Putin—the suzerain, the supreme ruler—with the head of his enemy as a sign of loyalty and obeisance. The day after the assassination, Putin sent a telegram to Nemtsov's mother. "Everything will be done," he wrote, "to give the organizers and perpetrators of the cowardly and cynical murder the punishment they deserve." A few days later, he spoke at a meeting of the Interior Ministry, saying that high-profile crimes with political overtones should be thoroughly investigated: "We must finally rid Russia of shame and tragedies like the one we recently experienced and saw," Putin continued, "I mean the audacious murder of Boris Nemtsov right in the centre of the capital."[35]

And then Putin disappeared for a fortnight. Some newspapers reported that he was furious about what had happened. Others noted that he did not even show up to events in which his participation had been announced. "I believe he gave *carte blanche* to the special services to investigate this murder, and then he was told that the thread led to the Chechen president, and this may have affected him very strongly," political strategist Stanislav Belkovsky speculated at the time. If that was the case, Putin did, indeed, have a lot to think about. To refuse the odious present handed to him would mean that he would have to change the government in Chechnya and the order established there. To accept it would mean to humiliate his own special services, and to share responsibility for one of the worst political murders in Russian history.

Soon everything became clearer. In April, lawyers for Zhanna Nemtsova, considered by the court to be an injured party, began to notice that the investigators were becoming increasingly reluctant to deal with them. On 16 April, speaking in a television talk with the public, Putin commented for the first time on the progress of the investigation. He said that there might not be someone who ordered the murder, and, if there was, he might not be found. This meant that he had made his decision: the investigation into Nemtsov's murder would be focused on the perpetrators, putting Kadyrov and his inner circle out of harm's way.

In late April, Krasnov was replaced by another investigator. "This is dismissal by promotion," Prokhorov said. A special department for particularly important cases was set up specifically for Krasnov in the Investigative Committee.[36] He headed the investigation team into Nemtsov's murder for just two months in all.

In autumn 2016, five natives of Chechnya were put on trial: Dadayev, the Gubashev brothers, former policeman and bodyguard Temirlan Eskerkhanov and engineer Hamzat Bakhayev, who lived with the Gubashev brothers outside Moscow. Eskerkhanov and Bakhayev were accused of aiding and abetting: they collected information about Nemtsov and drove the killers. But no biological traces of Bakhayev were found in the flats on Veyernaya, and the Nemtsov family considered his guilt unproven. Nikolai Tutevich replaced Krasnov as the new head of the investigation team attempted to bring charges against

Ruslan Geremeyev *in absentia* and put him on the wanted list, but twice the authorities stopped him with the pretext that there were not sufficient grounds. Tutevich was not surprised. He already had experience investigating murders that led to Kadyrov, and he knew the rules of the game. After all, he investigated the notorious assassination of Ruslan Yamadayev in central Moscow in September 2008. In that case, the perpetrators were jailed, but the people who ordered the murder were never found.

Ruslan Geremeyev remained a witness, but he was never questioned. In the course of the trial, the lawyer Prokhorov asked one of the investigators why this was. The investigator said he went to see Geremeyev in Chechnya to bring him in for interrogation, but no one answered the door. The lawyers' attempts to summon Zolotov, to whom the North Battalion formally reported, Adam Delimkhanov, Suleiman Geremeyev (in addition to telephone billing records, an electronic key to his room at the President Hotel[37] was found in a flat on Veyernaya Street) and Kadyrov himself came to nothing, as might be expected. "We have not been able to convince the investigation team to question Kadyrov in these [six years since the murder]," Zhanna Nemtsova said. She has no doubt that Kadyrov knew about the preparations for her father's murder. "I don't think that special operations like that can be conducted without him, especially if they involve Chechen residents, and most especially those who serve in the North Battalion. And besides, things like this are simply impossible without Kadyrov. I think his role is much broader."[38]

Ruslan Mukhudinov was put on the wanted list. Investigators and later the Moscow District Military Court would eventually name him as both the organizer and the person who ordered Nemtsov's murder. He is alleged to have hired all five defendants to kill Nemtsov for fifteen million roubles, although it is believed he wasn't acting alone but together with some unidentified accomplices. However, in order to find them, Mukhudinov had to be found, and he had disappeared. But why would Ruslan Geremeyev's driver and assistant kill Nemtsov? What was his motive? Vadim Prokhorov explained the court's position: "The court answered, 'This is a separate case. Wait until we find Mukhudinov or someone among the other suspects, and then we'll ask them.'"[39]

Apparently Mukhudinov's case was separated into another criminal proceeding for this purpose.

The five people arrested in the Nemtsov murder case in summer 2017 were sentenced to long prison terms. Zaur Dadayev received the harshest sentence: twenty years in prison. Another three years later, in November 2020, *Mediazona* uncovered other possible accomplices to Nemtsov's murder who were not put on trial. They include another policeman from Chechnya and Adam Delimkhanov's personal assistant. Mukhudinov was never found, and the people who ordered Nemtsov's murder have gone unpunished.

"It's very dangerous to say, 'I plan to live a long life.' That was my father's phrase," Zhanna said. "But I'd like to live to see the day."[40]

# EPILOGUE

## Five Years Later: 2020

### Putin bets on Zelensky

No matter how relentlessly Putin fought Ukraine, he always lost. In 2004, he had to accept that Viktor Yushchenko was president. In 2014, he first lost Euromaidan and then was unable to break off Eastern Ukraine. But Putin's obsession with Ukraine did not dissipate over the years; it just grew stronger. He would not stop. Nemtsov was still alive when Putin decided he had finally got his way.

"To all intents and purposes, the official authorities in Kyiv have agreed to carry out deep-going constitutional reforms in order to satisfy well-known requests for independence—whatever it's called: decentralization, autonomization, federalization—of certain regions of their country," he triumphantly told journalists on 17 February 2015 to explain the meaning of the Minsk Agreements that Ukraine had just signed.[1] This was ten days before the shots were fired on the Moskvoretsky Bridge. The Minsk Agreements were meant to turn Ukraine into a confederation. The Donbas territories, which were occupied by Russia at that time, would formally return to Ukraine, but at the same time would be granted full independence from Kyiv. They would have their own army and police, an open border with Russia, the right to conduct independent trade with Russia, and the right to block Kyiv's key decisions in international relations. This would paralyse Ukraine as a state.

After the Ukrainian defeat in Debaltseve, Poroshenko had no choice. Ukraine was unable to stand up to Russia on the battlefield, and Western leaders had declined to provide Kyiv with military aid. Poroshenko had signed the Minsk Agreements at gunpoint. Even if Putin didn't send his military to storm Kyiv, the risk of losing all of Donbas and other territories in the east was too great.

Seven years later, when the war was already underway, Angela Merkel would explain that she had pushed Ukraine to negotiate the Minsk Agreements so that the country had time to build up its military. But she certainly wasn't planning for the long haul. At that point, both Western leaders and Poroshenko wanted to stop the war as soon as possible. In fact, Poroshenko was even trying to fulfil the Minsk Agreements. He was looking for language that suggested some kind of compromise in that murky, loophole-filled text. Putin watched as the West caved in to his ambitions and believed that this time Ukraine would not slip through his fingers.

But he was wrong again. In August 2015, the first vote on the law granting special status to Donbas led to violence outside the Rada—a grenade thrown by protesters killed four National Guard officers protecting the building and injured dozens of others—and then to a fight inside the hall of the Rada. The ruling coalition was on the verge of a split.

At this point, Poroshenko realized that the implementation of the Minsk Agreements would most likely lead to a grave political crisis.

The bill never made it to the second reading. The Minsk Agreements were unenforceable. Diplomats on both sides spent several more years looking for sections of the text and interpretations that let them act as they wished. Which should be done first—conduct elections in the occupied territories and then give Ukraine control over the border? Or the other way around? And so on. But the main contradiction was impossible to overcome: either Ukraine was a sovereign state or it wasn't—and there wasn't a third option. Kyiv continued to discuss options with Moscow, but Putin was getting tired of waiting: Poroshenko was just stalling. Ukraine rejected the idea of peace at any price. Public opinion polls showed that the majority of Ukrainians considered peace on the basis of the Minsk Agreements to be a betrayal of national interests.

In 2019, Poroshenko had already gone into the presidential elections as the mouthpiece for the hopes and aspirations of the patriotic camp and the candidate who would build up the national army. His election campaign had been focused on fighting the Russian threat. The Kremlin wanted his rival, Volodymyr Zelensky, to win, figuring that if they couldn't pressure Poroshenko, they could Zelensky. Zelensky, the young showman, actor and stand-up comedian who had created the most successful satirical show in Ukraine, appeared in Ukrainian politics out of the blue. Many Ukrainians didn't vote for him but for his screen image in the popular TV series *Servant of the People*, which had been airing for three years by then. In the show, Zelensky played an honest history schoolteacher who won the election by a considerable margin.

Ukrainians were tired of living in an in-between state of neither war nor peace, tired of the endless hassling over the Minsk Agreements. Born in Kryvyi Rih in Eastern Ukraine, Zelensky went to the polls with the slogan of peace with Russia. He sincerely wanted to negotiate peace with Putin, but he had neither the political experience nor a plan. Ukrainian journalist Vitaly Portnikov wrote that Zelensky "had the naïve hope that if he met with Vladimir Putin, he would explain everything to him and the war would end."[2]

In Moscow, they thought Zelensky would be a pushover. Not long before, he had been entertaining the Moscow public on the New Year's television show—how could he possibly withstand Putin's pressure? Putin lured the inexperienced Zelensky into a trap. He met him halfway on the issue of prisoner exchanges and gave the illusion that a deal was possible.

After the only face-to-face meeting between Putin and Zelensky, in Paris in December 2019, the press called it a draw: Zelensky did not lose, but Putin did not win. This was the breaking point. Zelensky finally saw Putin for who he was without any illusions. At the press conference, Zelensky clearly stated that Donbas and Crimea were part of Ukraine, and that he would not amend the constitution with special rights for the occupied part of Donbas. Putin's response was also clear. He said that the key issue was to "enshrine in the [Ukrainian] constitution the special status of Donbas on a permanent basis."[3] They were in a deadlock.

No one knows when Putin decided that he would send tanks to Kyiv. What is known is that the Kremlin had considered it before the war in Donbas. In 2015, some of Putin's generals and advisers lamented that he had stopped instead of going all the way. In Paris, Putin realized that Zelensky was not ready to hand him the keys to Ukraine. And then, three months later, in March 2020, there was another scandal over the Minsk Agreements. Dmitry Kozak, the deputy head of Putin's administration and Moscow's negotiator, and Andriy Yermak, the head of the Ukrainian president's office and Ukraine's negotiator, agreed to create a kind of advisory council, which, the Ukrainian press found out, was to include representatives of the occupied territories of Donbas. The news was a bombshell in Kyiv. Zelensky was accused of betrayal, and the Ukrainian security service even opened a criminal case against Yermak. The Minsk Agreements were finally buried once and for all. It's likely that this is when Putin began to think seriously about war.

Any military operation requires preparation—political, organizational and financial. But in spring 2020, Putin had no time for that. He was occupied with another matter that was of utmost importance to him. There was still one obstacle to having infinite power in Russia: the constitution. The Yeltsin constitution still in force prohibited him from seeking another presidential term. The constitution had to be changed.

## Russia turns towards tyranny

Many years later, no one could say for sure why the word "consecutive" appeared in the article of the constitution limiting presidential powers to two terms, which allowed Vladimir Putin to run for a third term in 2012 after a break. Yeltsin's opponents later insisted that in 1993, when the future constitution was being discussed, Yeltsin's team had very consciously included unlimited presidential terms. In fact, they accused the team of steamrolling it in. This is unlikely. In 1993, it would not have occurred to anyone to plan Yeltsin's return to the Kremlin in 2004. Some historians are inclined to believe that the situation was the opposite. The word "consecutive" was written by Yeltsin's aides in order to guarantee the transition of power: not only is the president's power limited to two terms, but the terms must also be consecutive. If Yeltsin leaves, he cannot return. At the time this was a symbolic concession to the opposition in the Yeltsin camp: in practice, it did not change anything.

When Putin returned to the Kremlin in 2012, he interpreted the word "consecutive" literally: no one could serve more than two terms consecutively, but it would be possible to serve more than two terms non-consecutively. The first time around, Putin solved this problem by handing the presidency to Dmitry Medvedev. But what would he do in 2024, when his third and fourth terms would end? Would he change places with someone else again?

It was common knowledge that Putin had been quite nervous the first time he and Medvedev traded places; he was not going to try the experiment a second time. His only choice was to change the constitution.

People who personally knew Putin well warned that he had no intention of sharing even a fraction of his power with anyone and would simply strike the two-term limit from the constitution. They thought he might use the pretext that this rule infringed on citizens' rights. Why shouldn't the people be able to keep the president if they wanted him to continue to rule? But no one believed he would do this; it would be an explicit step towards dictatorship. Journalists and political analysts expected Putin to take a different path—inventing a new position for himself and running the country in a new capacity.

As far back as April 2019, Vyacheslav Volodin, who was then speaker of the State Duma, suddenly began suggesting that the parliament should be more actively involved in forming the government, hinting that the constitution ought to be amended. He did this so that Putin could cite it later. Indeed, the question suddenly came up out of nowhere at his annual press conference in December 2019 a few days after his meeting with Zelensky in Paris. Putin answered, "I know that there are discussions about this. Aren't changes to the constitution overdue? Could the powers of parliament, government and president be redistributed?"

Yes, it is possible, he continued, "after comprehensive preliminary work and a serious discussion in society—and even then it must be done with great responsibility." Since it was being discussed, he suggested striking out the word "consecutive" from the provision on two presidential terms, saying that it "confuses some of our political analysts and public figures."⁴ Clearly a special operation was underway. But what exactly was he up to?

There was still no answer to this question even after the New Year holidays, when in his annual address to the Duma Putin announced a sweeping constitutional reform. Some amendments, such as giving the president the right to dismiss judges of the Constitutional and Supreme Courts, sounded the death knell for the independent judiciary. Other amendments would diminish the rights of the government, such as giving the president the right to dismiss the prime minister without having to dismiss the entire cabinet. (Putin had already burnt himself on this constitutional provision in 2004 when he fired Mikhail Kasyanov, and he was making sure this wouldn't catch him up in the future.) The third amendment moved the "independent" (on paper) municipal power to the vertical of federal power. Soon there was an amendment to subordinate the Prosecutor General's Office to the Kremlin completely by taking away the Federation Council's responsibility to approve the appointment and dismissal of the person in that position (as if the shadow of Prosecutor General Yury Skuratov—whose dismissal in 1999 Vladimir Putin had to deal with personally while still serving as head of the FSB—was still hovering over Russia). At the same time, there was a proposal to give the Duma the right to participate in the appointment of ministers, as Volodin had requested. But given a parliament that was absolutely loyal to Putin—and that was, to all intents and purposes, appointed, not elected—this amendment would have no effect.

However, all these amendments did not clarify how exactly the main issue—the extension of Putin's power—would be resolved. In fact, on the contrary, they only muddied the water. Putin also proposed to enshrine the status of the State Council in the constitution. In the early aughts, the Kremlin had removed governors from the Federation Council and moved them to this advisory body. Observers thought they'd found what Putin was up to. He seemed to have decided to make the State Council the superstructure over the system of power. After he left the presidency in 2024, he'd control everything from the council as either a monarch or a new version of the Soviet-era General Secretary—as "the father of the nation." But then why did the other amendments strengthen the role of the president in the system of power? And what levers of power would the future State Council—or rather, the one who would head it—use to control affairs in the country? There were no answers to these questions.

Meanwhile, in order to show that the entire society was involved in the process, the Kremlin formed a working group of famous athletes, artists, military men, doctors and teachers to finalize the constitution. In this way amendments appeared to be proposed by the people: to prohibit gay marriage, to honour the memory of the nation's ancestors, to prohibit expropriation of Russia's territories, to declare the Russian language essential to state development, and so on. There was also the obviously popular amendment on mandatory indexation of pensions.

The vector of all these changes was obvious. Vladimir Putin was bringing the constitution in line with reality—and hammering the final nail into the coffin of Yeltsin's legacy. Russia was now officially, on paper, ceasing to be the democracy that Yeltsin's Russia had once long ago dreamt of becoming. Thirty years before, it had seemed that the democratic revolution had ushered in the ideas of freedom, individual rights and the responsibility of the government to society. These amendments to the constitution eliminated those ideas. "I am really frightened. We are clearly on our way to an anti-democratic, repressive-suppressive order," historian Yury Pivovarov wrote in his assessment of the proposed amendments. "Once again, it is not the individual, the citizen who is the measure of things, but 'national groups', 'historical truth', etc. Once again, we are returning to the times of an 'official national identity' that has been 'enriched' by the terrible experience of the twentieth century."[5]

By the beginning of March, there were already more than two hundred amendments, but the main question remained unanswered: what's next? How does Putin stay in power? He waved off suggestions to abolish term limits altogether, saying that, no, the country needs the transition of power. But, he continued, it would be needed later, in the future. "Now, perhaps, stability and the orderly development of the country are more important."[6]

He wasn't going anywhere, but how would his presence be justified? None of the scenarios discussed—an heir as in Kazakhstan, an ayatollah as in Iran, a party politburo as in China before Xi Jinping—were realistic. The amendments to the constitution had already passed their first reading in the Duma, and the date of the national vote had already been set for 22 April. The law did not require the vote: the amendments would have been considered adopted after approval in the Duma, regional parliaments and the Federation Council. But Putin insisted on a popular vote because it was important for him to include the people as co-authors of the constitutional reform, as if it were not his personal arbitrary decision but the desire of the society as a whole. And yet, there was still no answer to the main question.

It all became clear on 10 March, during the second reading of the amendments. According to the rules of parliament, amendments should be prepared in advance, but they could also be introduced and put to a vote right in the hall. That's what they did. The Kremlin entrusted the key amendment to deputy Valentina Tereshkova, the first woman cosmonaut who had been tasked with delivering speeches at the Communist Party congresses back in the days of Brezhnev. "Why are we bending over backwards or trying to come up with artificial constructs?"[7] Tereshkova asked the deputies. The incumbent president should simply be allowed to run again. An hour later, Putin explained from the same parliamentary rostrum that it was not necessary to abolish the limit of two presidential terms altogether, but since Russia would have a new constitution, they could start counting his terms anew. If the Constitutional Court didn't object, he wasn't against it either.

And so, in the end Putin chose the easiest path—zeroing out his presidential terms—and his move to include the State Council in the constitution and the other amendments had just been a cover operation. His new terms as president would end in 2036, when, at the age of eighty-eight, he would have served out his two (and this time final) terms in office.

The date didn't matter. Putin was staying for ever. He was committing a constitutional coup, going the way of Alexander Lukashenko, who had changed the Belarusian constitution in 1996 and nullified his presidency on that basis. That meant that the political regime in Russia was changing, though not as rapidly as it had been in Belarus twenty-five years earlier. But it was also transitioning from a sovereign democracy into fully fledged tyranny.

Putin was in a hurry. He was conducting the most important special operation of his entire rule, and it had to happen quickly so that no one would have time to think about it. On 10 March, Tereshkova introduced her amendment, and a month and a half later, on 22 April, the vote would take place.

But life got in the way. The world was hit by the Coronavirus epidemic. By the beginning of March, the virus had spread around the world, and the numbers of people who were ill—and the number of dead—were skyrocketing in America and Europe. Countries closed borders, flights were cancelled, sports events and conferences were called off, and museums and movie theatres were closed. On 9 March, Italy went into lockdown; on 11 March, the World Health Organization officially declared it a pandemic.

The first cases were registered in Moscow on 2 March and in St Petersburg on 5 March. By the middle of the month, the government realized that Russia was facing an epidemic, but Putin initially hoped that the referendum would take place as he had arranged at the end of April. On 25 March, he was forced to concede the inevitable and move the vote to July. At the same time, Putin abruptly changed his mode of communication with the outside world. He went into self-isolation, a state that he is still in today. From that moment on, he would surround himself exclusively with loyal aides and servants, and anyone who had to be in his presence would have to endure two weeks of quarantine. Putin postponed the vote on the amendments, but he didn't want to get involved with the fight against Covid; on the contrary, he distanced himself from the epidemic. The state completely failed in its measures to control the epidemic. If quarantine helped, it didn't help enough. The propaganda to discredit Western vaccines ultimately ended up discrediting vaccination in general: Putin never showed himself being vaccinated, and, as a result of all this, people didn't trust the government or doctors and refused to be vaccinated. Local authorities falsified statistics. The Coronavirus epidemic in Russia turned into a real catastrophe: from April 2020 to December 2021, excess deaths in the country would exceed one million people.

The epidemic would last almost two years, but Putin couldn't wait that long. The most important act was still not accomplished:

extending his power. He was not ready to take another time-out. The referendum on the amendments was rescheduled for the week of 25 June–1 July 2020. It was clear that the epidemic would not subside by that time, but that didn't bother Putin; he was already resentful for lost time. More than a week before the vote, he announced that Russia was "coming out of the coronavirus pandemic confidently and with minimal losses."[8]

There were two problems with the amendments, however. The first was that the most important amendment—to zero out presidential terms for Putin—did not enjoy enthusiastic public support. Polls showed that public opinion was split in two. That's roughly how people answered the question of whether they want Putin to be president after 2024: forty-six per cent said yes; forty per cent said no.[9]

The Kremlin realized that Tereshkova's amendment was the most unpopular up for a vote. That's why it was buried among dozens of other amendments, and only one question was on the referendum: "Do you approve the changes to the constitution of the Russian Federation?"

The second problem was that Putin needed strong popular support for his amendments. He was cementing his status as supreme ruler for years and decades to come. In the concept of his rule, the people were now a unified and indivisible loyal mass with no room for dissent. Everyone must be in favour, as it was under Stalin. Putin said so before the vote—he said he was convinced that the amendments to the constitution were "supported by the absolute majority of our citizens."[10]

The Kremlin sent voting targets everywhere in the country: the majority of registered voters had to favour the amendments, not just the majority of people who came to the polls. There had never before been an election like this. It lasted for a week, ballot boxes were brought directly to workplaces, and the CEC's recommendations on Coronavirus prevention made it possible to vote anywhere, from playgrounds to buses and benches in front of apartment buildings.

Putin got the result he wanted: 68 per cent voted in favour of the amendments with a turnout of 78 per cent; that is, 57.7 million people, almost 53 per cent of all voters in the country. He won more votes than in the last presidential election, and this despite plummeting approval ratings, a Coronavirus epidemic and a severe economic crisis. "Scholars who study Russian election statistics believe the nationwide vote on constitutional amendments was the most unfair since 2000," *Meduza* wrote. Sergei Shpilkin, an expert in electoral statistics, estimated that of the 57.7 million votes cast in favour of the new constitution, almost half—about 25 million—were simply faked.[11] But the deed was done. Putin had achieved omnipotence. His hands were untied.

## How Navalny defeated Putin again

There was a reason why the amendments to the constitution to nullify presidential terms had to be pushed through the vote quietly: Putin had been losing popularity for the past two years. In summer 2018, confidently re-elected for a fourth term, he raised the retirement age, and his rating, which had soared after the annexation of Crimea, instantly fell back to pre-Crimean levels. The society monolith that had immediately appeared in spring 2014 now disappeared just as quickly. In May 2020, a month before the vote, Putin's support rating fell to a historic low; it had been lower only at the beginning of his rule. Protest sentiment and the demand for change were on the rise again. The wind was once again filling the opposition's sails.

Alexei Navalny was full of plans. Less than a year before, in September 2019, he again defeated the government, this time in the Moscow parliamentary elections. Independent candidates such as Ilya Yashin were not allowed to participate. Tens of thousands of Muscovites took to the streets, and the protest was suppressed with unprecedented brutality. But Navalny was not discouraged. In each district of Moscow, Navalny's headquarters identified the most popular candidates from the mainstream opposition who were still allowed to run in the elections. They urged people to vote for them.

This was the same tactic that Navalny had used in the 2011 elections when he called for votes for the mainstream opposition against United Russia. The only difference was that in the Moscow parliamentary elections it was not parties competing against each other but specific candidates. The idea was the same, though: since there was no real choice in the elections, Navalny would try to break the system from within; that is, if United Russia candidates lost to oppositional candidates within the system, the government would be dealt a severe blow. Navalny branded his project Smart Voting. "There is a range of people in the mainstream opposition, but they can't act collectively with other candidates," Navalny explained. "So we need to unite them forcibly from below."[12]

Dissatisfaction with the authorities was growing. Many Muscovites were outraged that opposition candidates were not allowed to participate in the elections, and so this tactic again brought Navalny success. In the Moscow parliament, candidates from the loyal opposition won twenty out of forty-five seats. "The Moscow City Duma elections were won by Navalny and his Smart Voting," *Vedomosti* wrote.[13] They certainly were. The anti-Putin protest was able to affect the legislative body of Russia's largest and most important city. For Putin, this was the most serious defeat on the home front since December 2011, when United Russia essentially lost the election. The reaction was immediate: the Investigative Committee took charge of checking donations to Navalny's Anti-Corruption Foundation, law enforcement officers raided Navalny's headquarters and associated activists across the country, the foundation was branded a "foreign agent", and financial authorities blocked the bank accounts of the foundation as well as those of Navalny and his family.

Meanwhile, Navalny was about to introduce Smart Voting in all the elections across the country. Navalny cited mathematical calculations showing that the candidates he supported got an average of nineteen per cent more votes. He saw that the authority of the government was declining. As soon as Covid restrictions were lifted, he began to act. In July 2020, in the far eastern city of Khabarovsk, for weeks in the city's streets thousands of citizens protested the sudden arrest of their governor, Sergei Furgal—another clear sign of the growing protest mood in the country. Other major cities in Siberia—Novosibirsk, Tomsk and Omsk—were scheduled to hold local elections in September. In recent years, Navalny had investigated high-profile people, mostly from Putin's entourage. This time he lowered the bar. "Investigations can be subordinated to political goals," explained Maria Pevchikh, leader of the investigative team at Navalny's headquarters. "That year there were elections to city councils, and we thought, 'This year, let's try to film Navalny doing an investigation about people nobody knows.'" So Navalny travelled to Siberia to expose local corrupt officials and United Russia leaders as a way of supporting independent candidates. Later, he called the plan "Killing United Russia with Smart Voting."[14]

Navalny and his associates flew to Novosibirsk on 14 August. On 17 August, they were already in Tomsk, shooting an investigative film to show how the leader of the local branch of United Russia controlled almost the entire municipal system of the city. On his trips, Navalny was usually bothered by the police and pro-government activists sent by the security services. There was none of that in Tomsk. "The trip was remarkably comfortable," recalls Navalny's press secretary, Kira Yarmysh. "Every time we filmed Alexei on the street, there was a line of people who wanted to take pictures with him."[15] Shooting lasted two days. Part of the team stayed in Tomsk to finish the investigation while Navalny flew on. The next stop on his investigative tour was Kazan, the capital of Tatarstan, but on Thursdays he always did a live broadcast on YouTube from a small studio in his Moscow office. It was Thursday, 20 August. Navalny flew to Moscow.

The plan was to fly the following Monday from Moscow to Kazan, where he'd meet up with his associates from Tomsk.

The flight was an early one. At 6.00 a.m. Navalny, his aide Ilya Pakhomov and Kira Yarmysh met in the lobby of their hotel in Tomsk and drove to the airport. As soon as the plane left the ground, Navalny turned on *Rick and Morty* on Netflix as usual, Yarmysh opened a book, and Pakhomov fell asleep. About twenty minutes after take-off, Navalny suddenly closed his laptop and turned to Yarmysh sitting next to him. He said he wasn't feeling well, and could she talk to him because he needed to concentrate on the sound of a human voice. Yarmysh looked up and turned to Navalny. He was green.

"I began to retell him the plot of the book," Yarmysh recalled. "He responded normally. A stewardess was just passing by with the drinks cart, and I asked if he wanted water. He shifted his gaze to the cart and looked that way for longer than necessary. Then he said he was going to the restroom."[16]

About ten minutes later, there was an announcement that a doctor was needed. Yarmysh turned around, saw the line at the toilet and woke

Pakhomov. He went to find out what was going on and returned five minutes later, bug-eyed with horror: Navalny was lying unconscious on the floor.

Later, Navalny remembered everything that had happened before he lost consciousness. He remembered sitting in his seat when he suddenly felt very strange: nothing hurt, but it was as if he were dying. He remembered going to the bathroom, sitting down and realizing that he had to get up or he would never get out of there. "The closest description is the Dementor in *Harry Potter*," Navalny later recalled. "Rowling writes that 'the Dementor kisses you, you are not hurt, but life goes out of you'. It's a consuming sensation: I'm about to die." The only thing Navalny had time to say on his way out of the restroom was, "I've been poisoned. I'm going to die." With these words, he lay down under the feet of the stewards at the back of the plane. "The last thing I remember hearing was: 'Man, don't pass out.'"[17]

The flight attendants could do nothing with the unconscious Navalny, and the pilots decided to land the plane (saving his life, as it came out later). After forty minutes, the Tomsk–Moscow flight made an emergency landing in the Siberian city of Omsk. The ambulance arrived very quickly, and the emergency doctors gave Navalny an injection of atropine—not least because Kira Yarmysh had insisted on it. The ambulance doctors found out who they were bringing in when they started filling out paperwork. But Yarmysh thought that at first they didn't realize who their new patient was. Navalny was brought to the intensive care unit of Omsk Hospital No. 1 around 10 a.m. Omsk time. After about another forty minutes, Yarmysh was informed that Navalny had fallen into a coma.

## The battle to save Navalny

On the plane, Kira Yarmysh had already realized that Navalny had been poisoned in an assassination attempt. Alcohol and drugs had nothing to do with it; it was poisoning, she told the ambulance doctors on the way to the hospital. At the hospital, she demanded that the police be called. A policeman on call arrived quickly; at the same time, men in suit jackets appeared in the hospital. They started asking questions, asking where Navalny's things were. The hospital's chief toxicologist, who had promised to return soon with the results of his tests, disappeared and never reappeared. After spending an hour and a half in the hospital, Yarmysh realized that local law enforcement—and probably the doctors—were trying to cover up the traces of the crime on orders from above. And what were they doing with Navalny inside? Was he still alive? Navalny's wife Yulia had already taken off from Moscow and was on her way to Omsk, along with the foundation's director, Ivan Zhdanov. "I was scared to land," she later recalled. "I was afraid to see the text messages. So I told Vanya [Zhdanov]: 'Go ahead and read them, and I'll know what's going on by your reactions.'"[18]

When Navalnaya and Zhdanov flew into Omsk at 3.00 p.m., the local hospital was already at the centre of international news and was filled with officials, police and FSB officers. A representative of the hospital had already gone to the press twice, but both times he said nothing concrete: "Poisoning is being considered as one of the possible causes." Navalny's associates understood that the doctors were scared and forbidden to say what they suspected was wrong with him. At first, Yulia was not allowed to visit her husband in the intensive care unit and was asked to show her marriage certificate because the stamp in her passport was not enough. But they finally let her in. Navalny was in a coma and hooked up to a ventilator. "He had muscle cramps," Yulia said later. "He was thrashing around like in the film *Alien*, and it was terrifying."[19]

Some time passed. Yulia and Yarmysh couldn't get anything definite from the doctors. Meanwhile, they were surrounded by police officers preventing them from leaving the hospital until they gave them the luggage Navalny had flown with from Tomsk. Why? "You'll only get it if you arrest me," Yulia told them. The police did not dare to detain her. By about 7.00 p.m. Navalny's associates, Maria Pevchikh and Georgy Alburov, who had remained behind in Tomsk, arrived in Omsk. They quickly decided what to do: take Navalny to a European clinic as soon as possible. Just about that time, Angela Merkel confirmed that Navalny would be accepted in Germany, and a medical plane was found to transport Navalny to the Charité clinic in Berlin. The plane left Nuremberg at

4.00 a.m. Omsk time; it would arrive in Omsk the next day, 21 August, at 11.00 a.m. Navalny could be sent to Germany around noon.

At 8.00 a.m. Navalny's associates rushed to the hospital. A group of doctors sent from Moscow to Omsk by the Russian Ministry of Health to assess Navalny's condition had arrived and was already meeting. Anaesthesiologist Alexander Polupan arrived in Omsk at the request of Navalny's friends, and he, too, was included in the group. He later recalled a detail that he didn't pay much attention to at the time: in the hospital, the Moscow doctors were asked to wear disposable gowns, even though they were each wearing their own medical uniforms, and there was a special woman at Navalny's bedside who made sure that everyone wore gloves and immediately took them off when they left the bed.

Polupan and other participants in the group had no doubts whatsoever. Of course, Navalny was transportable, and they'd put him on board as soon as the plane arrived. Polupan wrote to Yuila that he could and should be transported. Doctors were already preparing the documents for transportation, and Navalny's friends were looking for an ambulance with resuscitation equipment to take him to the airport. But suddenly the situation changed. Polupan received a call from his superiors. A decision had been made at the top that Navalny could not be taken anywhere. He had to tell Navalny's relatives that the patient was not transportable, and, if he didn't, he'd face serious consequences. When the medical plane with the German crew landed in Omsk, representatives of the hospital were already explaining to the press that Navalny could not be transported. "Yulia wrote to me with the question: 'Has something changed?' I suggested we go outside for a smoke and talk there... I briefly told her that the patient was transportable, but a decision had been made in Moscow to forbid it."[20]

Those were the most terrifying hours, Maria Pevchikh recalled: "From around noon until the late evening on 21 August, it was a battle against the system, the essence of Putin's Russia." Navalny was nearby, so close they could reach out and touch him, there was a plane waiting on the runway, but nothing could be done. FSB officers were everywhere, blocking the way—even using physical violence. "You realize that you are losing," Pevchikh later said. "You're helpless, and then they'll come out and say that they could not save him."[21]

The struggle continued into the night. Navalny's evacuation to Germany became the world's top story. This is not a hospital, but a prison, human-rights activists said. A political assassination is taking place live on air, journalists shouted. European leaders called Putin, demanding that Navalny be released from the hospital. Yulia Navalnaya demanded the same from Putin in an open letter.

At 10.00 p.m., doctors suddenly agreed to the move. "We were sitting in our office at the hospital when a call came from the Kremlin, and they said to let the patient go," someone who worked at the Omsk hospital recalled later. "Everyone exhaled with relief."[22] But the crew of the medical plane was already required by regulation to rest, and so the plane with Navalny in a coma did not leave for Berlin until the next morning.

## New rules of the game

Soviet chemists synthesized a derivative of the military nerve poison Novichok from the 1970s until the late 1980s. In the 1990s, Russia signed the Chemical Weapons Convention, and Russian authorities repeatedly claimed that production of chemical poisons stopped in the late 1980s. Vil Mirzayanov, a chemist involved in the development of Novichok who published its formula in 2008, later claimed that testing continued into the early 1990s.

But the Russian word Novichok entered the broader global vernacular—like the Soviet-era words sputnik and perestroika—decades later and thanks to Vladimir Putin.

In March 2018, Novichok poisoned former Russian spy Sergei Skripal, who was exposed as a double agent in Russia and jailed before being released to Britain as part of a spy swap. Along with Skripal, his daughter Yulia, who had come to visit him that day, also fell into a coma. Both eventually survived, but how well they survived the consequences of poisoning has not been made public. The assassins, quickly identified by British security services as GRU officers, applied poison to the front door handle of Skripal's home in the British town of Salisbury.

The poisoning was an enormous international scandal. Putin, of course, denied his involvement in the attempted assassination of the Skripals, but made it clear that he saw nothing wrong with it: "Skripal is a traitor to his homeland," he said, "just a scumbag."[23] No one thought Russian intelligence would dare to undertake such a special operation without Putin's knowledge.

By the time of the assassination attempt on the Skripals, the Russian intelligence services had already earned a reputation as experts in the use of poisons. Back in 2002, during the second Chechen war, *Kommersant* newspaper told how FSB officers killed Saudi field commander al-Khattab, an associate of Basayev's, with the help of a poisoned letter: "The FSB decided to use the experience of the 1930s and 1940s, when Soviet security services frequently used poisons to eliminate people. But they replaced poison with the most modern toxic substance."[24] In 2006, former FSB officer Alexander Litvinenko was killed in London with radioactive polonium. In 2015, Bulgarian businessman and arms exporter Emilian Gebrev fell into a coma in Sofia after contact with Novichok. Twice, in 2015 and 2017, Vladimir Kara-Murza was hospitalized in a very serious condition with similar symptoms, but at the time no one could prove anything.

Navalny's associates immediately remembered the Skripals. On the morning of 20 August, after learning that Navalny had been poisoned, Maria Pevchikh and his other friends remaining in Tomsk rushed to his hotel room to collect potential evidence: trash, toiletries, towels, and so on. "Novichok sounded like a joke. It was too much," Pevchikh recalled.[25] In her archive of video footage from that day, there are still shots of her wearing gloves and a mask (Pevchikh had carried one with her since Covid) while holding a water bottle and telling her associate Georgy Alburov to open the window because there might be fumes while Alburov waves his hand dismissively: there's clearly nothing in the bottle. Pevchikh took the bottle along with everything else when she and Yulia Navalnaya flew Alexei to Germany. The bottle would be proof that Navalny was poisoned in the hotel: it still bore traces of Novichok.

Navalny was brought to the Charité clinic. The diagnosis was established instantly. It was not difficult to determine that it was poisoning by organophosphate, that is, the substance that is contained in Novichok. A week later, Angela Merkel announced that Navalny had been poisoned by Novichok, and within the next two weeks this fact was confirmed by three independent European laboratories. Leonid Volkov recalls Navalny's reaction when he came out of his coma, regained consciousness and was told what had happened:

"Alexei, don't worry, it was an assassination attempt. Putin tried to kill you with Novichok."

"No shit?! That's so dumb!" Navalny replied.[26]

For their part, Russian propagandists offered all sorts of versions: there was no poisoning—it was an attack of pancreatitis; or it was the homemade Siberian hooch that Navalny drank the day before; or his blood sugar dropped because he was on a diet; or he was poisoned on the plane to Germany or at the Charité clinic; or it was Khodorkovsky's doing; or Pevchikh did it.

Navalny could have swallowed the Novichok himself, Putin explained to Macron. "Oh, sure, I whipped up some Novichok in the kitchen. Quietly sipped it from a flask on the aeroplane. And then I fell into a coma," Navalny joked from the clinic. "To die in an Omsk hospital and end up in an Omsk morgue, where the cause of death would be determined as 'lived long enough'—that was the ultimate goal of my cunning plan. But Putin outplayed me. He can't be fooled. In the end, like a fool, I lay in a coma for eighteen days, but I didn't get what I wanted."[27] Macron called Putin on 14 September, a week after Navalny came out of his coma. As the newspaper *Le Monde* wrote, Macron did not accept this version. Novichok could not have been made by a private citizen, he told Putin.

In the history of political assassinations and attempts in Russia, Navalny's poisoning stands apart. In the assassination attempts on Skripal and Litvinenko, one could see the logic of interdepartmental relations inside the Russian security services. This was a sinister tradition—punishing people the FSB considered traitors. The investigation into Nemtsov's murder led to Ramzan Kadyrov's palace. Putin was politically responsible for it, but he could easily deny having anything to do with it. This time Putin became a hostage to his own subterfuge. Novichok is a convenient murder weapon because it is usually impossible to establish the cause of death and therefore the fact of an assassination attempt. A person suddenly dies, and no one knows why. But Novichok can only be made under the auspices and supervision of the special services, and if its traces are found, they lead to the very top floor of the Russian government. In the case of the assassination attempt on Navalny—a politician known to the entire country—the traces led straight to Vladimir Putin's office.

In any case, everything already pointed to the state's involvement in the assassination attempt. Surveillance footage was missing from the hotel in Tomsk. Despite his demands, Navalny was never given back the clothes he was wearing on the flight to Moscow. In the Omsk hospital, Navalny's family was never given his medical records. And the Investigative Committee, despite the obvious fact of the crime and the demands of the international community, refused to open a criminal case. It was obvious why: if a case were opened, it would have been easier for the victim's lawyers to get access to all the evidence. Besides, the murder of Nemtsov showed that even if you sabotage the official investigation, it still leads to those who organized and carried out the assassination.

In the end, there was no need for an official investigation. Navalny soon found the killers himself—or, rather, he helped to find them. The European investigative group Bellingcat and the fluent Russian-speaking journalist Christo Grozev, who specializes in working with open data, had already investigated how Flight MH17 had been shot down in summer 2014 in the skies above Ukraine, and how Russian artillery participated in the fighting in Donbas. In 2018, he and his group identified the GRU officers who poisoned the Skripals, and then identified the specific scientific centre in Moscow where Novichok had been developed since 2010. Grozev began to investigate who the institute scientists were talking to by phone. He was surprised at how quickly he was able to figure out the names of specific FSB officers who had followed Navalny everywhere since the beginning of 2017, confirmed by air-travel data. Then he wrote to Navalny: "Alexei, it looks like we know who wanted to kill you."[28]

In 2021, Bellingcat and Grozev presented a list of Russian activists who had been the targets of FSB assassins over the last few years, including activists in the North Caucasus and Russian provinces. (Vladimir Kara-Murza was on this list, and in three other cases the assassination attempts had been successful.) But Navalny's speech in December 2020 was historic—and groundbreaking. "Hi, this is Navalny. I know who wanted to kill me. I know where they live. I know where they work. I know their real names. I know their aliases. I have their photographs."[29] On 14 December, the investigation was published simultaneously by Navalny, Bellingcat, *Der Spiegel* and CNN.

Right before publication—it would have been too late afterwards—Navalny took another step: he called the killers himself. At first, he simply asked, "Hello, can you tell me why you wanted to kill me?" The men immediately hung up on him. Then he changed tactics. He began to introduce himself as a member of the Security Council, who was preparing a report and needed to clarify something. A special app falsified the phone number that came up for the respondent. "The calculation is simple. Someone gets a call at seven in the morning. He sees a familiar office number, picks up the phone and starts talking," Navalny explained.[30] And one of the men he called, Konstantin Kudryavtsev, a military chemist from the FSB Institute of Forensic Sciences (a technical specialist, not an operative) fell into this trap, even though he was surprised he was being asked these questions over an open line. He said he had processed Navalny's clothes after the poisoning. "They told me to work on his underwear, on the inside," he said. So it turned out that the poison had been applied to his underpants. When asked why the operation failed, Kudryavtsev said that they "calculated everything correctly", but "the situation was not in our favour"—that is, the pilots quickly landed the plane.

It was unbelievable. Grozev and Pevchikh, who were sitting next to Navalny, could not believe their ears: a participant in the special operation to kill Navalny—and then to cover up the traces of the crime—was himself confirming the conclusions of their investigation. It was indeed a confession of guilt, straight from the heart. Navalny had defeated Putin once again.

The significance of all these events—the failed assassination attempt on Navalny and his successful investigation—cannot be overemphasized. "This investigation closes the circle of the entire history of Putin's system," political scientist Alexander Morozov immediately wrote.[31] When he came to power, Vladimir Putin put the concepts of traitor and enemy at the core of his power: he would show no mercy for traitors, but he respected enemies and would not destroy his political opponents just because they were his political opponents. But it turned out that, with the transformation of sovereign democracy into tyranny, the rules of the game had changed: the FSB's special department for political assassinations worked around the clock, seven days a week, and the head of state personally approved an assassination attempt on an opposition leader.

As soon as Navalny came out of his coma, both his family and his team knew that he'd go back to Russia. But first he was discharged from the hospital and moved from Berlin to Freiburg for rehabilitation. His associates set up a small office there and began working on a new investigation about an enormous palace that had been under construction for Putin on the Black Sea near Gelendzhik since the mid-aughts. At the end of December, Navalny was about to fly home. He decided to fly after the holidays and bought a ticket for 17 January. What would happen? How would he be met? His headquarters considered options. Would they put him in jail right away? Would he be put under house arrest? As he prepared to return home, he knew he wouldn't be allowed a quiet life. But, as he thought about all this, he missed the most important thing: Putin was preparing to invade Ukraine.

On the evening of 17 January 2021, Navalny flew to Moscow and was arrested at border control.

Three years and one month later, on 16 February 2024, at 2.30 p.m. in Moscow, the Russian prison service announced that convict Alexei Navalny "felt unwell after a walk, lost consciousness, and died despite the colony medical staff's efforts to resuscitate him."

At first, it was impossible to believe he'd been killed in prison. He had already survived a Novichok poisoning; it was as if he had defeated death once and had been living under a charm ever since. He should have become the Russian Nelson Mandela—the leader who would outlive and dismantle the regime that tormented him and repressed the entire nation.

But it quickly became clear: Navalny was gone. For millions of people, this was a personal disaster, a tragedy. That evening, the programming on the TV Rain channel—now operating from exile in Amsterdam—was a spontaneous memorial service.

Why did he suddenly die, even though the day before—captured on a recording of his video court appearance—he looked healthy, laughing and joking with the bailiffs and judges? Why was his body not released to his mother for several days? Six months later, investigators from the Russian independent journal *Insider* proved that the official documents pertaining to Navalny's death had been edited. In 2025 Yulia Navalnaya announced that independent analysis of tissue samples smuggled out of the prison showed he'd been poisoned. In his memoirs, Navalny writes that, during one of his last visits to prison in the spring of 2022, he discussed the following scenario with his wife Yulia:

"...if everything starts falling apart, they'll bump me off at the first sign the regime is collapsing. They'll poison me."

"I know," she said with a nod, in a voice that was calm and firm. "I was thinking that myself."[32]

Navalny gave Putin too much credit. Putin did not wait for his regime to begin to crumble. He was most likely driven by a desire for revenge. After Navalny escaped death the first time he was poisoned, he exposed his killers and made a mockery of Putin and the FSB poisoners.

But even after his return and arrest in January 2021, Navalny was much more than Putin's personal enemy. For three years, he was kept behind bars in inhumane conditions—starved, denied medical care, deprived of visits—and spent almost one of those three years in solitary confinement. But his social media posts—witty and humorous as always—were full of determination. And his speeches in court after each sentence were filled with faith in the people and the future of Russia. He addressed his executioners and judges, asking why they were wasting their lives as lackeys of murderers and corrupt officials when "it's better to live in a free and prosperous country than a corrupt and poor one." And then he appealed to the people: "You don't have to go to prison [...], but everyone must make some kind of sacrifice, everyone must make some effort [...], [so that] together we can bring closer the Beautiful Russia of the Future."[33]

Putin's invasion of Ukraine turned Russia into a full-scale dictatorship, leaving people with a simple alternative: shut up—or go to jail.

The political activists who decided to stay in Russia and speak out now faced years-long prison terms. Vladimir Kara-Murza, who was Boris Nemtsov's close associate, was arrested in April, less than two months after the war started. He was charged with treason for speaking out against Putin's regime at international public events and sentenced to twenty-five years in prison. It was as if the accusation and the jail term had come straight from Stalin's era.

Ilya Yashin, Boris Nemtsov's apprentice and longtime friend, was arrested in July and was sentenced to eight and a half years for "spreading false information" about Putin's war. Hundreds of others across Russia who dared to speak out were jailed, too. (Ultimately, Yashin and Kara-Murza, along with several other Russian political prisoners, would be freed and sent to the West through a prisoner exchange a few months after Navalny's death.)

Born out of obsession and ambition, the war with Ukraine also proved to be a way to strengthen Putin's grip at home: no need to respect rules anymore, no need for propriety. In Russia's journey, this was the final stop.

Nemtsov's career was an embodiment of this Russian drama. Gorbachev's perestroika brought freedom and opportunity. It opened the door for Nemtsov and his aspiration to create a new future in which Russia would become a civilized democratic state. The Yeltsin era facilitated his political rise towards the highest reaches of power, but it left him holding an empty bag in the end. Under Putin, Nemtsov, as the leader of Russian opposition, faced growing intimidation followed by harassment, arrests and finally murder.

In 2015, the assassination of Nemtsov marked the end of the Russian democratic project. Yet there was still hope embodied in Navalny, who took on the mantle as the leader of national resistance and reinvented how to do politics under the tightening grip of Putin's tyranny. For millions of Russians, Navalny—even when he was in jail—was a moral authority and a beacon shining a ray of light through the deepening night of Putin's rule. For many, hope died on 16 February 2024.

# ENDNOTES

## Prologue

1 Vladimir Putin, speech delivered on 18 March 2021, https://www.youtube.com/watch?v=WQ0fXYxatc06 accessed January 2025.
2 Informal CIS Summit, 20 December 2019, http://kremlin.ru/events/president/news/62376, accessed January 2025.
3 Valdai Discussion Club, 21 October 2021, https://ru.valdaiclub.com/events/posts/articles/vladimir-putin-xviii-ezhegodnoe-zasedanie-mezhdunarodnogo-diskussionnogo-kluba-valday-stenogramma/, accessed January 2025.
4 Ibid.
5 Vladimir Putin, press conference held on 23 December 2021, https://www.youtube.com/watch?v=-IaYAh0TpXY, accessed January 2025.
6 M. Kimmage and M. Kofman. 'Russia Won't Let Ukraine Go Without a Fight', *Foreign Affairs*, 22 November 2021, https://www.foreignaffairs.com/articles/ukraine/2021-11-22/russia-wont-let-ukraine-go-without-fight, accessed January 2025.
7 M. Fishman, *And So On*, TV Rain, 3 December 2021, https://tvrain.tv/teleshow/fishman_vechernee_shou/srabotaet_li_ultimatum_putina-543289, accessed January 2025.
8 M. Fishman, *And So On*, TV Rain, 11 February 2022, https://tvrain.tv/teleshow/fishman_vechernee_shou/delo_idet_k_vojne-547658/, accessed January 2025.

## Chapter 1

1 L. Aron, *Roads to the Temple: Truth, Memory, Ideas, and Ideals in the Making of the Russian Revolution*, New Haven, Yale University Press, 2012, [ebook].
2 From the author's interview with Nikolai Ashin, June 2019.
3 B. Nemtsov, 'Khochu umeret, katayas na vindserfinge', *Moskovsky komsomolets*, 29 December 2006.
4 B. Nemtsov, *Ispoved buntarya*, Moscow, Partizan, 2007, p. 11.
5 Interview with Boris Nemtsov, *Leninskaya smena*, February 1990.
6 I. Eidman, 'O netochnosti v biografii moyego brata Borisa Nemtsova', Obozrevatel.com, 1 March 2015.
7 From the author's interview with Lev Tsimring, June 2019.

8   D. Nemtsova, 'O syne', *Novaya gazeta*, 5 February 2016.
9   Yegor Vereshchagin, 'Neizvestny Nemtsov', *Sovershenno sekretno*, 17 March 2015.
10  From the author's interview with Lev Tsimring, June 2019.
11  From the author's interview with Alexander Kotyusov, June 2019.
12  From the author's interview with Pavel Chichagov, June 2019.
13  From the author's interview with Natalia Lapina, April 2019.
14  From the author's interview with Lev Tsimring, June 2019.
15  M. Ryutova, 'Molodoi Nemtsov: 'Ya smogu proiti po kanatu cherez propast', *Troitsky variant*, 23 March 2016.
16  From the author's interview with Lev Tsimring, June 2019.
17  From the author's interview with Raisa Nemtsova, September 2019.
18  Ibid.
19  Ibid.
20  A. Grachev, *A.S. Gorbachev*, Moscow, Vagrius, 2001.
21  From the author's interview with Pavel Chichagov, June 2019.
22  From the author's interview with Stanislav Dmitriyevsky, June 2019.
23  From an interview with Boris Nemtsov on Ekho Moskvy, 4 March 2013 (site destroyed by Russian government).
24  From the author's interview with Stanislav Dmitriyevsky, June 2019.
25  B. Nemtsov, 'Pochemu ya protiv AST', *Gorkovsky rabochy*, 2 July 1988.
26  From the author's interview with Askhat Kayumov, June 2019.
27  Ye. Odintsova, Facebook, 18 June 2019.
28  'Akademik Andrei Sakharov: my ne vprave derzhat lyudei v strakhe', *Leninskaya smena*, 13 October 1988.
29  Anatoly Chernyayev, *Sovmestny iskhod. Dnevnik dvukh epokh*, Moscow, ROSSPEN, 2009, p. 365.
30  B. Yeltsin, *Ispoved na zadannuyu temu*, Moscow, Ogonyok-Variant, 1990, p. 1.
31  Ibid, p. 37.
32  B. Nemtsov, op. cit., p. 12.
33  From the author's interview with Nikolai Ashin, June 2019.
34  From the author's interview with Viktor Lysov, June 2019.

# Chapter 2

1  G. Shakhnazarov, *S vozhdyami i bez nikh*, Moscow, Vagrius, 2001, p. 388.
2  A. Sakharov, *Gorkii, Moskva, dalee vezde. Vosnominaniya*, Moscow, Prava cheloveka, 1996.
3  Ye. Gaidar, *Dni porozhenii i pobed*, Moscow, Vagrius, 1997, p. 71.
4  See M. Zezin, O. Malyshev, F. Malkhozov, R. Pikhoi, *Chelovek peremen. Issledovaniye politicheskoi biografii Borisa Yeltsina*, Moscow, Novy khronograf, 2011, p. 199.
5  The letter was registered by the Yuzhkuzbassugol Corporation on 2 February 1989 and then published by the former deputy to the USSR Parliament, Teimuraz Avaliani.
6  Ye. Gaidar, *Gibel imperii: uroki dlya sovremennoi Rossii*, Moscow, ROSSPEN, 2006, p. 157.

7 *Sakharovskiye chteniya. Otchyot*, 27 January 1990. From the archives of the A.D. Sakharov House Museum, Nizhny Novgorod.
8 From the author's interview with Lev Tsimring, June 2019.
9 *Leninskaya smena*, 20 January 1990.
10 N. Zvereva, *Pryamoi efir. V kadre i za kadrom*, Moscow, Alpina Non-Fiction, 2012.
11 From the author's interview with Valery Kulikov, June 2019.
12 B. Nemtsov, *Ispoved buntarya*, p. 12.
13 From the author's interview with Pavel Chichagov, June 2019.
14 From the author's interview with Lev Tsimring, June 2019.
15 From the author's interview with Nina Zvereva for the film *The Man Who Was Too Free*, 2015.
16 From an interview with Boris Nemtsov in *Leninskaya smena*, February 1990.
17 From the author's interview with Pavel Chichagov, June 2019.
18 From the author's interview with Nina Zvereva for the film *The Man Who Was Too Free*, 2015.
19 G. Shakhnazarov, op. cit., p. 388.
20 B. Minayev, *Yeltsin*, Moscow, Molodaya gvardiya, 2014, p. 227.
21 A. Grachev, *A.S. Gorbachev*, Moscow, Vagrius, 2001.
22 Speech by Valentin Rasputin at the Congress of People's Deputies of the RSFSR, 1 June 1989. https://www.svoboda.org/a/vasin-hod-anatoliy-strelyanyy-o-myatezhe-protiv-myatezha/31411780.html, accessed April 2023.
23 Speech by Boris Yeltsin at the Congress of People's Deputies of the RSFSR 22 May 1990, https://yeltsin.ru/archive/paperwork/8610, accessed April 2023.
24 B. Minayev, op. cit. p. 234.
25 Interview with Boris Yeltsin, May 1990.
26 B. Nemtsov, op. cit., p. 16.
27 From an interview with Boris Yeltsin in the archives of the Boris Yeltsin Presidential Center.
28 From the author's interview with Pavel Chichagov, July 2019.
29 From the author's interview with Alexander Lyubimov, October 2019.
30 G. Shakhnazarov, op. cit. p. 383.
31 B. Yeltsin, *Zapiski prezidenta*, Moscow, Ogonyok Publishers, 1994, p. 33.
32 From an interview with Boris Nemtsov in *Leninskaya smena*, June 1990.
33 From the author's interview with Sergei Shakhrai, June 2019.
34 *Leninskaya smena*, 22 August 1990.
35 From the author's interview with Viktor Khlystun, June 2019.
36 B. Nemtsov, *Provintsial*, Moscow, Vagrius, 1997.
37 Ye. Gaidar, op. cit., p. 74.
38 From the author's interview with Grigory Yavlinsky, September 2019.
39 Ibid.
40 W. Taubman, *Gorbachev: His Life and Times*, New York, W.W. Norton and Company, 2017, [ebook].
41 M. Mironov, 'Razgovor s Sergeyem Akeksashenko o 90-kh i ne tolko', Ekho Moskvy, 10 September 2018 (site destroyed by Russian government).
42 Ye. Gaidar, op. cit., p. 75.

43 From a speech by Boris Yeltsin at the Second Session of the Supreme Council of the RSFSR, 16 October 1990, https://yeltsin.ru/archive/paperwork/9294, accessed April 2023.
44 L. Sukhanov, *Kak Yeltsin stal prezidentom. Zapiski pervogo pomoshchnika*, Moscow, Eksmo: Algoritm, 2011, p. 84.
45 From the author's interview with Viktor Aksyuchits, September 2017.
46 From a television interview with Boris Nemtsov, 19 February 1991.
47 From an interview by Nina Pributkovskaya, 'Molodoi Nemtsov', 31 May 1991.
48 P. Aven, A. Kokh, *Revolyutsiya Gaidara. Istoriya reform 90-kh iz pervykh ruk*, Moscow, Alpina Publisher, 2015, p. 125.

## Chapter 3

1 B. Yeltsin, op. cit., p. 34.
2 Yeltsin's speech after taking the presidential oath of office, 10 July 1991, https://yeltsin.ru/archive/audio/8968, accessed April 2023.
3 J. Matlock, *Autopsy on an Empire: The American Ambassador's Account of the Collapse of the Soviet Union*, New York, Random House, 199, pp. 541–42.
4 A. Chernyayev, *1991 god. Dnevnik pomoshchnika prezidenta SSSR*, Moscow, Terra, 1997, p. 83.
5 A. Chernyayev, *Sovmestny iskhod. Dnevnik dvukh epokh*, Moscow, ROSSPEN, 2009.
6 W. Taubman, loc. cit.
7 I. Lozo, *Avgustovsky putch 1991 goda. Kak eto bylo*, Moscow, Rosspen, 2014. p. 160.
8 Ye. Gaidar, *Dni porozhenii i pobed*, p. 81.
9 From the author's interview with Sergei Shakhrai, August 2016.
10 A. Lebed, *Za derzhavu obidno*, Moscow, Moskovskaya pravda, 1995.
11 Yu. Baturin, A. Ilin, V. Kadatsky et al., *Epokha Yeltsina. Ocherki politicheskoi istorii*, Moscow, Vagrius, 2001, p. 147.
12 From the author's interview with Alexander Lyubimov, October 2019.
13 From the author's interview with Lev Ponomaryov, October 2019.
14 From the author's interview with Sergei Shakhrai, June 2019.
15 From the author's interview with Viktor Aksyuchits, September 2017.
16 I. Lozo, loc. cit.
17 Loc.cit.
18 B. Nemtsov, loc. cit.
19 Interfax, 20 August 1991.
20 A. Nezhny, 'Nad bezdnoi', *Ogonyok* 37, September 1991.
21 I. Lozo, op. cit., p. 248.

## Chapter 4

1 From the author's interview with Lev Ponomaryov, October 2019.
2 P. Aven, 'Vo glave FSB Chubais prinyos by ne menshe polzy, chto na privatizatsii', *Forbes*, 2 March 2010.

3   P. Aven, A. Kokh, op. cit., p. 54.
4   From the author's interview with Lev Ponomaryov, October 2019.
5   Loc. cit.
6   From Yeltsin's speech to the Supreme Soviet, December 1991, https://www.youtube.com/watch?v=y6u-Adxkq8o, accessed 24 April 2023.
7   B. Yeltsin, op. cit., p. 156.
8   B. Minayev, op. cit., p. 326.
9   T. Colton, *Yeltsin: A Life*, New York, Basic Books, 2011, [ebook].
10  From the author's interview with Viktor Khlystun, June 2019.
11  Transcript of cabinet meeting 15 November 1991, *Istoriya novoi Rossii*, http://ru-90.ru/content/заседания-правительства-рсфср-15-ноября-1991-года-0, accessed 25 April 2023.
12  V. Sheinis, *Vzlyot i padeniye parlamenta: perelomnye gody v rossiiskoi politike*, Moscow, R. Elinin Publishing House, 2005, vol. 1, p. 530.
13  B. Yeltsin, loc. cit.
14  Yeltsin's Address to the Fifth Congress of People's Deputies of the RSFSR on 28 October 1991, *Istoriya novoi Rossii*, http://ru-90.ru/content/выступление-президента-рф-бн-ельцина-на-v-съезде-народных-депутатов-рсфср-28-октября---2-ноя, accessed 25 April 2023.
15  *Moskovskiye novosti*, 17 November 1991.
16  Loc. cit.
17  N. Popov, 'Likhiye 90-e. Kakim bylo obshchestvennoye mneniye v epokhu Yeltsina', *Kapital strany*, 28 November 2015.
18  From Nikos Sidiroupulos's interview with Gavriil Popov, December 2004, Moskovskoye obshchestvo grekov, https://www.greekmos.ru/gavriil_popov, accessed 15 January 2024.
19  Russian Public Opinion Research Center poll, July 1991.
20  Boris Nemtsov's speech at a rally 19 August 2012, https://nemtsov-most.org/2016/08/19/boris-nemtsov-right-now-the-heirs-of-the-state-emergency-committee-are-in-power-they-hate-freedom, accessed 16 August 2023.
21  Quoted in Ye. Gaidar, op. cit., p. 132.
22  B. Nemtsov on Ekho Moskvy, 23 December 2009 (site destroyed by Russian government).
23  Ye. Gaidar, op. cit., p. 134.
24  *Moskovskiye novosti*, 8 December 1991.
25  Alexander Rutskoi's speech in Barnaul, 30 November 1991.
26  'V 60 let vstretimsya. I ya vam rasskazhu'. Interview with Boris Nemtsov 1992, *Novaya gazeta*, 21 February 2018.
27  'Pri karernom roste ne dolzhno toshnit'. Interview with Boris Nemtsov in *Ogonyok*, 9 March 2015.
28  From the author's interview with Alexander Minzhurenko, November 2019.
29  *Nizhegorodsky rabochy*, 15 October 1991.
30  From the author's interview with Nikolai Ashin, June 2019.
31  From the author's interview with Alexander Minzhurenko, November 2019.
32  *Nizhegorodsky rabochy*, 15 October 1991.
33  From the author's interview with Alexander Minzhurenko, November 2019.
34  From the author's interview with Tatyana Grishina, June 2019.

**35** *Leninskaya smena*, 25 November 1991.
**36** From the author's interview with Sergei Shakhrai, June 2019.
**37** Poll by the Sociological Research Center, 9–10 October 1991, *Nizhegorodsky rabochy*.
**38** Boris Nemtsov on the television programme *V gostyakh u Dmitriya Gordona*, March 2008.
**39** *Leninskaya smena*, 1 December 1991.
**40** From the author's interview with Grigory Yavlinsky for the film *The Man Who Was Too Free*, 2015.

# Chapter 5

**1** From Yegor Gaidar and Anatoly Chubais's visit to Nizhny Novgorod in 1992, reported by Nina Zvereva.
**2** A. Chubais, ed., *Privatizatsiya po-rossiiski*, Moscow, Vagrius, 1999, p. 101.
**3** IFC, Small-Scale Privatization in Russia: The Nizhny Novgorod Model, July 1992, https://documents.worldbank.org/en/publication/documents-reports/documentdetail/142531468336002246/a-city-officials-guide, accessed 25 April 2023.
**4** From the author's interview with Dmitry Bednyakov, June 2019.
**5** O. Bessarab, O. Ryabov et al., *Kak my otkryvali gorod*, Nizhny Novgorod, Knigi, 2009, p. 102.
**6** *Nizhegorodsky rabochy*, 13 January 1992.
**7** From the author's interview with Pavel Chichagov, June 2019.
**8** Yeltsin Center, *B. Yeltsin v Nizhnem Novgorode i Nizhegorodskoi oblasti*, archive materials.
**9** A. Chubais, ed., loc. cit.
**10** 'In Memory of Yegor Gaidar', Ekho Moskvy, 16 December 2009 (site destroyed by Russian government).
**11** From the author's interview with Pavel Chichagov, 4 June 2019.
**12** A. Chubais, ed., op. cit., p. 98.
**13** From the author's interview with Anatoly Chubais, August 2017.
**14** From the author's interview with Dmitry Bednyakov, June 2019.
**15** *The Washington Post*, 16 March 1992.
**16** *Los Angeles Times*, 5 April 1992.
**17** From the author's interview with Anatoly Chubais, August 2017.
**18** From the author's interview with Dmitry Bednyakov, June 2019.
**19** From the author's interview with Grigory Yavlinsky for the film *The Man Who Was Too Free*, 2015.
**20** From the author's interview with Dmitry Bednyakov, June 2019.
**21** Ye. Gaidar, op. cit., p. 156.
**22** Interview with Boris Nemtsov, *Moskovskiye novosti*, 19 July 1992.
**23** From the author's interview with Grigory Yavlinsky for the film *The Man Who Was Too Free*, 2015.
**24** *Kommersant*, 6 May 1994.
**25** 'In Memory of Yegor Gaidar', Ekho Moskvy, 16 December 2009 (site destroyed by Russian government).
**26** From the author's interview with Pavel Chichagov, June 2019.

27 From the author's interview with Alexander Kotyusov, June 2019.
28 From the author's interview with Vladimir Sedov, June 2019.
29 'In Memory of Yegor Gaidar', Ekho Moskvy, 16 December 2009 (site destroyed by Russian government).
30 O. Bessarab, O. Ryabov et al., op. cit., p. 159.
31 A. Tarasov, *Millioner. Ispoved pervogo kapitalista novoi Rossii*, Moscow, Vagrius, 2004.
32 B. Nemtsov, *Ispoved buntarya*, p. 148.
33 From the author's interview with Igor Maskayev, February 2018.
34 From the author's interview with Viktor Khlystun, June 2019.
35 V. Uzun, '20 let. Agrarnaya reforma: "Ostavlyat kolkhozy v prezhnem vide bylo nelzya"', *Krestyanin*, 23 June 2010.
36 From the author's interview with Yury Lebedev, June 2019.
37 'Boris Nemtsov: istoriya vslyota i padeniya', *Kstovo.ru*, 6 March 2015.
38 Quoted from *Kommersant Vlast* 28, 21 July 2003.
39 From the author's interview with Oleg Sysuyev for the Film *The Man Who Was Too Free*, 2015.
40 N. Lisitsyna, 'Vystrel v spinu. Vspominaya Borisa Nemtsova', *Nizhny seichas*, 3 March 2015.
41 From the author's interview with Yury Lebedev, June 2019.
42 From the author's interview with Alexander Lyubimov, October 2019.

# Chapter 6

1 V. Sheinis, op. cit., vol. 2, p. 58.
2 Ye. Gaidar, op. cit., p. 163.
3 Ruslan Khasbulatov meeting with Italian senators, 13 January 1992.
4 *Kommersant Vlast* 103, 20 January 1992.
5 Ye. Gaidar, op. cit., p. 165.
6 *Moskovskiye novosti*, 19 April 1992.
7 From the author's interview with Sergei Filatov, February 2020.
8 Loc. cit.
9 *Izvestiya*, 8 April 1992.
10 From an interview with Yegor Gaidar in *Moskovskiye novosti*, January 1992.
11 See A. Nechayev, *Rossiya na perelome. Otkrovenniye zapiski pervogo ministra ekonomiki*, Moscow, Rus-Olimp, Astrel, 2010.
12 Ye. Gaidar, op. cit., p. 180.
13 A. Nechayev, op. cit., p. 404.
14 Ye. Gaidar, op. cit., p. 185.
15 V. Sheinis, op. cit., p. 125.
16 *Moskovskiye novosti*, December 1992.
17 V. Sheinis, op. cit., p. 167.
18 Op. cit., p. 168.
19 Yu. Baturin, A. Ilin, V. Kadatsky et al., op. cit., p. 250.
20 Op. cit., p. 251.

21 *Izvestiya*, 7 December 1992.
22 Ye. Gaidar, op. cit., p. 213.
23 Op. cit., p. 215.
24 From the author's interview with Sergei Filatov, February 2020.
25 RF Ministry of Security Analysis, 'Varianty razvitiya krizisa vlasti osenyu 1993 g.', from the Yeltsin Center Archives, March 1993.
26 Ibid.
27 'Deistviya generala de Gollya v krizisnoi politicheskoi situatsii vo Frantsii', from the Yeltsin Center archives, March 1993.
28 Yu. Baturin, A. Ilin, V. Kadatsky et al., op. cit., p. 291.
29 B. Yeltsin, loc. cit.
30 O. Moroz, *Khronika liberalnoi revolyutsii*, Moscow, Raduga, 2003.
31 V. Sheinis, op. cit., p. 271.
32 O. Poptsov, 'Khronika vremyon "Tsarya Borisa"', Moscow, Sovershenno sekretno, 1996.
33 Ye. Gaidar, op. cit., p. 239.
34 *Nezavisimaya gazeta*, 27 April 1993.
35 *Moskovskiye novosti*, 2 May 1993.
36 V. Sheinis, op. cit., p. 339.
37 *Nezavisimaya gazeta*, 5 May 1993.

# Chapter 7

1 K. Rogov, 'Krizis perekhoda. Oktyabr 1993-go i uroki makroistorii', *InLiberty*, 6 October 2018, https://www.inliberty.ru/magazine/issue8, accessed 24 July 2023.
2 Quoted in Yu. Baturin, A. Ilin, V. Kadatsky et al., op. cit., p. 347.
3 V. Sheinis, op. cit., p. 474.
4 From the author's interview with Sergei Filatov, February 2020.
5 *Izvestiya*, 27 July 1993.
6 Loc. cit.
7 From the author's interview with Sergei Filatov, February 2020.
8 From the author's interview with Lev Ponomaryov, October 2019.
9 Loc. cit.
10 Yu. Baturin, A. Ilin, V. Kadatsky et al., op. cit., p. 345.
11 Loc. cit., p. 349.
12 V. Sheinis, op. cit., p. 510.
13 Loc. cit., p. 509.
14 B. Yeltsin, op. cit., p. 329.
15 From the author's interview with Nina Zvereva for the film *The Man Who Was Too Free*, 2015.
16 Loc. cit.
17 A. Kulikov, *Tyazhyolyye zvyozdy*, Moscow, Voina i mir buks, 2002.
18 Ye. Gaidar, op. cit., p. 247.
19 B. Yeltsin, op. cit., p. 340.
20 From the author's interview with Sergei Filatov, February 2020.

21  From Nina Zvereva's video chronicles.
22  V. Bessarab, O. Ryabov et al., op. cit., p. 365.
23  From Nina Zvereva's video chronicles.
24  B. Nemtsov, loc. cit.
25  Nina Zvereva's video chronicles.
26  *Izvestiya*, 25 September 1993.
27  A. Kulikov, loc. cit.
28  *Kommersant*, 24 September 1993.
29  N. Zheleznova, A. Panova, A. Surkov et al., *Moskva. Osen-93. Khronika protivostoyaniya*, Moscow, Respublika, 1995, p. 86.
30  O. Moroz, loc. cit.
31  S. Filatov, *Sovershenno nesekretno*, Moscow, Vagrius, 2000.
32  A. Orlov, *Osen 93-go. Chyornyye steny Belogo doma*, Moscow, Veche, 2014.
33  From the author's interview with Sergei Filatov, February 2020.
34  Interview with Boris Nemtsov in the show *Pryamaya rech*, Volga Television Station, 4 October 2003.
35  B. Nemtsov, loc. cit.
36  V. Sheinis, op. cit., p. 532.
37  Yu. Voronin, *Strenozhennaya Rossiya. Politiko-ekonomichesky portret Yeltsinisma*, Moscow, Respublika, 2003.
38  V. Sheinis, op. cit., p. 528.
39  B. Yeltsin, op. cit., p. 350.
40  *Nezavisimaya gazeta*, 29 September 1993.
41  From the author's interview with Sergei Filatov, February 2020.
42  Loc. cit.
43  Loc. cit.
44  'Peregovory v Svyato-Danilovom monastyre. Stenogramma', in N. Zheleznova, A. Panova, A. Surkov et al., op. cit., p. 346.
45  A. Kulikov, loc. cit.
46  From the author's interview with Sergei Filatov, February 2020.
47  A. Kulikov, loc. cit.
48  B. Yeltsin, op. cit., p. 362.
49  Ye. Gaidar, op. cit., p. 260.
50  N. Zheleznova, A. Panova, A. Surkov et al., op. cit., p. 397.
51  Op. cit., pp. 603–4.
52  See memoirs by Yeltsin, Filatov, Korzhakov and Grachev.
53  B. Yeltsin, op. cit., p. 365.
54  S. Filatov, loc. cit.
55  P. Aven, A. Kokh, op. cit., p. 355.
56  O. Moroz, *Tak kto zhe rasstrelyal parlament?*, Moscow, Olimp, 2007.
57  This fact was confirmed in talks with two interviewees and was also related by P. Aven and A. Kokh in *Revolyutsiya Gaidara*.
58  P. Aven, A. Kokh, op. cit., p. 357.
59  N. Zheleznova, A. Panova, A. Surkov et al., op. cit., p. 600.
60  *Kommersant*, 5 October 1993.

61 P. Aven, A. Kokh, op. cit., p. 356.
62 *Kommersant*, 5 October 1993.
63 Interview with Boris Nemtsov in the show *Pryamaya rech*, Volga Television Station, 4 October 2003.
64 Yu. Baturin, A. Ilin, V. Kadatsky et al., op. cit., p. 369.
65 Ye. Gaidar, op. cit., p. 264.
66 V. Sheinis, op. cit., p. 566.
67 Interview with Boris Nemtsov for the project '1993. Vosstaniye v zashzhitu Konstitutsii', 15 February 2012, https://nemtsov-most.org/tag/расстрел-парламента-1993, accessed 24 July 2023.

# Chapter 8

1 From the author's interview with Oleg Sysuyev for the film *The Man Who Was Too Free*, 2015.
2 V. Gelman, S. Rivera, 'Governing Nizhny Novgorod. Boris Nemtsov as a regional leader', in *Soviet and Post-Soviet Politics and Society*, p. 181, 2018.
3 From the author's interview with Olga Smirnova, April 2020.
4 B. Nemtsov, op. cit., p. 29.
5 A. Chubais, ed., op. cit., p. 54.
6 From Nina Zvereva's interview with Boris Nemtsov, October 1994.
7 S. Lozinsky, *Voskhozhdeniye. Fotokniga o nizhegorodskom gybernatore Borise Nemtsove*, Nizhny Novgorod, Promis, 1998, p. 28.
8 From the author's interview with Mikhail Fridman for the film *The Man Who Was Too Free*, 2015.
9 Loc. cit.
10 Loc. cit.
11 Loc. cit.
12 *Kommersant Vlast*, 6 December 1993.
13 From Nemtsov's speech during the conflict with Vidyayev, February 1994.
14 V. Bessarab, O. Ryabov, et al., op. cit., p. 303.
15 From the author's interview with Pavel Chichagov, June 2019.
16 *Kommersant Vlast*, 28 August 1994.
17 From the author's interview with Pavel Chichagov, June 2019.
18 'Nizhegorodskiye reformy v izlozhenii gubernatora', from Nina Zvereva's archive, January 1995.
19 Quoted at N. Rozontova, 'Sidet i zhdat Nemtsov ne mog', *Koza press*, 9 October 2019.
20 'Nizhegorodskiye reformy v izlozhenii gubernatora', from Nina Zvereva's archive.
21 From the author's interview with Yury Lebedev, June 2019.
22 'Nizhegorodskiye reformy v izlozhenii gubernatora', from Nina Zvereva's archive.
23 From the author's interview with Yury Lebedev, June 2019.
24 From the author's interview with Olga Smirnova, April 2020.
25 From the author's interview with Dmitry Bednyakov, June 2019.

26 From the author's interview with Viktor Lysov, June 2019.
27 *Kommersant*, 29 March 1994.
28 D. Degtev, D. Zybov, *B. Nemtsov. Slishkom neizvestny chelovek*, Moscow, Tsentr-poligraf, 2017, p. 154.
29 From the author's interview with Viktor Lysov, June 2019.
30 From the author's interview with Dmitry Bednyakov, June 2019.
31 Loc. cit.
32 Loc. cit.
33 'Nizhegorodskiye reformy v izlozhenii gubernatora', from Nina Zvereva's archive.
34 From Nina Zvereva's video archive.
35 B. Nemtsov, loc. cit.
36 'Pri karernom roste ne dolzhno toshnit', interview with Boris Nemtsov in *Ogonyok*, 9 March 2015.
37 Ibid.
38 Quoted at V. Kostikov, *Roman c prezidentom. Zapiski press-sekretarya*, Moscow, Vagrius, 1997.
39 B. Nemtsov, loc. cit.
40 V. Kostikov, loc. cit.
41 From Nina Zvereva's video archive, October 1994.
42 V. Kostikov, loc. cit.
43 V. Gelman, S. Rivera, loc. cit.

# Chapter 9

1 Told to the author by Franz Klitsnevich, who heard it from Yazov.
2 'Dmitry Yazov. V razvale Sovetskogo Soyuza vinovata ne tolko pyataya kolonna', *Nezavisimaya gazeta*, 26 February 2020.
3 D. Gakayev, 'Put k chechenskoi revolyutsii', in *Chechnya i Rossiya. Obshchestva i gosudarstva*, Moscow, Polinform-Talburi, 1999.
4 Loc. cit.
5 Quoted at 'Nezamechenny perevorot Dudayeva', *Znak.com*, 6 September 2016.
6 From the author's interview with Musa Muradov, November 2018.
7 *Nezavisimaya gazeta*, 12 November 1991.
8 'On obozhal zhizn', *Gazeta.ru*, 28 February 2015.
9 A. Kulikov, loc. cit.
10 'Yesli Rossiya oslabnet, to zapylaet ves Kavkaz', *Lenta.ru*, 24 December 2015.
11 A. Tarasov, loc. cit.
12 A. Lieven, *Chechnya. Tragediya rossiiskoi moshchi*, Moscow, Universitet Dmitriya Pozharskogo, Russky fond sodeistviya obrazovaniyu i nauke, 2019.
13 'Spetzproyekt. Pevaya voina', *Kommersant*, 13 December 2014.
14 From the author's interview with Sergei Filatov, February 2020.
15 *The New Times*, 8 December 2014.
16 'Dzhokhar Dudayev. Ya ne znayu kakoi put Rossii nuzhen', *Kommersant*, 1 September 1998.

17 Miriam Vakhidova quoting Deinekin.
18 A. Lieven, loc. cit.
19 From the author's interview with Sergei Filatov, February 2020.
20 Ye. Savostyanov, *Demokrat-Kontrrazvedchik*, Moscow, Radiosoft, 2020, p. 448.
21 *Kommersant*, 31 August 1994.
22 *Kommersant*, 30 November 2019.
23 *Delovaya pressa*, 19 December 2002.
24 B. Yeltsin's speech on 8 September 1995 to Russian and international media, https://yeltsin.ru/archive/act/41867, accessed 26 April 2023.
25 B. Yeltsin, *Presidentskii Marafon*, Moscow, AST, 2000.
26 Ye. Savostyanov, op. cit., p. 469.
27 A. Kulikov, op. cit.
28 P. Grachev, 28 November 1994, https://ria.ru/20110417/365652355.html, accessed 26 April 2023.
29 P. Grachev, 'Menya naznachili otvetstvennym za voinu', *Trud*, 15 March 2001.
30 *Aleksandr Cherkasov o pervoi chechenskoi voine, Yeltsinmedia*, http://www.yeltsinmedia.com/interviews/cherkasov, accessed 4 December 2023.
31 From the author's interview with Andrei Kozyrev, June 2020.
32 From the author's interview with Stanislav Dmitriyevsky, June 2019.
33 Loc. cit.
34 A. Antipov, *Lev Rokhlin. Zhizn i Smert Generala*, Moscow, Eksmo-Press, 1998.
35 *Aleksandr Cherkasov o pervoi chechenskoi voine, Yeltsinmedia*, http://www.yeltsinmedia.com/interviews/cherkasov, accessed 4 December 2023.
36 *The New Times*, 8 December 2014.
37 *Itogi*, NTV, 1 January 1995.
38 From the author's interview with Nina Zvereva for the film *The Man Who Was Too Free*, 2015.
39 V. Kiselyov, *Nizhegorodtsy na chechenskoi voine*, Nizny Novgorod, 2000.
40 From the author's interview with Andrei Belyaninov, July 2020.
41 From the author's interview with Igor Kalyapin, June 2019.

# Chapter 10

1 A. Klimentyev, 'Prishyol v meriyu, vse byli dovolny', *Komsomolskaya pravda Nizhny Novgorod*, 30 March 2018.
2 A. Klimentyev, *Mezhdu vlastyu i turmoi*, St Petersburg, Sarov, 2008, p. 28.
3 Op. cit., p. 29.
4 'Nezavisimoye analiticheskoye obozreniye', Nizhny Novgorod, 19 April 2006.
5 *Kommersant*, 28 July 1995.
6 From the author's interview with Alexander Kotyusov, June 2019.
7 O. Bessarab, O. Ryabov et al., op. cit., p. 129.
8 Andrei Belyaninov, [video report], 1995.
9 From the author's interview with Olga Smirnova, April 2020.
10 Ibid.

11  From the author's interview with Vladimir Sedov, June 2019.
12  Andrei Belyaninov, *Istoriya odnogo kredita*, Set NN, 1995.
13  A. Klimentyev, loc. cit.
14  *Novaya gazeta*, 9 June 1998.
15  O. Bessarab, O. Ryabov et al., op. cit., p. 106.
16  From the author's interview with Alexander Lyubimov, October 2019.
17  *Playboy Magazine*, March 1995.
18  H. Kurtz, 'Media Notes: Zhirinovsky Hot to Trotsky. Russian Proposes Orgy to Playboy Interviewer', *The Washington Post*, 30 January 1995, https://www.washingtonpost.com/archive/lifestyle/1995/01/31/media-notes/8d4b5d64-ec92-4811-8a01-90156ba29a46, accessed 7 January 2024.
19  O. Bessarab, O. Ryabov et al., op. cit., p. 109.
20  M. Berger, O. Proskurinina, *Krest Chubaisa*, Moscow, Kolibri, 2008, p. 196.
21  Loc. cit.
22  A. Lieven, *Fenomen. Shtrikhi k portretu Eduarda Rosselya*, Yekaterinburg, Bank Kulturnoi informatsii, 2007, p. 163.
23  From an interview of Boris Nemtsov by the studio Nizhegorosky meridian, 6 October 1994.
24  Local Government of Nizhegorodskoi oblasti, No.1, 1995.
25  *Kommersant*, 28 November 1995.
26  V. Gelman, S. Rivera, 'Governing Nizhny Novgorod: Boris Nemtsov as a Regional Leader', in A. Makarychev, A. Yatsyk, ed., *Boris Nemtsov and Russian Politics: Power and Resistance*, Ibidem-Verlag, Stuttgart, 2018.
27  Commentary by B. Yeltsin, 13 January 1996, www.kommersant.ru/doc/390624, accessed 20 July 2023.
28  O. Bessarab, O. Ryabov et al., op. cit., p. 111.
29  Text of Boris Nemtsov's letter to Boris Yeltsin, https://nemtsov-most.org/2017/08/11/nemtsov-for-many-months-in-a-row-in-chechnya-without-ceasing-blood-is-flowing, accessed 18 July 2023.
30  From the author's interview with Stanislav Dmitriyevsky, June 2019.
31  O. Bessarab, O. Ryabov et al., loc. cit.
32  Boris Nemtsov on the show *Geroi dnya*, NTV, 29 January 1996, www.yeltsinmedia.com/events/jan-29-1996, accessed 18 July 2023.
33  B. Doktorov, A. Oslon, Ye. Petrenko, *Epokha Yeltsina: mneniya rossiyan. Sotsiologicheskiye ocherki*, Moscow, Public Opinion Fund, 2002, p. 137.
34  Loc. cit.
35  *Obshchaya gazeta*, 4 April 1996.
36  O. Bessarab, O. Ryabov et al., op. cit., p. 111.
37  Boris Nemtsov on the show *Geroi dnya*, NTV, 29 January 1996, www.yeltsinmedia.com/events/jan-29-1996, accessed 18 July 2023.
38  From the author's interview with Emil Pain, May 2020.
39  'Pri karernom roste ne dolzhno toshnit', interview with Boris Nemtsov in *Ogonyok*, 9 March 2015.
40  From the author's interview with Ivan Kladnitsky, June 2019.
41  Loc. cit.

42. Boris Nemtsov's Speech, 12 March 1996.
43. 'Poslanie Prezidenta Federalnomu sobraniyu', 23 February 1996, www.kremlin.ru/acts/bank/36349, accessed 18 July 2023.
44. *Kommersant*, 18 April 1996.
45. A. Lieven, *Chechnya*.
46. B. Minayev, op. cit., p. 594.
47. 'Pri karernom roste ne dolzhno toshnit', interview with Boris Nemtsov in Ogonyok, 9 March 2015.
48. B. Nemtsov. 'Muzhskoi razgovor s Dmitriem Gordonom', December 2008, www.youtube.com/watch?v=NpVzD0yRimY, accessed 18 July 2023.
49. From the author's interview with Emil Pain, May 2020.
50. *The New Times*, 12 April 2007.
51. Loc. cit.
52. *Itogi*, NTV, 30 May 1996.
53. From the author's interview with Emil Pain, May 2020.
54. Loc. cit.
55. Statement by Vyacheslav Tikhomirov, commander of the Combined Forces in Chechnya, 25 May 1996.
56. *Aleksandr Cherkasov o pervoi chechenskoi voine*, Yeltsinmedia, http://www.yeltsinmedia.com/interviews/cherkasov, accessed 4 December 2023.
57. *Kommersant*, 3 September 1996.
58. G. Troshev, *Moya voina. Chechensky dnevnik okopnogo generala*, Moscow, Vagrius, 2001.
59. *The New Times*, 12 April 2007.
60. Loc. cit.

## Chapter 11

1. *Geroi dnya*, NTV, 22 January 1996, http://www.yeltsinmedia.com/events/jan-22-1996, accessed 17 July 2023.
2. Ye. Gaidar, op. cit., p. 316.
3. Op. cit., p. 304.
4. Yegor Gaidar press conference, 13 February 1996.
5. From the author's interview with Alfred Kokh for the film *The Man Who Was Too Free*, 2015.
6. Boris Yeltsin's speech in Yekaterinburg, 15 February 1996.
7. M. Mironov, loc. cit.
8. From the author's interview with Leonid Nevzlin, May 2018.
9. D. Hoffman, *The Oligarchs: Wealth and Power in the New Russia*, New York, Public Affairs, 2010, [ebook].
10. From the author's interview with Anatoly Chubais, September 2020.
11. From the author's interview with Sergei Filatov, February 2020.
12. From an interview with Alexander Korzhakov in *Biznes-gazeta*, 19 June 2016.
13. From the author's interview with Valentin Yumashev for the film *The Man Who Was Too Free*, 2015.

14 Mikhail Khodorkovsky, 'Svoboda slova formiruetsya ne vnutri otdelnykh SMI', *Yeltsinmedia*, http://www.yeltsinmedia.com/interviews/khodorkovsky, accessed 18 July 2023.
15 D. Hoffman, loc. cit.
16 From the author's interview with Yevgeny Kiselyov for the film *The Man Who Was Too Free*, 2015.
17 M. Khodorkovsky, N. Gevorkyan, *Prison and Freedom*, Moscow, Govard Rork/Howard Roark Publishers, 2012, p. 134.
18 Quoted at D. Hoffman, loc. cit.
19 From the author's interview with Vladimir Gusinsky, October 2020.
20 *Geroi dnya*, NTV, 22 January 1996, http://www.yeltsinmedia.com/events/jan-22-1996, accessed 17 July 2023.
21 *Kommersant*, 17 June 1997.
22 A. Oslon, 'Kak v 1996 godu Analiticheskaya gruppa sdelala oprosy sotsialnym faktom', *Polit.ru*, 25 September 2006.
23 From the author's interview with Vladimir Gusinsky, October 2020.
24 Yegor Gaidar speaking in Nizhny Novgorod, quoted in *The Man Who Was Too Free*, 2015.
25 From the author's interview with Viktor Yaroshenko, September 2020.
26 *Itogi*, NTV, 10 March 1996.
27 Loc. cit.
28 M. Khodorkovsky, N. Gevorkyan, op. cit., p. 135.
29 From the author's interview with Mikhail Fridman for the film *The Man Who Was Too Free*, 2015.
30 *Kommersant*, 12 March 1996.
31 Loc. cit.
32 A. Kulikov, loc. cit.
33 B. Nemtsov, *Provintsial v Moskve*, loc. cit.
34 S. Filatov, loc. cit.
35 M. Kramer, 'Rescuing Boris,' *Time Magazine*, 24 June 2001, https://content.time.com/time/magazine/article/0,9171,136204,00.html, accessed 18 July 2023.
36 D. Hoffman, op. cit., p. 337.
37 B. Yeltsin, loc. cit.
38 A. Kulikov, op. cit.
39 Loc. cit.
40 *Izvestiya*, 23 May 2006.
41 Yu. Baturin, A. Ilin, V. Kadatsky et al., op. cit., p. 562.
42 From the author's interview with Vladimir Gusinsky, October 2020.
43 Yu. Baturin, A. Ilin, V. Kadatsky et al., op. cit., p. 559.
44 *Kommersant*, 17 June 1997.
45 A Oslon, loc. cit.
46 Ye. Gaidar, op. cit., p. 320.
47 Op. cit., p. 321.
48 From Yeltsin's speech at a congress of supporters, 8 April 1996.
49 *Izvestiya*, 6 February 1996.
50 Yu. Baturin, A. Ilin, V. Kadatsky et al., op. cit., p. 567.
51 I. Petrovskaya, 'Predvybornaya lovushka dlya TV', *Izvestiya*, 19 April 1996.

52 L. Hockstader, 'Yeltsin paying top ruble for positive news coverage', *The Washington Post*, 30 June 1996, https://www.washingtonpost.com/archive/politics/1996/06/30/yeltsin-paying-top-ruble-for-positive-news-coverage/fdc11c69-66ba-4385-98a6-77493ad8c211, accessed 18 July 2023.
53 B. Yeltsin, loc. cit.
54 From the author's interview with Grigory Yavlinky, August 2019.
55 From the author's interview with Viktor Lysov, June 2019.
56 *Chas pik*, ORT, 4 June 1996.
57 Loc. cit.
58 From the author's interview with Tatyana Yumasheva for the film *The Man Who Was Too Free*, 2015.
59 P. Aven, *Vremya Berezovskogo*, Moscow, Corpus, 2018, p. 248.
60 The author has a copy.
61 From the *Biznes-gazeta* interview with Alexander Korzhakov, 19 June 2016.
62 A. Goldfarb, 'Korobka iz-pod kseroksa. Pervaya bitva silovikov i liberalov', *Snob.ru*, 18 June 2015.
63 From the author's interview with Anatoly Chubais, August 2017.
64 Loc. cit.
65 *Ogonyok*, 29 October 2000.
66 Loc. cit.
67 Quoted at D. Hoffman, loc. cit.
68 B. Yeltsin, loc. cit.
69 V. Mikhailov, 'Demokratizatsiya Rossii. Razlichnaya skorost v regionakh', *Osobaya zona: vybory v Tatarstane*, Ulyanovsk, 2000.
70 Yeltsin's television address, 4 July 1996.
71 *Izvestiya*, 7 July 1996.

## Chapter 12

1 *Kommersant*, 18 October 1996.
2 As told by a source who worked in the Kremlin at the time.
3 *Kommersant*, 23 October 1996.
4 From the author's interview with Sergei Dubinin, August 2017.
5 *Ogonyok*, 16 March 1997.
6 From the author's interview with Sergei Zverev, July 2017.
7 *Ogonyok*, 16 March 1997.
8 From Dmitry Gordon's interview with Boris Nemtsov, 2008.
9 From the author's interview with Mikhail Fridman for the film *The Man Who Was Too Free*, 2015.
10 From the author's interview with Valentin Yumashev for the film *The Man Who Was Too Free*, 2015.
11 B. Yeltsin, loc. cit.
12 Loc. cit.
13 From Dmitry Gordon's interview with Boris Nemtsov, 2008.

14 Loc. cit.
15 From the author's interview with Tatyana Yumasheva for the film *The Man Who Was Too Free*, 2015.
16 B. Nemtsov, *Ispoved buntarya*, op. cit., p. 29.
17 From the author's interview with Mikhail Fridman for the film *The Man Who Was Too Free*, 2015.
18 *Geroi dnya bez galstuka*, NTV, 1997.
19 From the author's interview with Yury Lebedev, June 2019.
20 Loc. cit.
21 Loc. cit.
22 From the author's interview with Alfred Kokh for the film *The Man Who Was Too Free*, 2015.
23 *Kommersant*, 23 March 1997.
24 From the author's interview with Anatoly Chubais, August 2017.
25 *Itogi*, NTV, March 1997.
26 *Kommersant*, 5 March 1998.
27 B. Fyodorov, *Pytayas ponyat Rossiyu*, St Petersburg, Limbus Press, 2000.
28 From the author's interview with Oleg Vyugin, August 2017.
29 Loc. cit.
30 'Nemtsov — geroi marta', Public Opinion Foundation Database, 4 April 1997, nemtsov-most.org/2017/03/03/fom-1997-boris-nemtsov-a-hero-in-march, accessed 4 January 2024.
31 From the author's interview with Gleb Pavlovsky, August 2017.
32 From the author's interview with Yury Lebedev, June 2019.
33 *Kommersant*, 17 March 1997.
34 B. Yeltsin, loc. cit.
35 From the author's interview with Oleg Sysuyev for the film *The Man Who Was Too Free*, 2015.
36 From the author's interview with Yuly Dubov, July 2017.
37 Yu. Luzhkov, *Moskva i zhizn*, Moscow, E Publishers, 2017.
38 B. Nemtsov, *Provintsial v Moskve*, loc. cit.
39 From the author's interview with Oleg Sysuyev for the film *The Man Who Was Too Free*, 2015.
40 Loc. cit.
41 B. Nemtsov, *Ispoved buntarya*, op. cit., p. 146.
42 From the author's interview with Oleg Sysuyev for the film *The Man Who Was Too Free*, 2015.
43 From the author's interview with Sergei Yastrzhembsky for the film *The Man Who Was Too Free*, 2015.
44 From the author's interview with Yakov Urinson, July 2017.
45 A. Chubais, ed., op. cit., p. 297.
46 M. Berger, O. Proskurina, op. cit., p. 44.
47 'Istoriya "ottsa" Gazproma: ot bezgranichnoi vlasti do zabveniya na pensii', *Forbes*, September 2012.
48 'Istoriya o tom, kak chut ne ukrali Gazprom', Boris Nemtsov's LiveJournal, 18 September 2012.

49  From the author's interview with Viktor Aksyuchts, September 2017.
50  V. Panyushkin, M. Zygar, *Gazprom. Novoye russkoye oruzhiye*, Moscow, Zakharov Publishers, 2008.
51  From the author's interview with Boris Nadezhdin, August 2017.
52  A. Goldfarb, *Sasha, Boris, Volodya... A Murder History*, New York, AGC/Grani, 2011.
53  From the author's interview with Alexander Goldfarb, November 2020.
54  *Kommersant Vlast*, 25 April 2000.
55  A. Goldfarb, loc. cit.
56  V. Panyushkin, M. Zygar, loc. cit.

# Chapter 13

1  'Sovershenno sekretno', 15 November 1996, http://www.yeltsinmedia.com/events/nov-15-1996, accessed 19 July 2023.
2  From the author's interview with Igor Malashenko, February 2018.
3  From the author's interview with Vladimir Gusinsky, October 2020.
4  From the author's interview with Igor Malashenko, February 2018.
5  Loc. cit.
6  From the author's interview with Vladimir Gusinsky, October 2020.
7  Loc. cit.
8  From the author's interview with Alfred Kokh, May 2018.
9  Loc. cit.
10  Loc. cit.
11  From the author's interview with Igor Malashenko, February 2018.
12  From the author's interview with Anatoly Chubais, August 2017.
13  *Kommersant Vlast*, 20 May 1997.
14  A. Chubais, ed., op. cit., p. 283.
15  From the author's interview with Igor Malashenko, February 2018.
16  *Kommersant*, 13 March 1998.
17  *Novaya gazeta*, 1 December 1997.
18  From the author's interview with Valentin Yumashev for the film *The Man Who Was Too Free*, 2015.
19  Loc. cit.
20  D. Hoffman, loc. cit.
21  From the author's interview with Sergei Zverev, July 2017.
22  P. Aven, op. cit., p. 391.
23  From the author's interview with Sergei Zverev, July 2017.
24  From the author's interview with Igor Malashenko, February 2018.
25  *Novosti*, ORT, 26 July 1997.
26  P. Aven, loc. cit.
27  *Novaya gazeta*, August 1997.
28  From the author's interview with Vladimir Grigoryev, November 2020.
29  Loc. cit.

30 B. Nemtsov, op. cit., p. 25.
31 Loc. cit.
32 From the author's interview with Igor Malashenko, February 2018.
33 Sergei Dorenko's programme on ORT, 14 March 1998, https://www.youtube.com/watch?v=EdtEv8G-NTw, accessed 19 July 2023.
34 *Nezavisimaya gazeta*, 13 September 1997.
35 *Kommersant*, 11 October 1997.
36 From the author's interview with Vladimir Gusinsky, October 2020.
37 From a *Yeltsinmedia* interview of Valentin Yumashev, www.yeltsinmedia.com/interviews/yumashev, accessed 19 July 2023.
38 Speech by Anatoly Chubais, September 1997, www.carnegieendowment.org/files/BorisYeltsinandHisRegime.pdf, accessed 4 January 2024.
39 From the author's interview with Oleg Sysuyev for the film *The Man Who Was Too Free*, 2015.
40 A. Petrova, S. Klimova, 'Fond Obshchestvennoye mneniye', 11 September 1997.
41 Statement by B. Yeltsin in Strasbourg, 10 October 1997, www.svoboda.org/a/24100581.html, accessed 5 January 2024.
42 From the author's interview with Tatyana Yumasheva for the film *The Man Who Was Too Free*, 2015.
43 Loc. cit.
44 Speech by Gennady Seleznyov in the State Duma 14 October 1997.
45 From the author's interview with Sergei Dubinin, August 2017.
46 Text of address was given to the author by Viktor Aksyuchits.
47 From the author's interview with Viktor Aksyuchits, September 2017.
48 *Kommersant*, 28 October 1997.
49 B. Yeltsin, loc. cit.
50 Boris Nemtsov's interview to the Yeltsin Center, 9 October 2015, https://yeltsin.ru/news/boris-nemcov-chubays-byl-ne-takoy-otvyaznyy-kak-ya, accessed 20 July 2023.
51 Aleksandr Minkin's interview on Ekho Moskvy, 12 November 1997.
52 'School for Scandal: The Burning of a Russian Crusader', *The New York Times*, 30 November 1997, https://www.nytimes.com/1997/11/30/weekinreview/school-for-scandal-the-burning-of-a-russian-crusader.html, accessed 20 July 2023.
53 A. Ostrovsky, *Govorit i pokazyvaet Rossiya*, Moscow, Corpus, 2019, p. 319.
54 From the author's interview with Vladimir Grigoryev, November 2020.
55 Loc. cit.
56 *Novaya gazeta*, 1 December 1997.
57 G. Soros, *The Crisis of Global Capitalism: Open Society Endangered*, New York, PublicAffairs, 1998, as quoted in *Kommersant*, 25 April 2000.
58 From the author's interview with Igor Malashenko, February 2018.
59 From the author's interview with Yevgeny Kiselyov for the film *The Man Who Was Too Free*, 2015.
60 *Nezavisimaya gazeta*, 30 September 1997.
61 Nizhegorodskoye televideniye NNTV, spring 1998.
62 Ekho Moskvy, 5 November 1997.
63 *Kommersant*, 17 March 1998.

64 From the author's interview with Yevgeniya Albats for the film *The Man Who Was Too Free*, 2015.
65 *Kommersant*, 17 March 1998.
66 From the author's interview with Irina Khakamada for the film *The Man Who Was Too Free*, 2015.
67 *Nezavisimaya gazeta*, 17 March 1998.
68 Loc. cit.

## Chapter 14

1 'Pokoyaniye. Materialy pravitelstvennoi komissii po izucheniyu voprosov, svyazannykh s isledovaniyem i perezakhoroneniem ostankov Rossiiskogo Imperatora Nikolaya II i chlenov ego semi', Moscow, 1998, p. 64, docs.historyrussia.org/ru/nodes/58368-pokayanie-materialy-pravitelstvennoy-komissii-po-izucheniyu-voprosov-svyazannyh-s-issledovaniem-i-perezahoroneniem-ostankov-rossiyskogo-imperatora-nikolaya-ii-i-chlenov-ego-semi, accessed 20 July 2023.
2 B. Yeltsin, loc. cit.
3 From the author's interview with Viktor Aksyuchits, September 2017.
4 From the author's interview with Vladimir Solovyev, November 2021.
5 Loc. cit.
6 S. Lozinsky, *Voskhozhdeniye. Fotokniga o nizhegorodskom gubernatore Borise Nemtsove*, Nizhny Novgorod, Promis, 1998, p. 137.
7 From the author's interview with Viktor Aksyuchits, September 2017.
8 From the author's interview with Vladimir Solovyev, November 2021.
9 Loc. cit.
10 Loc. cit.
11 N. Yeltsina, *Lichnaya zhizn*, Moscow, Sindbad, 2017, p. 296.
12 Ye. Moryzev, 'Boris Efimovich Nemtsov. Intervyu Litpromu', 2 March 2015, litprom.ru/thread62567.html, accessed 5 January 2024.
13 From the author's interview with Sergei Dubinin, August 2017.
14 *Izvestiya*, 17 July 2002.
15 Boris Yeltsin's television address, 16 July 1998, yeltsin.ru/archive/video/51551, accessed 20 July 2023.
16 From Boris Yeltsin's address at the burial of the imperial remains, 17 July 1998, www.youtube.com/watch?v=LQJDMp_ORlA, accessed 5 January 2024.
17 A. Mitchina, 'Svyashchennii sinod perenyos priznanie ostankov tsarskoi semi Romanovykh', *UralPolit*, 18 April 2022, uralpolit.ru/news/urfo/18-04-2022/255359, accessed 6 January 2024.

## Chapter 15

1 From an interview with the author in October 2017.
2 Loc. cit.

3 *Kommersant Vlast*, 23 June 1998.
4 *Kommersant Vlast*, 23 June 1998.
5 From the author's interview with Valentin Yumashev, December 2020.
6 From the author's interview with Sergei Dubinin, August 2017.
7 From the author's interview with Yakov Urinson, July 2017.
8 Boris Yeltsin, loc. cit.
9 From the author's interview with Alfred Kokh, May 2018.
10 T. Colton, loc. cit.
11 From the author's interview with Viktor Lysov, June 2019.
12 From the author's interview with Boris Nedezhdin, August 2017.
13 From the author's interview with Yevgeniya Albats for the film *The Man Who Was Too Free*, 2015.
14 *Nezavisimaya gazeta*, March 1998.
15 *Kommersant*, 4 June 1998.
16 Sergei Aleksashenko, *Bitva za rubl. Vzglyad uchastnika sobytii*, Moscow, Vremya Publishers, 2008.
17 From the author's interview with Oleg Vyugin, August 2017.
18 M. Gilman, *No Precedent, No Plan: Inside Russia's 1998 Default*, Boston, MIT Press, 2010.
19 Interview with Nemtsov, 'Za defolt v otvete nasha "zamechatelnaya" Gosduma', from V. Solovyev, *Russkaya ruletka. Zametki na polyakh noveishei istorii*, 5 October 1999, www.nemtsov-most.org/2021/06/23/nemtsov-our-wonderful-state-duma-is-responsible-for-the-default, accessed 5 January 2024.
20 *Kommersant*, 30 June 1998.
21 From Vladimir Solovyev's interview with Boris Nemtsov, 5 October 1999.
22 M. Gilman, *Defolt, kotorogo moglo ne byt*, Moscow, Vremya Publishers, 2008.
23 G. Soros, 'The Only Way for Russia to End Its Crisis', *Financial Times*, 13 August 1998, https://www.georgesoros.com/1998/08/13/the-only-way-for-russia-to-end-its-crisis, accessed 22 July 2023.
24 From the author's interview with Sergei Dubinin, August 2017.
25 Loc. cit.
26 From the author's interview with Mikhail Khodorkovsky, July 2017.
27 *Kommersant*, 17 October 1998.
28 From the author's interview with Sergei Dubinin, August 2017.
29 Quoted on *Itogi*, NTV, 12 August 2008.
30 *Kommersant*, 19 January 1999.
31 *Kommersant*, 17 November 1998.
32 Loc. cit.
33 From Dmitry Gordon's interview with Viktor Chernomyrdin, 2010.
34 *Kommersant*, 25 August 1998.
35 Ye. Primakov, *Vosem mesyatsev plyus*, Moscow, Mysl, 2002.

# Chapter 16

1 From the author's interview with Alfred Kokh for the film *The Man Who Was Too Free*, 2015.

2 From an interview with Sergei Tsyplyayev to Online812.ru, 13 July 2016.
3 A. Sobchak, *Dyuzhina nozhei v spinu*, Moscow, Vagrius, 1999.
4 From an interview by 812Online.ru with Sergei Tsyplyayev, 13 July 2016.
5 From the author's interview with Alfred Kokh for the film *The Man Who Was Too Free*, 2015.
6 From Igor Shadkhan's interview with Vladimir Putin in 1996.
7 Loc. cit.
8 P. Aven, op. cit., p. 423.
9 From the film *Delo Sobchaka*, directed by Vera Krichevskaya, 2018.
10 Outtakes from Vera Krichevskaya's film *Delo Sobchaka*.
11 From the author's interview with Gleb Pavlovsky, August 2017.
12 N. Gevorkyan, N. Timakova, A. Kolesnikov, *First Person: An Astonishingly Frank Self-Portrait by Russia's President Vladimir Putin*, tr. C. Fitzpatrick, New York, PublicAffairs, [ebook].
13 S. Röbel, W. Tietze, 'Russian President's Years in Germany Seem Less Exciting Than the Stories', *Spiegel International*, 7 June 2023, www.spiegel.de/international/germany/were-vladimir-putin-s-years-in-germany-less-thrilling-than-the-stories-a-178de140-b799-472d-83bc-5e3b1adf65b2, accessed 4 January 2024.
14 *Kommersant*, 4 August 1998.
15 From the author's interview with Oleg Sysuyev for the film *The Man Who Was Too Free*, 2015.
16 *Kommersant*, 30 July 1998.

# Chapter 17

1 Valentin Yumashev, 'My glotnuli svobody i otravilis eyu', *Moskovsky komsomolets*, 31 January 2011.
2 'Doveryayut li rossiyane pravitelstvu i ego glave', Fond Obshchevennoye mneniye, 25 February 1999.
3 From the author's interview with Sergei Stepashin, December 2017.
4 Ye. Primakov, loc. cit.
5 From the author's interview with Sergei Dubinin, August 2017.
6 Yury Skuratov, *Variant drakona*, Moscow, Detektiv-press, 2002.
7 S. LaFraniere, 'Yeltsin Linked to Bribe Scheme', *The Washington Post*, 8 September 1999, p. A1.
8 P. Aven, op. cit., p. 447.
9 Transcription of the session of the Federation Council, 17 March 1999, council.gov.ru/media/files/41d44e65cce75f5265d0.doc, accessed 24 July 2023.
10 *Kommersant*, 19 March 1999.
11 Yury Skuratov writes about this in his memoirs, *Kremlyovskiye podryady. Poslednyeye delo genpropkurora* (2013).
12 B. Yeltsin, loc. cit.
13 Loc. cit.
14 From the author's interview with Sergei Stepashin, December 2017.

15 From the author's interview with Yevgeny Kiselyov, April 2018.
16 *Kommersant*, 5 June 1999.
17 *Kommersant Vlast*, 11 May 1999.
18 From the author's interview with Gleb Pavlovsky, August 2017.
19 *Kommersant*, 15 June 1999.
20 From an interview for *Snob* with Sergei Stepashin on 15 April 2016.
21 From the author's interview with Igor Malashenko, February 2018.
22 Loc. cit.
23 B. Nemtsov, op. cit., p. 53.
24 Quoted at L. Mlechin, *KGB. Predsedateli organov bezopasnosti. Rassekrechennyye sudby*, Moscow, Tsentropoligraf, 2006.
25 From the author's interview with Gleb Pavlovsky, August 2017.
26 From the author's interview with Sergei Stepashin, December 2017.
27 Loc. cit.
28 Ye. Primakov, loc. cit.
29 *Kommersant*, 6 August 1999.
30 From Pyotr Aven's interview with Alexander Voloshin in P. Aven, op. cit., p. 444.
31 From the author's interview with Boris Nadezhdin, August 2017.
32 See A. Lieven, loc. cit.
33 Among others, Abbaz Osmayev writes about this in his article 'Obshchevstvenno-politicheskaya situatsiya v Chechenskoi Respublike v 1996-1999 gg.', *Izvestiya Altaiskogo gosudarstvennogo universiteta*, 2008.
34 *Nezavisimaya gazeta*, 14 January 2000.
35 Vladimir Putin's address to the Federation Council 17 September 1999, council.gov.ru/media/files/41d44e65cce75f5265d0.doc., accessed 24 July 2023.
36 *Kommersant*, 22 September 1999.
37 E. Pain, 'Vtoraya chechenskaya voina i eyo posledstviya', *Istoriya novoi Rossii*, May 2000.
38 B. Doktorov, A. Oslon, Ye. Petrenko, op. cit., p. 310.
39 From the author's interview with Gleb Pavlovsky, August 2017.
40 B. Doktorov, A. Oslon, Ye. Petrenko, op. cit., p. 312.

## Chapter 18

1 From an Ekho Moskvy radio station interview with Boris Nemtsov, 4 March 2013.
2 B. Nemtsov, 'Ya ne khudzhii variant dlya Rossii', *Ogonyok*, 11 July, 1999.
3 From the author's interview with Irina Khakamada, June 2018.
4 From the author's interview with Alexander Kotyusov, June 2019.
5 *Izvestiya*, 28 November 1998.
6 From the author's interview with Anatoly Chubais, August 2017.
7 From the author's interview with Irina Khakamada, June 2018.
8 *Kommersant*, 25 May 1999.
9 *Kommersant Vlast*, 1 June 1999.
10 From the author's interview with Gleb Pavlovsky, August 2017.
11 From the author's interview with Pyotr Shchedrovitsky, January 2018.

12   From the author's interview with Irina Khakamada, June 2018.
13   From the author's interview with Irina Khakamada for the film *The Man Who Was Too Free*, 2015.
14   Quoted in *The Man Who Was Too Free*.
15   Loc. cit.
16   *Segognya*, 24 September 1999.
17   From the author's interview with Gleb Pavlovsky, August 2017.
18   From the author's interview with Valentin Zavadnikov, February 2018.
19   *Novosti*, NTV, 1 January 2000.
20   From the author's interview with Yevgenia Albats for the film *The Man Who Was Too Free*, 2015.
21   From the author's interview with Alfred Kokh for the film *The Man Who Was Too Free*, 2015.
22   *Izvestiya*, 13 November 1999.
23   Debate between Boris Nemtsov and Vladimir Zhirinovsky, Ekho Moskvy, 27 November 1999.
24   *Kommersant*, 8 June 1999.
25   Debate between Boris Nemtsov and Vladimir Zhirinovsky, Ekho Moskvy, 27 November 1999.
26   From the author's interview with Robert Skidelsky, May 2019.
27   *Novosti*,*ORT*, 13 December 1999,
28   V. Putin, *Ot pervogo litsa*, Moscow, Vagrius, 2000.
29   Loc. cit.
30   From Ksenia Sobchak's interview with Sergei Pugachyov on TV Rain in June 2015.
31   From the film *Svideteli Putina*, directed by Vitaly Mansky, 2018.
32   'Russia's Best Bet', *The New York Times*, 5 January 2000, https://www.nytimes.com/2000/01/05/opinion/russia-s-best-bet.html, accessed 24 July 2023.
33   Radio Liberty, 20 January 2000.
34   *Kommersant*, 9 February 2000.
35   *Kommersant*, 10 March 2000.
36   From an Ekho Moskvy interview with Boris Nemtsov on 11 February 2000.
37   From the film *Svideteli Putina*, directed by Vitaly Mansky, 2018.

# Chapter 19

1   A.V. Ulyukayev, *Pravy povorot*, Moscow, Strelyets, 1999.
2   *Ogonyok*, 9 April 2000.
3   From the author's interview with Igor Malashenko, February 2018.
4   Loc. cit.
5   From a *Novaya gazeta* interview with Mikhail Kasyanov, March 2014.
6   *Kommersant*, 20 July 1999.
7   From the author's interview with Yevgeny Kiselyov, August 2018.
8   Loc. cit.
9   NTV, 26 March 2000.

10 From the author's interview with Yevgeny Kiselyov, April 2018.
11 D. Hoffman, loc. cit.
12 From the author's interview with Igor Malashenko, February 2018.
13 *Kommersant Vlast*, 20 June 2000.
14 Sergei Dorenko's programme, ORT, 17 June 2000.
15 Loc. cit.
16 NTV, 17 June 2000.
17 *Kommersant Vlast*, 20 June 2000.
18 From the author's interview with Irina Khakamada for the film, *The Man Who Was Too Free*, 2015.
19 *Kommersant*, 14 July 2000.
20 Vladimir Putin's introductory speech at a meeting with businesspeople, 28 July 2000.
21 *Forbes*, 28 October 2010.
22 Boris Nemtsov's press conference, 28 July 2000.
23 From the author's interview with Yevgeny Kiselyov, April 2018.
24 From the author's interview with Alim Yusupov, April 2018.
25 *Kommersant*, 29 August 2000.
26 From the author's interview with Alexei Venediktov, April 2018.
27 From Larry King's interview with Vladimir Putin, CNN, 8 September 2000, http://edition.cnn.com/TRANSCRIPTS/0009/08/lkl.00.html, accessed 17 April 2023.
28 From the author's interview with Yevgeny Kiselyov, April 2018.
29 *Itogi*, NTV, 2 April 2001, https://www.youtube.com/watch?v=y9l4y6cPL6g, accessed 17 April 2001.
30 Loc. cit.
31 From the author's interview with Alfred Kokh, July 2018.
32 Loc. cit.
33 Loc. cit.

# Chapter 20

1 *Svoboda*, 15 April 1995.
2 *Kommersant Vlast*, 5 March 2002.
3 *Kommersant*, 19 March 2002.
4 V. Pribylovsky, 'Chto takoye "upravlyayemaya demokratiya": kontseptsiya, istoriya, rossiisky opyt', Informational-Analytical Centre Sova, 17 March 2005.
5 From the author's interview with Anatoly Lebedko, December 2018.
6 From the author's interview with Zinaida Gonchar, December 2018.
7 From the author's interview with Irina Khakamada for the film *The Man Who Was Too Free*, 2015.
8 From the author's interview with Anatoly Lebedko, December 2018.
9 From the author's interview with Irina Khakamada for the film *The Man Who Was Too Free*, 2015.
10 *Kommersant*, 24 October 2002.
11 Radio Liberty, 25 October 2002.

12 Dolnik A., Pilch R., 'The Moscow Theater Hostage Crisis: The Perpetrators, Their Tactics and the Russian Response', *International Negotiation* 8, 2003.
13 '*Nord-Ost pyat let spustya*', Ekho Moskvy, 24 October 2007.
14 From *Nord Ost: Condolence Book*.
15 REN TV, 24 October 2002.
16 From the author's interview with Irina Khakamada for the film *The Man Who Was Too Free*, 2015.
17 *Komsomolskaya pravda*, 23 October 2012.
18 A. Zaukha, *Moskva. Nord-Ost*, Moscow, Prava Cheloveka, 2009.
19 *Komsolmolskaya pravda*, 23 October 2012.
20 *K baryeru*, NTV, 23 October 2003.
21 *Moskovsky komsomolets*, 25 June 2004.
22 From the author's interview with Anatoly Chubais, August 2017.
23 '10 let Nord-Ostu. Rasledovaniya', *Novaya gazeta*, 22 October 2012.
24 Interfax, 29 October 2002.
25 *Kommersant*, 8 September 2001.
26 From the author's interview with Anatoly Chubais, August 2017.
27 Grigory Yavlinsky's blog, 25 October 2017.
28 'My ne uznayom, pochemu oni ne vzorvali zal', Radio Liberty, 23 October 2014.
29 *Vremya*, OPT, 26 October 2002.
30 From footage that was not used in Zosya Rodkevich's film *Moi drug Boris Nemtsov*, 2013.
31 Loc. cit.
32 From the author's interview with Alexei Venediktov, April 2018.
33 From the author's interview with Alexander Ryklin, December 2017.
34 Loc. cit.

## Chapter 21

1 A former Yukos employee quoted on condition of anonymity.
2 From the author's interview with Mikhail Khodorkovsky, April 2017.
3 From a conversation with a former Yukos employee.
4 From the author's interview with Mikhail Khodorkovsky, July 2017.
5 *Kommersant*, 16 December 2002.
6 M. Zygar, *All the Kremlin's Men: Inside the Court of Vladimir Putin*, New York, PublicAffairs, 2016, [ebook].
7 Ye. Gaidar, op. cit., p. 301.
8 Op. cit., p. 305.
9 From the author's interview with Leonid Nevzlin, May 2018.
10 From the author's interview with Mikhail Khodorkovsky, July 2017.
11 Grigory Yavlinsky's letter to Boris Nemtsov and Irina Khakamada, 28 January 2003.
12 From the author's interview with Grigory Yavlinsky for the film *The Man Who Was Too Free*, 2015.
13 Anatoly Chubais's speech to the SPS congress, 10 September 2003.
14 *Kommersant*, 28 September 2002.

15 *Yezhenedelny zhurnal*, 25 May 2003.
16 From the author's interview with Leonid Gozman, September 2017.
17 Vladimir Putin's annual press conference, 20 June 2003.
18 Survey by the Public Opinion Foundation, 19 December 2002.
19 From the author's interview with Yevgeny Malkin, October 2017.
20 From the author's interview with Irina Khakamada for the film *The Man Who Was Too Free*, 2015.
21 From the author's interview with Anatoly Chubais, August 2017.
22 From the author's interview with Yevgeny Malkin, October 2017.
23 Anatoly Chubais's speech to the SPS congress, 10 September 2003.
24 From the author's interview with Irina Khakamada for the film *The Man Who Was Too Free*, 2015.
25 From the author's interview with Oleg Sysuyev for the film *The Man Who Was Too Free*, 2015.
26 From the author's interview with Alfred Kokh, July 2018.
27 M. Khodorkovsky, N. Gevorkyan, op. cit., p. 364.
28 *Kommersant*, 21 August 2004.
29 *Forbes* (Russian edition), 3 July 2005.
30 From the author's interview with Leonid Nevzlin, May 2018.
31 From the author's interview with Vasily Shakhnovsky, April 2018.
32 From the author's interview with Mikhail Khodorkovsky, January 2020.
33 *Gosudarstvo i oligarkhiya*, Sovet po natsionalnoi strategii, 26 May 2003.
34 From the author's interview with Vasily Shakhnovsky, April 2018.
35 Told to the author by a source who worked in the Kremlin at the time.
36 From the author's interview with Mikhail Khodorkovsky, January 2020.
37 I. Zhegulyov, *Khod Tsaryom. Tainaya borba za vlast i vliyaniye v sovremennoi Rossii ot Yeltsina do Putina*, Moscow, Govard Rork/Howard Roark, 2022, p. 259.
38 M. Khodorkovsky, N. Gevorkyan, op. cit., p. 353.
39 Told to the author from a source who attended the meetings.
40 *Novaya gazeta*, 6 July 2016.
41 From the author's interview with Vasily Shakhnovsky, April 2018.
42 From the author's interview with Mikhail Khodorkovsky, July 2017.
43 M. Khodorkovsky, N. Gevorkyan, op. cit., p. 359.
44 I. Zhigulyov, op. cit., p. 260.
45 From the author's interview with Leonid Nevzlin, May 2018.
46 *Sobchak Live*, TV Rain, 12 April 2012.
47 *Kommersant*, 7 October 2003.
48 Voronezh Channel 4, 17 October 2003.
49 From the author's interview with Dmitry Zimin, June 2018.
50 From the author's interview with Anatoly Chubais, August 2017.
51 *Vedomosti*, 29 October 2003.
52 Meeting between Vladimir Putin and members of his cabinet, 27 October 2003.
53 *Kommersant*, 9 June 2003.
54 V. Pereverzin, *Zalozhnik. Istoriya menedzhera YUKOSa*, Moscow, Govard Rork/Howard Roark, 2013, p. 5.

55 M. Khodorkovsky, N. Gevorkyan, loc. cit.
56 NTV, 7 November 2003.
57 Loc. cit.
58 From the author's interview with Alfred Kokh, July 2018.
59 From the author's interview with Anatoly Chubais, August 2017.
60 Debates on *NTV,* 7 November 2003.
61 SPS leaders' press conference, 3 December 2003.
62 BBC Russian Service, 8 December 2003.
63 B. Nemtsov, *Ispoved buntarya*, op. cit., p. 68.
64 M. Kasyanov, *Bez Putina*, Moscow, Novaya gazeta, 2009, p. 233.
65 Loc. cit.

## Chapter 22

1 B. Nemtsov, op. cit., p. 189.
2 From the author's interview with Mikhail Prokhorov for the film *The Man Who Was Too Free*, 2015.
3 Loc. cit.
4 B. Nemtsov, op. cit., p. 176.
5 From the author's interview with Alexander Ryklin, December 2017.
6 Founding declaration of Committee-2018, 19 January 2004.
7 *Kommersant*, 19 January 2004.
8 *Apelsinovy sok*, NTV, 18 April 2004.
9 From the author's interview with Mikhail Fridman for the film *The Man Who Was Too Free*, 2015.
10 B. Nemtsov, op. cit., p. 120.
11 A briefing by Boris Nemtsov, 11 February 2004.

## Chapter 23

1 *Kommersant*, 27 April 2001.
2 N. Petrov, A. Ryabov, 'The Role of Russia in the Orange Revolution', in *Revolution in Orange: The Origins of Ukraine's Democratic Breakthrough*, Washington, Carnegie, 2006.
3 From an interview with Anatoly Chubais on Ekho Moskvy, 27 September 2003.
4 *Vedomosti*, 1 December 2004.
5 From the author's interview with Roman Bessmertny, September 2021.
6 From the author's interview with Viktor Pinzenik, July 2019.
7 From the author's interview with Viktor Yushchenko for the film *The Man Who Was Too Free*, 2015.
8 *Versii.com*, 14 November 2002.
9 UNIAN, 28 January 2005.
10 From the author's interview with Viktor Yushchenko for the film *The Man Who Was Too Free*, 2015.

11  Loc. cit.
12  From the author's interview with Mikhail Pogrebinsky, August 2018.
13  C. Rice, *No Higher Honor*, New York, Broadway Books, 2011, [ebook].
14  S. Pifer, *The Eagle and the Trident: U. S. — Ukraine Relations in Turbulent Times*, Washington, D.C., Brookings Institution Press, 2017, [ebook].
15  See T. Garton-Ash, T. Snyder, 'The Orange Revolution', *New York Review of Books*, 28 April 2005.
16  *Kommersant*, 27 October 2004.
17  From the author's interview with Oleg Rybachuk, July 2018.
18  Boris Nemtsov's speech on the Maidan, 22 November 2004.
19  From the author's interview with Viktor Yushchenko for the film *The Man Who Was Too Free*, 2015.
20  UNIAN, 28 January 2005.
21  *Kommersant*, 24 November 2004.
22  From the author's interview with Viktor Yushchenko for the film *The Man Who Was Too Free*, 2015.
23  REN TV, November 2004.
24  S. Pifer, loc. cit.
25  *Putin, Russia and the West*, BBC, 2012.
26  UNIAN, 28 January 2005.

# Chapter 24

1  From the author's interview with Oleg Rybachuk, July 2018.
2  From the author's interview with Alexander Vershbow, August 2018.
3  UNIAN, 28 January 2005
4  C. Rice, loc. cit.
5  M. Zygar, loc. cit.
6  Press Conference of Vladimir Putin, Silvio Berlusconi and George Robertson, Rome, 28 May 2002, www.kremlin.ru/events/president/transcripts/21925, accessed 10 April 2023.
7  A. Roxburgh, *The Strongman: Vladimir Putin and the Battle for Russia*, London, I.B.Tauris, 2011, [ebook].
8  *Yezhenedelny zhurnal*, 30 May 2002.
9  T. Graham, 'World Without Russia?', Jamestown Foundation Conference, 9 June 1999, https://carnegieendowment.org/1999/06/09/world-without-russia-pub-285, accessed 10 April 2023.
10  From the author's interview with Alexander Vershbow, August 2018.
11  Loc. cit.
12  P. Baker, S. Glasser, *Kremlin Rising. Vladimir Putin's Russia and the End of Revolution*, Scribner, New York, 2005, [ebook].
13  P. Baker, *Days of Fire: Bush and Cheney in the White House*, Knopf Doubleday Publishing Group, New York, 2013, [ebook].
14  From the author's interview with Alexander Vershbow, August 2018.
15  P. Baker, loc. cit.

16 *Breakfast with Frost*, BBC, news.bbc.co.uk/hi/english/static/audio_video/programmes/breakfast_with_frost/transcripts/putin5.mar.txt, accessed 5 January 2024.
17 'Putin: Rossiya pytalas stat "svoei" dlya Zapada, dazhe "zabrasyvala udochki" v NATO', TASS, 13 June 2023, tass.ru/politika/17996941, accessed 4 January 2024.
18 W. Clinton, 'I Tried to Put Russia on Another Path', *The Atlantic*, 7 April 2022, www.theatlantic.com/ideas/archive/2022/04/bill-clinton-nato-expansion-ukraine/629499, accessed 4 January 2024.
19 Vladimir Putin's speech on Beslan, 4 September 2004, kremlin.ru/events/president/transcripts/22589, accessed 2 June 2023.
20 *Svobodnaya pressa*, 20 January 2010.
21 *Novoye vremya*, 14 March 2005.
22 From the author's interview with Oleg Rybachuk, July 2018.
23 Loc. cit.
24 Loc. cit.
25 C. Rice, loc. cit.
26 Burns W. J., *The Back Channel*, New York, Random House Publishing Group, 2019, [ebook].
27 *Kommersant*, 7 April 2008.
28 From the author's interview with Ostap Semerak, March 2020.
29 From the author's interview with Mikhail Fridman for the film *The Man Who Was Too Free*, 2015.

## Chapter 25

1 *Ogonyok*, 25 July 2001.
2 *The New Times*, 8 October 2007.
3 holmogor.livejournal.com/1009707.html, 29 November 2004, accessed 14 June 2023.
4 b-nemtsov.livejournal.com/86229.html, 14 October 2010, accessed 14 June 2023.
5 *Komsomolskaya pravda*, 28 September 2004.
6 *Novaya gazeta*, 28 May 2008.
7 P. Baker, S. Glasser, loc. cit.
8 *Komsomolskaya pravda*, 20 August 2007.
9 L. Gudkov, 'Negativnaya identichnost. Obraz vraga v sovetskom totalitarnom iskusstve i literature. Stati, 1997–2002. Avtosky sbornik', *Novoye literaturnoye obozreniye*, Moscow, 2004.
10 A. Morozov, 'Konets fabriki obrazov', *Artkhronika*, July 2013.
11 M. Kasyanov, loc. cit.
12 *Kommersant*, 9 December 2005.
13 Loc. cit.
14 *Novaya gazeta*, 9 February 2006.
15 Alexandr Khinshtein's press conference, 7 February 2006.
16 'Russkaya volna 2006', Extreme.nnov.ru, February 2006.
17 *Shkola zlosloviya*, NTV, December 2005.
18 Da-Debaty, Moscow, 17 October 2006.

19 Loc. cit.
20 N. Yeltsina, op. cit., p. 296.
21 Putin's speech at the memorial service in the Kremlin, 25 April 2007.
22 *The New Times*, 30 April 2007.
23 Ekho Moskvy, 27 April 2007.
24 *Komsomolskaya pravda*, 8 December 2000.
25 N. Yeltsina, op. cit., p. 311.
26 M. Kasyanov, loc. cit.
27 Ekho Moskvy, 27 April 2007.
28 *B.N.*, a documentary film by Nikolai Svanidze, RTR, 2006.
29 United Russia party congress, 1 October 2007.
30 'Nemtsov prinyal Ulyanovsk za Meksiku', *Ulpressa*, 26 September 2007.
31 'Chyornaya kassa Kremlya', *The New Times*, 10 December 2007.
32 Loc. cit.
33 Vladimir Putin's meeting with members of the Valdai International Discussion Club, 14 September 2007.
34 Vladimir Putin speaking at a forum of supporters of United Russia, 21 November 2007.
35 *Kommersant*, 23 November 2007.
36 *Fontanka.ru*, 29 August 2007.
37 A. Gentelev, working materials for the film *Operation: Successor*, February 2008.
38 Ekho Moskvy, 2 December 2007.

## Chapter 26

1 *Kommersant Vlast*, 21 April 2008.
2 *Kommersant Vlast*, 8 August 2005.
3 O. Allenova, *Chechnya ryadom. Voina glazami zhenshchiny*, Moscow, Kommersant Publishing House, 2008.
4 Quoted from a source who participated in the meeting.
5 *Rossiiskaya gazeta*, 18 May 2004.
6 *Kommersant*, 27 June 2005.
7 *Kommersant*, 7 October 2003.
8 O.V. Allenova, loc. cit.
9 'Vospominaniya Ramzana Kadyrova. "Ya syn svoyeva ottsa i syn svoyevo naroda"', on VKontakte page 'Svetlaya pamyat Akhmata-Khadzhi Kadyrova'.
10 Loc. cit.
11 *Moskovsky komsomolets*, 24 January 2007.
12 *Novaya gazeta*, 13 May 2004.
13 Quote from one of Kadyrov's acquaintances.
14 *Moskovsky komsomolets*, 14 February 2005.
15 O.V. Allenova, loc. cit.
16 *Novaya gazeta*, 14 August 2003.
17 *Novaya gazeta*, 13 May 2004.
18 *Novaya gazeta*, 21 June 2004.

19  Told to the author by Natalia Estemirova.
20  Vladimir Putin's Press Conference in Dresden, 10 October 2006.
21  *Russian Newsweek*, 20 July 2009.
22  *Novaya gazeta*, 15 September 2014.
23  *Kommersant*, 20 November 2006.
24  *Kommersant*, 23 November 2006.
25  *Kommersant Vlast*, 21 April 2008.
26  *Russian Newsweek*, 25 August 2008.
27  *Novaya gazeta*, 24 November 2008.
28  RIA Novosti, 1 February 2010.

# Chapter 27

1  From Dmitry Gordon's interview with Boris Nemtsov, 17 April 2009.
2  Anatoly Chubais's address to the SPS congress, 15 November 2008.
3  Loc. cit.
4  Boris Nemtsov's address to the SPS congress, 15 November 2008.
5  *Kommersant*, 13 February 2008.
6  B. Nemtsov, V. Milov, 'Putin. Itogi. Nezavisimy ekspertny doklad', Moscow, Solidarnost, 2008, www.putin-itogi.ru/doklad, accessed 27 July 2023.
7  Loc. cit.
8  *Vedomosti*, 20 December 2010.
9  *Financial Times*, 30 November 2011.
10  B. Nemtsov, V. Milov, loc. cit.
11  From the author's interview with Nadezhda Mityushkina, February 2019.
12  From the author's interview with Ilya Yashin, December 2018.
13  Loc. cit.
14  Loc. cit.
15  Finparty, 26 April 2011.
16  From the author's interview with Anastasia Faizullina, February 2019.
17  *Kommersant*, 21 April 2009.
18  Roman Udot, LiveJournal, 24 April 2009.
19  Vladimir Putin's address to the council on the Development of Physical Education and Sports, 23 March 2009, kremlin.ru/catalog/persons/88/events/3523, accessed 27 July 2023.
20  'Sochi. Vybory mera', Public Opinion Foundation, April 2009, www.bd.fom.ru/pdf/sochi_vybory.pdf, accessed 4 January 2024.
21  Ilya Yashin, LiveJournal, 7 April 2009.
22  'Sochi. Vybory mera, spetsvypusk', Public Opinion Foundation, 22 April 2009.
23  Loc. cit.
24  From the author's interview with Konstantin Doroshka, November 2018.
25  From the author's interview with Olga Shorina, November 2018.
26  Georgy Boos's address to the meeting of Gossovet 22 January 2010.
27  From the author's interview with Konstantin Doroshka, November 2018.

## Chapter 28

1. Comments by Yury Shevchuk on Pushkin Square, Moscow, 22 August 2010.
2. *Samara.ru*, 3 December 2010.
3. Boris Nemtsov, LiveJournal, 20 August 2010.
4. *Izvestiya*, 16 December 2010.
5. *Gazeta.ru*, 14 December 2010.
6. From the author's interview with Vladimir Ryzhkov for the film *The Man Who Was Too Free*, 2015.
7. Ekho Moskvy v Samare, 2 December 2010.
8. Boris Nemtsov, LiveJournal, 29 July 2010.
9. From the author's interview with Vladimir Kara-Murza, April 2021.
10. The version about Surgutneftegaz was laid out in *The Insider*, 1 March 2017; the version about Rosneft was from *Kommersant*, 20 March 2006.
11. *Snob*, June 2011.
12. 'Suspect Lawsuits Target Russian Financial Firms', *Bloomberg Business Week*, 6 November 2008.
13. From the author's interview with Vladimir Kara-Murza, April 2021.
14. *Kommersant*, 18 November 2010.
15. *Kommersant*, 22 November 2010.
16. From the author's interview with Vladimir Kara-Murza, April 2021.
17. From the author's interview with Olga Shorina, November 2018.
18. B. Nemtsov, V. Milov, loc. cit.
19. Loc. cit.
20. Boris Nemtsov, LiveJournal, 24 September 2010.
21. *Zasekin.ru*, 3 October 2010.
22. *Rolling Stone*, 2010.
23. M. Kasyanov, loc. cit.
24. *Razgovor s Vladimirom Putinym*, 15 December 2011.
25. Interfax, 15 February 2011.
26. From the author's interview with Vladimir Ryzhkov for the film *The Man Who Was Too Free*, 2015.
27. *Kommersant*, 24 February 2011.
28. Zh. Nemtsova, *Doch svoego ottsa*, Moscow, Bombora, 2022.
29. From the author's interview with Vladimir Ryzhkov for the film *The Man Who Was Too Free*, 2015.
30. *Gazeta.ru*, 17 January 2011.
31. From the author's interview with Zhanna Nemtsova for the film *The Man Who Was Too Free*, 2015.
32. Ekho Moskvy, 19 January 2011.

## Chapter 29

1 From the author's interview with Gleb Pavlovsky, May 2019.
2 *Kommersant*, 22 November 2010.
3 Loc. cit.
4 From a BBC Russian Service interview with Arkady Dvorkovich, 10 December 2010, www.bbc.com/russian/russia/2010/12/101210_dvorkovich_medvedev_comment, accessed 3 November 2023.
5 From the author's interview with Gleb Pavlovsky, May 2019.
6 J, Becker, S. Shane, 'Hillary Clinton, "Smart Power", and the Dictator's Fall', *The New York Times*, 27 February 2016, www.nytimes.com/2016/02/28/us/politics/hillary-clinton-libya.html?searchResultPosition=5, accessed 3 November 2023.
7 *Kommersant*, 21 March 2011.
8 M. McFaul, *From Cold War to Hot Peace*, Boston, Houghton Mifflin Harcourt, 2018, [ebook].
9 *Moskovskiye novosti* used this formulation, citing a source in the Kremlin, 19 March 2011.
10 From Putin's speech at Votkinsky Factory, 21 March 2011, inosmi.ru/20110329/167857490.html, accessed 4 November 2023.
11 Announcement by Dmitry Medvedev, 21 March 2011, regnum.ru/news/1385989, accessed 7 November 2023.
12 Dmitry Medvedev's press conference, 18 May 2011, kremlin.ru/events/president/news/11259, accessed 7 November 2023.
13 *Nezavisimaya gazeta*, 18 May 2011.
14 M. McFaul, loc. cit.
15 Loc. cit.
16 M. Zygar, loc. cit.
17 From the author's interview with Gleb Pavlovsky, May 2019.
18 From a speech by Dmitry Medvedev at the United Russia congress, 24 September 2011, www.1tv.ru/news/2011-09-24/113566-vystuplenie_d_medvedeva_i_v_putina_na_vtorom_dne_s_ezda_partii_edinaya_rossiya_polnaya_versiya, accessed 8 November 2023.

## Chapter 30

1 *Afisha*, 11 July 2011.
2 Loc. cit.
3 *Vedomosti*, 17 November 2011.
4 From the author's interview with Ilya Krasilshchik, November 2018.
5 *Afisha*, 17 October 2011.
6 *Bolshoi gorod*, 5 October 2011.
7 *Afisha*, 15 September 2011.
8 Alexei Navalny, LiveJournal, 6 June 2013.
9 From the author's interview with Pyotr Miloserdov, February 2021.
10 *Lenta.ru*, 4 November 2011.

11  Alexei Navalny, LiveJournal, 9 June 2008.
12  Manifesto of the NAROD movement, 27 June 2007, www.apn.ru/publications/article17321.htm, accessed 5 December 2023.
13  From the author's interview with Alexei Navalny, November 2018.
14  From the author's interview with Pyotr Miloserdov, February 2021.
15  *Lenta.ru*, 4 November 2011.
16  From the author's interview with Alexei Navalny, November 2018.
17  *Vedomosti*, 30 December 2009.
18  From the author's interview with Leonid Volkov, February 2021.
19  From the author's interview with Alexei Navalny, November 2018.
20  *Esquire*, December 2011.

# Chapter 31

1  Debates at the The Last Autumn forum, 2 October 2011.
2  Loc. cit.
3  Loc. cit.
4  *Kommersant*, 8 November 2011.
5  Loc. cit.
6  Levada Center, 'Rossiya posle vyborov', 21 October 2011.
7  *Russian Newsweek*, 18 October 2009.
8  A. Buzin, 'Devolyutsiya rossiiskikh vyborov v kartinakh, ili kak na vyborakh pobedit Gaussa', Ekho Moskvy, 8 December 2012.
9  S. Shpilkin, 'Statisticheskoye issledovaniye resulatatov rossiiskikh vyborov 2007–2009', *trvscience.ru*, www.trv-science.ru/2009/10/statisticheskoe-issledovanie-rezultatov-rossijskix-vyborov-2007-2009-gg, accessed 14 December 2023.
10  *Vedomosti*, 13 October 2011.
11  Dmitry Medvedev's comment to the press, 4 December 2011.
12  Tarasfedoseev.livejournal.com, 5 December 2011.
13  A. Dashevsky's Facebook page, 5 December 2011.
14  *Forbes*, 11 March 2012.
15  Radio Kommersant, 4 December 2012.
16  From the author's interview with Ilya Yashin, December 2018.
17  Alexei Navalny, LiveJournal, 5 December 2011.
18  *Lenta.ru*, 6 December 2011.
19  From the author's interview with Vladimir Ryzhkov for the film *The Man Who Was Too Free*, 2015.
20  From the author's interview with Nadezhda Mityushkina, February 2019.
21  *OpenSpace.ru*, 7 December 2011.
22  From the author's interview with Ilya Klishin, March 2019.
23  Ilya Krasilshchik's Facebook page, 7 December 2011.
24  From the author's interview with Ilya Krasilshchik, November 2018.
25  From the author's interview with Alexei Venediktov, February 2019.
26  From the author's interview with Sergei Parkhomenko, November 2017.

27 *Novaya gazeta*, 10 December 2016.
28 *Razgovor s Vladimirom Putinym*, 15 December 2011, https://rg.ru/2011/12/15/stenogramma.html, accessed 15 December 2023.
29 *Kommersant*, 15 December 2011.
30 *Forbes*, 13 December 2011.
31 From the author's interview with Alexei Navalny, November 2018.

## Chapter 32

1 *Razgovor s Vladimirom Putinym*, 15 December 2011, rg.ru/2011/12/15/stenogramma.html, accessed 16 December 2023.
2 *The New Times*, 3 December 2012.
3 'Vystupleniye Vladimira Putina na stadione v Luzhnikakh 23 fevralya 2012', 23 February 2012.
4 From the author's interview with Gennady Gudkov, April 2019.
5 'Doklad Obshchestvennoi komissii o sobytiyakh na Blolotnoi ploshchadi 6 maya 2012 goda', OVD, ovd.info/documents/2013/12/18/doklad-mezhdunarodnoy-komissii-o-sobytiyah-na-bolotnoy-ploshchadi-6-maya-2012, accessed 17 December 2023.
6 From the author's interview with Gennady Gudkov, April 2019.
7 Loc. cit.
8 Loc. cit.
9 From the author's interview with Sergei Udaltsov, April 2019.
10 Radio Liberty, 7 May 2012.
11 From the author's interview with Gennady Gudkov, April 2019.
12 Twitter account of Alexander Sidyakin, 15 May 2012.
13 From the Investigative Committee's press release, 11 May 2012.
14 Boris Nemtsov's speech at a rally, 12 June 2012.
15 Information from Ilya Yashin.
16 RIA Novosti, 27 June 2012.
17 From the author's interview with Ilya Yashin, December 2018.
18 *Vedomosti*, 26 October 2012.

## Chapter 33

1 Speech by Yevgeny Urlashov at a rally in Yaroslavl, 19 June 2013, https://vk.com/video-49570890_168530565, accessed 15 April 2023.
2 From the author's interview with Vladimir Ryzhkov for the film *The Man Who Was Too Free*, 2015.
3 From the author's interview with Mikhail Prokhorov for the film *The Man Who Was Too Free*, 2015.
4 *76.ru*, 22 May 2013.
5 Ilya Yashin's speech at a rally in Yaroslavl, 16 July 2013.
6 *V gostyakh u Putina*, NTV, 7 October 2012.

7 Loc. cit.
8 From Leonid Parfyonov's interview with Alexei Navalny, 26 January 2013.
9 *Izvestiya*, 12 April 2013.
10 Loc. cit.
11 *Lenta.ru*, 18 July 2013.
12 *Kirovsky reporter*, 18 July 2013.
13 Vladimir Putin at the Youth Forum Seligar-2013, 2 August 2013, https://ria.ru/20130802/953978793.html, accessed 17 April 2023.
14 From the author's interview with Vasily Tsependa, January 2021.
15 From the author's interview with Sergei Balabayev, February 2021.
16 *Yezhdnevny zhurnal*, 5 September 2013.
17 *The New Times*, 2 September 2013.
18 From the author's interview with Zhanna Nemtsova for the film *The Man Who Was Too Free*, 2015
19 From the author's interview with Alexei Navalny, November 2018.
20 *Lenta.ru*, 18 July 2013.
21 Yulia Navalnaya's speech at the rally, 6 September 2013, https://www.youtube.com/watch?v=euy2FguOfos, accessed 16 April 2023.
22 Alexei Navalny at a meeting with votes, 30 August 2013, https://tvrain.tv/teleshow/prjamaja_linija/mer_i_moskvichi_na_voprosy_izbiratelej_otvechaet_aleksej_navalnyj-351155, accessed 17 April 2023.
23 'Kandidatam kapayut protsenty', Levada Center, 2 September 2013, https://www.levada.ru/2013/09/02/kandidatam-kapayut-protsenty/, accessed 14 April 2023.
24 *The New Times*, 16 September 2013.
25 TV Rain, 10 September 2013.
26 *Ulitsa Moskovskaya*, 13 April 2015.
27 From the author's interview with Sergei Balabayev, February 2021.
28 From the author's interview with Alexei Navalny, November 2018.

# Chapter 34

1 'Pyaty srok. Kakim budet novy politichesky kurs Rossii', *Inliberty*, 18 March 2018, www.inliberty.ru/magazine/issue1, accessed 22 April 2023.
2 Vladimir Putin's address at the Valdai Club, 19 September 2013, rg.ru/2013/09/19/stenogramma-site.html, accessed 12 April 2023.
3 Vladimir Putin's address to the Federal Assembly, 12 December 2012, www.kremlin.ru/events/president/news/17118, accessed 22 April 2023.
4 R. Adzhubei, 'Khrushchev znal o zagovore', *RG.ru*, rg.ru/2004/10/14/doch.html, accessed 4 January 2024.
5 Vladimir Putin's address to the 43rd Munich Security Conference, 10 February 2007, www.youtube.com/watch?v=hQ58Yv6kP44, accessed 4 January 2024.
6 *V gostyakh u Putina*, NTV, 7 October 2012, www.ntv.ru/video/355540, accessed 22 April 2023.
7 From the author's interview with Sergei Chapnin, May 2023.

8 'Strakh drugogo. Problema gomofobii v Rossii', Levada Center, 12 April 2013, www.levada.ru/2013/03/12/strah-drugogo-problema-gomofobii-v-rossii, accessed 23 April 2023.
9 *Izvestiya*, 4 October 2011.
10 *The New Times*, 29 August 2019.
11 *Zerkalo nedeli*, 22 November 2011.
12 *Zerkalo nedeli*, August 2013.
13 From the author's interview with a source who participated in the discussions.
14 *Kommersant*, 11 November 2013.
15 *Kyiv Post*, 29 November 2013.
16 *V gostyakh u Gordona*, TV Channel 112, 13 April 2017.
17 G. Chizhov, ed., *Perelomnyye gody. Stranitsty ukrainskoi revolyutsii*, Kyiv, Laurus, 2018, p. 79.
18 Op. cit., p. 130.
19 S. Koshkina, *Maidan. Nerasskazannaya istoriya*, Kyiv, Bright Star Publishing, 2015.
20 Valdai Forum, 24 October 2014.
21 E. Nakashima, 'Inside a Russian Disinformation Campaign in Ukraine in 2014', *The Washington Post*, 25 December 2017, www.washingtonpost.com/world/national-security/inside-a-russian-disinformation-campaign-in-ukraine-in-2014/2017/12/25/f55b0408-e71d-11e7-ab50-621fe0588340_story.html, accessed 6 January 2024.
22 M. Zygar, *Vsya kremlyovskaya rat*, Moscow, Intellektualnaya literatura, 2016, p. 345.

# Chapter 35

1 From the author's interview with Nadezhda Mityushkina, February 2019.
2 From journalists' interview with Boris Nemtsov at the Ukrainian embassy in Moscow, December 2013.
3 From the author's interview with Ilya Yashin, December 2018.
4 *Novaya gazeta*, 1 March 2014.
5 From the author's interview of Alexei Navalny, November 2018.
6 *Novaya gazeta*, 1 March 2014.
7 Boris Nemtsov, LiveJournal, 2 March 2014.
8 Boris Nemtsov, LiveJournal, 7 March 2014.
9 Loc. cit.
10 Rosbalt, 14 April 2014.
11 Radio Liberty, 20 April 2014.
12 Ksenia Sobchak, Twitter, 14 April 2014.
13 From the author's interview with Vladimir Kara-Murza, 22 April 2021.
14 Boris Nemtsov, LiveJournal, 30 December 2021.
15 From the author's interview with Vladimir Bukovsky for the film *The Man Who Was Too Free*, 2015.
16 Vladimir Putin's address at the All-Russian People's Front Mediaforum, 24 April 2014.
17 'Russia-Ukraine: Dialog', Kyiv, 25 April 2014.
18 Boris Nemtsov, speech in Kyiv, 25 April 2014.

19 Radio Liberty, 30 April 2014.
20 Loc. cit.
21 From *RussiaWeek*'s interview with Boris Nemtsov, 26 April 2014.
22 Pyaty kanal, April 2014.
23 On the sidelines of 'Russia-Ukraine: Dialog', Kyiv, 25 April 2014.
24 Alexander Gordon, interview with Boris Nemtsov, April 2014.
25 Loc. cit.
26 Boris Nemtsov, Facebook page, 28 May 2014.
27 Boris Nemtsov, Facebook page, 30 May 2014.
28 Rina Naumova-Davis, LiveJournal, 2 June 2014.
29 Rina Naumova-Davis, LiveJournal, 22 August 2014.
30 Jennifer Rankin, 'Three Men Found Guilty of Murdering 298 People in Shooting Down of MH17', *Guardian*, 17 November 2022.
31 *Pskovskaya guberniya*, 25 August 2014.
32 Radio Liberty, 3 September 2014.
33 Loc. cit.
34 Boris Nemtsov, speech at a Moscow rally, 9 September 2014.
35 Vyacheslav Volodin, meeting with participants in the Valdai Discussion Club, 23 October 2014.
36 Radio Liberty, 25 November 2014.
37 Boris Nemtsov, blog on Ekho Moskvy website, 16 November 2014.
38 *Meduza*, 21 November 2014.
39 Zosya Rodkevich, *Moi drug Boris Nemtsov*, [film], 2016.
40 Ekho Moskvy, 5 September 2014.

# Chapter 36

1 Rally at a stadium in Grozny, 28 December 2014.
2 *Novaya gazeta*, 15 March 2021.
3 M. Galeotti, 'US Takes on the Russian Organized Crime "Brothers' Circle." Who?', *In Moscow's Shadows*, 26 July 2011, https://inmoscowsshadows.wordpress.com/2011/07/26/us-takes-on-the-russian-organized-crime-brothers-circle-who.
4 *Novaya gazeta*, 26 February 2016.
5 *Novaya gazeta*, 15 March 2021.
6 Ramzan Kadyrov, Instagram, December 2014.
7 Boris Nemtsov, blog on Ekho Moskvy website, 9 January 2015.
8 Ramzan Kadyrov, Instagram, 8 January 2014.
9 Zh. Nemtsova, loc. cit.
10 Loc. cit.
11 Loc. cit.
12 Author's interview with Lyudmila Shabuyeva, January 2021.
13 Ramzan Kadyrov, Instagram, 8 March 2015.
14 Alexei Navalny, blog post, 28 January 2015.
15 Boris Nemtsov, Facebook page, 12 February 2015.

16 Boris Nemtsov, Facebook page, 15 February 2015.
17 'Press-konferentsiya organizatorov marsha "Vesna"', *Nemtsov most*, 20 February 2015, nemtsov-most.org/2019/02/20/the-chronicle-of-that-february-preparing-the-march-spring-press-conference, accessed 20 January 2023.
18 Alexei Navalny, blog post, 19 February 2015.
19 From the author's interview with Olga Shorina, November 2018.
20 'Kak ubivali Nemtsova', *Mediazona*, 1 March 2021, zona.media/chronicle/nemtsov-chronicle, accessed 20 January 2023.
21 'Reportazh s suda po dely ob ubiistsve Nemtsova', *Nemtsov most*, 23 November 2016, nemtsov-most.org/2016/11/23/geremeeva-it-was-necessary-for-the-organization-to-attract, accessed 19 January 2023.
22 'Kak ubivali Nemtsova', loc. cit.
23 Boris Nemtsov, Facebook page, 27 February 2015.
24 Ekho Moskvy, 27 February 2015.
25 Loc. cit.
26 From Dmitry Gordon's interview with Anna Duritskaya, 25 November 2020, www.youtube.com/watch?v=AK3hfLjhahg, accessed 20 January 2023.
27 Zh. Nemtsova, op. cit.
28 From the author's interview with Oleg Sysuyev for the film *The Man Who Was Too Free*, 2015.
29 From a *Meduza* interview with Zhanna Nemtsova, 24 February 2021.
30 From material on the interrogation of Shadid Gubashev, April 2015, www.svoboda.org/a/28438374.html, accessed 20 January 2023.
31 *Novaya gazeta*, 24 February 2016.
32 *Novaya gazeta*, 13 March 2015.
33 Loc. cit.
34 *Novaya gazeta*, 24 February 2016.
35 Putin's speech to the collegium of the Ministry of Internal Affairs, 4 March 2015, www.kremlin.ru/events/president/news/47776/audios, audio accessed 14 January 2023.
36 From the author's interview with Vadim Prokhorov, May 2021.
37 'Neizvestniye ubiitsy Nemtsova', *Mediazona*, 20 November 2020.
38 Voice of America, 27 February 2021.
39 *Kavkazsky uzel*, 27 June 2017.
40 *Nastoyashcheye vremya*, 27 February 2020.

# Epilogue

1 Vladimir Putin's briefing in Budapest, 17 February 2015, http://special.kremlin.ru/events/president/transcripts/47706, accessed January 2025.
2 Radio Liberty interview with Vitaly Portnikov, 5 June 2020, https://www.radiosvoboda.org/a/zelenskii-poroshenko-ermak-putin/30654710.html, accessed January 2025.
3 Press conference in Paris with Vladimir Putin, Volodymyr Zelensky, 10 December 2019, http://www.en.kremlin.ru/events/president/transcripts/62277/videos, accessed January 2025.

4 Vladimir Putin, press conference, 19 December 2019, https://www.youtube.com/watch?v=cotHVrVzmaE.
5 Ekho Moskvy, 6 March 2020.
6 Vladimir Putin, speech delivered on 6 March 2020, http://www.kremlin.ru/events/president/transcripts/comminity_meetings/62953/audios, accessed January 2025.
7 Valentina Tereshkova, speech addressed to the State Duma, 10 March 2020, https://www.interfax.ru/russia/698440, accessed January 2025.
8 Interview with Vladimir Putin, 14 June 2020, https://meduza.io/news/2020/06/14/putin-rossiya-vyhodit-iz-epidemii-koronavirusa-s-minimalnymi-poteryami-a-v-ssha-tak-ne-proishodit, accessed January 2025.
9 Levada Center, 27 March 2020, https://www.levada.ru/2020/03/27/obnulenie-prezidentskih-srokov/, accessed January 2025.
10 Comment by Vladimir Putin, 12 June 2020, https://www.rbc.ru/politics/12/06/2020/5ee3573e9a794734fb65f5bb, accessed January 2025.
11 D. Kuznets, 'Na golosovanii po popravkam mogli byt samyye bolshyye falsifikatsii v noveishei istorii. Sergei Shpilkin schitayet, chto "za" golosovalo okolo 30% rossiyan', *Meduza*, 3 July 2020, https://meduza.io/feature/2020/07/03/na-golosovanii-po-popravkam-mogli-byt-samye-bolshie-falsifikatsii-v-noveyshey-istorii-sergey-shpilkin-schitaet-chto-za-progolosovalo-okolo-30-rossiyan, accessed January 2025.
12 Alexei Navalny, blog post, 9 September 2019.
13 P. Aptekar and M. Zheleznova, 'Kto vyigral vybory', *Vedomosti*, 10 September 2019, https://www.vedomosti.ru/opinion/articles/2019/09/10/810876-viigral-vibori, accessed January 2025.
14 Yury Dud, interview with Alexei Navalny, 6 October 2020, https://www.youtube.com/watch?v=vps43rXgaZc&t=3311s, accessed January 2025.
15 From the author's interview with Kira Yarmysh, April 2023.
16 Loc. cit.
17 Yury Dud, interview with Alexei Navalny, 6 October 2020, loc. cit.
18 Loc. cit.
19 Loc. cit.
20 Svetlana Reuter, 'V avguste 2020 goda Navalnogo otravili boevym yadom…', *Meduza*, 23 March 2023, https://meduza.io/feature/2023/03/23/v-avguste-2020-goda-navalnogo-otravili-boevym-yadom-reanimatolog-aleksandr-polupan-byl-v-gruppe-vrachey-kotorye-pytalis-postavit-emu-diagnoz, accessed January 2023.
21 From the author's interview with Maria Pevchikh, May 2023.
22 A. Zverev and G. Stolyarov, 'Russian Paramedics' Accounts Challenge Moscow's Explanations for Navalny's Coma – sources', Reuters, 14 September 2020, https://www.reuters.com/article/us-russia-politics-navalny-health-exclus/exclusive-russian-paramedics-accounts-challenge-moscows-explanation-for-navalnys-coma-sources-idUSKBN265298/, accessed January 2025.
23 'Putin nazval Skripalya predatelem rodiny i podonkom', RBC, 3 October 2018, https://www.rbc.ru/politics/03/10/2018/5bb4b5ae9a79473137d9379c, accessed January 2025.
24 S. Bugrov, 'Khattab uvyol za soboi v mogilu boevikov i chekistov', *Kommersant*, 3 October 2002, https://www.kommersant.ru/doc/340124, accessed January 2025.
25 From the author's interview with Maria Pevchikh, May 2023.

26  Alexei Navalny, Instagram, 22 September 2020.
27  Daniel Roher, *Navalny*, [film], 2022.
28  Loc. cit.
29  Alexei Navalny, blog post, 14 December 2020.
30  Alexei Navalny, blog post, 21 December 2020.
31  Alexander Morozov, Facebook page, 16 December 2020.
32  A. Navalny, *Patriot: A Memoir*, New York, Knopf Doubleday Publishing Group, 2024, [ebook].
33  A. Navalny, 'Sovest i intellekt. Posledneye slovo Alekseya Navalnogo na sude po "ektremizmu"', https://navalny.com/p/6644.

# INDEX OF NAMES

Abdulatipov, Ramazan   131–32
Abramovich, Roman   211, 335, 337, 339, 341, 385, 421, 424, 434, 437
Achalov, Vladislav   59, 60, 126
Afanasyev, Yury   25, 26
Afonin, Vyacheslav   176, 177
Aksyuchits, Victor   44, 45, 59, 257, 279, 290, 292, 293
Akunin, Boris   603, 607
Albats, Yevgeniya   284, 301, 363, 392
Alekperov, Vagit   386, 437
Aleksashenko, Sergei   43, 208, 271, 305–7, 310–11
Alekseyeva, Lyudmila   524, 557, 560
Alexy II, Patriarch   130, 290, 293, 294
Alkhanov, Alu   520, 521
Allenova, Olga   517, 519, 521, 525
Andreyeva, Nina   15, 51
Andrianova, Anna   404, 405
Anikin, Valery   291, 349
Aronov, Igor   93–94
Aslakhanov, Aslambek   405, 416, 417
Aven, Pyotr   64, 268, 269, 338, 383
Avturkhanov, Umar   169–71

Baisarov, Movladi   524, 525
Bakov, Anton   510, 512
Balabayev, Sergei   640, 647
Bandera, Stepan   464, 680
Barayev, Movsar   403–5, 409, 410
Barsukov, Mikhail   123, 124, 199, 200, 227, 228, 230, 238, 319, 320

Basayev, Shamil   167, 175, 184, 185, 186, 192, 196, 199, 343, 344, 345, 402, 415, 516, 517, 518, 519, 522, 523, 722
Bednyakov, Dmitry   84, 87, 89, 150–53
Belkovsky, Stanislav   435, 436, 702
Belyaninov, Andrei   176, 181
Belykh, Nikita   509, 511, 512, 535, 584, 637
Bendukidze, Kakha   135, 387
Berezovsky, Boris   210–14, 221, 225–29, 230, 237, 238, 240, 241, 243, 248, 252, 258–69, 271, 273, 280–83, 286, 298, 300, 308, 312, 329, 335, 337, 339, 341, 343, 344, 354, 360, 361, 378, 379, 380, 381, 383, 384, 385, 387, 389, 390, 430, 434, 442, 538, 566, 210
Berger, Mikhail   256
Biden, Joe   575, 576
Blair, Tony   437, 458, 479
Bocharov, Mikhail   42, 541
Bonner, Yelena   19, 78
Boos, Georgy   548–54
Bordyuzha, Nikolai   330, 341
Borodin, Pavel   329, 330
Brezhnev, Leonid   11, 33, 104, 178, 179, 208, 288, 506, 564, 673, 712
Browder, Bill   560, 561
Bukovsky, Vladimir   560, 672–74
Burbulis, Gennady   64, 65, 67

771

## INDEX OF NAMES

Bush Jr., George W.   440, 458, 466, 478, 479, 481, 482, 487, 490, 495, 497, 573

Cherkasov, Alexander   172, 174, 201
Chernomyrdin, Viktor   109, 112, 124, 135, 137, 138, 145, 172, 185, 186, 191, 198, 205, 206, 210, 218, 220, 229, 239, 242, 243, 245, 246, 256–60, 271, 272, 278, 286, 294, 297–300, 302, 303, 306–9, 312–15, 318, 327, 357, 402
Chernyayev, Anatoly   20, 49
Chichagov, Pavel   11, 16, 29, 30–32, 37, 87, 91, 146, 147
Chirac, Jacques   213, 479
Chubais, Anatoly   64, 65, 83, 84, 86–88, 188, 205, 208, 209, 212–18, 219, 220–24, 227–31, 238–42, 245–47, 250–53, 255, 259, 262–69, 272–86, 298, 299, 301, 302, 306, 309–12, 315, 316, 319, 321, 325, 335, 337–39, 341–43, 351, 353–57, 359, 363–66, 372, 375, 383, 385, 396, 406–8, 425–27, 429–32, 440–41, 443–45, 459, 509, 511–12, 535–37, 543, 570, 583, 610
Clinton, Bill   154, 483
Colton, Timothy   67, 301

Dadayev, Zaur   689, 693–96, 699–700, 702, 704
Delimkhanov, Adam   525, 527, 686, 693, 701, 703–4
Dmitriyevsky, Stanislav   17, 173–76, 193
Dolnik, Adam   403–4, 411, 413
Dorenko, Sergei   269, 272, 283, 361–62, 380, 383–84, 390
Doroshok, Konstantin   550–51, 553

Dubinin, Sergei   240, 278, 282, 295, 299, 304, 306–7, 310–11, 328
Dudayev, Dzhokhar   75, 158–63, 165–76, 185–86, 191, 196–97, 199, 344, 516, 664
Duritskaya, Anna   668, 693–97
Dvorkovich, Arkady   574, 576–77, 579
Dyachenko, Tatyana   154, 213, 219–20, 229, 243, 269, 273, 298, 312, 325, 335, 337–38

Eismont, Maria   581, 590
Estemirova, Natalia   523–24

Filatov, Sergei   109–11, 122–24, 128, 130–33, 136, 167, 205, 210, 253
Fridman, Mikhail   143–45, 216, 240, 242, 244–45, 269, 286, 359, 383, 385, 439, 454–55, 488, 570
Fyodorov, Boris   247, 353

Gaddafi, Muammar   574–75, 578
Gaidar, Yegor   25, 27, 41, 43, 44, 54, 64–68, 73, 83, 84, 86–88, 90–93, 100–103, 105–9, 114, 123, 124, 134–35, 139, 147, 155, 174, 191, 204–6, 210, 212, 215, 222, 225, 240, 246, 251, 252, 257, 268, 301, 302, 311, 312, 315, 335, 353, 354, 357, 359, 365, 366, 376, 377, 425, 427–29, 463, 511, 535, 536, 541, 548, 610
Gakayev, Dzhabrail   160–61
Geremeyev, Artur   694, 699
Geremeyev, Ruslan   693–94, 699, 701, 703
Geremeyev, Suleiman   693, 701, 703
Gevorkyan, Natalia   371, 432, 443
Gilman, Martin   308, 310
Ginzburg, Vitaly   9, 12–13, 18

## INDEX OF NAMES

Glazyev, Sergei   444, 658
Gonchar, Viktor   396, 399
Gorbachev, Mikhail   5–6, 14–16, 19–21, 24–25, 27, 32–34, 38–40, 42–53, 57, 61–62, 64, 68, 75, 98, 102–3, 105, 115, 159–60, 163, 205, 315, 482, 608, 655, 728
Gorbenko, Alexander   606–7, 618
Govorukhin, Stanislav   231–32
Gozman, Leonid   429, 514, 535
Grachev, Andrei   15, 34
Grachev, Pavel   56, 124, 133, 135–38, 149, 171–73, 227
Gref, German   375–77, 435, 438
Grigoryev, Vladimir   270–71, 281, 295
Grishina, Tatyana   53, 77
Gromov, Alexei   565, 606
Gryzlov, Boris   402, 503
Gubashev, Anzor   695–96, 699–700, 702
Gubashev, Shadid   695–96, 699–700, 702
Gudkov, Gennady   614, 616–20, 624
Gudkov, Lev   233, 495
Gusinsky, Vladimir   135, 211–14, 219–21, 229, 238, 240, 261–69, 273–74, 281, 286, 299, 334, 338–39, 343–44, 354–55, 360, 362, 378–93, 434, 538, 672

Hitler, Adolf   462, 492, 584
Hoffman, David   209–10, 214, 218, 223, 267
Hollande, François   657–58

Ivanov, Sergei   531–32, 612
Ivanov, Viktor   394, 422

Jordan, Boris   267, 269, 392–93, 409, 414

Kadannikov, Vladimir   108–9, 246
Kadyrov, Akhmat   414–18
Kadyrov, Ramzan   515–27, 558, 677–78, 685–89, 693, 700–703, 723
Kalyapin, Igor   173–77, 686–87
Kara-Murza, Vladimir   560, 562, 672, 722, 725, 728
Kasparov, Gary   453, 513–14, 539, 542, 554, 584, 589, 590, 595, 615, 624
Kasyanov, Mikhail   380, 393, 402, 421–22, 438, 446–47, 455, 496–500, 507, 513, 557, 558, 560, 565–66, 580, 622, 631, 635, 710
Kazantsev, Viktor   403–4, 411
Khakamada, Irina   276–77, 285, 352–55, 357–60, 363, 365–66, 372, 386, 398–401, 405–8, 414, 425–26, 430–32, 443–45
Khalatnikov, Isaak   12–13
Khasbulatov, Ruslan   60, 69, 73, 87, 90, 101–8, 110–13, 115–16, 118–19, 122–23, 125–26, 129–33, 135, 138–39, 161–62, 164–65, 168–69, 395
Khinshtein, Alexander   497, 500
Khlystun, Viktor   41, 67–68, 72, 96
Khodorkovsky, Mikhail   135, 208, 210, 212–13, 216, 240, 274, 311, 359, 385, 419–26, 432–46, 448, 455, 481, 533, 560–61, 566–67, 571–72, 653, 672, 675, 688, 723
Kholmanskikh, Igor   613–14
Khrushchev, Nikita   52, 57, 506, 651
Kiriyenko, Segei   29, 246, 286, 297, 300–304, 306–15, 327, 335, 342, 352–59, 363–66, 372, 386, 427, 431
Klimentyev, Andrei   178–84, 187, 324

# INDEX OF NAMES

Klishin, Ilya   601–3, 607
Klyuyev, Andriy   465, 470
Kobzon, Iosif   406–7, 410
Kokh, Alfred   206, 245–46, 262–65, 269, 271–72, 274, 280–82, 300, 317, 364, 384, 390–94, 430–32, 443, 564, 672
Kolokoltsev, Vladimir   604, 606
Korzhakov, Alexander   65, 119, 121, 136, 155, 171, 195, 199–200, 205, 210, 212, 217–18, 220, 227–32, 238, 261, 319–20, 335, 379, 385
Kostikov, Vyacheslav   112, 155–56
Kotyusov, Alexander   10, 91, 180, 350–52
Kovalchuk, Yury   538, 563
Kozyrev, Andrei   172, 205
Krasilshchik, Ilya   581, 603, 607–9
Krasnov, Igor   700, 702
Krasnov, Mikhail   297–98
Krestyaninov, Yevgeny   151–52
Kryuchkov, Vladimir   48–53, 57, 59–62
Kuchma, Leonid   457–62, 465–67, 469, 473–75, 478, 482, 485–87
Kudrin, Alexei   246, 319, 363, 375, 435, 566, 613
Kulikov, Anatoly   122–23, 127, 132–33, 165, 171, 176, 217–21
Kulikovskaya-Romanova, Olga   289–92
Kutsyllo, Veronika   137–38

Lapina, Natalia   11–12
Lavrov, Sergei   578, 662, 687
Lebed, Alexander   55–56, 201–2, 226–29, 238, 241, 248, 351
Lebedev, Konstantin   625, 671
Lebedev, Platon   432–33, 437–38, 442, 443, 448, 567, 572

Lebedev, Yury   96, 99, 149, 237, 244–45, 249
Lebedko, Anatoly   398–400
Lenin, Vladimir   287, 291
Lesin, Mikhail   384, 387
Lieven, Anatol   166, 168, 197
Ligachev, Yegor   6, 15, 20, 21, 24
Limonov, Eduard   494, 584, 602, 605
Linshits, Igor   455–56, 498, 500, 672
Lisovsky, Sergei   228, 230, 269–71
Litvinenko, Alexander   501, 544, 722–23
Lozo, Ignaz   51, 59
Lukashenko, Alexander   395–400, 447, 458, 650, 684, 712
Lukyanov, Anatoly   48, 102
Luzhkov, Yury   131–32, 135, 189, 213, 218, 220, 248, 251–54, 261, 266, 295, 313–14, 328–31, 335, 339, 341, 345, 349, 351, 355–56, 360–62, 366, 369, 371, 379–80, 383, 385, 393, 397, 407, 492, 497, 540, 548, 551, 572, 580, 593
Lysov, Viktor   23, 44, 151–52, 225, 301
Lyubimov, Alexander   38, 58, 100, 184

McFaul, Michael   559, 575, 578
Magnitsky, Sergei   560–62, 649
Malashenko, Igor   213, 223, 228–30, 261–62, 264–65, 268, 272, 283, 337–39, 378–79, 382, 384–85, 387
Malkin, Yevgeny   429–31
Mamut, Alexander   423, 498
Mandela, Nelson   636, 726
Markov, Sergei   399–401
Maskhadov, Aslan   173, 191, 201, 344, 346, 364–65, 408, 410, 415, 515, 517–19, 522, 524

# INDEX OF NAMES

Matlock, Jack   48–50
Medvedchuk, Viktor   461–62, 465, 467, 470, 475, 658, 675
Medvedev, Dmitry   233, 372, 423, 461, 469, 477, 508, 514, 531–34, 536, 538–40, 552, 559, 563, 571–79, 581–82, 586, 591, 594, 597, 599–601, 606, 608, 612–13, 615, 635, 637, 649, 652, 654, 656, 709
Merkel, Angela   653, 657–59, 706, 719, 723
Mikhalkov, Nikita   98, 194, 508
Miller, Alexei   393, 434, 447
Miloserdov, Pyotr   583, 585
Milov, Vladimir   537–38, 550, 557, 563, 566–67
Minayev, Boris   33, 35, 198
Minkin, Alexander   269, 271, 280–81, 407
Minzhurenko, Alexander   75–77
Mironov, Sergei   447, 610, 614
Mityushkina, Nadezhda   539, 595, 601–2, 605–7, 665–67
Mladentsev, Andrei   93, 143
Morar, Natalia   510–11
Moroz, Oleg   112, 127, 137, 457, 469
Moroz, Oleksandr   457, 469
Morozov, Alexander   496, 726
Moskal, Hennadiy   659, 674
Mukhudinov, Ruslan   693, 699, 701, 703–4
Muradov, Musa   162, 167, 169

Nadezhdin, Boris   258, 260, 301, 342, 352
Narusova, Lyudmila   321–22
Navalnaya, Yulia   719, 721–22, 727
Navalny, Alexei   431, 504–5, 581–88, 590–91, 592, 595, 599–600, 609–10, 612, 614–15, 618–20, 622–24, 630, 633–39, 642–45, 647, 654, 666–67, 671, 683, 690–91, 694, 715–28
Nemtsov, Boris   7–23, 27–46, 53–62, 71–72, 74–79, 84–100, 114, 121–22, 124–26, 128, 138, 140, 142–56, 164–66, 175–96, 199, 201–7, 214–19, 225–26, 229, 237, 241–60, 266–67, 269–73, 275–80, 282–86, 291–96, 298–304, 308–9, 311–12, 315–16, 320–21, 324, 335, 339–40, 342–43, 349–59, 361, 363, 365–66, 368, 370–72, 375–78, 382–87, 391–93, 397–401, 406–14, 416–17, 425–32, 441, 443, 445–47, 451–56, 463–65, 471–76, 478–79, 484–85, 487–88, 494–98, 500, 502–7, 509–14, 533–48, 550–54, 556–60, 562–64, 566–71, 576, 580, 583–85, 588–90, 592, 595–96, 598–602, 604–11, 613–15, 618–24, 631–35, 637–49, 654, 665–78, 680–84, 687–99, 701–5, 723–24, 728
Nemtsova, Zhanna   698, 702–3
Nevzlin, Leonid   208, 385, 424–25, 432, 434, 438–39
Nicholas II   287, 289, 294–95, 619

Obama, Barack   533, 559, 573–75, 576–78
Odintsova, Yekaterina   19, 452
Oslon, Alexander   214, 222, 347
Ostrovsky, Arkady   273, 281
Ofitserov, Pyotr   637–38

Pain, Emil   163, 195, 197–200, 347
Pakhomov, Anatoly   544–45, 547–48

Pakhomov, Ilya   717–18
Pavlov, Valentin   45, 48, 50–51
Parkhomenko, Sergei   604, 606, 610
Patrushev, Nikolai   402, 422
Pavlovsky, Gleb   248, 322–24, 330, 336, 340, 347, 356, 361, 372, 572, 574, 579
Pereverzin, Vladimir   442–43, 533
Pichugin, Alexei   433, 438
Pifer, Steven   467, 475
Pilch, Richard   403–4, 411, 413
Politkovskaya, Anna   405, 410, 520, 522–24
Ponomaryov, Lev   58, 63–65, 68, 118–20
Popov, Gavriil   26, 48–50, 58, 70
Poroshenko, Petro   485, 679, 705–7
Potanin, Vladimir   207–9, 239–40, 246–47, 263–65, 267–69, 271–73, 281, 286, 385–86, 441, 451, 454, 684
Potapov, Vitaly   195–96
Primakov, Yevgeny   49, 205, 314–16, 326–37, 339–41, 347, 351, 355–56, 360–62, 369, 371, 379–80, 383, 385, 393, 397, 492
Prokhorov, Mikhail   451–52, 630–33
Prokhorov, Vadim   567, 678, 702–3
Pugin, Nikolai   146, 195
Putin, Vladimir   246, 317–25, 330–34, 336, 338–43, 346–47, 356, 361–72, 375–91, 393–448, 453–56, 459–62, 466–69, 474–75, 477–83, 485, 487–88, 491–98, 501, 503, 505–527, 531–53, 556, 558–59, 562–67, 569–74, 576–84, 587, 591, 594, 597–603, 606, 608–10, 612–18, 620–25, 630, 633–36, 638–39, 641, 644–87, 692, 694, 697, 699, 701–2, 705–16, 720–28

Raduyev, Salman   191–92
Rice, Condoleezza   466, 478, 487
Rivera, Sharon   142, 156, 191
Rodkevich, Zosya   683–84
Rogayev, Yevgeny   290, 292
Rogov, Kirill   117, 460, 494, 650
Rogozin, Dmitry   445, 503–5, 584
Rogozin, Georgy   227, 231
Rokhlin, Lev   173, 175
Romanovs, family   288–89, 291, 293, 295–96
Rostropovich, Mstislav   121, 213, 295
Rotenberg, Arkady   538, 563, 569
Rutskoi, Alexander   64, 70, 73, 102, 109–11, 123, 125–27, 130–31, 133, 135, 138–39, 163–64, 252, 548, 569
Ryabov, Geli   288, 292
Rybachuk, Oleh   470, 477, 485–86
Ryklin, Alexander   417, 453
Ryzhkov, Vladimir   557, 559, 566–69, 600, 605–7, 613, 632–33

Saidullayev, Malik   416–18
Sakharov, Andrei   18–21, 25–27, 33, 35, 78, 87, 121, 353, 363, 510, 610, 612–13, 621, 698
Saprykin, Yury   581–82, 643
Savostyanov, Yevgeny   49, 169–70
Sechin, Igor   422–24, 435, 438, 441, 447, 561
Sedov, Vladimir   92, 125, 182
Shaimiyev, Mintimer   341, 356
Shakhnazarov, Georgy   24, 32, 38
Shakhnovsky, Vasily   434–35, 438–39
Shakhrai, Sergei   39, 54, 59, 76, 78, 127, 131, 165
Shavanov, Beslan   693, 695–96, 699–700

# INDEX OF NAMES

Sheinis, Viktor   61, 68, 101, 107–8, 115, 118, 120–21, 128–29, 133, 140
Shevchenko, Yury   315, 321
Shevchuk, Yury   178, 556, 558, 603
Shkolnikova, Maria   401–2, 405–6
Shlosberg, Lev   679–80, 692
Shoigu, Sergei   361–62
Shorina, Olga   541, 551, 562, 680, 683, 692, 697
Shpilkin, Sergei   593–94, 598, 715
Sklyarov, Ivan   77–79, 93
Skuratov, Yury   219–20, 319–21, 328–33, 340, 378, 492, 710
Smirnova, Olga   142, 181–82
Sobchak, Anatoly   58, 70, 317–23, 342, 368, 538, 580, 701
Sobchak, Ksenia   580, 616, 621–24, 672
Sobyanin, Sergei   580, 635, 643–45
Solovyov, Vladimir   289, 290–93
Solzhenitsyn, Alexander   6, 400, 653
Soros, George   258–59, 265, 267–69, 282, 310, 467
Soskovets, Oleg   205, 212–18, 230
Stalin, Joseph   5–8, 52, 141, 160, 495, 506, 540, 714, 728
Stepashin, Sergei   169, 300, 328, 334, 336–41, 343–45, 356–57, 367, 380
Stetsko, Slava   464–65
Surkov, Vladislav   407, 421–22, 432, 436, 439, 444, 458, 491–96, 498–99, 508, 510, 512, 534, 536, 540, 544, 546, 551–53, 557–60, 562, 565, 569–70, 606, 612–14, 635, 660, 663, 675
Sysuyev, Oleg   98, 142, 246, 250, 252–54, 275, 291, 303, 316, 325, 332, 353–55, 386, 432, 698

Tarasov, Artyom   94, 166
Taubman, William   43, 50
Thatcher, Margaret   95, 98, 366, 623
Timchenko, Gennady   322, 538, 563, 569, 586
Troshev, Gennady   202, 517
Tsependa, Vasily   632, 640
Tsimring, Lev   10, 12–13, 28, 31
Tumanov, Vladimir   188, 219, 220
Tutevich, Nikolai   702–3
Tymoshenko, Yulia   469, 484–85, 655, 658

Udaltsov, Sergei   596, 602, 615, 618–20, 622, 624–25
Udaltsova, Anastasia   605, 607
Urinson, Yakov   255, 299, 303
Urlashov, Yevgeny   629–33, 640, 645
Ustinov, Vladimir   436, 438

Venediktov, Alexei   389, 414, 604, 606, 688, 689, 694
Vershbow, Alexander   433, 478, 480–81
Vidyayev, Boris   141–43, 145, 146, 151, 369
Volkov, Leonid   587, 694, 723
Volodin, Vyacheslav   612, 613, 614, 620, 635, 636, 682, 709, 710
Voloshin, Alexander   330–37, 340, 341, 371, 380, 402, 407, 409, 411, 422–24, 441, 461
Voronin, Yury   129, 131, 132
Vyugin, Oleg   248, 306
Vyakhirev, Rem   256, 257, 260, 339, 393

Yakemenko, Vasily   492–93, 560, 569
Yakovlev, Alexander   14–15, 50
Yakunin, Gleb   63, 65, 353
Yamadayev, Ruslan   517, 525–27, 703

Yamadayev, Sulim 515–17, 525–27
Yanayev, Gennady 53–54, 57
Yandarbiyev, Zelimkhan 160, 197–201, 404
Yashin, Ilya 513, 541–42, 557–58, 564, 599–601, 618, 621–24, 633, 638–41, 666, 683, 692, 697, 715, 728
Yastrzhembsky, Sergei 254, 276, 406
Yavlinsky, Grigory 41–44, 64, 79, 89–91, 126, 134, 150, 174, 186, 192, 194, 206, 224–26, 261, 278, 351, 357, 365, 372, 380, 405–9, 425–26, 580, 585
Yazov, Dmitry 48, 49, 51, 60–62, 158–59, 161
Yeltsin, Boris 6, 13, 20–21, 24–27, 32–33, 35–79, 84–86, 88–89, 92, 98, 100–140, 142, 145, 147, 152–56, 159, 163–65, 167–72, 184–233, 237–58, 260, 262, 264–66, 269, 271–80, 283–89, 291, 294–302, 304, 307, 309–42, 347, 350–52, 354, 356, 360–65, 367–72, 376, 378–81, 383, 385, 390, 396, 422, 425, 434, 441–46, 483, 488, 494, 497, 505–8, 519, 543, 565, 575, 642, 651, 667–68, 680, 698, 708–9, 711, 728

Yevstafyev A. V. 228–30
Yumashev, Valentin 210, 213, 219, 227–30, 238, 240, 242–43, 246, 266–67, 269, 273–74, 279–80, 291, 297–300, 311–12, 314–15, 320–21, 324–25, 327, 330–31, 335, 337–40, 352, 354, 372
Yumasheva, Tatyana *see* Dyachenko, Tatyana
Yurovsky, Yakov 287–93
Yushchenko, Viktor 458–59, 461–78, 484–88, 496–97, 705

Zhirinovsky, Vladimir 147, 172, 184, 186–87, 302, 324, 553, 591
Zavadnikov, Valentin 359, 363
Zavadsky, Dmitry 396, 399
Zavgayev, Doku 160–62
Zadornov, Mikhail 295, 311
Zverev, Sergei 240, 267–68
Zvereva, Nina 29, 31–32, 122, 154, 176
Zolotov, Viktor 701, 703
Zorkin, Valery 108, 111–12, 130–31
Zygar, Mikhail 424, 479, 579, 664
Zyuganov, Gennady 115, 156, 190–91, 204, 206, 210–18, 221–27, 231–34, 248, 299, 314, 320, 328, 347, 366, 395, 438, 614